T0202661

Lecture Notes in Computer Science   14773

Advanced Research in Computing and Software Science
Subline of Lecture Notes in Computer Science

More information about this series at https://link.springer.com/bookseries/558

Ludovic Levy Patey · Elaine Pimentel ·
Lorenzo Galeotti · Florin Manea
Editors

Twenty Years of Theoretical and Practical Synergies

20th Conference on Computability in Europe, CiE 2024
Amsterdam, The Netherlands, July 8–12, 2024
Proceedings

 Springer

Editors
Ludovic Levy Patey ⓘ
The Mathematics Institute of Jussieu
Paris, France

Elaine Pimentel ⓘ
University College London
London, UK

Lorenzo Galeotti
University of Amsterdam
Amsterdam, The Netherlands

Florin Manea ⓘ
University of Göttingen
Göttingen, Germany

ISSN 0302-9743   ISSN 1611-3349 (electronic)
Lecture Notes in Computer Science
ISBN 978-3-031-64308-8   ISBN 978-3-031-64309-5 (eBook)
https://doi.org/10.1007/978-3-031-64309-5

This Springer imprint is published by the registered company Springer Nature Switzerland AG
The registered company address is: Gewerbestrasse 11, 6330 Cham, Switzerland

If disposing of this product, please recycle the paper.

Preface

Computability in Europe 2024:
Twenty Years of Theoretical and Practical Synergies
Amsterdam, Netherlands
8–12 July 2024

The conference *Computability in Europe* (CiE) is organised yearly under the auspices of the Association CiE, a European association of mathematicians, logicians, computer scientists, philosophers, physicists, biologists, historians, linguistics and others interested in new developments in computability and their underlying significance for the real world. CiE promotes the development of computability-related science, ranging over mathematics, computer science and applications in various natural and engineering sciences, such as physics and biology, as well as related fields, such as philosophy and history of computing. CiE 2024 had as its motto *Twenty Years of Theoretical and Practical Synergies*, a nod to the history of the conference, which started in 2005 and actively promoted dialogue and collaboration between all communities interested in computability theory and its diverse aspects, while challenging the future conferences to follow the same path.

CiE 2024 was the 20th conference in the series, and the second one to take place in Amsterdam, where everything started. The conference was jointly organised by the Institute for Logic, Language and Computation (Universiteit van Amsterdam) and the Amsterdam University College (Universiteit van Amsterdam & Vrije Universiteit Amsterdam). The previous CiE conferences have been held in Amsterdam (The Netherlands) in 2005, Swansea (UK) in 2006, Siena (Italy) in 2007, Athens (Greece) in 2008, Heidelberg (Germany) in 2009, Ponta Delgada (Portugal) in 2010, Sofia (Bulgaria) in 2011, Cambridge (UK) in 2012, Milan (Italy) in 2013, Budapest (Hungary) in 2014, Bucharest (Romania) in 2015, Paris (France) in 2016, Turku (Finland) in 2017, Kiel (Germany) in 2018, Durham (UK) in 2019, Salerno (Italy – virtually) in 2020, Ghent (Belgium – virtually) in 2021, Swansea (UK) in 2022 and Batumi (Georgia) in 2023. Currently, the annual CiE conference is the largest international meeting focused on computability-theoretic issues. The proceedings, containing the best submitted papers, as well as extended abstracts of invited, tutorial, and special session speakers, for all these meetings are published in the Springer series *Lecture Notes in Computer Science*.

The CiE conference series is coordinated by the CiE Conference Series Steering Committee, consisting of Veronica Becher (Universidad de Buenos Aires), Liesbeth De Mol (Université de Lille), Gianluca Della Vedova (Executive Officer, Università degli Studi di Milano-Bicocca), Benedikt Löwe (Universities of Hamburg and Cambridge), Lila Kari (University of Waterloo), Florin Manea (Chair, University of Göttingen), Klaus Meer (BTU Cottbus-Senftenberg), Russell Miller (City University of New York), and Mariya Soskova (University of Wisconsin-Madison).

The Program Committee of CiE 2024 was chaired by Ludovic Levy Patey (CNRS, Université Paris-Cité) and Elaine Pimentel (University College London). The Committee, consisting of 29 members, selected the invited and tutorial speakers and the special session organisers, and they coordinated the reviewing process of all submitted contributions.

Structure and Program of the Conference

The Program Committee invited six speakers to give plenary lectures at CiE 2024: Arnold Beckmann (Swansea University, UK), Rod Downey (Victoria University of Wellington, New Zealand), Elvira Mayordomo (University of Zaragoza, Spain), Alexandre Miquel (Universidad de la República, Uruguay), Monika Seisenberger (Swansea University, UK) and Mariya Soskova (University of Wisconsin-Madison, USA). The conference also had two plenary tutorials, presented by Matthew Harrison-Trainor (University of Illinois Chicago, USA) and Sonja Smets (University of Amsterdam, The Netherlands).

In addition, the conference had six special sessions:

- Algorithmic Randomness and Kolmogorov Complexity.
  Organisers: Denis Hirschfeldt (University of Chicago) and Rupert Hölzl (Bundeswehr University Munich).
  Speakers: Jacob Fiedler (University of Chicago), Jun Le Goh (National University of Singapore), Satyadev Nandakumar (Indian Institute of Technology, Kanpur) and Alexander Shen (LIRMM, CNRS, University of Montpellier 2).
- Computable Aspects of Symbolic Dynamics and Tilings.
  Organisers: Benjamin Hellouin (LISN, Université Paris-Saclay) and Ilkka Törmä (University of Turku).
  Speakers: Martin Kutrib (Universität Gießen), Marcus Lohrey (Universität Siegen), Etienne Moutot (CNRS, I2M, Aix-Marseille University) and Matthieu Rosenfeld (LIRMM, University of Montpellier 2).
- Computing Knowledge: Computational Aspects of Epistemic Logics (HaPoC).
  Organisers: Marianna Girlando (ILLC, University of Amsterdam) and Ekaterina Kubyshkina (University of Milan).

Speakers: Alexandru Baltag (ILLC, University of Amsterdam), Nina Gierasimczuk (Danish Technical University), Roman Kuznets (Technische Universität Wien), Giuseppe Primiero (University of Milan) and Sonja Smets (ILLC, University of Amsterdam)

– Computational Methods in Evolutionary Biology (BiC).
  Organisers: Jasmijn Baaijens (Delft University of Technology) and Gianluca Della Vedova (Università degli Studi di Milano-Bicocca).
  Speakers: Simone Ciccolella (Università degli Studi di Milano-Bicocca), Hilje Doekes (Wageningen University & Research), Mareike Fischer (University of Greifswald) and David Moi (University of Lausanne).

– Quantum Computation.
  Organisers: Delaram Kahrobaei (QC The City University of New York) and Mehrnoosh Sadrzadeh (University College London).
  Speakers: Chris Heunen (University of Edinburgh), Ludovic Perret (Sorbonne University/LIP6), Stefano Pirandola (University of York) and Sonja Smets (University of Amsterdam).

– Computable Structure Theory.
  Organisers: Ekaterina Fokina (Vienna University of Technology) and Stefan Vatev (Sofia University).
  Speakers: Pavel Alaev (Novosibirsk State University), David Gonzalez (University of California, Berkeley), Karen Lange (Wellesley College) and Dino Rossegger (University of California, Berkeley).

Speakers in these special sessions were selected by the respective special session organisers and were invited to contribute papers to this volume.

CiE 2024 also included some satellite events organised by the following Amsterdam University College students: Djordje Djokovic, Ana-Catinca Mare and Diana Radovanovic.

Finally, a panel to celebrate 20 years of CiE was organised, with panel members: Arnold Beckmann, Peter van Emde Boas, Benedikt Löwe, Elvira Mayordomo, Andrea Sorbi, Mariya Soskova and Alexandra Soskova.

The members of the Program Committee of CiE 2024 selected for publication in this volume and for presentation at the conference 26 of the 43 non-invited submitted papers. Each paper received at least three reviews by the Program Committee and their subreviewers. In addition to the accepted contributed papers, this volume contains seven special session papers, one invited paper and a reproduction of Barry Cooper's paper: "If CiE Did Not Exist, It Would Be Necessary to Invent It", originally published in the first CiE proceedings (LNCS, volume 3526). The production of the volume would have been impossible without the diligent work of our expert referees, both Program Committee members and subreviewers. We would like to thank all of them for their excellent work.

Springer-Verlag generously funded this year a Best Student Paper Award, awarded to a paper authored solely by students. The winners of this award are the papers "Structures of Finite Punctual Dimension $n > 2$" by Ellen Hammatt and "Complexities of Theories of Profinite Subgroups of S_ω via Tree Presentations" by Jason Block.

All authors who have contributed to this conference are encouraged to submit significantly extended versions of their papers, with additional unpublished research content, to *Computability: The Journal of the Association CiE*.

The Steering Committee of the conference series CiE is concerned about the representation of female researchers in the field of computability. In order to increase female participation, the series started the Women in Computability (WiC) program in 2007. In 2016, after the new constitution of the Association CiE allowed for the possibility of creating special interest groups, a Special Interest Group named Women in Computability was established. Also since 2016, the WiC program is sponsored by ACM's Women in Computing. This program includes a workshop, the annual WiC dinner, the mentorship program and a grant program for young female researchers. The Women in Computability workshop continued in 2024, coordinated by Elvira Mayordomo.

The organisers of CiE 2024 would like to acknowledge and thank the following entities for their financial support (in alphabetical order): the *Amsterdam University College* (AUC), the *Association for Symbolic Logic* (ASL), the *Institute for Logic, Language and Computation* (ILLC), *Koninklijke Nederlandse Akademie van Wetenschappen* (KNAW) and *Nederlandse Organisatie voor Wetenschappelijk Onderzoek* (NWO). We would also like to acknowledge the support of the *Association Computability in Europe*.

We gratefully thank all the members of the Organising Committee of CiE 2024 for their work towards making the conference a successful event.

May 2024

Ludovic Levy Patey
Elaine Pimentel
Lorenzo Galeotti
Florin Manea

Organization

Program Committee Chairs

Levy Patey, Ludovic — CNRS, Université Paris-Cité, France
Pimentel, Elaine — University College London, UK

Steering Committee Chair

Manea, Florin — University of Göttingen, Germany

Organizing Committee Chair

Galeotti, Lorenzo — University of Amsterdam, Amsterdam University College, The Netherlands

Program Committee Members

Afshari, Bahareh — University of Gothenburg, Sweden
Aubrun, Nathalie — CNRS, Université Paris-Saclay, France
Béal, Marie-Pierre — Université Gustave Eiffel, France
van den Berg, Benno — University of Amsterdam, The Netherlands
Berndt, Sebastian — University of Lübeck, Germany
Bouyer-Decitre, Patricia — CNRS, France
Cai, Jin-Yi — University of Wisconsin-Madison, USA
Csima, Barbara — University of Waterloo, Canada
Della Vedova, Gianluca — University of Milano-Bicocca, Italy
Epstein, Leah — University of Haifa, Israel
Ferreira, Gilda — Universidade Aberta, Portugal
Forster, Yannick — Inria, France
Galeotti, Lorenzo — University of Amsterdam, Amsterdam University College, The Netherlands
Hoyrup, Mathieu — Inria, LORIA, France
Kari, Jarkko — University of Turku, Finland
Knight, Julia — University of Notre Dame, USA
Ladra, Susana — Universidade da Coruña, Spain
Lang, Timo — University College London, UK
Lange, Karen — Wellesley College, USA
Levy Patey, Ludovic — Université Paris-Cité, France
Manea, Florin — University of Göttingen, Germany
Melnikov, Alexander — Victoria University of Wellington, New Zealand
Naibo, Alberto — Université Paris 1 Panthéon-Sorbonne, France
Pimentel, Elaine — University College London, UK

Rojas, Cristobal   Universidad Católica, Chile
Schiaffonati, Viola   Politecnico di Milano, Italy
Shafer, Paul   University of Leeds, UK
Solomon, Reed   University of Connecticut, USA
Weiermann, Andreas   Ghent University, Belgium

Organising Committee Members

Bahareh Afshari   University of Gothenburg, Sweden
Luis Aguilar Suarez   Amsterdam University College, The Netherlands
Benno van den Berg   Universiteit van Amsterdam, The Netherlands
Andrea De Domenico   Vrije Universiteit Amsterdam, The Netherlands
Tamara Dobler   Vrije Universiteit Amsterdam, The Netherlands
Lorenzo Galeotti   Amsterdam University College, The Netherlands
Yurii Khomskii   Amsterdam University College, The Netherlands
Mattia Panettiere   Vrije Universiteit Amsterdam, The Netherlands
Benjamin Rin   Universiteit Utrecht, The Netherlands

Administrative Staff

Ingrid van Loon   AUC, The Netherlands
Peter van Ormondt   ILLC, The Netherlands
Marcus Smit   AUC, The Netherlands
Belinda Stratton   AUC, The Netherlands
Marco Vervoort   GreenLight Solutions, The Netherlands
Alexandra Zieglerová   ILLC, The Netherlands

Reviewers

Afshari, Bahareh   Ferreira, Gilda
Aubrun, Nathalie   Forster, Yannick
van den Berg, Benno   Franklin, Johanna
Berndt, Sebastian   Frittaion, Emanuele
Bouyer, Patricia   Galeotti, Lorenzo
Béal, Marie-Pierre   Gutin, Gregory
Cai, Jin-Yi   Harizanov, Valentina
Csima, Barbara   Hoyrup, Mathieu
Day, Joel   Kalimullin, Iskander
Della Vedova, Gianluca   Kari, Jarkko
Dolce, Francesco   Khomskii, Yurii
Draghici, Andrei   Knight, Julia
Dzhafarov, Damir   Ladra, Susana
Epstein, Leah   Lang, Timo
Faizrahmanov, Marat   Lange, Karen
Fazekas, Szilard   Le Houérou, Quentin

Leporati, Alberto
Levy Patey, Ludovic
Manea, Florin
Melnikov, Alexander
Mercas, Robert
Naibo, Alberto
Oliva, Paulo
Pimentel, Elaine
Pollett, Chris
Quaresmini, Camilla
Rojas, Cristobal
Rossegger, Dino
Salo, Ville
Sanders, Sam

Santos, Paulo
Schiaffonati, Viola
Shafer, Paul
Turetsky, Daniel
Sipos, Andrei
Solda, Giovanni
Solomon, Reed
Stephan, Frank
Tutu, Ionut
Weiermann, Andreas
Welch, Philip
Wu, Huishan
Yang, Yue

Invited Papers

Computing Knowledge: Computational Aspects of Epistemic Logics (HaPoC)

Marianna Girlando[1] and Ekaterina Kubyshkina[2]

[1] ILLC, University of Amsterdam, Science Park 107, 1098 XG Amsterdam,
Netherlands
m.girlando@uva.nl
[2] LUCI, PhilTech, University of Milan, Via Festa del Perdono, 7, 20122 Milan,
Italy
ekaterina.kubyshkina@unimi.it

Abstract. Epistemic logics offer formal tools to reason about epistemic attitudes, among which knowledge and belief, and they find key applications in different fields, most notably philosophy and artificial intelligence. This special session is dedicated to the investigation of the computational aspects of epistemic logics, shedding light on how advances in computing are reshaping our understanding of knowledge representation, reasoning, and decision-making. The primary objective of this session is to discuss the computational challenges within epistemic logic, establishing bridges between semantic frameworks, decidability questions and proof theoretical strategies emerging within epistemic logics. More specifically, we shall address key issues such as the development of robust tools for reasoning about epistemic attitudes, creating efficient methods for determining the logical consequences of a given set of knowledge or belief statements, and establishing frameworks for updating these statements based on newly acquired information.

The session is organized on behalf of the Association for the History and Philosophy of Computing (https://hapoc.org/).

Speakers:
Nina Gierasimczuk (Danish Technical University)
Roman Kuznets (TU Wien)
Sonja Smets & Alexandru Baltag (ILLC, University of Amsterdam)
Giuseppe Primiero (LUCI, PhilTech, University of Milan)

The Theory of Enumeration Degrees and Its Fragments

Mariya I. Soskova (ID)

University of Wisconsin–Madison, 480 Lincoln Dr, Madison, WI, 537206, USA
e-mail: soskova@wisc.edu
https://people.math.wisc.edu/~soskova/

Abstract. We survey a line of investigation into the theory of the enumeration degrees. Enumeration reducibility captures a model of computation based on positive information. We will focus on the theory of the associated degree structure in the language of partial orders and its fragments, built by restricting the quantifier complexity of statements. We will consider the local substructure of the enumeration degrees captured by the degrees that are computationally weaker than the Halting set. We consider how things change when we change the signature of the language.

Keywords: enumeration degrees · decidability · theory · fragments

This is the extended abstract of my talk for the conference CiE 2024 "Twenty years of theoretical and practical synergies". I will present a line of investigation into one aspect of the structure of the enumeration degrees–one that asks: how complicated is the theory of the structure. This line of investigation accompanies the study of every computability theoretic reducibility. It was carried out extensively for the Turing degrees. The enumeration degrees can be viewed as an extension of the Turing degrees. We will keep track of relevant result in both structures and point out aspects in which they differ.

The partial order of the enumeration degrees arises from the relation *enumeration reducibility*, introduced by Friedberg and Rogers [3] in 1959.

Definition 1. (Friedberg and Rogers [3]). *A set A is enumeration reducible to a set B (denoted by $A \leq_e B$) if there is a c.e. set Φ, such that*

$$ A = \Phi(B) = \{n : \exists u(\langle n, u \rangle \in \Phi \,\&\, D_u \subseteq B)\}, $$

where D_u denotes the finite set with code (canonical index) u under the standard coding of finite sets.

Equivalent forms of enumeration reducibility were actually introduced by several authors independently: see Kleene [7], Myhill [13], Uspensky [24], Selman [17]. The most common motivation for their introduction was to extend the notion of Turing reducibility to partial function. Scott [16] showed that enumeration reducibility on c.e. sets gives rise to a structure that interprets untyped lambda calculus, thus we can be confident that the reducibility provides a robust notion of computation that is intrinsically interesting.

To each reducibility we associate a degree structure in which we identify sets that are reducible to each other. The structure of the Turing degrees $\mathcal{D}_T$ has a natural embedding in the structure of the enumeration degrees $\mathcal{D}_e$: we map the Turing degree of a set A to the enumeration degree of the set $A \oplus \overline{A}$. In this sense we view $\mathcal{D}_e$ as an extension of $\mathcal{D}_T$.

This embedding is non-trivial and, in fact, the two structures are not even elementary equivalent. Spector [23] proved that the Turing degrees have minimal elements, while Gutteridge [5] showed that the enumeration degrees are downwards dense.

We focus on understanding the complexity of the sets of statements in the language of partial orders that are true in the Turing degrees and that are true in the enumeration degrees. We denote these sets by $Th(\mathcal{D}_T)$ and $Th(\mathcal{D}_e)$ and call them the *theory* of the degree structure. We will see that in each case these theories are maximally complex: as complicated as the theory Second order arithmetic. These results are due to Simpson [20] for $\mathcal{D}_T$ and to Slaman and Woodin [22] for $\mathcal{D}_e$. We will describe the general method of Slaman and Woodin [21] that codes models of arithmetic inside the degree structure and also comment on an alternative proof for the complexity of $Th(\mathcal{D}_e)$ that relies on the definability of the Turing degrees inside the enumeration degrees by Cai et al. [1].

The local structure of the enumeration degrees $\mathcal{D}_e(\leq 0'_e)$ consists of the interval degrees $[0_e, 0'_e]$. It contains as a substructure the image of the interval $[0_T, 0'_T]$, which constitutes the local structure of the Turing degree $\mathcal{D}_T(\leq 0'_T)$. It is a countable structure and its element have simple definitions in terms of the arithmetical hierarchy: the enumeration degrees of Σ_2^0 sets. Cooper [2] proved that $\mathcal{D}_e(\leq 0'_e)$ is dense, while Sacks [15] showed that minimal Turing degrees exist even in $\mathcal{D}_T(\leq 0'_T)$. The theories of the local structures are also maximally complex: each is computably isomorphic to first order arithmetic [4, 19].

In each of the cases above we may decide to restrict our attention to simpler statements: we will borrow notation from the arithmetical hierarch and say that a statement of the form $(\exists x_1)(\forall x_2)\ldots(Qx_n)\varphi$, where Q is the appropriate quantifier after $n - 1$ alternations and φ is quantifier free, a Σ_n formula. Π_n is defined similarly when we start with $\forall$. The Σ_n-Theory of a structure $\mathcal{D}$ consists of all Σ_n statements true in $\mathcal{D}$ and is denoted by Σ_n-$Th(\mathcal{D})$.

The Σ_1 theories of $\mathcal{D}_T$, $\mathcal{D}_e$, $\mathcal{D}_T(\leq 0'_T)$ and $\mathcal{D}_e(\leq 0'_e)$ are each decidable. They can be reformulated as a structural question asking which finite partial orders can be embedded in the structure. In each case the answer is all. And so at the one end, when we consider only existential statements, we have decidable theories. At the other, when we allow arbitrarily long quantifier alternations, we have highly undecidable theories. Naturally, we wonder where does decidability break down.

In all cases the Σ_3-theory of the degree structure is undecidable. We will review these results due to Lerman and Schmerl (see [11]) for the local and global Turing degrees and to Kent [6] for the local and global enumeration degrees. We will describe the Nies Transfer Method [14] that gives a general recipe on how to prove such results.

The question that remains is then what happens at level 2. In the Turing degrees both global [10, 18] and local [12] we have an algorithm to decide where a two-quantifier statement is true or not. The algorithm largely relies on a generalization of the existence of minimal degrees. In $\mathcal{D}_e$ and in $\mathcal{D}_e(\leq 0'_e)$ these questions remain open. We will discuss partial progress made towards such a solution and the obstacles ahead. The work discussed features in [9] and [8].

Finally we will consider how things change if we change the signature of the language: what happens if we add a function symbol for the jump operator, the skip operator, or the least upper bound operator.

Acknowledgements. The author is supported by NSF Grant No. DMS-2053848.

References

1. Cai, M., Ganchev, H.A., Lempp, S., Miller, J.S., Soskova, M.I.: Defining totality in the enumeration degrees. J. Amer. Math. Soc. **29**(4), 1051–1067 (2016)
2. Barry Cooper, S.: Partial degrees and the density problem. Part 2: The enumeration degrees of the Σ_2 sets are dense. J. Symb. Logic **49**, 503–513 (1984)
3. Friedberg, R.M., Rogers, H., Jr.: Reducibility and completeness for sets of integers. Z. Math. Logik Grundlag. Math. **5**, 117–125 (1959)
4. Ganchev, H., Soskova, M.: Interpreting true arithmetic in the local structure of the enumeration degrees. J. Symb. Logic **77**(4), 1184–1194 (2012)
5. Gutteridge, L.: Some results on enumeration reducibility. Ph.D. Dissertation, Simon Fraser University (1971)
6. Kent, T. F.: The Π_3-theory of the Σ_2^0-enumeration degrees is undecidable. J. Symb. Logic **71**(4), 1284–1302 (2006)
7. Kleene, S.C.: Introduction to metamathematics, p. 550 D. Van Nostrand Co., Inc., New York (1952)
8. Lempp, S., Slaman, T.A., Sorbi, A.: On extensions of embeddings into the enumeration degrees of the Σ_2^0-sets. J. Math Logic **05**(2), 247–298 (2005)
9. Lempp, S., Slaman, T.A., Soskova, M.I.: Fragments of the theory of the enumeration degrees. Adv. Math. **383** (2021)
10. Lerman, M.: Initial segments of the degrees of unsolvability. Ann. of Math. **93**(2), 365–389 (1971)
11. Lerman, M.: Degrees of Unsolvability. Perspectives in Mathematical Logic. Springer-Verlag, Berlin (1983). ISBN 3-540-12155-2
12. Lerman, M., Shore, R.A.: Decidability and invariant classes for degree structures. Trans. Amer. Math. Soc. **310**(2), 669–692 (1988)
13. Myhill, J.: Note on degrees of partial functions. J. Proc. Amer. Math. Soc. **12**, 519–521 (1961)
14. Nies, A.O.: Undecidable fragments of elementary theories. Algebra Univers. **35**(1), 8–33 (1996)
15. Sacks, G.E.: On the degrees less than $0'$. Ann. Math. **77**(2), 211–231 (1963)
16. Scott, D.: Lambda calculus and recursion theory. In: Kanger (ed.) Proceedings of the. Third Scandinavian Logic Symposium, pp. 154–193, North-Holland, Amsterdam (1975)

17. Alan L. Selman, Arithmetical reducibilities I, Z. Math. Logik Grundlag. Math. **17**, 335–350 (1971)
18. Shore, R.A.: On the $\forall\exists$-sentences of α-recursion theory, in Generalized recursion theory I. (Proc. Second Sympos., Univ. Oslo, Oslo, 1977), Stud. Logic Foundations Math. Vol. 94 (North-Holland, Amsterdam-New York), 331–353 (1978)
19. Shore, R.A.: The theory of the degrees below $0'$. J. Lond. Math. Soc. **24**, 1–14 (1981)
20. Simpson, S.G.: First-order theory of the degrees of recursive unsolvability. Ann. of Math. **105**(1), 121–139 (1977)
21. Slaman, T.A., Hugh Woodin, W.: Definability in degree structures. Preprint (2005). http://math.berkeley.edu/∼slaman/talks/sw.pdf
22. Slaman, T.A., Hugh Woodin, W.: Definability in the enumeration degrees. Arch. Math. Logic. **36**(4–5), 255–267 (1997)
23. Spector, C.: On degrees of recursive unsolvability. Ann. Math. **64**(2), 581–592 (1956)
24. Uspensky, V.A.: Russian translation of: H. Rogers, Jr., Theory of recursive functions and effective computability, Mir, p. 482 (1972)

Further Extensions of the Point to Set Principle[1]

Elvira Mayordomo (ID)

Departamento de Informática e Ingeniería de Sistemas, Instituto de Investigación
en Ingeniería de Aragón, Universidad de Zaragoza, Spain
elvira@unizar.es
http://webdiis.unizar.es/~elvira/

Abstract. Effective and resource-bounded dimensions were defined by Lutz in
[3] and [2] and have proven to be useful and meaningful for quantitative analysis
in the contexts of algorithmic randomness, computational complexity and fractal
geometry (see the surveys [1, 4, ?, ?] and all the references in them).

The point-to-set principle (PSP) of J. Lutz and N. Lutz [5] fully characterizes
Hausdorff and packing dimensions in terms of effective dimensions in the
Euclidean space, enabling effective dimensions to be used to answer open
questions about fractal geometry, with already an interesting list of geometric
measure theory results (see [9, 7] and more recent results in [8, 11–13].

In this talk I will review the point-to-set principles focusing on its recent
extensions to separable spaces [7] and to Finite-State dimensions [12], and
presenting open questions on the oracle and oracle access in PSP as well as
further application opportunities.

Keywords: algorithmic dimensions · finite-state dimension · geometric measure
theory · point-to-set principle

References

1. Downey, R.G., Hirschfeldt, D.R.: Algorithmic randomness and complexity. Springer-Verlag (2010)
2. Lutz, J.H.: Dimension in complexity classes. SIAM J. Comput. **32**(5), 1236–1259 (2003)
3. Lutz, J.H.: The dimensions of individual strings and sequences. Inf. Comput. **187** (1), 49–79 (2003)
4. Lutz, J.H.: Effective fractal dimensions. Math. Logic Q. **51**(1), 62_72 (2005)
5. Lutz, J.H., Lutz, N.: Algorithmic information, plane Kakeya sets, and conditional dimension. ACM Trans. Comput. Theory **10** (2018) (Article 7)

---

[1] Supported in part by Spanish Ministry of Science and Innovation grant PID2022-138703OB-I00 and by the Science dept. of Aragon Government: Group Reference T64_20R (COSMOS research group).

6. Lutz, J.H., Lutz, N., Mayordomo, E.: Dimension and the structure of complexity classes. Theory Comput. Syst. **67**, 473–490 (2023)
7. Lutz, J.H., Mayordomo, E.: Algorithmic fractal dimensions in geometric measure theory. In: Brattka, V., Hertling, P. (eds.) Handbook of Computability and Complexity in Analysis. Theory and Applications of Computability. Springer, Cham (2021). https://doi.org/10.1007/978-3-030-59234-9_8
8. Lutz, J.H.: The point-to-set principle, the continuum hypothesis, and the dimensions of Hamel bases. Computability (2022, to appear)
9. Lutz, J., Lutz, N.: Who asked us? How the theory of computing answers questions about analysis. In: Complexity and Approximation: In Memory of Ker-I Ko. Springer, ding-zhu du and jie wang (eds.) edn. (2020)
10. Mayordomo, E.: A point to set principle for finite-state dimension. Technical report. arXiv:2208.00157, Arxiv (2022)
11. Slaman, T.: On capacitability for co-analytic sets. New Zealand J. Math. **52**, 865–869 (2022)
12. Stull, D.M.: The dimension spectrum conjecture for planar lines. In: Bojańczyk, M., Merelli, E., Woodru, D.P. (eds.) ICALP 2022. Leibniz International Proceedings in Informatics (LIPIcs), vol. 229, pp. 133:1–133:20. Schloss Dagstuhl – Leibniz-Zentrum für Informatik, Dagstuhl, Germany (2022)
13. Stull, D.: Optimal oracles for point-to-set principles. In: Berenbrink, P., Monmege, B. (eds.) STACS 2022. Leibniz International Proceedings in Informatics (LIPIcs), vol. 219, pp. 57:1–57:17. Schloss Dagstuhl – Leibniz-Zentrum für Informatik (2022)

Uniform Distribution and Algorithmic Randomness

Jun Le Goh[1] (iD) and Manlio Valenti[2] (iD)

[1] National University of Singapore, Singapore, 119076
[2] Swansea University, Swansea, SA1 8EN, UK

Abstract. Koksma [3] proved that for almost every $x > 1$, the sequence of powers $(x^n)_n$ is uniformly distributed modulo one (UD for short). One might consider such x to be "random"; however, there are computable numbers x with this property (Levin [4]). Instead, we say x is random if for every *computable* nonzero c, $(cx^n)_n$ is UD. This definition is motivated by a stronger result of Koksma [3]: For every nonzero c, $(cx^n)_n$ is UD for almost every $x > 1$. We shall review related results by Avigad and Becher-Grigorieff [1, 2], followed by preliminary results on the effective content of Koksma's theorem and its associated notion of randomness.

Keywords: Uniform distribution · algorithmic randomness · computable analysis

References

1. Avigad, J.: Uniform distribution and algorithmic randomness. J. Symb. Logic **78**(1), 334–344 (2013)
2. Becher, V., Grigorieff, S.: Randomness and uniform distribution modulo one. Inf. Comput. **285**, 12 (2022). Paper No. 104857
3. Koksma, J.F.: Ein mengentheoretischer Satz über die Gleichverteilung modulo Eins. Compositio Math. **2**, 250–258 (1935)
4. Levin, M.B.: Effectivization of the Koksma theorem. Mat. Zametki **47**(1), 163–166 (1990)

Special Session at CiE 2024: Computable Aspects of Symbolic Dynamics and Tilings

Benjamin Hellouin de Menibus and Ilkka Törma

Symbolic dynamics is the study of discrete dynamical systems, especially those whose configurations can be described by finite or infinite sequences of letters or *symbols*, in one or more dimensions. Under this umbrella, we find traditional models of computation such as Turing machines; discrete models with dynamical or mathematical motivations, such as subshifts or tilings; and many examples that can be counted on both sides, such as cellular automata, sandpiles, automata networks, etc. It is natural, therefore, that this area is a fertile ground for the interaction of mathematics and the theory of computation, in addition to many other areas interested in these discrete models in computer science, statistical physics, etc.

It would be difficult to give a complete panorama of the answers and active questions related to computability and discrete mathematics in this topic. An underlying motivation is to further our understanding of the nature of computation: what does it mean for a system to be universal, especially when it doesn't have an unambiguous input or output? What impact does it have on the (un)decidability of its properties? Another recurring question relates to the *frontier of undecidability*: what properties make a problem go from undecidable to decidable, and how is it related to the computational properties of the system?

Many of these systems exhibit highly complex behaviours, structures or patterns, despite their simple descriptions; famous examples include the rule 110 elementary cellular automata, Langton's ant, etc. These phenomena have been described as emergent complexity, and the relationship between this *empiric* complexity of individual systems and their universality is a rich area of research.

On the other direction, the computability point of view brought, in many cases, a new light to questions that were historically studied with more traditional mathematical methods. This point of view is usually not only *computational*, in the sense that the object of interest is not an algorithm but, rather, the computability properties themselves. Complexity or computability classes are used to describe or characterise possible behaviours, and jumps in computational difficulty of problems uncover changes in the behaviour or properties of the system. As an example, a particularly active area relates the decidability of problems where configurations corresponds to words on a group and the algebraic and computational properties of that group.

We have invited speakers representing various points of view on symbolic dynamics – combinatorial, algebraic, algorithmical... – and we hope that you enjoy this panorama of our area of research.

How Much Pattern Complexity Can Help Us Solve the Domino Problem?

Etienne Moutot ⓘD

CNRS, Aix-Marseille Université, Marseille, France
etienne.moutot@math.cnrs.fr
https://emoutot.perso.math.cnrs.fr/

Abstract. The *domino problem* asks whether it is possible to tile an infinite space (for example a plane) using a given set of tiles. Easily decidable in dimension one, this problem becomes undecidable for dimensions two and higher [1]. In order to understand better the reasons why this problem becomes so hard in dimension two, one can look a "simpler" tilings, and try to understand when the domino problem becomes decidable again. One measure of complexity for tilings is the pattern complexity, which is the function counting the number of finite patterns of a given size that appear in the tiling.

In this talk, I will explain how the pattern complexity plays an important role in the (un)decidability of the domino problem, as we showed with Jarkko Kari that tilesets with "low enough" complexity will have a decidable domino problem [2]. Moreover, as soon as the complexity is higher that a given bound, it becomes undecidable as in the general case. These bounds are tightly linked to Nivat's conjecture about general colorings of $\mathbb{Z}^2$.

Keywords: Nivat's conjecture · Domino problem · Symbolic dynamics

The *domino problem* asks whether it is possible to tile an infinite space (for example a plane) using a given set of tiles. Easily decidable in dimension one, this problem becomes undecidable for dimensions two and higher [1].

In order to understand better the reasons why this problem becomes so hard in dimension two, one can look a "simpler" tilings, and try to understand when the domino problem becomes decidable again. One measure of complexity for tilings is the pattern complexity, which is the function counting the number of finite patterns of a given size that appear in the tiling.

In this talk, I will explain how the pattern complexity plays an important role in the (un)decidability of the domino problem, as we showed with Jarkko Kari that tilesets with "low enough" complexity will have a decidable domino problem [2]. Moreover, as soon as the complexity is higher that a given bound, it becomes undecidable as in the general case. These bounds are tightly linked to Nivat's conjecture about general colorings of $\mathbb{Z}^2$.

References

1. Berger, R.: The Undecidability of the Domino Problem. Memoirs of the American Mathematical Society, The American Mathematical Society (1966)
2. Kari, J., Moutot, E.: Decidability and periodicity of low complexity tilings. Theory of Computing Systems, October 2021. https://doi.org/10.1007/s00224-021-10063-8

Sufficient Conditions for Non-emptiness of a Subshift and Computability of Its Entropy

Matthieu Rosenfeld

LIRMM, CNRS, Université de Montpellier, France

Abstract. Given an integer d, a finite subset S of $\mathbb{Z}^d$ and an alphabet $\mathcal{A}$, a **pattern** p is an element of $\mathcal{A}^S$. A **configuration** is an element of $\mathcal{A}^{\mathbb{Z}^d}$, and we say that a pattern p of support S appears in a configuration $x \in \mathcal{A}^{\mathbb{Z}^d}$ at position $i \in \mathbb{Z}^d$ if for all $s \in S$, $x(i+s) = p(s)$. Given d, $\mathcal{A}$ and a set of **forbidden patterns** $\mathcal{F}$ the corresponding **subshift** is the set of configurations that avoid all the patterns of $\mathcal{F}$. These notions naturally generalize to any other group than $\mathbb{Z}^d$.

Fix d and $\mathcal{A}$, now consider the problem of deciding whether a subshift given by a set of forbidden patterns $\mathcal{F}$ is empty. Even when $\mathcal{F}$ is finite the problem is undecidable as soon as $d \geq 2$. On the other hand, if $\mathcal{F}$ is finite and $d = 1$ the problem is decidable, and the so-called topological entropy is even computable (using elementary results from automata theory and linear algebra). More generally, the question of characterizing the groups for which the problem is decidable when $\mathcal{F}$ is finite is still open. Now, if $\mathcal{F}$ is allowed to be infinite the question becomes more difficult even for $d = 1$. In this presentation, I will first present some element of context for this question. I will then focus on the case where $\mathcal{F}$ is allowed to be infinite, providing sufficient conditions on $\mathcal{F}$ for the subshift to be non-empty and for its topological entropy to be computable.

Reasoning about (Negative) Trust under Uncertainty

Francesca Doneda(iD), Francesco A. Genco(iD)
and Giuseppe Primiero(iD)

Logic, Uncertainty, Computation and Information Lab,
Department of Philosophy, University of Milan, Italy
{francesca.doneda,francesco.genco,giuseppe.primiero}
@unimi.it

Abstract. The notion of trust is a major player in many epistemic and computational contexts. It appears especially relevant in all those situations where verification or evaluation of knowledge is missing, not reachable or non-existent, and agents must rely on information received by others. This includes cases where expert knowers may not yet be able to ground their claims, and the public has to build an opinion by considering the dynamic of the information exchange. Formal logic approaches to this aim have been increasingly important and diverse in the last decades. Recently, the notion of negative trust has been formalized in terms of a proof theory and semantics [1]: this approach distinguishes between distrust, as the epistemic act of rejecting incoming contradictory information considered unreliable; and mistrust, as the epistemic act of updating one's own information state by removing previously held data in order to accommodate newly received information. A natural and important extension of such multi-agent contexts is where epistemic acts are performed under uncertainty, at several levels: the claims of the agents may be graded; information may reach agents with a certain degree of probability; and the degree of acceptance or rejection of the information received may not be binary. In this talk we present a logic of negative trust applied to uncertain judgements. We offer a proof theory and a relational semantics for which soundness and completeness results hold. Applications will focus on developing a ranking algorithm for trustworthiness evaluation under uncertainty, expanding on work presented in [2].

Keywords: Trust · Distrust · Mistrust · Trustworthiness · Uncertainty

References

1. G. Primiero, A logic of negative trust. J. Appl. Non Class. Logics **30**(3), 193–222 (2020)
2. G. Primiero, D. Ceolin, F. Doneda, A computational model for assessing experts' trustworthiness. J. Exp. Theor. Artif. Intell. https://doi.org/10.1080/0952813X.2023.2183272

Quantum Computating from Reversible Classical Computing

Chris Heunen

University of Edinburgh
chris.heunen@ed.ac.uk

Abstract. Quantum computations have two ingredients: unitary gates forming reversible circuits, and irreversible measurements. The theory of quantum computation is at heart therefore about how these ingredients combine. We will discuss two universal constructions modelling these ingredients in terms of rig categories. Together they give a semantics that is sound, complete, computationally universal, fully equational, and conceptually satisfying. (Based on joint work with Pablo Andres-Martinez, Jacques Carette, Robin Kaarsgaard, Neil Julien Ross, and Amr Sabry.)

Keywords: Quantum computing · Reversible computing · Semantics · Rig categories

References

1. Heunen, C., Kaarsgaard, R.: Quantum information effects. ACM Princ. Program. Lang. **6**, 1–27 (2022)
2. Carette, J., Heunen, C., Kaarsgaard, R., Sabry, A.: With a few square roots, quantum computing is as easy as Pi. ACM Princ. Program. Lang. **8**, 546–574 (2024)
3. Andres-Martinez, P., Heunen, C., Kaarsgaard, R.: Universal properties of partial quantum maps. In: Quantum Physics and Logic, Electronic Proceedings in Theoretical Computer Science, vol. 394, pp. 192–207 (2023)
4. Carette, J., Heunen, C., Kaarsgaard, R., Sabry, A.: The quantum effect: a recipe for Quantum Pi. arxiv:2302.01885 (2023)

Complexity of Well-Ordered Sets in an Ordered Abelian Group

Chris Hall[1], Julia Knight[2] and Karen Lange[3] (iD)

[1] Western University, London, ON, N6A 3K7, Canada
chall69@uwo.ca
[2] University of Notre Dame, Notre Dame, IN, 46556, USA
jlknight@nd.edu
[2] Wellesley College, Wellesley, MA, 02481, USA
karen.lange@wellesley.edu

We study the complexity of determining whether a well-ordered subset of an ordered abelian group has order type at least α. We focus on well-ordered subsets of ordered groups that arise naturally from the group operation, specifically the set of sums $A+B$ of two well ordered subsets A and B of a group G and the set of finite sums $[C]$ of elements from a well-ordered subset C of $G^{\geq 0}$. We measure complexity in the Borel and effective Borel hierarchies. Since the class of well orderings (and related classes) are not Borel, our results use Calvert's notions of complexity and completeness *within*. This work is joint with Chris Hall and Julia Knight.

Contents

Invited Papers

If CiE Did Not Exist, It Would Be Necessary to Invent It *

S. Barry Cooper(✉)

School of Mathematics, University of Leeds,, Leeds LS2 9JT, UK
pmt6sbc@leeds.ac.uk
http://www.maths.leeds.ac.uk/pmt6sbc

As it happens, "Computability in Europe" *was* invented, just over two years ago, and in a short time has grown beyond all expectations. But even though the surprise of finding together so many researchers into different aspects of computability has not worn off, **CiE** does represent a strand of scientific endeavour going back to the earliest times. Even before Euclid of Alexandria devised his algorithm for finding the greatest common divisor of two integers, human survival depended on the identification of *algorithmic content* in the everyday world. What distinguished Euclid, and successors like Newton, Leibniz, Frege, Peano, Babbage, Russell, Hilbert, Gödel and Turing, is the reaching for control over that content through theory and abstraction. Perhaps Albert Einstein had something like this in mind in 1950 when he wrote (p. 54 of *Out of My Later Years*, Philosophical Library, New York):

> "When we say that we understand a group of natural phenomena, we mean that we have found a constructive theory which embraces them."

What is peculiarly contemporary about **CiE** is the scrutiny it brings to bear on the *quest* for algorithmic content, something that was not possible before Turing and his fellow 1930s pioneers in the area.

Through the work of computability theorists, the search for algorithmic content goes beyond the ad hoc, and develops into an activity guided by an expanded *consciousness* of what we are doing. We can now explain why certain basic problems are harder than others. We can use our knowledge of logical structure and language to devise more efficient computer programs. We can relate the structures of computability theory to real-world situations, and find models which aid prediction, or make problems in making predictions mathematically explicit. And, the hope is, we can get enough insight into how physical systems 'compute' to ease us past the computational barriers our theory has brought to our notice. The questions surrounding 'New Computational Paradigms' are indeed fundamental ones. Answers, as so often in the past, will depend on the sort of mix of the practical and the theoretical that Alan Turing, if he were still with us, would have recognised, and found fascinating.

In current terminology, the scientific approach of **CiE** is interdisciplinary, approaching real-world problems from different perspectives and using diverse

---

* With Apologies to Voltaire.

© The Author(s), under exclusive license to Springer Nature Switzerland AG 2024
L. Levy Patey et al. (Eds.): CiE 2024, LNCS 14773, pp. 3–9, 2024.
https://doi.org/10.1007/978-3-031-64309-5_1

techniques. **CiE** seeks to bridge the theoretical divide between mathematics and computer science, and between computability theory and science, which are traceable back almost to the birth of computability theory in the mid-1930 s. Of course, the natural scientist of the Enlightenment would have had no problem with the so-called interdisciplinarity of **CiE**. It is only since the sixteenth and seventeenth centuries that scientific specialisms have solidified into exclusive disciplines, regulated by senior figures whose role it is to perseverate the assumptions and conventions of their areas, complete with their own technical priorities.

Even 'new paradigms' constitutes a project started by Turing — the natural scientist par excellence, at least to the computability theorist. On the one hand, the yawning gap between computation and the real-world played a key role in both his scientific and personal lives, just as it now dominates the work of **CiE**. This was a gap he was ever, both practically and conceptually, seeking to bridge, and many of his ideas anticipate current research. On the other hand, this was a preoccupation which took him — and now promises to take us — beyond the safe confines of what Thomas Kuhn calls 'normal science'. Here is how Kuhn describes normal science in his influential book *The Structure of Scientific Revolutions* (pp. 162–164 of the Third Edition, The University of Chicago Press, 1996):

> "Normally, the members of a mature scientific community work from a single paradigm or from a closely related set. ...once the reception of a common paradigm has freed the scientific community from the need constantly to re-examine its first principles, the members of that community can concentrate exclusively upon the subtlest and most esoteric of the phenomena that concern it. Inevitably, that does increase both the effectiveness and the efficiency with which the group as a whole solves new problems."

What has become problematic in many areas of science and the humanities is dealing with globally determined phenomena. Everywhere, we see nonlinear development, breakdown in inductive and predictive structures, computer simulation replacing mathematical solutions, and the puzzle of emergence of new relations in the midst of turbulence. We also see the ad hoc development of particular solutions to everyday problems which seem to challenge existing conceptual frameworks. And we have quite basic obstacles to raising the capabilities of present-day computers to the needs of the working scientist. All this is reflected in the wide variety of theoretical directions to be found within **CiE**. The aim is to bring a new understanding to existing developments, and to establish the sort of consciousness of computational issues upon which exciting new practical innovations can be based.

However, the reader coming to this volume for the weird and wonderful from today's scientific fringe will be disappointed. There are indeed contributions which acknowledge the extent to which the Turing machine paradigm is already shifting — see, for instance, Dina Goldin and Peter Wegner on *The Church-Turing Thesis: Breaking the Myth* — but this tends to be work which has gone through a long period of gestation, and received a measure of acceptance and respect within the computer science community. Here is how one of our reviewers of Goldin and Wegner's article described the situation:

"Fifty years ago the Turing Thesis was OK, now it is still OK provided we know to what computational scenario it should be related. If we are changing the scenario (as the practice of computing prompts us), we have to update the notion of a Turing machine (or of any other fundamental model of computation) as well - that's all."

Of course, that may be 'all'. But extracting useful models from new computational situations, or — to approach things more theoretically — to develop new abstractions and make innovative real-world connections, is the essence of the challenge. So we also see here papers dealing with more overtly mathematical extensions of the standard Turing model of computation, such as infinite time Turing machines — see Joel Hamkins on *Infinitary computability with infinite time Turing machines*, and the paper of Philip Welch — and, at the other extreme, a number of contributions dealing with natural computation. Membrane computing is represented by Gheorghe Păun (a seminal figure in this area), Marian Gheorghe et al., and Shankara Narayanan Krishna, and we have Paola Bonizzoni, Felice, and Mauri on DNA computing, and Natalio Krasnogor (with Gheorghe again, and others) on computational modelling of the important microbiological phenomenon of 'quorum sensing'. The resurgent topic of analog computers is touched on by Jérôme Durand-Lose, Giuseppe Trautteur (on *Beyond the Super-Turing Snare: Analog Computation and Virtual Digitality*) and Jeffery Zucker with John Tucker, and neural networks, another area with a long history, is represented by Angelo Cangelosi, and Krzysztof Michalak with Halina Kwasnicka. And, of course, quantum computation is a key topic at **CiE 2005** (where from Harry Buhrman we get just a taster from his talks). New paradigms of computation come in all shapes and sizes, and the growth of quantum computing reminds us that even quite modest improvements (theoretically speaking) in computing efficiency promise big changes in the world we live in.

Although a number of people associated **CiE** are involved with these different areas, most of us do not actually set out to *do* quantum computing, membrane computing, neural networks, evolutionary computation, and so on. The agenda is not so piecemeal. This is not computational tourism, the Readers Digest Condensed Books version, with the grown-ups head for the real thing — WCIT, CINC, CEC, and other myriad specialist meetings. The intervention of **CiE** is aimed at using logical and mathematical methods to reveal underlying structures and unities, to develop general frameworks and conceptual aids — to build the sort of theoretical and practical synergies which gave Turing and von Neumann such a key role in the early days of the first computing revolution. For example, one can recognise within most of the existing proposals for new computational paradigms a high degree of interactivity, as is picked up on in Goldin and Wegner's paper. One aspect of this is the importance now given to connectionist models of computation, anticipated by Turing himself in his discussion of 'unorganised machines' in his 1948 National Physical Laboratory Report *Intelligent* *machinery.* In 1988 Paul Smolensky observed in his influential *Behavioral and Brain Sciences* paper *On the proper treatment of connectionism* (p. 3) that:

> "There is a reasonable chance that connectionist models will lead to the development of new somewhat-general-purpose self-programming, massively parallel analog computers, and a new theory of analog parallel computation: they may possibly even challenge the strong construal of Church's Thesis as the claim that the class of well-defined computations is exhausted by those of Turing machines."

This kind of challenge is being met on a number of levels. On the one hand one has the work on neural networks and logic reported on by Artur Garcez in this volume, while on the other one has models based on computational reducibilities (such as that derived from Turing's oracle machines), which promises a new relevance to the sort of classical computability featuring in the contributions from Finkel, Harris, Kalimullin, Lewis, Angsheng Li, Selivanov, Soskov, Alexandra Soskova, and Terwijn (describing an interesting application of the Medvedev lattice). As our anonymous reviewer pointed out above, "Fifty years ago the Turing Thesis was OK, now it is still OK provided we know to what computational scenario it should be related." The world has not lost its algorithmic content, but there is needed a fundamental process of readjustment to new realities, involving full use of our powers of theoretical deconstruction of computationally complex environments. Relevant here is the paper of Udi Boker and Nachum Dershowitz. As one of our reviewers commented: "The subject of this paper is very central to the topic of the conference: How can we compare the computational power of different computational paradigms?". As already suggested, we can think of **CiE** as *computation with consciousness*, in the sense that there is a relatively high level of detachment and abstraction involved. Wonderful things can be achieved without consciousness. Bert Hölldobler and Edward O. Wilson's book on *The Ants* runs to over eight-hundred pages, and ants and similar biological examples have inspired new problem-solving strategies based on 'swarm intelligence'. But the limits to what a real-life ant colony can achieve are more apparent than those of more obviously conscious beings. As the constructors move in and tarmac over our richly structured ant colony, the ants have no hope of expanding their expertise to deal with such eventualities. For us algorithmic content gives rise to new emergent forms, which themselves become victim to our algorithmic appetites, and even the inevitable limits on this inductive process we hope to decode. Maybe it is going *too* far to think of **CiE** as the conscious and interventionist observers of the ant-like activities of our more ad hoc computational colleagues! But any sceptics might remember how Turing himself put even this aspect of the computational process under the mathematical microscope. When Turing says in his 1939 paper:

> "Mathematical reasoning may be regarded ...as the exercise of a combination of ...*intuition* and *ingenuity*. ...In pre-Gödel times it was thought by some that all the intuitive judgements of mathematics could be replaced by a finite number of ...rules. The necessity for intuition would then be

entirely eliminated. In our discussions, however, we have gone to the opposite extreme and eliminated not intuition but ingenuity, ..."

he is talking about what happens when one persistently transcends a particular context by iterating an overview, such as that of Gödel for first-order
Peano arithmetic. We can trace back to this paper the genesis of powerful proof-
theoretic methods which have both benefitted from, and fed back into, computability theoretic perspectives. One tends to think of computability as being
a language- independent notion, but the need to describe what is going on computationally reasserts the human dimension, and leads us to appropriate proof
theoretic hierarchies. This direction is represented here by *Proofs and Computation* Special Sessions contributors Ulrich Berger, Coquand, and Wainer (with
Geoff Ostrin), and by proof mining expert Ulrich Kohlenbach.

An important recent development has been the growth of proof complexity since the appearance of Sam Buss' thesis on *Bounded Arithmetic* back in
1985, showing that basic complexity classes could be allied with levels of relatively easily described proof theoretic hierarchies. And if ever there was an
area in need of new paradigms, it is computational complexity. There are, of
course, deep and intractable problems, basic to how we compute in the future,
for which no one seems to be able to even get close to a solution. The appearance of Yuri Matiyasevich and Yiannis Moschovakis (with the intriguing title
Recursion and complexity) on our list of authors reminds us of similarly basic
computational issues arising from traditional logical frameworks. Contributions
from Barra and Kristiansen, Ricardo Gavaldá (on computational learning theory), Gibson and Woods, Kristiansen again, Jack Lutz (on *The Dimension of
a Point: Computability Meets Fractal Geometry*), Peter Bro Miltersen, Victor
Mitrana et al., Pheidas and Vidaux, and Jacobo Torán give just an indication
of the great variety of output to be encountered.

Also to be found here are articles and abstracts dealing with real computation — another key topic at **CiE 2005** — an implicit acknowledgement of
gap between how the working scientist describes the universe in terms of real
numbers, and the way in which present-day computers are constrained to work
with discrete data. Richard Feynman may have commented, characteristically
provocative as ever, in a 1982 article on *Simulating physics with computers* in
the *International Journal of Theoretical Physics*:

"It is really true, somehow, that the physical world is representable in a
discretized way, and ...we are going to have to change the laws of physics."

But the practical realities which faced Feynman the scientist in dealing with
continuous mathematical models of physical systems have not changed. This area
also sees a variety of theoretical approaches to the practical problems involved,
some easily located within the familiar framework of what has been known as
recursive analysis, and others much more immediately geared to applications. At
the more applied end of the spectrum we have Edalat-Khanban-Lieutier, Amin
Farjudian, Lieutier, Pattinson, and Ning Zhong. More mathematical approaches,
including work on computable and c.e. reals, etc., show up in nice contributions

from George Barmpalias, Klaus Meer, Guohua Wu, Zheng Xizhong and Martin Ziegler. Korovina and Kudinov take us in the direction of computability over higher type continuous data, connecting up with more general and set theoretical work, such as that of Peter Kœpke, and Alexey Stukachev.

Amongst other important computational notions not yet mentioned are computable models (Hirschfeldt, Morozov), randomness (Reimann), reverse mathematics (Joseph Berger), and other riches too many to itemise in detail.

In the end, the overall impression is one of *normal science at its best* — in its particularities inventive, relevant and soundly based, but a confluence of perspectives exceeding the sum of its parts. This is the essence of most paradigm shifts in history. In retrospect we may recognise a particular 'eureka' moment, but closer inspection often reveals revolutionary new ideas *emerging* out of a number of contributory and seemingly unrelated developments. Only when the picture is focused and comprehensive enough one can one clearly distinguish both its failings and potentialities. As Kuhn says (p. 92):

> "...scientific revolutions are inaugurated by a growing sense, ...often restricted to a narrow subdivision of the scientific community, that an existing paradigm has ceased to function adequately in the exploration of an aspect of nature to which that paradigm itself had previously led the way."

Paradigm shifts are not easily come by. Their underlying ideas must be connected, justified, validated, formed in to a persuasive whole, through the detailed and selfless work of many people. Some of this work may be anticipatory, brave, but wrong, and in putting together this volume the editors have been all too aware of this. In particular cases, we have preferred to err on the side of caution. Again, this is a usual feature of paradigm shifts, and we hope our readers (and contributors) will understand this. We do believe **CiE** to provide a home for those exploring the developing real-world relevance of computability and complexity, and we hope this volume is a first sign of what we can achieve as a more coherent scientific community.

It is appropriate to give Thomas Kuhn the (almost) final word (pp. 167–168):

> "The very existence of science depends upon investing the power to choose between paradigms in the members of a special kind of community. Just how special that community must be if science is to survive and grow may be indicated by the very tenuousness of humanity's hold on the scientific enterprise. Every civilization of which we have records has possessed a technology, an art, a religion, a political system, laws, and so on. In many cases those facets of civilization have been as developed as our own. But only the civilizations that descend from Hellenic Greece have possessed more than the most rudimentary science. The bulk of scientific knowledge is a

product of Europe in the last four centuries. No other place and time has supported the very special communities from which scientific productivity comes."

Even if Europe is now but one part of an interconnecting global scientific community, computability continues to be an area in which the European contribution is something quite special.

Some Open Questions and Recent Results on Computable Banach Spaces

Rod Downey[1($\boxtimes$)], Noam Greenberg[1], and Long Qian[2]

[1] School of Mathematics and Statistics and Operations Research, Victoria University, P. O. Box 600, Wellington, New Zealand
{rod.downey,Noam.greenberg}@vuw.ac.nz
[2] Department of Mathematical Sciences, Carnegie Mellon University, Pittsburgh, USA
longq@andrew.cmu.edu

Abstract. We discuss some open questions and results in the geometry of computable Banach spaces.

1 Introduction

1.1 Banach Spaces

Recall that a normed vector space has associated with it a distance $d(x,y) = \|x - y\|$. If this is a complete metric space, it is called a Banach space. Banach spaces are fundamental to the field of functional analysis, and have extensive applications. The modern theory of computable Banach spaces likely began with the work of Pour-El and Richards [PER83] who showed how the effective theory gave insight into issues from classical physics. Brattka [Bra16] looked at the effective content of basic results from the area including the Open Mapping Theorem, the Closed Graph Theorem, and the Banach-Steinhaus Theorem, and Brattka [Bra16] and earlier Metakides-Nerode-Shore [MNS85] and others studied the important Hahn-Banach Theorem's computable content.

In this paper we will highlight some recent work concerning the algorithmic content of work around the geometry of Banach spaces, specifically those associated with bases, and decompositions.

We remark that the questions provide a fascinating "logician's eye view" of classical constructions, in that it seems that *all* of the classical constructions are insufficient to answer some of the basic questions such as the complexity of finding a Schauder basis.

1.2 Computable Banach Spaces

Going back to Turing, the fundamental concept of computable analysis is that of a computable real number r, which is one for which there is a computable

Dedicated to the memory of Barry Cooper. Research supported by the Marsden Fund of New Zealand, and based on Downey's Cooper Prize Lecture.

sequence of rationals (q_i) such that $|r - q_i| < 2^{-i}$. That is, there is a computable *fast Cauchy sequence* with limit r. Such a sequence is also known as a *Cauchy name* of r. The reader unfamiliar with modern computable analysis, might guess that a computable function on the reals is one effectively taking computable reals to computable reals, and this was Turing's [Tur36] intuition, but the modern "type 2" definition of a computable function on the reals, is one that acts effectively on *all* reals: it is a function $f: \mathbb{R} \to \mathbb{R}$, induced by a computable functional acting on fast Cauchy sequences, taking any Cauchy name of a real r and producing a Cauchy name of $f(r)$. Note that this definition means that all computable functions on the reals must be continuous, and, indeed, g is continuous iff it is computable relative to some oracle.

The notion of a *computable metric space* is a natural generalization of this approach. This is a complete metric space (X, d), equipped with a sequence of points (q_i), dense in X, restricted to which the metric is computable: that is, the reals $d(q_i, q_j)$ are computable, uniformly given i and j. Using the points (q_i) as analogs of the rational numbers, we can similarly define Cauchy names of points of X, and computable functions between computable metric spaces. Using this notion of computability, we can now define:

Definition 1. *A* computable Banach space *is a computable metric space equipped with a compatible, computable normed vector space structure. That is, addition, scalar multiplication, and the norm, are all computable functions.*

1.3 Generalized Computable Banach Spaces

One of the guiding principles in the study of effective (computable) structure theory is that most *natural* structures studied in classical mathematics have natural computable presentations. Here "natural" is vaguely defined, but we mean structures arising in, for example, applied mathematics or physics.

This is true for many Banach spaces. For example, Hilbert spaces have computable representations. Other examples include the spaces ℓ_n^p and ℓ^p for computable $p \geq 1$ ($\mathbb{R}^n$ equipped with the p-norm, and the space of p-summable infinite sequences of reals); more generally, $L^p(\Omega)$ spaces for a variety of measure spaces Ω; the space c_0 of infinite sequences of reals converging to 0; the space $C[0, 1]$ of continuous functions from the unit interval to $\mathbb{R}$ (equipped with the supremum norm; here as analogs of the rational numbers we can take a suitable sequence of polynomials). There are many other examples.

However, some very natural Banach spaces are missing from this list, starting with the space ℓ^∞ of bounded sequences of reals, equipped with the supremum norm. The problem is that this space is not *separable*, so even the underlying metric space cannot be given a computable structure, using the definition above. In some sense this does point at a deficiency in the definition, in that ℓ^∞ is surely a "natural" space. Researchers in computable analysis have defined more general representations of computable spaces (see Weihrauch [Wei00]). However, all continuous representations are necessarily restricted to separable spaces. Indeed,

Brattka [Bra16, Prop.:15.3] observed that there is no representation of ℓ^∞ providing the expected notion of computable points, and for which vector addition is computable. Brattka proposed to omit the norm, and rather, concentrate on convergence. He defined the notion of a *general computable normed space*, which is a represented space in which the operation taking (names of) fast converging Cauchy sequences to (a name of) the limit of the sequence, is a computable function on names. The natural representation of ℓ^∞ is a general computable normed space.

The reason this notion is particularly interesting is that the theory of Banach spaces is replete with results involving the *dual* space. If B is a computable and hence separable Banach space, then its dual is not necessarily separable, but as Brattka [Bra16] showed, it is always a general computable Banach space. The non-computability of the dual space is a great impediment to the development of theory of computable Banach spaces. It means that alternative methods must be found to replace classical arguments using the dual, as we will see, for instance, in the proof of Theorem 8.

We remark that sometimes, the dual space is computable, such as in the finite dimensional case, and more generally, when the space has a well-behaved basis. We will discuss bases in Sect. 3 below. We mention here that Brattka and Dillhage [BD07] have a number of results when a space has a nice computable basis ("shrinking" for instance; see [BD07, Cor.:5.9]). We believe that this area is rife with interesting questions.

Question 1. Suppose that B is a computable Banach space. Under what circumstances is the dual of B computable? Suppose that X is a general computable Banach space. Under what circumstances is it isomorphic to the dual of a computable Banach space? More generally, develop the theory of general computable Banach spaces.

We also remark that while the norm of a dual space may not be computable, the dual of a computable Banach space has a natural representation in which the norm of an element is (uniformly) left-c.e. in the name. This is because the unit sphere of a computable Banach space is a computable closed (located) set. It may be interesting to investigate this as an alternative or an added requirement to general computable spaces.

2   Some Classical Effectivity Results

Some of the best known results in computable Banach space theory are due to Pour-El and Richards e.g. [PER83,PER89]. One of the classic results was to effectivize the classical theorem that an operator on a Banach space is continuous iff it is bounded.

Theorem 1 (Pour-El and Richards [PER83]). *Let X, Y be computable Banach spaces, and (e_i) be a computable sequence in X whose linear span is dense. Let $T : X \to Y$ be a linear operator with closed graph whose domain* *contains* $\{e_i\}$ *and such that the sequence* $(T(e_i))$ *is computable in* Y. *Then* T *maps every computable element of its domain onto a computable element of* Y *if and only if* T *is bounded.*

Theorem 1 has many applications. For example, it shows that the indefinite integral of a computable function $f \in C[a, b]$ is computable. It also can be used to give a proof of a Theorem of Myhill that there exists computable functions in $C[a, b]$ which have continuous derivatives, but whose derivatives are not computable.

From the point of computable structure theory, being an analytic structure defined via a computable dense sequence means that we can code up the structures via countable (computable) information, and hence the usual methods and questions from computable structure theory (such as e.g. Ash-Knight [AK00]) apply. Indeed, this is the thesis of a recent book [DMNar], which gives a unified view of computable structure theory, both countable and analytic.

For example, now we can think of computable Banach spaces as c.e. sets and hence associate indices to the structures. We can then look at, for example, the complexity of isomorphism and classification. Whilst this is not the main business of the present paper, we mention some recent results of this ilk.

As well as Banach spaces, computable metric spaces, computable locally compact topological groups, and the like, have been investigated. For example, Melnikov and Nies [MN13] showed that *compact* computable metric spaces could be classified by a Π_3^0 effective formula and all were Δ_3^0 categorical, and hence were relatively simple to classify logically, whereas Nies and Solecki [NS15] proved that the characterisation problem for computable *locally* compact metric spaces is Π_1^1-complete, meaning that it is as hard as *any* isomorphism problem for countable structures. Associated results are reported in the survey [DM20].

Various families of Banach spaces have been studied in this way. For example, computable Lebesgue spaces have a Π_3^0 characterization [BMM], and $C[0, 1]$ also has an arithmetical characterization [FHD+20]. The general classification problem is hard.

Theorem 2 (Downey and Melnikov [DM23]). *The isomorphism problem for computable Banach spaces is* Σ_1^1-*complete.*

Proof (sketch). The upper bound is Σ_1^1 since it is sufficient to state that there is an isometry that works for special points, maps zero to zero, and is, furthermore, surjective (these properties are closed). The well-known Mazur-Ulam theorem asserts that every isometry with these properties has to be linear. Completeness follows from the Σ_1^1-completeness for Boolean algebras, as follows. First, uniformly produce the computably compact Stone space $\widehat{B}$ of a given Boolean algebra B, and then consider $C(\widehat{B}; \mathbb{R})$ whose computable Banach space structure can be produced uniformly effectively [BHTM21] from the compact presentation of the space. It is well-known that the homeomorphism type of the compact domain determines the linear isomorphism type of the resulting space, and vice versa (this is Banach-Stone duality). This gives the Σ_1^1-completeness. $\square$

14   R. Downey et al.

We remark that Ferenczi, Louveau and Rosendal [FLR09] showed a similar result in the context of Borel equivalence relations. Their construction is direct.

Question 2 (Melnikov). For each n, is there Δ^0_{n+1}-categorical but not Δ^0_n-categorical Banach space? Same for Polish groups.

A somewhat related question concerns the (Anderson-)Kadets (Kadec) Theorem [Kad66] which states that *any two infinite dimensional separable Banach spaces are homeomorphic as* topological *spaces, and hence homeomorphic to* $\mathbb{R}^{\mathbb{N}}$. The result is also true for a more general class called Fréchet spaces.

Question 3. Is Kadets' Theorem true effectively?

The published proofs all involve complex methods involving duality and the effectivity is by no means clear.

3   The Geometry of Computable Banach Spaces

We turn to the main concern of this paper. The theory of finite dimensional vector spaces revolves around the notion of a basis, specifically a *Hamel basis* where every element is a *finite* linear combination of basis elements. In Banach spaces, the picture is again murky. If B is an infinite dimensional Banach space then every Hamel basis must be uncountable. But spaces like ℓ^p are in some sense coded by countable information. One of the main basis notions for Banach spaces is the following.

Definition 2 (Schauder [Sch28]). *Let X be a Banach space. A sequence $(x_i)_{i\in\mathbb{N}} \in X^{\mathbb{N}}$ is a Schauder basis of X if for all $x \in X$, there is a unique sequence of coefficients $(a_i)_{i\in\mathbb{N}} \in \mathbb{R}^{\mathbb{N}}$ such that*

$$\sum_{i=1}^{\infty} a_i x_i = x$$

A sequence that is the Schauder basis of the closure of its linear span is called a basic sequence.

We emphasise that a Schauder basis is a *sequence* so that order counts. The standard unit vectors for ℓ^p give a Schauder basis as is every orthonormal basis of a Hilbert space. Haar [Haa10] gave a Schauder basis for $L^p(0,1)$ for $1 \le p < \infty$.

Note that every Banach space with a basis must be separable, and in his famous book [Ban32], Banach asked if every separable Banach space has a Schauder basis. There was a huge effort towards solving the basis problem. As a part of the effort, many important properties regarding the geometry of Banach spaces were identified; especially those that were implied by the existence of a Schauder basis. In this paper we will look at some of these concepts and questions of effectivity concerning these geometric considerations.

It was only after 40 years that Banach's question was solved by Per Enflo [Enf73], and he did this by showing that there was a Banach space without something called *the approximation property* (Definition 6), which is a consequence of having Schauder basis. In his PhD Thesis, Bosserhof proved that Enflo's example can be made computable.

Theorem 3 (Bosserhof [Bos08]). *There is a computable copy of Enflo's example, and hence there is a computable Banach space without the approximation property and hence without a Schauder basis.*

Our fundamental question is the following:

Question 4. What is the complexity of having a basis? Specifically, what is the complexity of the index set of computable Banach spaces that have a basis?

To establish an upper bound on this complexity, we need the following fundamental fact about Schauder bases.

Lemma 1 (Banach e.g. in [Ban32]). *Let X be a Banach space and $(x_i)_{i\in\mathbb{N}} \subseteq X$ a sequence of nonzero elements. Then (x_i) is a basis of X if and only if:*

1. *There is a constant $K \in \mathbb{R}$ such that for all $n, m \in \mathbb{N}$ with $m < n$, for all sequences of scalars $(a_i)_{i\in\mathbb{N}}$, we have*

$$\left\|\sum_{i=1}^{m} a_i x_i\right\| \leqslant K \left\|\sum_{i=1}^{n} a_i x_i\right\|$$

2. *The finite linear span of $(x_i)_{i\in\mathbb{N}}$ is dense in X.*

The proof of the harder direction of Lemma 1 consists of considering the projections $\{S_i\}_{i\in\mathbb{N}}$ associated with the basis (x_i), defined by $S_k\left(\sum_{i=0}^{\infty} \alpha_i x_i\right) = \sum_{i=0}^{k} \alpha_i x_i$. Then (1) is equivalent to requiring the value $\sup_i \|S_i\|$ to be finite. To show the lemma, define the alternate norm $\|\cdot\|_b$ on X by $\left\|\sum_{i=0}^{\infty} \alpha_i x_i\right\|_b = \sup_n \left\|\sum_{i=0}^{n} \alpha_i x_i\right\|$. Note that this is well-defined as $\left(\sum_{i=0}^{n} \alpha_i x_i\right)_n \to \sum_{i=0}^{\infty} \alpha_i x_i$, so $\|\cdot\|_b$ is finite on any $v \in X$. Furthermore, $\|\cdot\|_b$ is indeed a norm on X, and $\|v\| \leq \|v\|_b$ for all $v \in X$. In fact, it is not hard to show that $(X, \|\cdot\|_b)$ is complete as well. An application of the open mapping theorem then proves that the norms $\|\cdot\|, \|\cdot\|_b$ are equivalent. Lemma 1 leads to the following fundamental concept.

Definition 3. *Let X be a Banach space and $(x_i)_{i\in\mathbb{N}}$ be a basis of X, and $\{S_i\}_{i\in\mathbb{N}}$ its associated sequence of projections. The* basis constant *of (x_i), denoted as $bc\left((x_i)\right)$, is the value $\sup_i \|S_i\|$. Note that $bc\left((x_i)\right)$ is equivalent to the infimum of all K that satisfies the requirements of Lemma 1. The basis constant of the space X, denoted $bc(X)$, is the infimum of basis constants across all of its bases. We set $bc(X) = \infty$ if X has no basis.*

The reader unfamiliar with Banach spaces might think that, like Hilbert spaces, there is always a Schauder basis with constant 1 if there is a basis. Such a basis is called *monotone*. Unfortunately, Szarek [Sza83] showed that there is a *finite* dimensional space which does *not* has a basis with basis constant 1, and in fact, there are finite-dimensional spaces with arbitrarily large basis constant. Recently, Ruofei Xie proved that Szarek's [Sza87] construction can be made effective.

Theorem 4 (Xie [Xie24]). *For each k, for sufficiently large n, there is a computable norm on $\mathbb{R}^n$ whose associated basis constant is greater than k.*

For finite dimensional spaces things are somewhat nice:

Lemma 2 (Bosserhof [Bos08]). *Let X be a computable Banach space, and $\{x_0, \ldots, x_n\}$ be a computable sequence of independent points. Then $bc(x_0, \ldots, x_n)$ is computable, uniformly in $\{x_0, \ldots, x_n\}$.*

Proof. Let $[x_0, \ldots, x_n]$ denote the space spanned by the points. Since the basis constant is the maximum of the norms of the associated projections, it suffices to observe that given an operator on a finite-dimensional computable Banach space, we can compute its norm. To do this, we use the fact that the unit ball of a finite-dimensional Banach space is compact, and if the space is computable, then the unit ball is computably compact. The maximum of a real-valued function on a computably compact set is computable, uniformly.   □

The following improves an earlier result of Bosserhof [Bos08] who observed that basis constants of finite dimensional spaces are right c.e.

Lemma 3. *Let X be a computable Banach space, and $\{x_0, \ldots, x_n\}$ be a computable sequence of linearly independent points. Then $bc([x_0, \ldots, x_n])$ is computable. Furthermore, this is uniform in $\{x_0, \ldots, x_n\}$.*

Note that here we are computing the basis constant of the space, not of the particular basis.

Proof. Denote $D = [x_0, \ldots, x_n]$, and let $(v_i)_{i \leq n}$ be an arbitrary sequence of elements in D. By definition, we may write $v_i = \sum_{j=0}^{n} \alpha_{i,j} x_j$, so the sequence $(v_i)_{i \leq n}$ is uniquely characterised by the sequences of coefficients

$$\alpha_{0,0}, \alpha_{0,1}, \ldots, \alpha_{0,n}, \alpha_{1,0}, \ldots, \alpha_{n,0}, \ldots, \alpha_{n,n}$$

Furthermore, as scalar scaling preserves the basis constant of $(v_i)_{i \leq n}$, we can assume without loss of generality that $\sum_{i=0}^{n} \sum_{j=0}^{n} |\alpha_{i,j}| = 1$. Consider the natural mapping $f : (\mathbb{R}^{n \times n}, \|\cdot\|_1) \to D^n$ given by $f((\alpha_{i,j})_{i,j \leq n}) = \left(\sum_{j=0}^{n} \alpha_{i,j} x_j \right)_i$. Under this mapping, we can naturally regard each basis of D as an element in the image. Therefore, the basis constant of D is equivalent to the minimum of basis constants on f's image. Now note that $\sum_{i=0}^{n} \sum_{j=0}^{n} |\alpha_{i,j}| = 1$ is an effectively compact subset of $(\mathbb{R}^{n \times n}, \|\cdot\|_1)$ and that f is a computable mapping. As with maxima, the minimum of a real-valued computable function on a computably compact set is computable.   □

The proof of Lemma 1 combined with 3 shows that if I give you a computable Schauder basis of a Banach space, then we can approximate the basis constant via the sequence of finite dimensional projections, and hence have the following.

Lemma 4. *Let X be a computable Banach space and $(x_i)_{i\in\mathbb{N}}$ a computable basis of X; then $bc((x_i))$ is a left-c.e. real.*

This result has an easy converse.

Theorem 5. *For any $\alpha \in \mathbb{R}$ that is left-c.e and $\alpha \geq 1$, there is Banach space X with basis $(e_i)_{i\in\mathbb{N}}$ such that $bc((e_i)_{i\in\mathbb{N}}) = \alpha$.*

Proof. In fact, we will show that it is sufficient to have $X = c_0$. Let $(e_i)_{i\in\mathbb{N}}$ denote the standard basis, the idea is to replace blocks of $\{e_i, e_{i+1}\}$ by $\{e_i + e_{i+1}, e_i + \beta_i e_{i+1}\}$, where β_i is some parameter in $\mathbb{Q}$. And since $bc(e_i + e_{i+1}, e_i + \beta_i e_{i+1})$ is simply a computable function continuous in β_i, we can choose β_i so that $bc(e_i + e_{i+1}, e_i + \beta_i e_{i+1}) = \alpha_i$, where (α_i) is a computable sequence of rationals increasing to α. Since the blocks are disjoint, the basis constants of the prefixes of the modified basis will form the sequence $\{\alpha_0, \alpha_1, \ldots\}$. □

It is also possible to use a coding argument to show that if a computable Banach space X has a basis of Turing degree $\mathbf{a}$ then it has one of every degree $\geq \mathbf{a}$. Roughly speaking we can prove this by showing that a Schauder basis can be replaced by one using the ideal points defining the underlying computable metric space structure.

Question 5. Let X be a computable Banach space with basis. What is the complexity of $bc(X)$? What if X has a computable basis?

Theorem 6 (Bosserhof [Bos08]). *There is a computable Banach space with a Schauder basis, but no computable Schauder basis.*

Question 6. Suppose that computable X has no computable Schauder basis but does have a basis. What complexity basis does it have?

Question 7 (Bosserhof [Bos08]). Suppose that a computable Banach space X has a monotone Schauder basis. Must X have a computable Schauder basis?

Bosserhof's construction gives a computable presentation of a Banach space with a basis and no computable one. It leaves open the question:

Question 8. Is there a computable Banach space X with a basis such that no computable presentation of X has a computable basis? Is having a computable basis presentation dependent amongst computable presentations?

Theorem 7 ([Qia21]). *The index set of computable Banach spaces with computable Schauder bases is Σ_3^0-complete.*

A theorem attributed to Mazur shows that every infinite dimensional Banach space (separable or otherwise) has a an infinite dimensional subspace with a Schauder basis. If we restrict ourselves to the linear structure, the computable analogue of Mazur's theorem fails: there is a computable, infinite-dimensional vector space, all of whose computable independent subsets are finite (Metakides and Nerode [MN77]). However, in the normed context, Mazur's theorem has a computable version.

Theorem 8. *Let X be an infinite dimensional computable Banach space, then there is a computable basic sequence in X.*

The proof of this theorem (given in the appendix) relies on methods quite distinct from the classical case, which heavily uses duality. Note that it leaves the following question open.

Question 9. Suppose that X is a general computable infinite dimensional Banach space. Does X have an infinite basic sequence? More generally, how complicated are the basic sequences in X?

Returning to the general basis question, the characterisation in terms of basis constants shows that the index-set of computable Banach spaces with bases is Σ_1^1. Is this set Σ_1^1-complete? We can prove Π_3^0-hardness, but this leaves an enormous gap.

One of the reasons this question is difficult, is that the known constructions of spaces without bases do so by producing spaces without other properties, that follow from having a basis, but are each weaker than having a basis. In most cases, these properties are known to be arithmetical, and so these constructions cannot be used to show Σ_1^1-completeness of having a basis. In turn, the complexity of having each of these properties is interesting in its own right, and in most cases is still open. We mention three such properties here; for more details, see [Qia21, JL01].

Definition 4 (Schauder decomposition). *Let X be a Banach space. A Schauder decomposition (SD) of X is an infinite sequence $(Z_i)_{i \in \mathbb{N}}$ of closed subspaces of X such that for all $x \in X$, there exists an unique sequence $(z_i)_{i \in \mathbb{N}}$, $z_i \in Z_i$ such that*

$$x = \sum_{i=1}^{\infty} z_i.$$

A Schauder decomposition where the spaces Z_i are all finite dimensional is called a finite dimensional Schauder decomposition (FDD).

If a Banach space X has a Schauder basis $(e_i)_{i \in \mathbb{N}}$, we can think of X being decomposed into one-dimensional spaces of the form $X = \mathrm{span}(e_0) \oplus \mathrm{span}(e_1) \oplus \dots$. Schauder decompositions are then equivalent to requiring X to be decomposed into *closed subspaces* in the form $X = M_1 \oplus M_2 \oplus M_3 \oplus \dots$, where the spaces M_i are no longer required to be one-dimensional. Finite dimensional Schauder decompositions simply enforces the spaces $\{M_i\}$ to be finite dimensional. Szarek [Sza87] proves these properties are strictly weaker than having a Schauder basis.

Definition 5 (Local basis structure). *Let X be a Banach space. X is said to have the* local basis structure *(LBS) if there is some constant $K \in \mathbb{R}$ such that for any finite dimensional subspace $B \subset X$, there exists a finite dimensional space $L \subset X$ such that $B \subseteq L$ and $bc(L) \leq K$.*

X having the local basis structure means it can be *approximated* by a sequence of finite dimensional subspaces, where each one of them have a "nice" basis of low basis constant. It accords with the intuition that we can build a Schauder basis by finite extension, in the same way we build a Hamel basis in the finite dimensional case. It is not unreasonable to wonder if LBS in fact *equivalent* to having a basis. Since it might seem that we can always build a basis using LBS by inductively extending the current "basis elements" $\{b_0, \ldots, b_n\}$ to a bigger space $E \supseteq \mathrm{span}\{b_0, \ldots, b_n\}$ which still has a bounded basis constant. However, the problem with this line of reasoning is that while we are guaranteed $bc(E) \leq K$ for some universal constant K, this only means that *some* basis of E has a low basis constant. It might be the case that no basis of E which extends the current "candidate basis" $\{b_0, \ldots, b_n\}$ has its basis constant bounded by K. As it turns out, this is indeed the case as shown by the original construction by Enflo in [Enf73], which has LBS yet lacks any basis. The locality of LBS is the reason that the associated index set is Σ_3^0, and indeed, this simplicity, together with the techniques required for Theorem 4, gives us the only known completeness result in this area:

Theorem 9 (Xie[Xie24]). *The index-set of computable Banach spaces with the local basis structure is Σ_3^0-complete.*

Definition 6 (Approximation property).

1. *Let X be a Banach space. X is said to have the* approximation property *(AP) if for all compact sets K, for all $\epsilon > 0$, there is a finite rank operator T on X such that $(\forall x \in K)\,(\|Tx - x\| < \epsilon)$.*
2. *Let X be a Banach space. X is said to have the* bounded approximation property *(BAP) if there is a $\lambda \geq 1$ such that for all compact sets K, for all $\epsilon > 0$, there is a finite rank operator T on X such that $(\forall x \in K)\,(\|Tx - x\| < \epsilon)$ and $\|T\| \leq \lambda$.*

Szarek's construction produces a space with the bounded approximation property (and a finite-dimensional decomposition) but which does not have the local basis structure.

For index-sets, we have the following bounds. For a property X, let X_I denote the index-set of computable Banach spaces with property X.

Theorem 10.

1. $\Pi_3^0 \leq BASIS_I \leq \Sigma_1^1$.
2. $\Pi_3^0 \leq BAP_I \leq \Sigma_4^0$.
3. $\Pi_3^0 \leq AP_I \leq \Pi_1^1$.
4. $\Pi_3^0 \leq FDD_I \leq \Sigma_1^1$.
5. $\Pi_3^0 \leq SD_I \leq \Sigma_1^1$.

The reader can see that there are *many* gaps in the classifications. The open question is to close them.

We remark that there are many varieties of Schauder bases [Meg98, Sin70, Sin81], such as monotone, shrinking, absolute, etc., and their complexity is mostly open (see [BD07]). There are also other notions of basis, such as *Markushevich basis*, which seem completely unexplored from a computability-theoretical perspective. For example, every separable Banach space has a Markushevich basis ([Mar43] even a "strong" one Terenzi [Ter94])), but we have no idea of this result's effective content. Hajek et al. [HSVZ08] is a good reference.

A Appendix-Some Proofs

A.1 Proof of Theorem 8

To prove Theorem 8, we will first need the following classical lemma. This proof is taken from [Qia21].

Lemma 5 (Mazur). *Let X be an infinite dimensional Banach space, $B \subset X$ be a finite-dimensional subspace, and $\epsilon > 0$. Then there is an $x \in X$ with $\|x\| = 1$ so that*
$$\|y\| \leq (1 + \epsilon) \|y + \lambda x\|$$
for all $y \in B, \lambda \in \mathbb{R}$. In fact, x can be chosen so that this inequality is strict whenever $\|y\|, \lambda \neq 0$.

When working with separable Banach spaces, this lemma can be slightly strengthened so that we only have to deal with the dense elements.

Lemma 6. *In Lemma 5, further suppose that X is a separable Banach space and that $(q_i)_{i \in \mathbb{N}}$ is dense in the unit sphere of X. We can require the desired $x \in X$ to be some element from (q_i).*

Proof. Let X be some separable Banach space, and let $(q_i)_{i \in \mathbb{N}}$ be dense in the unit sphere of X. Let $B \subset X$ be some finite-dimensional subspace and $\epsilon > 0$ be some pre-determined constant. Further denote $x \in X$ to be some element that satisfies the requirements as given by Lemma 5 with $\|x\| = 1$. Note that by homogeneity ($y \in B \iff \frac{y}{\lambda} \in B$) it is sufficient to find some $z \in (q_i)$ which satisfies
$$\|y\| \leq (1 + \epsilon) \|y + z\|$$
for all $y \in B$. As $x \notin B$, we have that $\delta_x = \min_{y \in B} \|x + y\|$ is both well-defined and positive. Let $z \in X$ be any element where $\|z\| = 1$, since $\|y + x\| \leq \|y + z\| + \|x - z\|$, we have
$$\delta_x = \min_{y \in B} \|y + x\| \leq \delta_z + \|x - z\|$$

From the inequality above, we can choose some z sufficiently close to x with $\|z\| = 1$ so that $\|x - z\| \leq \epsilon(1 + \epsilon)^{-1}\delta_z$, we show that this choice works
$$\|y\| \leq (1 + \epsilon) \|y + x\| = (1 + \epsilon) \|y + x - z + z\|$$

$$\leq (1+\epsilon)\left(\|y+z\| + \|x-z\|\right) \leq (1+\epsilon)\left(\|y+z\| + \epsilon(1+\epsilon)^{-1}\delta_z\right)$$

And by definition of δ_z, we get that

$$(1+\epsilon)\left(\|y+z\| + \epsilon(1+\epsilon)^{-1}\delta_z\right) \leq (1+\epsilon)\|y+z\| + \epsilon\|y+z\|$$

$$= (1+2\epsilon)\|y+z\|$$

Since Lemma 5 works for all values of ϵ, the conclusion follows. In fact, the exact same argument shows that we can always choose the desired $x \in X$ to be some computable point when X is a computable Banach space. $\qquad\square$

We are now ready to prove Theorem 8.

Proof (Proof of Theorem 8). In light of Lemmas 6 and 2, we can simply carry out the classical construction. Fix some sequence of computable reals $(\epsilon_i)_{i\in\mathbb{N}}$ such that $\prod_{i=0}^{\infty}(1+\epsilon_i) < \infty$. We will construct a basic sequence $(u_i)_{i\in\mathbb{N}}$ inductively. Having constructed $u_0, \ldots, u_n$, find some x in the effective dense sequence for X such that $\mathrm{bc}(u_0, \ldots, u_n, x) \leq \prod_{i=0}^{n+1}(1+\epsilon_i)$. The existence of such an element is guaranteed by Lemma 6. Furthermore, this process is computable as the basis constants are computable. $\qquad\square$

A.2   Complexity of Computable Basis

Whilst we don't have space to prove all of the claims in the paper, we will give a brief sketch of how to prove Σ_3^0 completeness of the index sets of computable Banach spaces with computable bases. In doing so, we also sketch the ideas used by Bosserhof [Bos08] as per [Qia21]. Below, let BASIS_C denote the index-set of computable Banach spaces that have a computable Schauder basis.

Theorem 11. *BASIS_C is Σ_3^0 complete.*

We first introduce the construction used in [Bos08]. Let Z denote the Banach space constructed in [Dav73] that lacks the approximation property. It was proven in [Bos08] that this space is computable and also exhibits the local basis property.

Theorem 12 ([Bos08]). *There exists a computable Banach space without AP but has LBS.*

In particular, this implies that Z can be approximated by a sequence of "nice" subspaces.

Theorem 13 ([Bos08]). *There is a computable linearly independent sequence $(x_i)_{i\in\mathbb{N}} \subseteq Z$, a computable increasing function $\sigma : \mathbb{N} \to \mathbb{N}$ and an universal constant C such that $[x_0, \ldots] = Z$ and*

$$(\forall n \in \mathbb{N})(\mathrm{bc}([x_0, \ldots, x_{\sigma(n)}]) < C)$$

We first need the following definitions.

Definition 7 ([Bos08]). *For any $n \in \mathbb{N}$, Z_n is defined as:*

$$Z_n = [x_0, \ldots, x_{\sigma(n)}]$$

where $(x_i)_{i \in \mathbb{N}}$ is given by Theorem 13. For any $\tau : \mathbb{N} \to \mathbb{N}$, the Banach space Y_τ is defined as:

$$Y_\tau = \big(\oplus_i Z_{\tau(i)}\big)_{c_0}$$

which is the sequence space where norms of elements within each sequence tends to 0, and the norm on the sequence is the supremum norm on the elements.

An important feature of this space is that it has a basis. Intuitively, as the columns have universally bounded basis constants, we can simply "join up" the bases of the columns in the larger space, and the resulting sequence will be a basis.

Lemma 7 ([Bos08]). *The space Y_τ as defined in Definition 7 has a basis for any $\tau : \mathbb{N} \to \mathbb{N}$.*

The key idea is that Y_τ is a Banach space with basis, however each of its components can be made arbitrarily "large" such that no computable sequence can span it. For the sake of simplicity, also denote $Y = (\oplus_i Z)_{c_0}$. The following lemma is crucial.

Lemma 8 ([Bos08]). *For any basic sequence $(y_i)_{i \in \mathbb{N}} \in Y^{\mathbb{N}}$ and $n \in \mathbb{N}$, we have*

$$\text{emb}^n(Z) \nsubseteq [y_0, y_1, \ldots]$$

Where $\text{emb}^n : Z \to Y$ is the map defined by

$$\text{emb}^n(x) = (0, \ldots, 0, x, 0, \ldots) \in Y$$

mapping $x \in Z$ to n-th position of a sequence that is otherwise entirely zero.

There is also a natural computability structure on the space Y_τ for certain classes of τ.

Definition 8. *A function $\tau : \mathbb{N} \to \mathbb{N}$ is* lower semicomputable *if there is a c.e set $A \subseteq \mathbb{N}$ such that*

$$\tau(n) = \sup\{k \in \mathbb{N} : \langle n, k \rangle \in A\}$$

for all $n \in \mathbb{N}$.

Lemma 9 ([Bos08]). *For any $\tau : \mathbb{N} \to \mathbb{N}$ that is lower semicomputable, the constructed space Y_τ equipped with the dense set $\{\text{emb}^j(x_i)\}_{i \leq \sigma(\tau(j)), j \in \mathbb{N}}$ is a computable Banach space.*

Finally, to construct a computable Banach space without any computable basis, it is sufficient to construct some lower semicomputable τ such that Y_τ does not contain any computable basis. Furthmore, by Lemma 8 and Theorem 13, we can construct τ by directly diagonalising against all computable basic sequences. The following is due to [Bos08], although presented in a slightly different fashion.

Lemma 10 ([Bos08]). *There is a lower semicomputable function $\psi : \mathbb{N}^3 \to \mathbb{N}$ such that for all $n, k, i \in \mathbb{N}$, if ϕ_n computes a basic sequence $(y_i)_{i \in \mathbb{N}} \in Y^{\mathbb{N}}$ with basis constant smaller than k, we have*

$$emb^i(Z_{\psi(n,k,i)}) \not\subseteq [y_0, \ldots]$$

Corollary 1 ([Bos08]). *There exists a computable Banach space without computable basis.*

Proof. By Lemmas 9 and 10, define $\tau : \mathbb{N} \to \mathbb{N}$ by

$$\tau(\langle n, k \rangle) = \psi(n, k, \langle n, k \rangle)$$

The resulting space Y_τ is a computable Banach space where $\tau(\langle n, k \rangle)$ is large enough so that $emb^{\langle n,k \rangle}(Z_{\tau(\langle n,k \rangle)})$ is not spanned by ϕ_n (if it is a basic sequence with basis constant smaller than k). This implies that the space Y_τ cannot be spanned by any computable basic sequence[1], and therefore lacks basis. $\square$

It is worth noting that although the space constructed in Corollary 1 has no computable basis, it is unclear how uncomputable the bases are.

Question 10. Let Y_τ be the space used in the proof of Corollary 1 that was constructed by [Bos08]. What are the corresponding Turing degrees for the bases in this space?

Using Lemma 1, it is easy to see that having a computable basis is Σ_3^0, and hence we need following lemma to show completeness.

Lemma 11. *Recall the construction carried out in Lemma 7. If τ is a computable function, then Y_τ contains a computable basis.*

Proof. As the basis constant of $Z_{\tau(i)}$ is uniformly bounded by some constant C, there is some basis $(a_{i,j})_{j \leq \sigma(\tau(i))}$ with basis constant smaller than C for each $Z_{\tau(i)}$. It was proved in [Bos08] that the natural embedding of these bases into Y_τ (i.e. $\{emb^i(a_{i,j}) | i \in \mathbb{N}, j \leq \sigma(\tau(i))\}$) forms a basis for Y_τ. We will show that this is actually computable when τ is computable. If τ is computable, the sequence

$$x_0, x_1, \ldots, x_{\sigma(\tau(i))}$$

will be computable as well since $(x_i)_{i \in \mathbb{N}}$ and σ are both computable. Therefore, the rational span of the sequence will be computable as well. By continuity, we can therefore effectively find some basis that lies in the rational span of $(x_i)_{i \leq \sigma(\tau(i))}$ with basis constant smaller than C. As this procedure is uniform, it gives a computable basis in Y_τ. $\square$

We are now ready to prove Theorem 11.

---

[1] Note that any computable sequence in Y_τ is also a computable sequence in Y, so it is sufficient to diagonalise against computable sequences in Y.

Proof (Proof of Theorem 11). BASIS$_C \in \Sigma_3$ essentially follows from Lemma 1, it remains to show that BASIS$_C$ is Σ_3 hard. It is a well known fact that for any set $A \in \Sigma_3$, there is a computable function $g : \mathbb{N}^2 \to \mathbb{N}$ such that

$$x \in A \iff (\exists y)(W_{g(x,y)} \text{ is infinite })$$

For all $x \in \mathbb{N}$, we construct a lower semicomputable function $h : \mathbb{N} \to \mathbb{N}$ in stages. Let $\{\psi_s\}$ be some computable enumeration of the function ψ constructed in Lemma 10. We also define the function $C : \mathbb{N} \to \mathbb{N}$, initially $C_0(n) = n$ for all $n \in \mathbb{N}$. $C(n)$ indicates the computable sequence that is diagonalised against at n. Initialise the construction by setting $h_s = 0$. At stage s, the following is carried out for each $n \le s$.

- If $C(n) = -1$, do nothing. Otherwise:
- Enumerate $W_{g(x,C(n)),s}$. If a new element is enumerated, set $C(k)$ to $C(k-1)$ for all $k > n + |W_{g(x,C(n)),s}|$ and $C(n + |W_{g(x,C(n)),s}|)$ to -1.
- View $C(n)$ as a pair $\langle a, b \rangle$ and set $h_s(n)$ to $\max(h_{s-1}(n), \psi_s(a,b,n))$.

Finally we define h as $h = \lim_{s\to\infty} h_s$. This is the end of the construction, we now verify its validity.

Lemma 12. *The function h constructed is indeed a lower semicomputable function.*

Proof. The constructed sequence $\{h_s\}$ is clearly a computable enumeration of h. So it remains to verify that $\{h_s\}$ converges. For any $n \in \mathbb{N}$, we have $C(n) \le n$. Therefore $h_s(n) \le \max_{\langle a,b\rangle \le n} \psi(a,b,n)$ for all s, and since $(h_s(n))_s$ is monotone, this implies convergence. $\square$

We now show that the constructed h has the desired properties.

Lemma 13. *In addition to h being lower semicomputable, it also exihibit the following properties*

- *If $x \in A$, h is computable (although this might be non-uniform).*
- *If $x \notin A$, Y_h contains no computable basis.*

Proof. Suppose $x \in A$, thus there is some y such that $W_{g(x,C(y))}$ is infinite. By the construction, this means that

$$-1 = C(y+1) = C(y+2) = C(y+3) = \dots$$

Therefore, to compute $h(k)$ for any $k > y$, we just have to run the computable construction for finitely many steps until $C(k) = -1$, in which case the current value of $h(k)$ will be its final value. And since there are only finite many values $h(k)$ for $k \le y$, this can be computed non-uniformly. Hence, h is a computable function.

Now suppose $x \notin A$, in which case $W_{g(x,y)}$ is finite for all $y \in \mathbb{N}$. We will show that for all $\langle a, b \rangle \in \mathbb{N}$, there is some $n \in \mathbb{N}$ where $C(n) = \langle a, b \rangle$, implying that

$h(n) \geq \psi(a, b, n)$ and therefore Y_h cannot contain any computable basis. At each stage s of the construction, there will be some index i_s where $C_s(i_s) = \langle a, b \rangle$. So it suffices to show that $(i_s)_s$ eventually stabilises. But by the construction, i_s can only increase when some new element has been enumerated in $W_{g(x,C(k))}$ for some $C(k) < \langle a, b \rangle$. And since $\{k : C(k) < \langle a, b \rangle\}$ is finite, and each set of the form $W_{g(x,y)}$ is finite as well, i_s can only increase for a finite number of steps until it eventually converges, and the proof is complete. $\square$

Therefore, as the construction of h is uniform in x, we have established a reduction from an arbitrary Σ_3 set to BASIS_C, proving that BASIS_C is indeed Σ_3 hard. $\square$

References

[AK00] Ash, C., Knight, J.: Computable Structures and the Hyperarithmetical Hierarchy. Studies in Logic and the Foundations of Mathematics, vol. 144. North-Holland Publishing Co., Amsterdam (2000)

[Ban32] Banach, S.: Théorie des opérations lin'eaires. Z subwencji Funduszu kultury narodowej, Warszawa (1932)

[BD07] Brattka, V., Dillhage, R.: On computable compact operators on computable Banach spaces with bases. Math. Logic Q. **53**(4–5)):345–364 (2007)

[BHTM21] Bazhenov, N., Harrison-Trainor, M., Melnikov, A.: Computable stone spaces (2021)

[BMM] Brown, T., McNicholl, T., Melnikov, A.: On the complexity of classifying Lebesgue spaces, submitted

[Bos08] Bosserhoff, V.: Computable functional analysis and probabilistic computability. Universität der Bundeswehr München, Thesis (2008)

[Bra16] Brattka, V.: Computability of Banach Space Principles. FernUniversität, Hagen (2016)

[Dav73] Davie, A.M.: The approximation problem for Banach spaces. Bull. Lond. Math. Soc. **5**(3), 261–266 (1973)

[DM20] Downey, R.G., Melnikov, A.G.: Computable analysis and classification problems. In: Anselmo, M., Della Vedova, G., Manea, F., Pauly, A. (eds.) CiE 2020. LNCS, vol. 12098, pp. 100–111. Springer, Cham (2020). https://doi.org/10.1007/978-3-030-51466-2_9

[DM23] Downey, R., Melnikov, A.: Computably compact spaces. Bull. Symb. Logic **29**, 170–263 (2023)

[DMNar] Downey, R., Melnikov, A., Ng, K.M.: Computable Structure Theory: A Unified Approach. Springer, Cham, to appear

[Enf73] Enflo, P.: A counterexample to the approximation problem in Banach spaces. Acta Math. **130**, 309–317 (1973)

[FHD+20] Franklin, J., Hölzl, R., Day, A., Khoussainov, B., Melnikov, A., Ng, K.M.: Continuous functions and effective classification (2020)

[FLR09] Ferenczi, V., Louveau, A., Rosendal, C.: The complexity of classifying separable Banach spaces up to isomorphism. J. Lond. Math. Soc. **79**(2), 323–345 (2009)

[Haa10] Haar, A.: Zur theorie der orthogonalen funktionensysteme. Math. Ann. **69**(3), 331–371 (1910)

[HSVZ08] Hajek, P., Santalucía, V., Vanderwerff, J., Zizler, V.: Biorthogonal Systems in Banach Spaces. Springer, Cham (2008)

[JL01] Johnson, W.B., Lindenstrauss, J.: Handbook of the Geometry of Banach Spaces, vol. 1. Elsevier (2001)

[Kad66] Kadets, M.: Proof of the topological equivalence of all separable infinite dimensional Banach spaces. Funktsional'nyi Analiz i Ego Prilozheniy **1**(1), 61–70 (1966)

[Mar43] Markushevich, A.: On a basis in the wide sense for linear spaces. Dokl. Akad. Nauk **41**, 241–244 (1943)

[Meg98] Megginson, R.: An Introduction to Banach Spaces. Springer, Cham (1998)

[MN77] Metakides, G., Nerode, A.: Recursively enumerable vector spaces. Ann. Math. Logic **11**(2), 147–171 (1977)

[MN13] Melnikov, A.G., Nies, A.: The classification problem for compact computable metric spaces. In: Bonizzoni, P., Brattka, V., Löwe, B. (eds.) CiE 2013. LNCS, vol. 7921, pp. 320–328. Springer, Heidelberg (2013). https://doi.org/10.1007/978-3-642-39053-1_37

[MNS85] Metakides, G., Nerode, A., Shore, R.: Recursive limits on the Hahn-Banach theorem. In: Errett Bishop: Reflections on Him and His Research, San Diego, California, Contemporary Mathematics, vol. 39, pp. 85–91. American Mathematical Society, Providence (1985)

[NS15] Nies, A., Solecki, S.: Local compactness for computable polish metric spaces is Π_1^1-complete. In: Beckmann, A., Mitrana, V., Soskova, M. (eds.) CiE 2015. LNCS, vol. 9136, pp. 286–290. Springer, Cham (2015). https://doi.org/10.1007/978-3-319-20028-6_29

[PER83] Pour-El, M., Richards, I.: Computability and noncomputability in classical analysis. Trans. Am. Math. Soc. **275**(2), 539–560 (1983)

[PER89] Pour-El, M., Richards, I.: Computability in Analysis and Physics. Perspectives in Mathematical Logic, Springer, Berlin (1989)

[Qia21] Qian, L.: Computability-theoretic complexity of effective Banach spaces. Master's thesis, Victoria University of Wellington (2021)

[Sch28] Schauder, J.: Eine eigenschaft des haarschen orthogonalsystems. Math. Z. **28**, 317–320 (1928)

[Sin70] Singer, I.: Bases in Banach Spaces, I. Springer, Cham (1970)

[Sin81] Singer, I.: Bases in Banach Spaces, II. Springer, Cham (1981)

[Sza83] Szarek, S.J.: The finite dimensional basis problem with an appendix on nets of Grassmann manifolds. Acta Math. **151**, 153–179 (1983)

[Sza87] Szarek, S.J.: A Banach space without a basis which has the bounded approximation property. Acta Math. **159**, 81–98 (1987)

[Ter94] Terenzi, P.: Every separable Banach space has a bounded strong norming biorthogonal sequence which is also a Steinitz basis. Studia Math. **111**, 207–222 (1994)

[Tur36] Turing, A.M.: On computable numbers, with an application to the entscheidungsproblem (with correction. 43(1937) 544–546. Proc. Lond. Math. Soc. **42**, 230–265 (1936)

[Wei00] Weihrauch, K.: Computable Analysis. Texts in Theoretical Computer Science. An EATCS Series. Springer, Berlin (2000). An introduction

[Xie24] Xie, R.: Computability and randomness. Ph.D. thesis, Victoria University of Wellington (2024)

Kolmogorov Complexity
as a Combinatorial Tool

Alexander Shen$^{(\boxtimes)}$ (ID)

LIRMM, Univ Montpellier, CNRS, Montpellier, France
`alexander.shen@lirmm.fr,sasha.shen@gmail.com`
`https://lirmm.fr/~ashen`

Abstract. Kolmogorov complexity is often used as a convenient language for counting and/or probabilistic existence proofs. However, there are some applications where Kolmogorov complexity is used in a more subtle way. We provide one (somehow) surprising example where an existence of a winning strategy in a natural combinatorial game is proven (and no direct proof is known).

Keywords: Kolmogorov complexity · Combinatorial games · Experts aggregation

1 Introduction

It is well known that Kolmogorov complexity is a useful tool for proving combinatorial statements; the entire Chap. 6 (*The Incompressibility Method*) of the classical Li–Vitányi textbook [1] is devoted to applications of this type—too numerous to mention them here. A typical application of the incompressibility method can be described as follows. We want to prove the existence of an object x in some class X such that x has some property $P(x)$. For that we show that every object $x \in X$ *not* having this property is compressible (has small Kolmogorov complexity) while most of the objects in X are incompressible.

A toy example: most undirected graphs with n vertices have complexity about $n^2/2$ (for each pair of vertices we need to specify whether there is an edge between them), but graphs that have clique or independent set S of large size k have shorter descriptions. Indeed, we do not need to consider individually all the pairs in S (about $k^2/2$ bits economy), it is enough to specify S itself (k vertices, $\log n$ bits per vertex), so if $k \gg \log n$ we get a shorter description (since $k^2 \gg k \log n$). Therefore, n-vertex graphs of maximal complexity have no cliques or independent sets of size $O(\log n)$—so we have proven the existence of graphs without large cliques and independent sets.

This argument is essentially a counting argument showing that the number of graphs that have a large clique or independent set is much smaller than the total number of graphs with n vertices. Many other applications of Kolmogorov complexity can be translated to a counting argument in the same way (which

L. Levy Patey et al. (Eds.): CiE 2024, LNCS 14773, pp. 27–31, 2024.
https://doi.org/10.1007/978-3-031-64309-5_3

does not mean, of course, that Kolmogorov complexity is not needed: a useful language is very important). More generally, we may use probability with respect to some non-uniform distribution instead of counting to estimate Kolmogorov complexity. For example, to prove the law of large numbers we may note that if the frequency of ones in a bit string x deviates from $1/2$, one can use skewed Bernoulli distribution and the relation between Kolmogorov complexity $C(x)$ and a priori probability of x (or just arithmetic coding) to show that the string is compressible. In other proofs we use a distribution on the outputs of some probabilistic algorithm and show that with high probability the algorithm produces an object we are looking for (otherwise the sequence of random bits used by the algorithm is compressible). Two proofs of this type are reproduced and discussed in [9]: the compressibility proof of (a special case of the) Lovász local lemma and the "tetris" proof of the existence of a sequence that avoids forbidden factors.

Are there other applications of Kolmogorov complexity to combinatorics[1] that do not follow this scheme? Can we reformulate these arguments without Kolmogorov complexity or at least find some other arguments that do not use complexity?

Here are some examples of this type:

- Levin's lemma from [2, Section 4.2] says that there exists a binary sequence such that all its sufficiently long factors are almost incompressible. This is the complexity version of a statement about forbidden factors and can be proven using Lovász local lemma (see [7]). The original Levin's proof involves multiple uses of the Kolmogorov–Levin formula for complexity of pairs, so its translation into combinatorial language is difficult; however, the combinatorial argument given by Rosenfeld [6] (see also Muchnik's argument in [10, p. 259]) can be considered (at some extent) as a combinatorial counterpart of Levin's argument in a much more general setting with much stronger bounds.
- There exists a simple proof of Loomis–Whitney inequality using Kolmogorov complexity (see [10, Section 8.8 and Chap. 10]); the complexity argument again uses the Kolmogorov–Levin formula for complexity of pairs several times, so its combinatorial translation is difficult. However, the proof can be reformulated easily in terms of Shannon entropy.
- A combinatorial result saying that every multidimensional set can be covered by a small number of "almost uniform" subsets can be derived from the classification of tuples according to their "complexity profile" in a quite straightforward way, see [10, p. 333, Lemma and its proof]. It is unclear how this argument can be translated into a combinatorial or probabilistic language—however, a combinatorial proof of a stronger version of this result exists [3].

---

[1] *Disclaimer*: we do not consider applications of Kolmogorov complexity to *infinite* objects—e.g., point-to-set principle in geometric measure theory or the notion of K-trivial sequence in recursion theory; see also other examples in [8].

There is one more example of a complexity result where more advanced tools are used, and its combinatorial corollary for which a combinatorial proof is not known (though a weaker result can be proved directly).

2   New Example

This complexity statement deals with combinatorial rectangles that are simple with respect to each its element. A set $R \subset \mathbb{B}^n \times \mathbb{B}^n$ (pairs of n-bit strings) is a *combinatorial rectangle* if $R = U \times V$ for some $U, V \subset \mathbb{B}^n$. For every finite set A of constructive objects let $i(A) = \min_{x \in A} C(A|x)$, where $C(A|x)$ is the conditional Kolmogorov complexity of A given x. Intuitively speaking, sets A with small $i(A)$ are classes of "good classifications": any equivalence class A for an equivalence relation of small complexity has small $i(A)$, since we can find A given the relation and arbitrary element of A.

Theorem 1 (Romashchenko, Zimand, lemma 4.6 in [5] adapted to one rectangle).

$$C(R) \geqslant C(R|x) + C(R|y) - O(\log n + i(R))$$

for every combinatorial rectangle $R \subset \mathbb{B}^n \times \mathbb{B}^n$ and every its element $(x, y) \in R$.

The original motivation for this result was the communication complexity setting where R is the combinatorial rectangle that corresponds to some transcript of the communication protocol for inputs x and y. However, it is a general complexity statement that can be proven using the complexity version of artificial independence trick ("copy lemma") used to prove non-Shannon inequalities (see, e.g., [10, Section 10.13] for more details).

To get a combinatorial translation, we can use Muchnik's game interpretation of Kolmogorov complexity results described in [4]. We do not describe the details, just formulate the result in terms of a winning strategy for a simple game. The game field is $\mathbb{B}^n \times \mathbb{B}^n$; two players alternate. The first player provides a sequence of disjoint combinatorial rectangles in $\mathbb{B}^n \times \mathbb{B}^n$. After a new rectangle is chosen, the second player replies by labeling this rectangle as "horizontal" or "vertical". The games continues for $T = ab$ moves (where a and b, as well as some factor k, are parameters of the game), and the second player wins if every horizontal line $\mathbb{B}^n \times \{y\}$ intersects at most ka horizontal rectangles, and every vertical line $\{x\} \times \mathbb{B}^n$ intersects at most kb vertical rectangles.

Theorem 2. *For some polynomial $p(n)$, the second player has a winning strategy in this game for all n, a, b and $k = p(n)$.*

Alexander Kozachinskiy and Tomasz Steifer (personal communication) noted that this game has a interesting version in terms of opinions' aggregation. Imagine a group of people traveling in a train. At every stop the train conductor comes and ask passengers whether they want the heating to be on or off (till the next stop). Some people want it on, some other want it off, some do not care and are happy with both options. Every decision of the conductor makes some passengers unhappy (those who wanted the opposite option), and this is unavoidable if there are conflicting requests, but the conductor wants to minimize the *maximal unhappiness* among passengers. (The unhappiness of a passenger is the number of her requests that were not fulfilled.) This can be difficult: for example, if two passengers have conflicting requests all the time (on every stop), then for t stops at least one of them has unhappiness at least $t/2$ (for obvious reasons). However, the following result is true for some polynomial p:

Theorem 3 (Kozachinskiy–Steifer). *If every pair of passengers has a conflict at most once, then the conductor can guarantee that the maximal unhappiness after t stops does not exceed $\sqrt{t} \cdot p(\log n)$ where n is a number of passengers.*

This statement can be reduced to the rectangle game. Informally speaking, the game board consists of passenger pairs, and for each stop we consider a combinatorial rectangle

(people who want the heating) × (people who do not want the heating),

the requirement about conflicts guarantees that the rectangles are disjoint, and vertical/horizontal labeling of rectangles corresponds to the on/off actions.

Kozachinskiy and Steifer found a combinatorial proof of a weaker version of this result, with $t^{2/3}$ instead of $\sqrt{t}$, using some modification of Littlestone–Warmuth weighted majority algorithm. Their proof provides an explicit (and computationally simple) strategy for the conductor while the complexity argument gives only the existence proof without any complexity bound (except for a trivial one that corresponds to the exhaustive search).

Constants in the Definition of Complexity

Finally, let us make some general remarks about complexity approach to combinatorics. The Kolmogorov complexity function is defined up to $O(1)$ additive terms: when we change the optimal programming language used in its definition, the numerical value of the complexity changes, but the changes are bounded by a constant that depends only on the two programming languages that we compare. This seems unavoidable, and people are accustomed to it. However, if we prove a combinatorial corollary that does not mention the complexity explicitly, we would like to be more explicit about the constant.

In the simplest applications of the incompressibility method this is not a problem: we construct some decompressor (that does not even need to be universal) and note that all the "bad objects" (e.g., the graphs with large clique or independent set) are compressible in this sense, while most graphs are incompressible (the later statement is valid for *every* decompressor and does not involve unknown constants). However, in more advanced arguments, for example when we use the Kolmogorov–Levin formula for complexity of pairs, this simple trick does not work. In these arguments we also get an $O(\log n)$ term that often translates to polynomial factors in the combinatorial setting, and the constant in the $O(\log n)$ notation can be quite big. Fortunately, this constant does not depend on the choice of the programming language, but $O(1)$ terms do, so to get a specific bound directly from the argument we need to fix a universal programming language and actually write programs involved in the proofs using this language. This is boring and most probably gives unreasonable large constants. Maybe one can choose some special programming language to minimize the efforts (and/or constants)?

Let us note also that in some arguments (e.g., for the Loomis–Whitney argument, and for the arguments with randomized algorithms mentioned above) the constants in the definition of Kolmogorov complexity do not matter (since the construction used in the argument includes some asymptotic reasoning).

Acknowledgments. The author is grateful to Alexander Kozachinskiy and Tomasz Steifer for the permission to include their unpublished results, and to the participants of the Kolmogorov seminar and LIRMM colleagues (especially Andrei Romashchenko and Matthieu Rosenfeld) for interesting discussions. This study was supported by ANR (grant ANR-21-CE48-0023 FLITTLA).

Disclosure of Interests. The author has no competing interests to declare that are relevant to the content of this article.

References

1. Li, M., Vitányi, P.: An Introduction to Kolmogorov Complexity and Its Applications. TCS, Springer, New York (2008). https://doi.org/10.1007/978-0-387-49820-1
2. Durand, B., Levin, L., Shen, A.: Complex tilings. J. Symb. Log. **73**(2), 593–613 (2008)
3. Alon, N., Newman, I., Shen, A., Tardos, G., Vereshchagin, N.: Partitioning multi-dimensional sets in a small number of "uniform" parts. Eur. J. Comb. **28**(1), 134–144 (2007)
4. Muchnik, A.A., Mezhirov, I., Shen, A., Vereshchagin, N.: Game interpretation of kolmogorov complexity. arXiv:1003.4712 (2010)
5. Romashchenko, A., Zimand, M.: An operational characterization of mutual information in algorithmic information theory. J. ACM **66**(5), 1–42 (2019). https://doi.org/10.1145/3356867
6. Rosenfeld, M.: Finding lower bounds on the growth and entropy of subshifts over countable groups. arXiv:2204.00394 (2022)
7. Rumyantsev, A.Y., Ushakov, M.A.: Forbidden substrings, kolmogorov complexity and almost periodic sequences. In: Durand, B., Thomas, W. (eds.) STACS 2006. LNCS, vol. 3884, pp. 396–407. Springer, Heidelberg (2006). https://doi.org/10.1007/11672142_32
8. Shen, A.: Kolmogorov complexity as a language. In: Kulikov, A., Vereshchagin, N. (eds.) CSR 2011. LNCS, vol. 6651, pp. 105–119. Springer, Heidelberg (2011). https://doi.org/10.1007/978-3-642-20712-9_9
9. Shen, Alexander: Compressibility and probabilistic proofs. In: Kari, Jarkko, Manea, Florin, Petre, Ion (eds.) CiE 2017. LNCS, vol. 10307, pp. 101–111. Springer, Cham (2017). https://doi.org/10.1007/978-3-319-58741-7_11
10. Shen, A., Uspensky, V.A., Vereshchagin, N.: Kolmogorov complexity and algorithmic randomness. American Mathematical Society (Mathematical Surveys and Monographs, volume 220 (2019). https://www.lirmm.fr/~ashen/kolmbook-eng-scan.pdf

Cellular Automata: Communication Matters

Martin Kutrib$^{(\boxtimes)}$ and Andreas Malcher

Institut für Informatik, Universität Giessen, Arndtstr. 2, 35392 Giessen, Germany
{kutrib,andreas.malcher}@informatik.uni-giessen.de

Abstract. We consider systems of a huge number of interacting finite automata as massively parallel systems. The finite automata (also called cells) are arranged as one-dimensional array and work synchronously at discrete time steps. Naturally, the communication between the cells is necessary for non-trivial computations and, in fact, the amount of communication matters. Here, we focus mainly on measuring the amount of communication quantitatively by the number of messages sent by the cells. Recent results on the computational capacity as well as on decidability problems in such restricted cellular automata are discussed. In particular, fundamental types of communication are considered and the questions of how much communication is necessary to accomplish a certain task and of whether there are communication hierarchies are addressed. Since even for systems with drastically bounded communication many properties are undecidable, another question is to what extent the systems have to be limited in order to regain decidable properties. We present some selected results on these topics and want to draw attention to the overall picture and to some of the main ideas involved.

1 Introduction

Parallel computational models are appealing and widely used in order to describe, understand, and manage parallel processes occurring in real life. One principal task in order to employ a parallel computational model in an optimal way is to understand how cooperation of several processors is organized optimally. How much communication is necessary for a computation? To answer these questions, it is essential to know which communication and which amount of communication must or should take place between several processors. From the viewpoint of energy and the costs of communication links, it would be desirable to communicate a minimal number of times with a minimum amount of information transmitted. On the other hand, it would be interesting to know how much communication is necessary in a certain parallel model to accomplish a certain task.

Here, we consider the parallel computational model of cellular automata which are linear arrays of identical copies of deterministic finite automata, where the single nodes, which are called cells, are homogeneously connected to their both immediate neighbors. They work synchronously at discrete time steps. In the general case, in every time step the state of each cell is communicated to its

L. Levy Patey et al. (Eds.): CiE 2024, LNCS 14773, pp. 32–43, 2024.
https://doi.org/10.1007/978-3-031-64309-5_4

neighbors. That is, on the one hand, the state is sent regardless of whether it is really required, and on the other hand, the number of bits sent is determined by the number of states. The latter question has been dealt with in [14, 15, 26–28, 31], where the bandwidth of the inter-cell links is bounded by some constant being independent of the number of states. The former question concerns the amount of communication necessary for a computation, where the communication is quantitatively measured by counting the number of messages sent by the cells. Bounds on the sum of all communications of a computation as well as bounds on the maximal number of communications that may appear between each two cells are considered (see, for example, [19–21].

Reducing the number of communications in such a way that each two neighboring cells may communicate constantly often only, leads to devices which also still can accept non-context-free (even non-semilinear) languages. Moreover, almost all of their decidability questions are undecidable. An interesting additional restriction is to consider inputs of a certain form only. For such bounded languages it is known that in other computational models, such as certain variants of multi-head finite automata, undecidable problems become decidable. However, all commonly investigated decidability questions remain undecidable for communication-restricted real-time one-way cellular automata accepting bounded languages. Thus, the resource communication makes the model in a way inherently complex since even a limitation to a very small amount of communication does not reduce the computational complexity of the model's undecidability problems.

In the next section, we present some basic notions and definitions, and introduce the classes of communication bounded cellular automata. Examples of constructions for important types of languages are presented. Then, in Sect. 3 some computational capacity aspects are investigated, where an infinite strict hierarchy depending on the bound on the total number of communications during an computation is shown. Since the proof methods used in connection with the number of state changes in [29, 30] apply also for the devices in question we adapt and summarize some of the known results.

Section 4 is devoted to discussing decidability problems. We consider the weakest non-trivial device, that is, real-time one-way cellular automata where each two neighboring cells may communicate constantly often only. By reduction of Hilbert's tenth problem, several problems turn out to be undecidable. In particular, also the question of whether or not a given real-time one-way cellular automaton belongs to the weakest class of cellular automata with sparse communication is undecidable.

2 Preliminaries and Definitions

The reader is assumed to be familiar with the basic notions of automata theory as contained, for example, in [7, 8]. We denote the set of *non-negative integers* by $\mathbb{N}$. An *alphabet* Σ is a non-empty finite set, its elements are called *letters* or *symbols*. We write Σ^* for the set of all words over the finite alphabet Σ. The *empty word* is denoted by λ, and $\Sigma^+ = \Sigma^* \setminus \{\lambda\}$. The *reversal* of a word w is denoted by w^R and for the *length* of w we write $|w|$. We use $\subseteq$ for *inclusions* and $\subset$ for *strict inclusions*.

A cellular automaton is a linear array of identical deterministic finite state machines, the cells. Except for the leftmost cell and rightmost cell each one is connected to its both nearest neighbors. We identify the cells by positive integers. The state transition depends on the current state of each cell and on the messages that are currently sent by its neighbors. The possible messages are formalized as a set of possible communication symbols. The messages to be sent by a cell depend on its current state and are determined by so-called communication functions. The two outermost cells receive a boundary symbol on their free input lines once during the first time step from the outside world. Subsequently, these input lines are never used again. By providing a set of communication symbols, the definition is more general than really needed in the following, since here we are interested in the number of messages sent only. However, the definition allows also to restrict the bandwidth of the communication links by bounding the set of communication symbols and, thus, fits well to the devices investigated in [14, 15, 17, 26–28, 31].

More precisely, a *cellular automaton* (CA) is a system $\langle S, F, A, B, \#, b_l, b_r, \delta \rangle$, where S is the finite, nonempty set of *cell states*, $F \subseteq S$ is the set of *accepting states*, $A \subseteq S$ is the nonempty set of *input symbols*, B is the set of *communication symbols*, $\# \notin S$ is the *boundary symbol*, $b_l, b_r \colon (S \cup \{\#\}) \to B \cup \{\bot\}$ are *communication functions* which determine the information *to be sent* to the left and right neighbors, where $\bot$ means *nothing to send*, and $\delta \colon (B \cup \{\bot\}) \times S \times (B \cup \{\bot\}) \to S$ is the *local transition function*.

Let M be a CA. A *configuration* of M at time $t \geq 0$ is a description of its global state, which is actually a mapping $c_t \colon \{1, 2, \dots, n\} \to S$, for $n \geq 1$. The operation starts at time 0 in a so-called *initial configuration*. For a given input $w = a_1 a_2 \cdots a_n \in A^+$ we set $c_{0,w}(i) = a_i$, for $1 \leq i \leq n$. During the course of its computation a CA steps through a sequence of configurations, whereby successor configurations are computed according to the global transition function Δ: Let c_t, $t \geq 0$, be a configuration. Then its successor configuration $c_{t+1} = \Delta(c_t)$ is as follows. For $2 \leq i \leq n - 1$,

$$c_{t+1}(i) = \delta(b_r(c_t(i-1)), c_t(i), b_l(c_t(i+1))),$$

and for the leftmost and rightmost cell we set $c_1(1) = \delta(b_r(\#), c_0(1), b_l(c_0(2)))$, $c_{t+1}(1) = \delta(\bot, c_t(1), b_l(c_t(2)))$, for $t \geq 1$, and $c_1(n) = \delta(b_r(c_0(n-1)), c_0(n), b_l(\#))$, $c_{t+1}(n) = \delta(b_r(c_t(n-1)), c_t(n), \bot)$, for $t \geq 1$. Thus, the global transition function Δ is induced by δ (Fig. 1).

Fig. 1. A two-way cellular automaton.

Now, instances of problems to be solved with a cellular automaton can be encoded as strings with a finite number of different symbols. So, the input data supplied to CA are strings of symbols. The output can be encoded in binary. Therefore, a computation can be decomposed into parallel processes, one for each bit of the output. Then each process computes a function that maps the input to YES or NO. In this way, each process is a binary decider. Hence, a string that is evaluated to YES is said to be accepted, and the set of all accepted strings is called a *formal language*.

An input w is accepted by a CA M if at some time i during the course of its computation the leftmost cell enters an accepting state. The *language accepted by* M is denoted by $L(M)$. Let $t\colon \mathbb{N} \to \mathbb{N}$, $t(n) \geq n$, be a mapping. If all $w \in L(M)$ are accepted with at most $t(|w|)$ time steps, then M is said to be of time complexity t.

An important subclass of cellular automata are so-called *one-way cellular automata* (OCA), where the flow of information is restricted to one way from right to left. For a formal definition it suffices to require that b_r maps all states to $\bot$, and that the leftmost cell does not receive the boundary symbol during the first time step (Fig. 2).

Fig. 2. A one-way cellular automaton.

In the following we consider the impact of communication in cellular automata. The communication is measured by the number of messages sent by the cells. It is understood that whenever a communication symbol not equal to $\bot$ is sent, a communication takes place. Here we do not distinguish whether either or both neighboring cells use the link. More precisely, the number of communications between cell i and cell $i+1$ up to time step t is defined by

$$\text{com}(i,t) = |\{\, j \mid 0 \leq j < t \text{ and } (b_r(c_j(i)) \neq \bot \text{ or } b_l(c_j(i+1)) \neq \bot) \,\}|.$$

For computations we now distinguish the maximal number of communications between two cells and the total number of communications. Let $c_0, c_1, \ldots, c_{t(|w|)}$ be the sequence of configurations computed on input w by some cellular automaton with time complexity $t(n)$, that is, the *computation on* w. Then we define

$$\text{mcom}(w) = \max\{\, \text{com}(i, t(|w|)) \mid 1 \leq i \leq |w| - 1 \,\} \text{ and}$$

$$\text{scom}(w) = \sum_{i=1}^{|w|-1} \text{com}(i, t(|w|)).$$

Let $f\colon \mathbb{N} \to \mathbb{N}$ be a mapping. If all $w \in L(M)$ are accepted with computations where $\text{mcom}(w) \leq f(|w|)$, then M is said to be *max communication bounded by f.* Similarly, if all $w \in L(M)$ are accepted with computations where scom(w) $\leq f(|w|)$, then M is said to be *sum communication bounded by f.* In general, it is not expected to have tight bounds on the exact number of communications but tight bounds on their numbers in the order of magnitude. For the sake of readability we denote the class of CA that are max communication bounded by some function $g \in O(f)$ by MC(f)-CA, where it is understood that f gives the order of magnitude. In addition, we use the notation *const* for functions from $O(1)$. Corresponding notations are used for OCA and sum communication bounded CAs and OCA (SC(f)-CA and SC(f)-OCA).

The family of all languages which are accepted by some device X with time complexity t is denoted by $\mathscr{L}_t(X)$. In the sequel we are particularly interested in fast computations and call the time complexity $t(n) = n$ *real time* and write $\mathscr{L}_{rt}(X)$.

3   The Impact of Communication on the Computational Capacity

A simple example that shows the principal idea of limiting the maximal number of communications appearing between each two cells to a *constant* deals with signals as follows.

Example 1. The language $\{\, a^n b^n \mid n \geq 1 \,\}$ belongs to $\mathscr{L}_{rt}(\mathsf{MC}(const)\text{-}\mathsf{OCA})$.

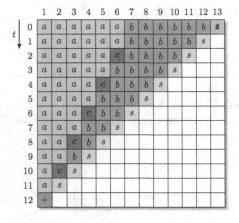

The idea of the construction is to establish two left-moving signals. See Fig. 3. The rightmost cell can identify itself by receiving a message from the sole border cell. It sends a signal s with maximum speed to the left. The unique cell which has an a in its input and has a right neighbor with a b in its input can identify itself as well if any cell initially communicates its input to the left. It sends a signal c with speed $1/2$ to the left. When both signals meet in a cell, an accepting state is entered. Clearly, each cell communicates only finitely often. ∎

Fig. 3. A real-time MC(*const*)-OCA accepting a^6b^6. The red cells c sketch the trace of the signal c, the state $+$ is accepting.

The construction of the example can be generalized as long as signals are used that require only constantly many messages for each cell. Note that there are more complex signals whose speed depends on the time, for example, logarithmically [2,3,13,22].

Generalizations of the above construction show that the border to non-context-free languages can be crossed. In particular, the non-context-free languages $\{\, a^n b^n c^n \mid n \geq 1 \,\}$, $\{\, a^n b^m c^n d^m \mid n, m \geq 1 \,\}$, and $\{\, a_1^n a_2^n \cdots a_k^n \mid n \geq 1 \,\}$, for $k \geq 3$ and different symbols $a_1, a_2, \ldots, a_k$, are accepted by real-time MC(*const*)-OCA as well.

However, the language $\{\, a^n b^{n_1} c^m b^{n_2} \mid n, m \geq 1 \wedge n_1, n_2 \geq 0 \wedge n_1 + n_2 = n \,\}$ is an example for which the technique of suitable signals having an appropriate speed cannot be applied, since the block of c's may be arbitrarily large. Similar arguments apply for the languages $\{\, a^n w \mid n \geq 1 \wedge w \in (b^* c^*)^k b^* \wedge |w|_b = n \,\}$, $k \geq 0$. However, they nevertheless can be accepted by some MC(*const*)-OCA [19], which shows that even one-way cellular automata that obey the real-time restriction and whose cells communicate constantly often, respectively, have a computational capacity that is not bounded from above by context-free languages. Can we push the upper bound further? All of the languages considered so far are either semilinear or non-bounded. So, a natural question is whether there is a non-semilinear and bounded language belonging to $\mathscr{L}_{rt}$(MC(*const*)-OCA). In contrast to many other computational devices, for example certain multi-head finite automata, parallel communicating finite automata, and certain parallel communicating grammar systems, the question can be answered in the affirmative. This is shown by the next example [20].

Example 2. The language $L = \{\, a^n b^{n+\lfloor \sqrt{n} \rfloor} \mid n \geq 1 \,\}$ belongs to the family $\mathscr{L}_{rt}$(MC(*const*)-OCA).

In [22], a CA is constructed such that cell n enters some fixed state q exactly at time step $2n + \lfloor \sqrt{n} \rfloor$, and at most n cells are used for the computation. In fact, the CA constructed is actually an OCA. Additionally, each cell performs only a finite number of communication steps. Thus, the CA constructed is an MC(*const*)-OCA. Now, an MC(*const*)-OCA accepting L implements this construction on the a-cells of some input $a^n b^m$. Thus, the leftmost cell enters state q at time step $2n + \lfloor \sqrt{n} \rfloor$. Additionally, in the rightmost cell a signal s with maximum speed is sent to the left. When this signal arrives in an a-cell exactly at a time step at which the cell would enter the state q, the a-cell changes to an accepting state instead. So, if $m = n + \lfloor \sqrt{n} \rfloor$, then s arrives at time $2n + \lfloor \sqrt{n} \rfloor$ at the leftmost cell and the input is accepted. In all other cases the input is rejected. Clearly, the OCA constructed is an MC(*const*)-OCA. ∎

In order to identify the computational power of communication bounded real-time devices more generally, we first inherit some results from [29,30], where two-way cellular automata are considered for which the number of proper state changes is bounded. By applying the technique of saving communication steps by storing the last signal received in the state and to interpret an arriving $\perp$ suitably [19], it is not hard to see that such a device can be simulated by the corresponding communication bounded device. Whether or not state change bounded devices are strictly weaker than communication bounded ones is an open problem. However, we inherit the following relationships.

Theorem 3. *1.* $\mathscr{L}_{rt}$(MC(*const*)-CA) $\subset$ $\mathscr{L}_{rt}$(SC(n)-CA).
2. REG $\subset$ $\mathscr{L}_{rt}$(MC(*const*)-CA) $\subset$ $\mathscr{L}_{rt}$(MC($\sqrt{n}$)-CA) $\subset$ $\mathscr{L}_{rt}$(MC(n)-CA).
3. $\mathscr{L}_{rt}$(MC(*const*)-CA) $\subset$ NL.

Next, we turn to an infinite strict hierarchy of real-time SC(f)-CA families [19]. The ingredient for the top of the hierarchy is the mirror language $\{\,wcw^R \mid w \in \{a,b\}^+\,\}$.

Theorem 4. *Let $f\colon \mathbb{N} \to \mathbb{N}$ be a function. If $f \in o(n^2/\log(n))$, then language $L = \{\,wcw^R \mid w \in \{a,b\}^+\,\}$ is not accepted by any real-time SC(f)-CA.*

What is the idea of the proof of this result from [19]?

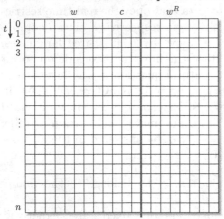

Assume that L is accepted by some real-time SC(f)-CA. First, prove that in an accepting computation on wcw^R there is some cell to the right of the center cell c that can send at most $r \in O(|w|/\log(|w|))$ messages. Second, estimate the number of possibilities for some r communications between two cells in real-time computations (see Fig. 4). These are at most $\binom{n}{r}(((|B|+1)^2 - 1)^r \leq 2^{k_0 \log(n)r} \leq \sqrt{2^{|w|}}$ possibilities. Third, conclude that there are two different words w and w' for which the communications are the same and derive a contradiction from it.

Fig. 4. Space-time-diagram for the proof idea of Theorem 4. The communication across the red line is considered. (Color figure online)

For all $i \geq 1$, the witness languages that separate the levels of the hierarchy are $L_i = \{\,w\$^{\varphi_i(|w|)-2|w|}w^R \mid w \in \{a,b\}^+\,\}$ defined by the function $\varphi_i\colon \mathbb{N} \to \mathbb{N}$ where $\varphi_1(n) = 2^n$, and $\varphi_i(n) = 2^{\varphi_{i-1}(n)}$, for $i \geq 2$.

Language L_i is accepted by some real-time SC($n\log^{[i]}(n)$)-CA, but cannot be accepted by any real-time SC(f)-CA if $f \in o((n\log^{[i]}(n))/\log^{[i+1]}(n))$.

Now, $n\log^{[i+1]}(n) \in o((n\log^{[i]}(n))/\log^{[i+1]}(n))$ yields the infinite strict communication hierarchy.

Theorem 5. *Let $i \geq 0$ be an integer. Then $\mathscr{L}_{rt}(SC(n\log^{[i+1]}(n))\text{-CA})$ is strictly included in $\mathscr{L}_{rt}(SC(n\log^{[i]}(n))\text{-CA})$.*

4 Decidability

By reduction of Hilbert's tenth problem, it is shown that several problems are undecidable for real-time MC($const$)-OCA [19]. Hilbert's tenth problem is to decide whether a given polynomial $p(x_1, x_2, \ldots, x_n)$ with integer coefficients has an integral root. That is, to decide whether there are integers $\alpha_1, \alpha_2, \ldots, \alpha_n$ such that $p(\alpha_1, \alpha_2, \ldots, \alpha_n) = 0$. By several technical observations it turns out that it is sufficient to consider such polynomials of the form

$$p(x_1, x_2, \ldots, x_n) = t_1(x_1, x_2, \ldots, x_n) + \cdots + t_r(x_1, x_2, \ldots, x_n)$$

where each $t_j(x_1, x_2, \ldots, x_n)$ is of the form

$$t_j(x_1, x_2, \ldots, x_n) = s_j x_1^{i_{j,1}} x_2^{i_{j,2}} \cdots x_n^{i_{j,n}}$$

with all $i_{j,k}$ positive. Now, the idea of the reduction is as follows. For a given polynomial $p(x_1, x_2, \ldots, x_n)$ with integer coefficients that has the above form, languages $L(t_j)$, for every term t_j, are defined that evaluate the terms t_j. The next step is to simulate an evaluation of the given polynomial p. To simulate an evaluation of p, the evaluations of the single terms have to be put together. This is done by constructing a language $\tilde{L}(p) = \bigcap_{j=1}^{r} \tilde{L}(t_j)^R$ from languages $\tilde{L}(t_j)$ which, in turn, are constructed from $L(t_j)$ by concatenations and some regular languages. Finally, from $\tilde{L}(p)$ another language $L(p)$ is constructed which is empty if and only if $p(x_1, x_2, \ldots, x_n)$ has no solution in the non-negative integers. In a long proof it is shown that $L(p)$ belongs to $\mathscr{L}_{rt}(\mathsf{MC}(const)\text{-OCA})$ [19]. So, emptiness is undecidable for $\mathscr{L}_{rt}(\mathsf{MC}(const)\text{-OCA})$. From the undecidability of the emptiness further undecidable problems are derived by standard techniques.

Theorem 6. *Emptiness, finiteness, infiniteness, equivalence, inclusion, regularity, and context-freeness are undecidable for real-time* $\mathsf{MC}(const)\text{-OCA}$.

Moreover, even the restrictions themselves are not decidable: Given some real-time $\mathsf{MC}(const)\text{-OCA}$ M', we define the language $\{a^{|w|}w \mid w \in L(M')\}$, which is accepted by a real-time OCA M, so that M is an $\mathsf{MC}(const)\text{-OCA}$ if and only if the language is finite.

Theorem 7. *It is undecidable for an arbitrary real-time* OCA *whether it is a real-time* $\mathsf{MC}(const)\text{-OCA}$.

So, even for the weakest non-trivial device with limited messages, that is, for real-time $\mathsf{MC}(const)\text{-OCA}$ all the mentioned properties are undecidable.

An approach often investigated and widely accepted is to consider a given type of device for special purposes only, for example, for the acceptance of languages having a certain structure or form. From this point of view it is natural to start with unary languages (for example, [1, 4, 12, 23, 24]). For general real-time one-way cellular automata it is known that they accept only regular unary languages [25]. Since the proof is constructive, we derive that the borderline between undecidability and decidability has been crossed. Let us, therefore, generalize unary languages to bounded languages. A language L over some alphabet $\{a_1, a_2, \ldots, a_k\}$ is said to be *bounded*, if $L \subseteq a_1^* a_2^* \cdots a_k^*$. For several devices it is known that they accept non-semilinear languages in general, but only semilinear bounded languages. Since for semilinear sets several properties are decidable [6], constructive proofs lead to decidable properties for these devices in connection with bounded languages [5, 9–11].

So, it is natural to consider decidability problems for $\mathsf{MC}(const)\text{-OCA}$) accepting bounded languages. However, Example 2 revealed already that there are non-semilinear bounded languages accepted by some $\mathsf{MC}(const)\text{-OCA}$). This already indicates that questions of decidability must at least be difficult. In fact, in [16] it has been shown that also with this additional restriction none of the problems becomes decidable as long as the number of messages allowed is not too small.

Theorem 8. *Emptiness, finiteness, infiniteness, equivalence, inclusion, regularity, and context-freeness are undecidable for arbitrary real-time* $SC(n)$-*OCA and* $MC(\log(n))$-*OCA accepting bounded languages.*

4.1 Cellular Automata with Minimal Communication

So far, we imposed restrictions on the number of communications only. Next, we measure the amount of communication also qualitatively by considering the bandwidth, that is, the number of different messages available, of the communication links between cells and bound it by some constant being independent of the number of states. This approach fits well to the devices investigated in [14, 15, 17, 26–28, 31].

Let $k \geq 1$ be the number of different communication symbols. Then we denote the class of CA which have at most k communication symbols and which are max communication bounded by some function f by $MC(f)$-CA_k. Corresponding notation is used for OCA and sum communication bounded CA and OCA. ($SC(f)$-CA_k and $SC(f)$-OCA_k).

The undecidability results already presented immediately raise the question for the status of decidability problems when the communication of cellular automata is drastically reduced to its minimum, but kept still enough to have non-trivial devices. To this end, we combine both approaches. Clearly, if there is no communication between two cells the array is split into two parts that work independently of each other. By the definition of acceptance, the right part is useless. So, to identify the minimum of communication, each two adjacent cells are allowed to communicate constantly often only. Moreover, only one possible message is provided, the information flow is one-way, and the time complexity is bounded to real time. That is, we consider the class of real-time $MC(const)$-OCA_1. These devices characterize the regular languages for unary alphabets. For non-unary alphabets non-context-free languages can be accepted [18, 20]. So, the computations are non-trivial.

Example 9. There is a real-time $MC(const)$-OCA_1 M that accepts a non-regular language. More precisely, only two messages per cell are used.

We describe the computation of M on inputs of the form $a^n b c^m$. The acceptance of the language is governed by two signals. During the first time step the rightmost cell receives the message sent by the boundary symbol and identifies itself to be the rightmost cell. During the second time step the cell with input symbol b (b-cell) sends the message. In this way, the unique a-cell with right neighboring b-cell can identify itself. Subsequently, the a-cell sends the message with speed $1/2$, and the rightmost cell sends the message with maximal speed to the left. So, the slow signal starts at time step 2 in the rightmost a-cell, takes $2n - 2$ further time steps to reach the leftmost cell, and thus stays at time steps $2n$ and $2n + 1$ in the leftmost cell. The fast signal is set up at time step 1 and takes $n + m$ further time steps to reach the leftmost cell. When both signals meet in a cell, that is, $n + m + 1 = 2n + 1$, an accepting state is entered. Therefore, the leftmost cell accepts if and only if $n = m$. Moreover, each cell sends at most two messages, and can be set up to send no more messages even for inputs of another form.

Now assume that the language accepted by M is regular. Since regular languages are closed under intersection, so is the language $L(M) \cap a^*bc^* = a^nbc^n$, which is non-regular but context free. From the contradiction the non-regularity of $L(M)$ follows. ∎

Turning to our key question for the status of decidability problems for MC($const$)-OCA$_1$, we present a lemma which relates languages accepted by MC($const$)-OCA with languages accepted by MC($const$)-OCA$_1$ [18].

Lemma 10. *Let* $M = \langle S, F, A, B, \#, b_l, \delta \rangle$ *be a real-time MC($const$)-OCA and* $\$ \notin A$ *be a new symbol. Then a real-time MC($const$)-OCA$_1$ M' accepting the language* $\{ w \$^{(|B|+2)(|w|+1)}v \mid v \in \{ \$, A(A \cup \{\$\})^* \}, w \in L(M) \}$ *can effectively be constructed.*

It is straightforward to generalize this lemma to cellular automata with two-way communication. Furthermore, since the construction increases the number of communication steps per cell only linearly, it is easy to see that the construction also works for SC(f)-CA and MC(f)-CA, where f is not necessarily a constant function.

By Lemma 10, now the undecidable problems known for MC($const$)-OCA can be reduced to problems of MC($const$)-OCA$_1$.

Theorem 11. *Emptiness, finiteness, infiniteness, equivalence, inclusion, regularity, and context-freeness are undecidable for real-time MC($const$)-OCA$_1$.*

Clearly, the undecidability carries over to, for example, MC($const$)-CA$_k$ with two-way communication and the models SC(n)-OCA$_k$ and SC(n)-CA$_k$.

The undecidability results for real-time SC(n)-OCA and MC($\log n$)-OCA accepting bounded languages cannot be translated directly to the corresponding automata with one communication symbol by using the construction of Lemma 10, since the construction does not preserve the boundedness of the languages. However, if we allow an additional communication symbol, then we obtain undecidability results also for bounded languages accepted by real-time SC(n)-OCA$_2$ and MC($\log n$)-OCA$_2$ [20].

Let us finally dive into the $const$. The undecidability proof for real-time MC($const$)-OCA is by reduction of Hilbert's tenth problem, where the precise number of communications per cell is not known. Recently, the constant could be made more precise. It is shown in [21] that the emptiness problem is undecidable for real-time MC($const$)-CA, where the constant number of communications is at most four, even on a unary input alphabet. In the same paper, it is shown that again four communications are enough to obtain the undecidability of emptiness for real-time MC($const$)-OCA that accept bounded languages which are subsets of a^*b^*. Then, the undecidability of finiteness, infiniteness, inclusion, equivalence, and regularity could be shown as well.

These undecidability results are in a way optimal with respect to the structure of the languages accepted, in particular, when compared with the languages used in the proofs for Theorems 6 and 8. In case of real-time MC($const$)-CA we obtain undecidability already for unary languages and at least four communications and in case of real-time MC($const$)-OCA we obtain undecidability for languages in a^*b^* and at least four communications, whereas it is known that real-time OCA on unary languages accept only regular languages (see, for example, [25]) for which all discussed decidability questions are decidable.

Finally, it is again undecidable to determine whether or not a given real-time OCA performs a finite number of communications per cell [21].

Theorem 12. *It is undecidable for an arbitrary real-time OCA M and some $i \geq 4$ whether or not M is a real-time MC($const$)-OCA, where the number of communications is at most i.*

Again, these results hold in case of two-way communication as well.

Corollary 13. *It is undecidable for an arbitrary real-time CA M and some $i \geq 4$ whether or not M is a real-time MC($const$)-CA, where the number of communications is at most i.*

References

1. Book, R.V.: Tally languages and complexity classes. Inform. Control **26**, 186–193 (1974)
2. Buchholz, T., Kutrib, M.: Some relations between massively parallel arrays. Parallel Comput. **23**, 1643–1662 (1997)
3. Buchholz, T., Kutrib, M.: On time computability of functions in one-way cellular automata. Acta Inform. **35**, 329–352 (1998)
4. Chrobak, M.: Finite automata and unary languages. Theor. Comput. Sci. **47**, 149–158 (1986)
5. Csuhaj-Varjú, E., Dassow, J., Kelemen, J., Păun, G.: Grammar Systems: A Grammatical Approach to Distribution and Cooperation. Gordon and Breach (1984)
6. Ginsburg, S.: The Mathematical Theory of Context-Free Languages. McGraw Hill (1966)
7. Harrison, M.A.: Introduction to Formal Language Theory. Addison-Wesley (1978)
8. Hopcroft, J.E., Ullman, J.D.: Introduction to Automata Theory, Languages, and Computation. Addison-Wesley (1979)
9. Ibarra, O.H.: Simple matrix languages. Inform. Control **17**, 359–394 (1970)
10. Ibarra, O.H.: A note on semilinear sets and bounded-reversal multihead pushdown automata. Inform. Process. Lett. **3**, 25–28 (1974)
11. Ibarra, O.H.: Reversal-bounded multicounter machines and their decision problems. J. ACM **25**, 116–133 (1978)
12. Klein, A., Kutrib, M.: Cellular devices and unary languages. Fund. Inform. **78**, 343–368 (2007)
13. Kutrib, M.: Cellular automata and language theory. In: Meyers, R. (ed.) Encyclopedia of Complexity and System Science, pp. 800–823. Springer, New York (2009). https://doi.org/10.1007/978-0-387-30440-3_54
14. Kutrib, M., Malcher, A.: Fast cellular automata with restricted inter-cell communication: computational capacity. In: Navarro, G., Bertossi, L., Kohayakawa, Y. (eds.) TCS 2006. IIFIP, vol. 209, pp. 151–164. Springer, Boston, MA (2006). https://doi.org/10.1007/978-0-387-34735-6_15

15. Kutrib, M., Malcher, A.: Fast iterative arrays with restricted inter-cell communication: constructions and decidability. In: Královič, R., Urzyczyn, P. (eds.) MFCS 2006. LNCS, vol. 4162, pp. 634–645. Springer, Heidelberg (2006). https://doi.org/10.1007/11821069_55
16. Kutrib, M., Malcher, A.: Bounded languages meet cellular automata with sparse communication. In: Dassow, J., Pighizzini, G., Truthe, B. (eds.) Descriptional Complexity of Formal Systems (DCFS 2009), pp. 211–222. Otto-von-Guericke-Universität Magdeburg (2009)
17. Kutrib, M., Malcher, A.: Computations and decidability of iterative arrays with restricted communication. Parallel Process. Lett. **19**, 247–264 (2009)
18. Kutrib, M., Malcher, A.: On one-way one-bit O(one)-message cellular automata. Electron. Notes Theor. Comput. Sci. **252**, 77–91 (2009)
19. Kutrib, M., Malcher, A.: Cellular automata with sparse communication. Theor. Comput. Sci. **411**, 3516–3526 (2010)
20. Kutrib, M., Malcher, A.: One-way cellular automata, bounded languages, and minimal communication. J. Autom. Lang. Comb. **15**, 135–153 (2010)
21. Kutrib, M., Malcher, A.: Iterative arrays with finite inter-cell communication. Nat. Comput. **21**, 3–15 (2022)
22. Mazoyer, J., Terrier, V.: Signals in one-dimensional cellular automata. Theor. Comput. Sci. **217**, 53–80 (1999)
23. Mereghetti, C., Pighizzini, G.: Optimal simulations between unary automata. SIAM J. Comput. **30**, 1976–1992 (2001)
24. Pighizzini, G., Shallit, J.: Unary language operations, state complexity and Jacobsthal's function. Int. J. Found. Comput. Sci. **13**, 145–159 (2002)
25. Seidel, S.R.: Language recognition and the synchronization of cellular automata. Tech. Rep. 79-02, Department of Computer Science, University of Iowa, Iowa City (1979)
26. Umeo, H.: Linear-time recognition of connectivity of binary images on 1-bit inter-cell communication cellular automaton. Parallel Comput. **27**, 587–599 (2001)
27. Umeo, H., Kamikawa, N.: A design of real-time non-regular sequence generation algorithms and their implementations on cellular automata with 1-bit inter-cell communications. Fund. Inform. **52**, 257–275 (2002)
28. Umeo, H., Kamikawa, N.: Real-time generation of primes by a 1-bit-communication cellular automaton. Fund. Inform. **58**, 421–435 (2003)
29. Vollmar, R.: On cellular automata with a finite number of state changes. Computing **3**, 181–191 (1981)
30. Vollmar, R.: Some remarks about the 'efficiency' of polyautomata. Int. J. Theoret. Phys. **21**, 1007–1015 (1982)
31. Worsch, T.: Linear time language recognition on cellular automata with restricted communication. In: Gonnet, G.H., Viola, A. (eds.) LATIN 2000. LNCS, vol. 1776, pp. 417–426. Springer, Heidelberg (2000). https://doi.org/10.1007/10719839_41

Membership Problems in Infinite Groups

M. Lohrey[(✉)] [iD]

University of Siegen, Siegen, Germany
lohrey@eti.uni-siegen.de
https://www.eti.uni-siegen.de/ti/mitarbeiter/lohrey/

Abstract. We review results for various kinds of membership problems
(subgroup membership, submonoid membership, rational subset membership, knapsack problem) in infinite groups.

Keywords: group theory · membership testing · rational sets

1 Algorithmic Membership Problems in Groups

Short Historic Outline. The investigation of membership problems in algorithmic group theory can be traced back to a paper of Markov from 1947 [47]. Markov proved that it is undecidable whether a given matrix A from the group $\mathsf{SL}_4(\mathbb{Z})$ of 4-dimensional integer matrices of determinant 1 can be written as a product (of arbitrary length) of other given matrices $A_1, \ldots, A_k \in \mathsf{SL}_4(\mathbb{Z})$. In the terminology that we introduce below, Markov showed that the *submonoid membership problem* for the matrix group $\mathsf{SL}_4(\mathbb{Z})$ is undecidable. Markov's work initiated extensive research on various algorithmic problems in low-dimensional matrix (semi)groups; see [5,16,37,51] for more recent work. Moreover, he introduced membership problems to group theory.

In general, a membership problem for a group G asks whether a given element $g \in G$ belongs to a given subset $S \subseteq G$. In order to get a well-defined decision problem, one has to restrict the input set S to a class of subsets having finitary representations. In Markov's case S is the submonoid generated by given matrices $A_1, \ldots, A_k \in \mathsf{SL}_4(\mathbb{Z})$. From a group theoretic perspective, it is also natural to consider the subgroup generated by the given matrices $A_1, \ldots, A_k \in \mathsf{SL}_4(\mathbb{Z})$. This leads to the *subgroup membership problem* for $\mathsf{SL}_4(\mathbb{Z})$, which is still undecidable by a result of Mihaĭlova [48]. Actually, Mihaĭlova proved that the subgroup membership problem is undecidable for the direct product of two free groups of rank 2, which is a subgroup of $\mathsf{SL}_4(\mathbb{Z})$. Following the work of Mihaĭlova, the subgroup membership problem has been studied in many different classes of groups; some of the results will be mentioned in the main part of this survey.

Whereas the subgroup membership problem is a restriction of the submonoid membership problem, one also finds a generalization of the submonoid membership problem in the literature. The class of *rational subsets* of a group G is the smallest class that can be obtained from finite subsets of G using three set operations: union, product (i.e., $S \cdot T = \{gh : g \in S, h \in T\}$ for subsets $S, T \subseteq G$)

L. Levy Patey et al. (Eds.): CiE 2024, LNCS 14773, pp. 44–59, 2024.
https://doi.org/10.1007/978-3-031-64309-5_5

and Kleene star $\langle S \rangle^*$, where $\langle S \rangle^*$ is the submonoid generated by S (often it is denoted by S^*). Alternatively, one can define rational subsets of G using finite automata whose transitions are labelled with elements of G. Clearly, a rational subset of a finitely generated group G has a finitary representation (by a regular expression or an automaton) which makes the *rational subset membership problem* well-defined. The rational subset membership problem can be traced back to a paper of Benois from 1969 [7], where she proved decidability for free groups. Gilman [23] independently rediscovered Benois' approach in 1984 and extended it to groups with a monadic confluent presentation. Grunschlag showed in 1999 that decidability of the rational subset membership problem is preserved by finite extensions and proved decidability for finitely generated abelian groups based on classical work of Eilenberg and Schützenberger. Kambites, Silva, and Steinberg took up the work of Grunschlag and showed in 2007 that rational subsets membership is decidable for the fundamental group of a graph of groups with finite edge groups and vertex groups with decidable rational subset membership problems [29]. This paper marks the starting point for a deeper investigation of the rational subset membership problem in many different classes of groups; see the main part of this survey for results obtained after 2007. In 2014, Myasnikov, Nikolaev and Ushakov introduced with the *knapsack problem* another special case of the rational subset membership problem [49]. It generalizes the classical knapsack problem over the cyclic group $\mathbb{Z}$ to a non-commutative setting.

Group Theoretic Setting. Before we introduce the above mentioned problems formally, we first set up the group theoretical context. Consider a group G. For a subset $\Sigma \subseteq G$ we denote with $\langle \Sigma \rangle$ the *subgroup* generated by Σ. It is the smallest subgroup (with respect to inclusion) of G that contains Σ. We will also consider the *submonoid* $\langle \Sigma \rangle^* \subseteq G$ and *subsemigroup* $\langle \Sigma \rangle^+ \subseteq G$ generated by Σ. Note that $\langle \Sigma \rangle^*$ ($\langle \Sigma \rangle^+$) is the set of all finite products $a_1 a_2 \cdots a_n \in G$ with $a_1, \ldots, a_n \in \Sigma$ and $n \geq 0$ ($n \geq 1$). A group G is *finitely generated* (f.g. for short) if there is a finite subset $\Sigma \subseteq G$ such that $G = \langle \Sigma \rangle$. In this situation, we say that Σ is a finite generating set of G. W.l.o.g. one can assume that for every $a \in \Sigma$, the inverse a^{-1} also belongs to Σ. For convenience, we will always assume this. It implies that $\langle \Sigma \rangle = \langle \Sigma \rangle^* = G$, i.e., there is a surjective monoid homomorphism $\pi : \Sigma^* \to G$ with $\pi(a) = a$ for all $a \in \Sigma$ (Σ^* is the free monoid generated by Σ) that we call the *evaluation homomorphism*. We also say that the word $w \in \Sigma^*$ represents the group element $\pi(w)$. For $g \in G$ we also write $|g|$ for the minimal length of a word in $\pi^{-1}(g)$. Here, we assume a fixed $\pi : \Sigma^* \to G$. We only deal with f.g. groups in this survey.

Formal Definition of the Membership Problems. We now define the computational problems that will be considered in this survey. For this we fix a f.g. group G together with an evaluation homomorphism $\pi : \Sigma^* \to G$ with Σ finite. Formally, the algorithmic problems that we introduce below depend on the choice of π. On the other hand, for the decidability and computational complexity of each of the following problems, the concrete choice of the set of generators only plays a minor role. If we take another generating set, the resulting problem is equivalent to the original problem with respect to logspace reductions.

Subgroup membership problem for G, SGM(G) for short:
- Input: words $w, w_1, \ldots, w_n \in \Sigma^*$
- Question: Does $\pi(w)$ belong to the subgroup $\langle \pi(w_1), \ldots, \pi(w_n) \rangle$?

The subgroup membership problem is also known as the generalized word problem or occurrence problem. It naturally generalizes to submonoids:

Submonoid membership problem for G, SMM(G) for short:
- Input: words $w, w_1, \ldots, w_n \in \Sigma^*$
- Question: Does $\pi(w)$ belong to the submonoid $\langle \pi(w_1), \ldots, \pi(w_n) \rangle^*$?

One might also consider the *subsemigroup membership problem* by replacing the submonoid $\langle \pi(w_1), \ldots, \pi(w_n) \rangle^*$ by the subsemigroup $\langle \pi(w_1), \ldots, \pi(w_n) \rangle^+$. But there is no real difference between the submonoid and the subsemigroup membership problem: For all $g \in G$ and $S \subseteq G$ we have $g \in \langle S \rangle^+$ iff $gh^{-1} \in \langle S \rangle^*$ for some $h \in S$. Vice versa, $g \in \langle S \rangle^*$ iff $g \in \langle S \rangle^+$ or $g \in \langle 1 \rangle^+$.

The submonoid membership problem can be further generalized to the rational subset membership problem. For a nondeterministic finite automaton $\mathcal{A}$ over an alphabet Σ we write $L(\mathcal{A}) \subseteq \Sigma^*$ for the language accepted by $\mathcal{A}$.

Rational subset membership problem for G, RatM(G) for short:
- Input: word $w \in \Sigma^*$ and a nondeterministic finite automaton $\mathcal{A}$ over the alphabet Σ
- Question: Does $\pi(w)$ belong to $\pi(L(\mathcal{A}))$?

The subsets $\pi(L(\mathcal{A})) \subseteq G$ with $\mathcal{A}$ a nondeterministic finite automaton are exactly the rational subsets of G defined above. Since for a rational subset $S \subseteq G$ and an element $g \in G$ the set $g^{-1}S$ is rational too, one can restrict to the case $w = \varepsilon$ (i.e., $\pi(w) = 1$) in the rational subset membership problem. The same restriction imposed on the subsemigroup membership problem defines the so-called *identity problem*:

Identity problem for G, Id(G) for short:
- Input: words $w, w_1, \ldots, w_n \in \Sigma^*$
- Question: Does 1 belong to the subsemigroup $\langle \pi(w_1), \ldots, \pi(w_n) \rangle^+$?

The identity problem was first studied by Choffrut and Karhumäki [14] for matrix groups. Bell and Potapov proved that the identity problem is undecidable for $SL_4(\mathbb{Z})$ [6], whereas the problem is NP-complete for $GL_2(\mathbb{Z})$ [5].

Another special case of the rational subset membership problem that has received a lot of attention in recent years is the *knapsack problem*:

Knapsack problem for G, $\mathsf{KS}(G)$ for short:
- Input: words $w, w_1, \ldots, w_n \in \Sigma^*$
- Question: Does $\pi(w)$ belong to $\langle \pi(w_1) \rangle^* \langle \pi(w_2) \rangle^* \cdots \langle \pi(w_n) \rangle^*$?

In other words, $\mathsf{KS}(G)$ is the membership problem for products of cyclic submonoids. A natural variant is the membership problem for products of cyclic subgroups. It can be reduced to $\mathsf{KS}(G)$, since $\langle g \rangle = \langle g \rangle^* \langle g^{-1} \rangle^*$.

The most general problem that we consider is *context-free membership*:

Context-free membership problem for G, $\mathsf{CFM}(G)$ for short:
- Input: word $w \in \Sigma^*$ and a context-free grammar $\mathcal{G}$ over the alphabet Σ
- Question: Does $\pi(w)$ belong to $\pi(L(\mathcal{G}))$?

In Sects. 2–10 we will give an overview on decidability and complexity results for the above mentioned problems in different classes of groups. We assume that the reader has some basic knowledge in group theory, computability, complexity theory and formal language theory. Occasionally, we use group presentations to describe groups. For a finite alphabet Γ and set of relators $R \subseteq (\Gamma \cup \Gamma^{-1})^*$ we write $\langle \Gamma \mid R \rangle$ for the corresponding group; it is the quotient of the free group $F(\Gamma)$ by the normal closure of R. For better readability we also write relators as equations: an equation $u = v$ corresponds to the relator uv^{-1}.

There are two related surveys on membership problems in group theory: [17,35]. The paper [35] focuses on rational subset membership. The present survey can be seen as an updated version of [35]. The more recent work [17] of Dong focuses on algorithmic problems for subsemigroups of groups including the subsemigroup membership problem and the identity problem. References on the complexity of word problems can be found in [38].

2   Virtually Abelian Groups

A group is *virtually abelian* if it has an abelian subgroup of finite index. In these groups, most algorithmic problems are decidable, and this holds also for membership problems:

Theorem 1. $\mathsf{CFM}(G)$ *is decidable for every f.g. virtually abelian group* G.

Proof (sketch). For the case that G is f.g. abelian, one can use Parikh's theorem to reduce $\mathsf{CFM}(G)$ to $\mathsf{RatM}(G)$. Since G is abelian, $\mathsf{RatM}(G)$ is decidable [25]. It therefore suffices to show that if G is a finite-index subgroup of H and $\mathsf{CFM}(G)$

is decidable, then also CFM(H) is decidable. One can show this with the same arguments used for rational subset membership in [35]. The crucial facts used in [35] are: (i) the word problem (viewed as the set of all words that represent the group identity) of H can be obtained by a rational transduction from the word problem for G and (ii) the class of rational languages is closed under rational transductions. But (ii) also holds for context-free languages [9, Cor. 4.2].   □

3   Free Groups and Groups Containing Free Monoids

To the knowledge of the author, the earliest result on the rational subset membership problem is due to Benois:

Theorem 2 ([7]). RatM(F) *is decidable for every f.g. free group F and can be solved in polynomial time.*

The context-free membership problem is undecidable for free groups of rank at least two. In fact, the following more general result holds (note that the free group of rank 2 contains a copy of the free monoid $\{a, b\}^*$):

Theorem 3. *If a f.g. group G contains a copy of a free monoid $\{a, b\}^*$ then* CFM(G) *is undecidable.*

Proof. Assume that the free monoid $\{a, b\}^*$ is a submonoid of G. In particular, we assume that $a, b \in G$. We reduce Post's correspondence problem (PCP) to CFM(G). Let $\Pi = \{(u_i, v_i) : 1 \leq i \leq k\}$ be an instance of PCP with $u_i, v_i \in \{a, b\}^*$. Consider the context-free grammar $\mathcal{G}$ with the productions $S \to u_i v_i^{-1}$ and $S \to u_i S v_i^{-1}$ for $1 \leq i \leq k$. We have $1 \in \pi(L(\mathcal{G}))$ iff Π has a solution.   □

Rosenblatt proved that a f.g. solvable group is either virtually nilpotent or contains a copy of $\{a, b\}^*$ [56]. Hence, the context-free membership problem for a f.g. solvable group that is not virtually nilpotent is undecidable.

4   Hyperbolic Groups

Hyperbolic groups are f.g. groups whose Cayley graph satisfies a certain condition that is motivated from hyperbolic geometry (geodesic triangles are δ-thin for a constant $\delta > 0$). They are one of the most important classes of groups in geometric group theory and have some nice algorithmic properties; for instance the word and conjugacy problem can be solved in linear time. In contrast, the subgroup membership problem is much harder by the following result of Rips:

Theorem 4 ([53]). *There is a hyperbolic group G with* SGM(G) *undecidable.*

Positive results are known for the knapsack problem in hyperbolic groups. The complexity class LogCFL consists of all languages that are logspace-reducible to a context-free language; it is a subset of P $\cap$ DSPACE($\log^2 n$).

Fig. 1. From left to right: the graphs P3, P4, C4 and C5.

Theorem 5 ([36,49]). *For every hyperbolic group G, $\mathsf{KS}(G)$ is decidable and belongs to the complexity class* LogCFL.

It is shown in [49] for every hyperbolic group G there is a polynomial $p(x)$ such that if $g \in \langle g_1 \rangle^* \langle g_2 \rangle^* \cdots \langle g_n \rangle^*$ for $g, g_1, \ldots, g_n \in G$ then there exist exponents $e_1, \ldots, e_n \in \mathbb{N}$ such that $g = g_1^{e_1} g_2^{e_2} \cdots g_n^{e_n}$ and $e_i \leq p(|g| + |g_1| + \cdots + |g_n|)$ for all i. This allows to reduce the knapsack problem for G to the *acyclic rational subset membership problem* for G, where the input automaton must be acyclic. The latter problem is shown to be in LogCFL in [36] using a result from [12] saying that context-sensitive languages where all productions are length increasing (so-called growing-context sensitive languages) can be accepted by nondeterministic one-way Turing machines working in polynomial time and logarithmic space and equipped with an additional pushdown store (the space used on the pushdown store does not count to the logarithmic space bound). These machines define LogCFL even without the one-way restriction. The word problem for a hyperbolic is known to be growing context-sensitive [38]. It is also shown in [36] that the knapsack problem for the free group F_2 of rank two is already LogCFL-complete.

Decidability of the identity problem for hyperbolic groups seems to be open.

5   Graph Groups

Let (Γ, I) be a finite graph, where Γ is the set of nodes and $I \subseteq \Gamma \times \Gamma$ is the symmetric and irreflexive edge relation. In the following we just speak of a graph. Figure 1 shows some graphs that will appear below. The *graph group* $\mathsf{G}(\Gamma, I)$ is the finitely presented group $\langle \Gamma \mid ab = ba \text{ for all } (a,b) \in I \rangle$. Graph groups are also known as right-angled Artin groups. They are linear; therefore their word problems can be solved in logspace. For the subgroup membership problem the situation is quite complicated. Note that $F_2 \times F_2$ (the direct product of two free groups of rank 2) is isomorphic to $\mathsf{G}(C4)$. Mihaĭlova proved the following:

Theorem 6 ([48]). $\mathsf{SGM}(\mathsf{G}(C4)) = \mathsf{SGM}(F_2 \times F_2)$ *is undecidable.*

A positive decidability result is known for chordal graphs, i.e., graphs that do not contain a cycle of length at least four as an induced subgraph.

Theorem 7 ([30]). $\mathsf{SGM}(\mathsf{G}(\Gamma, I))$ *is decidable if the graph* (Γ, I) *is chordal.*

In [30], Theorem 7 is stated as a corollary of a more general result saying that the subgroup membership problem is decidable for the fundamental group of a graph of groups where all vertex and edge groups are polycyclic-by-finite. An alternative proof of this result was given in [40].

A characterization of those graph groups having a decidable subgroup membership problem is not known. In particular, it is open, whether G(C5) has a decidable subgroup membership problem. For the rational subset membership problem and the submonoid membership problem, an exact characterization of the decidable cases is known. Graphs that neither contain P4 nor C4 as an induced subgraph are also known as *transitive forests*.

Theorem 8 ([39]). *Let (Γ, I) be a graph. The following are equivalent:*

- (Γ, I) *is a transitive forest.*
- SMM$(G(\Gamma, I))$ *is decidable.*
- RatM$(G(\Gamma, I))$ *is decidable.*

For the undecidability part of Theorem 8, it suffices to show that SMM(G(P4)) and SMM(G(C4)) are undecidable. The latter follows from Theorem 6. Undecidability of SMM(G(P4)) is shown in [39] by using a result on trace monoids from [1]. Trace monoids can be viewed as the monoid counterparts of graph groups. Given a finite graph (Γ, I) as above, the corresponding trace monoid M(Γ, I) is the quotient of the free monoid Σ^* by the congruence generated by all pairs (ab, ba) with $(a, b) \in I$. Rational subsets of M(Γ, I) are defined as for groups. The *disjointness problem* for rational subsets of M(Γ, I) asks whether $K \cap L \neq \emptyset$ for two given rational subsets $K, L \subseteq$ M(Γ, I). It is shown in [1] that the disjointness problem for rational subsets of M(Γ, I) is decidable if and only if (Γ, I) is a transitive forest. Finally, note that $K \cap L \neq \emptyset$ for $K, L \subseteq$ M(Γ, I) if and only if $1 \in KL^{-1}$, where KL^{-1} is viewed as a rational subset of the graph group G(Γ, I). This shows in particular that RatPM(G(P4)) is undecidable. Finally, RatPM(G(P4)) is reduced to SMM(G(P4)) in [39].

The decidability part in Theorem 8 was further refined by Haase and Zetzsche who determined the complexity of RatM$(G(\Gamma, I))$ for transitive forests:

Theorem 9 ([27]). *Let (Γ, I) be a transitive forest. Then* RatM$(G(\Gamma, I))$ *is*

- NL-*complete if (Γ, I) is a clique,*
- P-*complete if (Γ, I) is a disjoint union of at least two cliques, and*
- NP-*complete if (Γ, I) contains an induced P3, i.e., (Γ, I) is not transitive.*

The uniform version of the rational subset membership problem for graph groups, where the transitive forest (Γ, I) is part of the input is NEXPTIME-*complete.*

For the NEXPTIME upper bound in the uniform case, where the transitive forest (Γ, I) is part of the input, Haase and Zetzsche show that the rational subset membership problem is equivalent to the satisfiability problem for existential Presburger arithmetic extended by the star operator. The star operator applied to a set $S \subseteq \mathbb{N}^k$ yields the submonoid of the additive monoid $(\mathbb{N}^k, +)$ generated by S. It is shown in [27] that the satisfiability problem for existential Presburger arithmetic with the star operator is NEXPTIME-complete. In addition, if the nesting depth of the star operator in the input formula is bounded by a fixed constant then the satisfiability problem becomes NP-complete (and hence has the same complexity as the satisfiability problem for existential Presburger arithmetic without the star operator). This yields the NP upper bound in Theorem 9. For the NP lower bound, the subset sum problem is reduced to $\mathsf{RatM}(F_2 \times \mathbb{Z})$.

A characterization similar to Theorem 9 is also known for the knapsack problem. The complexity class TC^0 is a very small class within LogCFL. It is captured by the problem of counting the number of 1's in a bit string.

Theorem 10 ([45]). $\mathsf{KS}(\mathsf{G}(\Gamma, I))$ *is decidable for every graph* (Γ, I) *and is*

- TC^0-*complete if* (Γ, I) *is a clique,*
- LogCFL-*complete if* (Γ, I) *is a transitive forest but not a clique, and*
- NP-*complete if* (Γ, I) *is not a transitive forest.*

For the NP upper bound the line of arguments in [45] goes as follows: Consider a graph group $G = \mathsf{G}(\Gamma, I)$. It is shown in [45] that if $g \in \langle g_1 \rangle^* \langle g_2 \rangle^* \cdots \langle g_n \rangle^*$ for $g, g_1, \ldots, g_n \in G$ then there exist $e_1, \ldots, e_n \in \mathbb{N}$ such that $g = g_1^{e_1} g_2^{e_2} \cdots g_n^{e_n}$ and every e_i is exponentially bounded in $|g| + |g_1| + \cdots + |g_n|$. One can therefore nondeterministically guess in polynomial time the binary encodings of exponents $e_1, \ldots, e_n$. It then remains to verify whether $g = g_1^{e_1} g_2^{e_2} \cdots g_n^{e_n}$ holds. This is an instance of the so-called compressed word problem for the graph group G, which can be solved in polynomial time [34]. The LogCFL upper bound in Theorem 10 for the case that (Γ, I) is a transitive forest, follows the same line of arguments that was sketched for hyperbolic groups in Sect. 4.

Let us also mention that the uniform knapsack problem for graph groups, where the graph is part of the input, is NP-complete by a recent result form [44].

6 Nilpotent Groups and Polycyclic Groups

Polycyclic groups are solvable groups where every subgroup is finitely generated. Mal'cev proved in [46] the following result (see [2] for an alternative proof):

Theorem 11 ([46]). $\mathsf{SGM}(G)$ *is decidable for every polycyclic group* G.

To the knowledge of the author, the complexity of the subgroup membership problem for polycyclic groups is open. For the smaller class of f.g. nilpotent groups, the complexity is very low:

Theorem 12 ([50]). $\mathsf{SGM}(G)$ *belongs to* TC^0 *for every f.g. nilpotent group* G.

Recently, the identity problem for nilpotent groups attracted a lot of attention. Dong [19] showed that the identity problem is decidable for all nilpotent groups of class at most 10. Shafrir then solved the general case:

Theorem 13 ([57]). $\mathsf{Id}(G)$ *belongs to* P *for every f.g. nilpotent group* G.

The main ingredient in [57] is the following result, where $G' = [G, G]$ is the commutator subgroup of G: If G is a f.g. nilpotent group and M is a submonoid of G such that MG' is a finite index subgroup of G then M is also a finite index subgroup of G. Moreover, if $MG' = G$ then $M = G$. For the case that M is a subgroup G this was known before. Shafrir combines this result with linear programming techniques (Farkas' lemma) to prove Theorem 13. With similar techniques, one can show Theorem 13 also using [10, Proposition 2.5], whose proof will appear in a forthcoming paper of Bodart, Ciobanu, and Metcalfe.

Somehow surprisingly, the knapsack problem and the submonoid membership problem are in general undecidable already for nilpotent groups of class 2. The following two results can be shown using reductions from Hilbert's 10th problem.

Theorem 14 ([54]). *There is a f.g. class-2 nilpotent group G with* SMM(G) *undecidable.*

Theorem 15 ([32]). *There is a f.g. class-2 nilpotent group G with* KS(G) *undecidable.*

For nilpotent groups of small *Hirsch length* further decidability were recently shown by Shafrir. The Hirsch length $h(G)$ of a nilpotent group G is the sum of the ranks of all the successive abelian factor groups in the lower central series.

Theorem 16 ([58]). KS(G) *is decidable for every f.g. nilpotent group G with* $h([G, G]) = 1$, *which means that* $[G, G] \cong \mathbb{Z} \times A$ *for a finite abelian group A.*

The proof of Theorem 16 is based on a short reduction of KS(G) to the problem of whether a system consisting of (i) a single quadratic Diophantine equation plus (ii) an arbitrary number of linear equations has an integer solution. Decidability of this special case of Hilbert's 10th problem is shown in [20, 24].

Theorem 17 ([58]). SMM(G) *is decidable for every f.g. nilpotent group G with* $h([G, G]) \leq 2$.

Shafrir uses a result of Bodart [10] that allows to reduce membership in a submonoid $M \subseteq G$ (for G a f.g. nilpotent group) to membership in products $\langle S_1 \rangle^* \langle S_2 \rangle^* \cdots \langle S_n \rangle^*$, where all S_i are finite and are contained in a subgroup $H \leq G$ with $h([H, H]) < h([G, G])$. Here, H depends on M. Then Shafrir shows, using a combinatorial lemma on integer sequences with bounded gaps, that in a f.g. nilpotent group H with $h([H, H]) = 1$, every f.g. submonoid is effectively a product of cyclic submonoids. Hence, the product $\langle S_1 \rangle^* \langle S_2 \rangle^* \cdots \langle S_n \rangle^*$ can be replaced by a product of cyclic submonoids, which allows to apply Theorem 16.

Theorems 16 and 17 generalize previous results for Heisenberg groups $H_n(\mathbb{Z})$ from [32] (for knapsack) and [15] (for submonoid membership). The Heisenberg group $H_n(\mathbb{Z})$ consists of all n-dimensional upper triangular integer matrices such that all diagonal entries are 1 and all non-diagonal entries that are not in the top-most row or the right-most column are 0. Note that $[H_n(\mathbb{Z}), H_n(\mathbb{Z})] \cong \mathbb{Z}$; therefore Theorems 16 and 17 apply. For $n = 3$, even rational subset membership is decidable by the following result of Bodart.

Theorem 18 ([10]). RatM$(H_3(\mathbb{Z}))$ *is decidable.*

Bodart proved this result by reducing $\mathsf{RatM}(H_3(\mathbb{Z}))$ to $\mathsf{KS}(H_3(\mathbb{Z}))$. For this he shows that every rational subset of $H_3(\mathbb{Z})$ is effectively the image of a *bounded* regular language L. A language is called bounded if it is contained in a set $w_1^* w_2^* \cdots w_k^*$ for words $w_1, \ldots, w_k$. One finally obtains a finite number of knapsack instances from a classical result of formal language theory saying that a regular language is bounded iff it is a finite union of languages $v_0 w_1^* v_1 w_2^* \cdots v_{k-1} w_k^* v_k$.

It is open, whether Theorem 18 generalizes to all Heisenberg groups $H_n(\mathbb{Z})$. It is also open whether $\mathsf{CFM}(H_3(\mathbb{Z}))$ is decidable. We have already observed that every f.g. solvable group that is not virtually nilpotent has an undecidable context-free membership problem (Sect. 3). It is known that every f.g. virtually nilpotent group that is not virtually abelian contains a copy of $H_3(\mathbb{Z})$ [28, proof of Theorem 12]. We obtain the following conditional characterization: assuming that $\mathsf{CFM}(H_3(\mathbb{Z}))$ is undecidable, a f.g. solvable group G is virtually abelian if and only if $\mathsf{CFM}(G)$ is decidable.

7 Metabelian Groups

A group G is *metabelian* if its commutator subgroup $[G, G]$ is abelian.

Theorem 19 ([3,55]). $\mathsf{SGM}(G)$ *is decidable for every f.g. metabelian group* G.

Both papers [3,55] actually show a more general result: if G is f.g. abelian-by-nilpotent then $\mathsf{SGM}(G)$ is decidable. The complexity of the subgroup membership problem for metabelian groups seems to be open. For the identity problem, Dong showed the following result. The proof is very involved and combines techniques from convex geometry, graph theory, algebraic geometry, and number theory:

Theorem 20 ([18]). $\mathsf{Id}(G)$ *is decidable for every f.g. metabelian group* G.

Theorems 19 and 20 are all general positive results for membership problems in f.g. metabelian groups that the author is aware of. On the side of undecidability, the following is known.

Theorem 21 ([42,43]). *There are f.g. metabelian groups* G *with* $\mathsf{SMM}(G)$ *undecidable. Examples are the wreath product* $\mathbb{Z} \wr \mathbb{Z}$ *and the free metabelian group* M_2 *generated by two elements.*

Undecidability of $\mathsf{SMM}(M_2)$ is shown in [43] by a reduction from a tiling problem for the Euclidean plane, whereas undecidability of $\mathsf{SMM}(\mathbb{Z} \wr \mathbb{Z})$ is shown in [43] by a reduction from the halting problem for 2-counter machines.

Also the knapsack problem is in general undecidable for f.g. metabelian groups by Theorem 15, because nilpotent groups of class two are metabelian. On the other hand, free metabelian groups have a decidable knapsack problem; this is a special case of Theorem 26 below. Also the knapsack problem for $\mathbb{Z} \wr \mathbb{Z}$ is decidable. This follows from a more general result: $\mathsf{KS}(G)$ is decidable for every co-context-free group G [32]. A f.g. group G with the evaluation homomorphism $\pi : \Sigma^* \to G$ is co-context-free if the co-word problem $\{w \in \Sigma^* : \pi(w) \neq 1\}$ is context-free [28]. The wreath product $\mathbb{Z} \wr \mathbb{Z}$ is co-context-free [28, Theorem 10]. Another interesting example of a co-context-free group is Thompson's group F.

8   Wreath Products

We mentioned above that $\mathsf{SMM}(\mathbb{Z} \wr \mathbb{Z})$ is undecidable [43]. In the same paper, the following positive result was shown:

Theorem 22 ([43]). *If G is a finite group and H is a f.g. virtually free group then $\mathsf{RatM}(G \wr H)$ is decidable.*

The proof of this result in [43] uses techniques from the theory of well-quasi orders. Due to this, the algorithm in [43] is not primitive recursive.

It seems to be difficult to extend Theorem 22 beyond the case where H is virtually free. For $\mathbb{Z}^2 = \mathbb{Z} \times \mathbb{Z}$ the following undecidability result is shown in [42] using a tiling problem.

Theorem 23 ([42]). *If $G \neq 1$ is a f.g. group then $\mathsf{RatM}(G \wr \mathbb{Z}^2)$ is undecidable.*

In contrast to Theorem 23, Shafrir showed the following result:

Theorem 24 ([52]). *If G is finite and abelian then $\mathsf{SMM}(G \wr \mathbb{Z}^2)$ is decidable.*

Shafrir's proof can be found in the Bachelor thesis [52], which is based on an unpublished draft of Shafrir. He shows that for any wreath product $W = G \wr \mathbb{Z}^2$ with G finite, $\mathsf{SMM}(W)$ can be reduced to $\mathsf{SGM}(W)$. If, in addition, G is abelian then W is metabelian and $\mathsf{SGM}(W)$ is decidable by Theorem 19.

Together, Theorems 23 and 24 yield examples of groups G where $\mathsf{RatM}(G)$ is undecidable but $\mathsf{SMM}(G)$ is decidable. The existence of such groups solved an open problem from [41], where it is shown that if G is a f.g. group with more than one end then there is a computable reduction from $\mathsf{RatM}(G)$ to $\mathsf{SMM}(G)$. Bodart [10] recently gave another example of a group G, where $\mathsf{RatM}(G)$ is undecidable but $\mathsf{SMM}(G)$ is decidable. His example is a f.g. nilpotent group G of class 2.

A corollary of these results is that decidability of the submonoid membership problem is not preserved by free products (in contrast to subgroup membership and rational subset membership): If it would be, then $\mathsf{SMM}(G * \mathbb{Z})$ would be decidable, where G is such that $\mathsf{RatM}(G)$ is undecidable and $\mathsf{SMM}(G)$ is decidable. Since $G * \mathbb{Z}$ has infinitely many ends, $\mathsf{RatM}(G * \mathbb{Z})$ and hence $\mathsf{RatM}(G)$ would be decidable by [41], which is a contradiction.

A characterization of the class of wreath products $G \wr H$ with a decidable knapsack problem can be found in [8]. The characterization is a bit technical and uses knapsack variants for G and H; we refer the reader to [8].

9   Solvable Groups

Metabelian groups are exactly the solvable groups of derived length 2. There is no hope to get decidability results for arbitrary solvable groups of derived length 3: Kharlampovich constructed a finitely presented solvable group of derived length 3 with an undecidable word problem [31]. For the subgroup membership problem, undecidability is already encountered for free solvable groups. Let $S_{c,r}$ be the free solvable group of derived length c generated by r elements.

Theorem 25 ([59]). $\mathsf{SGM}(S_{3,2})$ *is undecidable.*

The knapsack problem for free solvable groups turns out to be easier:

Theorem 26 ([21]). *For every* $c, r \geq 2$, $\mathsf{KS}(S_{c,r})$ *is decidable and* NP-*complete.*

The proof of Theorem 26 exploits the Magnus embedding theorem that allows to embed a free solvable group into an iterated wreath product $\mathbb{Z}^m \wr (\mathbb{Z}^m \wr (\mathbb{Z}^m \cdots))$. For such a wreath product one can show that if $g \in \langle g_1 \rangle^* \langle g_2 \rangle^* \cdots \langle g_n \rangle^*$ then $g = g_1^{e_1} g_2^{e_2} \cdots g_n^{e_n}$, where every $e_i \in \mathbb{N}$ is exponentially bounded in $|g| + |g_1| + \cdots + |g_n|$.

Solvable matrix groups are another important class of solvable groups with a more amenable algorithmic theory. Note that by Tits alternative a f.g. matrix group is either virtually solvable or contains a copy of the free group of rank 2.

Theorem 27 ([33]). $\mathsf{SGM}(G)$ *is decidable for every f.g. virtually solvable matrix group over the field of algebraic numbers.*

Theorem 28 ([11]). $\mathsf{Id}(G)$ *is decidable for every f.g. virtually solvable matrix group over the field of algebraic numbers.*

Theorem 28 generalizes the decidability statement in Theorem 13. The proof of Theorem 28 extends some of the key results from [10,18,57].

10   Baumslag-Solitar Groups

For $p, q \geq 1$, the *Baumslag-Solitar group* $\mathsf{BS}_{p,q} = \langle a, t \mid t^{-1} a^p t = a^q \rangle$ is a one-relator group that was introduced by Baumslag and Solitar in [4], where they showed that $\mathsf{BS}_{2,3}$ is non-Hopfian (i.e., $\mathsf{BS}_{2,3}$ is isomorphic to a proper quotient of $\mathsf{BS}_{2,3}$). The word problem for every Baumslag-Solitar group $\mathsf{BS}_{p,q}$ can be solved in logarithmic space. The following result is a corollary of a more general result from [30] that has already mentioned after Theorem 7.

Theorem 29 ([30]). $\mathsf{SGM}(\mathsf{BS}_{p,q})$ *is decidable for all for* $p, q \geq 1$.

The groups $\mathsf{BS}_{1,q}$ is also metabelian, so $\mathsf{Id}(\mathsf{BS}_{1,q})$ is decidable by Theorem 20. In addition, the following two positive results hold:

Theorem 30 ([13]). $\mathsf{RatM}(\mathsf{BS}_{1,q})$ *for* $q \geq 2$ *is* PSPACE-*complete.*

Theorem 31 ([22]). $\mathsf{KS}(\mathsf{BS}_{1,q})$ *for* $q \geq 2$ *is* NP-*complete.*

In their proof of Theorem 30 the authors use a particular word representation of elements of $\mathsf{BS}_{1,q}$, which they call the pointed expansion. It is well known that $\mathsf{BS}_{1,q}$ is isomorphic to the semidirect product $\mathbb{Z}[1/q] \rtimes \mathbb{Z}$, where $\mathbb{Z}[1/q]$ is the additive group of all rationals of the form $z q^i$ where $z, i \in \mathbb{Z}$ and $\mathbb{Z}$ acts on $\mathbb{Z}[1/q]$ by $j \cdot z q^i = z q^{i+j}$ for $i, j, z \in \mathbb{Z}$. Hence, one can represent an element $g \in \mathsf{BS}_{1,q} \cong \mathbb{Z}[1/q] \rtimes \mathbb{Z}$ by a pair $(\pm a_k a_{k+1} \cdots a_0 {\scriptstyle\bullet} a_{-1} a_{-2} \cdots a_{-\ell}, i)$, where $\pm a_k a_{k+1} \cdots a_0 \bullet a_{-1} a_2 \cdots a_\ell$ is the q-ary representation of the $\mathbb{Z}[1/q]$-part (hence, $a_k, \ldots, a_{-\ell} \in [0, q-1]$) and $i \in [-\ell, k]$ is the $\mathbb{Z}$-part. Uniqueness of this representation can be obtained by choosing the interval $[-\ell, k]$ minimal. The pointed expansion of G is then obtained by taking the word $\pm a_k a_{k+1} \cdots a_0 \bullet a_{-1} a_{-2} \cdots a_{-\ell}$ and marking a_i with a special marker. The main result of [22] states that for a rational subset $S \subseteq G$ the set $\mathsf{pe}(S)$ of all pointed expansions of elements from S is effectively a regular language. Moreover, from a given automaton for S one can construct in polynomial space a certain succinct description of an automaton for $\mathsf{pe}(S)$. This suffices in order to get the PSPACE upper bound in Theorem 30. The PSPACE lower bound is shown by a reduction from the intersection nonemptiness problem for finite automata.

For the proof of Theorem 31, $\mathsf{KS}(\mathsf{BS}_{1,q})$ is reduced in [22] to the existential fragment of Büchi arithmetic. Büchi arithmetic is the first-order theory of the structure $(\mathbb{Z}, +, \geq, 0, V_q)$, where V_q is the function that maps the the integer n to the largest power of q that divides n. Here, $q \geq 2$ is a fixed integer. The existential fragment of Büchi arithmetic was shown to be in NP in [26].

Let us finally remark that since $\mathsf{BS}_{1,q}$ contains a copy of the free submonoid $\{a, b\}^*$ ($\mathsf{BS}_{1,q}$ is solvable but not virtually nilpotent), the context-free subset membership problem for $\mathsf{BS}_{1,q}$ is undecidable.

11 Open Problems

We conclude with a list of open problems. Some of them were already mentioned in the main part of the paper.

1. Is $\mathsf{CFM}(H_3(\mathbb{Z}))$ decidable?
2. Is there any non-virtually-abelian group G such that $\mathsf{CFM}(G)$ is decidable?
3. Is $\mathsf{RatM}(H_n(\mathbb{Z}))$ decidable for all n?
4. Is $\mathsf{Id}(G)$ decidable for every hyperbolic group G?
5. For which graph groups G is $\mathsf{SGM}(G)$ decidable?
6. Is $\mathsf{RatM}(\mathsf{BS}_{p,q})$ decidable for all p, q? What about $\mathsf{SMM}(\mathsf{BS}_{p,q})$?
7. Is $\mathsf{SGM}(\mathsf{SL}_3(\mathbb{Z}))$ decidable? What about $\mathsf{Id}(\mathsf{SL}_3(\mathbb{Z}))$ and $\mathsf{KS}(\mathsf{SL}_3(\mathbb{Z}))$?
8. Is there a group G such that $\mathsf{SMM}(G)$ is decidable and $\mathsf{KS}(G)$ is undecidable?
9. Is SMM (RatM) decidable for fundamental groups of closed orientable two-dimensional manifolds of genus at least two?

References

1. Aalbersberg, I.J., Hoogeboom, H.J.: Characterizations of the decidability of some problems for regular trace languages. Math. Syst. Theory **22**, 1–19 (1989)
2. Avenhaus, J., Wißmann, D.: Using rewriting techniques to solve the generalized word problem in polycyclic groups. In: Proceedings of the ISSAC 1989, pp. 322–337. ACM (1989)
3. Baumslag, G., Cannonito, F.B., Miller, C.F., III.: Computable algebra and group embeddings. J. Algebra **69**, 186–212 (1981)

4. Baumslag, G., Solitar, D.: Some two-generator one-relator non-Hopfian groups. Bull. Am. Math. Soc. **68**(3), 199–201 (1962)
5. Bell, P.C., Hirvensalo, M., Potapov, I.: The membership problem for subsemigroups of GL2(Z) is NP-complete. Inf. Comput. **296**, 105132 (2024)
6. Bell, P.C., Potapov, I.: On the undecidability of the identity correspondence problem and its applications for word and matrix semigroups. Int. J. Found. Comput. Sci. **21**(6), 963–978 (2010)
7. Benois, M.: Parties rationnelles du groupe libre. Comptes rendus de l'Académie des sciences, Sér. A **269**, 1188–1190 (1969)
8. Bergsträßer, P., Ganardi, M., Zetzsche, G.: A characterization of wreath products where Knapsack is decidable. In: Proceedings of the STACS 2021. LIPIcs, vol. 187, pp. 11:1–11:17. Schloss Dagstuhl - Leibniz-Zentrum für Informatik (2021)
9. Berstel, J.: Transductions and context–free languages. Teubner (1979)
10. Bodart, C.: Membership problems in nilpotent groups (2024). http://arxiv.org/abs/2401.15504
11. Bodart, C., Dong, R.: The identity problem in virtually solvable matrix groups over algebraic numbers (2024). http://arxiv.org/abs/2404.02264
12. Buntrock, G., Otto, F.: Growing context-sensitive languages and Church-Rosser languages. Inf. Comput. **141**, 1–36 (1998)
13. Cadilhac, M., Chistikov, D., Zetzsche, G.: Rational subsets of Baumslag-Solitar groups. In: Proceedings of the ICALP 2020. LIPIcs, vol. 168, pp. 116:1–116:16. Schloss Dagstuhl - Leibniz-Zentrum für Informatik (2020)
14. Choffrut, C., Karhumäki, J.: Some decision problems on integer matrices. RAIRO Theor. Inform. Appl. **39**(1), 125–131 (2005)
15. Colcombet, T., Ouaknine, J., Semukhin, P., Worrell, J.: On reachability problems for low-dimensional matrix semigroups. In: Proceedings of the ICALP 2019. LIPIcs, vol. 132, pp. 44:1–44:15. Schloss Dagstuhl - Leibniz-Zentrum für Informatik (2019)
16. Diekert, V., Potapov, I., Semukhin, P.: Decidability of membership problems for flat rational subsets of GL(2, Q) and singular matrices. In: Proceedings of the ISSAC 2020, pp. 122–129. ACM (2020)
17. Dong, R.: Recent advances in algorithmic problems for semigroups. ACM SIGLOG News **10**(4), 3–23 (2023)
18. Dong, R.: Semigroup algorithmic problems in metabelian groups (2023). http://arxiv.org/abs/2304.12893
19. Dong, R.: The identity problem in nilpotent groups of bounded class. In: Proceedings of the SODA 2024, pp. 3919–3959. SIAM (2024)
20. Duchin, M., Liang, H., Shapiro, M.: Equations in nilpotent groups. Proc. Am. Math. Soc. **143**, 4723–4731 (2015)
21. Figelius, M., Ganardi, M., Lohrey, M., Zetzsche, G.: The complexity of knapsack problems in wreath products. In: Proceedings of the ICALP 2020. LIPIcs, vol. 168, pp.126:1–126:18. Schloss Dagstuhl - Leibniz-Zentrum für Informatik (2020)
22. Ganardi, M., Lohrey, M., Zetzsche, G.: Knapsack and the power word problem in solvable Baumslag-Solitar groups. Int. J. Algebra Comput. **33**(3), 617–639 (2023)
23. Gilman, R.H.: Computations with rational subsets of confluent groups. In: Fitch, J. (ed.) EUROSAM 1984. LNCS, vol. 174, pp. 207–212. Springer, Heidelberg (1984). https://doi.org/10.1007/BFb0032843
24. Grunewald, F., Segal, D.: On the integer solutions of quadratic equations. J. Reine Angew. Math. **569**, 13–45 (2004)
25. Grunschlag, Z.: Algorithms in geometric group theory. Ph.D. thesis, University of California at Berkley (1999)

26. Guépin, F., Haase, C., Worrell, J.: On the existential theories of Büchi arithmetic and linear p-adic fields. In: Proceedigns of the LICS 2019, pp. 1–10. IEEE (2019)
27. Haase, C., Zetzsche, G.: Presburger arithmetic with stars, rational subsets of graph groups, and nested zero tests. In: Proceedings of the LICS 2019, pp. 1–14. IEEE (2019)
28. Holt, D.F., Rees, S., Röver, C.E., Thomas, R.M.: Groups with context-free co-word problem. J. Lond. Math. Soc. **71**(3), 643–657 (2005)
29. Kambites, M., Silva, P.V., Steinberg, B.: On the rational subset problem for groups. J. Algebra **309**(2), 622–639 (2007)
30. Kapovich, I., Weidmann, R., Myasnikov, A.: Foldings, graphs of groups and the membership problem. Int. J. Algebra Comput. **15**(1), 95–128 (2005)
31. Kharlampovich, O.: A finitely presented solvable group with unsolvable word problem. Izvestiya Ak. Nauk, Ser. Math. **45**(4), 852–873 (1981)
32. König, D., Lohrey, M., Zetzsche, G.: Knapsack and subset sum problems in nilpotent, polycyclic, and co-context-free groups. In: Algebra and Computer Science. Contemporary Mathematics, vol. 677, pp. 138–153. AMS (2016)
33. Kopytov, V.M.: Solvability of the problem of occurrence in finitely generated soluble groups of matrices over the field of algebraic numbers. Algebra Logic **7**(6), 388–393 (1968)
34. Lohrey, M.: The Compressed Word Problem for Groups. Springer, Cham (2014)
35. Lohrey, M.: The rational subset membership problem for groups: a survey. In: Proceedings of the Groups St Andrews 2013. London Mathematical Society Lecture Note Series, vol. 422, pp. 368–389 (2016)
36. Lohrey, M.: Knapsack in hyperbolic groups. J. Algebra **545**, 390–415 (2020)
37. Lohrey, M.: Subgroup membership in GL(2,Z). Theory Comput. Syst. (2023)
38. Lohrey, M.: Parallel complexity in group theory. In: Languages and Automata: GAGTA BOOK 3. De Gruyter, to appear
39. Lohrey, M., Steinberg, B.: The submonoid and rational subset membership problems for graph groups. J. Algebra **320**(2), 728–755 (2008)
40. Lohrey, M., Steinberg, B.: An automata theoretic approach to the generalized word problem in graphs of groups. Proc. Am. Math. Soc. **138**, 445–453 (2010)
41. Lohrey, M., Steinberg, B.: Submonoids and rational subsets of groups with infinitely many ends. J. Algebra **324**(4), 970–983 (2010)
42. Lohrey, M., Steinberg, B.: Tilings and submonoids of metabelian groups. Theory Comput. Syst. **48**(2), 411–427 (2011)
43. Lohrey, M., Steinberg, B., Zetzsche, G.: Rational subsets and submonoids of wreath products. Inf. Comput. **243**, 191–204 (2015)
44. Lohrey, M., Stober, F., Weiß, A.: The power word problem in graph products. Theory Comput. Syst. (2024). https://doi.org/10.1007/s00224-024-10173-z
45. Lohrey, M., Zetzsche, G.: Knapsack in graph groups. Theory Comput. Syst. **62**(1), 192–246 (2018)
46. Mal'cev, A.I.: On homomorphisms onto finite groups. Am. Math. Soc. Translations Series **2**(119), 67–79 (1983)
47. Markov, A.: On certain insoluble problems concerning matrices. Dokl. Akad. Nauk SSSR **57**, 539–542 (1947)
48. Mihaĭlova, K.A.: The occurrence problem for direct products of groups. Math. USSR Sbornik **70**, 241–251 (1966). English translation
49. Myasnikov, A., Nikolaev, A., Ushakov, A.: Knapsack problems in groups. Math. Comput. **84**, 987–1016 (2015)
50. Myasnikov, A., Weiß, A.: Parallel complexity for nilpotent groups. Int. J. Algebra Comput. **32**(5), 895–928 (2022)

51. Potapov, I., Semukhin, P.: Decidability of the membership problem for 2×2 integer matrices. In: Proceedings of the SODA 2017, pp. 170–186. SIAM (2017)
52. Potthast, F.: Submonoid membership for wreath products. Bachelor thesis, University of Siegen (2020)
53. Rips, E.: Subgroups of small cancellation groups. Bull. Lond. Math. Soc. **14**, 45–47 (1982)
54. Roman'kov, V.A.: Undecidability of the submonoid membership problem for free nilpotent group of class $l \geq 2$ of sufficiently large rank. Izvestiya Math. **87**(4), 798–816 (2023)
55. Romanovskiĭ, N.S.: The occurrence problem for extensions of abelian groups by nilpotent groups. Sibirsk. Mat. Zh. **21**, 170–174 (1980)
56. Rosenblatt, J.M.: Invariant measures and growth conditions. Trans. Am. Math. Soc. **193**, 33–53 (1974)
57. Shafrir, D.: A saturation theorem for submonoids of nilpotent groups and the identity problem (2024). http://arxiv.org/abs/2402.07337
58. Shafrir, D.: Bounded generation of submonoids of Heisenberg groups (2024). https://arxiv.org/pdf/2405.05939
59. Umirbaev, U.U.: The occurrence problem for free solvable groups. Sibirskiĭ Fond Algebry i Logiki. Algebra i Logika **34**(2), 211–232, 243 (1995)

Communication Modalities

Roman Kuznets[✉] [iD]

TU Wien, Vienna, Austria
roman@logic.at

Abstract. Epistemic analysis of distributed systems is one of the biggest successes among applications of logic in computer science. The reason for that is that agents' actions are necessarily guided by their knowledge. Thus, epistemic modal logic, with its knowledge and belief modalities (and group versions thereof), has played a vital role in establishing both impossibility results and necessary conditions for solvable distributed tasks. In distributed systems, knowledge is largely attained via communication. It has been standard in both distributed systems and dynamic epistemic logic to treat incoming messages as trustworthy, thus, creating difficulties in the epistemic analysis of byzantine distributed systems where faulty agents may lie. In this paper, we argue that handling such communication scenarios calls for additional modalities representing the informational content of messages that should not be taken at face value. We present two such modalities: *hope* for the case of fully byzantine agents and *creed* for non-uniform communication protocols in general.

Keywords: Distributed systems · Modal logic · Epistemic logic · Byzantine agents

1 Introduction

In their paper *On the Unusual Effectiveness of Logic in Computer Science* [14], Halpern et al. list "the deployment of epistemic logic to reason about knowledge in multi-agent systems" as one of the "areas of computer science on which logic has had a definite and lasting impact" and support their thesis with multiple examples. This should come as no surprise since knowledge is inextricably linked with action. Moses [22] recently formalized this in the form of the *Knowledge of Preconditions Principle* (KoP):

Knowledge of Preconditions Principle. If φ is a necessary condition for agent i performing action α, then $K_i\varphi$ (i.e., agent i's knowledge of φ) is also a necessary condition for agent i performing action α.

The logic commonly used to reason about knowledge is *epistemic modal logic* [16], with its semantics of *Kripke models* consisting of possible worlds.

This research was funded by the Austrian Science Fund (FWF) project ByzDEL (P33600).

L. Levy Patey et al. (Eds.): CiE 2024, LNCS 14773, pp. 60–71, 2024.
https://doi.org/10.1007/978-3-031-64309-5_6

According to this semantics, knowledge is limited by how well agents are able to pinpoint the real world among the many worlds they consider possible: the fewer possibilities considered, the more the agent knows.

This semantics is adapted to the specific needs of distributed systems in the *runs and systems framework* [8], with global states of the distributed system playing the role of possible worlds and with each agent's local states determining what this agent considers possible. As a result, all global states where the agent has the same local state are indistinguishable for the agent, resulting in rather strong properties of knowledge, including factivity (whatever is known must be true), as well as positive and negative introspection (the agent knows what it knows and what it does not know). In modal terms, this corresponds to (the multimodal version of) logic S5.

While the form of messages in distributed systems is not restricted, it is assumed that agents interpret each message they receive based on the common a priori knowledge of the *joint protocol*, i.e., of the protocols of each agent. This assumption of common a priori knowledge of the protocols is akin to the common knowledge of the model pointed out by Artemov as an assumption in epistemic modal logic in general [1]. In particular, it completely abstracts away any difficulties of interpreting messages correctly.

The other side of this coin, however, is that it is not clear how to interpret messages that are not sent according to a pre-determined protocol. A prominent example of this can be found in *byzantine distributed systems*, i.e., distributed systems with *fully byzantine* agents [20], i.e., agents that can arbitrarily deviate from their protocols. In particular, a fully byzantine agent can send any message at any time, independent of both its local state and its (correct) protocol. Thus, it should come as no surprise that, until recently, the standard epistemic analysis of distributed systems did not extend to byzantine distributed systems.[1]

Providing the epistemic analysis of distributed systems with fully byzantine agents was the goal of the project "ByzDEL: Reasoning about Knowledge in Byzantine Distributed Systems" funded by the Austrian Science Fund (FWF) that Roman Kuznets led in TU Wien with Ulrich Schmid as the co-PI. In this paper, we report (some of) the findings of our team.

The difficulty of interpreting a message in byzantine systems is that the recipient must consider the possibility of the sender being faulty. With faulty agents able to lie, there seems to be no increase in the recipient's knowledge. And yet distributed protocols work for byzantine systems. One of the basic observations is that, under the common assumption of having at most f byzantine agents, receiving the same message from $f + 1$ distinct agents is sufficient to guarantee the message veracity. But counting is not part of epistemic modal logic, making it hard to explain this increase in knowledge in the modal language of knowledge.

---

[1] There were papers about knowledge in "byzantine" or "fault-tolerant" distributed systems, such as [7,15,24], but the types of failures there is restricted to crashes and/or omissions, meaning that all messages are still sent according to the pre-determined protocol.

One of the byzantine distributed problems we analyzed was the Firing Rebels with Relay [9], which is related to both the Byzantine Firing Squad by Burns and Lynch [2] and the consistent broadcasting primitive Srikanth and Toueg [29], the latter used for fault-tolerant clock synchronization and byzantine synchronous consensus. In the course of this analysis [11], we discovered a new modality we called *hope* H_i. In this paper, we show that $H_i\varphi$ represents exactly the informational content of receiving message φ from agent i and argue that the language with both knowledge and hope modalities for each agent is the right language for the epistemic analysis of byzantine distributed systems.

In byzantine systems, a message is either taken at face value or ignored, depending on whether the sender is correct or byzantine. However, many communicative situations call for a more nuanced way of interpreting information than all or nothing. For instance, the quantity maxim of Grice [13] may allow to extract additional information from the message by considering what could have been said but was not. To address such more complex types of communication we propose a generalization of hope modality that we call *creed*.

The paper is structured as follows. In Sect. 2, we recall the standard representation of knowledge in distributed systems via the runs and systems framework and the resulting logic S5 for the knowledge modality. In Sect. 3, we show how our analysis of byzantine distributed systems forces to relativize knowledge to the agent's correctness, resulting in the so-called modality of belief as defeasible knowledge. In Sect. 4, we discuss our novel hope modality for representing information obtained by communication in byzantine distributed systems. In Sect. 5, we introduce the creed modality that generalizes hope and can be used to describe communication in *heterogeneous distributed systems*, with more complex agent types than just correct and byzantine. Finally, in Sect. 6, we provide conclusions.

2   Knowledge Modality

As already mentioned, Kripke models are the standard tool for semantic reasoning about modality in general and *knowledge modality* in particular. Throughout the paper, we assume that there is a finite set $A = \{1, \ldots, n\}$ of *agents* denoted $i, j, a, b, \ldots$ and a countably infinite set Prop of (*propositional*) *atoms* denoted $p, q, p_1, \ldots$

Definition 1 (Multi-agent Kripke models). *A Kripke model for the set A of agents is a tuple $M = \langle S, \mathcal{R}, V \rangle$ that consists of a non-empty set S of (possible) worlds, a function $\mathcal{R}: A \to 2^{S \times S}$ mapping each agent $i \in A$ to a binary accessibility relation $\mathcal{R}_i \subseteq S \times S$ on S, and a valuation function $V: \text{Prop} \to 2^S$ mapping each atom $p \in \text{Prop}$ to a set $V(p) \subseteq S$ of worlds where p is true.*

The truth of a formula φ from the grammar $\varphi ::= p \mid \neg\varphi \mid (\varphi \wedge \varphi) \mid K_i\varphi$ with $p \in \text{Prop}$ and $i \in A$ is recursively defined as follows: for a world $s \in S$, we have $M, s \vDash p$ iff $s \in V(p)$, classical boolean connectives, and $M, s \vDash K_i\varphi$ iff $M, t \vDash \varphi$ whenever $s\mathcal{R}_i t$.

For a given interpreted system I consisting of a set R of runs, the corresponding Kripke model is constructed as follows:

Definition 2 (Runs and systems). *If R is the set of runs of a given distributed system, then its* global states *can be represented by pairs (r, t) of a run $r \in R$ and time instance $t \in \mathbb{N}$, meaning that the set of possible worlds $S := R \times \mathbb{N}$. It is assumed that, for each global state (r, t) each agent $i \in A$ is in its* local state *$r_i(t)$. The accessibility relations $\sim_i$ are defined based on local states: $(r, t) \sim_i (r', t')$ iff $r_i(t) = r_i'(t')$. The resulting Kripke model $\langle R \times \mathbb{N}, \sim, V \rangle$ describes the knowledge of agents.*

It is easy to see that these $\sim_i$ are equivalence relations, hence, the logic for reasoning about knowledge in distributed systems ends up being (multi-modal) S5. In particular, it validates factivity $\mathsf{t} : K_i\varphi \rightarrow \varphi$, positive introspection $4 : K_i\varphi \rightarrow K_iK_i\varphi$, and negative introspection $5 : \neg K_i\varphi \rightarrow K_i\neg K_i\varphi$ for each agent $i \in A$. (See [12] for details.)

Applying the Kripke definition of knowledge to an interpreted system I yields

$$I, r, t \vDash K_i\varphi \qquad \Longleftrightarrow \qquad \Big(r_i(t) = r_i'(t') \quad \Longrightarrow \quad I, r', t' \vDash \varphi \Big). \qquad (1)$$

Thus, agent i's local state $r_i(t)$ determines what i knows at global state (r, t) (modulo the a priori assumptions about the whole system). This explains why programming can be done based on agents' local states, despite it creating the erroneous impression of agent's knowledge not being taken into account, in seeming violation of the Knowledge of Preconditions Principle (KoP). It is this model of knowledge (1) that was so successful in analyzing fault-free distributed systems [8].

As already mentioned in the introduction, this model does not easily translate to byzantine distributed systems, with the exception of certain types of so-called *benign* faults, e.g., crashes and omissions [7,15,24]. This exception can also be explained via KoP. Recall that actions are determined by knowledge, which is determined by the local state. Both crashes and (send) omissions represent the type of byzantine behavior involving a faulty agent *not* doing something assigned by the protocol, rather than *doing* something in violation of the protocol. With no actions performed differently, no need arises to modify how knowledge is modeled in runs and systems, nor the agent's local state.[2] By contrast, if a faulty agent can perform a different action, it is not clear how to reflect this in its knowledge and local state. This becomes especially obvious when considering *fully byzantine* agents that can perform any action. How does their knowledge determine their arbitrary actions? Does it mean that their knowledge should be inconsistent, which would be incompatible with the logic of knowledge S5?

One of our first achievements [17,18] was a new framework extending the runs and systems framework with machinery for handling fully byzantine agents without losing the modeling of knowledge according to (1). Without getting into all the technical details of our solution [19,26], the main idea behind it was to decouple the arbitrary actions of faulty agents from their knowledge. In our

---

[2] One could point out that inaction could be viewed as a kind of action, but temporary inaction is how asynchrony is modeled in distributed systems, and the same methodology applies here more or less as is.

framework, all faulty actions are perpetrated by the (adversarial aspect of the) environment. Thus, a faulty agent retains its knowledge according to (1) but loses the control of its actions.

Another barrier we had to overcome stemmed from the tension between the factivity of S5 knowledge and the necessity to represent faulty sensors and, more generally, to give faulty agents the ability to be mistaken. This was solved by shifting the knowledge corruption to the level of local states. In order to enable agents to be wrong, our framework imbues the environment with the ability to falsify events, actions, and/or messages and to record these "fake" events into the agent's local state. The result is that the agent's knowledge is subjectively factive, in compliance with S5, but may not match the objective reality, e.g., the agent may subjectively "know" that it has received a particular message even though in reality no such message was ever sent. Of course, to ensure overall logical consistency, that requires to drop the a priori assumption that every received message must have been sent, which is routinely made in distributed systems with at most crash and omission failures.

To summarize, by extending runs and systems framework to the case of fully byzantine agents, which may have false memories, lie, and violate their protocol, our framework [17–19] finally provided a model for analyzing knowledge of agents in fully byzantine distributed systems, while retaining the traditional S5 logical properties of knowledge.

Paradoxically, one of the first results of this analysis made it clear that knowledge is too strong to be used for triggering actions in byzantine environments. For instance, a natural trigger for an agent's action would be some triggering event. However, we showed [18] that the subjective nature of the factivity of agents' knowledge has the following consequence: in a fully byzantine distributed system, no agent (correct or faulty) can know that a particular event took place objectively. We proved this by formalizing the infamous *brain in a vat* thought experiment [25] in our framework and showing that in any global state (r, t) each agent i has an indistinguishable global state (r', t') where i is a "brain in a vat," i.e., all actions and events recorded in i's local state $r_i(t) = r_i'(t')$ are fake in run r': none of them took place. The inability to distinguish (r, t) from (r', t') precludes agent i from knowing in run r that any action or event took place, even if all agents are correct in run r. Moreover, this result applies to a wide range of distributed systems, both asynchronous [18] and synchronous [27].

This result might seem quite devastating in light of KoP. How can an agent react to a triggering event if the agent cannot know that such an event happened?

3   Belief Modality

The solution is known at least since [21], where Moses proposed to define a *belief modality* as knowledge relativized to the agent's correctness.[3] In our language, this modality is represented by

$$B_i\varphi := K_i(correct_i \to \varphi), \tag{2}$$

---

[3] Albeit in a slightly different language involving *indexical sets*.

where $correct_i \in \mathsf{Prop}$ are finitely many designated propositional atoms, one per agent, with truth value determined by whether agent i is correct or not. Later in [23], Moses and Shoham dubbed this modality *belief as defeasible knowledge* and axiomatized it as K45 with two additional axioms:

$$correct_i \rightarrow (B_i\varphi \rightarrow \varphi) \quad \text{and} \quad B_i correct_i, \quad (3)$$

where K45 means that B_i has positive and negative introspection but not necessarily factivity. However, the first additional axiom means that B_i is factive for correct agents. Consequently, if a correct agent i performs an action based on $B_i\varphi$, then φ is guaranteed to hold. While this may not hold true for a faulty agent i, those actions do not have to follow the protocol anyway. As a result, in a fully byzantine distributed system, the way to program a reaction to a triggering event φ is to use $correct_i \rightarrow \varphi$ as a trigger instead. While knowledge $K_i\varphi$ is not achievable [18, 27], belief $B_i\varphi = K_i(correct_i \rightarrow \varphi)$ may be, and it results in the same actions for correct agents.

The necessity to replace knowledge $K_i\varphi$ with belief $B_i\varphi$ in byzantine distributed systems is the first conclusion we formally derived in our framework.

However, while belief enables one to describe agent's actions, it is not sufficient to explain how agents learn by communication. The problem lies in the ability of byzantine agents to lie: if agent i receives a message φ from agent j and considers a possibility that this message is a lie, what can i learn? Were j guaranteed to be truthful, then $K_j\varphi$ would be a precondition for sending φ in fault-free systems per KoP, from which φ would follow by factivity. As just discussed, the precondition in byzantine scenarios would be the weaker $B_j\varphi$, which is also factive for a correct j. Yet, when the truthfulness assumption is removed, in particular, in the case of j being fully byzantine, then even $B_j\varphi$ becomes too strong. In fact, since a faulty j can send any message independent of its knowledge, the informational content of φ would be non-existent, i.e., trivial.

But communication is the main tool for solving distributed tasks. If agents cannot learn from messages, then how does communication help solve the task?

4 Hope Modality

We propose the answer to this question in the form of the *hope modality* [10]

$$H_i\varphi \quad := \quad correct_i \rightarrow B_i\varphi \quad = \quad correct_i \rightarrow K_i(correct_i \rightarrow \varphi).$$

This modality emerged naturally in our analysis of the distributed task we called Firing Rebels with Relay (FRR) [11], which is an asynchronous variant of the Byzantine Firing Squad problem [2] and is closely related to the consistent broadcasting primitive [29]. Only later did we understand the proper meaning of hope.

$H_j\varphi$ is precisely the informational content of a message φ received from agent j in a byzantine distributed system. Indeed, as we just discussed, two options should be considered while interpreting φ: agent j is either correct or faulty. If j is correct, then $B_j\varphi$ is the precondition for sending φ; if j is faulty, then the precondition is trivial, i.e., $\top$. Collecting both possibilities, one concludes

$$(correct_j \to B_j\varphi) \wedge (\neg correct_j \to \top) \qquad \leftrightarrow \qquad H_j\varphi. \qquad (4)$$

The first axiomatization of hope, in the style of Moses–Shoham [23] was obtained by Fruzsa in 2019 [10]: hope is axiomatized as K45 plus the same two axioms (3) with hope $H_i\varphi$ replacing belief $B_i\varphi$, plus one more additional axiom

$$\neg correct_i \to H_i\varphi.$$

Both Moses–Shoham's axiomatization of belief and Fruzsa's initial axiomatization of hope lack the substitution property: e.g., substituting an arbitrary formula φ for $correct_i$ in the axiom $H_i correct_i$ yields $H_i\varphi$. Validating all $H_i\varphi$ would have trivialized the hope modality, and would have rendered all communication useless. Thus, the logic of hope in [10] is not a normal modal logic.

Fortunately, an alternative axiomatization of hope [4] can remove this obstacle. It turns out that expressing the correctness atoms through hope as

$$correct_i := \neg H_i \bot, \qquad (5)$$

produces an equivalent representation of hope that is axiomatized as KB4, i.e., a normal modal logic with axiom 4 for positive introspection as earlier and with b : $\varphi \to H_i \neg H_i \neg \varphi$ replacing 5.

So far we discussed four syntactic constructs to be used for describing reasoning about *knowledge and communication* in byzantine distributed systems: **knowledge modalities** for preconditions of actions; **correctness atoms** for determining whether an agent is correct or faulty; **belief modalities** for weaker preconditions of actions in byzantine settings; **hope modalities** for the informational content of messages. In view of (5) and (2) it is clear that knowledge and hope modalities for each agent suffice. As shown in [4], correctness atoms cannot be expressed through knowledge. It, therefore, follows from (5) that neither can hope.

Thus, we posit that, at a minimum, a language suitable for reasoning about knowledge and communication in byzantine distributed systems should contain knowledge and hope modalities for each agent.

Definition 3 (Axiomatization of knowledge and hope [4]). *The logic* KH *of knowledge and hope has the following axioms and inference rules:*

all propositional tautologies

$\mathsf{d}_{\to}^H$: $H_i \neg H_i \bot$ $\qquad$ k^K : $K_i(\varphi \to \psi) \to (K_i\varphi \to K_i\psi)$

$\qquad\qquad\qquad\qquad$ 4^K : $K_i\varphi \to K_i K_i\varphi$

$\qquad\qquad\qquad\qquad$ 5^K : $\neg K_i\varphi \to K_i \neg K_i\varphi$

$\qquad\qquad\qquad\qquad$ t^K : $K_i\varphi \to \varphi$

MP: $\dfrac{\varphi \quad \varphi \to \psi}{\psi}$ $\qquad$ Nec^K: $\dfrac{\varphi}{K_i\varphi}$

$\qquad$ kh : $\quad H_i\varphi \leftrightarrow \left(\neg H_i \bot \to K_i(\neg H_i \bot \to \varphi)\right)$

Kripke models for this logic are a simple generalization of models from Definition 1 that has two accessibility relations per agent:

Definition 4 (Kripke models for knowledge and hope [4]). *A Kripke model for knowledge and hope for the set A of agents is a tuple $M = \langle S, \mathcal{K}, \mathcal{H}, V \rangle$ that consists of a set $S \neq \varnothing$, a valuation function $V \colon$ Prop $\rightarrow 2^S$, and functions $\mathcal{K}, \mathcal{H} \colon A \rightarrow 2^{S \times S}$ mapping each agent $i \in A$ to binary accessibility relations $\mathcal{K}_i$ and $\mathcal{H}_i$ on S respectively such that each $\mathcal{K}_i$ is an equivalence relation (reflexive, transitive, and symmetric), each $\mathcal{H}_i$ is a partial equivalence relation (transitive and symmetric), and, in addition, $\mathcal{H}_i \subseteq \mathcal{K}_i$ for each $i \in A$ and $s\mathcal{K}_i t$ implies $s\mathcal{H}_i t$ whenever $s\mathcal{H}_i s'$ and $t\mathcal{H}_i t'$ for some worlds s' and t' for each $i \in A$.*

The truth of a formula φ from the grammar $\varphi ::= p \mid \neg\varphi \mid (\varphi \wedge \varphi) \mid K_i\varphi \mid H_i\varphi$ with $p \in$ Prop and $i \in A$ is the same as in Definition 1 except $M, s \vDash K_i\varphi$ iff $M, t \vDash \varphi$ whenever $s\mathcal{K}_i t$, with the new clause $M, s \vDash H_i\varphi$ iff $M, t \vDash \varphi$ whenever $s\mathcal{H}_i t$.

We illustrate how to model communication in byzantine distributed systems:

Example 5. It is standard in distributed systems to restrict the number of byzantine agents to at most f for some $0 \leq f \leq n$. Indeed, such a restriction is typically necessary for the distributed task at hand to be solvable, with $n \geq 2f + 1$ or $n \geq 3f + 1$ being a common necessary condition. In light of (5), this can be formalized as

$$Byz_f := \bigvee_{\substack{G \subseteq A \\ |G| = n - f}} \bigwedge_{i \in G} \neg H_i \bot.$$

Using the standard group notion of mutual hope $E_G^H \varphi := \bigwedge_{i \in G} H_i \varphi$ for a group $G \subseteq A$ of agents, we can derive factivity of mutual hope for sufficiently large groups: whenever $|G| \geq f + 1$,

$$\mathsf{KH} + Byz_f \quad \vdash \quad E_G^H \varphi \rightarrow \varphi. \tag{6}$$

As simple as the derivation of (6) might seem, it faithfully formalizes the process of learning in byzantine distributed systems: if the same message is received from $f + 1$ distinct agents, then one of them must be correct, ensuring the veracity of the message.

Other examples formalizing specifications of byzantine systems by knowledge and hope, as well as other properties derived using the logic from Definition 4 can be found in [4].

More syntactic constructs may be added to the logic of knowledge and hope as needed. For instance, our analysis of the FRR problem [11] is done in a language with the addition of temporal modality $\Diamond\varphi$ for "φ holds at some point in the future" and a mixed temporal–epistemic fixpoint group modality $C^{\Diamond H}\varphi$ of *eventual common hope*. Another example can be found in [5], where dynamic operators in the style of Dynamic Epistemic Logic [6] are used to (self-)correct agents.

One last thing to discuss about hope is the origins of the name. Initially, hope was chosen as an attitude similar to but weaker than belief. Indeed, in our logic,

KH $\vdash B_i\varphi \to H_i\varphi$. However, it is reasonable to ask whether one would actually say "hope" in colloquial speech in the same situations where our hope modality is employed. Here is one such example. It often happens that, meeting someone familiar after a long break, I may not be sure about the name of their child. Say, the name "Florian" comes to mind, but it might also be "Miro." I clearly do not *know* it is Florian. But, in fact, my memory may be so fuzzy that I cannot even say that I *believe* it to be Florian: it may be more that, in my mind, it is, say, Florian with 85% probability. Sometimes, in such situations, I still venture, in the name of politeness, to ask about Florian, *hoping* that I got the name right. And that is the meaning of hope that our hope modality embodies.

5   Creed Modality

The breakdown of hope from (4) underscores the all-or-nothing dichotomy of correct/faulty agents: correct agents are completely trusted, while faulty agents are completely distrusted. The same approach, however, can also be applied in less discriminating circumstances. In this section, we show how hope can be generalized from byzantine distributed systems, where agents are either correct or faulty, to *heterogeneous distributed systems* where agents may belong to several different types with each type communicating in its own way that need not be fully known to other agent types. We start by illustrating the utility of this approach by solving one of Smullyan's puzzles [28, Puzzle 28].

Example 6 (Knights and knaves [3]). All inhabitants of an island are either *knights* who always tell the truth or *knaves* who always lie. Agents a and b are two of these inhabitants. Agent a makes the following statement: "At least one of us two is a knave." What are a and b?

Here we have two types of agents: knights and knaves. Thinking of utterances as actions that have preconditions, we can reformulate the definition of these two types as follows: the precondition for agent j saying φ is

- φ, and, according to KoP, $K_j\varphi$ for a knight;
- $\neg\varphi$, and, according to KoP, $K_j\neg\varphi$ for a knave.

Consequently, the analog of (4) for agent j's utterance of φ would in this case be

$$(knight_j \to K_j\varphi) \wedge (knave_j \to K_j\neg\varphi),$$

where $knight_j$ and $knave_j$ are atoms that, like $correct_j$ for hope, signify the type of agent j. The above statement of agent a can be formalized in this language as $\varphi := knave_a \vee knave_b$. Accordingly, the informational content of this φ amounts to

$$\left(knight_a \to K_a(knave_a \vee knave_b)\right) \wedge \left(knave_a \to K_a\neg(knave_a \vee knave_b)\right). \quad (7)$$

Using normal modal reasoning, factivity of knowledge, and the puzzle's a priori assumption $knight_j \leftrightarrow \neg knave_j$, we can easily derive $knight_a \wedge knave_b$ from (7). This provides the answer to the puzzle: a is a knight while b is a knave.

In this vein, we defined *creed modality* [3] as a generalization of hope:

$$\mathbb{C}_a^{L\backslash S}\varphi := S_a \rightarrow K_a f_{LS}(\varphi)$$

where L is the type of the listening agent, S is a possible type the speaking agent a might have, and $f_{LS}(\varphi)$ is the strongest precondition for speaking φ by an S-type agent that L-type agents are aware of. Using creed, an L-type agent can extract the following informational content from a message φ of agent a:

$$\mathbb{C}_a^{L\backslash S_1}\varphi \wedge \cdots \wedge \mathbb{C}_a^{L\backslash S_k}\varphi$$

where $S_1, \ldots, S_k$ are all the agent types the listener thinks a may belong to.

6   Conclusions

In this paper, we have proposed the minimal language needed to reason about knowledge and its increase via communication in byzantine distributed systems. This language should include, for each agent, knowledge modality to describe preconditions for this agent's actions and hope modality to describe what other agents learn from this agent's messages. Hope modality first appeared in the epistemic analysis of a particular distributed task, a simplified version of consistent broadcasting, further proving its indispensability for reasoning about knowledge and communication in distributed systems with fully byzantine agents.

Looking beyond hope, we have shown the first glimpse of how to logically model communication among agents of different types and different communication strategies, the situation that is to become more and more widespread as distributed systems grow both in size and in complexity. The research into this novel creed modality is only in its initial stages.

Acknowledgement. This paper summarizes a particular strain of the results obtained within the framework of the Austrian Science Fund (FWF) project ByzDEL (P33600). Many people contributed to our research project and shared their ideas and expertise over the years, whether officially or unofficially participating in or simply collaborating with the project. Some are cited. Others collaborated on other topics or contributed in less visible but nevertheless tangible and crucial ways. I will provide an alphabetical list of people involved in the project in all these various capacities, to whom I am immensely thankful for joining me on this exciting ride: Giorgio Cignarale, Hans van Ditmarsch, Stephan Felber, Patrik Fimml, Krisztina Fruzsa, Lucas Gréaux, Yoram Moses, Laurent Prosperi, Sergio Rajsbaum, Rojo Randrianomentsoa, Hugo Rincón Galeana, Thomas Schlögl, Ulrich Schmid, Thomas Studer, and Tuomas Tahko.

References

1. Artemov, S.: Observable models. In: Artemov, S., Nerode, A. (eds.) LFCS 2020. LNCS, vol. 11972, pp. 12–26. Springer, Cham (2020). https://doi.org/10.1007/978-3-030-36755-8_2
2. Burns, J.E., Lynch, N.A.: The Byzantine firing squad problem. In: Preparata, F.P., (ed.) Parallel and Distributed Computing. Advances in Computing Research: A Research Annual, vol. 4, pp. 147–161. JAI Press (1987)
3. Cignarale, G., Kuznets, R., Rincon Galeana, H., Schmid, U.: Logic of communication interpretation: how to not get lost in translation. In: Sattler, U., Suda, M. (eds.) FroCoS 2023. LNCS, vol. 14279, pp. 119–136. Springer, Cham (2023). https://doi.org/10.1007/978-3-031-43369-6_7
4. van Ditmarsch, H., Fruzsa, K., Kuznets, R.: A new hope. In: Fernández-Duque, D., Palmigiano, A., Pinchinat, S., (eds.) Advances in Modal Logic, vol. 14, pp. 349–369. College Publications (2022). http://www.aiml.net/volumes/volume14/22-vanDitmarsch-Fruzsa-Kuznets.pdf
5. van Ditmarsch, H., Fruzsa, K., Kuznets, R., Schmid, U.: A logic for repair and state recovery in byzantine fault-tolerant multi-agent systems. In: Proceedings of IJCAR 2024: International Joint Conference on Automated Reasoning. Lecture Notes in Computer Science. Springer (2024, in press). https://doi.org/10.48550/arXiv.2401
6. van Ditmarsch, H., van der Hoek, W., Kooi, B.: Dynamic Epistemic Logic. Synthese Library, vol. 337. Springer, Dordrecht (2007). https://doi.org/10.1007/978-1-4020-5839-4
7. Dwork, C., Moses, Y.: Knowledge and common knowledge in a Byzantine environment: crash failures. Inf. Comput. **88**(2), 156–186 (1990). https://doi.org/10.1016/0890-5401(90)90014-9
8. Fagin, R., Halpern, J.Y., Moses, Y., Vardi, M.Y.: Reasoning About Knowledge. MIT Press, Cambridge (1995). https://doi.org/10.7551/mitpress/5803.001.0001
9. Fimml, P.: Temporal-epistemic logic in Byzantine message-passing contexts. Master's thesis, TU Wien, Vienna, Austria (2017). https://doi.org/10.34726/hss.2017.38943
10. Fruzsa, K.: Hope for epistemic reasoning with faulty agents! In: Pavlova, A., Pedersen, M.Y., Bernardi, R. (eds.) ESSLLI 2019. LNCS, vol. 14354, pp. 93–108. Springer, Cham (2023). https://doi.org/10.1007/978-3-031-50628-4_6
11. Fruzsa, K., Kuznets, R., Schmid, U.: Fire! In: Halpern, J., Perea, A., (eds.) Proceedings of the Eighteenth Conference on Theoretical Aspects of Rationality and Knowledge, Beijing, China, June 25–27, 2021. Electronic Proceedings in Theoretical Computer Science, vol. 335, pp. 139–153. Open Publishing Association (2021). https://doi.org/10.4204/EPTCS.335.13
12. Garson, J.: Modal logic. In: Zalta, E.N., Nodelman, U., (eds.) The Stanford Encyclopedia of Philosophy. Metaphysics Research Lab, Stanford University, Spring 2023 edition (2023). https://plato.stanford.edu/archives/spr2023/entries/logic-modal/
13. Grice, H.P.: Logic and conversation. In: Cole, P., Morgan, J.L., (eds.) Speech Acts. Syntax and Semantics, vol. 3, pp. 41–58. Brill (1975). https://doi.org/10.1163/9789004368811_003
14. Halpern, J.Y., Harper, R., Immerman, N., Kolaitis, P.G., Vardi, M.Y., Vianu, V.: On the unusual effectiveness of logic in computer science. Bull. Symbolic Logic **7**(2), 213–236 (2001). https://doi.org/10.2307/2687775

15. Halpern, J.Y., Moses, Y., Waarts, O.: A characterization of eventual Byzantine agreement. SIAM J. Comput. **31**(3), 838–865 (2001). https://doi.org/10.1137/S0097539798340217
16. Hintikka, J.: Knowledge and Belief: An Introduction to the Logic of the Two Notions. Cornell University Press (1962)
17. Kuznets, R., Prosperi, L., Schmid, U., Fruzsa, K.: Causality and epistemic reasoning in byzantine multi-agent systems. In: Moss, L.S., (ed.) Proceedings of the Seventeenth Conference on Theoretical Aspects of Rationality and Knowledge, Toulouse, France, 17–19 July 2019. Electronic Proceedings in Theoretical Computer Science, vol. 297, pp. 293–312. Open Publishing Association (2019). https://doi.org/10.4204/EPTCS.297.19
18. Kuznets, R., Prosperi, L., Schmid, U., Fruzsa, K.: Epistemic reasoning with byzantine-faulty agents. In: Herzig, A., Popescu, A. (eds.) FroCoS 2019. LNCS (LNAI), vol. 11715, pp. 259–276. Springer, Cham (2019). https://doi.org/10.1007/978-3-030-29007-8_15
19. Kuznets, R., Prosperi, L., Schmid, U., Fruzsa, K., Gréaux, L.: Knowledge in Byzantine message-passing systems I: Framework and the causal cone. Technical Report TUW-260549, TU Wien (2019). https://publik.tuwien.ac.at/files/publik_260549.pdf
20. Lamport, L., Shostak, R., Pease, M.: The Byzantine Generals Problem. ACM Trans. Program. Lang. Syst. **4**(3), 382–401 (1982). https://doi.org/10.1145/357172.357176
21. Moses, Y.: Resource-bounded knowledge. In: Vardi, M.Y., (ed.) Proceedings of the Second Conference on Theoretical Aspects of Reasoning About Knowledge, pp. 261–275. Morgan Kaufmann (1988). https://dl.acm.org/doi/abs/10.5555/1029718.1029741
22. Moses, Y.: Relating knowledge and coordinated action: the Knowledge of Preconditions principle. In: Ramanujam, R., (ed.) Proceedings Fifteenth Conference on Theoretical Aspects of Rationality and Knowledge, Carnegie Mellon University, Pittsburgh, USA, June 4–6, 2015. Electronic Proceedings in Theoretical Computer Science, vol. 215, pp. 231–145. Open Publishing Association (2016). https://doi.org/10.4204/EPTCS.215.17
23. Moses, Y., Shoham, Y.: Belief as defeasible knowledge. Artif. Intell. **64**(2), 299–321 (1993). https://doi.org/10.1016/0004-3702(93)90107-M
24. Moses, Y., Tuttle, M.R.: Programming simultaneous actions using common knowledge. Algorithmica **3**(1–4), 121–169 (1988). https://doi.org/10.1007/BF01762112
25. Pessin, A., Goldberg, S.: The Twin Earth Chronicles: Twenty Years of Reflection on Hilary Putnam's "The Meaning of 'Meaning;". M. E. Sharpe (1995). https://doi.org/10.4324/9781315284811
26. Schlögl, T.: An extension framework for epistemic reasoning in byzantine distributed systems. Master's thesis, TU Wien, Vienna, Austria (2020). https://doi.org/10.34726/hss.2020.69444
27. Schlögl, T., Schmid, U., Kuznets, R.: The persistence of false memory: brain in a vat despite perfect clocks. In: Uchiya, T., Bai, Q., Marsá Maestre, I. (eds.) PRIMA 2020. LNCS, vol. 12568, pp. 403–411. Springer, Cham (2021). https://doi.org/10.1007/978-3-030-69322-0_30
28. Smullyan, R.M.: What Is the Name of This Book? — The Riddle of Dracula and Other Logical Puzzles. Prentice–Hall (1978)
29. Srikanth, T.K., Toueg, S.: Optimal clock synchronization. J. ACM **34**(3), 626–645 (1987). https://doi.org/10.1145/28869.28876

Algorithmic Aspects of Left-Orderings of Solvable Baumslag–Solitar Groups via its Dynamical Realization

Meng-Che "Turbo" Ho[1], Khanh Le[2], and Dino Rossegger[3(✉)]

[1] Department of Mathematics, California State University, Northridge, Northridge, USA
turbo.ho@csun.edu
[2] Department of Mathematics, Rice University, Houston, USA
khanh.le@rice.edu
[3] Institut für Diskrete Mathematik und Geometrie, Technische Universität Wien, Vienna, Austria
dino.rossegger@tuwien.ac.at
https://sites.google.com/view/turboho,
https://sites.google.com/view/khanhqle, https://drossegger.github.io

Abstract. We answer a question of Calderoni and Clay [4] by showing that the conjugation equivalence relation of left orderings of the Baumslag-Solitar groups $BS(1,n)$ is hyperfinite for any n. Our proof relies on a classification of $BS(1,n)$'s left-orderings via its one-dimensional dynamical realizations. We furthermore use the effectiveness of the dynamical realizations of $BS(1,n)$ to study algorithmic properties of the left-orderings on $BS(1,n)$.

1 Introduction

A group G is *left-orderable* if there is a linear ordering $\prec$ on the elements of G such that for all $f, g, h \in G$, $g \prec h$ implies $fg \prec fh$. We refer to such a linear ordering as a *left-ordering* of G. The study of (left-)orderable groups has a long tradition in mathematics starting with the work of Dedekind and Hölder in the late 19th and early 20th century. Dedekind famously characterized the real numbers as a complete bi-orderable Abelian group and Hölder showed that

Part of this research was performed during Summer 2022 while Ho and Rossegger were visiting the Mathematical Sciences Research Institute (MSRI), now becoming the Simons Laufer Mathematical Sciences Institute (SLMath), which is supported by the National Science Foundation (Grant #DMS-1928930). Ho and Rossegger wish to thank the American Institute of Mathematics for stimulating this research and providing the venue for the discussion of part of this work. The work of Ho was partially supported by the National Science Foundation under Grant #DMS-2054558. The work of Le was partially supported by the AMS-Simons Travel Grant. The work of Rossegger was supported by the European Union's Horizon 2020 Research and Innovation Programme under the Marie Skłodowska-Curie grant agreement No. 101026834 - ACOSE.

L. Levy Patey et al. (Eds.): CiE 2024, LNCS 14773, pp. 72–84, 2024.
https://doi.org/10.1007/978-3-031-64309-5_7

any Archimedean ordered group is isomorphic to an additive subgroup of the reals with their standard ordering. These fundamental results led to an influx of interest in orderable groups and established their theory as a cornerstone of group theory; see [18] for a treatment of the classical theory.

While most studies of orderable groups employed algebraic methods, there is a strong connection with one-dimensional dynamics. Indeed, a group is left-orderable if and only if it acts faithfully on the real line by orientation preserving homeomorphisms [14] (see also Sect. 2.1). Motivated by this observation, Navas [21] systematically applied dynamical ideas to study orderable groups and give new proofs of results previously obtained by algebraic methods, as well as new results. He gave a new dynamical proof of the fact that LO(F_n), the space of left-orderings of the non-abelian free group of rank n, is homeomorphic to the Cantor set if $n \geq 2$ [21, Theorem A], and of the result of Linnell which states that the number of left-orderings of a group is either finite or uncountable [21, Theorem C]. Since then one-dimensional dynamics has become an important tool in orderable group theory with many applications. Generalizing Navas's approach, Rivas proved that for all left-orderable groups G and H, the free-product $G * H$ has no isolated left-orderings [24, Theorem A]. In [19, Theorem 1.1] dynamics was used to find new examples of groups with isolated left-orderings, and in [23, 25] characterizations of left-orderings of various solvable groups were obtained.

These developments have led to various natural questions about the space of left-orderings of groups, LO(G). Of particular interest to this paper is a question by Deroin, Navas, and Rivas [10, Question 2.2.11] that asks if the conjugation equivalence relation of G on LO(G) is standard. This question has attracted the interest of Calderoni and Clay [3] who initiated the study of the conjugation equivalence of orderings on a fixed group G in the setting of descriptive set theory.

Among other groups, Calderoni and Clay studied the space of linear orders of solvable Baumslag-Solitar groups [4]. Baumslag-Solitar groups are introduced in [1] as an example of non-Hopfian groups, and have served as important examples and counterexamples in group theory [2, Chapter 5]. In particular, the solvable Baumslag-Solitar groups admit nice structural properties and thus provide useful test cases for theories and techniques.

The main contribution of our paper is in this context: We show that the conjugation equivalence relation of the solvable Baumslag-Solitar group $BS(1, n)$ is hyperfinite for every n. This answers a question posed by Calderoni and Clay [4].

The algorithmic aspects of left-orderable groups have also seen attention in the past, mainly focusing on the complexity of orderings of computable groups [8, 9, 12, 16] and their reverse mathematics [27, 28]. In Sect. 4, we explore how a group's dynamics can be used to study algorithmic properties of its orderings, using $BS(1, n)$ as an example. Our main result shows that the index sets of orderings that are conjugates of a given ordering with irrational base point is Σ_3^0-complete. Our proof relies on the dynamical realizations of $BS(1, n)$ and the machinery developed in prior sections.

Before we prove the main results of this paper we review the main tools used in their proofs and give the necessary definitions to formally state our results.

2   Left-Orderable Groups, Their Dynamical Realizations, and E_{lo}

A left ordering $\prec$ on a group G induces a partition of G into disjoint subsets

$$P^+ = \{g \in G \mid g \succ id\}, P^- = (P^+)^{-1} = \{g \in G \mid id \succ g\} \text{ and } \{id\}$$

where P^+ is called the *positive cone* of the left-ordering $\prec$. Notice that the reverse order $\prec^*$, defined as $g \prec^* h$ if and only if $h \prec g$, is also a left-ordering of G with associated positive cone P^-. It is not hard to see that the positive cones on G are precisely the subsets $P \subseteq G$ satisfying

$$P \cap P^{-1} = \varnothing, \, PP \subseteq P \text{ and } P \cup P^{-1} \cup \{id\} = G.$$

Moreover, every positive cone gives rise to an associated left-ordering $\prec_P$ via

$$g \prec_P h \iff g^{-1}h \in P$$

and thus we get a bijection between positive cones and left-orderings on G.

The collection of all positive cones P of G forms a closed subspace, $\mathrm{LO}(G)$, via the subspace topology of 2^G and is thus a Polish space [26]. Given any positive cone $P \in \mathrm{LO}(G)$ and any element $g \in G$, the set $P^g = \{p^g = g^{-1}pg : p \in P\}$ defines a positive cone on G. Consequently, the group G acts on $\mathrm{LO}(G)$ via conjugation simply by defining $g(P) = P^{g^{-1}}$ for all $g \in G$ and $P \in \mathrm{LO}(G)$. It is not hard to see that the action of G on $\mathrm{LO}(G)$ is continuous and, in fact, computable uniformly in G.

Remark 1. A countable group G is *computable* if its domain and group operation are computable. We can assume that the domain of G is all of ω and thus view positive cones $P \subset G$ as subsets of the natural numbers and 2^G simply as 2^ω. Then the above comment that the action of G on $\mathrm{LO}(G)$ is *computable uniformly in G* means that there is a Turing operator Φ such that

$$\Phi(G, P; g) = g(P) \text{ for all left-orderable groups G, positive cones P, and} g \in G.$$

2.1   Dynamical Realizations

Although left-orderability is an algebraic concept, it has a deep connection to one-dimensional dynamics. In particular, the left-orderable countable group can be characterized in dynamical terms.

Theorem 1 (*[14, Theorem 6.8]*). *Let G be a countable group. Then the following are equivalent:*

1. G is left-orderable.

2. G acts faithfully on the real line by orientation preserving homeomorphisms, i.e., there is a faithful representation $\gamma : G \to \mathrm{Homeo}_+(\mathbb{R})$.

Let us elaborate on Theorem 1. Given an embedding D of G into $\mathrm{Homeo}_+(\mathbb{R})$ and a dense sequence $(x_1, \dots)$ in $\mathbb{R}$, we can obtain a positive cone $P_D = P_D(x_1, \dots)$ as follows: we define $g \in P_D$ if, for the least i such that $D(g)(x_i)$ is not a fixed point, $D(g)(x_i) > x_i$. The proof of the reverse implication that G is left-orderable implies that G embeds into $\mathrm{Homeo}_+(\mathbb{R})$ is effective. In particular, given a left-ordering on G, there is an associated group action of G on the real line, called a *dynamical realization* of G, constructed as follows. Fix a left-ordering $\prec$ on G and, since G is countable, fix an enumeration of the elements of $G = (g_0, g_1, \dots)$. We define a map $t : G \to \mathbb{R}$ that preserves $\prec$, namely,

$$t(g) < t(h) \iff g \prec h,$$

by defining $t : G \to \mathbb{R}$ inductively starting with $t(g_0) = 0$ and

$$t(g_i) = \begin{cases} \max\{t(g_0), \dots t(g_{i-1})\} + 1 & \text{if } (\forall j < i) g_j \prec g_i \\ \min\{t(g_0), \dots t(g_{i-1})\} - 1 & \text{if } (\forall j < i) g_i \prec g_j \\ \frac{t(g_m) + t(g_n)}{2} & \text{if } g_i \in (g_m, g_n),\ m, n < i \text{ and } (\forall j < i) g_j \notin (g_m, g_n) \end{cases}$$

Then we can define an action of G on $t(G)$ via $g(t(g_i)) = t(gg_i)$ and extend this action continuously to the closure $\overline{t(G)}$. Finally, we extend the action to $\mathbb{R} \setminus \overline{t(G)}$ by affine maps to obtain a faithful orientation-preserving action of G on $\mathbb{R}$ and a faithful representation $D : G \to \mathrm{Homeo}^+(\mathbb{R})$. By construction, this action

- has no global fixed point unless G is the trivial group, and
- the orbit of 0 is free; i.e., the stabilizer of 0 under this action is trivial.

These two properties characterize the dynamical realization up to topological semiconjugacy. In particular, we have

Lemma 1 ([21, Lemma 2.8]). *Let $\prec_1$ be a left-ordering on a non-trivial countable group G, and let D_1 be a dynamical realization of $\prec_1$. Let D_2 be an action of G on $\mathbb{R}$ by orientation-preserving homeomorphisms such that*

- *D_2 has no global fixed point, and*
- *the orbit of 0 is free.*

If $\prec_2$ is a left-ordering on G defined by

$$g \prec_2 h \Leftrightarrow D_2(g)(0) < D_2(h)(0),$$

then the two left-orderings $\prec_1$ and $\prec_2$ coincide if and only if D_2 is topologically semiconjugate to D_1 relative to 0. That is, there exists a continuous non-decreasing surjective map $\varphi : \mathbb{R} \to \mathbb{R}$ such that $D_1(g) \circ \varphi = \varphi \circ D_2(g)$ for all $g \in G$ and that $\varphi(0) = 0$[1].

---

[1] The condition that φ fixes the origin was not stated in [21], but was used in the proof as pointed out in [20, Lemma 3.7].

Remark 2. Topological semiconjugacy is not an equivalence relation as φ could collapse some intervals to points. The lemma above says that among all actions satisfying the two conditions, the dynamical realization is "minimal".

It follows that a different choice of enumeration of G yields a different action that is topologically semiconjugate to D. Therefore, we may speak of the dynamical realization of a left-ordering on G without referencing the enumeration of G. From the dynamical realization, we can also recover the original positive cone P on G and its conjugate.

Proposition 1. *Suppose that D is a dynamical realization of a left-ordering P of G. Let $t : G \to \mathbb{R}$ be the order-preserving map used in the construction of D. Then for any $h \in G$, we have*

$$P^h = \{g \in G : D(g)(t(h^{-1})) > t(h^{-1})\}.$$

Proof. When $h = id$, we have

$$P = \{g \in G : D(g)(t(id)) > t(id)\}$$

since t is an order-preserving map. In general, we have

$$
\begin{aligned}
P^h &= \{h^{-1}gh : g \in P\} \\
&= \{h^{-1}gh : D(g)(t(id)) > t(id)\} \\
&= \{f \in G : D(hfh^{-1})(t(id)) > t(id)\} \\
&= \{f \in G : D(f)(t(h^{-1})) > t(h^{-1})\}.
\end{aligned}
$$

$\square$

An application of the dynamical realization that is useful for this paper is an effective classification of the left-orderings on the solvable Baumslag–Solitar group $BS(1, n)$ [23, Theorem 4.2]. We will review this classification in Sect. 3.

2.2   Descriptive Set Theory and E_{lo}

For a fixed group G, the conjugation action of G on $LO(G)$ defines an orbit equivalence relation, denoted E_{lo}^G, where

$$P \, E_{lo}^G \, Q \Leftrightarrow \exists g \in G, g(P) = Q.$$

When G is countable, every equivalence class of E_{lo}^G (or just E_{lo} if G is clear from context) is countable.

Equivalence relations where each equivalence class is countable are called *countable equivalence relations* and are a major topic in descriptive set theory, where the complexity of equivalence relations is measured using Borel reducibility $\leq_B$. The structure of the quasi-order of countable Borel equivalence relations under Borel reducibility is complicated and its investigation is an active research area, see [17] for an overview of developments. Let us mention three benchmark equivalence relations:

1. The *identity relation* on 2^ω, id^{2^ω}, is the least complicated equivalence relation among countable equivalence relations on uncountable spaces. The equivalence relations reducible to id^{2^ω} are called *smooth*.

2. The equivalence relation of eventual equality on 2^ω,

$$x \, E_0 \, y \iff \exists m (\forall n > m) x(n) = y(n)$$

is the archetypical non-smooth *hyperfinite* equivalence relation (i.e., an increasing union of equivalence relations having only finite classes). By [15] every hyperfinite equivalence relation is either bi-reducible with E_0 or smooth.

3. The orbit equivalence relation S of the shift action of F_2 on 2^{F_2} is *universal* for countable Borel equivalence relations, i.e., every other countable Borel equivalence relation is Borel reducible to it.

While the interval (id^{2^ω}, E_0) is trivial, the interval between E_0 and S is known to be extremely complicated.

A fundamental result due to Feldman and Moore [13] shows that the countable equivalence relations are precisely the orbit equivalence relations of Borel actions of countable groups. One major conjecture in the area, known as Weiss's conjecture, aims to shed light on which groups cannot have complicated orbit equivalence relations. It states that every Borel action of an amenable group has a hyperfinite orbit equivalence relation. So far this conjecture has not been fully confirmed and only partial results are known with the latest advance made in [7].

Deroin, Navas, and Rivas [10] asked if LO(G) modulo the action of G is standard, which is equivalent to asking if E_{lo}^G is smooth. Calderoni and Clay generalized this to studying the complexity of equivalence relations E_{lo}^G under Borel reductions [3–5]. They showed that E_{lo} is universal for free products of countable left-orderable groups and not smooth for many groups, including the Baumslag–Solitar group BS($1, n$) and the Thompson's group F. They also showed that $E_{lo}^{\mathrm{BS}(1,2)}$ is hyperfinite. It is still open if there is a group G with E_{lo}^G being *intermediate*, namely, strictly between E_0 and S. There are also other closely related orbit equivalence relations, including the action of Aut(G) on the Archimedean ordering of $\mathbb{Z}^n$ or $\mathbb{Q}^n$. In [6, Theorem 1.1], it was shown that the orbit equivalence relation of Aut($\mathbb{Q}^2$) on the space of Archimedean orderings of $\mathbb{Q}^2$ is not smooth. Extending this result, Poulin showed that the action of Aut($\mathbb{Q}^n$) on LO($\mathbb{Q}^n$) is not hyperfinite when $n \geq 3$ [22, Corollary 1.3].

In the next section, we use the affine action of BS($1, n$) on $\mathbb{R}$ to show that the $E_{lo}^{\mathrm{BS}(1,n)}$ is hyperfinite for every n (Theorem 3), answering a question of Calderoni and Clay [5, Question 4.2]. While this result does follow from Weiss's conjecture, the conjecture has not been confirmed for BS($1, n$), $n > 2$. In any case, we believe that our proof is of interest as it is quite elementary compared to known proofs of parts of Weiss's conjecture. Furthermore, the result determines exactly the complexity of the conjugation action of BS($1, n$) on LO(BS($1, n$)) which is of interest from the orderable group theory perspective.

3 $E_{lo}^{\mathrm{BS}(1,n)}$ is Hyperfinite

The solvable Baumslag–Solitar group $\mathrm{BS}(1,n)$, given by the presentation

$$\langle a, b : b^{-1}ab = a^n \rangle,$$

is an important example in group theory. The normal closure $\langle\langle a \rangle\rangle$ of a is abstractly isomorphic to $\mathbb{Z}[1/n]$, the subgroup of $\mathbb{Q}$ generated by $1/n, 1/n^2, 1/n^3, \ldots$, via an isomorphism sending a to 1 and $b^k a b^{-k}$ to $1/n^k$ for every $k \in \mathbb{Z}$. Abusing notation, we will write elements of $\langle\langle a \rangle\rangle$ as a^r where $r \in \mathbb{Z}[1/n]$. The quotient of $\mathrm{BS}(1,n)$ by the normal closure of a is the infinite cyclic group generated by the image of b. Therefore, $\mathrm{BS}(1,n)$ fits into a (split) short exact sequence

$$0 \to \mathbb{Z}[1/n] \to \mathrm{BS}(1,n) \to \mathbb{Z} \to 0,$$

and admits the semidirect product structure $\mathrm{BS}(1,n) = \langle\langle a \rangle\rangle \rtimes \langle b \rangle$. The elements of G have the normal forms $a^r b^s$ where $r \in \mathbb{Z}[1/n]$ and $s \in \mathbb{Z}$. As a warm-up, we first recall a well-known construction of left-orderings using a short exact sequence.

Proposition 2. *Let K and H be left-orderable groups equipped with positive cones $P_K \subset K$ and $P_H \subset H$. Consider the following short exact sequence of groups:*

$$1 \to K \to G \xrightarrow{\pi} H \to 1$$

The set $P_G := \{g \in G \mid \pi(g) \in P_H\} \cup P_K$ defines a positive cone of G.

To order $\mathrm{BS}(1,n)$, we observe that there are exactly two orderings on $\mathbb{Z}[1/n]$ and $\mathbb{Z}$: the ordering coming from the standard ordering on $\mathbb{R}$ and its reversal. Applying Proposition 2, we get four left-orderings on $\mathrm{BS}(1,n)$. The positive cones of these four left-orderings are:

- $P_\infty^{++} = \{a^r b^s : s > 0 \vee (s = 0 \wedge r > 0)\}$,
- $P_\infty^{+-} = \{a^r b^s : s > 0 \vee (s = 0 \wedge r < 0)\}$,
- $P_\infty^{-+} = \{a^r b^s : s < 0 \vee (s = 0 \wedge r > 0)\}$,
- $P_\infty^{--} = \{a^r b^s : s < 0 \vee (s = 0 \wedge r < 0)\}$,

We note that all four left-orderings above are conjugation invariant. In other words, they are all bi-orderings on $\mathrm{BS}(1,n)$ and the action of $\mathrm{BS}(1,n)$ on $\mathrm{LO}(\mathrm{BS}(1,n))$ fixes these four bi-orderings. However, $\mathrm{BS}(1,n)$ admits other left-orderings not coming from Proposition 2. To study $E_{lo}^{\mathrm{BS}(1,n)}$, we will review the classification of all left-orderings on $\mathrm{BS}(1,n)$ for any integer $n \geq 2$ due to Rivas [23, Theorem 4.2]. Note that although Rivas stated the classification of left-orderings only for $\mathrm{BS}(1,2)$, his proof works without modification for any positive integer n. The proof for arbitrary positive integers n is also presented in [10].

A different source of left-orderings on $BS(1, n)$ comes from the affine action of $BS(1, n)$ on $\mathbb{R}$. Consider the action of $BS(1, n)$ on $\mathbb{R}$ given by $\rho : BS(1, n) \to \mathrm{Aff}^+(\mathbb{R})$ where

$$\rho(a)(x) = x + 1 \quad \text{and} \quad \rho(b)(x) = x/n.$$

It is a straightforward computation that this action is faithful.

Lemma 2 *[23, page 10]. Let $x \in \mathbb{R}$. If $x \in \mathbb{Q}$, then the stabilizer $Stab_\rho(x) \cong \mathbb{Z}$. If x is not in $\mathbb{Q}$, then the stabilizer $Stab_\rho(x)$ is trivial.*

Proof. First, we observe that the stabilizer of any point must be either trivial or isomorphic to $\mathbb{Z}$. Under ρ, the normal closure of a acts by translation and has no fixed points. Therefore, if the stabilizer of some point on $\mathbb{R}$ is nontrivial, it must be mapped injectively into the quotient $BS(1, n)/\langle\langle a \rangle\rangle \cong \mathbb{Z}$. Since ρ is a faithful representation, the nontrivial stabilizer must be isomorphic to $\mathbb{Z}$.

For any $r \in \mathbb{Z}[1/n]$ and $s \in \mathbb{Z}$, we have

$$\rho(a^r b^s)(x) = n^{-s}x + r.$$

If $s \neq 0$, then the affine map above has a fixed point which must be rational. Now suppose that $x = p/q \in \mathbb{Q}$. We want to find $r \in \mathbb{Z}[1/n]$ and $s \in \mathbb{Z}$ such that

$$n^s \frac{p}{q} + r = \frac{p}{q}$$

Let $q = dq'$ and $p' = np/d$ where $d = \gcd(q, n)$. The previous equation is equivalent to

$$n^s \frac{np}{dq'} + nr = \frac{np}{dq'} \quad \text{or} \quad (n^s - 1)\frac{p'}{q'} = -nr$$

Since n and q' are relatively prime, q' is in the (multiplicative) group of units of $\mathbb{Z}/n\mathbb{Z}$, so we can find $s \in \mathbb{N} \setminus \{0\}$ such that q' divides $n^s - 1$. Now we set

$$r = -\frac{n^s - 1}{q'}\frac{p'}{n} \in \mathbb{Z}[1/n]$$

since $p' \in \mathbb{Z}$. Therefore $\rho(a^r b^{-s})$ fixes p/q. $\quad\square$

It follows that if $\varepsilon \in \mathbb{R} \setminus \mathbb{Q}$, then each of the following subsets defines a positive cone on $BS(1, n)$:

- $P_\varepsilon^+ = \{g : \rho(g)(\varepsilon) > \varepsilon\}$,
- $P_\varepsilon^- = \{g : \rho(g)(\varepsilon) < \varepsilon\}$

When $\varepsilon \in \mathbb{Q}$, we define the following four positive cones.

- $Q_\varepsilon^{++} = \{g : (\rho(g)(\varepsilon) > \varepsilon) \vee (\rho(g)(\varepsilon) = \varepsilon \wedge \rho(g)(\varepsilon + 1) > \varepsilon + 1)\}$
- $Q_\varepsilon^{+-} = \{g : (\rho(g)(\varepsilon) > \varepsilon) \vee (\rho(g)(\varepsilon) = \varepsilon \wedge \rho(g)(\varepsilon + 1) < \varepsilon + 1)\}$
- $Q_\varepsilon^{-+} = \{g : (\rho(g)(\varepsilon) < \varepsilon) \vee (\rho(g)(\varepsilon) = \varepsilon \wedge \rho(g)(\varepsilon + 1) > \varepsilon + 1)\}$
- $Q_\varepsilon^{--} = \{g : (\rho(g)(\varepsilon) < \varepsilon) \vee (\rho(g)(\varepsilon) = \varepsilon \wedge \rho(g)(\varepsilon + 1) < \varepsilon + 1)\}$

Theorem 2. ([23, **Theorem 4.2**], [10]). P_ε^+ and P_ε^- for $\varepsilon \in \mathbb{R} \backslash \mathbb{Q}$, Q_ε^{++}, Q_ε^{+-}, Q_ε^{-+}, and Q_ε^{--} for $\varepsilon \in \mathbb{Q}$, and the 4 positive cones P_∞^{++}, P_∞^{+-}, P_∞^{-+}, and P_∞^{--} corresponding to bi-orderings are all distinct and contain all the left-orderings on $\mathrm{BS}(1, n)$.

Recall that for a left-orderable group G, a faithful action $D : G \to \mathrm{Homeo}_+(\mathbb{R})$ and a dense sequence $x_1, \cdots \in \mathbb{R}$ one can recover an ordering $P_D(x_1, \dots)$ as mentioned after Theorem 1. Theorem 2 tells us that by using the action ρ of $\mathrm{BS}(1, n)$ on $\mathbb{R}$, one can classify all the bi-orderings by considering the first elements $\varepsilon = x_1$ of dense sequences in $\mathbb{R}$. Thus, given a positive cone P of the form P_ε^+, P_ε^-, P_∞°, or Q_ε° where $\circ \in \{++, --, +-, -+\}$ we refer to ε as the *base point* of P and P^+, P^-, P°, and Q° as its type.

We observe that given some $g \in \mathrm{BS}(1, n)$, $\varepsilon \in \mathbb{R}$, and $\circ \in \{+, -, ++, +-, -+, --\}$, we have $T_\varepsilon^\circ = (T_{g(\varepsilon)}^\circ)^{g^{-1}}$, where $T \in \{P, Q\}$. In particular, ε is rational if and only if $g(\varepsilon)$ is rational and $\mathbb{Q}$ is a countable $\mathrm{BS}(1, n)$-invariant subset. Thus, the conjugation equivalence of the positive cones is Borel equivalent to the orbit equivalence relation of $\mathrm{BS}(1, n) \curvearrowright \mathbb{R}$.

Theorem 3. *The orbit equivalence relation E generated by the affine action* $\mathrm{BS}(1, n) = \langle a, b \mid b^{-1} a b = a^n \rangle \curvearrowright \mathbb{R}$ *via $a(x) = x+1$ and $b(x) = nx$ is hyperfinite.*

Proof. We will reduce E to E_t, the tail equivalence relation, defined on n^ω by $A E_t B$ if $\exists p, q \forall k\ A(p+k) = B(q+k)$. This suffices as the tail equivalence relation is hyperfinite by [11, Section 8].

The reduction $f : \mathbb{R} \to n^\omega$ is given by sending $x \in \mathbb{R}$ to the base n expansion of the fractional part $\{x\}$ of x. To show this is a reduction, let $x, y \in \mathbb{R}$. Assume first that $x\ E_{lo}^{\mathrm{BS}(1,n)}\ y$, so there is some $g \in \mathrm{BS}(1, n)$ such that $g(x) = y$. Assuming $g = a^r b^s$ such that $r \in \mathbb{Z}[1/n]$ and $s \in \mathbb{Z}$, we have $y = g(x) = a^r b^s(x) = n^{-s} x + r$. As $r \in \mathbb{Z}[1/n]$, we can multiply the equation by a power of n to get $n^p y = n^q x + t$, where $p, q \in \mathbb{N}$ and $t \in \mathbb{Z}$. Since t is an integer, we have $\{n^p y\} = \{n^q x\}$. However, in base n, $\{n^q x\}$ can be obtained from $\{x\}$ by truncating the first q digits and shifting the decimal point by q places, and similarly for $\{y\}$ and $\{n^p y\}$. Thus, $\{n^p y\} = \{n^q x\}$ implies that $\{x\}\ E_t\ \{y\}$.

Conversely, assume $\{x\}\ E_t\ \{y\}$ in base n. Then there are some $q, p \in \mathbb{N}$ such that for every k, the $(q + k)$-th decimal place of $\{x\}$ is the same as the $(p + k)$-th decimal place of $\{y\}$. Thus, we have $\{n^q x\} = \{n^p y\}$, namely, there is some $t \in \mathbb{Z}$ with $n^p y = n^q x + t$, or equivalently $y = n^{q-p} x + t/n^p$. This means $y = g(x)$ with $g = a^{t/n^p} b^{p-q}$, so $x\ E\ y$. This shows that f is indeed a reduction. $\qquad \square$

It follows that $E_{lo}^{\mathrm{BS}(1,n)}$ is hyperfinite, and [5] showed that $E_{lo}^{\mathrm{BS}(1,n)}$ is not smooth.

Corollary 1. $E_{lo}^{\mathrm{BS}(1,n)} \sim_B E_0$.

4 Computability of Dynamical Realizations

Given a left-ordering of G, it is straightforward to see that the left-ordering (considered as a relation on G) and the corresponding positive cone (considered as a subset of G) are Turing equivalent. It is thus natural to ask if this equivalence extends to the dynamical realization of the left-ordering. We will soon see that this is the case for $BS(1, n)$.

Towards this fix an enumeration of the dyadic rational numbers $\mathbb{Q}_2$ and recall that a real number $r \in \mathbb{R}$ is *left-c.e.* if its left cut is c.e., i.e., the set $\{q < r : q \in \mathbb{Q}_2\}$ is computably enumerable. If both its left cut and right cut are c.e., then we say that it is *computable*.

Proposition 3. *Let P be a left-ordering of $BS(1, n)$, then P is Turing equivalent to its base point. Furthermore, the reductions are uniform in the type.*

Proof. We non-uniformly fix the type of P. We will assume that the type is P^+ with the construction easily adaptable to work for other types. We enumerate a right cut of its base point ε. For every $q \in \mathbb{Q}_2$ we enumerate P and whenever we see $g = a^r b^s \in P$ such that $\rho(g)(q) = n^{-s}q + r > q$ we enumerate q into C. Say $n^{-s}x + r > x$, then $x > \frac{-r}{n^{-s}-1}$, and so $\rho(g)(\varepsilon) > \varepsilon$ if and only if for every $q > \varepsilon$, $\rho(g)(q) > q$. Thus, C_q is a right cut of ε. Similarly, we can enumerate a left cut.

Similarly, say we can compute a left cut L and right cut R of ε and are given a type T. We will give a proof assuming that $T = P^+$. The proof can be easily adapted to work for other types. For $q \in Q_2$, we can compute whether $g \in T_q$. By the affineness of ρ we have that

$$g \in P_\varepsilon^+ \iff (\exists q \in R)\rho(g)(q) > q \iff (\forall q \in R)\rho(g)(q) \geq q.$$

Hence, we can compute P_ε^+ from its right cut. □

For G a left-orderable computable group and P a computable positive cone of G the following canonical index sets appear.

$$I(G) = \{e : W_e \text{ is a positive cone}\}$$
$$I(P, G) = \{e : W_e \, E_{lo} \, P\}$$

By definition the set $I(G) \in \Pi_2^0$ as membership in a c.e. set is Σ_1^0. Similarly, it can be seen that $I(P, G) \in \Sigma_3^0$.

Proposition 4. *Let G be an infinite computable group with a computable left-ordering. Then $I(G)$ is Π_2^0-complete.*

Proof. We reduce Inf to $I(G)$. Fix a computable positive cone P and an index e so that $W_e = P$. Given n, we build a total computable function f so that $W_{f(n)} = P$ if and only if $n \in$ Inf. To do this, we enumerate W_n in stages $W_{n,s}$, and, whenever $W_{n,s+1} \neq W_{n,s}$ with $k = |W_{f(n),s+1}|$, we define $W_{f(n),s+1} = W_{e,k}$. The resulting set $W_{f(n)}$ is clearly c.e. and $n \in$ Inf if and only if $W_{f(n)} = W_e = P$. □

Theorem 4. *1. $I(P_\infty^\circ, BS(1, n))$ is Π_2^0-complete for every $\circ \in \{++, --, +-, -+\}$.*
2. $I(P_\varepsilon^\circ, BS(1, n))$ is Σ_3^0-complete for every computable $\varepsilon \in \mathbb{R}\backslash\mathbb{Q}$ and $\circ \in \{+, -\}$.

Proof. The proof for Item 1. is analogous to the proof of Proposition 4.

We prove the Σ_3^0-hardness of $I(P_\varepsilon^\circ, \mathrm{BS}(1,n))$ for a fixed computable $\varepsilon \in \mathbb{R} \backslash \mathbb{Q}$. That $I(P_\varepsilon^\circ, \mathrm{BS}(1,n)) \in \Sigma_3^0$ follows easily from the definition. Given a Σ_3^0 set S we may assume that there is a computable function $g : \omega^2 \to \omega$ such that

$$n \in S \iff \exists y W_{g(n,y)} \in \mathrm{Inf}.$$

We may also assume that for every $k \in \omega$ there are infinitely many y with $|W_{g(n,y)}| > k$.

Given n, we will define a left cut $C_{f(n)}$ in stages as follows. We let $C_{f(n)}^0 = \emptyset$ and at every stage s we choose some $y < s$ and extend $C_{f(n)}^s$ with the goal to make $C_{f(n)}$ a left cut of a real number δ_y. Furthermore, every y will define natural numbers k_y and l_y when it acts at a stage s. Every δ_y will differ from ε at only finitely many digits in their base n expansions and $\delta_0 = \varepsilon$ with $k_0 = l_0 = 0$. The construction is a classical finite injury construction where higher priority "requirements" (i.e., smaller y) will initialize the work of larger y. At the start of the construction, all y are initialized.

Assume we are at stage $s + 1$ and that y_0 is least with $W_{g(x,y_0),s+1} \neq W_{g(x,y_0),s}$. Let y_1 be the y that acted at stage s. If y_0 has been initialized since it last acted or has never acted before, do the following:

Set $k_{y_0} = k_{y_1} + 1 = \langle p, q \rangle$. By induction we can assume that $\{n^r \delta_{y_1}\} = \{n^r \varepsilon\}$ for some $r \in \omega$. If $p \neq q$, then since ε is irrational $n^p \delta_{y_1} \neq n^q \varepsilon$. Hence, there must be some least $i > r$ such that the $(p+i)$-th bit of $\{\delta_{y_1}\}$ is not equal to the $(q+i)$th bit of ε. We declare $\delta_{y_0} = \delta_{y_1}$ and $l_{y_0} = \max\{l_{y_1}, p+i\}$.

Now, if $p = q$, then we consider the least $r > \max\{p, l_{y_1}\}$ such that $\delta_{y_1} - n^{-r} \in (\max C_{f(n)}^s, \delta_{y_1})$ and the r-th decimal place of δ_{y_1} is nonzero, let $\delta_{y_0} = \delta_{y_1} - n^{-r}$ and set $l_{y_0} = r$. Note that the first $r - 1$ decimal digits of δ_{y_0} and δ_{y_1} are the same.

At last, no matter if y_0 was initialized at the start of this stage or not, let

$$C_{f(n)}^{s+1} = C_{f(n)}^s \cup \{q_i\}$$

where $q_i \in \mathbb{Q}_2$ is least in an enumeration of $\mathbb{Q}_2$ with $q_i < \delta_{y_0}$ and initialize all lower priority requirements. This finishes the construction.

Let $C_{f(n)} = \lim_s C_{f(n)}^s$. We claim that this is a left cut. Indeed, if $q \in C_{f(n)}$ at some stage s_0, then we have $\delta_y[s] > \max(C_{f_n}^s) \geq q$ for $y \in \omega$ and $s > s_0$.[2] As infinitely often some y will act, any $q' < q$ will eventually be enumerated into $C_{f(n)}$, making it a left cut.

If $n \in S$, let y_0 be the least such that $W_{g(n,y_0)} \in \mathrm{Inf}$. Then there is a stage s_0 such that y_0 is never initialized again. As every $y > y_0$ defines $\delta_y[s] \leq \delta_{y_0}$ at every $s > s_0$ and y_0 acts infinitely often $\delta = \delta_{y_0}$ has left cut $C_{f(n)}$. Furthermore, as mentioned in the construction, $\{n^r \delta_{y_0}\} = \{n^r \varepsilon\}$ for some $r \in \omega$. From Proposition 3 we get a positive cone P_δ° and as can be seen in the proof of Theorem 3, $P_\delta^\circ \, E_{lo}^{\mathrm{BS}(1,n)} \, P_\varepsilon^\circ$.

---

[2] Following Lachlan $\delta_y[s]$ is the value of δ_y at stage s.

On the other hand, suppose $n \notin S$, so that all $W_{g(n,y)}$ are finite. Given y, let s_y be the stage after which y is never initialized again. Then, by the construction $C_{f(n)}$ is the left cut for $\delta = \lim_y \delta_y[s_y]$ and $\{k_y[s_y] : y \in \omega\} = \omega$. Thus, there cannot be p, q such that $n^p \delta = n^q \varepsilon$. This is the case because if $k_y[s_y] = \langle p, q \rangle$, then it is ensured at stage s_y that $n^p \delta \neq n^q \varepsilon$ since $\{\delta\} \restriction l_y[s_y] = \{\delta_y[s_y]\} \restriction l_y[s_y]$ and already this finite part witnessed that $n^p \delta \neq n^q \varepsilon$. Hence, $\{\delta\} \not\equiv_t \{\varepsilon\}$ and for the positive cone P_δ° we get from Propositon 3, $P_\delta^\circ \not\equiv_{lo}^{BS(1,n)} P_\varepsilon^\circ$.   □

Question 1. What is the complexity of $I(Q_\varepsilon^\circ, BS(1, n))$ for $\varepsilon \in \mathbb{Q}$ and $\circ \in \{++, --, +-, -+\}$?

References

1. Baumslag, G., Solitar, D.: Some two-generator one-relator non-Hopfian groups. Bull. Am. Math. Soc. **68**, 199–201 (1962). https://doi.org/10.1090/S0002-9904-1962-10745-9
2. Bonanome, M.C., Dean, M.H., Dean, J.P.: A sampling of remarkable groups. Compact Textbooks in Mathematics, Birkhäuser/Springer, Cham (2018).https://doi.org/10.1007/978-3-030-01978-5. Thompson's, self-similar, Lamplighter, and Baumslag-Solitar
3. Calderoni, F., Clay, A.: Borel structures on the space of left-orderings. Bull. Lond. Math. Soc. **54**(1), 83–94 (2022). https://doi.org/10.1112/blms.12559
4. Calderoni, F., Clay, A.: The Borel complexity of the space of left-orderings, low-dimensional topology, and dynamics. arXiv preprint arXiv:2305.03927 (2023)
5. Calderoni, F., Clay, A.: Condensation and left-orderable groups. arXiv preprint arXiv:2312.04993 (2023)
6. Calderoni, F., Marker, D., Motto Ros, L., Shani, A.: Anti-classification results for groups acting freely on the line. Adv. Math. **418**, Paper No. 108938, 45 (2023). https://doi.org/10.1016/j.aim.2023.108938
7. Conley, C.T., Jackson, S.C., Marks, A.S., Seward, B.M., Tucker-Drob, R.D.: Borel asymptotic dimension and hyperfinite equivalence relations. Duke Math. J. **172**(16), 3175–3226 (2023). https://doi.org/10.1215/00127094-2022-0100
8. Darbinyan, A.: Computability, orders, and solvable groups. J. Symb. Log. **85**(4), 1588–1598 (2020). https://doi.org/10.1017/jsl.2020.34
9. Darbinyan, A., Steenbock, M.: Embeddings into left-orderable simple groups. J. London Math. Soc. Second Ser. **105**(3), 2011–2045 (2022). https://doi.org/10.1112/jlms.12552
10. Deroin, B., Navas, A., Rivas, C.: Groups, orders, and dynamics (2016). http://arxiv.org/abs/1408.5805, https://doi.org/10.48550/arXiv.1408.5805
11. Dougherty, R., Jackson, S., Kechris, A.S.: The structure of hyperfinite Borel equivalence relations. Trans. Am. Math. Soc. **341**(1), 193–225 (1994). https://doi.org/10.2307/2154620
12. Downey, R.G., Kurtz, S.A.: Recursion theory and ordered groups. Ann. Pure Appl. Logic **32**, 137–151 (1986). https://doi.org/10.1016/0168-0072(86)90049-7
13. Feldman, J., Moore, C.C.: Ergodic equivalence relations, cohomology, and von Neumann algebras. I. Trans. Am. Math. Soc. **234**(2), 289–324 (1977). https://doi.org/10.2307/1997924

14. Ghys, É.: Groups acting on the circle. Enseignement Math. **47**(3/4), 329–408 (2001)
15. Harrington, L.A., Kechris, A.S., Louveau, A.: A Glimm-Effros dichotomy for Borel equivalence relations. J. Am. Math. Soc. 903–928 (1990)
16. Harrison-Trainor, M.: Left-orderable computable groups. J. Symb. Log. **83**(1), 237–255 (2018). https://doi.org/10.1017/jsl.2017.19
17. Kechris, A.: The theory of countable Borel equivalence relations. Preprint (2019)
18. Kopytov, V.M., Medvedev, N.Y.: Right-Ordered Groups. Springer, Heidelberg (1996)
19. Malicet, D., Mann, K., Rivas, C., Triestino, M.: Ping-pong configurations and circular orders on free groups. Groups Geom. Dyn. **13**(4), 1195–1218 (2019). https://doi.org/10.4171/ggd/519
20. Mann, K., Rivas, C.: Group orderings, dynamics, and rigidity. Ann. Inst. Fourier (Grenoble) **68**(4), 1399–1445 (2018). http://aif.cedram.org/item?id=AIF_2018_68_4_1399_0
21. Navas, A.: On the dynamics of (left) orderable groups. Univ. de Grenoble Ann. l'Inst. Fourier **60**(5), 1685–1740 (2010). https://doi.org/10.5802/aif.2570
22. Poulin, A.: Borel complexity of the isomorphism relation of Archimedean orders in finitely generated groups. arXiv preprint arXiv:2403.11326 (2024)
23. Rivas, C.: On spaces of Conradian group orderings. J. Group Theory **13**(3), 337–353 (2010). https://doi.org/10.1515/JGT.2009.053
24. Rivas, C.: Left-orderings on free products of groups. J. Algebra **350**, 318–329 (2012). https://doi.org/10.1016/j.jalgebra.2011.10.036
25. Rivas, C., Tessera, R.: On the space of left-orderings of virtually solvable groups. Groups Geom. Dyn. **10**(1), 65–90 (2016). https://doi.org/10.4171/GGD/343, https://doi-org.ezproxy.rice.edu/10.4171/GGD/343
26. Sikora, A.S.: Topology on the spaces of orderings of groups. Bull. London Math. Soc. **36**(4), 519–526 (2004). https://doi.org/10.1112/S0024609303003060
27. Solomon, R.: $\Pi_1^1 - CA_0$ and order types of countable ordered groups. J. Symb. Log. **66**(1), 192–206 (2001). https://doi.org/10.2307/2694917
28. Solomon, R.: Π_1^0 classes and orderable groups. Ann. Pure Appl. Log. **115**(1–3), 279–302 (2002). https://doi.org/10.1016/S0168-0072(01)00097-5

Hybrid Maximal Filter Spaces

David Gonzalez (✉) ⓘD

University of California, Berkeley, CA 94720, USA
david_gonzalez@berkeley.edu

Abstract. We introduce a new way of encoding general topology in second order arithmetic that we call hybrid maximal filter (hybrid MF) spaces. This notion is a modification of the notion of a proper MF space introduced by Montalbán. We justify the shift by showing that proper MF spaces are not able to code most topological spaces, while hybrid MF spaces can code any second countable MF space. We then answer Montalbán's question about metrization of well-behaved MF spaces to this shifted context. To be specific, we show that in stark contrast to the original MF formalization used by Mummert and Simpson, the metrization theorem can be proven for hybrid MF spaces within ACA_0 instead of needing $\Pi_2^1 - CA_0$.

Keywords: General topology · Maximal filter space · Reverse mathematics · Computable structures

1 Introduction

In this article we explore the concept of general topology in second order arithmetic through a new lens. Because a topology is naturally described as a third order object, it is not clear how to formalize its study in second order arithmetic. The usual approach involves restricting to topologies with structure that allows you to see the topology in a second order way. The most well studied approach looks at separable, complete metric spaces (see: [1,2] Chap. 10). However, many theorems of topology lack meaning in this setting. For example, metrization and the study of not completely metrizable spaces (like order topologies) are totally excluded.

To remedy the lack of expressive power of metric spaces, there have been two main explored approaches. The first is studying countable second-countable (CSC) spaces (eg. [3,10]). In this setting everything is countable, so all aspects of the topological space can be captured using only second order arithmetic. This system has the obvious disadvantage that it only describes countable spaces. In particular, it is not a good place to study notions such as connectivity.

The second approach is studying countably based maximal filter (MF) spaces (e.g. [7]). It is this second approach that we focus on in this article. Here, a topological space is encoded by a partially ordered set. Each basic open is given by an element in this partially ordered set, and the points of the space are

L. Levy Patey et al. (Eds.): CiE 2024, LNCS 14773, pp. 85–99, 2024.
https://doi.org/10.1007/978-3-031-64309-5_8

given by maximal filters in the partially ordered set. A point is said to be in a basic open if the element corresponding to that open set is an element of the point as a maximal filter. This approach has the advantage of defining a broad class of topological spaces that includes all separable, complete metric spaces and many spaces that are not metrizable (exactly classified in [8]). MF spaces as formalized here do have some undesirable properties. For example, saying a subset of a partially ordered set is a maximal filter can be as difficult as requiring $\Pi_1^1 - \mathrm{CA_0}$ (this is not explicitly noted [7], but we will see a short proof of it later based on those results). In other words, it may take $\Pi_1^1 - \mathrm{CA_0}$ to declare that a set encodes a point in your space. For this reason, it can be difficult to compute relatively simple topological properties in the MF space setting. For example, Mummert and Simpson [7] showed that the set of pairs of opens such that the closure of the first is contained in the second may need $\Pi_2^1 - \mathrm{CA_0}$ to compute.

The above results are striking in the high complexity they achieve. They also bring up a potential concern. The difficulty of recording basic topological relations may hide the combinatorial core of a theorem or make a construction seem overly difficult to describe. In this, results proven in the setting of MF spaces leave a stone unturned: what would the complexity of the result be without these descriptive difficulties surrounding basic topological notions like point and containment. For example, the well known result of the metrization theorem being equivalent to $\Pi_2^1 - \mathrm{CA_0}$ in MF spaces [7] ought to be far simpler if we were in a setting where basic notions were easier to compute.

The coding of an object is often an innocuous part of computability theory. This is not the case with MF spaces; there are apparent difficulties with the chosen coding. It is for this reason that alternate codings ought to be explored, especially if they result in different outcomes for the descriptive complexity of objects like a complete metric on the space. This is what led Montalbán to propose the notion of proper MF spaces, and what leads us to investigate the notion of hybrid MF spaces.

In the next sections we will give the necessary background on reverse mathematics and MF spaces. After this we will study proper MF spaces in general to justify the definition of hybrid MF spaces. Next we will give a proof of the metrization theorem for hybrid MF spaces in $\mathrm{ACA_0}$. The last section will feature some complexity calculations and suggestions for future work.

2   Background on Reverse Math

Reverse mathematics aims to calibrate a proof to a particular subsystem of second order arithmetic. Over a weak base system a typical argument shows that a mathematical theorem implies a stronger system and vice versa. We mention the following systems in this paper (listed from weakest to strongest). $\mathrm{RCA_0}$ contains Δ_1^0 comprehension and Σ_1^0 induction. In other words, it allows only for the definitions of computable objects. $\mathrm{ACA_0}$ contains arithmetical comprehension and arithmetical induction. This allows for the definition of arithmetical objects. $\Pi_1^1 - \mathrm{CA_0}$ is $\mathrm{ACA_0}$ along with Π_1^1 comprehension. $\Pi_2^1 - \mathrm{CA_0}$ is $\mathrm{ACA_0}$

along with Π_2^1 comprehension. There are many texts that go over the definitions of these subsystems in detail (see e.g. [2, 11]).

While RCA_0 is occasionally mentioned, ACA_0 is base system for this paper. This base system is unusually strong, but this is typical when working with MF spaces. The reason for this is that in [5] it was shown that the existence of a maximal filter in a poset is equivalent to ACA_0. As our spaces will be coded by maximal filters in a poset, it is difficult to account for the case where there are no maximal filters at all. Furthermore, typical objects like upward closures of sets in a poset cannot be calculated without ACA_0 and this is needed constantly. In short, one cannot give an honest formalization of MF spaces outside of ACA_0.

Our main result concerns metrization, and it is proven in our base system. We do not produce a reversal, as such an endeavor is not common when working in a base system.

One could understand the metrization result through a more structural lens. The result in [7] shows that given a regular MF space there is a metric on it, but this metric necessarily uses Π_2^1 sets in its definition. Our metrization result is proven in ACA_0, so shows that any regular hybrid MF space (a concept defined later) has a metric on it and this metric is arithmetically defined. In short, the subsystems of second order arithmetic used in this context can be understood as bounds on the complexity of defining additional metric structure on a given topological space.

3 Background on MF Spaces

This section aims to give the definitions regarding MF spaces established in [7] that will also be used in this article. There will also be definitions of a few needed terms from general topology.

Definition 1. *Fix a partially ordered set P. A pre-filter on P is a non-empty subset R with the property that for every $x, y \in R$ there is a $z \in R$ with $z \geq x$ and $z \geq y$. A filter on P is a pre-filter that is upwards closed. A maximal filter is a filter that is not strictly contained in any filter.*

Given $S \subseteq P$ we let $\text{ucl}(S)$ denote the upwards closure of S. Note that if S is a pre-filter then $\text{ucl}(S)$ is a filter. We use the concept of maximal filters to defined a maximal filter space.

Definition 2. *Let P be a countable partially ordered set. $MF(P)$ is the set of maximal filters on P. Every $p \in P$ codes a basic open set*

$$N_p := \{m \in MF(P) | p \in m\}.$$

A general open set is given by $U \subseteq P$ as follows

$$N_U := \bigcup_{p \in U} N_p.$$

These open sets are called the poset topology on $MF(P)$

Note that in ACA_0 one can show that the N_U are closed under unions and finite intersections. In particular, it is justified to call these sets a topology. Note also that we can code closed sets with the code for the open set that represents its complement. Concepts that can be defined in a general topological space carry the same definitions in this context based on the open sets N_U. For example, $m \in \mathrm{cl}(N_U)$ if every $q \in m$ has a common extension with some $p \in U$.

The metrization theorem concerns regular spaces.

Definition 3. *An MF space is regular if for every $x \in MF(P)$ and $p \in P$ with $x \in N_p$ there is a $q \in P$ with $n \in N_q$ and $cl(N_q) \subseteq N_p$.*

We will also mention the more technical notion of strong regularity.

Definition 4. *An MF space is strongly regular if there is a sequence of subsets $\langle D_p | p \in P \rangle$ with the property that $N_p = \bigcup_{q \in R_p} N_q$ and $cl(N_q) \subseteq N_p$ whenever $q \in D_p$.*

Given a strongly regular space, and $p \in P$ we will always use D_p to denote the set in the definition above. In a classical sense it is not difficult to see that all regular spaces are strongly regular. In fact, one can make this observation in $\Pi_2^1 - \mathrm{CA}_0$ (see [7] Lemma 4.1). One only must enumerate the set p, q such that $\mathrm{cl}(N_q) \subseteq N_p$. One of the central insights of [7] is that this set of pairs can in fact be Π_2^1-complete. In other words, showing strong regularity from regularity requires the strength of $\Pi_2^1 - \mathrm{CA}_0$. This insight is what ultimately leads to showing that the following metrization theorem is equivalent to $\Pi_2^1 - \mathrm{CA}_0$.

Definition 5. *MFMT is the statement that every regular MF space is homeomorphic to a complete separable metric space.*

The notion of homeomorphism between an MF space and a complete separable metric space is similar to the one we use in Definition 9. It is not central to this exposition, so we omit the exact notion used in [7] here.

We will briefly mention the notion of a *normal* topological space which is one in which every pair N_p, N_q with $\mathrm{cl}(N_q) \cap \mathrm{cl}(N_p) = \emptyset$ has r, t such that $\mathrm{cl}(N_q) \subseteq N_r$, $\mathrm{cl}(N_p) \subseteq N_t$ and $N_t \cap N_r = \emptyset$.

The final topology definition that will be used is that of paracompactness.

Definition 6. *A cover of a topological space is point finite if every point in the space has a neighborhood that only intersects finitely many of the elements of the cover. A topological space is paracompact if every cover admits a point finite subcover.*

The fact that every complete metric space is paracompact was formalized as Theorem II.7.2 in [11]. We will return to this notion when it is needed at the end of the final section.

4   Proper MF Spaces and Hybrid MF Spaces

Montalbán [6] made the following definition.

Definition 7. *A partial order P defines a proper MF space if for $p, q \in P$, $p \leq q$ if and only if $N_p \subseteq N_q$ and if p and q are comparable there is an $r \in P$ such that $N_r = N_p \cap N_q$.*

The hope was that these sorts of spaces would be easier to work with than general MF spaces. In particular, every MF space would be codeable as a proper MF space, but issues like definability of points would be simplified. This is what prompted Montalbán in [6] to ask his 15th question: what is the reverse mathematical strength of the complete metrization of proper MF spaces?

Unfortunately, we observe below that the notion of a proper MF space is not a suitable formulation for further study. Contrary to the suspicions of Montalbán, proper MF spaces cannot code every MF space.

In the proposition below we use $p \wedge q$ to denote the r such that $N_r = N_p \cap N_q$ in the proper MF space.

Proposition 1. *The topology of a proper MF space given by the elements of its poset is a clopen basis.*

Proof. Let P be the partial order that gives rise to the MF space. Consider a basic open set coded by $y \in P$. Say there is a maximal filter $M \subseteq P$ with $M \in \partial(N_y)$. Consider the set

$$N := \{p \in P | p \in M \vee \exists m \in M \ p = m \wedge y\}.$$

First note that N does not contain the empty set. This is because every open set containing M must intersect N_y. Therefore, any $m \in M$ has a non-empty meet with y.

We claim that N is a pre-filter. Note that for $m, n \in M$, we have that $m \wedge y, n \wedge y \in N$ so $(m \wedge y) \wedge (n \wedge y) = (m \wedge n) \wedge y \in N$ as $m \wedge n \in M$. Similarly, $m, n \wedge y \in N$ so $m \wedge (n \wedge y) = (m \wedge n) \wedge y \in N$ as $m \wedge n \in M$. Of course, $m \wedge n \in M \subseteq N$. This means that ucl($N$) is a filter. Note that ucl(N) contains M. By maximality of M, this means that $M = $ ucl(N). In particular, $y \in M$ and therefore $M \in N_y$.

This means that the boundary of N_y is contained in N_y, and therefore it is closed.

Example 1. $[0, 1]$ is not a proper MF space.

This follows from Proposition 1 and the fact that $[0, 1]$ is connected, so it cannot have a clopen basis.

One method that this example discounts for finding posets including meet that code a particular topological space is taking the meet-semilattice of open sets given to us by the basis of the topology. More explicitly, if we take the standard countable basis for $[0, 1]$ of rational radius balls with rational centers, this meet-semilattice of open sets does not code $[0, 1]$ in the sense of an MF space. For example, the set of opens containing $1/2$ is not a maximal filter. In fact, it can be extended to a maximal filter in two different ways. Either the open rational intervals ending in $1/2$ can be added or the open rational intervals starting with $1/2$ can be added. It can be observed that this topology is quite distinct from that of $[0,1]$ as every rational number is duplicated in this way.

This excursion leads us to the conclusion that the basic open sets in an MF space actually serve two distinct roles that cannot be unified into a single object:

1. Like in all spaces, they encode topological information via a lattice of open sets,
2. They code points via maximal filters on a selected subposet of the above lattice.

In many cases the subposet cannot be a an induced subposet as in the example above. Either this, or the subposet lacks meets or joins. The lattice and poset are actually quite far apart from each other. It seems natural then that a more complete description and encoding of an MF space should actually include both of these objects and how they interact.

This leads to the following "hybrid" approach to the definition of an MF space in second order arithmetic.

Definition 8. *A hybrid MF space is a pseudo-complemented distributive lattice $(L, \leq_L, \wedge, \vee, 0, 1, ^c)$ with a distinguished subposet $(P, \leq_p)$ such that:*

1. *$x \leq_L y$ for $x, y \in P$ if and only if every maximal filter in P containing x also contains y.*
2. *Every non-zero element $x \in L$ is $\leq_L$ above infinitely many elements of P. For ease of notation we call this set $B(x) \subseteq P$.*
3. *$x \leq_L y$ for $x, y \in L$ if and only if $B(x) \subseteq B(y)$.*
4. *$B(x \wedge y) = B(x) \cap B(y)$.*
5. *$B(x \vee y) = B(x) \cup B(y)$.*
6. *If $B(x \wedge y) = \emptyset$ then $x \wedge y = 0$.*
7. *If every maximal filter passes through $B(x \vee y)$ then $x \vee y = 1$.*
8. *$B(x^c)$ is the set of all y such that $x \wedge y = 0$.*

We say that a maximal filter M is in a basic open $p \in P$ if $p \in M$. For $x \in L$ we say that M is in x if there is some $p \in P$ with $x \geq_L p$ and $p \in M$. M is contained union of basic open sets coded by $W \subseteq L$ if there is an $x \in W$ with M in x.

It can be shown that any partial order P can be upgraded to a hybrid MF space using $\Pi^1_2 - \mathrm{CA}_0$. The most difficult portion is the definition of $\leq_L$ among the elements of P. The definition given above is naturally Π^1_2 as $\leq_L = \{(x,y) | \forall M \subseteq P\ MaxFilt(M) \to (x \in M \to y \in M)\}$ and $MaxFilt(M)$ is Π^1_1.

To be concrete, it is not difficult to define a hybrid MF representation of the previously problematic space $[0,1]$. L is given by the collection of unions of finitely many rational subintervals of $[0,1]$. P is given by the rational subintervals of $[0,1]$. $\leq_P$ is given by the relation that states that the closure of a an interval sits inside the larger interval (i.e. the right and left end points are contained in the larger interval). Lemma 4.2 of [7] demonstrates that this representation as an ordinary MF space is as desired. $\leq_L$ is defined by containment which is easily computable. $\wedge, \vee, 0, 1$ and ^{c} are similarly easy to compute.

The following is essentially immediate from the work of Mummert and Simpson (e.g. it follows from Lemma 3 below).

Lemma 1 (*[7]*). *The statement that every partial order P can be extended to a hybrid MF-space is equivalent over ACA_0 to $\Pi_2^1 - CA_0$.*

The question now becomes what sort of results can be proven in the hybrid formalism. In the next section we explore Montalbán's 15th question from [6] in the hybrid context. We assess the strength of the metrization theorem in a setting where basic topological definitions are easily definable, as Montalbán desired.

However, before we move forward we note here some basic properties of the pseudo-complement that will prove helpful later on. Note that the definition of pseudo-complement can be naturally extended to open sets coded by reals. We let $U^c = \{p \in L | \forall q \in U q \vee p = 0\}$, a set definable in ACA_0. All of these properties are provable in ACA_0. In fact, the proof is quite straightforward and precisely the same as Lemma 4.5 in [7] (a more detailed treatment can be found in [9] Lemma 4.3.11).

Lemma 2 (*ACA_0*). *Fix an open set U coded by a real number in a hybrid MF space.*

1. *The entire space is a disjoint union of $cl(U)$ and U^c. In particular, every point is in exactly one of these sets.*
2. *There is no point in both U and $cl(U^c)$.*

We will use the above lemma freely in the proofs of the next section.

5 Metrization

In MF spaces, there is a deep difference between regular spaces and the made-for-reverse-math notion of strongly regular spaces. In fact, showing that regular spaces are strongly regular is equivalent to $\Pi_2^1 - CA_0$. In hybrid MF spaces, this distinction does not exist and can be seen in the base theory of ACA_0.

Lemma 3 (*ACA_0*). *Every regular hybrid MF space is strongly regular.*

Proof. We only need to form the set of $p, q \in P$ such that $cl(N_p) \subseteq N_q$. This is easily done by checking the condition $p^c \vee q = 1$.

Another previously discussed aspect of MF spaces is that it is difficult to define the set of points. In general, the points are Π_1^1 to define.

Lemma 4. *The predicate $MaxFilt(X)$ which states that X is a maximum filter in a poset is Π_1^1 in general.*

Proof. In [7] they show that the set of p, q such that $\mathrm{cl}(N_q) \subseteq N_p$ can be Π_2^1 complete. We can write this set in terms of the $MaxFilt(X)$ predicate as follows:

$$\mathrm{cl}(N_q) \subseteq N_p \iff \forall X \left(MaxFilt(X) \wedge \forall \ell \in X \exists r \; r \geq \ell \wedge r \geq q \right) \to p \in X.$$

If the above is Π_2^1 complete then $MaxFilt(X)$ must be strictly Π_1^1.

The above is true even if we restrict to case of regular spaces, the matter of interest in the metrization theorem. A major contrast in the hybrid approach is that the set of points is definable in the base theory of ACA_0 due to the following observation.

Lemma 5 *(RCA_0). There is an arithmetic formula that is true exactly on the maximal filters of a given regular hybrid MF space.*

Proof. We claim that a subset of P is a maximal filter if and only if it is a filter and for any $p \in P - M$ one of the following 2 cases hold:

1. there is an $m \in M$ such that $p \wedge m = \emptyset$,
2. for every $r \in D_p$ there is an $n \in M$ such that $r \wedge n = \emptyset$.

We first show that if one of these conditions hold of every $p \in P - M$, then M is maximal. If M was not maximal, there would be a maximal filter N containing some point $p \in P - M$. If Condition 1 holds of this point, then N cannot be a filter as there is $p, m \in N$ with no common extension. This is an immediate contradiction. Say instead that Condition 2 holds of the point p. As the $r \in D_q$ cover N_p by construction, in order theoretic terms, any maximal filter containing p must contain one of the $r \in D_q$. Therefore, N contains one of these r. However, N cannot contain such an r as there is an $n \in M$ such that $r \wedge n = \emptyset$.

We now show that if M is maximal then one of these conditions holds. If M is maximal, then it is a point in the space, and p represents an open set that does not contain M. It is immediate that Condition 1 holds exactly when M is not in the closure of N_p. Therefore, we need to check that if M is in the boundary of N_p, then Condition 2 holds. Consider an $r \in D_p$. As $\mathrm{cl}(N_r) \subseteq N_p$, $M \notin \mathrm{cl}(N_r)$. Therefore, there is $n \in M$ such that $r \wedge n = \varnothing$, as desired.

We will use the arithmetic definition of maximal filter moving forward in the proof.

We now prove metrizability in the hybrid setting. The outline of the proof is similar to the one in [7], but there are differing details throughout. These details are critical as they move the complexity of the proof down from $\Pi_2^1 - \mathrm{CA}_0$ to ACA_0. We start with the regularity implies normality lemma.

Lemma 6 *(ACA_0). Let X be a hybrid MF space. There are functionals ν_1, ν_2 with the following property. If U and V are open subsets of X and $cl(U) \cap cl(V) = \emptyset$, then $\nu_1(U, V)$ and $\nu_2(U, V)$ are disjoint open subsets of X such that $cl(U) \subseteq \nu_1(U, V)$ and $cl(V) \subseteq \nu_2(U, V)$.*

Proof. For an open set W, let $\{e(W, n)\}_{n \in \omega}$ be an enumeration of the union of D_p for $p \in W$ in increasing order. Let

$$U(n) = e(U^c, n) \cap \bigcap_{i \le n} (e(V^c, i))^c$$

$$V(n) = e(V^c, n) \cap \bigcap_{i \le n} (e(U^c, i))^c$$

be the corresponding elements of L.

Define

$$\nu_1(U, V) = \{V(n)\}_{n \in \omega},$$

$$\nu_2(U, V) = \{C(n)\}_{n \in \omega}.$$

The classical proof that these functionals have the desired properties now goes through in ACA_0. To be specific, let $x \in \text{cl}(U)$. As $\text{cl}(U) \cap \text{cl}(V) = \emptyset$, this means that $x \in e(V^c, n)$ for some n. Furthermore, if $x \notin e(U^c, i)^c$ this means that every open set containing x intersects $e(U^c, i)$. However, this means that $x \in \text{cl}(U^c, i) \subseteq U^c$. This is a contradiction to the fact that $x \in \text{cl}(U)$. Therefore, $x \in V(n)$ for some n. A similar and symmetric proof demonstrates this point for V.

To see that the two open sets are disjoint, note that if $x \in U(n)$ for some n it is in $e(U^c, n)$ and each of the $(e(V^c, i))^c$ for $i \le n$. This means that x is not in $V(m)$ for $m \le n$ as $(e(U^c, m))^c \cap e(U^c, m) = \emptyset$. Furthermore, x is not in $V(m)$ for $m \ge n$ as $(e(V^c, m))^c \cap e(V^c, m) = \emptyset$. This completes the proof.

Lemma 7 *(ACA_0).* *Fix $p \in P$ and $q \in R_p$. Let D be the set of dyadic rational numbers in the interval $[0, 1]$. There is a map $g_{p,q}$ from D to coded open subsets of X such that $g_{p,q}(0) = \{q\}$, $g_{p,q}(1) = \{p\}$, and $\text{cl}(g_{p,q}(k)) \subseteq g_{p,q}(k')$ whenever $k < k'$.*

Proof. Let $U_0 = \{q\}$ and $U_1 = \{p\}$. We define the rest of the U_k for dyadic k by induction. Throughout the induction we will maintain that for dyadic rationals $k < k'$, $\text{cl}(U_k) \subseteq U_{k'}$. Let us note that this is an arithmetic condition. In particular, we can check if $U_k^c \cup U_{k'} = 1$. This means that we can preform our induction within ACA_0.

We assume that the map has already been defined for all dyadic k with reduced form $\frac{a}{2^m}$. We show how to define the map on dyadic ℓ with reduced form $\frac{b}{2^{m+1}}$. Select $k < k'$ with reduced form $\frac{a}{2^m}$ that are the closest to ℓ. We have that $\ell = \frac{k+k'}{2}$. By induction, we assume that $\text{cl}(U_k) \subseteq U_{k'}$. In other words, we have that $\text{cl}(U_k) \cap \text{cl}(U_{k'}^c) = \emptyset$, as otherwise there would be a point in both $U_{k'}$ and $U_{k'}^c$. This means that we define the U_ℓ as $U_\ell = \nu_1(U_k, U_{k'}^c)$. By the previous lemma this can be done in ACA_0. Furthermore, we are guaranteed that $\text{cl}(U_k) \subseteq U_\ell$. Lastly, we claim that $\text{cl}(U_\ell)$ is contained in $U_{k'}$. Note that $\nu_2(U_k, U_{k'}^c)$ is an open disjoint from U_ℓ by construction. Furthermore, $\nu_2(U_k, U_{k'}^c)$ contains the closure of $U_{k'}^c$. Therefore, every point not in $\nu_2(U_k, U_{k'}^c)$ must be in $U_{k'}$, and in particular every point in U_ℓ is in $U_{k'}$ as required.

The next three results have arguments that are quite similar to those found in [7] (and indeed they are also quite similar to the classical arguments). There are not many details different from the argument for ordinary MF spaces and hybrid MF spaces because the arguments produced in [7] already go through at the lower complexity level of ACA_0. The proofs of these intermediate lemmas are still produced here, but not in full detail; one ought to examine [7] Lemmas 4.7–4.10 or [9] Lemmas 4.3.12, 4.3.13, and 4.3.18 for further details.

Lemma 8 *(ACA_0). There is a sequence $\langle f_{p,q} | p \in P, q \in R_p \rangle$ of continuous functions from $P \to [0, \infty)$ such that for all $p \in P$ and $q \in R_p$ we have $f_{p,q}(N_q) = 0$ and $f_{p,q}(X - N_p) = 1$.*

Proof. We can form the set $\langle g_{p,q} | p \in P, q \in R_p \rangle$ for all p and q by the previous lemma. We extend $g_{p,q}$ to all positive dyadic rationals by letting $g_{p,q}(k)$ be the whole space if $k > 1$. As in the previous lemma, U_k is meant to indicate the open set coded by $g_{p,q}(k)$. Let

$$f_{p,q} = \inf\{k \in D^+ | x \in U_k\}.$$

It is clear that these $f_{p,q}$ satisfy the desired conclusion. This can be executed in ACA_0. $f_{p,q}(x) < k$ if and only if there is some $k' < k$ with $x \in U_{k'}$ if and only if there is $r \in P$ with $r \in x \cap U_{k'}$. To see $f_{p,q}(x) > k$ you similarly check for a $k'' > k$ with $x \in U_{k''}^c$ which can be seen by looking for an $r \in P$ with $r \in x \cap U_{k''}^c$. This is enough to define the output of f.

From this, we get the desired metrizability.

Proposition 2 *(ACA_0). Every hybrid MF space is metrizable.*

Proof. Reindex the function from the above lemma to be f_n and let

$$d(x,y) = \sum_{n \in \omega} 2^{-n} |f_n(x) - f_n(y)|.$$

The classical proof of Uryshon's metrization theorem is straightforward and shows that this is a metric.

At this point we pause to note that the above development answers Question 4.1 from [7], in a certain sense. They ask what can be said about the reverse mathematical strength of stating that every strongly regular MF space has a (not necessarily complete) metric. By moving to a different representation meant to easily capture topological notions like strong regularity, we are able to show this in the base theory of ACA_0. Or course, in a stricter sense their question remains open.

We now wish to show that hybrid MF spaces are completely metrizable. It is in fact this theorem that was shown in [7] to be equivalent to $\Pi_2^1 - CA_0$.

We use the following lemma to demonstrate this, which states that in RCA_0 every G_δ subset of a completely metrizable space is completely metrizable.

Lemma 9 *(RCA$_0$). If (U_i) is a sequence of open sets in a complete, separable metric space $(\hat{A}, D)$, the there is a complete metric d' such on $\bigcap_i U_i$ that agrees with the subspace topology on $\bigcap_i U_i$. Furthermore, if $D \subseteq \bigcap_i U_i$ is computable and dense then this topology is canonically isomorphic to $\hat{D}$.*

Proof. This follows from the classical proof see e.g. [4] Theorem 3.11. More details for the context of reverse mathematics can be found in [9] Lemma 4.3.18.

Given a hybrid MF space X we let $A \subseteq X$ be a computable dense set definable in ACA$_0$. Note that this can be found; given non-empty $p \in P$ we find a maximal filter containing p by recursion. Let $p_0 = p$, and let p_{i+1} be the least element of P that has non-zero intersection with $p_0, \cdots, p_i$ and non-zero intersection with some sequence of elements in $D_{p_0} \times \cdots \times D_{p_i}$. By Lemma 5 this is enough to guarantee that we build a maximal filter in the limit. We show first that X is isometrically embeddable in $\hat{A}$, the completion of A, and then we show that the image of this embedding is G_δ.

To formalize the idea of a continuous map between an MF space and a metric space we take the following definition.

Definition 9. *A continuous function code F between a hybrid MF space based on the poset P and a complete metric space given by a dense set A is given by a set of pairs $\langle p, \langle a, r \rangle \rangle \in P \times A \times \mathbb{R}$. F induces a partial function from $MF(P)$ to $\hat{A}$. We say that F is defined at $m \in MF(P)$ if for every sequence of elements in $m_i \in m$ there is $\langle m_i, \langle a_i, r_i \rangle \rangle \in F$ with $r_i \to 0$. Furthermore, for every such $\langle m_i, \langle a_i, r_i \rangle \rangle \in F$ with $r_i \to 0$, the a_i are a Cauchy sequence in the same equivalence class. In this case we say that F sends m to this unique equivalence class of Cauchy sequences. A coded continuous function is one that is a total function induced by a continuous function code.*

It is not too difficult to see in ZFC that every continuous function between a hybrid MF space and a complete metric space is induced by such a code. It is enough to check that given such a function f, $\{\langle p, \langle a, r \rangle \rangle \in P \times A \times \mathbb{R} | f(N_p) \subseteq B_r(a)\}$ is a continuous function code for f.

Lemma 10 *(ACA$_0$). If X is a metrizable countably based hybrid MF space, there is a separable complete metric space $\hat{A}$ and a continuous, open bijection h between X and a dense subset of A. Furthermore, h is an isometry.*

Proof. Define the metric d on X with Proposition 2. Let A be a countable dense subset of X. For each $p \in P$,

$$diam(p) := \sup\{d(a, b) | a, b \in A \cap N_p\}.$$

Let H be the set of all $\langle p, \langle a, r \rangle \rangle$ such that $diam(p) < r$ and $a \in N_p$.

Consider m a maximal filter in P. We first find a $\langle m_i, \langle a_i, r_i \rangle \rangle \in H$ with $r_i \to 0$. Let b_i be a sequence of points in A that converge to m. Because X is metrizable, there is some $p \in m$ such that $diam(p) \leq 2^{-n-1}$. Let $b_{i(n)}$ be such that $b_{i(n)} \in N_p$. This yields that $\langle m_i, \langle b_i, 2^{-n} \rangle \rangle \in H$. As n was arbitrary this gives the needed sequence.

Now consider two distinct $\langle m_i, \langle a_i, r_i \rangle \rangle, \langle m'_i, \langle a'_i, r'_i \rangle \rangle \in H$. Say that $r_i \to 0$ and $r'_i \to 0$ and they are both decreasing without loss of generality. By definition, $d(a_i, m) < r_i$ and $d(a'_i, m) < r'_i$. This means that for all $j \geq i$ $d(a_i, a_j) < 2r_i$ and $d(a'_i, a'_j) < 2r'_i$. Or, what is the same, the sequences are Cauchy. Furthermore, $d(a_i, a'_i) < r_i + r'_i$ and therefore tends to 0 too. This means that the sequences a_i and a'_i must be in the same equivalence class as desired.

It is clear that the h that H codes is an isometry because it is an isometry on the dense set A shared between the spaces. As h is an isometry, it is open on its dense image.

We will also use the Paracompactness Lemma from Theorem II.7.2 in [11].

Lemma 11 *(RCA$_0$). Given a complete, separable metric space (A, d), there is a computable functional Φ that, given a sequence of opens U_i, returns a point finite refinement V_i*

Theorem 1 *(ACA$_0$). Every hybrid MF space is completely metrizable.*

Proof. We wish to construct a sequence of open subsets of $\hat{A}$ that witness that $\mathrm{im}(h)$ from Lemma 10 is G_δ. From here we will appeal to Lemma 9 to complete the proof.

By our previous results, we obtain a metric d on X that induces the topology, along with a set of witnesses R_p for $p \in P$ for the strong regularity of X. We construct countable sequences of open sets and will form a tree of these sequences. The odd entries in the sequences, denoted W_i, will be themselves sequences of balls in the metric topology centered on $a \in A$. The even entries will be elements $q_i \in P$ that represent basic open sets in the MF topology. In this notation, the sequences will look like $(W_0, q_0, \cdots, W_n, q_n)$ or $(W_0, q_0, \cdots, q_n, W_{n+1})$. To define the precise tree we are working with, we put the following restrictions on the sequences:

1. For every i and q_i, there is a basic open ball B enumerated in W_i such that $N_q \subseteq B$.
2. For every i, $q_{i+1} \leq_P q_i$.
3. For every i, $\mathrm{diam}(q_i) < 2^{-i}$.
4. W_0 is an element of the point finite refinement of the canonical $B(a, 1)_{a \in A}$ covering of X.
5. W_{i+1} is an element of the point finite refinement of the cover of the element W_i given by the set of N_{q_i} such that the q_i satisfy Conditions 1–3.

It is clear that Conditions 1–4 are arithmetic. Condition 5 is also arithmetic, but requires more explanation. In the statement of Condition 5, it is implicitly assumed that the set of N_{q_i} satisfying Conditions 1–3 cover W_i. We start by showing this. Consider a point $x \in W_i$. Take a point $a \in A$ with $d(x, a) < 2^{-i}$. The set $B(a, 2^{-i}) \cap W_i$ is open, and is therefore a union of N_r for $r \in P$. In particular, for some c with $N_c \subseteq B(a, 2^{-i}) \cap W_i$, $x \in N_c$. If $i > 0$, then the W_i

came from a point finite refinement of q_{i-1}, so, $W_i \subseteq N_{q_{i-1}}$. This means that, considering x as a filter, $q_{i-1}, c \in x$. Take q_i to be a common extension of q_{i-1} and c. It can now be see that $x \in N_{q_i}$ with all of the desired properties.

Strictly speaking, we can only apply the paracompactness functional to balls in the space, not the opens given by the maximal filter space. That being said, we can obtain a description for N_q in terms of balls arithmetically, which fixes this issue. In particular, given N_q, let

$$U_q = \{B | \exists p \in R_q \ B \cap A \subseteq N_p \cap A\}.$$

Mummert shows that $N_q = \bigcup_{B \in U_q} B$ in Lemma 4.3 of [7]. In terms of reverse mathematics, when we say "the point finite refinement of the cover of the element W_i given by the set of N_{q_i} such that..." we precisely mean "the point finite refinement of the cover of the element W_i given by the set of U_{q_i} such that...".

With this, it should be clear that the above conditions are well defined and, in fact, arithmetic. Because the satisfaction of these properties is determined locally by looking at the preceding elements in the finite sequence, it is clear that the sequences satisfying the conditions form a countable tree definable in ACA_0. We call this tree T. We now define the open sets C_i as the union of the $2i + 1$st level of T. We claim that $\operatorname{im}(h) = \bigcap_i C_i$.

We first show that $\operatorname{im}(h) \subseteq \bigcap_i C_i$. Given $x \in \operatorname{im}(h)$, we show that $\forall i \ x \in C_i$ by induction. C_0 is a cover by definition so it contains x. By the argument above, if $x \in C_i$ because $x \in W_i$, there is an extension q_i with $x \in N_{q_i}$. Furthermore, because the paracompactness functional maintains covers, x must be in some W_{i+1}. Therefore, $x \in C_{i+1}$ as desired.

We now show that $\bigcap_i C_i \subseteq \operatorname{im}(h)$. Fix $z \in \bigcap_i C_i$. We form the tree, T_z, which contains all sequences $(W_0, \cdots, W_n)$ that are odd projections from elements of T with $x \in W_n$. T_z is infinite as there are arbitrarily long paths, because $z \in C_i$ for all i. However, T_z is finitely branching. By construction, once you fix W_i the possible extensions form a point finite cover, so only finitely many of them contain z. This means that only finitely many of these extensions are in T_z, as we claimed. By Konig's Lemma there is an infinite path through the tree $(W_i)_{i \in \omega}$. By definition, $z \in \bigcap_i W_i$. This corresponds to a sequence q_i in the even projection from the tree T with $z \in \bigcap_i q_i$. Note that the q_i are arbitrarily small, so $\bigcap_i q_i$ has only one point. Now consider $m = \operatorname{ucl}_L((q_i)_{i \in \omega}) \subseteq P$. It is not difficult to see that m is a filter. We now show that it is maximal. If it was not maximal, there would be an $r \in P - m$ with $c \in D_r$ such that for all $i \ c \wedge q_i \neq \emptyset$. Let $\varepsilon = d(\bar{N}_c, \bar{N}_r^c)$, positive by regularity. Take i with $2^{-i} < \varepsilon$ and note that $q_i \leq_L r$. Therefore, $r \in m$, a contradiction. This gives that the image of m under h must be z. Therefore, $z \in \operatorname{im}(h)$, as desired.

Lemma 9 completes the proof.

6 Some Complexity Calculations and Future Work

We define a map which demonstrates a few interesting complexity calculations. These calculations suggest directions for future work.

Definition 10. *Given a tree $\mathcal{T} \subseteq \mathbb{N}^{<\mathbb{N}}$ we define $\Phi(\mathcal{T}) \subseteq (\mathbb{N} \cup \{*\})^{<\mathbb{N}}$ where $*$ is a symbol not among $\mathbb{N}$. We take $\Phi(\mathcal{T}) = \{\sigma^\frown * \,|\, \sigma \in \mathcal{T}\} \cup \mathcal{T}$.*

Note that given a tree, we can understand it as a partial ordering via the inclusion relation. In particular, every tree also codes an MF space. Furthermore, in ACA_0 this MF space can be extended to a hybrid MF space. It is easy to confirm $\leq_P$ and $\leq_L$ coincide as the maximal filters are the maximal paths through the tree and the points in the tree just contain each path that includes them. One can then extend the structure to include $0, 1, \wedge, \vee, ^c$ in a direct way. In what follows, we consider trees as a hybrid MF space in the manner described above.

Lemma 12. *Every $\mathcal{T} \subseteq \mathbb{N}^{<\mathbb{N}}$ represents a regular topology.*

Proof. It was observed above that $\leq_P$ and $\leq_L$ coincide in the topology of $\mathcal{T}$. Furthermore, it can be confirmed that given $\sigma, \tau \in \mathcal{T}$ their meet is the longest common initial segment of σ and τ. The meet is of σ and τ are then inside of the poset P. This means that $\mathcal{T}$ represents a proper MF space. By Proposition 1, this means that the basis is clopen.

In other words for $x \in N_p$, it is enough to note that $\mathrm{Cl}(N_p) \subseteq N_p$ to see that there is a witness to regularity for the pair x, p (namely p itself).

Proposition 3. *The set of discrete, regular hybrid MF spaces is $\mathbf{\Pi}_1^1$ complete.*

Proof. First we note that there is a $\mathbf{\Pi}_1^1$ definition. Being discrete for a regular space is equivalent to saying there are no limit points; in other words, no sequence of points converges to any particular point. This can be expressed as

$$\forall X, \{Y_i\}_{i \in \omega} \left(\bigwedge\!\!\!\bigwedge MaxFilt(Y_i) \wedge MaxFilt(X) \right) \to \exists p \in P \; p \in X \wedge \bigwedge\!\!\!\bigwedge p \notin Y_i.$$

By Lemma 5 , $MaxFilt(X)$ can be expressed as an arithmetic formula, so the above expression is Π_1^1 in P as desired.

We now note that $\Phi(\mathcal{T})$ is discrete if and only if $\mathcal{T}$ is well-founded. Note that if $\mathcal{T}$ is well-founded, so is $\Phi(\mathcal{T})$. In any well-founded tree the maximal filters are finite, and are therefore isolated by the unique maximal string in the filter. Therefore, any well-founded tree gives rise to a discrete space. If $\mathcal{T}$ is not well-founded let A be a path in T. It is straightforward to confirm that A is a limit point of $(A \upharpoonright n)^\frown *$, so $\Phi(\mathcal{T})$ is not discrete.

The above calculation is made exact by the fact that $MaxFilt(X)$ can be expressed as an arithmetic formula. It does not yield a similar result with ordinary MF spaces as the given definition of discreteness would be Π_2^1 in P. This is a good example of how moving to the hybrid formalism can allow for greater expressive power in a way that facilitates calculations above the level of ACA_0. The same comments apply to the example below.

Proposition 4. *The set of covers of a regular hybrid MF spaces are $\mathbf{\Pi}_1^1$ complete.*

Proof. First we note that there is a Π^1_1 definition. To say that a set of opens $\{p_i\}_{i\in\omega}$ covers a space is to say every maximal filter contains one of these points. This can be expressed as

$$\forall X \; MaxFilt(X) \to \bigvee p_i \in X.$$

By Lemma 5 , $MaxFilt(X)$ can be expressed as an arithmetic formula, so the above expression is Π^1_1 in $\{p_i\}_{i\in\omega}$ as desired.

We now note that $\{\sigma^\frown * | \sigma \in \mathcal{T}\}$ covers $\Phi(\mathcal{T})$ if and only if $\mathcal{T}$ is well-founded. If $\mathcal{T}$ is well-founded the maximal filters in $\Phi(\mathcal{T})$ are all maximal finite segments. By construction, these all end in $*$; i.e. there is a point in the filter among $\{\sigma^\frown * | \sigma \in \mathcal{T}\}$. Therefore, $\{\sigma^\frown * | \sigma \in \mathcal{T}\}$ covers $\Phi(\mathcal{T})$. If $\mathcal{T}$ is If $\mathcal{T}$ is not well-founded let A be a path in T. It is straightforward to confirm that A is a point in $\Phi(\mathcal{T})$ that is not within $\{\sigma^\frown * | \sigma \in \mathcal{T}\}$.

This proposition begins to aim at the theory of compactness in which covers play a central role. The following remains an open and motivating question for further development of this area.

Question 1. What is the reverse mathematical strength of the one point compactification theorem?

References

1. Brown, D.K.: Notions of closed subsets of a complete separable metric space in weak subsystems of second-order arithmetic. In: Logic and Computation (Pittsburgh, PA, 1987). Contemporary Mathematics, vol. 106, pp. 39–50. American Mathematical Society, Providence (1990)
2. Dzhafarov, D.D., Mummert, C.: Reverse Mathematics–Problems, Reductions, and Proofs. Theory and Applications of Computability. Springer, Cham (2022). https://doi.org/10.1007/978-3-031-11367-3
3. Dorais, F.G.: Reverse mathematics of compact countable second-countable spaces (2011). https://arxiv.org/abs/1110.6555
4. Kechris, A.S.: Classical Descriptive Set Theory. Graduate Texts in Mathematics, vol. 156. Springer, New York (1995). https://doi.org/10.1007/978-1-4612-4190-4
5. Lempp, S., Mummert, C.: Filters on computable posets. Notre Dame J. Formal Logic **47**(4), 479–485 (2006)
6. Montalbán, A.: Open questions in reverse mathematics. Bull. Symb. Logic **17**(3), 431–454 (2011)
7. Mummert, C., Simpson, S.G.: Reverse mathematics and Π^1_2 comprehension. Bull. Symb. Log. **11**(4), 526–533 (2005)
8. Mummert, C., Stephan, F.: Topological aspects of poset spaces. Michigan Math. J. **59**(1), 3–24 (2010)
9. Mummert, C.: On the reverse mathematics of general topology. ProQuest LLC, Ann Arbor (2005). Thesis (Ph.D.)–The Pennsylvania State University
10. Shafer, P.: The strength of compactness for countable complete linear orders. Computability **9**(1), 25–36 (2020)
11. Simpson, S.G.: Subsystems of Second Order Arithmetic. Perspectives in Logic, 2nd edn. Cambridge University Press, Cambridge; Association for Symbolic Logic, Poughkeepsie (2009)

Inversion in P-Computable Fields

Pavel Alaev$^{(\boxtimes)}$ [ID]

Novosibirsk State University and Sobolev Institute of Mathematics SB RAS, Novosibirsk, Russia
alaev@math.nsc.ru

Abstract. We consider fields computable in polynomial time (P-computable). We prove that under some assumptions about a P-computable field $(A, +, \cdot)$ of characteristic 0, there exists a P-computable field $(B, +, \cdot) \cong (A, +, \cdot)$, in which x^{-1} is not a primitive recursive function. In particular, this holds for the field $\mathbb{Q}$ of rational numbers.

Keywords: computability · polynomial computability · computable structure · field

1 Introduction

If Σ is a finite alphabet, then Σ^* denotes the set of all words in this alphabet. If $x \in \Sigma^*$ then $|x|$ is the length of x. A function $f : A \to \Sigma^*$, where $A \subseteq (\Sigma^*)^n$, is called *computable in polynomial time* (in short, P-*computable*) if the computing time of $f(x_1, \ldots, x_n)$ on a Turing machine can be estimated by a polynomial of $\max_{i \leqslant n}\{|x_i|\}$. Such functions can be considered as a theoretical attempt to define the concept of a fast computable function.

In this paper, we consider P-computable structures. Let $\mathcal{A} = (A, L^A)$ be a structure of a finite signature L. We say that $\mathcal{A}$ is P-*computable* if $A \subseteq \Sigma^*$ for some finite alphabet Σ, and A and all functions and predicates in L^A are P-computable. A structure $\mathcal{A}$ is called a P-*computable presentation* of a structure $\mathcal{B}$ if $\mathcal{A}$ is P-computable and $\mathcal{A} \cong \mathcal{B}$. This definition can be found, for example, in [1].

Let $\mathcal{A} = (A, +, \cdot)$ be a P-computable field in the signature with two operations. What can we say about the complexity of the operation $x \mapsto x^{-1}$ in $\mathcal{A}$, where $0^{-1} = 0$? Clearly, it is computable, since $x^{-1} = \mu y\,[\,y \in A\,\&\,x \cdot y = 1\,]$ for $x \neq 0$. It is shown here that we cannot assert anything more under sufficiently weak assumptions about the field $\mathcal{A}$ of characteristic 0. Namely, there exists a P-computable structure $\mathcal{B} \cong \mathcal{A}$, in which x^{-1} is not a primitive recursive function. This means that P-computable fields in the signatures of $(+, \cdot)$ and in $(+, \cdot, ^{-1})$ are significantly different objects.

In particular, these assumptions hold for the standard binary presentation of the field $\mathbb{Q}$, and we can assert that there is a P-computable field $\mathcal{B} \cong (\mathbb{Q}, +, \cdot)$, in which the operation x^{-1} is not primitive recursive, i.e., cannot be computed by an algorithm with any explicit estimates for its working time.

L. Levy Patey et al. (Eds.): CiE 2024, LNCS 14773, pp. 100–109, 2024.
https://doi.org/10.1007/978-3-031-64309-5_9

We note that in some sense an opposite result was proved in [2]. For every P-computable field $\mathcal{A} = (A, +, \cdot)$, there exists a P-computable field $\mathcal{C} = (C, +, \cdot) \cong \mathcal{A}$, in which the operation x^{-1} is also P-computable.

In [3], similar facts were established for the class of groups. Every P-computable group $\mathcal{A} = (A, \cdot)$ is isomorphic to a P-computable group $\mathcal{C} = (C, \cdot)$, in which the operation x^{-1} is P-computable, and if its center $Z(\mathcal{A})$ contains an element a of infinite order, then under some additional assumptions $\mathcal{A}$ is isomorphic to a P-computable group $\mathcal{B} = (B, \cdot)$, in which x^{-1} is not primitive recursive.

Below in Sect. 2, we formulate some basic definitions and prove several auxiliary arithmetic facts. Section 3 is devoted to the proof of the main theorem.

2 Arithmetic in Structures with Linear Growth

By 1^x we denote the word $11 \ldots 1$ of length x, and by $\mathrm{bin}(x) \in \{0, 1\}^*$, where $x \in \omega$, denote the standard representation of x in the binary number system. If $x < 0$ then $\mathrm{bin}(x) = 0\mathrm{bin}(-x)$. Let $\mathrm{Tal}(\omega) = \{0\} \cup \{1^x \mid x \geqslant 1\}$. The writing $\log k$ denotes $\log_2 k$, $\lceil y \rceil$ is the result of rounding a number $y \in \mathbb{R}$ up, and $[y]$ is the integer part of y.

As a basic computing device, we use multi-tape Turing machines described in [4]. A function $f : A \to \Sigma^*$ is *computable* on a machine T, where $A \subseteq (\Sigma^*)^n$, if T obtains words $x_1, \ldots, x_n$ on the first n tapes, and stops after a finite number of steps by writing down the word $f(x_1, \ldots, x_n)$ on the $(n+1)$th tape. If the number of steps for every $\langle x_1, \ldots, x_n \rangle \in A$ is estimated as $P(\max_{i \leqslant n}\{|x_i|\})$, where $P(t) \in \mathbb{N}[t]$ is a polynomial, then we say that f is computable in polynomial time. It is known that this notion does not depend on the choice of a particular Turing machine.

Using an appropriate natural numbering $\gamma : \omega \to \Sigma^*$, we can also define the notion of a *primitive recursive function* $f : A \to \Sigma^*$. Every function whose computing time is estimated by an explicit and meaningful formula lies in the class of p.r.f.

The definition of a P-computable structure $\mathcal{A} = (A, L^A)$ of a finite signature L has been mentioned in the introduction. We say that $\mathcal{A}$ is a *structure with linear growth* (see [3]) if for every n-place operation $f \in L^A$ and every $x_1, \ldots, x_n \in A$ the evaluation

$$|f(x_1, \ldots, x_n)| \leqslant c(|x_1| + \ldots + |x_n| + 1)$$

holds, where c is a constant. This condition can be replaced by $|f(x_1, \ldots, x_n)| \leqslant c(\max_{i \leqslant n}\{|x_i|\} + 1)$.

For example, it is easy to verify that the standard binary presentation of the field $\mathbb{Q}$ with the universe $\{\mathrm{bin}(x) * \mathrm{bin}(y) \mid x, y \in \mathbb{Z}, y > 0, \text{ and } (x, y) = 1\}$ is a P-computable structure with linear growth, since $|\mathrm{bin}(x)| = [\log x] + 1$ for $x \geqslant 1$. Here $* \notin \{0, 1\}$. Apparently, the class of P-computable structures with linear growth is a much more suitable object for the practice than the class of all P-computable structures.

General information about fields can be found in [5]. In this article, we practically do not use the general field theory, except for some basic facts.

Lemma 1. *Let $\mathcal{A} = (A,+)$ be a P-computable structure with an associative operation $+$, in which $|a + b| \leqslant d \cdot \max\{|a|,|b|,1\}$ for $a,b \in A$, where $d \geqslant 1$ is a constant. Suppose that $a_1,\dots,a_k \in A$, where $k \geqslant 1$, $|a_i| \leqslant M$ for $i \leqslant k$, and $M \geqslant 1$. Then the following hold*
   a) $|a_1 + a_2 + \dots + a_k| \leqslant d^{\lceil \log k \rceil} M \leqslant d k^{\log d} M$;
   b) *the word $a_1 + a_2 + \dots + a_k$ can be computed from the word $a_1 * a_2 * \dots * a_k$ in time equal to a polynomial of kM.*

Proof. This is obvious for $k = 1$. Let $k \geqslant 2$. We prove a) by induction on k and at the same time describe an algorithm for computing the word $a' = a_1 + a_2 + \dots + a_k$. First, consider the case $k = 2n$. Then $\log k = 1 + \log n$. We replace the word $a_1 * a_2 * \dots * a_k$ by $b_1 * b_2 * \dots * b_n = (a_1+a_2)*(a_3+a_4)*\dots*(a_{k-1}+a_k)$. Then $|b_i| \leqslant dM$ for $i \leqslant n$, and $|a'| \leqslant d^{\lceil \log n \rceil} \cdot dM = d^{\lceil \log k \rceil} M$ by induction hypothesis.

Let $k = 2n + 1$. Then $\lceil \log k \rceil = \lceil \log(k+1) \rceil = 1 + \lceil \log(n+1) \rceil$. Again we replace $a_1 * \dots * a_k$ by $b_1 * \dots * b_{n+1} = (a_1+a_2)*(a_3+a_4)*\dots*(a_{k-2}+a_{k-1})*a_k$. By induction hypothesis $|a'| \leqslant d^{\lceil \log(n+1) \rceil} \cdot dM = d^{\lceil \log k \rceil} M$.

The last inequality in a) follows from the fact that $d^{\lceil \log k \rceil} \leqslant d^{1+\log k} = d \cdot d^{\log k} = d \cdot 2^{\log d \cdot \log k} = d k^{\log d}$.

b): we can assume that $a+b$ is computed in $\mathcal{A}$ in time $\max\{|a|,|b|,2\}^p$, where $p \geqslant 1$ is a constant. Let $M_1 = \max\{d^{\lceil \log k \rceil} M, 2\}$. As shown above, $|a_i + a_{i+1} + \dots + a_j| \leqslant M_1$ for each $1 \leqslant i \leqslant j \leqslant k$. We show by induction on $k \geqslant 1$ that in this case a' can be found from the word $a_1 * \dots * a_k$ in $c k M_1^p$ steps, where $c \geqslant 1$ is a constant. The statement is obvious for $k = 1$.

Let $k = 2n$. The above transition from $a_1 * \dots * a_{2n}$ to $b_1 * \dots * b_n$, is performed in $c_0 n M_1^p$ steps if the constant c_0 is large enough. The specified condition is also met for the set $b_1, \dots, b_n$, hence, the transition $b_1 * \dots * b_n \mapsto a'$ is performed in $c n M_1^p$ steps. If $c \geqslant c_0$ then we get $c k M_1^p$ steps in total.

Let $k = 2n + 1$. The transition $a_1 * \dots * a_{2n+1} \mapsto b_1 * \dots * b_{n+1}$ again takes $c_0 n M_1^p$ steps, since we just need to copy a_{2n+1} to b_{n+1}, and $|a_{2n+1}| \leqslant M_1 \leqslant M_1^p$. The transition $b_1 * \dots * b_{n+1} \mapsto a'$ requires $c(n+1)M_1^p$ steps, and we get $c(2n+1)M_1^p$ steps if $c \geqslant c_0$. □

If $\mathcal{A} = (A,+,\cdot)$ is a ring with unity 1^A, then the standard notation n^A means $\underbrace{1^A + 1^A + \dots + 1^A}_{n}$ for $n \geqslant 0$, and $-((-n)^A)$ for $n < 0$. Sometimes we just write n instead of n^A.

Lemma 2. *Let $\mathcal{A} = (A,+,\cdot)$ be a P-computable associative ring with unity in which $|a + b|, |a \cdot b| \leqslant d \cdot \max\{|a|,|b|,1\}$ for $a,b \in A$, where $d \geqslant 1$ is a constant, and let $M = \max\{|-1^A|,|0^A|,|1^A|,|2^A|,|3^A|\}$. If $n \geqslant 2$ then*
   a) $|n^A| \leqslant d^{2\lceil \log(\lceil \log n \rceil) \rceil} M \leqslant (2\lceil \log n \rceil)^{2 \log d} M$;
   b) *the word n^A can be computed in polynomial time from the word $bin(n)$, and in linear time from the word 1^n.*

Proof. a): we prove the first inequality. First, consider the case $n = 2^k$, $k \geqslant 1$. Then $n^A = \underbrace{2^A \cdot 2^A \cdot \ldots \cdot 2^A}_{k}$ and $|n^A| \leqslant d^{\lceil \log k \rceil} M$ by Lemma 1, where $k = \log n = [\log n]$.

Now we suppose that $n \geqslant 2$ is an arbitrary number and $n = 2^{k_1} + 2^{k_2} + \ldots + 2^{k_s}$, where $k_1 > k_2 > \ldots > k_s \geqslant 0$ and $k_1 \geqslant 1$. In this case $2^{k_1} \leqslant n < 2^{k_1+1}$, $[\log n] = k_1$, and $s \leqslant k_1 + 1$. First, we assume that $s \leqslant k_1$. Then $|2^{k_i}| \leqslant d^{\lceil \log k_1 \rceil} M$ for $i \leqslant s$, and $|n^A| \leqslant d^{\lceil \log s \rceil} \cdot d^{\lceil \log k_1 \rceil} M \leqslant d^{2\lceil \log k_1 \rceil} M$ by the same Lemma 1.

If $s = k_1 + 1$ then $n = 2^{k_1} + (-1)$, $|2^{k_1+1}| \leqslant d^{\lceil \log(k_1+1) \rceil} M$, and $|n^A| \leqslant d^{\lceil \log(k_1+1) \rceil + 1} M$. If $k_1 \geqslant 3$ then $\lceil \log(k_1 + 1) \rceil + 1 \leqslant \lceil \log k_1 \rceil + 2 \leqslant 2\lceil \log k_1 \rceil$. If $k_1 = 1$ then $n = 3$ and $|n^A| \leqslant M$. If $k_1 = 2$ then $n = 7 = 2^2 + 3$, $|2^2| \leqslant dM$, and $|n^A| \leqslant d^2 M$.

The second inequality follows from the fact that $d^{2\lceil \log t \rceil} \leqslant d^{2(1 + \log t)} = 2^{2 \log d (1 + \log t)} = (2t)^{2 \log d}$, where $t = [\log n]$.

b): Lemma 1 implies that the transition $1^k \mapsto (2^k)^A$ for $k \geqslant 1$ is performed in $O(k^p)$ steps, where $p \geqslant 1$ is a constant. We suppose that a word $\mathrm{bin}(n) = \varepsilon_k \varepsilon_{k-1} \ldots \varepsilon_1 \varepsilon_0$ is given, where $\varepsilon_i \in \{0, 1\}$ for $i \leqslant k$, and $n = \varepsilon_k 2^k + \ldots + \varepsilon_1 2 + \varepsilon_0$. Then $k = [\log n]$. The set $b_k * b_{k-1} * \ldots * b_0$, where $b_i = (\varepsilon_i 2^i)^A$, can be found in $O((k+1)k^p)$ steps. In addition, $|b_i| \leqslant dk^{\log d} M$ for $i \leqslant k$. Using Lemma 1 again, we find $n^A = b_k + \ldots + b_0$ in time of the form $O(k^{p_1})$, where p_1 is a constant.

If the input of algorithm is a word 1^n, then it is not difficult to find the word $\mathrm{bin}(n)$ in linear time as follows. Passing through 1^n, we find ε_0 and $1^{[n/2]}$, then ε_1 and $1^{[n/4]}$, etc. Next, the computing time of n^A is estimated as $c[\log n]^{p_1}$, which is less than n for $n \geqslant n_0$. We have received a linear estimate for the working time. $\square$

In Lemmas 1 and 2, we consider P-computable structures with linear growth. Note that these estimates for the computing time of n^A can be obtained only with estimating $|n^A|$.

Lemma 3. *Let $\mathcal{A} = (A, +, \cdot)$ be a P-computable associative ring with unity, in which the evaluation $|n^A| \leqslant c_0 (\log n)^p$ holds for all $n \geqslant 2$, where $c_0, p \geqslant 1$ are constants. Then point b) in Lemma 2 again holds, i.e., the word n^A can be computed from a word $\mathrm{bin}(n)$, $n \geqslant 0$, in polynomial time.*

Proof. First, we consider the case $n = 2^k$, where $k \geqslant 1$. The algorithm from Lemma 1 for computing $b_k = (2^k)^A$ looks as follows: we form the word $a_1 * a_2 * \ldots * a_k$, where $a_i = 2^A$, and use induction on k. We may assume that the number p in this formulation is equal to p in the proof of Lemma 1. If $1 \leqslant i \leqslant j \leqslant k$ then $|a_i \cdot a_{i+1} \cdot \ldots \cdot a_j| = |(2^{(j-i)})^A| \leqslant c_0 k^p = M_1$. In the proof of Lemma 1, we noted that in this case $a' = (2^k)^A$ can be computed in ckM_1^p, i.e., in $cc_0^p k^{p^2+1}$ steps.

Now we can repeat the argument from b) of Lemma 2. $\square$

3   Fields with Slow Inversion Operation

Theorem 1. *Suppose that $\mathcal{A} = (A, +, \cdot)$ is a P-computable field of characteristic 0 such that the following hold*

a) $(A, +)$ *is a structure with linear growth;*

b) $|n^A| \leqslant c_0(\log n)^d$ *for* $n \geqslant 2$, *where* c_0, d *are constants.*

Then there exists a P-computable field $\mathcal{B} = (B, +, \cdot) \cong A$, *in which the operation* $x \mapsto x^{-1}$ *is not primitive recursive.*

In addition, $B = \mathrm{Tal}(\omega)$ *and there is a computable isomorphism* $g : \mathcal{B} \to A$.

Proof. Let $A \subseteq \Sigma^*$, where Σ is a finite alphabet. We may assume that $|a| \geqslant 2$ for all $a \in A$, and $|0^A| = |1^A| = 2$. This can be achieved by a small transformation of A, which does not violate a) and b)).

Then we may assume that $a + b$ and $a \cdot b$ are computed in A in time $\max\{|a|, |b|\}^d$, and in addition $|a + b| \leqslant d \cdot \max\{|a|, |b|\}$. This will become true if we sufficiently increase d. In particular, $|a \cdot b| \leqslant \max\{|a|, |b|\}^d$.

By $A[u]$ we denote the set of all polynomials of the form $E(u) = a_n u^n + \ldots + a_1 u + a_0$, where $a_i \in A$ for $i \leqslant n$, and $a_n \neq 0$ for $n \neq 0$. Then $n = \deg(E(u))$. We consider $A[u]$ as a ring $(A[u], +, \cdot)$ with the standard operations of addition and multiplication. Identifying an element $a \in A$ with the polynomial a of degree 0, we may assume that A is a subring of $A[u]$. The polynomial $E(u)$ is encoded by the word $a_n * a_{n-1} * \ldots * a_1 * a_0$, where $* \notin \Sigma$.

We evaluate some standard operations on polynomials in this situation. Let $E(u) = a_n u^n + \ldots + a_1 u + a_0$ and $F(u) = b_k u^k + \ldots + b_1 u + b_0$, where $|a_i|, |b_i| \leqslant M$ and $n, k \leqslant 2^t$. Suppose that $H(u) = E(u) \cdot F(u) = c_m u^m + \ldots + c_1 u + c_0$. Then $m \leqslant n + k \leqslant 2^{t+1}$ and $c_s = a_0 b_s + a_1 b_{s-1} + \ldots + a_s b_0$, where $a_i = 0$ for $i > n$, $b_i = 0$ for $i > k$, $s \leqslant 2^{t+1}$, and the number of summands does not exceed $2^t + 1$. We have that $|a_i b_j| \leqslant M^d$ and $|c_s| \leqslant d \cdot 2^{(t+1)\log d} M^d$, and the computing time for one c_s can be estimated as $O((2^{t+1} M^d)^p)$, where p is fixed, by Lemma 1. The time of computing $E \cdot F$ from E, F has the same form.

Since it is easier to add polynomials than to multiply, a similar estimate holds for $E(u) + F(u)$.

Now we describe a construction. We construct the following set of finite objects by induction on $t \in \omega$. At the end of step t, we define a majorant $n_t = 2^{c^t}$, where the constant $c \geqslant 2$ is defined below, a finite set $S_t \subseteq A[u]$, the finite set $B_t = \{1^1, 1^2, \ldots, 1^{n_t}\}$, and a bijection $g_t : B_t \to S_t$. All these objects are encoded by one word

$$W_t = g_t(1^1) \perp g_t(1^2) \perp \ldots \perp g_t(1^{n_t}),$$

where $*, \perp \notin \Sigma$, and the code of a polynomial $g_t(1^i)$ is specified above. The inclusion $g_t \subseteq g_{t+1}$, generally speaking, does not hold here. During the construction, the following conditions are met for every $t \in \omega$:

1) if $E \in S_t$ then $\deg(E) \leqslant 2^t$;

2) if $E \in S_t$ and $E = a_n u^n + \ldots + a_1 u + a_0$, then $|a_i| \leqslant n_t$ for $i \leqslant n$;

3) $g_{2t} \subseteq g_{2t+1}$;

4) $S_{2t} + S_{2t} \subseteq S_{2t+1}$ and $S_{2t} \cdot S_{2t} \subseteq S_{2t+1}$;

5) there is a ring homomorphism $h : A[u] \to A[u]$ such that $h \circ g_t \subseteq g_{t+1}$;

6) there is an algorithm (one for all t) that, given W_t, finds W_{t+1} in polynomial time.

At the end of work, we put $B = \bigcup_{t \in \omega} B_t = \{1^x \mid x \geqslant 1\}$, and define operations on B as follows: if $1^x, 1^y, 1^z \in B_t$ and $g_t(1^x) + g_t(1^y) = g_t(1^z)$ for some $t \in \omega$, then $1^x + 1^y = 1^z$, and if $g_t(1^x) \cdot g_t(1^y) = g_t(1^z)$, then $1^x \cdot 1^y = 1^z$. The definition does not depend on the choice of t, since if $g_t(1^x) + g_t(1^y) = g_t(1^z)$ and $h \circ g_t \subseteq g_{t+1}$, where $h : A[u] \to A[u]$ is a homomorphism, then $h(g_t(1^x) + g_t(1^y)) = h(g_t(1^z))$ and $g_{t+1}(1^x) + g_{t+1}(1^y) = g_{t+1}(1^z)$. The condition cannot be true for two different z, since g_t is injective. The existence of such z is shown below.

From 1) and 2) it follows that $|W_t| \leqslant ((n_t + 1)(2^t + 1) + 1)n_t \leqslant P(n_t)$, where $P(n) \in \mathbb{N}[n]$ is a polynomial with natural coefficients, since $2^t \leqslant n_t$. We show that $(B, +, \cdot)$ is a P-computable structure. Let the input of algorithm be words 1^x and 1^y. Show how to compute $1^x + 1^y$. We may assume that $y \leqslant x$. If $x \leqslant n_0$ then the number of such pairs is finite. We consider only the case $n_0 < x$.

Using condition 6), we start to compute the words $W_0, W_1, \ldots$ step by step, until find t and W_{t+1} such that $1^x \in B_{t+1} \setminus B_t$. Then $n_t < x \leqslant n_{t+1}$. We have that $|W_t| \leqslant P(n_t) \leqslant P(x)$. Similarly, $|W_i| \leqslant P(x)$ for all $i \leqslant t$. Suppose that the computing time of W_{i+1} from W_i is estimated as $Q(|W_i|)$, where $Q(n) \in \mathbb{N}[n]$. Then the total computing time for the whole sequence of words can be estimated as $x \cdot Q(P(x))$, since $t \leqslant n_t < x$. The condition $1^x \in B_i$ is checked in linear time, and W_{t+1} can be found from 1^x in polynomial time. Next, we also find W_{t+2}.

Let $t + 1$ be even. Then $1^x, 1^y \in \mathrm{dom}(g_{t+1})$, and by 3) and 4) there exists $1^z \in \mathrm{dom}(g_{t+2})$ such that $g_{t+2}(1^z) = g_{t+1}(1^x) + g_{t+1}(1^y) = g_{t+2}(1^x) + g_{t+2}(1^y)$. Using W_{t+2}, we find $g_{t+2}(1^x)$ and $g_{t+2}(1^y)$, add them in $A[u]$, and find the corresponding element $g_{t+2}(1^z)$ in W_{t+2}, thereby obtaining $1^z = 1^x + 1^y$. This is a polynomial algorithm due to the estimates above.

If $t + 1$ is odd, then we need to additionally compute W_{t+3} and make one step to the right, replacing $t + 1$ with $t + 2$ in the previous argument.

We fix a natural order $\leqslant$ on Σ^*, comparing words first by length, and then lexicographically. Then $\Sigma^* = \{u_0 < u_1 < u_2 < \ldots\}$. We formulate a few more conditions. If $t \in \omega$ then

7) for every $x \geqslant 1$, there is t such that $g_t(1^x) \in A$;
8) if $g_t(1^x) \in A$ then $g_t(1^x) = g_{t_1}(1^x)$ for all $t_1 \geqslant t$;
9) if the word u_t is in A, then $u_t \in S_{2t+1}$.

We show that when these conditions are met, the constructed structure $\mathcal{B} = (B, +, \cdot)$ is isomorphic to $\mathcal{A}$. We construct $g : \mathcal{B} \to \mathcal{A}$ as follows: if $1^x \in B$ and $g_t(1^x) \in A$ for some $t \in \omega$, then put $g(1^x) = g_t(1^x)$. Points 7) and 8) imply that this definition is correct.

It is easy to show that g is an isomorphism. We check, for example, injectivity. If $1^x, 1^y \in B$ and $x \neq y$, then there is t such that $1^x, 1^y \in B_t$ and $g_t(1^x), g_t(1^y) \in A$. Then $g(1^x) = g_t(1^x) \neq g_t(1^y) = g(1^y)$. Surjectivity follows from 9).

For $t = 0$, we put $n_0 = 2^{c^0} = 2$ and $S_0 = \{0^A, u\}$. Then $g_0 : \{1^1, 1^2\} \to S_0$ is some bijection.

It remains to find an algorithm that constructs W_{t+1} from W_t, respecting all the conditions 1) – 9), and in addition provides that the operation x^{-1} in $\mathcal{B}$ is not primitive recursive. We shortly describe the main idea of proof. When we want to meet a requirement R_k specified below, we build $\mathcal{B}$ as a finite fragment of the ring $A[u]$, permanently adding new sums and products of already constructed polynomials. This fragment contains the polynomial u, and we are waiting for the moment when the value of the p.r.f. $\pi_k(u)$ is computed. After that, we isomorphically embed the constructed fragment into A, substituting some integer from A instead of u so that $\pi_k(u)$ turns out to be different from u^{-1}. This ensures that π_k is not the operation x^{-1} in $\mathcal{B}$. First, we consider the simpler case.

Case 1: t is even. Then $g_t \subseteq g_{t+1}$ and 5) is met with $h = \mathrm{id}_{A[u]}$. We need to perform 4) and 9), respecting 1) and 2). Let $E(u), F(u)$ be two polynomials in the word W_t, $E(u) = a_n u^n + \ldots + a_1 u + a_0$, and $F(u) = b_k u^k + \ldots + b_1 u + b_0$. To get $H(u) = E(u) \cdot F(u) = c_m u^m + \ldots + c_1 u + c_0$, we need to compute each coefficient $c_s = a_0 b_s + a_1 b_{s-1} + \ldots + a_s b_0$. Since $n, k \leqslant 2^t$, $m \leqslant 2^{t+1}$. As noted above, $|a_i b_j| \leqslant n_t^d$ and $|c_s| \leqslant d \cdot 2^{(t+1) \log d} n_t^d$, and the computing time of each c_s is evaluated as $O((2^{t+1} n_t^d)^p)$.

To meet 2), we need the estimate $|c_s| \leqslant n_{t+1}$, which reduces to the inequality $2^{(t+2) \log d} \cdot 2^{dc^t} \leqslant 2^{c^{t+1}}$, or $(t + 2) \log d + dc^t \leqslant c^{t+1}$, which is equivalent to $\frac{t+2}{c^t} \log d + d \leqslant c$. Since $\frac{t+2}{c^t} \leqslant 2$ as $c \geqslant 2$, the required evaluation holds if $2 \log d + d \leqslant c$.

Next, the computing time of one coefficient c_s is a polynomial of n_t, since $t + 1 \leqslant c^t$ and $2^{t+1} \leqslant n_t$. The number of such coefficients does not exceed $2^{t+1} + 1$, and the number of pairs $\langle E, F \rangle$, where $E, F \in S_t$, is equal to n_t^2. Since $n_t \leqslant |W_t|$, we can create a list of all polynomials $E \cdot F$, where $E, F \in S_t$, in polynomial time. The same is true for a list $E + F$, where $E, F \in S_t$.

It remains to sort this list and add to W_t its elements that are not there, forming W_{t+1} and S_{t+1}. In addition, going through all the words $u_0, u_1, \ldots$, we find $u_{t/2}$, check the condition $u_{t/2} \in A$, and if it is true and $u_{t/2}$ is not yet included in W_{t+1}, add it there. Since $|u_i| \leqslant i$, this is a polynomial operation.

The number of new elements in $S_{t+1} \setminus S_t$ does not exceed $2n_t^2 + 1$. To realize the condition $|S_{t+1}| = n_{t+1}$, it is necessary to have that $n_{t+1} - n_t \geqslant 2n_t^2 + 1 \Leftrightarrow n_t^c \geqslant 2n_t^2 + n_t + 1$. Since $n_t \geqslant 2$, this is true for $c \geqslant 4$.

Suppose that S_{t+1} has n' elements at the moment. If $n' < n_{t+1}$ then we add additional $n_{t+1} - n'$ elements from A to S_{t+1}. For this, we make the list of all elements $1^A * 2^A * \ldots * n_{t+1}^A$. If $k \leqslant n_{t+1}$ then k^A can be found by Lemma 3 in time of the form $O(c^{tp})$, where p is a constant. Since $c^t \leqslant n_t$, the list will be created in polynomial time. We choose $n_{t+1} - n'$ elements from it that are not yet in W_{t+1}, and add them. The word W_{t+1} is constructed.

If $k \leqslant n_{t+1}$ then $|k^A| \leqslant c_0 (\log n_{t+1})^d = c_0 c^{d(t+1)}$. To meet 2), we need the condition $|k^A| \leqslant n_{t+1}$, i.e., $c_0 c^{d(t+1)} \leqslant 2^{c^{t+1}}$, or $\log c_0 + d(t + 1) \log c \leqslant c^{t+1}$. It is true for sufficiently large c.

Case 2: t is odd. Now we don't need to worry about conditions 3), 4), and 9). The basic idea is that we either extend g_t to g_{t+1}, as in Case 1, or choose a number $n \geqslant 1$, construct the homomorphism $h : A[u] \to A$, $h(E(u)) = E(n^A)$, put $g_t' = h \circ g_t$, and then expand g_t' to g_{t+1}, in addition placing the polynomial u to S_{t+1}. Then 1), 5), and 8) are met, since $h(a) = a$ for $a \in A$. If the replacement of g_t by $h \circ g_t$ will occur infinitely often, then 7) will also be met.

Thus, we only need to keep track of 2) and, most difficult of all, ensure the injectivity of $h \circ g_t$. We discuss how this can be achieved. Suppose that the number n is selected and $h(g_t(1^x)) = h(g_t(1^y))$ for $x \neq y$. Let $g_t(1^x) = E(u)$ and $g_t(1^y) = F(u)$. Then n^A is a root of the polynomial $E(u) - F(u)$. The number of pairs $\langle E(u), F(u) \rangle$, where $E(u) \neq F(u)$, does not exceed $n_t^2 - n_t$, and for each such pair, $E(u) - F(u)$ has at most 2^t roots in $\mathcal{A}$. We make the list of elements $1^A * 2^A * \ldots * m^A$, where $m = 2^t n_t^2$, and for each $n \leqslant m$, compute all the values $E(n^A)$, where $E(u) \in S_t$. There exists $n \leqslant m$ for which all these values will be different, and it is the desired number. We need to understand that this search takes polynomial time. Fix $E(u) = a_k u^k + \ldots + a_1 u + a_0 \in S_t$ and $n \leqslant m$, and estimate the computing time of $E(n^A)$.

Let $s \leqslant k$. Then $s \leqslant 2^t$ and $|(n^s)^A| \leqslant c_0 (\log n^{2^t})^d \leqslant c_0 2^{dt} (\log m)^d \leqslant c_0 2^{dt} (\log n_t^3)^d = c_0 \cdot 3^d (2c)^{dt} = c_1 (2c)^{dt} \leqslant c_1 n_t^{2d}$, where $c_1 = c_0 \cdot 3^d$, since $m \leqslant n_t^3$.

Therefore, $|a_s (n^s)^A| \leqslant c_1^d n_t^{2d^2} = M$, and $|E(n^A)| \leqslant d^t M$ by Lemma 1.

To compute $E(n^A)$, we can create the list $\mathrm{bin}(1) * \mathrm{bin}(n) * \mathrm{bin}(n^2) * \ldots * \mathrm{bin}(n^k)$, where each next element is obtained by multiplying $\mathrm{bin}(n^s)$ by $\mathrm{bin}(n)$ in the ordinary binary arithmetic. Since $|\mathrm{bin}(n^s)| \leqslant 1 + \log n^s = 1 + s \log n \leqslant 1 + s \log m \leqslant 1 + s \log n_t^3 = 1 + 3 s \log n_t \leqslant 1 + 3(2c)^t \leqslant 1 + 3 n_t^2$, the list is generated in polynomial time. Then we use Lemma 3 to find the list $1^A * n^A * (n^2)^A * \ldots * (n^k)^A$, and compute $E(n^A)$ using Lemma 1.

Hence, computing the whole set $\{E(n^A) \mid E(u) \in S_t\}$ and searching for repetitions in it also takes polynomial time, and the same is true for going through all $n \leqslant m \leqslant n_t^3$.

To meet 2), we in addition need the estimate $|E(n^A)| \leqslant n_{t+1}$. The above estimate can be rewritten as $|E(n^A)| \leqslant n_t^e$, where e is a constant. If $c \geqslant e$ then $n_t^e \leqslant n_t^c = n_{t+1}$.

Now we describe the key element of the construction. Let $\{\pi_k(x)\}_{k \in \omega}$ be a computable numbering of all 1-place p.r.f. from ω to ω. This means that the function $F(k, x) = \pi_k(x)$ is computable, and $\pi_k(x)$ is a p.r.f. for every fixed $k \in \omega$. There is a Turing machine T that, given words $1^k, 1^x$, finds $1^{\pi_k(x)}$. We denote by $\pi_{k,t}(x)$ the result of the work of T after t steps, i.e., $\pi_{k,t}(x) \uparrow$ if the result has not yet been computed, and $\pi_{k,t}(x) = y$ if the result is 1^y. To find $\pi_{k,t}(x)$, we start T on the words $1^k, 1^x$ and create a counter 1^t on a separate tape, which decreases by 1 at each step of the work. After computing $\pi_{k,t}(x)$, we clear all used tapes. If $\pi_{k,t}(x) \downarrow = y$ then $y \leqslant t$.

In addition to all conditions above, we meet the following series of requirements during the construction

R_k: the function $1^x \mapsto 1^{\pi_k(x)}$ is not equal to the operation $(1^x)^{-1}$ in the field $(B, +, \cdot)$,

where $k \in \omega$. The requirements $R_0, R_1, \ldots$ are performed in turn. At the end of a step t, some requirement R_k is current, and $R_0, R_1, \ldots, R_{k-1}$ are met. At the end of step 0, the current requirement is R_0.

Now we suppose that at the end of the step t, the current requirement is R_k. The construction is arranged so that the polynomial u always is in S_t. Therefore, there is $1^{x_t} \in B_t$ such that $g_t(1^{x_t}) = u$. Suppose that $\pi_{k,t}(1^{x_t})\uparrow$. Then we construct W_{t+1} exactly as in Case 1: assume that $g_t \subseteq g_{t+1}$, and complete W_t to W_{t+1} with elements from the list $1^A * 2^A * \ldots * n_{t+1}^A$, i.e., really do nothing.

Suppose that $\pi_{k,t}(1^{x_t})\downarrow= 1^y$. We declare the requirement R_k met and make R_{k+1} current. If $1^y \notin B$, i.e., $y = 0$, then R_k is obviously met, and we again expand g_t to g_{t+1}.

Let $y > 0$. Then $y \leqslant t$ and $1^y \in B_t$. Let $g_t(1^y) = F(u) \in S_t$. It is the case where we start the above search for n and replace g_t by g_t'. Then $g_{t+1}(1^{x_t}) = g(1^{x_t}) = n^A$, and $g_{t+1}(1^y) = g(1^y) = F(n^A)$. If 1^{x_t} and 1^y are inverse in $\mathcal{B}$, then $n^A \cdot F(n^A) = 1$, i.e., n^A is a root of the polynomial $H(u) = uF(u) - 1$. Therefore, n must be chosen so that it is false.

This means that in the above search algorithm for n, we need to additionally compute $H(n^A)$ and check the condition $H(n^A) \neq 0$. The number of roots of $H(u)$ does not exceed $2^t + 1$, all estimates above for the time of computing $H(n^A)$ again hold, and it is sufficient to go through all $n \leqslant m$.

Having constructed g_t', we then extend it to $g_{t+1} : B_{t+1} \to S_{t+1}$, acting as in Case 1, and add u to S_{t+1}. The construction is finished.

Every requirement R_k becomes current at some moment, and then will be met, since $\pi_k(x)$ is defined everywhere. It follows that 7) is performed and the construction works correctly. The function g is computable, since to get $g(1^x)$, we need to find the first step t such that $g_t(1^x) \in A$.

As a result, we construct the structure $\mathcal{B}$ with universe $\{1^x \mid x \geqslant 1\}$, which can be easily replaced by $\mathrm{Tal}(\omega)$. The theorem is proved. $\square$

Note that the proof of this theorem did not use the condition that $\{\pi_k(x)\}_{k \in \omega}$ is the sequence of all p.r.f. The only fact we need is the uniform computability of this sequence. In the construction, we can diagonalize against any class of functions having such a numbering. For example, against all p.r.f. with a fixed computable oracle.

Theorem 2. *Suppose that $\mathcal{A} = (A, +, \cdot)$ is a P-computable field of characteristic 0 with linear growth. Then the statement of Theorem 1 again holds, i.e., there exists a P-computable field $\mathcal{B} = (B, +, \cdot) \cong \mathcal{A}$, in which the operation $x \mapsto x^{-1}$ is not primitive recursive.*

In addition, $B = \mathrm{Tal}(\omega)$ and there is a computable isomorphism $g : \mathcal{B} \to \mathcal{A}$.

Proof. This is a direct corollary of Theorem 1 and Lemma 2. $\square$

As mentioned above, Theorem 2 can be applied to the standard binary presentation of the field $(\mathbb{Q}, +, \cdot)$. An interesting question is whether it is possible to find the structure $\mathcal{B}$ in Theorem 2 which also has linear growth, if we remove the condition $B = \mathrm{Tal}(\omega)$.

Acknowledgments. This study was supported by the Russian Science Foundation (grant No. 23-11-00170), https://rscf.ru/project/23-11-00170.

Disclosure of Interests. The author has no competing interests to declare that are relevant to the content of this article.

References

1. Cenzer, D., Remmel, J.: Polynomial time versus recursive models. Ann. Pure Appl. Logic **54**(1), 17–58 (1991)
2. Alaev, P.: Inversion operations in algebraic structures. Computability **12**(4), 315–322 (2023)
3. Alaev, P.E.: Complexity of the inversion operations in groups. Algebra Log. **62**(2), 103–118 (2023)
4. Aho, A.V., Hopcroft, J.E., Ullman, J.D.: The Design and Analysis of Computer Algorithms. Addison-Wesley, Reading (1974)
5. Van der Waerden B.L.: Algebra I. Springer, Heidelberg (1971)

Regular Papers

On the Computational Properties
of Weak Continuity Notions

Sam Sanders[(⊠)]

Department of Philosophy II, RUB Bochum, Bochum, Germany
sasander@me.com
https://sasander.wixsite.com/academic

Abstract. The properties of continuous functions are *very* well-studied in computability theory and related areas. As it happens, there are **many** *decompositions of continuity*, which take the form

continuity ↔ [weak continuity notion A + weak continuity notion B],

for certain spaces and where the weak continuity notions are generally independent. In this paper, we investigate the properties of some of these weak continuity notions in Kleene's computability theory based on S1–S9. Interestingly, certain weak continuity notions can be analysed fully with rather modest means (Kleene's quantifier $\exists^2$), while others can be analysed with powerful tools (Kleene's quantifier $\exists^3$), but not with weaker oracles. In particular, *finding the supremum on the unit interval* is possible using $\exists^2$ for certain weak continuity notions, while for others the italicised operation is computable in $\exists^3$ but *not in weaker oracles*.

1 Introduction

1.1 Motivation and Overview

The computational properties of continuous functions are *very* well-studied in computability theory and related areas [2,16,19,33]. Now, there are dozens, if not hundreds, of *decompositions of continuity*, a few examples of which are:

continuity ↔ quasi-continuity + graph continuity ([26]),   (E)

  ↔ α-continuity + $\mathcal{A}$-continuity ([31]),

  ↔ pre-continuity + $\mathcal{B}$-continuity ([32]) (or: $\mathcal{AB}$-continuity [7]),

  ↔ α-continuity + $D(c, \alpha)$-continuity ([24]) (or: C-continuity [11]),

  ↔ s-continuity + strong $\mathcal{B}$-continuity ([6]),

  ↔ almost cont. (Husain) + almost cont. (Stallings) + not Cesàro type ([29]),

  ↔ Young condition + closed graph ([5]),

  ↔ peripheral continuity + closed graph ([8]).

This research was supported by the *Klaus Tschira Boost Fund* (grant nr. GSO/KT 43) and RUB Bochum.

© The Author(s), under exclusive license to Springer Nature Switzerland AG 2024
L. Levy Patey et al. (Eds.): CiE 2024, LNCS 14773, pp. 113–125, 2024.
https://doi.org/10.1007/978-3-031-64309-5_10

These are valid for certain spaces and generally independent with rather basic counterexamples. A (fuller) historical overview may be found in [6,8,34]. Baire provides an early (first?) decomposition of continuity involving upper and lower semi-continuity circa 1899 in [1, §46, p. 71]. We note that 54C08 is the AMS code for *weak and generalised continuity*, i.e. this is not a fringe topic.

In this paper, we study the computational properties of *basic* operations, like finding the supremum, for most of the weak continuity notions from (E) on the unit interval. We work in Kleene's computability theory based on S1–S9 to which Sect. 1.2.1 furnishes a brief introduction.

Certain of the above weak continuity notions can be analysed fully with relatively weak oracles like Kleene's quantifier $\exists^2$, while others require powerful oracles like Kleene's quantifier $\exists^3$ (see Sect. 1.2.2 for these functionals). To be absolutely clear, $\exists^2$ can compute $\sup_{x \in [0,1]} f(x)$ for $f : [0,1] \to \mathbb{R}$ satisfying either: *α-continuity*, *s-continuity*, *$\mathcal{A}$-continuity*, or *$\mathcal{AB}$*-continuity (Theorem 8). On the other hand, computing $\sup_{x \in [0,1]} f(x)$ for $f : [0,1] \to \mathbb{R}$ satisfying the following weak continuity notions can be done using $\exists^3$ but not using weaker oracles: (restrictions of) *graph continuity*, (strong) *$\mathcal{B}$-continuity*, *C-continuity*, *$D(c,\alpha)$-continuity*, *the Young condition and variations*, *almost continuity* (Husain), *precontinuity*, or '*not of Cesàro type*' (Theorems 5, 6, 11, 10, 13). We stress the considerable difference in computational power of $\exists^2$ and $\exists^3$, as the former decides *arithmetical* formulas, while the latter decides *second-order* ones.

Finally, we have chosen the supremum as our object of study as the latter (together with the infimum) allows us to decide or witness many other properties. In particular, in light of the below proofs, one can obtain similar results for functionals deciding properties like continuity (everywhere or almost everywhere), Riemann integrability, the Darboux property, boundedness, et cetera. These results contribute to the topic of [27], namely exploring the abyss[1] in Kleene's computability theory between $\exists^2$ and $\exists^3$. A possible explanation for this 'abyss' phenomenon may be found in Sect. 2.4.

1.2   Preliminaries and Definitions

We briefly introduce Kleene's *higher-order computability theory* in Sect. 1.2.1. We introduce some essential axioms (Sect. 1.2.2) and definitions (Sect. 1.2.3). A full introduction may be found in e.g. [20, §2] or [16]. Since Kleene's computability theory borrows heavily from type theory, we shall often use common notations from the latter; for instance, the natural numbers are type 0 objects, denoted n^0 or $n \in \mathbb{N}$. Similarly, elements of Baire space are type 1 objects, denoted $f \in \mathbb{N}^{\mathbb{N}}$ or f^1. Mappings from Baire space $\mathbb{N}^{\mathbb{N}}$ to $\mathbb{N}$ are denoted $Y : \mathbb{N}^{\mathbb{N}} \to \mathbb{N}$ or Y^2. An overview of this kind of notations can be found in e.g. [16,22].

---

[1] Rathjen states in [25] that Π_2^1-CA$_0$ *dwarfs* Π_1^1-CA$_0$ and Martin-Löf talks of a *chasm* and *abyss* between these two systems in [18], all in the context of ordinal analysis. Since the difference between $\exists^2$ and $\exists^3$ amounts to the difference between ACA$_0$ and Z$_2$ (see [28] for these systems), we believe 'abyss' to be apt.

1.2.1 Kleene's Computability Theory

Our main results are in computability theory and we make our notion of 'computability' precise as follows.

(I) We adopt ZFC, i.e. Zermelo-Fraenkel set theory with the Axiom of Choice, as the official metatheory for all results, unless explicitly stated otherwise.

(II) We adopt Kleene's notion of *higher-order computation* as given by S1–S9 (see [16, Ch. 5]) as our official notion of 'computable' for total objects.

(III) Kleene's notion of S1–S9-computability can be extended to partial objects. We adopt the (standard) approach from [22].

We mention that S1–S8 are rather basic and merely introduce a kind of higher-order primitive recursion with higher-order parameters. The real power comes from S9, which essentially hard-codes the *recursion theorem* for S1–S9-computability in an ad hoc way. By contrast, the recursion theorem for Turing machines is derived from first principles in [30].

On a historical note, it is part of the folklore of computability theory that many have tried (and failed) to formulate models of computation for objects of all finite types and in which one derives the recursion theorem in a natural way. For this reason, Kleene ultimately introduced S1–S9, which were initially criticised for their aforementioned ad hoc nature, but eventually received general acceptance. Now, Dag Normann and the author have introduced a new computational model based on the lambda calculus in [22] with the following properties:

- S1–S8 is included while the 'ad hoc' scheme S9 is replaced by more natural (least) fixed point operators,
- the new model exactly captures S1–S9 computability for total objects,
- the new model accommodates 'computing with partial objects',
- the new model is more modular than S1–S9 in that sub-models are readily obtained by leaving out certain fixed point operators.

We refer to [16,22] for a thorough overview of higher-order computability theory.

1.2.2 Some Comprehension Functionals

In Turing-style computability theory, computational hardness is measured in terms of where the oracle set fits in the well-known comprehension hierarchy. For this reason, we introduce some axioms and functionals related to *higher-order comprehension* in this section. We are mostly dealing with *conventional* comprehension here, i.e. only parameters over $\mathbb{N}$ and $\mathbb{N}^{\mathbb{N}}$ are allowed in formula classes like Π_k^1 and Σ_k^1.

First of all, the functional φ^2, also called *Kleene's quantifier* $\exists^2$, as in $(\exists^2)$ is discontinuous[2] at $f = 11 \ldots$.

---

[2] Note that $\varphi(11\ldots) = 1$ and $\varphi(g) = 0$ for $g \neq_1 11\ldots$ by the definition of $(\exists^2)$, i.e. $\lambda f.\varphi(f)$ is discontinuous at $f = 11 \ldots$ in the usual 'epsilon-delta' sense.

$$(\exists\varphi^2 \leq_2 1)(\forall f^1)\big[(\exists n)(f(n) = 0) \leftrightarrow \varphi(f) = 0\big]. \tag{$\exists^2$}$$

Related to ($\exists^2$), the functional μ^2 in (μ^2) is called *Feferman's μ*

$$(\exists\mu^2)(\forall f^1)\big([(\exists n)(f(n) = 0) \rightarrow [f(\mu(f)) = 0 \wedge (\forall i < \mu(f))(f(i) \neq 0)] \tag{μ^2}$$
$$\wedge [(\forall n)(f(n) \neq 0) \rightarrow \mu(f) = 0]\big).$$

We have ($\exists^2$) $\leftrightarrow$ (μ^2) over Kohlenbach's base theory [14], while $\exists^2$ and μ^2 are also computationally equivalent. Hilbert and Bernays formalise considerable swaths of mathematics using only μ^2 in [12, Supplement IV].

Secondly, the functional S^2 in (S^2) is called *the Suslin functional* [14].

$$(\exists S^2 \leq_2 1)(\forall f^1)\big[(\exists g^1)(\forall n^0)(f(\overline{g}n) = 0) \leftrightarrow S(f) = 0\big]. \tag{S^2}$$

By definition, the Suslin functional S^2 can decide whether a Σ_1^1-formula as in the left-hand side of (S^2) is true or false. We similarly define the functional S_k^2 which decides the truth or falsity of Σ_k^1-formulas.

Thirdly, the following functional E^3 clearly computes $\exists^2$ and S_k^2 for any $k \in \mathbb{N}$:

$$(\exists E^3 \leq_3 1)(\forall Y^2)\big[(\exists f^1)(Y(f) = 0) \leftrightarrow E(Y) = 0\big]. \tag{$\exists^3$}$$

The functional E^3 from ($\exists^3$) is also called *Kleene's quantifier* $\exists^3$, and we use the same (by now obvious) convention for other functionals. Hilbert and Bernays introduce a functional ν^3 in [12, Supplement IV], and the latter is essentially $\exists^3$ which also provides a witness like the aforementioned functional ν_n does.

1.2.3 Some Definitions

We introduce some definitions needed in the below, mostly stemming from mainstream mathematics. We note that subsets of $\mathbb{R}$ are given by their characteristic functions (Definition 1), where the latter are common in measure and probability theory.

First of all, we make use of the usual definition of (open) set, where $B(x, r)$ is the open ball with radius $r > 0$ centred at $x \in \mathbb{R}$.

Definition 1 [Set]

- Subsets A of $\mathbb{R}$ are given by their characteristic function $F_A : \mathbb{R} \rightarrow \{0, 1\}$, i.e. we write $x \in A$ for $F_A(x) = 1$ for all $x \in \mathbb{R}$.
- We write '$A \subset B$' if we have $F_A(x) \leq F_B(x)$ for all $x \in \mathbb{R}$.
- A set $O \subset \mathbb{R}$ is *open* if $x \in O$ implies that there is $k \in \mathbb{N}$ with $B(x, \frac{1}{2^k}) \subset O$.
- A set $C \subset \mathbb{R}$ is *closed* if the complement $\mathbb{R} \setminus C$ is open.

– For $S \subset \mathbb{R}$, int(S), ∂S, and $\overline{S}$ are the *interior*, *boundary*, and *closure* of S.

No computational data/additional representation is assumed in the previous definition. As established in [21,22], one readily comes across closed sets in basic real analysis (Fourier series) that come with no additional representation.

Secondly, we need the following (classes of) functionals from [21,22], where the second item witnesses that the unit interval is uncountable.

Definition 2

– The functional $\Omega_b : (\mathbb{R} \to \mathbb{R}) \to \mathbb{R}$ is defined for $X \subset \mathbb{R}$ with at most one element. For such sets, $\Omega_b(X) = 0$ if and only if X is empty.
– Any $\Phi : ((\mathbb{R} \to \mathbb{R}) \times (\mathbb{R} \to \mathbb{N})) \to \mathbb{R}$ is called a *Cantor realiser* in case $\Phi(A, Y) \notin A$ for non-empty $A \subset [0,1]$ and $Y : [0,1] \to \mathbb{N}$ injective on A.
– A *weak Cantor realiser* is a Cantor realiser that requires Y to be surjective.

As shown in [21], no weak Cantor realiser is computable in any S_k^2. By the first cluster theorem in [21], Ω_b computes a Cantor realiser, assuming $\exists^2$.

2   Main Results

2.1   Graph Continuity

We study the computational properties of *graph continuity* from (E). We show that the associated supremum functional computes Ω_b from Sect. 1.2.3 while related functionals exhibit similar hardness. It is a straightforward exercise to show that all functionals in this section are computable in $\exists^3$.

Definition 3. For $f : \mathbb{R} \to \mathbb{R}$, we have the following definitions:

– the *graph* of f is defined as $G(f) = \{(x, y) \in \mathbb{R} \times \mathbb{R} : f(x) =_{\mathbb{R}} y\}$,
– f is *graph continuous* if there is a continuous $g : \mathbb{R} \to \mathbb{R}$ with $G(g) \subset \overline{G(f)}$,
– f is *quasi-continuous* at $x_0 \in \mathbb{R}$ if for $\epsilon > 0$ and an open neighbourhood U of x_0, there is a non-empty open $G \subset U$ with $(\forall x \in G)(|f(x_0) - f(x)| < \varepsilon)$.
– f is *cliquish* at $x_0 \in \mathbb{R}$ if for $\epsilon > 0$ and an open neighbourhood U of x_0, there is a non-empty open $G \subset U$ with $(\forall y, z \in G)(|f(y) - f(z)| < \varepsilon)$.

As shown in [23,27], $\exists^2$ computes $\sup_{x \in [0,1]} f(x)$ for quasi-continuous f. Despite the close relation to cliquishness (see [27, §2.1]), the supremum functional $\lambda f. \sup_{x \in [0,1]} f(x)$ restricted to cliquish f, is not computable in any S_k^2.

First of all, Theorem 4 right below suggests that graph continuity is a fairly 'universal' notion. Moreover, the generality of Theorem 4 is vast compared to the resources needed to establish it. Indeed, a cliquish function on the reals is the sum of two quasi-continuous functions [3,4,17], but no functional S_k^2 can compute the latter from the former in general by [27, Theorem 8].

Theorem 4. *Given any* $f : \mathbb{R} \to \mathbb{R}$, $\exists^2$ *computes graph continuous* $f_0, f_1 : \mathbb{R} \to \mathbb{R}$ *such that* $f(x) = f_0(x) + f_1(x)$.

Proof. The proof from [9, Theorem 1] goes through as follows: let A, B be countable dense sets in $\mathbb{R}$ with $A \cap B = \emptyset$, e.g. $A = \mathbb{Q}$ and $B = \{q + \pi : q \in \mathbb{Q}\}$ works. Now define $f_0, f_1 : \mathbb{R} \to \mathbb{R}$ as follows:

$$f_0(x) := \begin{cases} 0 & x \in A \\ f(x) & x \in B \\ f(x)/2 & \text{otherwise} \end{cases} \quad \text{and } f_1(x) := \begin{cases} f(x) & x \in A \\ 0 & x \in B \\ f(x)/2 & \text{otherwise} \end{cases}$$

and note that $f = f_0 + f_1$. Since A and B are dense, the 'zero everywhere function' g_0 is such that $G(g_0) \subset \overline{G(f_i)}$ for $i \leq 1$, i.e. f_0, f_1 are graph continuous. Note that the complement of A is also dense, including as it does B. $\square$

Secondly, one cannot replace 'quasi-continuity' in (E) by 'cliquish' as shown in [26]. Nonetheless, the combination 'cliquish + graph continuous' still implies that the function is equal to some continuous function *on a dense subset* [26, Cor. 3]. Despite the close connection between cliquish and quasi-continuous, the difference between (E) and the aforementioned result for cliquishness is significant as is clear from Theorem 5. In particular, computing the supremum for cliquish functions is hard [27, Theorem 8], and this remains so if we additionally assume graph continuity.

Theorem 5. *The following are not computable in any S_k^2:*

- *any functional $\Phi : ((\mathbb{R} \to \mathbb{R}) \times \mathbb{R}^2) \to \mathbb{R}$ such that for cliquish and graph continuous $f : [0,1] \to \mathbb{R}$, $\Phi(f, p, q) = \sup_{x \in [p,q]} f(x)$.*
- *any functional $\Psi : (\mathbb{R} \to \mathbb{R}) \to \mathbb{R}$ such that for cliquish and graph continuous $f : [0,1] \to \mathbb{R}$, there exists dense $A \subset [0,1]$ and continuous $g : [0,1] \to \mathbb{R}$ with $f(x) = g(x)$ for $x \in A$, such that $\Psi(f) \in A$.*

In particular, each of the items computes a Cantor realiser (given $\exists^2$).

Proof. Fix non-empty $A \subset [0,1]$ and let $Y : [0,1] \to \mathbb{N}$ be injective on A. The following function $f : [0,1] \to \mathbb{R}$ is readily seen to be cliquish:

$$f(x) := \begin{cases} \frac{1}{2^{Y(x)+1}} & \text{in case } x \in A \\ 0 & \text{otherwise} \end{cases} . \tag{1}$$

Indeed, for fixed $\varepsilon > 0$ and $x \in [0,1]$, there are only finite many $x_0, \ldots, x_k \in [0,1]$ such that $f(x_i) > \varepsilon$ for $i \leq k$. Thus, choosing an open ball around x that excludes x_i for $i \leq k$, the definition of cliquishness is satisfied. Moreover, for the zero everywhere function $g_0 : [0,1] \to \mathbb{R}$, we have $G(g_0) \subset \overline{G(f)}$ as the complement of countable sets is dense, i.e. f is also graph-continuous.

For the first item, since A is non-empty, $\sup_{x \in [0,1]} f(x) = \frac{1}{2^{n_0}} = f(y_0)$ for some $n_0 \in \mathbb{N}$ and $y_0 \in A$ by the definition of f in (1). Now use $\exists^2$ to check whether $\sup_{x \in [0,\frac{1}{2}]} f(x) = \frac{1}{2^{n_0}}$ or not. Hence, we have learnt the first bit in the binary expansion of y_0; continuing in this fashion, we find the entire expansion of the latter. Repeating this process, we can enumerate A and Cantor's diagonal argument provides $y \notin A$, as required for a Cantor realiser. We note (once and for all) that the diagonal argument is computable (and efficient) by [10].

For the second item, the function g from the definition of graph continuity is *unique* if f is cliquish by [26, Theorem 2]. Thus, for f as in (1), g from Definition 3 must be the zero everywhere function g_0, i.e. $\Psi(f)$ must satisfy $f(\Psi(f)) = g_0(\Psi(f)) = 0$. By the definition of f, $f(\Psi(f)) = 0$ implies $\Psi(f) \notin A$, as required. □

Thirdly, we have the following corollary showing that 'effectivising' the definition of graph continuity does not resolve the computational hardness. We refer to the function g from Definition 3 as a *modulus* (of graph continuity).

Theorem 6. *Given* $\exists^2$, *the following computes* Ω_b:

any functional $\Phi : ((\mathbb{R} \to \mathbb{R})^2 \times \mathbb{R}^2) \to \mathbb{R}$ *such that for graph continuous* $f : [0, 1] \to \mathbb{R}$ *and modulus* g, $\Phi(f, g, p, q) = \sup_{x \in [p,q]} f(x)$.

Proof. First of all, fix $X \subset [0, 1]$ with at most one element and define $g_X : [0, 1] \to \mathbb{R}$ as follows:

$$g_X(x) := \begin{cases} 1 & \text{if } (\exists q \in \mathbb{Q})(x + q \in X) \\ 0 & \text{otherwise} \end{cases}. \tag{2}$$

Use $\exists^2$ to verify that X contains no rational and note that g_X from (2) is such that $([0, 1] \times \{0\}) \subset \overline{G(g_X)}$ as $((\mathbb{Q} \cap [0, 1]) \cup \{0\}) \subset G(g_X)$. In particular, the everywhere zero function $g_0 : [0, 1] \to \{0\}$ is a modulus for g_X; the previous sentence holds regardless of whether $X = \emptyset$.

Secondly, observe that $X = \emptyset \leftrightarrow \sup_{x \in [0,1]} g_X(x) = 0$, i.e. given the supremum functional from the theorem (and $\exists^2$), we can decide if $X = \emptyset$; thus, we have obtained Ω_b as required. □

In conclusion, basic properties of graph continuous functions can be said to be *hard to compute* as no S_k^2 suffices. By contrast, the 'complementary' notion of quasi-continuity from (E) can be handled using $\exists^2$.

2.2 Topological Weak Continuity

We investigate the computational properties of various weak continuity notions from (E) that mostly stem from topology. It is a straightforward exercise to show that all functionals in this section are computable in $\exists^3$.

First of all, continuous functions are characterised topologically by the inverse image of open sets being open. Weakening the latter requirement yields weak continuity notions, as in the following definition.

Definition 7 (Weak continuity I). Let $f : [0, 1] \to \mathbb{R}$ and $S \subset \mathbb{R}$ be given,

- S is *semi-open* if $S \subset \overline{\text{int}(S)}$ and semi-closed if $\text{int}(\overline{S}) \subset S$.
- S is an *α-set* in case $S \subset \text{int}\left(\overline{\text{int}(S)}\right)$,

- S is *regular closed* in case $S = \overline{\text{int}(S)}$,
- S is an *$\mathcal{A}$-set* if $S = O \cap C$ for open O and regular closed C,
- S is an *$\mathcal{AB}$-set* if $S = O \cap C$ for open O and semi-closed semi-open C,
- f is *s-continuous*[3] if for any open $G \subset \mathbb{R}$, $f^{-1}(G)$ is semi-open,
- f is *α-continuous* if for any open $G \subset \mathbb{R}$, $f^{-1}(G)$ is an α-set,
- f is *$\mathcal{A}$-continuous* if for any open $G \subset \mathbb{R}$, $f^{-1}(G)$ is an $\mathcal{A}$-set.
- f is *$\mathcal{AB}$-continuous* if for any open $G \subset \mathbb{R}$, $f^{-1}(G)$ is an $\mathcal{AB}$-set.

An *s*-continuous function is cliquish by (the proof of) [15, Theorem 13].

Secondly, the weak continuity functions from Definition 7 are relatively tame.

Theorem 8. *The functional $\exists^2$ computes* $\sup_{x \in [p,q]} f(x)$ *for* $p, q \in [0,1]$ *in case* $f : [0,1] \to \mathbb{R}$ *is either α-, s-, $\mathcal{A}$-, or $\mathcal{AB}$-continuous.*

Proof. First of all, for $S \subset [0,1]$ an α-set, we have the following, by definition:

$$S \neq \emptyset \to \text{int}(S) \neq \emptyset \to (\exists x \in [0,1], N \in \mathbb{N})(B(x, \tfrac{1}{2^N}) \subset S) \to (\exists r \in \mathbb{Q} \cap [0,1])(r \in S).$$

Hence, $\exists^2$ suffices to decide if an α-set S is empty or not. Similarly, fix $q \in \mathbb{R}$ and α-continuous $f : [0,1] \to \mathbb{R}$ and suppose $(\exists x \in [0,1])(f(x) > q)$. Now fix $k_0 \in \mathbb{N}$ and $x_0 \in [0,1]$ such that $f(x_0) - \tfrac{1}{2^{k_0}} > q$. Moreover for $G_0 = B(x_0, \tfrac{1}{2^{k_0}})$, $f^{-1}(G_0)$ is an α-set and non-empty (as $x_0 \in G_0$). Hence, there is $r_0 \in \mathbb{Q} \cap [0,1]$ in $f^{-1}(G_0)$ by the previous. By definition, this implies $f(r_0) > q$ and we obtain

$$(\exists x \in [0,1])(f(x) > q) \leftrightarrow (\exists r \in [0,1] \cap \mathbb{Q})(f(r) > q). \tag{3}$$

i.e. $\exists^2$ suffices to decide whether $(\exists x \in [0,1])(f(x) > q)$. In this way, one readily finds the supremum of f, which could be the special value $+\infty$ using the usual interval-halving technique. The same proof goes through for the other continuity notions. In particular, if $S \neq \emptyset$ is regular closed, then $\text{int}(S)$ is non-empty. □

Thirdly, the following notions appear side by side with Definition 7 in the literature.

Definition 9 (Weak continuity II). Let $f : [0,1] \to \mathbb{R}$ and $S \subset \mathbb{R}$ be given,

- S is a *t-set* in case $\text{int}(S) = \text{int}(\overline{S})$,
- S is a *Q-set* in case $\text{int}(\overline{S}) = \overline{\text{int}(S)}$),
- S is *pre-open* in case $S \subset \text{int}(\overline{S})$,
- S is an *α^*-set* in case $\text{int}(S) = \text{int}\left(\overline{\text{int}(S)}\right)$,
- S is a *$D(c,\alpha)$-set* in case $\text{int}(S) = S \cap \text{int}\left(\overline{\text{int}(S)}\right)$,
- S is a *C-set* in case $S = O \cap A$ where A is an α^*-set and O is open,
- S is a *$\mathscr{B}$-set* if $S = O \cap T$ where T is a *t*-set T and O is open,
- S is a *strong $\mathscr{B}$-set* if $S = O \cap T$, T is a semi-closed Q-set, and O is open,
- f is *$\mathscr{B}$-continuous* if for any open $G \subset \mathbb{R}$, if $f^{-1}(G)$ is a $\mathscr{B}$-set,
- f is *strongly $\mathscr{B}$-continuous* if for any open $G \subset \mathbb{R}$, $f^{-1}(G)$ is a strong $\mathscr{B}$-set,

---

[3] We use 's-continuity' as the full name was used by Baire for a different notion.

- f is *pre-continuous* if for any open $G \subset \mathbb{R}$, $f^{-1}(G)$ is pre-open,
- f is *C-continuous* if for any open $G \subset \mathbb{R}$, $f^{-1}(G)$ is a *C*-set,
- f is *D(c, α)-continuous* if for any open $G \subset \mathbb{R}$, $f^{-1}(G)$ is a $D(c, \alpha)$-set.

Fourth, most of the weak continuity notions from Definition 9 give rise to Cantor realisers, but seemingly not Ω_b, even if we drop the 'cliquish' condition. In particular, (2) does not satisfy any of the weak continuity notions in Definition 9.

Theorem 10. *Given $\exists^2$, the following computes a Cantor realiser:*

any functional $\Phi : ((\mathbb{R} \to \mathbb{R}) \times \mathbb{R}^2) \to \mathbb{R}$ such that for cliquish $f : [0,1] \to \mathbb{R}$ satisfying Γ, $\Phi(f, g, p, q) = \sup_{x \in [p,q]} f(x)$,

where Γ is either: (strong) $\mathcal{B}$-continuity, C-continuity, or $D(c, \alpha)$-continuity.

Proof. Fix $A \subset [0,1]$ and $Y : [0,1] \to \mathbb{N}$ such that the latter is injective on the former, i.e. A is countable. Use μ^2 to remove any rationals from A if necessary and let $(q_n)_{n \in \mathbb{N}}$ be a fixed enumeration of $\mathbb{Q} \cap [-1,1]$. Now define $\tilde{A} \subset (0,1)$ as follows: $y \in \tilde{A}$ if and only if there is $q \in \mathbb{Q} \cap [-1,1]$ and $n \in \mathbb{N}$ such that

$$y + q \in A \wedge Y(y + q) = n \wedge \tfrac{1}{2^{n+1}} \leq y < \tfrac{1}{2^n} \tag{4}$$

and the number q is the rational with minimal index in the enumeration $(q_n)_{n \in \mathbb{N}}$ satisfying (4). We now define a variation of (1) that is more suitable for our purposes. Indeed, define $\tilde{f} : [0,1] \to \mathbb{R}$ as follows:

$$\tilde{f}(x) := \begin{cases} \frac{1}{2^{n+1}} & x \in \tilde{A} \wedge \frac{1}{2^{n+1}} \leq x \leq \frac{1}{2^n} \\ 0 & x \notin \tilde{A} \end{cases} \tag{5}$$

Trivially, $\tilde{f}$ is cliquish. We now show that $\tilde{f}$ is $\mathcal{B}$-continuous. To this end, let $G \subset \mathbb{R}$ be open and consider the following three cases.

- If $0 \in G$, then $\tilde{f}^{-1}(G)$ is '$[0,1]$ minus a finite set', which is open. Note that $T = [0,1]$ is a *t*-set by definition.
- If $0 \notin G$ and $(\exists N \in \mathbb{N})(\forall n \geq N)(\frac{1}{2^n} \notin G)$, then $f^{-1}(G)$ is finite and hence a *t*-set. The ambient space $[0,1]$ is open (in itself).
- If $0 \notin G$ and $(\forall N \in \mathbb{N})(\exists n \geq N)(\frac{1}{2^n} \in G)$, then the closure of $f^{-1}(G)$ is included in $\tilde{A} \cup \{0\}$, which has empty interior, i.e. $f^{-1}(G)$ is a *t*-set.

By the previous case distinction, $\tilde{f}$ is $\mathcal{B}$-continuous. As in the proof of Theorem 5, we can find an enumeration of $\tilde{A}$, and hence of A; this yields $y \notin A$ by Cantor's diagonal argument, as required. To show that $\tilde{f}$ is *strongly* $\mathcal{B}$-continuous, one proceeds in exactly the same way. Indeed, the above case distinction goes through for '*t*-set' replaced by 'semi-closed *Q*-set'.

Finally, the function $\tilde{f}$ from (5) is also *C*-continuous, as follows. Let $G \subset \mathbb{R}$ be open and consider the following three cases.

- If $0 \in G$, then $\tilde{f}^{-1}(G)$ is '$[0,1]$ minus a finite set', which is open. Note that $A = [0,1]$ is an α^*-set by definition.

- If $0 \notin G$ and $(\exists N \in \mathbb{N})(\forall n \geq N)(\frac{1}{2^n} \notin G)$, then $f^{-1}(G)$ is finite and hence an α^*-set. The ambient space $[0,1]$ is open (in itself).
- If $0 \notin G$ and $(\forall N \in \mathbb{N})(\exists n \geq N)(\frac{1}{2^n} \in G)$, then the closure of $f^{-1}(G)$ is included in $\tilde{A} \cup \{0\}$, which has empty interior, i.e. $f^{-1}(G)$ is an α^*-set.

By the previous case distinction, $\tilde{f}$ is C-continuous. If we can find the supremum of $\tilde{f}$ on any interval, we can find an enumeration of $\tilde{A}$, and hence of A; this yields $y \notin A$ by Cantor's diagonalisation argument, as required. The same case distinction goes through for $D(c,\alpha)$-continuity as finite sets as well as $\tilde{A} \cup \{0\}$ are $D(c,\alpha)$ sets, essentially by definition.   □

Fifth, we have the following theorem showing that pre-continuity stands out.

Theorem 11. *Given $\exists^2$, the following functional computes Ω_b:*

any functional $\Phi : (\mathbb{R} \to \mathbb{R}) \to \mathbb{R}$ such that for pre-continuous $f : [0,1] \to \mathbb{R}$ and
$$p, q \in [0,1], \ \Phi(f) = \sup_{x \in [p,q]} f(x).$$

Proof. Fix $X \subset [0,1]$ which has at most one element and recall $g_X : [0,1] \to \mathbb{R}$ from (2). To show that this function is pre-continuous, the case where $X = \emptyset$ is trivial. In case $X \neq \emptyset$, fix open $G \subset \mathbb{R}$. In case $1 \in G$ or $0 \in G$, $\overline{f^{-1}(G)} = [0,1]$, which shows that $f^{-1}(G)$ is pre-open in this case. In case $0, 1 \notin G$, $f^{-1}(G) = \emptyset$, which is also (pre-)open. Hence, g_X is pre-continuous and $0 < \sup_{x \in [0,1]} g_X(x)$ is equivalent to $X \neq \emptyset$, as required for Ω_b.   □

2.3   Historical and Other Weak Continuity Notions

We investigate the computational properties of most of the remaining weak continuity notions from (E). It is a straightforward exercise to show that all functionals in this section are computable in $\exists^3$. Some go back more than a hundred years, like Young's condition (see [35]).

Definition 12 (Weak continuity III). *For $f : [0,1] \to \mathbb{R}$, we say that*

- *f is almost continuous (Husain) if for any $x \in [0,1]$ and open $G \subset \mathbb{R}$ containing $f(x)$, the set $\overline{f^{-1}(G)}$ is a neighbourhood of x,*
- *f has the Young condition in case for $x \in [0,1]$ there are sequences $(x_n)_{n \in \mathbb{N}}, (y_n)_{n \in \mathbb{N}}$ on the left and right of x with the latter as limit and $\lim_{n \to \infty} f(x_n) = f(x) = \lim_{n \to \infty} f(y_n)$,*
- *for f satisfying the Young condition, a Young modulus is a functional $\Phi_f : \mathbb{R} \to (\mathbb{N} \to \mathbb{R})^2$ such that for any $x \in \mathbb{R}$, $\Phi(x) = ((x_n)_{n \in \mathbb{N}}, (y_n)_{n \in \mathbb{N}})$ are the sequences in the Young condition.*
- *f is peripherally continuous if for any $x \in [0,1]$ and open intervals U, V with $x \in U, f(x) \in V$, there is an open $W \subset U$ with $x \in W$ and $f(\partial(W)) \subset V$.*
- *for peripherally continuous f, a modulus is any Ψ_f such that $\Psi_f(x, U, V) = W$ as in the previous item.*
- *f is said to be of Cesàro type if there are non-empty open $U \subset [0,1], V \subset \mathbb{R}$ such that for all $y \in V$, $U \subset \overline{f^{-1}(y)}$.*

Secondly, we again obtain Ω_b based on the notions in Definition 12.

Theorem 13. *Given $\exists^2$, the following functional computes Ω_b:*

any functional $\Phi : (\mathbb{R} \to \mathbb{R}) \to \mathbb{R}$ such that for $f : [0,1] \to \mathbb{R}$ satisfying Γ and
$$p, q \in [0,1], \ \Phi(f) = \sup_{x \in [p,q]} f(x),$$

where Γ is either almost continuity (Husain), 'not of Cesàro type', the Young condition, or peripheral continuity (the latter two also with a modulus).

Proof. Fix $X \subset [0,1]$ with at most one element and recall g_X from (2). To show that g_X is almost continuous (Husain), note that $1 \in G$ or $0 \in G$ implies $\overline{f^{-1}(G)} = [0,1]$, which is a neighbourhood of any point. To show that g_X is *not of Cesàro type*, note that the latter notion expresses that for all non-empty open $U \subset [0,1], V \subset \mathbb{R}$ there is $y \in V$ with $U \not\subset \overline{f^{-1}(y)}$. Since V is open, we can always choose $y \neq 0, 1$, yielding $g_X^{-1}(y) = \emptyset$, implying that the function g_X from (2) is not of Cesàro type. By definition, g_X has the Young condition regardless whether $X = \emptyset$. A Young modulus for g_X is $\Phi(x) := ((x - \frac{1}{2^n})_{n \in \mathbb{N}}, (x + \frac{1}{2^n})_{n \in \mathbb{N}})$. The Young condition is equivalent to peripheral continuity [8, Theorem 2.1] on $\mathbb{R}$, but one also readily observes that g_X satisfies the latter. For a modulus (of peripheral continuity), the only non-trivial case for $\Psi_f(x, U, V)$ is that the latter needs to be $(x - \frac{1}{2^n}, x + \frac{1}{2^n}) \subset U$ in case $x \in X$. $\square$

In conclusion, basic properties of weak continuity functions as in Definition 12 can be said to be *hard to compute* as no S_k^2 suffices.

2.4   Second-Order-ish Mathematics

We finish this paper with a conceptual section explaining the above results.

First of all, quasi-continuity from Definition 3 satisfies the following heuristic:

for any $x \in \mathbb{R}$ and quasi-continuous $f : \mathbb{R} \to \mathbb{R}$, the function value $f(x)$ can be approximated using only $f(q)$ for all $q \in \mathbb{Q}$.

One can of course replace the rationals by any other 'nice' countable dense set, but the point remains: while there are *many*[4] quasi-continuous functions, the function values can be approximated using a *second-order* set, namely $f(q)$ for all $q \in \mathbb{Q}$. In this light, it is immediate that (3) holds for quasi-continuous functions, explaining why $\exists^2$ computes $\sup_{x \in [0,1]} f(x)$ for quasi-continuous f (see e.g. [23]). What is important to note here is that the **third-order** left-hand side of (3) is equivalent to the **second-order** right-hand side. For this reason, we refer to quasi-continuous functions as *second-order-ish*: they *are* third-order objects but also 'sort of second-order', as they have nice 'second-order approximations'. Thanks to the latter, $\exists^2$ (or S^2) suffices to witness the associated properties.

Secondly, continuous functions are of course second-order-ish, which is the very idea underlying the second-order coding of continuous functions, going

---

[4] If $\mathfrak{c}$ is the cardinality of $\mathbb{R}$, there are $2^{\mathfrak{c}}$ non-measurable quasi-continuous $[0,1] \to \mathbb{R}$-functions and $2^{\mathfrak{c}}$ measurable quasi-continuous $[0,1] \to [0,1]$-functions (see [13]).

back to Kleene. However, many *large*[4] classes of *discontinuous* functions are also second-order-ish, including those in Definition 7, although this is somewhat obscured by the topological definitions. By contrast, *cliquish* functions as in Definition 3 do **not** necessarily satisfy the above approximation property, i.e. they are **not** second-order-ish; the same holds for graph continuity, pre-continuity, almost continuity (Husain), the Young condition, and 'not of Cesàro type'. We believe that an essential property of **non**-second-order-ish functions is that 'second-order approximations' like in e.g. (3) are **not** possible in general, explaining why Kleene's quantifier $\exists^3$ computes $\sup_{x \in [0,1]} f(x)$ but S_k^2 does not.

Finally, the previous two paragraphs explain the results in this paper in an informal way. As suggested by one of the anonymous referees, one would like to formalise the definition of 'second-order-ish function'. A problem with such a formalisation is in which logical system this purported definition should be formulated. In particular, whether countable choice should be allowed or not.

Acknowledgement. We thank the anonymous referees for their helpful comments.

References

1. Baire, R.: Sur les fonctions de variables réelles. Ann. di Mat. 1–123 (1899)
2. Bishop, E.: Foundations of Constructive Analysis. McGraw-Hill, New York (1967)
3. Borsík, J., Doboš, J.: A note on real cliquish functions. Real Anal. Exch. **18**(1), 139–145 (1992/93)
4. Borsík, J.: Sums of quasicontinuous functions defined on pseudometrizable spaces. Real Anal. Exch. **22**(1), 328–337 (1996/97)
5. Das, A., Nesterenko, V.: On decomposition of continuity, B-quasicontinuity and closed graph. Topol. Appl. **263**, 325–329 (2019)
6. Dontchev, J.: Strong $\mathscr{B}$- sets and another decomposition of continuity. Acta Math. Hungar. **75**(3), 259–265 (1997)
7. Dontchev, J.: Between $\mathscr{A}$- and $\mathscr{B}$- sets. Math. Balkanica **12**(3–4), 295–302 (1998)
8. Gibson, R.G., Natkaniec, T.: Darboux like functions. Real Anal. Exch. **22**(2), 492–533 (1996/97)
9. Grande, Z.: Sur les fonctions A-continues. Demonstr. Math. **11**(2), 519–526 (1978). (French)
10. Gray, R.: Georg Cantor and transcendental numbers. Amer. Math. Monthly **101**(9), 819–832 (1994)
11. Hatir, E., Noiri, T., Yüksel, S.: A decomposition of continuity. Acta Math. Hungar. **70**(1–2), 145–150 (1996)
12. Hilbert, D., Bernays, P.: Grundlagen der Mathematik. II, Zweite Auflage. Die Grundlehren der mathematischen Wissenschaften, Band 50. Springer (1970)
13. Holá, Ľ.: There are $2^\mathfrak{c}$ quasicontinuous non Borel functions on uncountable Polish space. Results Math. **76**(3), 11 (2021). Paper No. 126
14. Kohlenbach, U., Higher order reverse mathematics. In: Reverse Mathematics, vol. 2005. Lecture Notes in Logic 21, pp. 281–295. ASL (2001)
15. Levine, N.: Semi-open sets and semi-continuity in topological spaces. Amer. Math. Monthly **70**, 36–41 (1963)
16. Longley, J., Normann, D.: Higher-Order Computability. Theory and Applications of Computability. Springer, Heidelberg (2015). https://doi.org/10.1007/978-3-662-47992-6

17. Maliszewski, A.: On the sums of Darboux upper semicontinuous quasi-continuous functions. Real Anal. Exch. **20**(1), 244–249 (1994/95)
18. Martin-Löf, P.: The Hilbert-Brouwer controversy resolved? In: One Hundred Years of Intuitionism (1907–2007), pp. 243–256 (1967)
19. Normann, D.: Recursion on the Countable Functionals. Lecture Notes in Mathematics, vol. 811. Springer, Heidelberg (1980). https://doi.org/10.1007/BFb0098600
20. Normann, D., Sanders, S.: On the uncountability of ℝ. J. Symb. Log. 43 (2022). https://doi.org/10.1017/jsl.2022.27
21. Normann, D., Sanders, S.: Betwixt Turing and Kleene. In: Artemov, S., Nerode, A. (eds.) LFCS 2022. LNCS, vol. 13137, pp. 236–252. Springer, Cham (2022). https://doi.org/10.1007/978-3-030-93100-1_15
22. Normann, D., Sanders, S.: On the computational properties of basic mathematical notions. J. Log. Comput. 18 (2022). https://doi.org/10.1093/logcom/exac075
23. Normann, D., Sanders, S.: The biggest five of reverse mathematics. J. Math. Log. 56 (2023). https://doi.org/10.1142/S0219061324500077
24. Przemski, M.: A decomposition of continuity and α- continuity. Acta Math. Hungar. **61**(1–2), 93–98 (1993)
25. Rathjen, M.: The art of ordinal analysis. In: International Congress of Mathematicians, vol. II. European Mathematical Society, Zürich (2006)
26. Sakálová, K.: On graph continuity of functions. Demonstr. Math. **27**(1), 123–128 (1994)
27. Sanders, S.: The non-normal abyss in Kleene's computability theory. In: Della Vedova, G., Dundua, B., Lempp, S., Manea, F. (eds.) CiE 2023. LNCS, vol. 13967, pp. 37–49. Springer, Cham (2023). https://doi.org/10.1007/978-3-031-36978-0_4
28. Simpson, S.G.: Subsystems of Second Order Arithmetic. Perspectives in Logic, vol. 2. CUP (2009)
29. Smith, B.D.: An alternate characterization of continuity. Proc. Amer. Math. Soc. **39**, 318–320 (1973)
30. Soare, R.I.: Recursively Enumerable Sets and Degrees. Perspectives in Mathematical Logic. Springer, Heidelberg (1987)
31. Tong, J.C.: A decomposition of continuity. Acta Math. Hungar. **48**(1–2), 11–15 (1986)
32. Tong, J.C.: On decomposition of continuity in topological spaces. Acta Math. Hungar. **54**(1–2), 51–55 (1989)
33. Weihrauch, K.: Computable Analysis. Springer, Berlin (2000)
34. Hatice Yalvaç, T.: Decompositions of continuity. Acta Math. Hungar. **64**(3), 309–313 (1994)
35. Young, W.H.: A theorem in the theory of functions of a real variable. Rendiconti del Circolo Matematico di Palermo **XXIV**, 187–192 (1907)

On Arithmetical Numberings in Reverse Mathematics

Nikolay Bazhenov[1] , Marta Fiori-Carones[1(✉)] , and Manat Mustafa[2]

[1] Sobolev Institute of Mathematics, Novosibirsk, Russia
bazhenov@math.nsc.ru, marta.fioricarones@outlook.it
[2] Nazarbayev University, Astana, Kazakhstan
manat.mustafa@nu.edu.kz

Abstract. The paper analyzes the strength of some statements of the theory of numberings from the point of view of reverse mathematics and Weihrauch reducibility. For a countable family S, a numbering is a surjection acting from the set of natural numbers onto S. The following types of numberings have been extensively studied in the literature: Friedberg, positive, and minimal numberings.

Fix $n \geq 2$. After formalizing the needed notions in the language of second-order arithmetic, we prove that, over RCA_0, ACA_0 is equivalent to the principle stating the existence of a (not necessarily Σ_n-computable) Friedberg numbering ν for any infinite Σ_n^0-computable family. Over $\mathsf{RCA}_0 + \mathsf{I}\Sigma_2$, ACA_0 is also equivalent to a similar principle for positive numberings ν. On the other hand, $\mathsf{RCA}_0 + \mathsf{I}\Sigma_2$ is sufficient to prove the existence of a minimal numbering for any infinite Σ_n^0-computable family. The reverse mathematics thus underlines a distinction between the considered types of numberings: intuitively, 'being Friedberg' and 'being positive' are internal properties of a numbering, while 'being minimal' is a more global property. The paper also includes a brief study of the Weihrauch reducibility strength for the existence of Friedberg numberings.

Keywords: Reverse mathematics · Theory of numberings · Friedberg numbering · Arithmetical numbering · Weihrauch reducibility

1 Introduction

This paper aims to analyze the strength of some statements of the theory of numberings from the point of view of reverse mathematics and Weihrauch reducibility. Given a countable family $\mathcal{S}$, a *numbering* is a surjective function $\nu\colon \mathbb{N} \to \mathcal{S}$; that is, ν indexes (with possible repetitions) all elements of $\mathcal{S}$. One of the first important applications of numberings was provided by Gödel: he used an enumeration of formulae of a certain language to embed the metatheory into the theory of arithmetic. The systematic investigations of computability-theoretic properties of numberings go back to the works of Kleene [18] and Rogers [23] in the West, and Kolmogorov and Uspenskii [19] in the USSR. We refer to the

© The Author(s), under exclusive license to Springer Nature Switzerland AG 2024
L. Levy Patey et al. (Eds.): CiE 2024, LNCS 14773, pp. 126–138, 2024.
https://doi.org/10.1007/978-3-031-64309-5_11

monograph [11] and the surveys [3,12] for the background on the (classical) theory of numberings.

The classical theory mainly deals with families S whose elements are computably enumerable (or Σ_1) subsets of the set of natural numbers ω. From the very beginning, the following three types of numberings have played a key role in the research area.

(i) A numbering ν is called *Friedberg* if $\nu(k) \neq \nu(l)$ for all $k \neq l$. The name is an homage to the work of Friedberg [13], where he constructed a uniform enumeration without repetitions for the family of all c.e. sets.

(ii) A numbering ν is *positive* if the set $\{(k,l) : \nu(k) = \nu(l)\}$ is c.e. Observe that every Friedberg numbering is positive.

(iii) In order to introduce our third type of numberings, we need to recall the notion of *reducibility* between numberings. A numbering ν is *reducible* to another numbering μ, denoted by $\nu \leq \mu$, if there exists a total computable function $f(x)$ such that $\nu(k) = \mu(f(k))$ for all $k \in \omega$. As usual, numberings ν and μ are *equivalent* (denoted by $\nu \equiv \mu$) if $\nu \leq \mu$ and $\mu \leq \nu$. A numbering ν of a family S is *minimal* if every numbering μ of S satisfies the following: if $\mu \leq \nu$, then $\mu \equiv \nu$. It is known that every positive numbering is minimal.

Informally, one can notice that there is a clear distinction between the three types of numberings. In a way, the properties 'being Friedberg' and 'being positive' are *internal* to the numbering itself (i.e., they do not depend on a comparison with other numberings). On the other hand, 'being minimal' is a *global* property: indeed, a numbering ν can be declared minimal only when compared with the other numberings of the same family. So, the notion of minimality depends on the definition of reducibility between numberings.

The current paper aims to analyze some results about Friedberg, positive, and minimal numberings within the framework of reverse mathematics. In particular, our work will discuss some facts related to the distinction described above. Firstly, we recall the necessary definitions.

Let S be a countable family of subsets of ω. A numbering ν of S is *computable* (or $\Sigma_1 - computable$) if the set $\{(k,y) : y \in \nu(k)\}$ is c.e. Before the second half of 1990s, researchers mainly worked with computable numberings (see Sect. 4 for some known results in this area).

Goncharov and Sorbi [15] introduced a general framework for *generalized computable* numberings. Here we give only their definition for numberings computable in the arithmetical hierarchy.

Definition 1 (Definition 2.2 in [15]). *Let n be a non-zero natural number, and let ν be a numbering of a family S whose elements are subsets of ω. The numbering ν is called $\Sigma_n - computable$ if there exists a total computable function $g(x)$ such that for any $k, y \in \omega$, we have $y \in \nu(k)$ if and only if the standard model of first-order arithmetic satisfies $\Psi_{g(k)}(y)$. Here $\Psi_{g(k)}$ denotes the formula (in the language of arithmetic) having number $g(k)$ in a fixed Gödel numbering of all Σ_n-formulas.*

This definition admits an equivalent, computability-theoretic characterization: a numbering ν is Σ_n-computable if and only if the set $\{(k, y) : y \in \nu(k)\}$ is Σ_n (Proposition 2.1 in [15]). Most of the subsequent works in numbering theory used the second characterization. Nevertheless, Definition 1 almost immediately provides a natural way to formalize the theory of numberings (at least, for the arithmetical hierarchy) within the framework of reverse mathematics. See Sect. 3 for the formal exposition.

Reverse mathematics and Weihrauch reducibility provide two, different but comparable, frameworks, where it is possible to compare theorems from almost all areas of mathematics, thus creating a hierarchy between them. The main monographs are [17, 24], and [9].

Despite a large body of literature on the theory of numberings (and its connections with other branches of logic), this theory has not been analyzed yet from the reverse-mathematical point of view. To the best of our knowledge, as a unique exception, we mention the paper [20] by Li, where she considered the strength of the mentioned above result of Friedberg (i.e., the existence of a Friedberg Σ_1-computable numbering for the family of all c.e. sets). This result can be formalized fully *within first-order arithmetic*, since c.e. sets can be naturally viewed as numbers through their indices. Thus, it is possible to analyze how much induction is needed to prove the theorem of Friedberg. Li [20] proved that this principle is equivalent to $I\Sigma_2$, over $\mathsf{PA}^- + \mathsf{B}\Sigma_2$.

In this paper, we choose a different, more flexible approach: we work in RCA_0, and our formalizations are given via formulas in second-order arithmetic. This allows us to easily formalize the main notions of the theory of arithmetical numberings [1, 15]. As usual, a family S is called $\Sigma_n^0 - computable$ if it admits a Σ_n^0-computable numbering (or Σ_n^0-numbering, for short).

Our paper is arranged as follows. Section 2 contains the necessary preliminaries. In Sect. 3 we give the exposition of our framework: in RCA_0, we formally define Friedberg, positive, and minimal Σ_n^0-numberings.

In Sect. 4, we discuss the distinction mentioned above: Friedberg and positive numberings vs. minimal numberings. Let $n \geq 2$. On one hand, over RCA_0, the system ACA_0 is equivalent to the principle stating the existence of a Friedberg numbering ν for any infinite Σ_n^0-computable family (Theorem 1). In addition, over $\mathsf{RCA}_0 + I\Sigma_2$, ACA_0 is also equivalent to a similar principle for positive numberings ν (Corollary 1). On the other hand, the principle, stating the existence of a minimal numbering for any infinite Σ_n^0-computable family, is weaker: this principle is provable in $\mathsf{RCA}_0 + I\Sigma_2$ (Theorem 3).

In Sect. 5, after introducing the needed preliminaries on Weihrauch degrees, we calibrate the Weihrauch complexity of the following multivalued functions Fr_n: given a Σ_n^0-definition (with a second-order parameter A) encoding a numbering ν of an infinite family S, Fr_n outputs a Σ_1^0-definition (with *another* second-order parameter B) encoding a Friedberg numbering μ of S. See Sect. 5 for the formal details. We prove that $\mathsf{Fr}_n <_{\mathsf{W}} \mathsf{Fr}_{n+1}$ (Proposition 1 and Corollary 3).

2   Preliminaries

Reverse mathematics is a research program, which dates back to the 1970s (see [14]), whose goal is to find the exact axiomatic strength of theorems from different areas of mathematics. It deals with statements about countable, or countably representable, structures, using the framework of the formal system of second-order arithmetic Z_2.

With the notation Σ_n^0 we denote the usual arithmetical formulae sliced depending on the number of alternations of quantifiers; recall that these formulae may contain second-order parameters. With the notation Σ_n we denote a Σ_n^0-formula with *no* second-order parameters.

The subsystems of second-order arithmetic are obtained by limiting the comprehension and induction axioms of Z_2 to specific classes of formulae. We mention only the two subsystems we are going to use in this paper: RCA_0 is the weak base theory with comprehension for Δ_1^0-definable sets and with induction limited to Σ_1^0-formulae; ACA_0 extends RCA_0 allowing for definitions of sets by arithmetical comprehension (from which follows arithmetical induction too). We recall that adding to RCA_0 induction for Σ_n^0-formulae (i.e., $I\Sigma_n^0$), for any $n \geq 2$, one gets a non-collapsing hierarchy of subsystems below ACA_0.

Let $(M, \mathcal{X}) \vDash RCA_0$ be a model, and let $Y \subseteq M$. We say that Y is a $\Sigma_n^0 -$ *definable set*, or simply a $\Sigma_n^0 - set$, if there is a Σ_n^0-formula $\varphi(x)$ such that Y is precisely the set of elements satisfying φ. Σ_n-sets are defined in a similar way: they are those definable by Σ_n-formulae. Notice that Y *may not belong to* $\mathcal{X}$. If Y is a Δ_1^0-set, then clearly $Y \in \mathcal{X}$, so we call it simply a 'set'. The notions of Π_n^0- and Δ_n^0-sets are defined analogously.

We fix a suitable coding for formulae. For each $n \in \omega$, it is possible to define a Σ_n^0-formula $Sat_n(x, y, X)$ such that, provably in RCA_0, φ is a Σ_n^0-formula and $\varphi(y, X)$ holds if and only if $Sat_n(e, y, X)$ holds, for a code e of φ. For more details see Theorem 1.75 and Corollary 1.76 in [16]. Notice that, if φ is a Σ_n-formula, then $Sat_n(e, y) := Sat_n(e, y, \emptyset)$ is also Σ_n. Thanks to the predicate Sat_n, one can quantify (second- or first-order, depending on the existence of parameters) over Σ_n^0-formulae (Σ_n-formulae). Moreover, we can safely speak interchangeably about a formula or about its index e.

In our proofs, we use the following well-known result:

Lemma 1 (see, e.g., Lemma III.1.3 in [24]). *Over* RCA_0, ACA_0 *is equivalent to the following statement: for any* 1-1 *function* $g \colon \mathbb{N} \to \mathbb{N}$, *its range exists.*

The next result checks that an analogue of Lemma 3.2 of [25] holds for all levels of the arithmetical hierarchy.

Lemma 2. *Let* $n \geq 2$. *Over* $RCA_0 + B\Sigma_n^0$, $I\Sigma_n^0$ *is equivalent to the following statement: for any unbounded* Σ_n^0-set S *there exists (the graph of) an injective* Δ_n^0-*enumeration of* S.

3   The Main Framework

In the introduction, we have (informally) discussed the definitions of a numbering and of some important types of numberings. Note that a numbering itself, being a surjective function from $\mathbb{N}$ onto $\mathcal{S}$, with $\mathcal{S}$ at most countable family of subsets of $\mathbb{N}$, is a third-order object. In order to deal with these objects in reverse mathematics, we should firstly represent them through second-order objects.

Recall that Goncharov and Sorbi [15] generalized the classical notion of a computable (or Σ_1-) numbering to Σ_n-computable numberings (see Definition 1). This notion of a generalized computable numbering gives a straightforward possibility to represent a numbering ν as a second-order object (essentially, ν can be represented by a Σ_n^0-formula defining ν).

Definition 2 (RCA$_0$). *Let* $n \geq 1$ *be a natural number. A* Σ_n^0-*numbering* ν *is coded by a* Σ_n^0-*formula* $\psi(x, y)$ *(possibly, with set parameters) as follows: we have* $\nu(x) = \{y : \psi(x, y)\}$, *for* $x \in \mathbb{N}$.

Whenever we write 'Σ_n^0-numbering ν', this should be read as 'Σ_n^0-formula $\psi(x, y)$' (coding ν). This way, when we quantify over Σ_n^0-numberings, formally speaking, we are quantifying over Σ_n^0-formulae. (This is possible thanks to the predicate *Sat* discussed in the preliminaries.) For example, by the sentence "numberings ν and μ index the same family", we mean the following: $\forall x \exists z \forall y \, (\varphi(x, y) \leftrightarrow \psi(z, y))$ and $\forall x \exists z \forall y \, (\varphi(z, y) \leftrightarrow \psi(x, y))$, for the formulae φ and ψ encoding ν and μ, respectively.

Note 1. If a Σ_n^0-numbering ν is coded by a Σ_n^0-formula $\psi(x, y, A)$, where A is a set parameter, then we say that ν is a Σ_n^A-*numbering*.

With Definition 2 in mind, one can immediately define a Friedberg Σ_n^0-numbering in RCA$_0$. We also formalize the notion of a positive numbering:

Definition 3 (RCA$_0$). *A* Σ_n^0-*numbering* ν *is* positive *if there exists a* Σ_1-*formula* $\theta(x, y)$ *such that:* $\forall x \forall y \, (\nu(x) = \nu(y) \leftrightarrow \theta(x, y))$.

Recall that in the classical theory of numberings, a numbering ν is positive iff the set $\{(k, l) : \nu(k) = \nu(l)\}$ is c.e., that is definable by a Σ_1^0-formula in the minimal ω-model of RCA$_0$. We emphasize that in the above definition, the defining formula is required to be Σ_1, that is *without second-order parameters*. This is due to the fact that we want to maintain the property of 'being positive' as absolute, namely not relative to the second-order part of a model of RCA$_0$. Otherwise, a given Σ_n^0-numbering ν coded by a formula $\psi(x, y, A)$, where A is a second-order parameter, would be positive in a model whose second-order part contains the n-th Turing jump $A^{(n)}$.

We choose our notion of the *reduction* between numberings as a 'parameter-free' one. This better suits the definition given in the theory of numberings, and it is closer to the treatment of Turing reducibility in reverse mathematics (where $A \leq_T B$ if and only if there is an index $e \in \mathbb{N}$ such that $A = \varphi_e(B)$).

Definition 4 (RCA$_0$). *A Σ_n^0-numbering ν is reducible to a Σ_n^0-numbering μ, denoted by $\nu \leq \mu$, if there exists an index $e \in \mathbb{N}$ for a total computable (Δ_1) function $\varphi_e: \mathbb{N} \to \mathbb{N}$ such that $\forall k\,(\nu(k) = \mu(\varphi_e(k)))$.*

Definition 4 induces, in a natural way, the notion of a minimal Σ_n^0-numbering:

Definition 5 (RCA$_0$). *A Σ_n^0-numbering ν of a family $\mathcal{S}$ is minimal if for every Σ_n^0-numbering μ of $\mathcal{S}$, the condition $\mu \leq \nu$ implies $\nu \leq \mu$.*

The three considered types of Σ_n^0-numberings are related: each Friedberg numbering is positive, and each positive numbering is minimal. This holds true in the base system RCA$_0$.

4 Existence of Friedberg, Positive, and Minimal Numberings

Let $\mathcal{S}$ be an infinite family of Σ_n-subsets of ω. In the classical theory of numberings, it is known that in general, the existence of a positive Σ_n-numbering ν for $\mathcal{S}$ does not imply existence of a Friedberg Σ_n-numbering of $\mathcal{S}$. Similarly, the existence of a minimal Σ_n-numbering for $\mathcal{S}$ does not imply the existence of a positive Σ_n-numbering of $\mathcal{S}$. Here we refer to the following results:

(A) Pour-El and Putnam (Theorem 2 in [22]) constructed an infinite family $\mathcal{S}$ of finite sets such that $\mathcal{S}$ has a positive Σ_1-numbering, but $\mathcal{S}$ does not have Friedberg Σ_1-numberings. See also [10].
(B) Marchenkov [21] built a family $\mathcal{S}$ of c.e. sets such that $\mathcal{S}$ has a minimal Σ_1-numbering, but $\mathcal{S}$ does not have positive Σ_1-numberings.
(C) On the other hand, Goncharov and Sorbi (Proposition 2.7 in [15]) obtained the following result for every $n \geq 2$: if an infinite family $\mathcal{S}$ of Σ_n sets has a positive Σ_n-numbering, then $\mathcal{S}$ also admits a Friedberg Σ_n-numbering.
(D) Let $n \geq 2$. Badaev and Goncharov (Theorem 1 in [4]) proved the following: if an infinite family $\mathcal{S}$ of Σ_n sets admits a Σ_n-numbering, then $\mathcal{S}$ has infinitely many pairwise non-equivalent minimal Σ_n-numberings. In addition, Badaev and Goncharov (Corollary 4 in [5]) constructed an infinite family $\mathcal{F}$ which has a Σ_n-numbering, but does not admit a Friedberg Σ_n-numbering. Notice that by result (C), the family $\mathcal{F}$ also does not have positive Σ_n-numberings.

Motivated by these results, in this section we compare the reverse-mathematical strength of the principles that postulate the existence of a Friedberg, or positive, or minimal numbering for each infinite family $\mathcal{S}$. When comparing the mentioned results with the ones we obtain, it is important to remember that the (classical) theory of numberings essentially works within the standard model of first-order arithmetic.

In this section, we work only with numberings of *infinite* families $\mathcal{S}$. Firstly, we isolate two existence principles (Theorem 1 and Corollary 1) which are equivalent to ACA$_0$.

Theorem 1 (RCA₀). *Suppose that $n \geq 1$. Then ACA_0 is equivalent to the following statement: for any $A \subseteq \mathbb{N}$ and any Σ_n^A-numbering ν, there exist a set $B \subseteq \mathbb{N}$ and a Friedberg Σ_n^B-numbering μ such that ν and μ index the same family.*

Proof ($\Rightarrow$). For a Σ_n^0-formula $\psi(x, y, A)$ encoding ν, we define the following unbounded Σ_{n+1}^0-set:

$$X = \{e : \forall i < e\,(\nu(i) \neq \nu(e))\}$$
$$= \{e : \forall i < e\, \exists y\, [(\psi(i, y, A) \wedge \neg\psi(e, y, A)) \vee (\neg\psi(i, y, A) \wedge \psi(e, y, A))]\}. \tag{1}$$

As usual, the formula $\neg\psi(x, y, A)$ is equivalent to a formula of the form

$$\forall z_1\, \exists z_2\, \forall z_3 \ldots Q_n z_n\, \alpha(x, y, z_1, z_2, z_3, \ldots, z_n, A),$$

where α is a Δ_0^0-formula, and $Q_n = \forall$ for odd n, $Q_n = \exists$ for even n. Observe that ACA_0 proves the existence of the set

$$C = \{\langle x, y, z_1, z_2, \ldots, z_{n-1}\rangle : \exists z_n\, \alpha(x, y, z_1, z_2, \ldots, z_{n-1}, z_n, A)\}.$$

Then it is not hard to show that X is a Σ_n^0-set defined by a Σ_n^0-formula of the form $\theta(x, C)$.

By Lemma 2, $\mathsf{RCA}_0 + \mathsf{I}\Sigma_n^0$ proves that there exists an injective Δ_n^0-enumeration $\pi_X : \mathbb{N} \to \mathbb{N}$ such that $X = \mathrm{range}(\pi_X)$. In addition, the formula defining π_X uses the same second-order parameter C as the formula θ. We define a Σ_n^0-numbering μ via the formula $\xi(x, y, A \oplus C)$ as follows:

$$\xi(x, y, A \oplus C) := \exists z\, (\pi_X(x) = z \wedge \psi(z, y, A)).$$

Then μ is a Friedberg numbering of the family $\mathcal{S}$.

($\Leftarrow$). Let g be a 1-1 function from $\mathbb{N}$ to $\mathbb{N}$. By Lemma 1, it is sufficient to prove that the set $\mathrm{range}(g)$ exists. Our construction is based on the idea from Theorem 2 of [22]. It is enough to give a proof for the case of Σ_1^0-numberings. We define a Σ_1^0-numbering ν of a family $\mathcal{S}$ as follows:

$$\nu(2x) = \{2x\} \cup \{2x + 1 : \exists t(g(t) = x)\},$$
$$\nu(2x + 1) = \{2x + 1\} \cup \{2x : \exists t(g(t) = x)\}.$$

If $x \notin \mathrm{range}(g)$, then $\nu(2x) = \{2x\}$ and $\nu(2x + 1) = \{2x + 1\}$. If $x \in \mathrm{range}(g)$, then $\nu(2x) = \nu(2x + 1) = \{2x, 2x + 1\}$.

Now let μ be a Friedberg Σ_1^0-numbering of $\mathcal{S}$. Then the set $\mathrm{range}(g)$ is Π_1^0-definable: indeed, $x \notin \mathrm{range}(g)$ if and only if $\exists i\, \exists j\, [i \neq j \wedge 2x \in \mu(i) \wedge 2x + 1 \in \mu(j)]$. By Δ_1^0-comprehension, we deduce that the range of g exists. Theorem 1 is proved. □

The next result works *only for $n \geq 2$*. Indeed, compare this with result (A) given at the beginning of Sect. 4.

Theorem 2. *Suppose that $n \geq 2$. Then $\mathsf{RCA}_0 + \mathsf{I}\Sigma_2$ proves the following: the existence of a positive Σ_n^0-numbering for a family S implies the existence of a Friedberg Σ_n^0-numbering for S.*

Proof. Essentially, here we follow the outline of [15, Proposition 2.7]. Let $\varphi(x, y, A)$ be a Σ_n^0-formula encoding a positive Σ_n^0-numbering ν of a family S. Note that $\forall b \, \exists c > b \, \forall b' \leq b \, (\nu(c) \neq \nu(b'))$, since the numbering ν indexes an infinite family. Consider the formula $\psi(k) := \forall k' < k \, (\nu(k) \neq \nu(k'))$. Notice that ψ is Π_1, since ν is assumed to be positive. Let G be the Δ_2-graph of an injective enumeration of ψ, according to Lemma 2.

Define now a formula $\theta(x, y, A)$ as $\exists z \, (G(x, z) \wedge \varphi(z, y, A))$. Since $n \geq 2$, the formula θ is Σ_n^0. We claim that θ codes a Friedberg numbering μ of the family S.

To prove that the coded numbering is Friedberg, suppose on the contrary that $\forall y \, (\theta(k, y, A) \leftrightarrow \theta(k', y, A))$ for some $k < k' \in \mathbb{N}$ (that is $\mu(k) = \mu(k')$). By definition of θ, this implies that there are $z \neq z'$ so that $G(k, z)$, $G(k', z')$, and $\forall y \, (\varphi(z, y, A) \leftrightarrow \varphi(z', y, A))$. Without loss of generality, we may assume that $z < z'$. Then we have $\neg\psi(z')$, contradicting $G(k', z')$.

To finish, we prove that φ and θ code the same family. It is immediate to check that $\forall x \, \exists z \, \forall y \, (\theta(x, y, A) \leftrightarrow \varphi(z, y, A))$. Hence, we are left with checking that $\forall z \, \exists x \, \forall y \, (\theta(x, y, A) \leftrightarrow \varphi(z, y, A))$ holds too. Fix $z \in \mathbb{N}$, and let z' be minimal such that $\nu(z') = \nu(z)$ (maybe, $z' = z$). Let x be such that $G(x, z')$ (notice that such x exists, since G is the graph of an enumeration of ψ). Then $\forall y \, (\theta(x, y, A) \leftrightarrow \varphi(z', y, A))$ holds by the definition of θ. That is, $\forall y \, (\theta(x, y, A) \leftrightarrow \varphi(z, y, A))$, given that z and z' are ν-indices of the same set. $\qquad\square$

By combining Theorems 1 and 2, we obtain the following.

Corollary 1. *Let $n \geq 2$. Over $\mathsf{RCA}_0 + \mathsf{I}\Sigma_2$, the system ACA_0 is equivalent to the following principle: for any $A \subseteq \mathbb{N}$ and any Σ_n^A-numbering ν, there exist $B \subseteq \mathbb{N}$ and a positive Σ_n^B-numbering μ such that ν and μ index the same family.*

The results above prove that (under some additional assumptions) the existence of a Friedberg and of a positive Σ_n^0-numbering of a certain family share the same strength, for $n \geq 2$. Now we show that the existence of a minimal Σ_n^0-numbering, for $n \geq 2$, is weaker, since it is provable in $\mathsf{RCA}_0 + \mathsf{I}\Sigma_2$. This result underlines the difference between 'being Friedberg' and 'being positive', on one side, and 'being minimal', on the other side.

Theorem 3. *Let $n \geq 2$. Then $\mathsf{RCA}_0 + \mathsf{I}\Sigma_2$ proves the following principle: for any $A \subseteq \mathbb{N}$ and for any Σ_n^A-numbering ν, there exists a minimal Σ_n^A-numbering μ such that ν and μ index the same family.*

Recall that a Σ_1-set M is *maximal* if for any Σ_1-set $A \supseteq M$, either $A \setminus M$ is finite or $\mathbb{N} \setminus A$ is finite. The following theorem was proved in [7, Theorem 2].

Theorem 4 (*[7]*). *Over $\mathsf{RCA}_0 + \mathsf{B}\Sigma_2$, $\mathsf{I}\Sigma_2$ is equivalent to the existence of a maximal Σ_1-set.*

Theorem 3. *Let* $n \geq 2$. *Then* $\mathsf{RCA}_0 + \mathsf{I}\Sigma_2$ *proves the following principle: for any* $A \subseteq \mathbb{N}$ *and for any* Σ_n^A*-numbering* ν, *there exists a minimal* Σ_n^A*-numbering* μ *such that* ν *and* μ *index the same family.*

Proof. We follow the outline of the proof of Badaev and Goncharov (Theorem 1 in [4], see also Theorem 1.3 in [2]).

Let $\varphi(x, y, A)$ be a Σ_n^0-formula encoding a Σ_n^0-numbering ν. Let M be a maximal Σ_1-set, which is guaranteed to exist by Theorem 4, and let ψ be the Σ_1-formula defining M. Let $G(x, y)$ be the graph of an injective enumeration of the complement of M. By Lemma 2, one can choose G as a Δ_2-formula.

Define a formula $\theta(x, y, A)$ (encoding the numbering μ) as follows:

$$\exists z \, (G(z, x) \wedge \varphi(z, y, A)) \vee (\psi(x) \wedge \varphi(0, y, A)).$$

In other words, if our G is the graph of an enumeration h, then

$$\mu(x) = \begin{cases} \nu(h^{-1}(x)), & \text{if } x \in \mathbb{N} \setminus M, \\ \nu(0), & \text{if } x \in M. \end{cases}$$

Since $n \geq 2$, the formula θ is Σ_n^0.

We claim that θ codes a minimal Σ_n^0-numbering μ of the same family as ν. It is immediate to check that

$$\forall x \, \exists z \, \forall y \, (\theta(x, y, A) \leftrightarrow \varphi(z, y, A)).$$

To check that $\forall z \, \exists x \, \forall y \, (\theta(x, y, A) \leftrightarrow \varphi(z, y, A))$ holds, fix z. Notice that for each $z' \in \mathbb{N}$, there exists x such that $G(z', x)$, by the properties of G. Thus, we choose x such that $G(z, x)$, so that we have $\forall y \, (\theta(x, y, A) \leftrightarrow \varphi(z, y, A))$.

Now we prove that μ is minimal. Suppose that $\rho \leq \mu$, for some Σ_n^0-numbering ρ enumerating the same family as μ, that is there exists $e \in \mathbb{N}$ such that $\forall k \, (\rho(k) = \mu(\varphi_e(k)))$. Let g be a computable (Δ_1) function such that $M = \text{range}(g)$. Let $R = \text{range}(\varphi_e)$ (since R is a Σ_1-set, recall that R is treated as a Σ_1-formula). By the maximality of M, the Σ_1-set $R \cup M$ is such that either $(R \cup M) \setminus M$ is finite or $\mathbb{N} \setminus (R \cup M)$ is finite. The latter must hold, since there exist infinitely many $x \in R \setminus M$, given that μ and ρ are enumerating an infinite family $\mathcal{S}$.

Without loss of generality, one may assume that $\rho(0) = \nu(0)$. We define a partial function h acting from $\mathbb{N}$ to $\mathbb{N}$ such that, for each $x \in R \cup M$,

$$h(x) = \begin{cases} 0, & \exists y \, (g(y) = x \wedge \forall z < y \, (\varphi_e(z) \neq x)), \\ \min y \, [\varphi_e(y) = x], & \text{otherwise.} \end{cases}$$

It is easy to check that, for each $x \in R \cup M$, $\mu(x) = \rho(h(x))$. Since there are only finitely many $x \notin R \cup M$, one can extend the function h, so to obtain a total Δ_1-function witnessing the reduction $\mu \leq \rho$. $\qquad\square$

The proofs of Theorem 2 and of Theorem 3 also imply the following: in $\mathsf{RCA}_0 + \mathsf{I}\Sigma_2$, the existence of a positive Σ_1^0-numbering (respectively, a Σ_1^0-numbering) for a family $\mathcal{S}$ implies the existence of a Friedberg (respectively, minimal) Σ_2^0-numbering for $\mathcal{S}$.

In conclusion, we observe the following consequence of Theorem 3 and Corollary 1.

Corollary 2. *Let $n \geq 2$. Over $\mathsf{RCA}_0 + \mathsf{I}\Sigma_2$, ACA_0 is equivalent to the following: for any $A \subseteq \mathbb{N}$ and any minimal Σ_n^A-numbering ν, there exist $B \subseteq \mathbb{N}$ and a Friedberg Σ_n^B-numbering μ such that ν and μ index the same family.*

Some questions are left open in this section, regarding in particular the amount of induction needed to prove Theorem 2 and 3 and Corollary 1.

5   Weihrauch Complexity for Existence of Friedberg Numberings

The statement of Theorem 1 asserts that in ACA_0, for each Σ_n^0-numbering ν, there exists a Friedberg numbering of the same complexity for the same family. One can formulate a similar statement, but requiring that the resulting Friedberg numbering has *lower complexity* than the given numbering ν.

Consider, for example, the following statement: for each A and for each Σ_n^A-numbering, there exist a set B and a Friedberg Σ_1^B-numbering for the same family. In order to prove this, one can proceed with the same proof as for Theorem 1, just arguing that X from Eq. (1) is a Σ_1-set in $A^{(n)}$, so that one obtains a Friedberg Σ_1-numbering relative to $A^{(n)}$. Certainly, ACA_0 is enough to carry out such proof, since it proves the existence of any iteration of the jump.

Despite the fact that clearly more jumps are used depending on n, the system ACA_0 does not have a possibility to differentiate the strength of the different statements according to n. To this end, we use Weihrauch reducibility—we want to 'slice' the Weihrauch complexity for the existence of Friedberg numberings.

(i) Firstly, we recall the necessary preliminaries on the Weihrauch complexity. Here we give a notion of *Weihrauch reducibility*, which does not capture the full generality of Weihrauch reducibility, *but* this notion is equivalent to the general one when one restricts their attention to the Baire space, as done in this paper. The following definition was introduced in [8, Definition 1.5, Appendix A].

Definition 6. *Let $\mathsf{F}, \mathsf{G} \colon \subseteq \omega^\omega \rightrightarrows \omega^\omega$ be multi-valued functions.*

- F *is* Weihrauch reducible *to* G, $\mathsf{F} \leq_\mathsf{W} \mathsf{G}$, *if there are Turing functionals $\Phi, \Psi \colon \subseteq \omega^\omega \to \omega^\omega$ such that $\Phi(f) \in \operatorname{dom}(\mathsf{G})$ for all $f \in \operatorname{dom}(\mathsf{F})$ and $\Psi(\langle f, g \rangle) \in \mathsf{F}(f)$ for all $f \in \operatorname{dom}(\mathsf{F})$ and $g \in \mathsf{G}(\Phi(f))$.*
- F *is* strongly Weihrauch reducible *to* G, $\mathsf{F} \leq_\mathsf{sW} \mathsf{G}$, *if there are Turing functionals $\Phi, \Psi \colon \subseteq \omega^\omega \to \omega^\omega$ such that $\Phi(f) \in \operatorname{dom}(\mathsf{G})$ for all $f \in \operatorname{dom}(\mathsf{F})$ and $\Psi(g) \in \mathsf{F}(f)$ for all $f \in \operatorname{dom}(\mathsf{F})$ and $g \in \mathsf{G}(\Phi(f))$.*

A Δ_2^0-*presentation* of a function $g \colon \omega \to \omega$ is a function $f \colon \omega \times \omega \to \omega$ such that $\forall n \, (g(n) = \lim_s f(n,s))$. Let $\lim f = g$ denote that f is a Δ_2^0-presentation of g. One can similarly define Δ_n^0-presentations, for $n \geq 3$.

Recall that $\lim \colon \subseteq \omega^{\omega \times \omega} \to \omega^\omega$ is the following function.

- Input/instance: An $f \in \omega^{\omega \times \omega}$ such that $\lim f$ exists,
- Output/solution: $\lim f$.

Let $\mathsf{F} \colon \subseteq \omega^\omega \rightrightarrows \omega^\omega$ be a multi-valued function. The *jump* of F, denoted F', is the following multi-valued function.

- Input/instance: A Δ_2^0-presentation f of a $g \in \mathrm{dom}(\mathsf{F})$.
- Output/solution: An element of $\mathsf{F}(g)$.

For each n, $\mathsf{F}^{(n)} = (\mathsf{F}^{(n-1)})'$ (where $\mathsf{F} = \mathsf{F}^{(0)}$). For further background on the Weihrauch complexity, we refer to, e.g., the survey [6].

(ii) Secondly, we formalize our approach to Σ_n^0-numberings. Since a numbering ν is a map of the type $\omega \to 2^\omega$, we need to introduce a *representation* for numberings in the Baire space — that is a map $\delta \colon \subseteq \omega^\omega \to (2^\omega)^\omega$. Given a $p \in \mathrm{dom}(\delta) \subseteq \omega^\omega$, we describe how this p codes the corresponding numbering $\delta(p) \colon \omega \to 2^\omega$.

Our intuition here is as follows: a given Σ_n-formula can be treated as a Σ_1-formula with respect to the Δ_n^0-set $\emptyset^{(n-1)}$. Hence, our representation δ will be based on Δ_n^0-presentations of functions $g \colon \omega \to \omega$.

For finite strings σ and τ, the formula $\sigma \sqsubseteq \tau$ denotes that σ is an initial segment of τ.

Definition 7. *A Σ_n^0-coded numbering is a sequence $p \in \omega^\omega$ satisfying the following conditions:*

- $p = p_1 \oplus p_2$,
- *for each $k \in \omega$, $p_1(k) = \langle x, y, \sigma \rangle$ for some $x, y \in \omega$ and $\sigma \in \omega^{<\omega}$,*
- *for any $x, y \in \omega$, if there exists $k \in \omega$ such that $p_1(k) = \langle x, y, \sigma \rangle$ for some σ, then, for each $\tau \sqsupseteq \sigma$, there exists $m \in \omega$ such that $p_1(m) = \langle x, y, \tau \rangle$,*
- *p_2 is a Δ_n^0-presentation of a function $g \in \omega^\omega$, that is, $g(a) = \lim_{s_1} \ldots \lim_{s_{n-1}} p_2(\langle a, s_1, \ldots, s_{n-1} \rangle)$ for each $a \in \omega$.*

A numbering ν is represented by a Σ_n^0-coded numbering $p = p_1 \oplus p_2$ (where p_2 is a Δ_n^0-presentation of a function $g \in \omega^\omega$) if and only if for every $x \in \omega$,

$$\nu(x) = \{y \in \omega : \exists k \, \exists \sigma \sqsubseteq g \, (p_1(k) = \langle x, y, \sigma \rangle)\}.$$

In this case, for convenience, sometimes we call ν itself a Σ_n^0-coded numbering.

A Σ_n^0-coded numbering given in the definition above is constituted by two parts interleaved, p_1 and p_2. The former lists triples with certain constraints, and *per se* does not single out any concrete numbering. On the other hand, p_1 names a family of numberings, and a concrete numbering is recovered depending on the information given by p_2. Moreover, the complexity of the numbering is 'discharged' into p_2, following the idea to represent Σ_n^0-numberings as those 'Σ_1 in $\emptyset^{(n-1)}$'.

Definition 8. *Let $n \geq 1$. Then* $\mathsf{Fr}_n \colon \subseteq \omega^\omega \rightrightarrows \omega^\omega$ *is the following multi-valued function:*

- *Input/instance: a Σ_n^0-coded numbering ν of an infinite family,*
- *Output/solution: a Σ_1^0-coded Friedberg numbering μ of the same family.*

The next proposition is the main result of this section: we formally 'calibrate' the Weihrauch complexity for producing a Friedberg Σ_1^0-numbering (according to Definition 8).

Proposition 1. *For each n,* $\lim^{(n-1)} \equiv_{\mathrm{sW}} \mathsf{Fr}_n$.

Corollary 3. *For each n,* $\mathsf{Fr}_n <_{\mathrm{W}} \mathsf{Fr}_{n+1}$.

Acknowledgements. The work of Bazhenov and Fiori-Carones was supported by the Mathematical Center in Akademgorodok under the agreement No. 075-15-2022-281 with the Ministry of Science and Higher Education of the Russian Federation. The research of Bazhenov and Mustafa was funded by the Science Committee of the Ministry of Science and Higher Education of the Republic of Kazakhstan (Grant No. AP19676989). The research of Mustafa was supported by Nazarbayev University Faculty Development Competitive Research Grants 201223FD8823.

References

1. Badaev, S., Goncharov, S.: Computability and numberings. In: Cooper, S.B., Löwe, B., Sorbi, A. (eds.) New Computational Paradigms, pp. 19–34. Springer, New York (2008). https://doi.org/10.1007/978-0-387-68546-5_2
2. Badaev, S., Goncharov, S., Sorbi, A.: Completeness and universality of arithmetical numberings. In: Goncharov, S.S., Cooper, S.B. (eds.) Computability and Models. The University Series in Mathematics, pp. 11–44. Springer, New York (2003). https://doi.org/10.1007/978-1-4615-0755-0_2
3. Badaev, S.A., Goncharov, S.S.: The theory of numberings: open problems. In: Cholak, P., Lempp, S., Lerman, M., Shore, R. (eds.) Computability Theory and Its Applications, Contemporary Mathematics, vol. 257, pp. 23–38. American Mathematical Society, Providence (2000). https://doi.org/10.1090/conm/257/04025
4. Badaev, S.A., Goncharov, S.S.: Rogers semilattices of families of arithmetic sets. Algebra Log. **40**(5), 283–291 (2001). https://doi.org/10.1023/A:1012516217265
5. Badaev, S.A., Goncharov, S.S.: Generalized computable universal numberings. Algebra Log. **53**(5), 355–364 (2014). https://doi.org/10.1007/s10469-014-9296-3
6. Brattka, V., Gherardi, G., Pauly, A.: Weihrauch complexity in computable analysis. In: Handbook of Computability and Complexity in Analysis. TAC, pp. 367–417. Springer, Cham (2021). https://doi.org/10.1007/978-3-030-59234-9_11
7. Chong, C.T., Yang, Y.: Σ_2 induction and infinite injury priority argument, part I: maximal sets and the jump operator. J. Symb. Log. **63**(3), 797–814 (1998). https://doi.org/10.2307/2586713
8. Dorais, F.G., Dzhafarov, D.D., Hirst, J.L., Mileti, J.R., Shafer, P.: On uniform relationships between combinatorial problems. Trans. Am. Math. Soc. **368**(2), 1321–1359 (2016). https://doi.org/10.1090/tran/6465

9. Dzhafarov, D.D., Mummert, C.: Reverse Mathematics: Problems, Reductions, and Proofs. Springer, Heidelberg (2022). https://doi.org/10.1007/978-3-031-11367-3
10. Ershov, Y.L.: On computable enumerations. Algebra Log. **7**(5), 330–346 (1968). https://doi.org/10.1007/BF02219286
11. Ershov, Y.L.: Theory of Numberings. Nauka, Moscow (1977). In Russian
12. Ershov, Y.L.: Theory of numberings. In: Griffor, E.R. (ed.) Handbook of Computability Theory, Studies in Logic and the Foundations of Mathematics, vol. 140, pp. 473–503. North-Holland, Amsterdam (1999). https://doi.org/10.1016/S0049-237X(99)80030-5
13. Friedberg, R.M.: Three theorems on recursive enumeration. I. Decomposition. II. Maximal set. III. Enumeration without duplication. J. Symb. Log. **23**(3), 309–316 (1958). https://doi.org/10.2307/2964290
14. Friedman, H.: Some systems of second order arithmetic and their use. In: Proceedings of the International Congress of Mathematicians (Vancouver, B. C., 1974), vol. 1, pp. 235–242 (1975)
15. Goncharov, S.S., Sorbi, A.: Generalized computable numerations and nontrivial Rogers semilattices. Algebra Log. **36**(6), 359–369 (1997). https://doi.org/10.1007/BF02671553
16. Hájek, P., Pudlák, P.: Metamathematics of First-Order Arithmetic, Perspectives in Logic, vol. 3. Cambridge University Press, Cambridge (2017)
17. Hirschfeldt, D.R.: Slicing the Truth: On the Computable and Reverse Mathematics of Combinatorial Principles. World Scientific Publishing Co., Hackensack (2015)
18. Kleene, S.C.: Introduction to Metamathematics. Van Nostrand, New York (1952)
19. Kolmogorov, A.N., Uspenskii, V.A.: On the definition of an algorithm. Uspehi Mat. Nauk **13**(4), 3–28 (1958). In Russian
20. Li, W.: Friedberg numbering in fragments of Peano arithmetic and α-recursion theory. J. Symb. Log. **78**(4), 1135–1163 (2013). https://doi.org/10.2178/jsl.7804060
21. Marchenkov, S.S.: Existence of families without positive numerations. Math. Notes **13**(4), 360–363 (1973). https://doi.org/10.1007/BF01146576
22. Pour-El, M.B., Putnam, H.: Recursively enumerable classes and their application to recursive sequences of formal theories. Arch. Math. Logik Grundlagenforsch. **8**(3–4), 104–121 (1965). https://doi.org/10.1007/BF01976264
23. Rogers, H.: Gödel numberings of partial recursive functions. J. Symb. Logic **23**(3), 331–341 (1958). https://doi.org/10.2307/2964292
24. Simpson, S.G.: Subsystems of Second Order Arithmetic, 2nd edn. Cambridge University Press, Cambridge (2009)
25. Simpson, S.G., Yokoyama, K.: Reverse mathematics and Peano categoricity. Ann. Pure Appl. Logic **164**(3), 284–293 (2013). https://doi.org/10.1016/j.apal.2012.10.014

Two-Player Domino Games

Benjamin Hellouin de Menibus[1]([✉])[ID] and Rémi Pallen[2][ID]

[1] Université Paris-Saclay, CNRS, Laboratoire Interdisciplinaire des Sciences du
Numérique, 91400 Orsay, France
`hellouin@lisn.fr`
[2] Université Paris-Saclay, ENS Paris-Saclay, 91190 Gif-sur-Yvette, France
`remi.pallen@ens-paris-saclay.fr`
`https://lisn.upsaclay.fr/~hellouin`

Abstract. We introduce a 2-player game played on an infinite grid,
initially empty, where each player in turn chooses a vertex and colours
it. The first player aims to create some pattern from a target set, while
the second player aims to prevent it.

We study the problem of deciding which player wins, and prove that
it is undecidable. We also consider a variant where the turn order is
not alternating but given by a balanced word, and we characterise the
decidable and undecidable cases.

Keywords: Game · Tiling · Pattern · Computability · Symbolic
dynamics · Subshift · Tic-tac-toe

1 Introduction

We introduce the Domino game which is played on a grid $\mathbb{Z}^d$, initially empty.
Each player, in turn, picks a vertex for $\mathbb{Z}^d$ and a colour from a finite alphabet.
The first player A wins if some pattern from a finite target set is created, and
the second player B wins if this never happens. In particular, B wins only if the
game lasts forever.

Combinatorial games played on grids are extremely common, from chess to
go, and this game is strongly related to tic-tac-toe, gomoku, and their variants.
Studying such games on infinite grids is also a common topic – chess on an
infinite board [3,5], to give just an example – and brings specific computational
and game-theoretical challenges, such as deciding whether a player has a strategy
to win in finitely many moves. Even for relatively simple cases, such as tic-tac-
toe/gomoku where the target pattern consists of n crosses in a row, it is known
that A wins for $n = 5$ and loses for $n = 8$ [1,6] on an infinite grid, the intermediate
cases being well-known open questions.

This game is also motivated by symbolic dynamics: it is a two-player version
of the classical *Domino problem* that consists in deciding whether it is possible
to colour an infinite grid $\mathbb{Z}^d$ while avoiding a given set of patterns[1]. This problem

---

[1] The name "Domino game" has sometimes been used for the one-player version.

L. Levy Patey et al. (Eds.): CiE 2024, LNCS 14773, pp. 139–152, 2024.
https://doi.org/10.1007/978-3-031-64309-5_12

is known to be undecidable [2], so the two-player version was expected to be as well, but this game-theoretical perspective provides new questions to explore.

Several similar games have been studied, often under names such as "Domino game" or "tiling game": [4] is a seminal paper for tiling games in finite grids (see [11] for a survey), and [10] and follow-up papers for infinite grids. The main specificity of our variant is that players are not forced to play at a specific position at each turn.

In Sect. 3, we prove that the Domino game problem, which consists in deciding whether A has a winning strategy, is recursively enumerable-complete on infinite grids for $d \geq 2$, and in particular undecidable. We also show that, if A wins, then they have a strategy to win in bounded time (which is not the case in infinite chess, for example). In Sect. 4, we prove that a bounded-time variant is decidable. In Sect. 5, we consider a variant where the turn order is given by a word on $\{A, B\}$. For a given game, the set of turn order words where A wins is a subshift, similar to the *winning shift* in [10]. Our main result is a characterisation of which balanced turn orders make the Domino game problem decidable, often because one player always wins. We conclude with some additional remarks and open questions. Our undecidability proofs proceed by reduction to the classical Domino problem.

Those results shed new light on why it is so difficult to determine the winner for some concrete games, such as 6-in-a-row and 7-in-a-row tic-tac-toe.

2 Preliminaries

2.1 Subshifts

Let $\mathcal{A}$ be a finite set of colours called *alphabet*. A *configuration* on $\mathbb{Z}^d$ for $d > 0$ is an element $x \in \mathcal{A}^{\mathbb{Z}^d}$. A *cell* is an element $i \in \mathbb{Z}^d$ and a *tile* is a coloured cell $t \in \mathbb{Z}^d \times \mathcal{A}$. A *pattern* $p = (S, f)$ is given by a subset $S \subseteq \mathbb{Z}^d$ called the *support*, also denoted supp p, and a colouring $f \in \mathcal{A}^S$; equivalently, it is a disjoint set of tiles. The pattern is finite if S is finite, and $\emptyset$ denotes the empty pattern. A configuration x is also a pattern $(\mathbb{Z}^d, x)$. Given a pattern $p = (S, f)$ and $i \in S$, denote $p_i = f(i)$. The pattern $p' = (S', f')$ is a subpattern of p if $S' \subset S$ and $f|_{S'} = f'$.

For a set of finite patterns $\mathcal{F}$, we define

$$X_{\mathcal{F}} \stackrel{\Delta}{=} \{x \in \mathcal{A}^{\mathbb{Z}^d} \ : \ \forall p = (S, f) \in \mathcal{F}, \forall i \in \mathbb{Z}^d, \ (x_{|i+s})_{s \in S} \neq p\}$$

the set of configurations where no pattern from $\mathcal{F}$ appears. Such a set is called a *subshift*; if $\mathcal{F}$ is finite it is a *subshift of finite type (SFT)*. Patterns which have no subpattern in $\mathcal{F}$ are called *admissible*.

Let $d > 0$ and $E \subset \mathbb{Z}^d$. The *Domino problem* on E, DOMINO(E), is:

Input: A SFT $(\mathcal{A}, \mathcal{F})$ on $\mathbb{Z}^d$.
Question: Is there an admissible pattern p with supp$(p) = E$? In other words, is it possible to colour E without creating a pattern in $\mathcal{F}$?

2.2   Computability

A decision problem, such as the Domino problem above, is a function $I \to \{0,1\}$ where I (the input set) is countable. The following definitions depend on a choice of encoding $I \to \mathbb{N}$ for different input sets; since any reasonable encoding gives the same classes, we do not give explicit encodings in the paper. A decision problem R is in:

- Π_1^0 if there exists a decidable problem S such that $R(x) \Leftrightarrow \forall y\ S(x,y)$.
- Σ_1^0 if there exists a decidable problem S such that $R(x) \Leftrightarrow \exists y\ S(x,y)$.

We use *many-one reductions* to compare the computational complexity of decision problems. We denote $Q \leq P$ if there exists a computable function $f : \mathbb{N} \to \mathbb{N}$ such that $Q(x) \Leftrightarrow P(f(x))$ for all inputs x. A problem P is *C-hard* for a class C if $Q \leq P$ for all $Q \in C$. P is *C-complete* if P is C-hard and $P \in C$.

For example, Σ_1^0 is the class of recursively enumerable problems and the Domino problem on $\mathbb{Z}^d$, $d > 1$, is known to be Π_1^0-complete.

2.3   The Domino Game

Given $d > 0$, a subset $E \subseteq \mathbb{Z}^d$, an alphabet $\mathcal{A}$ and a finite set of finite patterns $\mathcal{F}$, we define the two-player *Domino game* $\Gamma(\mathcal{A}, \mathcal{F}, E)$.

The two players are denoted A and B. The state of the game at each turn, called *position*, is given by a pattern p with $\mathrm{supp}(p) \subset E$ together with a letter $\rho \in \{A, B\}$ indicating whose turn it is to play. In a given position $\alpha = (p, \rho)$, the current player ρ must play a *move* m. A move is either a pass (denoted $m = \mathrm{pass}$) or a choice of a cell $i \in E \setminus \mathrm{supp}\,p$ and a colour $a \in \mathcal{A}$ (denoted $m = (i, a)$). The new position is $\alpha' = (p', \overline{\rho})$ where:

- If $m = \mathrm{pass}$: $p' = p$.
- If $m = (i, a)$: $\mathrm{supp}\,p' = \mathrm{supp}\,p \cup \{i\}$, $p'_i = a$ and $p' = p$ on all other cells.
- $\overline{A} = B$ and $\overline{B} = A$ (alternate play).

We write $p \xrightarrow{m} p'$ when a move m changes a pattern p to a pattern p'.

A game starts from the position $\alpha_0 = (\emptyset, A)$, that is, every cell is uncoloured and A starts. A position (p, ρ) where some pattern from $\mathcal{F}$ appears in p is called *final*: the game ends and A wins. B wins if a final position never occurs. Therefore a *game* of length $\ell \in \mathbb{N}^* \cup \{\infty\}$ is a sequence of patterns $(p_t)_{t < \ell}$ such that:

- for all $t < \ell - 1$, there is a move m_t such that $p_t \xrightarrow{m_t} p_{t+1}$;
- if $t < \ell - 1$, p_t is not final;
- if $\ell < \infty$, either $p_{\ell-1}$ is final (A wins) or $\mathrm{supp}(p) = E$.

Notice that, if E is infinite, then B wins if and only if the game never ends.

2.4   Game Theory

Define inductively a position (p, ρ) to be *winning for A* (with value $v(p, \rho)$, which is an ordinal number) if:

- it is a final position (and $v(p, \rho) = 0$), or
- $\rho = A$, and there is a move $p \xrightarrow{m} p'$ with (p', B) winning for A (and $v(p, A) = \min v(p', B) + 1$, taken over all such moves), or
- $\rho = B$, and for all moves $p \xrightarrow{m} p'$, (p', A) is winning for A (and $v(p, B) = \sup v(p', A) + 1$, taken over all possible moves).

See [5] for more details on game values.

A *winning position for B* is a position which is not winning for A. The game is *winning for $\rho \in \{A, B\}$* if the *initial position* $(\emptyset, A)$ is winning for ρ. If the game is winning for A, the value of the game is the value of the initial position which may be infinite (as is the case with chess on an infinite grid [3,5]).

A *strategy* is a partial function[2] $\mathcal{S} : \mathcal{A}^{\mathcal{P}(E)} \to \mathcal{M}$, where $\mathcal{M}$ is the set of moves, such that $\mathcal{S}(p)$ is legal in p. We say that player ρ *applies a strategy* $\mathcal{S}_\rho$ during a game $(p_t)_{t<\ell}$ if $p_t \xrightarrow{\mathcal{S}_\rho(p_t)} p_{t+1}$ for every even t (if $\rho = A$), resp. every odd t (if $\rho = B$). A strategy $\mathcal{S}_\rho$ is a *winning strategy* for player ρ if ρ wins any game where ρ applies $\mathcal{S}_\rho$. It is easy to see that $\rho \in \{A, B\}$ has a winning strategy if and only if the initial position is a winning position for ρ.

3   Complexity of the Domino Game Problem

Definition 1 (The Domino game problem). *Given $d > 0$ and $E \subseteq \mathbb{Z}^d$, the Domino game problem on E, denoted* DGAME(E), *is defined as:*

Input: *A SFT $(\mathcal{A}, \mathcal{F})$ on $\mathbb{Z}^d$.*
Question: *Does A have a winning strategy for the game $\Gamma(\mathcal{A}, \mathcal{F}, E)$?*

Theorem 1. *The Domino game problem on $\mathbb{Z}^d$, $d > 1$, is Σ_1^0-complete, and in particular undecidable.*

We prove this result in two parts: Propositions 1 and 2.

3.1   Membership

Proposition 1. *For any $d > 0$,* DGAME($\mathbb{Z}^d$) *is in Σ_1^0.*

This follows from:

Lemma 1. *Let $(\mathcal{A}, \mathcal{F})$ be a SFT on $\mathbb{Z}^d$. B wins the game $\Gamma(\mathcal{A}, \mathcal{F}, \mathbb{Z}^d)$ if and only if B wins the game $\Gamma(\mathcal{A}, \mathcal{F}, [\![-n, n]\!]^d)$ for all $n \in \mathbb{N}^*$.*

---

[2] A strategy does not need to be defined on unreachable positions, e.g. infinite patterns.

Proof. If B has a winning strategy $\mathcal{S}$ for $\Gamma(\mathcal{A}, \mathcal{F}, \mathbb{Z}^d)$, $\mathcal{S}$ is also winning for $\Gamma(\mathcal{A}, \mathcal{F}, [\![-n, n]\!]^d)$ (passing when $\mathcal{S}$ outputs a move outside of $[\![-n, n]\!]^d$). Conversely, if B wins $\Gamma(\mathcal{A}, \mathcal{F}, [\![-n, n]\!]^d)$ which is a finite game, B has a *strongly winning* strategy $\mathcal{S}_n$, that is, applying the strategy wins the game from any winning position (not only the starting position).

To define a strategy $\mathcal{S}_\infty$ for $\Gamma(\mathcal{A}, \mathcal{F}, \mathbb{Z}^d)$ as a limit strategy of the sequence $(\mathcal{S}_n)$, since the space of possible moves $\mathbb{Z}^d \times \mathcal{A}$ is not compact, we consider pass as a point at infinity (one-point compactification). Concretely, $\mathcal{S}_\infty$ is a limit strategy of $(\mathcal{S}_n)$ if, and only if, on every pattern p:

- $\mathcal{S}_\infty(p) = (i, a)$ only if $\mathcal{S}_n(p) = (i, a)$ for infinitely many n;
- $\mathcal{S}_\infty(p) = \text{pass}$ only if $\mathcal{S}_n(p) = \text{pass}$ for infinitely many n, or if $\{\mathcal{S}_n(p) : n \in \mathbb{N}\}$ contains moves arbitrarily far from 0.

Notice that there may be multiple limit strategies. Let $(p_t)_{t \leq \ell}$, $\ell < \infty$ be the beginning of a game where B applies $\mathcal{S}_\infty$; we show that p_ℓ is not final, i.e. A cannot win. This is a finite sequence, so A played only in $[\![-n, n]\!]^d$ for some n.

The starting position p_0 is winning for B in $\Gamma(\mathcal{A}, \mathcal{F}, [\![-n, n]\!]^d)$, so p_1 is as well. By definition of $\mathcal{S}_\infty$, $\mathcal{S}_\infty(p_1)$ agrees with some strategy $\mathcal{S}_k(p_1)$ with $k \geq n$ when moves outside of $[\![-n, n]\!]^d$ are replaced by passes. $\mathcal{S}_k$ is strongly winning on $[\![-k, k]\!]^d$, so its restriction on $[\![-n, n]\!]^d$ is also strongly winning, and $p_2 = \mathcal{S}_\infty(p_1)$ is winning for B. Iterating this argument, we find that p_ℓ is winning for B, so p_ℓ is not final.

Corollary 1. *If the game $\Gamma(\mathcal{A}, \mathcal{F}, \mathbb{Z}^d)$ is winning for A, then it has a finite game value. In fact, A does not need to play outside $[\![-n, n]\!]^d$ for some n.*

The following result implies that there is no computable bound on n.

3.2   Hardness

Proposition 2. *For any $d > 0$, $\text{CODOMINO}(\mathbb{Z}^d) \leq \text{DGAME}(\mathbb{Z}^d)$. In particular, $\text{DGAME}(\mathbb{Z}^d)$ is Σ_1^0-hard when $d > 1$.*

Proof. We describe a computable transformation that to a SFT $(\mathcal{A}, \mathcal{F})$ on $\mathbb{Z}^d$ associates a SFT $(\mathcal{A}', \mathcal{F}')$ on $\mathbb{Z}^d$ such that $X_\mathcal{F} = \emptyset$ if and only if A has a winning strategy for the game $\Gamma(\mathcal{A}', \mathcal{F}', \mathbb{Z}^d)$.

Define $\mathcal{A}' = (\mathcal{A}^2 \times \{\leftarrow, \rightarrow\}) \cup \{\blacksquare\}$ (where $\blacksquare \notin \mathcal{A}$ is a fresh "black box" symbol). A colour $c \in \mathcal{A}' \backslash \{\blacksquare\}$ is given by $c = (\pi_1(c), \pi_2(c), \pi_3(c))$. Let $e_1 = (1, 0, \ldots, 0)$.

Let us define a notion of *interpretation*. Given a pattern p on the alphabet $\mathcal{A}'$, each cell i is *interpreted* by a set of colours $\iota_i(p)$ in $\mathcal{A}$ defined by:

- If $i \in \text{supp}(p)$ and $p_i \neq \blacksquare$, then $\pi_1 p_i \in \iota_i(p)$.
- If $i - e_1 \in \text{supp}(p)$ and $p_{i-e_1} \neq \blacksquare$ and $\pi_3 p_{i-e_1} = \rightarrow$, then $\pi_2 p_{i-e_1} \in \iota_i(p)$.
- If $i + e_1 \in \text{supp}(p)$ and $p_{i+e_1} \neq \blacksquare$ and $\pi_3 p_{i+e_1} = \leftarrow$, then $\pi_2 p_{i+e_1} \in \iota_i(p)$.

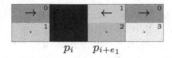

$$p_i \qquad p_{i+e_1}$$

Fig. 1. A pattern p on alphabet $\{0, 1, 2, 3, \blacksquare\}$, where $0, 1, 2, 3$ are represented by colors $\blacksquare^0, \blacksquare^1, \blacksquare^2, \blacksquare^3$, respectively. $\iota_i(p) = \{\blacksquare^0, \blacksquare^1\}$ and $\iota_{i+e_1}(p) = \{\blacksquare^2\}$.

Every cell has 0 to 3 interpretations. See Fig. 1 for an example.

By extension, for a pattern p' and $S \subset \mathbb{Z}^d$, define its set of interpretations $\iota_S(p')$ as the set of patterns $p \in \mathcal{A}^S$ such that $p \in \iota_S(p') \Leftrightarrow \forall i \in S, p_i \in \iota_i(p')$.

Assume without loss of generality that $\mathcal{F} \subset \mathcal{A}^{[\![-n,n]\!]^d}$ for some $n \in \mathbb{N}^*$. Let $\mathcal{F}'$ be the set of patterns $p' \in \mathcal{A}'^{[\![-n-1,n+1]\!]^d}$[3] such that $\iota_{[\![-n,n]\!]^d}(p') \subset \mathcal{F}$. We show that $X_{\mathcal{F}} = \emptyset$ if and only if A has a winning strategy for $\Gamma(\mathcal{A}', \mathcal{F}', \mathbb{Z}^d)$.

A cell i is said to be *surrounded* if $i - e_1$ and $i + e_1$ are coloured. Notice that, if a coloured surrounded cell has no interpretation (such as the center of $\blacksquare\blacksquare\blacksquare$), A eventually wins by playing around it until some pattern p' of support $[\![-n-1, n+1]\!]^d$ is created; $\iota_{[\![-n,n]\!]^d}(p') = \emptyset$, so $p' \in \mathcal{F}'$.

Assume that $X_{\mathcal{F}} = \emptyset$. We describe a winning strategy for A that maintains the following invariant: no cell has more than one interpretation, and every uncoloured cell has no interpretation.

First note that, assuming the invariant holds, if A plays $(i, \blacksquare)$ and i is surrounded, A wins since the cell i has no interpretation. Otherwise, B must play a tile at $i \pm e_1$ that gives an interpretation to i: if they do not and $i + e_1$ is not already coloured, A plays $(i + e_1, \blacksquare)$. Both i and $i + e_1$ have no interpretation, so A is able to create a surrounded cell with no interpretation next move and eventually wins. The other case is symmetric.

Notice that the move of B either loses quickly or provides an interpretation only to coloured cells that had no interpretation before, so such a move by A maintains the invariant.

The strategy of A is to play a $\blacksquare$ tile to a free cell closest to 0 unless B deviates as above. Let us prove that this strategy is winning for A.

By compactness, since $X_{\mathcal{F}} = \emptyset$, there exists an $m \in \mathbb{N}$ such that every pattern in $\mathcal{A}^{[\![-m,m]\!]^d}$ has a sub-pattern in $\mathcal{F}$. As a consequence, for any pattern $M \in \mathcal{A}'^{[\![-m-1,m+1]\!]^d}$, all interpretations in $\iota_{[\![-m,m]\!]^d}(M)$ contain a sub-pattern in $\mathcal{F}$. When A applies that strategy, some pattern p' from $\mathcal{A}'^{[\![-m-1,m+1]\!]^d}$ is eventually created. p' has a unique interpretation p, and p contains some subpattern $q \in \mathcal{F}$. Denoting $a + [\![-n,n]\!]^d = \text{supp}(q)$, the pattern $q' = p'|_{a+[\![-n-1,n+1]\!]}$ has a unique interpretation which is inadmissible. Therefore $q' \in \mathcal{F}'$ and A wins.

Assume that $X_{\mathcal{F}} \neq \emptyset$ and let $x \in X_{\mathcal{F}}$. We define a winning strategy for B based on the following invariant: before A plays, on every line of direction vector

---

[3] Choosing $[\![-n-1, n+1]\!] \times [\![-n,n]\!]^{d-1}$ as the support for forbidden patterns would be enough, but we made the support slightly larger for clarity.

e_1, every maximal connected set of uncoloured cells is either infinite or of even length. This invariant is true in the starting position $(\emptyset, A)$.

When A plays at (i, a), they split a maximal connected uncoloured set in two parts: one is even (possibly empty or infinite), the other is odd (nonempty, possibly infinite). If the odd set is to the right, B plays the colour $(x_{i+e_1}, x_i, \leftarrow)$ on the cell $i + e_1$, restoring the invariant. The other case is symmetric.

After B plays, every tile p_i admits the interpretation x_i. Since $x \in X_{\mathcal{F}}$, this gives an admissible interpretation to all patterns. This strategy is therefore winning for B.

4   Games with Bounded Time

In this section, we consider a variant where the number of turns is bounded.

Theorem 2. *The following problem is decidable: given $(\mathcal{A}, \mathcal{F}, E)$ and $T \in \mathbb{N}$, does A have a strategy to win the game $\Gamma(\mathcal{A}, \mathcal{F}, E)$ in T moves or less?*

In other words, we decide whether the game has value at most T. This cannot be proved by brute force since there are infinitely many moves in each position; still, the same phenomenon occurs e.g. for chess on infinite grids [3] for similar reasons. We will see that moves that are sufficiently far from other tiles are, in some sense, equivalent. We use the distance $d(i, j) = \sum_{k=1}^{d} |i_k - j_k|$ for $i, j \in \mathbb{Z}^d$.

We define a variant $\Gamma_T^{\omega}(\mathcal{A}, \mathcal{F}, E)$ whose positions are given by $((p^k)_{k \leq b}, \rho)$ where (p^k) is a finite sequence of patterns called *boards* and ρ is the current player. The initial position is $(\emptyset, A)$, where $\emptyset$ is the empty sequence. Possible moves are the following, where t denotes the number of the current turn:

- passing;
- adding a tile (i, a) to one of the boards p^k, if $d(i, \text{supp}(p^k)) \leq 2^{T-t}$;
- adding a new board $p^{b+1} = \{(0, a)\}$.

A position is final (and A wins) if a pattern from $\mathcal{F}$ appears on any board. After turn T, B wins if the position is not final.

Lemma 2. *The Domino game problem for the game Γ_T^{ω} is decidable.*

Proof. The number of turns is bounded and there are finitely many possible moves at each turn.

Lemma 3. *Assume for simplicity that all patterns of $\mathcal{F}$ are connected. There exists a transformation Θ from partial games for $\Gamma(\mathcal{A}, \mathcal{F}, \mathbb{Z}^d)$ to partial games for $\Gamma_T^{\omega}(\mathcal{A}, \mathcal{F}, \mathbb{Z}^d)$ of the same length. Furthermore, A wins $\Theta(g)$ if and only if A wins g.*

Proof. Denote $g = (p_t)_{t \leq T}$; we construct $\Theta(g) = ((p_t^k)_{k \leq b_t})_{t \leq T}$ by induction on t. We assign a vector $z_k \in \mathbb{Z}^d$ to each board p^k that is opened during the game $\Theta(g)$, and the following invariants will be preserved at each t:

1. $\mathrm{supp}(p_t) = \cup_{k \leq b_t}(z_k + \mathrm{supp}(p_t^k))$
2. $p_{t|z_k + \mathrm{supp}(p_t^k)} = p_t^k$.
3. $k \neq k' \Rightarrow d(z_k + \mathrm{supp}(p_t^k), z_{k'} + \mathrm{supp}(p_t^{k'})) > 2^{T-t}$.

If $t = 0$, then g and $\Theta(g)$ are the starting positions and all invariants hold.

If $0 < t \leq T$, let $g = g' \xrightarrow{m} p_t$, and define inductively $\Theta(g) = \Theta(g') \xrightarrow{m'} (p_t^k)_{k \leq b_t}$ as follows.

- If $m = \mathrm{pass}$, then $m' = \mathrm{pass}$.
- If $m = (i, a)$ and $d(i, \mathrm{supp}(p_{t-1})) > 2^{T-t}$, then m' opens a new board p^{b_t+1} and plays $(0, a)$. The new board is assigned the vector $z_{b_t+1} \stackrel{\Delta}{=} i$.
- If $m = (i, a)$ and $d(i, \mathrm{supp}(p_{t-1})) \leq 2^{T-t}$, then there is a unique k such that $d(i, z_k + \mathrm{supp}(p_{t-1}^k)) \leq 2^{T-t}$ by the first and third invariants. Then m' consists in playing $(i - z_k, a)$ on board p_t^k.

It is clear that Invariants 1 and 2 are preserved in each case. Invariant 3 is preserved for all boards k and k':

If m is on board k, then by construction

$$d(i, z_{k'} + \mathrm{supp}(p_{t-1}^{k'})) \geq d(z_k + \mathrm{supp}(p_{t-1}^k), z_{k'} + \mathrm{supp}(p_t^{k'})) - d(i, z_k + \mathrm{supp}(p_t^k))$$
$$> 2^{T-(t-1)} - 2^{T-t} = 2^{T-t}.$$

If m is on a different board,

$$\mathrm{supp}(p_t^k) = \mathrm{supp}(p_{t-1}^k) \text{ and } \mathrm{supp}(p_t^{k'}) = \mathrm{supp}(p_{t-1}^{k'}).$$

Patterns in $\mathcal{F}$ are assumed to be connected, and the invariants ensure that a connected pattern appears in p_T if and only if it appears in some board in $(p_T^k)_{k \leq b_T}$. Lemma 3 is proved.

Lemmas 2 and 3 imply Theorem 2 in the connected case, because A has a strategy to win $\Gamma(\mathcal{A}, \mathcal{F}, E)$ in T turns or less if and only if he wins on $\Gamma_T^\omega(\mathcal{A}, \mathcal{F}, E)$, which is decidable.

Indeed, Θ induces a transformation of strategies so that, if a strategy S is winning for A on $\Gamma(\mathcal{A}, \mathcal{F}, E)$ in T turns or less, then $\Theta(S)$ is winning for A on $\Gamma_T^\omega(\mathcal{A}, \mathcal{F}, E)$. Conversely, from a winning strategy S' on $\Gamma_T^\omega(\mathcal{A}, \mathcal{F}, E)$, it is easy to build a strategy S that is winning for A on $\Gamma(\mathcal{A}, \mathcal{F}, E)$ in T turns or less such that $\Theta(S) = S'$: S is entirely determined except for the choice of the z_k when a new board is opened, which can be given arbitrary values as long as they are far away from existing tiles.

The proof is easily adapted when patterns from $\mathcal{F}$ are not connected: let δ be the maximum diameter of a pattern from $\mathcal{F}$ and replace 2^{T-t} in Condition 3 by $\delta \cdot 2^{T-t}$. This ensure that all boards are always at least at distance δ from each other so that a forbidden pattern in g must be contained in a single board of $\Theta(g)$.

5   Non-alternating Play

We consider a variant where players do not play in alternation but according to a *turn order word* $s \in \{A, B\}^\omega$. The *non-alternating Domino game* $\Gamma_s(\mathcal{A}, \mathcal{F}, E)$ has the same rules as the standard Domino game $\Gamma(\mathcal{A}, \mathcal{F}, E)$, except that s_i is the current player at turn i. To keep track of the current player, positions are now given as (p, s), where p is a pattern, s_0 is the current player and every move shifts s by one letter.

For $d > 0$ and $s \in \{A, B\}^\omega$, the corresponding *non-alternating Domino game problem* NADGAME$_s(\mathbb{Z}^d)$ is defined as:

Input: A SFT $(\mathcal{A}, \mathcal{F})$ on $\mathbb{Z}^d$.
Question: Does A have a winning strategy for the game $\Gamma_s(\mathcal{A}, \mathcal{F}, \mathbb{Z}^d)$?

We begin with a few quick remarks.

Proposition 3. *Given $(\mathcal{A}, \mathcal{F}, E)$, the set of words s such that B wins the game $\Gamma_s(\mathcal{A}, \mathcal{F}, E)$ is a subshift.*

Proof. If A wins on $\Gamma_s(\mathcal{A}, \mathcal{F}, E)$, then the game value is finite, for the same reason as Corollary 1. Consequently, the winning strategy of A only depends on some prefix $s_{[0,t]}$. Let $W \subseteq \{A, B\}^*$ be the set of such prefixes on which A wins. Notice that if $w \in W$, then $vw \in W$ for any $v \in \{A, B\}^*$: starting at turn $|v| + 1$, A applies their winning strategy on w far away from existing tiles. Therefore B wins if, and only if, no pattern from W appears in s.

Proposition 4. *Given $d > 0$ and $w \in \{A, B\}^*$, NADGAME$_{wB^\omega}(\mathbb{Z}^d)$ is decidable.*

Proof. Use the same method as Theorem 2, noticing that A wins only if they win in $|w|$ moves or less.

Corollary 2. *If s is computable, NADGAME$_s(\mathbb{Z}^d)$ is recursively enumerable.*

Proof. If A wins, the game $\Gamma_s(\mathcal{A}, \mathcal{F}, \mathbb{Z}^d)$ has a finite value, so the problem is equivalent to finding $T \in \mathbb{N}$ such that A wins $\Gamma_{s_{[0,T]}B^\omega}(\mathcal{A}, \mathcal{F}, \mathbb{Z}^d)$.

Our main result covers the case where the turn order word is *balanced*.

Definition 2. *A word $s \in \{A, B\}^\omega$ is balanced if for all $i, j \in \mathbb{Z}$ and $n \in \mathbb{N}$, we have $|s_{[i,i+n]}|_A - |s_{[j,j+n]}|_A \in \{-1, 0, 1\}$.*

Balanced words are either ultimately periodic or Sturmian. They were first studied in [8]; see [7] (Chapter 2) for a modern exposition.

Proposition 5. *Let s be a balanced word. The number $\lim\limits_{n \to \infty} \frac{|s_{0,n}|_A}{n+1} \in [0, 1]$ exists and is called $f_A(s)$, the frequency of A in s.*

These games correspond to *Domino games with a budget*: from a budget b_i, A plays $\lfloor b_i \rfloor$ moves, B plays one move, and iterate with $b_{i+1} = b_i - \lfloor b_i \rfloor + \frac{f_A(s)}{1 - f_A(s)}$.

Theorem 3. *Let s be a balanced word.*

If $0 < f_A(s) \leq \frac{1}{2}$, then $co\text{DOMINO}(\mathbb{Z}^d) \leq \text{NADGAME}_s(\mathbb{Z}^d)$ *(and the problem is undecidable if $d \geq 2$). Otherwise,* $\text{NADGAME}_s(\mathbb{Z}^d)$ *is decidable.*

The rest of this section is devoted to proving this result case by case. For simplicity, we assume that all patterns in $\mathcal{F}$ are of support $[\![-n, n]\!]^d$.

Case $f_A(s) = 0$. There is at most one A in s, so this follows from Proposition 4.

Case $f_A(s) > \frac{1}{2}$. s contains infinitely many occurrences of AA. Since s is balanced, there is a bound k such that the distance between consecutive occurrences of AA is at most $2k + 1$.

For $c \in \mathbb{N}$, fix $v_n^c(k) = c(2k + 1)\frac{(k+1)^n - 1}{k}$. We prove by induction on n that for all pattern w composed by n cells and $\delta > 0$, A has a strategy such that, after $v_n^c(k)$ turns, there are c occurrences of w that are δ-isolated, that is, at distance δ from each other and all other tiles. The case $n = 0$ is trivial.

Take $\delta \in \mathbb{N}$, w composed by $n+1$ cells and w' some subpattern of w composed by n cells. By induction hypothesis, there is a strategy $\mathcal{S}$ so that, after $v_n^{c(k+1)}(k)$ turns, there are $c(k + 1)$ occurrences of w' that are $2\delta + 3$-isolated. Consider the following strategy:

1. during the first $v_n^{c(k+1)}(k)$ turns, apply $\mathcal{S}$.
2. during the next $c(2k + 1)$ turns, when A plays, A completes each occurrence of w' to an occurrence of w if possible, and passes otherwise.

Since s is balanced, B plays at most ck moves during the second phase. Since B cannot play at distance $\leq \delta$ of two occurrences in the same move, there are at least c occurrences of w that are still δ-isolated. This strategy took $v_n^{c(k+1)}(k) + c(2k + 1) = v_{n+1}^c(k)$ turns. This ends the induction.

A wins as long as $\mathcal{F} \neq \emptyset$ (which is decidable) by applying this strategy on $w \in \mathcal{F}$, $c = 1$ and $\delta = 1$.

Case $\frac{1}{2} \geq f_A(s) > \frac{1}{3}$. Since $f_A(s) \leq \frac{1}{2}$ and s is balanced, s contains at most one occurrence of the pattern AA. For clarity, we begin with the case where this does not occur. For a SFT $(\mathcal{A}, \mathcal{F})$, use the same reduction as in Proposition 2 (which corresponds to the case $s = (AB)^\omega$, with $f_A(s) = \frac{1}{2}$) to obtain $(\mathcal{A}', \mathcal{F}')$. We show that A wins on $\Gamma_s(\mathcal{A}', \mathcal{F}', \mathbb{Z}^d)$ if and only if $X_{\mathcal{F}} = \emptyset$, which implies $co\text{DOMINO}(\mathbb{Z}^d) \leq \text{NADGAME}_s(\mathbb{Z}^d)$.

When $X_{\mathcal{F}} \neq \emptyset$, B wins on $\Gamma_s(\mathcal{A}', \mathcal{F}', \mathbb{Z}^d)$ by applying the strategy outlined in the proof of Proposition 2 during all turns for B that come right after a turn for A, and passing on other turns.

When $X_{\mathcal{F}} = \emptyset$, we show that, for all m, A has a strategy to force the configuration to contain a pattern of length m with a single interpretation. This strategy wins for A for m large enough, just as in the proof of Proposition 2.

Since $\frac{1}{2} \geq f_A(s) > \frac{1}{3}$, BBB does not appear in s but ABA does, and the distance between consecutive occurrences of ABA is at most $3k + 2$ for some k.

By using the same technique as in the case $f_A(s) > \frac{1}{2}$, A forces the existence of c isolated areas where A played n moves and B played at most n moves in time $c(3k+2)\frac{(k+1)^n-1}{k}$. By only playing tiles ■, A forces this pattern to have at most one interpretation, which ends the proof.

We left the case of turn order words with a single occurrence of AA, that is, $B^{\{0,1\}}(AB)^*A(AB)^\omega$. We only give a proof sketch as this case is more tedious.

Put $\mathcal{A}' \triangleq \mathcal{A}^{11}\cup\{■\}$ and $e_1 = (1,0,\ldots,0)$. Given a pattern p on $\mathcal{A}'$, the tile at cell i "votes" for the interpretations of all tiles at cells $\{i+ke_1 : -5 \le k \le 5\}$ (a ■ tile does not vote) in the sense that the interpretation of i is the set of all colours that appear at least 4 times in the multiset $\{\pi_k p_{i+ke_1} : -5 \le k \le 5, \; p_{i+ke_1} \ne ■\}$. Again $\mathcal{F}'$ is the set of patterns p' such that $\iota_{[-n-5,n+5]^d}(p') \subset \mathcal{F}$.

If $X_\mathcal{F} = \emptyset$, A wins by playing only ■ and forcing a large pattern with a unique interpretation. Conversely, if $X_\mathcal{F} \ne \emptyset$, B chooses some $x \in X_\mathcal{F}$ and is able to force the interpretation x_i at every cell i, which we checked by computer enumeration of all local strategies for A.

Case $\frac{1}{3} \ge f_A(s) > 0$. Since s is balanced and $f_A(s) \le \frac{1}{3}$, there is no occurrence of the pattern AA and at most one occurrence of ABA. As above, we begin by the simpler case where there is no occurrence of ABA.

We reduce the codomino problem to the problem NADGAME$_s(\mathbb{Z}^d)$. Let $(\mathcal{A}, \mathcal{F})$ be a SFT. Let $\mathcal{A}' = \mathcal{A}^9 \cup \{■\}$.

Again, we define another notion of interpretation. Given a pattern p on $\mathcal{A}'$, each cell i is interpreted by the majority colour (with some arbitrary tiebreaker) in the multiset $\{\pi_k p_{i+ke_1} : -4 \le k \le 4, \; p_{i+ke_1} \ne ■\}$. A tile have no interpretation if all tiles in the neighbourhood are ■. Let $\mathcal{F}' \subseteq \mathcal{A}'^{[-n-4,n+4]^d}$ be the set of patterns p' such that $\iota_{[-n,n]^d} \subset \mathcal{F}$.

If $X_\mathcal{F} = \emptyset$, there exists by compactness an m such that no pattern in $\mathcal{A}^{[-m,m]^d}$ is admissible. Therefore all patterns in $\mathcal{A}'^{[-m-4,m+4]^d}$ have a subpattern in $\mathcal{F}'$. A wins by playing in $[-m-4,m+4]^d$ until a pattern from $\mathcal{F}'$ is created; notice that A plays infinitely often since $f_A(s) > 0$.

If $X_\mathcal{F} \ne \emptyset$, take $x \in X_\mathcal{F}$. We describe a strategy for B to play a majority of the tiles in $\{i+ke_1 : -4 \le k \le 4\}$ for every cell i, so B wins by choosing tiles such that each cell i has interpretation x_i. To make this clearer, we mark by a and b the cells where A and B play, respectively, and we show that B wins the game $\Gamma_s(\{a,b\}, \mathcal{F}_2, \mathbb{Z}^d)$ for $\mathcal{F}_2 = \{w \in \{a,b\}^9 : |w|_a \ge 5\}$. B uses the following strategy:

- if there is an uncoloured cell to the left or right of a tile a, B plays b there;
- if there is an uncoloured cell to the left of a pattern $baba$, B plays a b there;
- if there is an uncoloured cell to the right of a pattern $b(ba)^nb$ for $n \in \{3,4\}$, B plays b there;
- otherwise, B passes.

We can prove that the following invariants hold on every line before A plays:

1. Every a is in a pattern bab.
2. Every aba is in a pattern $bbaba$ or $b(ba)^nbb$ for $n \in \{3,4\}$.

After a move by A, B restores the invariants in two moves with this strategy. The pattern aa cannot appear by the first invariant. The only other problematic pattern from $\mathcal{F}_2$ is $abababab$, which violates the second invariant.

We left the case of words with a single occurrence of ABA. The same reduction works, using a neighbourhood of size 15 and $\mathcal{A}' = \mathcal{A}^{15} \cup \{\blacksquare\}$ rather than 9. B wins the game $\Gamma_s(\{a,b\}, \mathcal{F}_3, \mathbb{Z}^d)$ for $\mathcal{F}_3 = \{w \in \mathcal{A}_3^{15} : |w|_A \geq 8\}$ using a similar strategy. We check with a computer enumeration that the pattern $ababababababab$ cannot occur.

6   Remarks and Open Questions

Complexity of Winning Strategies. By Corollary 1, given a game $\Gamma(\mathcal{A}, \mathcal{F}, E)$ winning for A, there is a computable winning strategy for A. However, the same is not true for B.

Take a nonempty SFT whose configurations are all uncomputable [9]. Apply the reduction for Proposition 2 to get a game $\Gamma(\mathcal{A}', \mathcal{F}', \mathbb{Z}^d)$ where B has a winning strategy. A can apply the (computable) strategy provided in the same proof so that B avoids losing only if arbitrarily large admissible patterns are constructed; that is, we compute some $x \in X_{\mathcal{F}}$ from any winning strategy of B. Therefore A has a computable strategy which is not winning, but beats every computable strategy for B.

Variant Without Pass and Zugzwang. We consider a variant $\Gamma^*(\mathcal{A}, \mathcal{F}, E)$ where players are not allowed to pass. Proposition 2 holds in this variant as the proof does not require any player to pass, so the problem remains undecidable on $\mathbb{Z}^d$ for $d \geq 2$. However, the proof of Proposition 1 requires B to pass.

Question 1. Is the Domino game problem without passes Σ_1^0 (recursively enumerable)?

A does not benefit from passing, so any winning strategy for A in $\Gamma(\mathcal{A}, \mathcal{F}, E)$ also wins for $\Gamma^*(\mathcal{A}, \mathcal{F}, E)$. When $\mathcal{A} = \{0,1\}$ and $\mathcal{F} = \{000, 111\}$, the position $(\emptyset, B)$ is *Zugzwang*: B loses in Γ^* and wins in Γ by passing. However, can the winner depend on the variant in the starting position $(\emptyset, A)$?

Question 2. Is there a SFT $(\mathcal{A}, \mathcal{F})$ such that A wins in $\Gamma^*(\mathcal{A}, \mathcal{F}, E)$ and loses in $\Gamma(\mathcal{A}, \mathcal{F}, E)$?

Conjecture 1. Let $\mathcal{A}_n = \{0, \ldots, n\}$ and $\mathcal{F}_n = \{\text{palindromes of length } 2n + 1\} \cup \{iii : i \in \mathcal{A}_n\}$. $\Gamma^*(\mathcal{A}_n, \mathcal{F}_n, \mathbb{Z})$ is winning for A. We conjecture that $\Gamma(\mathcal{A}_n, \mathcal{F}_n, \mathbb{Z})$ is winning for B for n large enough.

A has a simple winning strategy for all games $\Gamma^*(\mathcal{A}_n, \mathcal{F}_n, \mathbb{Z})$ that we outline below. A also has a winning strategy for $\Gamma(\mathcal{A}_5, \mathcal{F}_5, \mathbb{Z})$ which is much more complicated and we do not think such strategies exist for all n.

1. On the empty position, play $(0,0)$.
2. If B plays (k,a) for some $k > 0$ (the other case is symmetric),
   (a) if $k-1$ contains a tile, play $(-k,a)$.
   (b) otherwise, play $(k+1,a)$. Next turn, play either $(k-1,a)$ or $(k+2,a)$.

If case 2(b) never occurs, then B and A fill progressively $[\![-n,n]\!]$ with a palindrome. Otherwise, the first time 2(b) occurs, the cell $k+2$ must be uncoloured (otherwise 2(b) would have occured earlier), so A makes a pattern aaa.

Question 3. Is there a SFT $(\mathcal{A},\mathcal{F})$ such that $\Gamma^*(\mathcal{A},\mathcal{F},\mathbb{Z}^d)$ is winning for A with an infinite game value?

For such an SFT, A would have a winning strategy, but for all $t \in \mathbb{N}$, B would have a strategy $\mathcal{S}_T$ to not lose before time T. This cannot happen for Γ by Corollary 1, so this would also answer Question 2. It may be also the case that $\Gamma^*(\mathcal{A},\mathcal{F},\mathbb{Z}^d)$ has some countable ordinal larger than ω as a game value.

Complexity for $d=1$. Since DOMINO($\mathbb{Z}$) is decidable, Proposition 2 says nothing for this case. The variant studied in [10], where players must play at prescribed positions, is decidable on $\mathbb{Z}$. The fact that, in our variant, players are allowed to play arbitrarily far from other tiles makes this case more challenging.

Conjecture 2. The Domino game problem is decidable on $\mathbb{Z}$.

Complexity in Bounded Space. Consider the Domino game problem for a finite subset whose size is given as input:

Input: An integer n given in unary and a SFT $(\mathcal{A},\mathcal{F})$ on $\mathbb{Z}^d$.
Question: Does A have a winning strategy for the game $\Gamma(\mathcal{A},\mathcal{F},[\![-n,n]\!]^d)$?

A brute-force algorithm solves this problem in polynomial space. The corresponding Domino problem on $[\![-n,n]\!]^d$ is known to be NP-complete (see the seed-free variant of the problem $TILING(n,n)$ in [11]), so this problem can be shown to be NP-hard by using the same reduction as for Proposition 2. We conjecture that the Domino game problem is strictly harder than the Domino problem in the finite case, similarly as for other variants [4]:

Conjecture 3. The finite Domino game problem is $PSPACE$-complete.

Domino Games on Groups. SFT can be defined on other finitely generated groups G, and we can play the Domino game on G as well. Proposition 1 holds by considering the Domino game problem on the central ball of radius n of the Cayley graph, assuming the word problem on G is decidable. The first part of Proposition 2 holds (coDOMINO(G) $\leq$ DGAME(G)) if G has an element with infinite order, so that every cell belongs to a copy of $\mathbb{Z}$.

Non-balanced Turn Order. This case seems more combinatorial and difficult. Arbitrary infinite words do not have densities, but even when they do, they are not sufficient to determine the decidability status. As long as a turn order word s contains occurrences of A^n for all n, the Domino game is always winning for A, and this can happen for any density $f_A(s)$. Therefore, for $f_A(s) \leq \frac{1}{2}$, the Domino game problem with turn order s may be decidable or undecidable. We conjecture that the first part of the proof of Theorem 3 can be adapted to show that:

Conjecture 4. The Domino game is always winning for A when the turn order word s satisfies $f_A(s) > \frac{1}{2}$.

Acknowledgements. The authors received financial support from IZES, an ANR project.

References

1. Allis, L.V., van den Herik, H.J., Huntjens, M.P.H.: Go-Moku solved by new search techniques. Comput. Intell. **12** (1996). https://doi.org/10.1111/j.1467-8640.1996.tb00250.x
2. Berger, R.: The Undecidability of the Domino Problem. Memoirs of the American Mathematical Society. American Mathematical Society (1966)
3. Brumleve, D., Hamkins, J.D., Schlicht, P.: The mate-in-n problem of infinite chess is decidable (2012)
4. Chlebus, B.S.: Domino-tiling games. J. Comput. Syst. Sci. **32**, 374–392 (1986). https://doi.org/10.1016/0022-0000(86)90036-X
5. Evans, C.D.A., Hamkins, J.D.: Transfinite game values in infinite chess (2014)
6. Hsu, W.Y., Ko, C.L., Chen, J.C., Wei, T.H., Hsueh, C.H., Wu, I.C.: On solving the 7,7,5-game and the 8,8,5-game. Theor. Comput. Sci. **815**, 79–94 (2020). https://doi.org/10.1016/j.tcs.2020.02.023
7. Lothaire, M.: Algebraic Combinatorics on Words, vol. 90. Cambridge University Press, Cambridge (2002)
8. Morse, M., Hedlund, G.: Symbolic Dynamics II: Sturmian Trajectories. Johns Hopkins University Press (1940)
9. Myers, D.: Nonrecursive tilings of the plane. II. J. Symb. Log. **39**, 286–294 (1974). https://doi.org/10.2307/2272641
10. Salo, V., Törmä, I.: Playing with subshifts. Fundam. Inform. **132**, 131–152 (2014). https://doi.org/10.3233/fi-2014-1037
11. Schwarzentruber, F.: The complexity of tiling problems. CoRR abs/1907.00102 (2019). http://arxiv.org/abs/1907.00102

Almost Sure OTM-Realizability

Merlin Carl[(✉)]

Institut für Mathematik, Europa-Universität Flensburg, Flensburg, Germany
`merlin.carl@uni-flensburg.de`

Abstract. Combining the approaches made in works with Galeotti and Passmann, we define and study a notion of "almost sure" realizability with parameter-free ordinal Turing machines (OTMs). In particular, we show that, in contrast to the classical case, almost sure realizability differs from plain realizability, while closure under intuitionistic predicate logic and realizability of Kripke-Platek set theory continue to hold.

1 Introduction

Kleene realizability is one of the most prominent interpretations for intuitionistic logic. However, by its reliance on Turing computability, it is limited to finite objects and procedures and not adapted to notions of generalized or "relaxed" effectivity, as described, e.g., in Hodges [9]. Therefore, a number of variants of Kleene realizability has been defined, among them one which is based on computability with Koepke's ordinal Turing machines (OTMs) [11] rather than Turing machines (see [7]). On the other hand, in [8], a "randomized" version of realizability was investigated, in which realizers are merely supposed to work with high probability relative to a random oracle. One of the results of [8] (Theorem 25) is that, due to Sacks' theorem (see, e.g., [6], Corollary 8.12.2), requiring random realizers to work with probability 1 leads back to classical realizability.

In this paper, we combine the two variants by considering a randomized version of OTM-realizability. Although the analogue of Sacks' theorem for OTMs is consistent with ZFC by ([5], Sects. 2.1 and 2.3), it turns out that randomized OTM-realizability with probability 1 is still different from "plain" OTM-realizability. This yields the notion of "almost sure OTM-realizability" (as-OTM-realizability).

We find that as-OTM-realizability enjoys similar features to the concept of OTM-realizability studied in [8]: In particular, we will show that as-OTM-realizability is sound for the deduction rules of intuitionistic predicate calculus and that all axioms of Kripke-Platek set theory are as-OTM-realizable, while some axioms of ZFC that go beyond KP are not. Thus, as-OTM-realizability at least captures Lubarsky's intuitionistic KP (IKP), see [10,12].

There does not seem to be a meaningful analogue of Lebesgue measurability, and thus of randomness, for domains that go beyond the real numbers, see, e.g. chapter 5 of [17].[1] Thus, our random oracles will be real numbers. Since the

---

[1] We thank Lorenzo Galeotti for pointing out this reference to us.

© The Author(s), under exclusive license to Springer Nature Switzerland AG 2024
L. Levy Patey et al. (Eds.): CiE 2024, LNCS 14773, pp. 153–165, 2024.
https://doi.org/10.1007/978-3-031-64309-5_13

random objects should be on par with the objects in the realm under consideration, we will restrict ourselves in this paper to statements about H_{ω_1}, the set of heriditarily countable sets, as precisely these sets can be encoded as real numbers.[2] Thus, unless stated otherwise, quantifiers will range over H_{ω_1} below. We recall that $(H_{\omega_1})^L = L_{\omega_1^L}$.

Most results in this paper are analogous to results obtained in joint work with Robert Passmann and Lorenzo Galeotti for (non-randomized) OTM-realizability [7] and randomized (classical) realizability [8], although our definition of randomized OTM-realizability differs in several respect from what a straightforward combination of these two approaches would look like.

2   Definitions and Basic Results

We briefly recall Koepke's OTMs (introduced in detail in [11]) for the sake of the reader; an OTM can be thought of as a Turing machine with a class-sized type of length On with time indexed by On, where the tape contents, the inner state and the head position are determined as the inferior limits of the sequence of earlier values at limit times.

For an OTM-program P, we write $P^x(y) \downarrow = z$ to indicate that P, when run on input y in the oracle x, halts with output z; if x or y are omitted, we mean the computation is started in the empty oracle or on the empty tape; if z is omitted, we mean that the computation stops without specifying the output. We fix a computable[3] enumeration $(P_i : i \in \omega)$ of OTM-programs. Moreover, we fix a natural enumeration $(\phi_i : i \in \omega)$ of $\in$-formulas and denote by $\lceil \phi \rceil$ the index of ϕ in this enumeration.

For x and y real numbers, we define $x \oplus y$ as $\{2i : i \in x\} \cup \{2j + 1 : j \in y\}$; more generally, for $x_0, ..., x_n$ real numbers, we define $\bigoplus_{i=0}^{0} x_i := x_0$ and $\bigoplus_{i=0}^{n} x_i := x_0 \oplus \bigoplus_{i=1}^{n} x_i$ for $n > 2$.

In order to pass sets as inputs to OTMs, these need to be encoded as sets of ordinals. This can be done as described in [3], Definition 2.3.18. However, since what we are after is a notion of realizability on sets, not set codes, we will require our programs to behave independently of the specific code given to them:

Definition 1. *An OTM-program P is coding-stable if and only if, for all sets $a_1, ..., a_n$, and all sets of ordinals $c_1^0, ..., c_n^0$ and $c_1^1, ..., c_n^1$ coding $a_1, ..., a_n$, $P^{c_1^0, ..., c_n^0}$ halts if and only if $P^{c_1^1, ..., c_n^1}$ does and moreover, if c^0 is the output of the first computation and c^1 is the output of the second computation, then c^0 and c^1 encode the same set.*

We say that P is safe if and only if, for all sets of ordinals x and y, $P^x(y)$ halts.

---

[2] Whether or not there is an interesting theory of OTM-realizability relative to random oracles on arbitrary sets is a question that we postpone to future work.

[3] More precisely, this means that the function mapping a program – regarded as a string – to its index should be recursive.

One of the technical advantages of coding stability is that we can abuse our notation and confuse sets with their codes in the discussion. Thus, when P is coding-stable and x, y are sets, we write $P^x(y)$ for the set coded by the output of P^x run with y on the input tape; in particular, this means that this computation halts.

The definition of as-OTM-realizability is adapted from the definition of "big realizability" in [8] to OTMs.

Definition 2. *Denote by $\mathfrak{P}(X)$ the power set of a set X. For $X \subseteq \mathfrak{P}(\omega)$, denote by $\mu(X)$ the Lebesgue measure of X, if it exists. Let $\mathcal{B}$ denote the set of $X \subseteq \mathfrak{P}(\omega)$ such that $\mu(X) = 1$.*

We will define what it means for a pair $(P, \vec{p}) = (P, (p_1, ..., p_n))$ to as-OTM-realize an $\in$-statement $\phi(\vec{x}, \vec{a})$, where $\vec{x}$ is a list of free variables and $\vec{a}$ is a list of set parameters. P will always be a safe and coding-stable OTM-program, while $p_1, ..., p_n$ will be a tuple of (codes for) hereditarily countable sets; for simplicity, we will assume that $p_1, ..., p_n$ are always real numbers.[4]

If $\phi(\vec{x}, \vec{a})$ contains free variables, then $(P, \vec{p}) \Vdash_{as}^{OTM} \phi(\vec{x}, \vec{a})$ if and only if $(P, \vec{p}) \Vdash_{as}^{OTM} \forall \vec{x} \phi(\vec{a})$, where the latter is defined as below.

We can thus focus on the case that ϕ does not contain free variables.

1. *If ϕ is atomic, then $(P, \vec{p}) \Vdash_{as}^{OTM} \phi(\vec{a})$ if and only if $\phi(\vec{a})$ is true.*
2. *If ϕ is $\psi_0 \wedge \psi_1$, then $(P, \vec{p}) \Vdash_{as}^{OTM} \phi(\vec{a})$ if and only if there is a set $\mathcal{O} \in \mathcal{B}$ such that, for all $x \in \mathcal{O}$, $P^{\vec{p}, \vec{a}, x}(i) \Vdash_{as}^{OTM} \psi_i(\vec{a})$ for $i \in \{0, 1\}$.*
3. *If ϕ is $\psi_0 \vee \psi_1$, then $(P, \vec{p}) \Vdash_{as}^{OTM} \phi(\vec{a})$ if and only if there is a set $\mathcal{O} \in \mathcal{B}$ such that, for all $x \in \mathcal{O}$, $P^{\vec{p}, \vec{a}, x}(0)$ terminates with output $i \in \{0, 1\}$ and $P^{\vec{p}, \vec{a}, x}(1) \Vdash_{as}^{OTM} \psi_i(\vec{a})$.[5]*
4. *If ϕ is $\psi_0 \rightarrow \psi_1$, then $(P, \vec{p}) \vdash_{as}^{OTM} \phi(\vec{a})$ if and only if, for every as-OTM-realizer s of $\psi_0(\vec{a})$, there is a set $\mathcal{O} \in \mathcal{B}$ such that, for all $x \in \mathcal{O}$, $P^{\vec{p}, \vec{a}, x}(s) \Vdash_{as}^{OTM} \psi_1(\vec{a})$.[6]*
5. *If ϕ is $\neg \psi$, then $(P, \vec{p}) \Vdash_{as}^{OTM} \phi(\vec{a})$ if and only if $(P, \vec{p}) \Vdash \phi \rightarrow (1 = 0)$.*
6. *If ϕ is $\exists y \psi(y)$, then $(P, \vec{p}) \Vdash_{as}^{OTM} \phi(\vec{a})$ if and only if there is $\mathcal{O} \in \mathcal{B}$ such that, for all $x \in \mathcal{O}$, we have:*

$$P^{\vec{p}, \vec{a}, x}(0) \Vdash_{as}^{OTM} \psi(P^{\vec{p}, \vec{a}, x}(1), \vec{a}).$$

7. *If ϕ is $\forall y \psi$, then $(P, \vec{p}) \Vdash_{as}^{OTM} \phi(\vec{a})$ if and only if, for every set b, there is $\mathcal{O}_b \in \mathcal{B}$ such that, for all $x \in \mathcal{O}_b$, we have that $P^{\vec{p}, \vec{a}, b, x} \Vdash \psi(b)$.*

---

[4] In order not to clutter our notation with iterated indices, the tuple of parameters will always consist of n entries, although, of course, the number of parameters is variable.

[5] Here, we deviate conceptually from the definition in [8] by allowing that, for different oracles, the disjuncts to be realized may also differ.

[6] Intuitively, the random real helping with the realization is only chosen after the evidence for the premise of the implication was obtained. This again deviates from the definition in [8].

Bounded quantifiers will be interpreted in the usual way – i.e., $\exists x \in a\phi(x)$ as $\exists x(x \in a \wedge \phi(x))$ and $\forall x \in a\phi(x)$ as $\forall x(x \in a \rightarrow \phi(x))$ – and interpreted accordingly using the above clauses.

In all clauses expect (1), some input ξ is given to the program. We call this a relevant input for $(P, \vec{p})$ and ϕ (thus, e.g. in the case of conjunction, the relevant input can be 0 or 1). For the sake of uniformity, we make the convention that the relevant input for atomic formulas is 0.

In the cases (2), (3) and (6), the set $\mathcal{O}$ is called a success set of $(P, \vec{p})$ for ϕ; in (4), (5) and (7), $\mathcal{O}_z$ is called a z-success set of $(P, \vec{p})$ for ϕ, denoted $succ^z_{(P,\vec{p})}(\phi)$. Again, in order to allow for a uniform treatment of all cases, we speak of the ξ-success set of $(P, \vec{p})$ for ϕ in all cases, where ξ is a relevant input. In the cases (2), (3) and (6), $succ^\xi_{(P,\vec{p})}(\phi)$ will thus not depend on ξ. By convention, $succ^\xi_{(P,\vec{p})}(\phi) = \mathfrak{P}(\omega)$ for atomic ϕ. The formula ϕ will not be mentioned if it is clear from the context, which is usually the case, in which case will talk about the ξ-success set of $(P, \vec{p})$ and drop the argument ϕ.

We say that a formula $\phi(\vec{a})$ with parameters $\vec{a}$ is as-OTM-realizable if and only if there is an OTM-program P such that $(P, \vec{a}) \Vdash^{OTM}_{as} \phi(\vec{a})$.[7]

Remark 3. Note that it is not OTM-decidable whether or not a program is an as-OTM-realizer. However, this is no different from classical realizability: Determining, e.g., determining whether a program P classically realizes $\forall x(x = x)$ is equivalent to determining whether P halts.

Dropping all mentions of oracles in this definition, one obtains the definition of *plain* OTM-realizability, a variant of which was discussed in [4], and another variant for infinitary logic in [7].

Remark 4. Besides requiring a success probability of 1, this definition also differs conceptually from the one used in [8] in the treatment of implication and universal quantification: The definition in [8] require an oracle that, with high probability, worked for all instances, while in the present setting, the oracle is only chosen *after* the instance. In our opinion, both versions have a certain intuitive appeal as an expression of the intuitive idea of "realizing relative to a random oracle": On the one hand, it may appear overly strict to insist on one oracle working for all instances. On the other hand, if one pictures applying an as-OTM-realizer to continuum many instances of a universally quantified formula by randomly picking a new oracle in each case, then intuitively, the chances of landing outside of the success set at least once may be large. However, it turns out the version presented here has much more convenient properties.

Lemma 5. *For each $\in$-formula ϕ and each tuple $\vec{p}$ of real numbers, the following are true:*

---

[7] Thus, the program is initially only allowed to access those parameters contained in the formula, but not others. Note, however, that, in the clause for implication, the as-OTM-realizers for the antecedent are allowed to use arbitrary parameters.

1. *The set of as-OTM-realizers of $\phi(\vec{p})$ is analytical in $\vec{p}$; in other words, the statement "$r \Vdash_{as}^{OTM} \phi(\vec{p})$ is Σ_n^1 in the parameter $\vec{p}$ for some $n \in \omega$.*
2. *For every relevant input ξ and every pair $\tau := (P, \vec{q})$ with P a safe and coding-stable OTM-program and $\vec{q}$ a parameter, $succ_\tau^\xi(\phi)$ is projective.*

Proof. We prove this by a simultaneous induction on formulas, ignoring the parameter $\vec{p}$.

- Suppose that ϕ is atomic. Then $r \Vdash_{as}^{OTM} \phi$ is equivalent to ϕ, which is Σ_1^0; thus, we have (1). Moreover, we have $\xi - succ_r(\phi) = \mathfrak{P}(\omega)$ whenever $r \Vdash_{as}^{OTM} \phi$, which is clearly projective.
- Suppose that ϕ is $(\psi_0 \wedge \psi_1)$. Then $r_{as}^{OTM} \Vdash_{as}^{OTM} \phi$ is equivalent to the statement "There exists a set $\mathcal{O}$ of measure 1 such that, for all $x \in \mathcal{O}$, there are OTM-computations $r^x(0) \downarrow = r_0$, $r^x(1) \downarrow = r_1$ satisfying $r_0 \Vdash_{as}^{OTM} \psi_0$ and $r_1 \Vdash_{as}^{OTM} \psi_1$". By induction, the statements $r_0 \Vdash_{as}^{OTM} \psi_0$ and $r_1 \Vdash_{as}^{OTM} \psi_1$ are Σ_n^1, for some $n \in \omega$. The existence of halting OTM-computations is also thus expressible, due to the fact that halting OTM-computations on real inputs will be countable, and thus themselves encodeable as real numbers. Finally, stating the existence of a set $\mathcal{O}$ of measure 1 amounts to stating that there is a null set $\overline{\mathcal{O}}$ such that the claim in question holds for all $x \notin \overline{\mathcal{O}}$; but the existence of a null set can be expressed as in the proof of Lemma 14 below by stating the existence of a real number coding an appropriate sequence of interval sequences. Thus, we have (1). To see (2), let $\tilde{r}$ be the OTM-program that, in the oracle x, simulates $r^x(i)$, for $i \in \{0, 1\}$. Thus, for all ξ, we have that $succ_r^\xi(\phi) = succ_{r_0}^\xi(\psi_0) \cap succ_{r_1}^\xi(\psi_1)$ is projective as an intersection of two projective sets.
- If ϕ is $(\psi_0 \vee \psi_1)$, we proceed as in the last case, replacing "and" with "or" in (1) and "$\cap$" with "$\cup$" in (2).

In the remaining cases, the techniques explained in the conjunction case can be straightforwardly applied, in combination with the respective inductive assumptions, to express the respective clauses of the definition in the desired way.

Lemma 6. *(Cf. [7], Lemma 22) There is an OTM-program $P_{eff-\Pi_2}$ that, for a true formula ϕ of the form $\forall x \exists y \psi$, where ψ is Δ_0, $P_{eff-\Pi_2}(\lceil \phi \rceil)$ outputs a plain OTM-realizer for ϕ which is also an as-OTM-realizer for ϕ.*

Consequently, the following are equivalent for such ϕ:

1. *ϕ is plainly OTM-realizable.*
2. *ϕ is as-OTM-realizable.*
3. *ϕ is true in H_{ω_1}.*

We observe that as-OTM-realizability differs from plain OTM-realizability:

Theorem 7. *There is an $\in$-sentence ϕ such that $\not\Vdash_{OTM} \phi$, but $\Vdash_{as-OTM} \phi$.*

Proof. The proof is an adaptation of the example for the case of randomized Turing-computability in [8], Theorem 14, which somewhat simplifies in the transfinite setting.[8]

---

[8] Also note that the example in [8] only guarantees a positive success probability, but not probability 1.

Let ϕ be the sentence stating the existence of an OTM-incomputable real number, i.e., "There is a real number x such that, for all natural numbers k and all ordinals α, the following holds: P_k does not halt in α many steps with output x".

It is clear that ϕ is not plainly OTM-realizable; for to realize ϕ, one would have to compute a real number x witnessing the existential statement on an OTM. However, if P_k was a program halting with output x after, say, α many steps, this would contradict the statement ϕ.

To see that ϕ is, however, as-OTM-realizable, note that there are only countably many OTM-computable real numbers (as there are only countably many OTM-programs), so that the set of OTM-incomputable real numbers has measure 1. For each such real number x, the remaining statement that for all $k \in \omega$, all ordinals α and all computations of P_k of length α, P_k does not terminate in α many steps with output x is of the form $\forall x \psi$, where ψ is Δ_0, so that we can apply Lemma 6.

We can generalize this argument somewhat:

Definition 8. *For a set x of ordinals, σ^x denotes the first stable ordinal relative to x, i.e., the minimal ordinal α such that $L_\alpha[x]$ is a Σ_1-submodel of $L[x]$.*[9]

We recall some basic information about the function $x \mapsto \sigma^x$.

Lemma 9. *Let x be a set of ordinals.*

1. *If x is a real number, σ^x is countable.*
2. *σ^x is the supremum of the halting times of parameter-free OTMs with oracle x.*
3. *σ^x is the supremum of the ordinals that have OTM-computable codes in the oracle x.*
4. *A set of ordinals y is OTM-computable relative to x if and only if $y \in L_{\sigma^x}[x]$.*

Proof. (1) is folklore. (2)–(4) are implicit in the work of Koepke and elaborated, e.g., in [3], proof of Lemma 3.5.2.

Corollary 10. *Let ψ be the statement "For each real number x, there is a real number y such that y is not OTM-computable from x". Then ψ is not OTM-realizable, but as-OTM-realizable.*

Proof. It follows immediately from Lemma 9.4 that ψ is not OTM-realizable, as setting $x = 0$ in ψ makes the ϕ from the proof of Theorem 7 a special case of ψ.

To see that ψ is as-OTM-realizable, note that, by Lemma 9.1, σ^x is a countable ordinal, so that $L_{\sigma^x}[x]$ is countable, which means that $\mu(\mathbb{R} \setminus L_{\sigma^b}[b]) = 1$. The rest works as in the proof of Theorem 7.

Assuming $V = L$, we can give an even more natural example, using Corollary 11 in [5], according to which, under $V = L$, the halting problem for OTMs is solvable by an OTM with a random oracle with probability 1.

---

[9] See, e.g., [1], Theorem 8.2.

Definition 11. *Let $a \subseteq \omega$.*

- *Define $h_0 := a$, $h_{n+1}^a := \{i \in \omega : P_i^{h_n^a} \downarrow\}$ for $n \in \omega$. We call h_n^a the n-th iterated OTM-halting problem relative to a or the n-th OTM-jump of a. If $a = \emptyset$, the superscript is dropped.*
- *Define $h^{as,a} := a$, $h_{n+1}^{as,a} := \{i \in \omega : \mu(\{x \subseteq \omega : P_i^{h_n^{as,a},x} \downarrow\}) = 1\}$ for $n \in \omega$. Thus, in particular $h_1^{as,a}$ is the set of OTM-programs that halt relative to a and a randomly chosen oracle x with probability 1. We call $h_i^{as,a}$ the i-th iterated as-OTM-halting problem relative to a.*

If $a = \emptyset$, the superscript is dropped.

Definition 12. *We say that $b \subseteq \omega$ is as-OTM-computable relative to $a \subseteq \omega$ if and only if there are an OTM-program P and a set $X \in \mathcal{B}$ such that, for all $x \in X$, $P^x(a) \downarrow = b$.*

We note that the jump operator works as expected:

Lemma 13. *Let $a \subseteq \omega$.*

1. *h_1^a is not OTM-computable relative to a.*
2. *$h_1^{as,a}$ is not as-OTM-computable relative to a.*

Proof. (1) is folklore and works exactly as for ordinary Turing machines.

The proof for (2) is also an easy adaptation of the usual argument, but since the involvement of the oracle set somewhat blurs the waters, we give the details for the sake of the reader.

So suppose that H as-OTM-computes h_1^{as} (we only deal with the unrelativized case, the relativization being straightforward). Thus, for all $i \in \omega$ there is a set $\mathcal{O}_{1,i} \in \mathcal{B}$ such that, for all $x \in \mathcal{O}_{1,i}$, $H^x(i)$ halts with output 1 if and only if P_i^y halts for all y from some measure 1 set, and otherwise with output 0. Since countable intersections of measure 1 sets are again of measure 1, we can – by replacing each $\mathcal{O}_{i,1}$ with the intersection of all these sets, if necessary – assume without loss of generality that all the $\mathcal{O}_{1,i}$ are all equal to a set $\mathcal{O}_1$. Modify H to $\hat{H}$ such that, for $i \in \omega$, some $X \in \mathcal{B}$ and all $x \in X$, $\hat{H}^x(i)$ halts if and only if it is not the case that $\mu(\{y \subseteq \omega : P_i^y(i) \downarrow\}) = 1$. Suppose that $\hat{H}$ is P_k and consider the set $S := \{x \subseteq \omega : \hat{H}^x(k) \downarrow\}$.

If $\mu(S) = 1$, then $P_k^y(k)$ halts for all elements of a measure 1 set, so, by definition of $\hat{H}$, $\hat{H}^x(k)$ does not halt for a measure 1 set of x, a contradiction, since $\hat{H}$ is P_k.

If S is not of measure 1 (i.e., not measurable or of smaller measure), then it is not the case that $P_k^x(k)$ halts for a measure 1 set of y, so $\hat{H}^y(k)$ should halt for a measure 1 set of y, again a contradiction.

Lemma 14. *The statement $\phi_{as\text{-}halts}(i)$ stating, for $i \in \omega$, that $\mu(\{x \subseteq \omega : P_i^{a,x} \downarrow\}) = 1$ is Σ_2 in the parameter a.*

Proof. $\phi_{\text{as-halts}}(i)$ can be reformulated as "There is a set $X \subseteq \mathfrak{P}(\omega)$ such that $\mu(X) = 0$ and, for all $x \notin X$, we have $P^{a,x} \downarrow$". A null set can be encoded as a countable sequence of countable sequences of rational intervals, which in turn can be encoded by a real number z. The statements that a given real number z codes a null set and, that a given real number x belongs to the coded set are Δ_1. Thus, the result follows.

Lemma 15. *Suppose that $V = L$. Then h_1^{as} is OTM-computable equivalent to Σ_2-truth in L_{ω_1}.*

Proof. One direction is immediate from Lemma 14.

Since negations of Σ_2-statements are Π_2, it suffices to show how to decide Π_2-statements. Hence, for the other reduction, let $\phi :\Leftrightarrow \forall y \exists z \psi(y, z)$, where ψ is Δ_0. Consider the OTM-program P that, in the oracle x, works as follows: Enumerate L until x appears, and let L_α be the first L-level in which it does. The level L_α is countable (and coded by a real number), so we can simultaneously run OTM-computations on all $a \in L_\alpha$ searching for some y such that $\psi(a, y)$; the computation will halt once such y have been found for all $a \in L_\alpha$. We claim that this computation halts for all x from a set of measure 1 if and only if ϕ is true in L_{ω_1}.

First, if ϕ holds in L_{ω_1}, then there is an appropriate y for any $a \in L_{\omega_1}$, which will eventually be found, causing the computation to halt.

On the other hand, suppose that the computation halts for all x from a set of measure 1. Then there are cofinally in ω_1 many L-levels such that corresponding witnesses for the existential quantifiers are found for all of their elements. Consequently, such witnesses exist for all elements of L_{ω_1}.

Lemma 16. *Suppose that $V = L$.*

1. *For every $a \subseteq \omega$ and every $n \in \omega$, h_n^x is as-OTM-computable.*
2. *Then the statement ϕ_h, given by "Every OTM-program halts or does not halt" is as-OTM-realizable (but not plainly OTM-realizable).*[10]
3. *More generally, for every $n \in \omega$, the statement "Every OTM-program in the oracle h_n halts or does not halt" is as-OTM-realizable.*

Proof. 1. Again, it is clear that ϕ_h is not OTM-realizable, since a realizer would map OTM-programs to pairs (i, r), the first component of which indicates whether or not the given program halts, thus solving the OTM-halting problem on an OTM.

Since $\mu(\mathbb{R} \cap (L \setminus L_\sigma)) = 1$, a randomly chosen real number x will, with probability 1, satisfy $x \notin L_\sigma$. Consider the OTM-program Q that enumerates L until it encounters x. If $x \notin L_\sigma$, this will have a halting time strictly bigger than σ. To decide, given an OTM-program P, whether or not P halts, run Q^x and P in parallel and, if P halts, halt with output 0, but if Q^x halts without P having halted, halt with output 1.

2. We use the same strategy noting that, with probability 1, the real number x will be such that h_n is contained in the minimal L-level that contains x.

---

[10] The proof follows the proof of Corollary 11 in [5].

3   Deduction Rules

We claim that the axioms and rules of intuitionistic predicate calculus, as found in [8], Definition 17, are sound for as-OTM-realizability in the following strong sense:

- If $\mathcal{A}(A_1, ..., A_n)$ is an axiom scheme using n propositional variables $A_1, ..., A_n$, then there is an OTM-program $P_{\mathcal{A}}$ which, on input $\lceil \phi_1 \rceil, ..., \lceil \phi_n \rceil$, computes an as-OTM-realizer for the instance $\mathcal{A}(\phi_1, ..., \phi_n)$.
- If $\{A_1, ..., A_n\} \vdash \mathcal{C}$ is a deduction rule ρ using n propositional variables $A_1, ..., A_n$, then there is an OTM-program P_{ρ} which, on input $(r_1, ..., r_n)$ with r_i an as-OTM-realizer for $\mathcal{A}_i$ for $i \in \{1, ..., n\}$, computes an as-OTM-realizer $r_{\mathcal{C}}$ for $\mathcal{C}$.

The proof will require some preparation. We note that, in terms of measure theory, there is no relevant difference between $\bigoplus_{i=0}^{n-1} x_i$ and $(x_0, ..., x_{n-1})$:

Lemma 17. *For each $n \in \omega$, the map $d_n : [0,1] \to [0,1]^n$ defined by $x \mapsto (x_0, ..., x_{n-1})$ where $x = \bigoplus_{i=0}^{n-1} x_i$ is a metric isomorphism for Lebesgue measure.*

Proof. The proof is a straightforward exercise in measure theory using Lemma 7.1.2 of [2], which we omit here for the sake of brevity. A detailed argument will appear in a forthcoming paper with Galeotti and Passmann.

We will thus freely confuse (x, y) and $x \oplus y$ below, and, more generally, $(x_1, ..., x_k)$ and $\bigoplus_{i=1}^{k} x_i$.

In order to guarantee the measurability of the occurring sets, we make a set-theoretical extra assumption. We do not know whether the below results hold in ZFC.

From now on, we assume projective determinacy (PD)[11]; in particular, this implies that all projective sets are Lebesgue measurable. By Lemma 5, this implies that success sets are always Lebesgue measurable.

Definition 18. *Let X be a set, and let $n \in \omega$. Moreover, for $i \in \{0, ..., n\}$, let $f_i : X^i \to \mathfrak{P}(X)$.[12] Then $\tilde{\bigotimes}_{i=0}^{n} f_i$ is defined as follows:*

$$\tilde{\bigotimes}_{i=0}^{n} f_i = \{(x_0, ..., x_n) : \forall i \leq n\, x_i \in f_i(x_0, ..., x_{i-1})\}.$$

We call $\tilde{\bigotimes}_{i=0}^{n} f_i$ the dependent product of $f_0, ..., f_n$.

Lemma 19. *1. Let $A \subseteq [0,1]^2$ be measurable, let $X \subseteq [0,1]$ have measure 1 (as a subset of $[0,1]$) and suppose that, for all $x \in X$, the set $A_x := \{y \in [0,1] : (x,y) \in A\}$ satisfies $\mu(A_x) = 1$ (as a subset of $[0,1]$). Then $\mu(A) = 1$.*

---

[11] Cf., e.g., [15].
[12] Note that we have $X^0 = \{\emptyset\}$. However, it is easier to directly think of f_0 as an element of $\mathfrak{P}(X)$, and this is what we will do below.

2. *More generally, let $n \in \omega$, $f_i : [0,1]^i \to \mathfrak{P}([0,1])$ for $i \in \{0,...,n\}$ such that the following holds for all $k \leq n - 1$: There is a $\mathcal{O}_k \subseteq [0,1]^k$ with $\mu(\mathcal{O}_k) = 1$ and $\mu(f_k(x_0,...,x_{k-1})) = 1$ for all $(x_0,...,x_{k-1}) \in \mathcal{O}_k$. Then $\mu(\tilde{\bigotimes}_{i=0}^n f_i) = 1$.*

Lemma 20. *The rules and axioms of intuitionistic first-order logic as given in [14] are sound for as-OTM-realizability.*

Proof. The proof is too long to be presented here. To show how the arguments work, we show here the proofs for one deduction rule and one axiom scheme as examples.

Rule: If a has no free occurences in ψ, then $\{\phi(a) \to \psi\} \vdash \exists a \phi(a) \to \psi$

Let as-OTM-realizers $r_\forall \Vdash^{\mathrm{OTM}}_{\mathrm{as}} (\phi(a) \to \psi)$ and $r_\exists \Vdash^{\mathrm{OTM}}_{\mathrm{as}} \exists a \phi(a)$ be given. Moreover, let $x \subseteq \omega$ be a real number. Finally, let ξ be a relevant input for ψ.

Our as-OTM-realizer Q is an as-OTM-program that, given this data, decomposes x into $x = \bigoplus_{i=0}^3 x_i$ and then computes $((r_\forall^{x_0}(r_\exists^{x_1}(1)))^{x_2}(r_\exists^{x_1}(0)))^{x_3}(\xi)$.

If x is such that $x_1 \in \mathrm{succ}_{r_\exists}$, we will have that $r_\exists^{x_1}(0) \Vdash^{\mathrm{OTM}}_{\mathrm{as}} \phi(r_\exists^{x_1}(1))$. Let $w := r_\exists^{x_1}(1)$. If moreover $x_0 \in \mathrm{succ}_{r_\forall}^w(1)$, then $r_1 := r_\forall^{x_0}(w) \Vdash^{\mathrm{OTM}}_{\mathrm{as}} \phi(w) \to \psi$. On the other hand, we have that $r_2 := r_\exists^{x_1}(0) \Vdash^{\mathrm{OTM}}_{\mathrm{as}} \phi(w)$. So, if $x_2 \in \mathrm{succ}_{r_1}^{r_2}$, then $r_3 := (r_\forall^{x_0}(r_\exists^{x_1}(1)))^{x_2}(r_\exists^{x_1}(0)) \Vdash^{\mathrm{OTM}}_{\mathrm{as}} \psi$. Thus, finally, if $x_3 \in \mathrm{succ}_{r_3}^\xi$, then $r_3^{x_3}(\xi)$ is as desired.

Again by Lemma 19, since the occuring success sets have measure 1 by definition of as-OTM-realizability, the set of x satisfying these conditions has measure 1.

Axiom Scheme: $(\phi \to \chi) \to ((\psi \to \chi) \to ((\phi \vee \psi) \to \chi))$

Let $r_{\phi \to \chi} \Vdash^{\mathrm{OTM}}_{\mathrm{as}} \phi \to \chi$ be given. Our procedure will map this to the OTM-program r which works as follows: Given $r_{\psi \to \chi} \Vdash^{\mathrm{OTM}}_{\mathrm{as}} \psi \to \chi$, output the OTM-program r' which has the following function: Given $r_{\phi \vee \psi} \Vdash^{\mathrm{OTM}}_{\mathrm{as}} \phi \vee \psi$, along with $x \subseteq \omega$, first compute $j := r_{\phi \vee \chi}^{x_0}(0)$. Then one of the following cases occurs:

1. If $j = 0$, compute $r_{\phi \to \chi}^{x_1}(r_{\phi \vee \psi}^{x_0}(1))$ and output it.
2. If $j = 1$, compute $r_{\psi \to \chi}^{x_1}(r_{\phi \vee \psi}^{x_0}(1))$ and output it.

If x is such that $x_0 \in \mathrm{succ}_{r_{\phi \vee \psi}}$, then $j \in \{0,1\}$ and $r_0 := r_{\phi \vee \psi}^{x_0}(1)$ will be an as-OTM-realizer of the j-th element of the disjunction $\phi \vee \psi$. If $j = 0$, and $x_1 \in \mathrm{succ}_{r_{\phi \to \chi}}^{r_0}$, then the the output $r_{\phi \to \chi}^{x_1}(r_0)$ will be an as-OTM-realizer of χ. Similarly if $j = 1$ and $x_1 \in \mathrm{succ}_{r_{\psi \to \chi}}^{r_0}$. Thus, for each $x_0 \in \mathrm{succ}_{r_{\phi \vee \psi}}$, the set of corresponding x_1 has measure 1. By Lemma 19, the set of x satisfying these conditions has measure 1.

4   Axioms of Set Theory

We now consider as-OTM-realizability of particular set-theoretical statements. It will turn out that all axioms of KP are as-OTM-realizable, while already Σ_2-comprehension is not. The axiom of replacement and the axiom of choice are as-OTM-realizable in their usual formulation, which, however, is due to the considerable deviation of the realizability interpretation from the classical semantics.

For the axiom schemes of induction, comprehension and collection, we interpret as-OTM-realizabilty in the same (strong) sense that we used for logical axioms when we prove that a certain statement is as-OTM-realizable; for negative results, we provide a concrete instance that fails to be as-OTM-realizable.

The next result, and its proof, are analogous to Theorem 43 of [8], where this was done for infinitary intuitionistic set theory.

Lemma 21. *1. The axioms of extensionality, empty set, pairing and union are as-OTM-realizable.*

2. The Δ_0-separation scheme is as-OTM-realizable.

3. The (full) collection scheme is as-OTM-realizable.

4. The induction scheme is OTM-realizable.

Note that, since $x \setminus y$ is easily computable from x and y, the as-OTM-realizability of Σ_n-separation is equivalent to that of Π_n-separation.

Lemma 22. *[Cf. [3], Proposition 9.4.4]*[13]

1. The as-OTM-realizability of the Σ_1-comprehension scheme (and, equivalently, that of the Π_1-comprehension scheme) is independent of ZFC.

2. (It is provable in ZFC that) the Σ_2-comprehension scheme (and, hence, the Σ_n-comprehension scheme and the Π_n-comprehension scheme for all $n \geq 2$) is not as-OTM-realizable.

Proof. 1. (a) Suppose first that $V = L$. Let $X \in L$ be a set, $\phi \equiv \exists y \psi(x, y)$ a Σ_1-formula. Since $X \in (H_{\omega_1})^L = L_{\omega_1}$, there is a (constructibly) countable ordinal α such that $X \subseteq L_\alpha$. Let $\beta := \sup\{\sigma^x : x \in X\}$, then $\beta < \omega_1^L$. It follows that (in L), we have $\mu(\mathbb{R} \cap (L \setminus L_\beta)) = 1$. Thus, if $\alpha(z)$ denotes the minimal α with $z \in L_\alpha$, then our randomly chosen real z will satisfy $\alpha(z) > \beta$ with probability 1.

Now, given $x \in X$, use z to calculate $L_{\alpha(z)}$ and search $L_{\alpha(z)}$ for a witness y for the statement $\exists y \psi(x, y)$. If such a y is found, x belongs to the specified subset. If no such y is found, then, as $\alpha(z) > \sigma^x$, none exists and x does not belong to the specified subset. Thus, the as-OTM-realizability of Σ_1-comprehension is consistent relative to ZFC.

(b) On the other hand, let M be a transitive model of ZFC such that, for each $x \subseteq \omega$, the set of real numbers generic for random forcing over $L[x]$ has measure 1. By Theorem 13 of [5], this implies that, in M, the analogue of Sacks' theorem holds for (parameter-free) OTMs: If $x \subseteq \omega$ is OTM-computable relative to all elements of a set of positive measure, then x is OTM-computable $(*)$. Let $r \Vdash_{as}^{OTM} \forall X \exists y \forall z (z \in Y \leftrightarrow (z \in X \wedge \phi(z)))$, where $\phi(z) :\Leftrightarrow P_z(0) \downarrow$. Take $X := \omega$. Then there is $\mathcal{O} \in \mathcal{B}$ such that, for

---

[13] We remark, however, that the argument is different, as the power set operator is not available in the present context.

all $a \in \mathcal{O}$, we have $r^a(\omega) = \{i \in \omega : P_i(0) \downarrow\}$, i.e., $r^a(\omega) = h_1$. By (*), h_1 is OTM-computable, a contradiction. Thus, in M, the Σ_1-comprehension axiom is not as-OTM-realizable.

2. To see that Σ_2-comprehension is not as-OTM-realizable, recall from Lemma 14 that the formula $\phi_{\text{as-halts}}(i)$, expressing "$P_i^x$ halts with probability 1" is Σ_2 and that, by Lemma 13 $h_1^{\text{as}} = \{i \in \omega : \phi_{\text{as-halts}}(i)\}$ is not as-OTM-computable. Thus, the instance of Σ_2-comprehension where X is ω and ϕ is $\phi_{\text{as-halts}}$ is not as-OTM-realizable.

Since H_{ω_1} does not even contain $\mathfrak{P}(\omega)$, the power set axiom cannnot be meaningfully considered in the present context.

Lemma 23. *The axiom of choice, formulated as*

$$\forall X (\forall y (y \in X \rightarrow \exists z z \in y) \rightarrow \exists F : X \mapsto \bigcup X \forall y \in X F(y) \in y),$$

is as-OTM-realizable.

Proof. Let $X \in H_{\omega_1}$, $r \Vdash_{\text{as}}^{\text{OTM}} \forall x(x \in X \rightarrow \exists y y \in x)$. Thus, for every $x \in X$, there is a set $\mathcal{O}_x \in \mathcal{B}$ such that, for all $a_0 \oplus a_1 := a \in \mathcal{O}_x$, we have that $(r^{a_0}(x))^{a_1}(1) \in x$. Since $X \in H_{\omega_1}$, X is countable, and so $\mathcal{O} := \bigcup_{x \in X} \mathcal{O}_x$ satisfies $\mu(\mathcal{O}) = 1$. Now, for all $a \in \mathcal{O}$ and all $x \in X$, we have that $(r^{a_0}(x))^{a_1}(1) \in x$, so we can let $F(x) = (r^{a_0}(x))^{a_1}(1)$, which will be as desired.

5   Conclusion and Further Work

We have shown that almost sure realizability with OTMs has the properties that one would expect a notion of set-theoretical realizability to have, while still differing from "plain" OTM-realizability; one could say that, set-theoretically, randomness is informative. Given that the axiom of choice is commonly regarded as highly non-constructive, the fact that the axiom of choice is realizable in this sense is somewhat counter-intuitive. This phenomenon, however, is well-known in constructive set theory. (See, however, [13] for the well-known, but questionable, claim that the axiom of choice is intuitionistically true, or even trivial.) For this reason, a number of formulations and variants of choice principles has been defined (see, e.g., [16]), and it would be worthwhile to see whether these are as-OTM-realizable. Moreover, there is a number of variants of our notion that warrant consideration: We mention here in particular the possibility of extending the realm of objects to the whole set-theoretical universe rather than just H_{ω_1}, allowing the OTMs to use ordinal parameters, and replacing the clauses for disjunction, implication and universal quantification with their uniform versions in the definition of as-OTM-realizability; it would also be interesting to see whether "realizability with probability > 0" has properties crucially different from "realizability with probability 1".

Acknowledgements. We thank our three anonymous referees for helpful suggestions for improving the presentation of the paper.

References

1. Barwise, J.: Admissible Sets and Structures. Perspectives in Logic. Cambridge University Press (2017). https://doi.org/10.1017/9781316717196
2. Bogachev, V.: Measure Theory, vol. 1. Physica-Verlag (2007)
3. Carl, M.: Ordinal Computability. An Introduction to Infinitary Machines, De Gruyter (2019)
4. Carl, M.: A Note on OTM-Realizability and Constructive Set Theories. Preprint. arXiv:1903.08945 (2019)
5. Carl, M., Schlicht, P.: Infinite computations with random oracles. Notre Dame J. Formal Logic **58**(2) (2017)
6. Downey, R., Hirschfeldt, D.: Algorithmic Randomness and Complexity. Springer, Cham (2010)
7. Carl, M., Galeotti, L., Passmann, R.: Realisability for infinitary intuitionistic set theory. Ann. Pure Appl. Logic **174**(6) (2023)
8. Carl, M., Galeotti, L., Passmann, R.: Randomising realizability. In: De Mol, L., Weiermann, A., Manea, F., Fernández-Duque, D. (eds.) CiE 2021. LNCS, vol. 12813, pp. 82–93. Springer, Cham (2021). https://doi.org/10.1007/978-3-030-80049-9_8
9. Hodges, W.: On the effectivity of some field constructions. In: Proceedings of the London Mathematical Society, pp. s3–32(1) (1976)
10. Iemhoff, R., Passmann, R.: Logics of intuitionistic Kripke-Platek set theory. Ann. Pure Appl. Logic **172**(10) (2021)
11. Koepke, P.: Turing computations on ordinals. Bull. Symb. Logic **11**(3) (2005). https://doi.org/10.2178/bsl/1122038993
12. Lubarsky, B.: IKP and friends. J. Symb. Logic **67**(4) (2002). https://doi.org/10.2178/jsl/1190150286
13. McCarty, C., Shapiro, S., Klev, A.: The axiom of choice is false intuitionistically (in most contexts). Bull. Symb. Logic **29**(1) (2023). https://doi.org/10.1017/bsl.2022.22
14. Moschovakis, J.: Intuitionistic logic. In: Zalta, E., Nodelman, U. (eds.) The Stanford Encyclopedia of Philosophy (2023). https://plato.stanford.edu/archives/sum2023/entries/logic-intuitionistic/. Accessed 05 Feb 2024
15. Martin, D., Steel, J.: A proof of projective determinacy. J. Am. Math. Soc. **2**(1) (1989)
16. Rathjen, M.: Choice principles in constructive and classical set theories. In: Chatzidakis, Z., Koepke, P., Pohlers, W. (eds.) Logic Colloquium 2002. Lecture Notes in Logic. Cambridge University Press (2006)
17. Wontner, N.: Views from a Peak. Generalisations and descriptive set theory. ILLC Dissertation Series DS-2023-NN (2023)

Learning Families of Algebraic Structures from Text

Nikolay Bazhenov[1,2] , Ekaterina Fokina[3] , Dino Rossegger[3] ,
Alexandra Soskova[4] , and Stefan Vatev[4(✉)]

[1] Sobolev Institute of Mathematics, Novosibirsk, Russia
`bazhenov@math.nsc.ru`
[2] Kazan Federal University, Kazan, Russia
[3] Institute of Discrete Mathematics and Geometry, Technische Universität Wien,
Vienna, Austria
`{ekaterina.fokina,dino.rossegger}@tuwien.ac.at`
[4] Faculty of Mathematics and Informatics, Sofia University, Sofia, Bulgaria
`{asoskova,stefanv}@fmi.uni-sofia.bg`

Abstract. We adapt the classical notion of learning from text to computable structure theory. Our main result is a model-theoretic characterization of the learnability from text for classes of structures. We show that a family of structures is learnable from text if and only if the structures can be distinguished in terms of their theories restricted to positive infinitary Σ_2 sentences.

Keywords: Algorithmic learning · Infinitary logic · Scott topology

1 Introduction

The classical algorithmic learning theory goes back to the works of Putnam [17] and Gold [12]. A learner M receives step by step more and more data (a finite amount at each step) about an object X to be learned, and M outputs a sequence of hypotheses that converges to a finitary description of X. The classical studies (up to the beginning of 2000s) mainly focused on learning for formal languages and for recursive functions, see the monograph [14].

Within the framework of computable structure theory, Stephan and Ventsov [19] initiated investigations of learnability for classes of substructures of a given computable structure $\mathcal{S}$. This approach was further developed, e.g., in the papers [11,13].

Fokina, Kötzing, and San Mauro [10] considered various classes $\mathfrak{K}$ of computable equivalence relations. For these $\mathfrak{K}$, they introduced the notions of *learnability from informant* (or **InfEx**-learnability) and *learnability from text* (**TxtEx**-learnability). The work [5] extended the notion of **InfEx**-learnability to arbitrary countable families of computable structures and obtained the following general model-theoretic characterization of **InfEx**-learnability. Let $\mathfrak{K} = \{\mathcal{A}_i : i \in \omega\}$ be a family of computable structures such that $\mathcal{A}_i \not\cong \mathcal{A}_j$ for $i \neq j$. Then

L. Levy Patey et al. (Eds.): CiE 2024, LNCS 14773, pp. 166–178, 2024.
https://doi.org/10.1007/978-3-031-64309-5_14

$\mathfrak{K}$ is learnable from informant if and only if there exists a family of infinitary Σ_2 sentences $\{\psi_i : i \in \omega\}$ such that

(†) for each i, $\mathcal{A}_i$ is the only member of $\mathfrak{K}$ satisfying ψ_i.

In turn, the results of [5] led to discovering some unexpected connections between **InfEx**-learnability and results from descriptive set theory, see [3].

The aim of this paper is to develop **TxtEx**-learnability for classes of countable structures. In Sect. 2, we introduce our new formal framework for classes of structures $\mathfrak{K}$: this approach allows us to simultaneously give both the known definition of **InfEx**-learnability and the new definition of **TxtEx**-learnability.

The main result of the paper (Theorem 3) shows that **TxtEx**-learnability admits a model-theoretic characterization similar to the characterization of **InfEx**-learnability discussed above: a family $\{\mathcal{A}_i : i \in \omega\}$ is **TxtEx**-learnable if and only if there exists a family of Σ_2^p sentences $\{\psi_i : i \in \omega\}$ satisfying (†).

After acceptance of this paper we noticed that Martin and Osherson [16] developed a framework similar to ours, albeit under different terminology. The most striking similarity is a syntactic characterization similar to ours (Item (3) in Theorem 3).

2   The Formal Framework

Let us consider structures $\mathcal{A}$ with domains a subset of ω. We consider computable signatures with $=$ and $\neq$. We shall denote by $\mathcal{D}(\mathcal{A})$ the basic diagram of $\mathcal{A}$, i.e., $\mathcal{D}(\mathcal{A})$ contains exactly the positive and negative atomic sentences true in $\mathcal{A}$, and by $\mathcal{D}_+(\mathcal{A})$ the positive atomic diagram of $\mathcal{A}$, i.e., $\mathcal{D}_+(\mathcal{A})$ contains only the positive atomic sentences true in $\mathcal{A}$.

For a signature L, by $Mod(L)$ we denote the set of all L-structures $\mathcal{A}$ with $dom(\mathcal{A}) \subseteq \omega$. If not specified otherwise, we assume that every considered class $\mathfrak{K} \subseteq Mod(L)$ is closed under isomorphisms.

First we need to introduce the components of our learning framework. Let $\mathfrak{K} \subseteq Mod(L)$ be a family which contains precisely κ isomorphism types, where $\kappa \leq \omega$, those are the types of L-structures $\mathcal{A}_i$, $i \in \kappa$.

- The *learning domain* (LD) is the collection of all copies $\mathcal{S}$ of the structures from $\mathfrak{K}$ such that $dom(\mathcal{S}) \subseteq \omega$, i.e.,

$$\mathrm{LD}(\mathfrak{K}) = \bigcup_{i \in \kappa} \{\mathcal{S} \in Mod(L) : \mathcal{S} \cong \mathcal{A}_i\}.$$

- The *hypothesis space* (HS) contains the indices i for $\mathcal{A}_i \in \mathfrak{K}$ (an index is viewed as a conjecture about the isomorphism type of an input structure $\mathcal{S}$) and a question mark symbol:

$$\mathrm{HS}(\mathfrak{K}) = \kappa \cup \{?\}.$$

- A *learner* M sees, stage by stage, some atomic facts about a given structure from $LD(\mathfrak{K})$. The learner M is required to output conjectures from $HS(\mathfrak{K})$. This is formalized as follows.

  Let Atm denote the set of (the Gödel numbers) of all positive and negative atomic sentences in the signature $L \cup \omega$ (in other words, positive and negative atomic facts about possible L-structures on the domain ω). The restriction of Atm to only positive atomic sentences is denoted by Atm_+. A *learner* M is a function from the set $(Atm)^{<\omega}$ (i.e., the set of all finite tuples of atomic facts) into $HS(\mathfrak{K})$.

- For an L-structure $\mathcal{S}$, an *informant* $\mathbb{I}$ for $\mathcal{S}$ is an arbitrary sequence $(\psi_0, \psi_1, \dots)$ containing elements from Atm and satisfying

$$\mathcal{D}(\mathcal{S}) = \{\psi_i : i \in \omega\}.$$

- For an L-structure $\mathcal{S}$, a *text* $\mathbb{T}$ for $\mathcal{S}$ is an arbitrary sequence $(\psi_0, \psi_1, \dots)$ containing elements from Atm_+ and satisfying

$$\mathcal{D}_+(\mathcal{S}) = \{\psi_i : i \in \omega\}.$$

- For $k \in \omega$, by $\mathbb{I} \upharpoonright k$ (respectively, $\mathbb{T} \upharpoonright k$) we denote the corresponding sequence $(\psi_i)_{i<k}$.

Definition 1 ([6])**.** *We say that the family $\mathfrak{K}$ is **InfEx**-learnable if there exists a learner M such that for any structure $\mathcal{S} \in \mathrm{LD}(\mathfrak{K})$ and any informant $\mathbb{I}_{\mathcal{S}}$ for $\mathcal{S}$, the learner eventually stabilizes to a correct conjecture about the isomorphism type of $\mathcal{S}$. More formally, there exists a limit*

$$\lim_{n \to \omega} M(\mathbb{I}_{\mathcal{S}} \upharpoonright n) = i$$

belonging to ω, and $\mathcal{A}_i$ is isomorphic to $\mathcal{S}$.

Recall that a structure $\mathcal{A} = (A; \sim)$ is an *equivalence structure* if $\sim$ is an equivalence relation on A. The paper [10] introduced the definition of **TxtEx**-learnability for equivalence structures. Here we generalize this definition to arbitrary structures.

Definition 2. *We say that the family $\mathfrak{K}$ is x**TxtEx**-learnable if there exists a learner M such that for any structure $\mathcal{S} \in \mathrm{LD}(\mathfrak{K})$ and any text $\mathbb{T}_{\mathcal{S}}$ for $\mathcal{S}$, the learner eventually stabilizes to a correct conjecture about the isomorphism type of $\mathcal{S}$. More formally, there exists a limit*

$$\lim_{n \to \omega} M(\mathbb{T}_{\mathcal{S}} \upharpoonright n) = i$$

belonging to ω, and $\mathcal{A}_i$ is isomorphic to $\mathcal{S}$.

In this paper, we give many examples of classes of equivalence structures. We use the notation $[\alpha_1 : \beta_1, \dots, \alpha_n : \beta_n]$, where $\alpha_i, \beta_i \leq \omega$, to denote the equivalence structure with precisely β_i-many equivalence classes of size α_i, for all $i = 1, \dots, n$ (and with no equivalence classes of other sizes).

Remark 1. The classes of equivalence structures $\mathcal{E} = \{[\omega : 1, n : 1] \mid n \geq 1\}$ and $\tilde{\mathcal{E}} = \{[\omega : \omega, n : \omega] \mid n \geq 1\}$ play an important role in this paper.

Remark 2. It is easy to observe that every **TxtEx**-learnable class is also **InfEx**-learnable (indeed, notice that an informant $\mathbb{I}$ for a structure $\mathcal{A}$ can be effectively transformed into a text $\mathbb{T}_I$ for this $\mathcal{A}$). Theorem 1.4 in [10] proves that the class $\mathfrak{K} = \{[\omega : 1], [\omega : 2]\}$ is **InfEx**-learnable, but not **TxtEx**-learnable.

3 Cantor-Continuous Embeddings

The Cantor space, denoted by 2^ω, can be represented as the collection of reals, equipped with the product topology of the discrete topology on the set $\{0, 1\}$. A basis for 2^ω is formed by the collection of $[\sigma] = \{f \in 2^\omega : \sigma \subset f\}$, for all finite binary strings σ. Here we will need the following characterization of the Cantor-continuous functions.

Proposition 1 (Folklore). *A function $\Psi : 2^\omega \to 2^\omega$ is Cantor-continuous if and only if there exists a Turing operator Φ_e and a set $A \in 2^\omega$ such that $\Psi(X) = \Phi_e(A \oplus X)$ for all $X \in 2^\omega$.*

Definition 3. *For $i \in \{0, 1\}$, let $\mathfrak{K}_i$ be a class of L_i-structures. A mapping Ψ is a Cantor-continuous embedding of $\mathfrak{K}_0$ into $\mathfrak{K}_1$, denoted by $\Psi : \mathfrak{K}_0 \leq_{\text{Cantor}} \mathfrak{K}_1$, if Ψ is Cantor-continuous and satisfies the following:*

1. *For any $\mathcal{A} \in \mathfrak{K}_0$, $\Psi(\mathcal{D}(\mathcal{A}))$ is the characteristic function of the atomic diagram of a structure from $\mathfrak{K}_1$. This structure is denoted by $\Psi(\mathcal{A})$.*
2. *For any $\mathcal{A}, \mathcal{B} \in \mathfrak{K}_0$, we have $\mathcal{A} \cong \mathcal{B}$ if and only if $\Psi(\mathcal{A}) \cong \Psi(\mathcal{B})$.*

When the embedding $\mathfrak{K}_0 \leq_{\text{Cantor}} \mathfrak{K}_1$ is given by a Turing operator Φ_e, then we say that $\mathfrak{K}_0$ is *Turing computable embeddable* into $\mathfrak{K}_1$, and we denote this by $\Phi_e : \mathfrak{K}_0 \leq_{tc} \mathfrak{K}_1$. The study of this notion was initiated in [7,15]. One of the main tools in proving results about the Turing computable embeddability is the following Pullback Theorem. Here the Σ_α^c formulas are the usual computable infinitary Σ_α formulas as defined in [1]. A $\Sigma_\alpha^{\text{inf}}$ formula is an infinitary Σ_α formula.

Theorem 1 (Pullback Theorem [15]). *Let $\Phi_e : \mathfrak{K} \leq_{tc} \mathfrak{K}'$. Then for any computable infinitary sentence φ' in the signature of $\mathfrak{K}'$, we can effectively find a computable infinitary sentence φ in the signature of $\mathfrak{K}$ such that for all $\mathcal{A} \in \mathfrak{K}$,*

$$\mathcal{A} \models \varphi \text{ if and only if } \Phi_e(\mathcal{A}) \models \varphi'.$$

Moreover, for a nonzero $\alpha < \omega_1^{CK}$, if φ' is Σ_α^c (or Π_α^c), then so is φ.

As noted in [5], Theorem 1, can be relativized to an arbitrary oracle X. By Proposition 1, we directly obtain the following non-effective version of Theorem 1.

Corollary 1 (Non-effective Pullback Theorem). *Let* $\Psi: \mathfrak{K} \leq_{\text{Cantor}} \mathfrak{K}'$. *Then for any infinitary sentence* φ' *in the signature of* $\mathfrak{K}'$, *there exists an infinitary sentence* φ *in the signature of* $\mathfrak{K}$ *such that for all* $\mathcal{A} \in \mathfrak{K}$,

$$\mathcal{A} \models \varphi \text{ if and only if } \Psi(\mathcal{A}) \models \varphi'.$$

Moreover, for a nonzero $\alpha < \omega_1$, *if* φ' *is* $\Sigma_\alpha^{\text{inf}}$ *(or* Π_α^{inf} *), then so is* φ.

4   Scott-Continuous Embeddings

The Scott topology, denoted by $\mathcal{P}(\omega)$, can be characterized as the product topology of the Sierpiński space on $\{0, 1\}$. The Sierpiński space on $\{0, 1\}$ is the topological space with open sets $\{\emptyset, \{1\}, \{0, 1\}\}$. A basis for $\mathcal{P}(\omega)$ is formed by the collection $[D] = \{A \subseteq \omega : D \subseteq A\}$, for all finite sets D.

Definition 4 (Case [8]). *A set* $A \in \mathcal{P}(\omega)$ *defines a* generalized enumeration operator $\Gamma_A : \mathcal{P}(\omega) \to \mathcal{P}(\omega)$ *if and only if for each set* $B \in \mathcal{P}(\omega)$,

$$\Gamma_A(B) = \{x : \exists v(\langle x, v \rangle \in A \ \& \ D_v \subseteq B)\}.$$

When $A = W_e$ for some c.e. set W_e, we write Γ_e instead of Γ_{W_e}, which is the usual enumeration operator as defined in [8] and [9], for example.

Proposition 2 (Folklore). *A mapping* $\Gamma : \mathcal{P}(\omega) \to \mathcal{P}(\omega)$ *is Scott-continuous if and only if* Γ *is a generalized enumeration operator.*

As a direct corollary of Proposition 2, the following characterization will be useful.

Corollary 2. *A mapping* $\Psi : \mathcal{P}(\omega) \to \mathcal{P}(\omega)$ *is Scott-continuous if and only if* Ψ *is*

(a) monotone, *i.e.,* $A \subseteq B$ *implies* $\Psi(A) \subseteq \Psi(B)$, *and*
(b) compact, *i.e.,* $x \in \Psi(A)$ *if and only if* $x \in \Psi(D)$ *for some finite* $D \subseteq A$.

We define Scott-continuous embedding for classes of structures as an analogue of the Cantor-continuous embedding from Definition 3. Here we take into consideration only the *positive* atomic diagram $\mathcal{D}_+(\mathcal{A})$ of a structure $\mathcal{A}$, and not the basic (positive and negative) atomic diagram $\mathcal{D}(\mathcal{A})$ as in [15].

Definition 5. *A mapping* Γ *is a* Scott-continuous embedding *of* $\mathfrak{K}_0$ *into* $\mathfrak{K}_1$, *denoted by* $\Gamma: \mathfrak{K}_0 \leq_{\text{Scott}} \mathfrak{K}_1$, *if* Γ *is Scott-continuous and satisfies the following:*

1. *For any* $\mathcal{A} \in \mathfrak{K}_0$, $\Gamma(\mathcal{D}_+(\mathcal{A}))$ *is the positive atomic diagram of a structure from* $\mathfrak{K}_1$. *This structure is denoted by* $\Gamma(\mathcal{A})$.
2. *For any* $\mathcal{A}, \mathcal{B} \in \mathfrak{K}_0$, *we have* $\mathcal{A} \cong \mathcal{B}$ *if and only if* $\Gamma(\mathcal{A}) \cong \Gamma(\mathcal{B})$.

If we consider enumeration operators Γ_e, we obtain an effective version of Definition 5. We say that Γ_e is a *positive computable embedding* of $\mathfrak{K}_0$ into $\mathfrak{K}_1$, and we denote it by $\Gamma_e \colon \mathfrak{K}_0 \leq_{pc} \mathfrak{K}_1$. Positive computable embeddings were first studied in [4]. To obtain an analogue of Theorem 1 for positive computable embeddings, we need to define a hierarchy of *positive* infinitary formulas.

Definition 6 ([4]). *Fix a countable signature L. For every $\alpha < \omega_1$ define the sets of Σ^p_α and Π^p_α L-formulas inductively as follows.*

– *Let $\alpha = 0$. Then:*
  - *the Σ^p_0 formulas are the finite conjunctions of atomic L-formulas.*
  - *the Π^p_0 formulas are the finite disjunctions of negations of atomic L-formulas.*
– *Let $\alpha = 1$. Then:*
  - *$\varphi(\bar{u})$ is a Σ^p_1 formula if it has the form*

$$\varphi(\bar{u}) = \mathbb{W}_{i \in I} \exists \bar{x}_i \psi_i(\bar{u}, \bar{x}_i),$$

where for each $i \in I$, $\psi_i(\bar{u}, \bar{x}_i)$ is a Σ^p_0 formula, I is countable.

  - *$\varphi(\bar{u})$ is a Π^p_1 formula if it has the form*

$$\varphi(\bar{u}) = \mathbb{A}_{i \in I} \forall \bar{x}_i \psi_i(\bar{u}, \bar{x}_i),$$

where for each $i \in I$, $\psi_i(\bar{u}, \bar{x}_i)$ is a Π^p_0 formula, I is countable.

– *Let $\alpha \geq 2$. Then:*
  - *$\varphi(\bar{u})$ is Σ^p_α formula if it has the form*

$$\varphi(\bar{u}) = \mathbb{W}_{i \in I} \exists \bar{x}_i (\xi_i(\bar{u}, \bar{x}_i) \wedge \psi_i(\bar{u}, \bar{x}_i)),$$

where for each $i \in I$, $\xi_i(\bar{u}, \bar{x}_i)$ is a $\Sigma^p_{\beta_i}$ formula and $\psi_i(\bar{u}, \bar{x}_i)$ is a $\Pi^p_{\beta_i}$ formula, for some $\beta_i < \alpha$ and I countable.

  - *$\varphi(\bar{u})$ is Π^p_α formula if it has the form*

$$\varphi(\bar{u}) = \mathbb{A}_{i \in I} \forall \bar{x}_i (\xi_i(\bar{u}, \bar{x}_i) \vee \psi_i(\bar{u}, \bar{x}_i)),$$

where for each $i \in I$, $\xi_i(\bar{u}, \bar{x}_i)$ is a $\Sigma^p_{\beta_i}$ formula and $\psi_i(\bar{u}, \bar{x}_i)$ is a $\Pi^p_{\beta_i}$ formula, for some $\beta_i < \alpha$ and I countable.

A similar hierarchy of positive infinitary formulas can be also found in [18], where it is used in connection with the α-th enumeration jump. This connection is the reason for the inclusion of both "positive" and "negative" in the definition of Σ^p_α-formulas for $\alpha > 2$. As usual, when we restrict to c.e. index sets I in the above definition, we obtain the hierarchy of *positive computable infinitary formulas*. For this hierarchy, we will use the notations Σ^{pc}_α and Π^{pc}_α.

Theorem 2 (Pullback Theorem [4]). *Let $\Gamma_e \colon \mathfrak{K} \leq_{pc} \mathfrak{K}'$. Then for any positive computable infinitary sentence φ' in the signature of $\mathfrak{K}'$, we can effectively find a positive computable infinitary sentence φ in the signature of $\mathfrak{K}$ such that for all $\mathcal{A} \in \mathfrak{K}$,*

$$\mathcal{A} \models \varphi \text{ if and only if } \Gamma_e(\mathcal{A}) \models \varphi'.$$

Moreover, for a nonzero $\alpha < \omega_1^{CK}$, if φ' is Σ_α^{pc} (or Π_α^{pc}), then so is φ.

Since Theorem 2 can be relativized, it is straightforward to obtain a non-effective version.

Corollary 3. *Let $\Gamma \colon \mathfrak{K} \leq_{\mathrm{Scott}} \mathfrak{K}'$. Then for any positive infinitary sentence φ' in the signature of $\mathfrak{K}'$, there exists a positive infinitary sentence φ in the signature of $\mathfrak{K}$ such that for all $\mathcal{A} \in \mathfrak{K}$,*

$$\mathcal{A} \models \varphi \text{ if and only if } \Gamma(\mathcal{A}) \models \varphi'.$$

Moreover, for a nonzero $\alpha < \omega_1$, if φ' is Σ_α^p (or Π_α^p), then so is φ.

5 Characterization of TxtEx-Learnability

Recall the class $\tilde{\mathcal{E}}$ from Remark 1. In this section, we obtain the following characterization of **TxtEx**-learning:

Theorem 3. *For a class $\mathfrak{K} = \{\mathcal{B}_i : i \in \omega\}$, the following are equivalent:*

*(1) The class $\mathfrak{K}$ is **TxtEx**-learnable.*
(2) $\mathfrak{K} \leq_{\mathrm{Scott}} \tilde{\mathcal{E}}$.
(3) There is a sequence of Σ_2^p sentences $\{\psi_i : i \in \omega\}$ such that for all i and j, $\mathcal{B}_j \models \psi_i$ if and only if $i = j$.

The proof of Theorem 3 is given as a sequence of lemmas.

$(1) \Rightarrow (2)$. For a finite sequence σ and an L-structure $\mathcal{A}$, we say that σ *is on* $\mathcal{D}_+(\mathcal{A})$ if σ is an initial segment of some text for the structure $\mathcal{A}$.

Proposition 3. *Let $\mathfrak{K}$ be a class of structures which is **TxtEx**-learnable by a learner M, and let $\mathcal{A}$ be a structure in $\mathfrak{K}$. For any finite σ on $\mathcal{D}_+(\mathcal{A})$, there exists an extension σ' of σ on $\mathcal{D}_+(\mathcal{A})$, such that for all τ on $\mathcal{D}_+(\mathcal{A})$, extending σ', $M(\sigma') = M(\tau)$.*

Proof. Assume that there exists σ on $\mathcal{D}_+(\mathcal{A})$ such that for all $\sigma' \succeq \sigma$, we can find $\tau \succ \sigma'$ such that $M(\sigma') \neq M(\tau)$. In this way it is clear that we can build an enumeration $\mathbb{T}$ of $\mathcal{D}_+(\mathcal{A})$ such that $\lim_{n \to \infty} M(\mathbb{T} \upharpoonright n)$ does not exist, and we obtain a contradiction. $\square$

Lemma 1. *For any **TxtEx**-learnable class $\mathfrak{K}$, $\mathfrak{K} \leq_{\mathrm{Scott}} \tilde{\mathcal{E}}$.*

Proof. For any finite enumeration $\sigma \in \omega^{<\omega}$ and ordinal $\alpha \leq \omega$, we define the auxiliary equivalence structure $\mathcal{A}_{\sigma,\alpha}$ with domain consisting of the elements $\{x_{\sigma,k} : k < \alpha\} \cup \{y_{\sigma,k} : k < \omega\}$ and $\mathcal{D}_+(\mathcal{A}_{\sigma,\alpha})$ saying that the elements $x_{\sigma,k}$ form an equivalence class of size at least α and the elements $y_{\sigma,k}$ form an equivalence class of size ω. Notice that $k \leq m$ implies $\mathcal{D}_+(\mathcal{A}_{\sigma,k}) \subseteq \mathcal{D}_+(\mathcal{A}_{\sigma,m})$.

Suppose M is a learner for the class $\mathfrak{K}$. We describe how the desired mapping Γ works. Given a finite set D, consider all finite enumerations σ of parts of D. First, we make sure that if $M(\sigma) = i$, then $\Gamma(D)$ contains the positive diagram of $\mathcal{A}_{\sigma,i+1}$. Second, if for some initial segment τ of σ, $M(\tau) \neq M(\sigma)$, then $\Gamma(D)$ contains the positive diagram of $\mathcal{A}_{\tau,\omega}$. More formally, let E_D be the set of all σ enumerating parts of D. Then $\Gamma(D)$ is the least set obeying the rules:

(1) $\bigcup_{\sigma \in E_D} \{\mathcal{D}_+(\mathcal{A}_{\sigma,i+1}) : M(\sigma) = i\} \subseteq \Gamma(D)$;
(2) $\bigcup_{\sigma \in E_D} \{\mathcal{D}_+(\mathcal{A}_{\tau,\omega}) : \tau \prec \sigma \ \& \ M(\tau) \neq M(\sigma)\} \subseteq \Gamma(D)$.

It is easy to see that Γ is motonone and compact, and hence Scott-continuous by Corollary 2.

Let $\mathcal{B}_i \in \mathfrak{K}$. We will show that $\Gamma(\mathcal{B}_i)$ is an equivalence structure of type $[\omega : \omega, i+1 : \omega]$. By Proposition 3, there are infinitely many σ on $\mathcal{D}_+(\mathcal{B}_i)$ such that $M(\sigma) = i$ and for all $\tau \succ \sigma$, $M(\tau) = i$. By the construction of Γ, $\Gamma(\mathcal{B}_i)$ contains infinitely many equivalence classes of size $i+1$. Assume that $\Gamma(\mathcal{B}_i)$ contains an equivalence class of a finite size $j+1 \neq i+1$. This can happen if there is a finite ρ on $D_+(\mathcal{B}_i)$ such that $M(\rho) = j$ and the equivalence structure $\mathcal{A}_{\rho,j+1}$ is a part of $\Gamma(\mathcal{B}_i)$. Again by Proposition 3, there exists an extension ρ' of ρ such that $M(\rho') = M(\tau)$ for all τ extending ρ'. Since M learns $\mathcal{B}_i$, we have $M(\rho') = i$. It follows by the construction of Γ that the equivalence structure $\mathcal{A}_{\rho,j+1}$ is extended to $\mathcal{A}_{\rho,\omega}$ in $\Gamma(\mathcal{B})$. □

(2)⇒(3). The next proposition shows the usefulness of Theorem 2 in giving a syntactic characterization of **TxtEx**-learnable classes.

Lemma 2. *Let $\mathfrak{K} = \{\mathcal{B}_i : i < \omega\}$ be a class such that $\Gamma \colon \mathfrak{K} \leq_{\mathrm{Scott}} \tilde{\mathcal{E}}$. Then there exist Σ_2^p sentences φ_i such that $\mathcal{B}_i \models \varphi_j$ if and only if $i = j$.*

Proof. Without loss of generality, we may assume that $\Gamma(\mathcal{B}_i)$ is an equivalence structure $\mathcal{A}_i$ of type $[\omega : \omega, i+1 : \omega]$. For $\mathcal{A}_i$, we have the infinitary Σ_2^p sentence

$$\varphi_i \overset{\text{def}}{=} \exists x_0 \cdots x_i \left[\bigwedge_{k \neq \ell \leq i} (x_k \sim x_\ell \ \& \ x_k \neq x_\ell) \ \& \ \forall y(\neg y \sim x_0 \vee \bigvee_{\ell \leq i} \neg y \neq x_\ell) \right]. \quad (1)$$

Notice that we assume that $\neq$ is in our signature, so $x_k \neq x_\ell$ is a positive atomic formula. By Theorem 2, we obtain Σ_2^p sentences for the structures $\mathcal{B}_i$ in $\mathfrak{K}$. □

(3)⇒(1). We give the final part of the proof:

Lemma 3. *Let $\mathfrak{K} = \{\mathcal{B}_i : i < \omega\}$. Suppose that there exist Σ_2^p sentences φ_i such that $\mathcal{B}_i \models \varphi_j$ if and only if $i = j$. Then $\mathfrak{K}$ is **TxtEx**-learnable.*

Proof. Without loss of generality, suppose that the Σ_2^p sentence φ_i has the form

$$\varphi_i = \exists \bar{x}_i \Big(\alpha_i(\bar{x}_i) \wedge \bigwedge_{j \in J_i} \forall \bar{y}_j \neg (\beta_{i,j}(\bar{x}_i, \bar{y}_j)) \Big),$$

where α_i and $\beta_{i,j}$ are positive atomic formulas, and J_i is a countable set. We will describe how the learner M for the class $\mathfrak{K}$ works.

Consider an arbitrary sequence σ of positive atomic formulas. We must determine the value of $M(\sigma)$. We find the least $\langle i, \bar{a} \rangle$ such that the Gödel code of $\alpha_i(\bar{a})$ is in the range of σ and no sentence of the form $\beta_{i,j}(\bar{a}, \bar{b}_j)$ is in the range of σ. Then we let $M(\sigma) = i$.

Suppose $\mathcal{A} \cong \mathcal{B}_i$ and consider some text $\mathbb{T}_\mathcal{A}$ for $\mathcal{A}$. Since $\mathcal{A} \models \varphi_i$, find the least tuple $\bar{a}$ such that $\mathcal{A} \models \alpha_i(\bar{a})$ and $\mathcal{A} \models \bigwedge_{j \in J_i} \forall \bar{y}_j \neg (\beta_{i,j}(\bar{a}, \bar{y}_j))$. It follows that the code of $\alpha_i(\bar{a})$ will appear in some initial segment of $\mathbb{T}_\mathcal{A}$ and none of the positive atomic sentences $\beta_{i,j}(\bar{a}, \bar{b}_j)$ will appear in $\mathbb{T}_\mathcal{A}$ for any $\bar{b}_j$ and any $j \in J_i$. It follows that $\lim_{n \to \infty} M(\mathbb{T}_\mathcal{A} \upharpoonright n) = i$.

Lemma 3 and Theorem 3 are proved. $\square$

The choice of the class $\tilde{\mathcal{E}}$ in Theorem 3 seems somewhat arbitrary. The statement of Theorem 3 suggests the following definition.

Definition 7. *A countably infinite class $\mathfrak{K}_0$ is **TxtEx**-complete if*

- *$\mathfrak{K}_0$ is **TxtEx**-learnable, and*
- *for any countable **TxtEx**-learnable class $\mathfrak{K}$, $\mathfrak{K} \leq_{\text{Scott}} \mathfrak{K}_0$.*

Corollary 4. *The class $\tilde{\mathcal{E}}$ is **TxtEx**-complete.*

6   TxtEx-Complete Classes

Consider a signature $L_{\text{st}} = \{<, =, \neq\} \cup \{P_i : i \in \omega\}$, where all P_i are unary. For each $i \in \omega$, we define a structure $\mathcal{A}_i$, where all $P_j^{\mathcal{A}_i}$ are disjoint infinite sets. In addition, for any two elements x, y, where $x \in P_j$ and $y \in P_k$ for $j \neq k$, x and y are incomparable under $<$. Let η denote the order type of the rationals, and, if $\mathcal{A}_{i,j}$ is the restriction of $\mathcal{A}_i$ to the elements in P_j, then define

$$\mathcal{A}_{i,j} \cong \begin{cases} \eta, & \text{if } i \neq j \\ 1 + \eta, & \text{if } i = j. \end{cases}$$

Let us denote $\mathfrak{K}_{\text{st}} = \{\mathcal{A}_i : i \in \omega\}$. This class is studied in [5], and by combining [5] with Corollary 1, the following characterization of **InfEx**-learnability is obtained.

Theorem 4 ([5]). *For a class $\mathfrak{K} = \{\mathcal{B}_i : i \in \omega\}$, the following are equivalent:*

*(1) The class $\mathfrak{K}$ is **InfEx**-learnable.*
(2) $\mathfrak{K} \leq_{\text{Cantor}} \mathfrak{K}_{st}$.

(3) There is a sequence of Σ_2^{inf} sentences $\{\psi_i : i \in \omega\}$ such that for all i and j, $\mathcal{B}_j \models \psi_i$ if and only if $i = j$.

This result suggests the following definition.

Definition 8. *We say that a class $\mathfrak{K}_0$ is **InfEx**-complete if*

- *$\mathfrak{K}_0$ is **InfEx**-learnable;*
- *for any **InfEx**-learnable class $\mathfrak{K}$, $\mathfrak{K} \leq_{\mathrm{Cantor}} \mathfrak{K}_0$.*

It follows that the class $\mathfrak{K}_{st}$ is **InfEx**-complete. Now we will show that $\mathfrak{K}_{st}$ is also **TxtEx**-complete (see Proposition 4 below). To do this, we borrow some ideas from [2] to get a series of ancillary facts.

Lemma 4. $\tilde{\mathcal{E}} \leq_{pc} \mathfrak{K}_{st}$.

Proof. For each number $k \geq 1$, consider the enumeration operator Γ_{e_k} (which takes an equivalence structure as an input), where the domain of the output structure is the set of non-empty tuples

$$D_k = \left\{ (x_0, \ldots, x_n) : \bigwedge_{i<n} x_i <_\mathbb{N} x_{i+1} \ \& \ |[x_i]_\sim| \geq k+1 \ \& \ |[x_n]_\sim| \geq k \right\},$$

where the ordering between the tuples is given by $\overline{x} \prec \overline{y}$ if and only if $\overline{x}$ is a proper extension of $\overline{y}$, or $x_i <_\mathbb{N} y_i$ for some index $i < \min\{|\overline{x}|, |\overline{y}|\}$.

If the input structure $\mathcal{A}$ has type $[\omega : \omega, \ k : \omega]$, then $\Gamma_{e_k}(\mathcal{A})$ is a linear ordering with a least element and no greatest element, and, if the input structure $\mathcal{A}$ has type $[\omega : \omega, \ m : \omega]$ for $m \neq k$, then $\Gamma_{e_k}(\mathcal{A})$ is a linear ordering with no least element and no greatest element.

Now, let Ψ_{a_k} be such that $\Psi_{a_k}(\mathcal{A})$ enumerates a copy of $1 + \eta$ in place of the elements enumerated by $\Gamma_{e_k}(\mathcal{A})$. At last, let $\Theta(\mathcal{A})$ enumerate the disjoint union of the structures $\Gamma_{e_k}(\mathcal{A})$ with P_k distinguishing the substructure enumerated by $\Gamma_{e_k}(\mathcal{A})$. It is now routine to check that $\tilde{\mathcal{E}} \leq_{pc} \mathfrak{K}_{st}$ via Θ. $\quad\square$

Lemma 5. $\mathfrak{K}_{st} \leq_{pc} \mathcal{E}$.

Proof. Suppose that the input structure $\mathcal{A}$ has domain $\{x_{k,i} : i, k \in \omega\}$, where $P_k^{\mathcal{A}} = \{x_{k,i} : i \in \omega\}$. We describe how the enumeration operator Γ_e works. The output structures of Γ_e will always have domain a subset of $\{y_{k,i}^j : k, i, j \in \omega\}$.

For any k, on input the finite diagram D_k describing a finite chain (inside $P_k^{\mathcal{A}}$) $x_{k,i_0} <_{\mathcal{A}} x_{k,i_1} <_{\mathcal{A}} \cdots <_{\mathcal{A}} x_{k,i_n}$, $\Gamma_e(D_k)$ is an infinite part of the output equivalence structure describing the following:

$$\bigwedge_{j<k} (y_{k,i_0}^j \sim y_{k,i_0}^{j+1}) \ \& \ \bigwedge_{\ell=1}^{n} \bigwedge_{j\in\omega} (y_{k,i_\ell}^j \sim y_{k,i_\ell}^{j+1}).$$

In other words, we associate with the current least element in the k-th linear ordering $P_k^{\mathcal{A}}$ an equivalence class of size $k + 1$, and with any other element in the k-th linear ordering we associate an infinite equivalence class.

Let $\mathcal{A}_k$ be the restriction of $\mathcal{A}$ to $P_k^{\mathcal{A}}$. If $\mathcal{A}_k \cong 1 + \eta$, then $\Gamma_e(\mathcal{A})$ will contain an equivalence class of size $k+1$, and all other equivalence classes will be infinite. □

Lemma 6. $\mathcal{E} \leq_{pc} \tilde{\mathcal{E}}$.

Proof. We define $\Gamma \colon \mathcal{E} \leq_{pc} \tilde{\mathcal{E}}$ is a straightforward manner: Γ essentially copies the input structure infinitely many times. □

By combining the previous three lemmas and Corollary 4 we obtain:

Proposition 4. *The classes $\mathcal{E}$, $\tilde{\mathcal{E}}$, and $\mathfrak{K}_{st}$ are* **TxtEx**-*complete.*

7   Applications

Recall that [10, Theorem 1.4] proves that the class $\mathfrak{K} = \{[\omega : 1], [\omega : 2]\}$ is **InfEx**-learnable, but not **TxtEx**-learnable. We give a new simple proof of this fact using **TxtEx**-complete classes.

Proposition 5. *The class $\mathfrak{K} = \{[\omega : 1], [\omega : 2]\}$ is* **InfEx**-*learnable, but not* **TxtEx**-*learnable.*

Proof. Towards a contradiction, assume that $\mathfrak{K}$ is **TxtEx**-learnable. A simple analysis of the proof of Lemma 1 shows that for the class $\mathfrak{K}_0 = \{[\omega : 1, 1 : 1], [\omega : 1, 2 : 1]\}$, we must have $\mathfrak{K} \leq_{\text{Scott}} \mathfrak{K}_0$ via some Scott-continuous operator Γ. Without loss of generality, suppose that for any structure $\mathcal{A}$ of type $[\omega : 1]$, $\Gamma(\mathcal{A})$ is an equivalence structure of type $[\omega : 1, 1 : 1]$.

Let b_0 be the element in $\Gamma(\mathcal{A})$ such that $|[b_0]_\sim| = 1$. By compactness, there is some finite part α of $\mathcal{A}$ for which $b_0 \in \Gamma(\alpha)$. Now, partition $\mathcal{A}$ into two infinite classes of infinite size such that α is contained entirely in one of the classes. In this way we produce a structure $\mathcal{A}'$ of type $[\omega : 2]$ which is a substructure (w.r.t. positive atomic facts) of $\mathcal{A}$. Since Scott-continuity implies monotonicity, $\Gamma(\mathcal{A}') \subseteq \Gamma(\mathcal{A})$. Since $b_0 \in \Gamma(\alpha)$ and α is a finite part of $\mathcal{A}'$, $b_0 \in \Gamma(\mathcal{A}')$. But since $\Gamma(\mathcal{A}')$ has type $[\omega : 1, 2 : 1]$, it follows that there is at least one element c_0 such that $\Gamma(\mathcal{A}') \models b_0 \sim c_0$. Since $\Gamma(\mathcal{A}') \subseteq \Gamma(\mathcal{A})$, it follows that $\Gamma(\mathcal{A}) \models b_0 \sim c_0$. We reach a contradiction with the fact that $|[b_0]_\sim| = 1$ in $\Gamma(\mathcal{A})$. □

It is natural to search for **TxtEx**-learnable classes which are not **TxtEx**-complete. Consider the class $\mathfrak{K} = \{\mathcal{A}_i : i \geq 1\}$, where $\mathcal{A}_i$ is an equivalence structure of type $[i : \omega]$. It is clear that $\mathfrak{K}$ is **TxtEx**-learnable, since for each structure $\mathcal{A}_i$ we have a distinguishing Σ_2^p sentence $\psi_i := \varphi_{i-1}$ taken from Eq. (1). To see that $\mathfrak{K}$ is not **TxtEx**-complete, it is enough to consider the following.

Proposition 6. $\{[\omega : 1, 1 : 1], [\omega : 1, 2 : 1]\} \nleq_{\text{Scott}} \{[1 : \omega], [2 : \omega]\}$.

Proof. Assume that $\Gamma\colon \{[\omega : 1, 1 : 1], [\omega : 1, 2 : 1]\} \leq_{\text{Scott}} \{[1 : \omega], [2 : \omega]\}$. Let $\mathcal{B}$ be an equivalence structure of type $[\omega : 1, 1 : 1]$ and $\mathcal{A}$ be a substructure (w.r.t. positive atomic facts) of $\mathcal{B}$ of type $[\omega : 1, 2 : 1]$. By the monotonicity of Scott-continuous operators, $\Gamma(\mathcal{A}) \subseteq \Gamma(\mathcal{B})$. But $\Gamma(\mathcal{A})$ is an equivalence structure of type $[2 : \omega]$ and $\Gamma(\mathcal{B})$ is an equivalence structure of type $[1 : \omega]$. We reach a contradiction by observing that $[2 : \omega]$ is not embeddable into $[1 : \omega]$. □

Assume that the class $\mathfrak{K}$ is **TxtEx**-complete, then $\mathcal{E} \leq_{\text{Scott}} \mathfrak{K}$. We can easily generalize the argument from Proposition 6 to reach a contradiction.

8 Further Discussion

Recall that the paper [3] explored some connections between **InfEx**-learnability and descriptive set theory. Here we elaborate more on this approach.

For $\alpha, \beta \in 2^\omega$, we define $\alpha\ E_0\ \beta$ if and only if $(\exists n)(\forall m \geq n)[\alpha(n) = \beta(n)]$. In [3], a class of structures $\mathfrak{K}$ is characterized as **InfEx**-learnable if and only if the isomorphism relation $\cong \restriction \text{LD}(\mathfrak{K})$ is (Cantor-)continuously reducible to the relation E_0 of eventual agreement on reals (i.e., there is a Cantor-continuous function Φ such that for all $\mathcal{A}, \mathcal{B} \in \mathfrak{K}\ \mathcal{A} \cong \mathcal{B}$ if and only if $\Phi(\mathcal{A})\ E_0\ \Phi(\mathcal{B})$).

Motivated by this result we formulate the following question.

Question 1. Characterize **TxtEx**-learnability in terms of Scott-continuous functions and familiar Borel equivalence relations.

Acknowledgements. The work of Bazhenov was supported by the Russian Science Foundation (project no. 24-11-00227). Fokina was supported by the Austrian Science Fund FWF through the project P 36781. Rossegger was supported by the European Union's Horizon 2020 Research and Innovation Programme under the Marie Skłodowska-Curie grant agreement No. 101026834—ACOSE. Soskova was supported by the European Union-NextGenerationEU, through the National Recovery and Resilience Plan of the Republic of Bulgaria, project no. BG-RRP-2.004-0008-C01. Vatev was supported by FNI-SU 80-10-180/17.05.2023.

References

1. Ash, C.J., Knight, J.F.: Computable Structures and the Hyperarithmetical Hierarchy. Studies in Logic and the Foundations of Mathematics, vol. 144. Elsevier Science B.V. (2000)
2. Bazhenov, N.A., Ganchev, H., Vatev, S.: Computable embeddings for pairs of linear orders. Algebra Logic **60**(3), 163–187 (2021). https://doi.org/10.1007/s10469-021-09639-7
3. Bazhenov, N., Cipriani, V., San Mauro, L.: Learning algebraic structures with the help of Borel equivalence relations. Theor. Comput. Sci. **951** (2023). https://doi.org/10.1016/j.tcs.2023.113762
4. Bazhenov, N., Fokina, E., Rossegger, D., Soskova, A.A., Vatev, S.V.: A Lopez-Escobar theorem for continuous domains (2023). http://arxiv.org/abs/2301.09940

5. Bazhenov, N., Fokina, E., San Mauro, L.: Learning families of algebraic structures from informant. Inf. Comput. **275**, 104590 (2020). https://doi.org/10.1016/j.ic. 2020.104590

6. Bazhenov, N., San Mauro, L.: On the Turing complexity of learning finite families of algebraic structures. J. Log. Comput. **31**(7), 1891–1900 (2021). https://doi.org/ 10.1093/logcom/exab044

7. Calvert, W., Cummins, D., Knight, J.F., Miller, S.: Comparing classes of finite structures. Algebra Logic **43**(6), 374–392 (2004). https://doi.org/10.1023/ B:ALLO.0000048827.30718.2c

8. Case, J.: Enumeration reducibility and partial degrees. Ann. Math. Logic **2**(4), 419–439 (1971). https://doi.org/10.1016/0003-4843(71)90003-9

9. Cooper, S.B.: Enumeration reducibility, nondeterministic computations and relative computability of partial functions. In: Ambos-Spies, K., Müller, G.H., Sacks, G.E. (eds.) Recursion Theory Week. LNM, vol. 1432, pp. 57–110. Springer, Heidelberg (1990). https://doi.org/10.1007/BFb0086114

10. Fokina, E., Kötzing, T., San Mauro, L.: Limit learning equivalence structures. In: Garivier, A., Kale, S. (eds.) Proceedings of the 30th International Conference on Algorithmic Learning Theory. Proceedings of Machine Learning Research, vol. 98, pp. 383–403. PMLR (2019)

11. Gao, Z., Stephan, F., Wu, G., Yamamoto, A.: Learning families of closed sets in matroids. In: Dinneen, M.J., Khoussainov, B., Nies, A. (eds.) WTCS 2012. LNCS, vol. 7160, pp. 120–139. Springer, Heidelberg (2012). https://doi.org/10.1007/978-3-642-27654-5_10

12. Gold, E.M.: Language identification in the limit. Inf. Control **10**(5), 447–474 (1967). https://doi.org/10.1016/S0019-9958(67)91165-5

13. Harizanov, V.S., Stephan, F.: On the learnability of vector spaces. J. Comput. Syst. Sci. **73**(1), 109–122 (2007). https://doi.org/10.1016/j.jcss.2006.09.001

14. Jain, S., Osherson, D., Royer, J.S., Sharma, A.: Systems that Learn. MIT Press, Cambridge (1999)

15. Knight, J.F., Miller, S., Vanden Boom, M.: Turing computable embeddings. J. Symb. Log. **72**(3), 901–918 (2007). https://doi.org/10.2178/jsl/1191333847

16. Martin, E., Osherson, D.: Scientific discovery on positive data via belief revision. J. Philos. Log. **29**(5), 483–506 (2000). https://doi.org/10.1023/A:1026569206678

17. Putnam, H.: Trial and error predicates and the solution to a problem of Mostowski. J. Symb. Log. **30**(1), 49–57 (1965). https://doi.org/10.2307/2270581

18. Soskov, I.: Degree spectra and co-spectra of structures. Ann. Sofia Univ. **96**, 45–68 (2004)

19. Stephan, F., Ventsov, Y.: Learning algebraic structures from text. Theor. Comput. Sci. **268**(2), 221–273 (2001). https://doi.org/10.1016/S0304-3975(00)00272-3

Structures of Finite Punctual Dimension $n > 2$

Ellen Hammatt[(✉)]

Victoria University of Wellington, Te Herenga Waka, Wellington, New Zealand
ellen.hammatt@vuw.ac.nz

Abstract. In this paper we prove the primitive recursive analogue of Goncharov's finite computable dimension n theorem [12,13]. In the case of structures with computable dimension $n > 2$, a certain elementary trick suffices. However in the primitive recursive case, this elementary trick no longer suffices. Our first theorem shows that a direct construction of structures of punctual dimension $n > 2$ is provably necessary. Our second theorem is a direct construction of these structures. This work extends the earlier result of Melnikov and Ng [18].

1 Introduction

In [17,20], Mal'cev and Rabin independently suggested that computable presented structures should be viewed up to computable isomorphism. Recall the following definition:

Definition 1. *A structure $\mathcal{A}$ is computable if it has a computable presentation which is a coding of $\mathcal{A}$ into universe $\mathbb{N}$ where all functions and relations in the language of $\mathcal{A}$ are computable on domain $\mathbb{N}$.*

We say a structure $\mathcal{A}$ is *computably categorical* if $\mathcal{A}$ has exactly one computable presentation up to computable isomorphism. Computably categorical structures have been classified in many common classes [2,11,19]. Remarkably, Goncharov discovered that there exist structures that have exactly two computable presentations up to computable isomorphism. We say that such a structure has computable dimension 2. Examples of structures with *computable dimension $n > 1$* exist among various classes of algebraic structures including, two-step nilpotent groups, fields, graphs and many other classes [13–15]. Note that each of these examples are complex and must be specifically constructed for this result. Properties of structures with finite computable dimension $n > 2$ and the complexity of their isomorphisms have also been studied more recently in [7,21]. These results have had a profound effect on the field. However, all of these proofs and techniques rely heavily on unbounded search. It is natural to ask whether these results remain true if we forbid unbounded search.

Mal'cev [17] also suggested to study primitive recursive structures:

L. Levy Patey et al. (Eds.): CiE 2024, LNCS 14773, pp. 179–191, 2024.
https://doi.org/10.1007/978-3-031-64309-5_15

Definition 2. *A structure $\mathcal{A}$ is primitive recursive if it has a primitive recursive presentation which is a coding of $\mathcal{A}$ into universe $M \subseteq \mathbb{N}$ where M is primitive recursive and all functions and relations in the language of $\mathcal{A}$ are primitive recursive on domain M.*

However, until [16] primitive recursive structures have been used mainly as a technical tool to study polynomial time structures. The systematic investigation of the primitive recursive content of mathematics was initiated in [16]. It was quickly discovered that novel techniques are often required to study structures with primitive recursive operations as defined below:

Definition 3 ([16]). *A structure $\mathcal{A}$ is punctual if it has a punctual presentation which is a coding of $\mathcal{A}$ into universe $\mathbb{N}$ where all functions and relations in the language of $\mathcal{A}$ are primitive recursive on domain $\mathbb{N}$.*

Note that the above definition is not the same as Definition 2. The domain of a punctual presentation must be all of $\mathbb{N}$. This ensures that there is no delay coded into the domain. We follow the convention established in [16] and adopt Definition 3 as our central notion. However, Definition 2 will play a technical role later in Sect. 2. Similar to the computable case we will view punctual presentations up to punctual isomorphism, which is defined as follows:

Definition 4. *Let $\mathcal{A}, \mathcal{B}$ be punctual presentations. An isomorphism $p : \mathcal{A} \to \mathcal{B}$ is a punctual isomorphism if p and p^{-1} are both primitive recursive.*

Note that the inverse of a primitive recursive function may not be primitive recursive.

Many results about punctual structures have been accumulated, see the surveys [3,10]. Notably, there are also applications of punctual structures in automatic structure theory [5] and to reverse mathematics [4]. Using techniques rather different from those in the computable case, in [18], Melnikov and Ng have established the following result:

Theorem 1 ([18]). *There is a structure with exactly two punctual presentations up to punctual isomorphism.*

Following the analogy in the computable case, we say that the structure from Theorem 1 has *punctual dimension* 2. Our principal goal is to extend this result to $n > 2$. For example, is there a structure of punctual dimension 4? In the computable case, the answer is elementary by taking the 'join' of two structures of computable dimension 2 and then observing that this structure has computable dimension 4 (folklore). Similar tricks can be used to produce examples of other finite computable dimensions. Our first result strongly suggests that using such 'tricks' in the punctual case is impossible:

Theorem 2. *For any infinite punctual structures $\mathcal{A}, \mathcal{B}$, the ordered and unordered joins of $\mathcal{A}$ and $\mathcal{B}$ have punctual dimension 1 or ∞.*

In Sect. 2 we will give the full proof in the case of the ordered join. Essentially the same proof works for the unordered join, this will be discussed in Sect. 2.2. This indicates that the results does not depend on the exact way of defining the join. Thus we strongly conjecture that, unlike in the computable case, a direct construction of punctual dimension $n > 2$ is necessary. We prove the following:

Theorem 3. *There is a structure $\mathcal{A}$ of punctual dimension n for each $n \in \mathbb{N}$.*

Our proof extends the techniques of [18]. In the case of punctual dimension $n > 2$ there are new conflicts that need to be overcome. For instance the 'recovery phase' needs careful attention. We leave open whether examples of punctual dimension 2 exist in common algebraic classes such as fields and groups. It is already known that such structures do not exist in the following classes: Boolean algebra, linear orders, unary structures and graphs [8, 16].

2   Punctual Dimension of the Join

In this section we prove Theorem 2. We split the proof into two cases, in the first subsection we prove this theorem for the ordered join and then we will prove it for the unordered join in the second subsection. Throughout this section, we will use $\mathcal{K}$ to denote a class of countable structures in a finite language.

2.1   Ordered Join

We define a formal notion of the ordered join of structures $\mathcal{A}$ and $\mathcal{B}$.

Definition 5. *Let $\mathcal{K}$ be a class of countable structures in a finite language. The ordered join of $\mathcal{A}, \mathcal{B} \in \mathcal{K}$ is the structure $\mathcal{A} \sqcup \mathcal{B}$ in the language of $\mathcal{K}$ augmented with a unary predicate U such that the following holds:*

- $\mathcal{A} \sqcup \mathcal{B} \upharpoonright_U \cong \mathcal{A}$,
- $\mathcal{A} \sqcup \mathcal{B} \upharpoonright_{\neg U} \cong \mathcal{B}$.

In the case of the ordered join the unary predicate distinguishes each 'side' of the join, so $\mathcal{A} \sqcup \mathcal{B}$ is not necessarily isomorphic to $\mathcal{B} \sqcup \mathcal{A}$. Let $\mathcal{C}$ be a structure of computable dimension 2, notice that with the above definition, $\mathcal{C} \sqcup \mathcal{C}$ has computable dimension 4. Now we work to show that in the punctual case this no longer works. The idea is that in the punctual case the overall structure can be punctual without each side being punctually enumerated. For example, we can produce a punctual presentation of $\mathcal{A} \sqcup \mathcal{B}$ with presentations of $\mathcal{A}$ and $\mathcal{B}$ that are not necessarily punctual. To formalise this notion, we define how to obtain a primitive recursive presentation of the join of $\mathcal{A}$ and $\mathcal{B}$, where $\mathcal{A}$ and $\mathcal{B}$ are primitive recursive presentations.

Definition 6. *Let $\mathcal{A}, \mathcal{B} \in \mathcal{K}$ be infinite primitive recursive structures. Let $\Phi(\mathcal{A}, \mathcal{B})$ be the primitive recursive presentation of $\mathcal{A} \sqcup \mathcal{B}$ such that:*

1. $\Phi(\mathcal{A}, \mathcal{B}) \upharpoonright_U \subseteq \{n \in \omega : n \text{ is even}\}$,
2. $\Phi(\mathcal{A}, \mathcal{B}) \upharpoonright_{\neg U} \subseteq \{n \in \omega : n \text{ is odd}\}$,
3. the map $\pi_0 : \mathcal{A} \rightarrow \{n \in \omega : n \text{ is even}\}$ where $\pi_0(x) = 2x$ is an isomorphism of $\mathcal{A}$ and $\Phi(\mathcal{A}, \mathcal{B}) \upharpoonright_U$,
4. the map $\pi_1 : \mathcal{B} \rightarrow \{n \in \omega : n \text{ is odd}\}$ where $\pi_0(x) = 2x+1$ is an isomorphism of $\mathcal{B}$ and $\Phi(\mathcal{A}, \mathcal{B}) \upharpoonright_{\neg U}$.

Notice that if $\mathcal{A}$ and $\mathcal{B}$ are punctual presentations, then $\Phi(\mathcal{A}, \mathcal{B})$ is a punctual presentation of $\mathcal{A} \sqcup \mathcal{B}$. The following lemma gives us a way to uniformly produce a punctual presentation from a primitive recursive presentation.

Lemma 1 (Alaev [1]). *Let $\mathcal{A}$ be a primitive recursive structure. Let h be an injective primitive recursive function such that $\operatorname{range} h \subseteq \operatorname{dom} \mathcal{A}$. Then $\mathcal{A}$ has a punctual presentation $\mathcal{B}$. Furthermore, we can uniformly produce a primitive recursive isomorphism $f : \mathcal{B} \rightarrow \mathcal{A}$ and its inverse $f^{-1} : \mathcal{A} \rightarrow \mathcal{B}$ which is primitive recursive on $\operatorname{dom} \mathcal{A}$.*

Proof. We build a punctual presentation $\mathcal{B} \cong \mathcal{A}$ along with $f : \mathcal{B} \rightarrow \mathcal{A}$. At stage s, do the following that applies:

- if $s \in \operatorname{dom} \mathcal{A}$ and $s \notin \operatorname{range} f[s-1]$ then define $f(s) = s$,
- otherwise, define $f(s) = h(i)$ for i least such that $h(i) \notin \operatorname{range} f[s-1]$ for $i \leq s$.

Then f has domain ω and range $\operatorname{dom} \mathcal{A}$ and induces a punctual presentation $\mathcal{B}$. Notice that f^{-1} is also primitive recursive on $\operatorname{dom} \mathcal{A}$ as $f^{-1}(n) \leq n$ by definition.

We give the analogue of Alaev's Lemma for pairs of structures.

Definition 7. *Let $\mathcal{A}, \mathcal{B}$ be primitive recursive structures. We say $(\mathcal{A}, \mathcal{B})$ is a punctual pair if there is an injective primitive recursive function g such that $\operatorname{range} g \subseteq \operatorname{dom} \mathcal{A} \cup \operatorname{dom} \mathcal{B}$.*

Lemma 2. *Let $(\mathcal{A}, \mathcal{B})$ be a punctual pair. Then we can uniformly obtain a punctual presentation $M(\mathcal{A}, \mathcal{B})$ of $\mathcal{A} \sqcup \mathcal{B}$ from $\Phi(\mathcal{A}, \mathcal{B})$ and g. Furthermore, we can uniformly produce a primitive recursive isomorphism $m : M(\mathcal{A}, \mathcal{B}) \rightarrow \Phi(\mathcal{A}, \mathcal{B})$ and its inverse m^{-1}, which is primitive recursive on $\operatorname{dom}(\Phi(\mathcal{A}, \mathcal{B}))$.*

Proof. Define $h(x) = 2g(x)$ if $g(x) \in \operatorname{dom} \mathcal{A}$, otherwise define $h(x) = 2g(x) + 1$. Since g is an injective primitive recursive function such that $\operatorname{range} g \subseteq \operatorname{dom} \mathcal{A} \cup \operatorname{dom} \mathcal{B}$, h is an injective primitive recursive function such that $\operatorname{range} h \subseteq \operatorname{dom} \Phi(\mathcal{A}, \mathcal{B})$. Then apply Lemma 1 to obtain $M(\mathcal{A}, \mathcal{B})$ and m as desired.

Now we prove Theorem 2 in the case of the ordered join. We will do this in three cases which depend on the punctual dimension of $\mathcal{A}$ and $\mathcal{B}$ and whether or not the structures are finitely generated. For the case that $\mathcal{A}$ and $\mathcal{B}$ are both finitely generated, we use the following lemma.

Lemma 3. *If $\mathcal{A}$ is finitely generated then $\mathcal{A}$ has punctual dimension 1 or ∞.*

Recall that $\mathcal{A} \leq_{pr} \mathcal{B}$ if there is a primitive recursive isomorphism $p : \mathcal{A} \to \mathcal{B}$. To prove Lemma 3 we use the following lemma.

Lemma 4. [6] *If a structure $\mathcal{A}$ is finitely generated then for any two punctual presentations of $\mathcal{A}$, $\mathcal{A}_1 <_{pr} \mathcal{A}_2$ there is a punctual presentation $\mathcal{A}_3$ so that $\mathcal{A}_1 <_{pr} \mathcal{A}_3 <_{pr} \mathcal{A}_2$.*

Proof (of Lemma 3). Suppose $\mathcal{A}$ has punctual dimension $n > 1$. As shown in [6], there is a $<_{pr}$-least punctual presentation of $\mathcal{A}$, call this presentation $\mathcal{B}$. Since $\mathcal{A}$ has punctual dimension $n > 1$, there must exist another presentation of $\mathcal{A}$ not punctually isomorphic to $\mathcal{B}$, call $\mathcal{C}$. It follows that there is primitive recursive $p : \mathcal{B} \to \mathcal{C}$, then by Lemma 4 $\mathcal{A}$ has punctual dimension ∞.

See [6] for example of finitely generated structures with punctual dimension ∞.

Now we give the proof of Theorem 2 in the case of the ordered join.

Proof. **Case 1.** Suppose $\mathcal{A}$ or $\mathcal{B}$ has punctual dimension ∞. Without loss of generality let $\mathcal{A}$ have punctual dimension ∞. Let $\mathcal{A}_1, \mathcal{A}_2, \ldots$ be punctual presentations of $\mathcal{A}$ that witness the infinite punctual dimension of $\mathcal{A}$. Fix some punctual presentation of $\mathcal{B}$ that we shall also denote as $\mathcal{B}$.

For each i, consider the primitive recursive structure $\Phi(\mathcal{A}_i, \mathcal{B})$ isomorphic to $\mathcal{A} \sqcup \mathcal{B}$. Since $\mathcal{A}_i$ and $\mathcal{B}$ are punctual for all i, so is $\Phi(\mathcal{A}_i, \mathcal{B})$. Let $\mathcal{M}_i = \Phi(\mathcal{A}_i, \mathcal{B})$. Suppose there are $i \neq j$ so that there is a punctual isomorphism $p : \mathcal{M}_i \to \mathcal{M}_j$. Then for $a \in \mathcal{A}_i$, $\pi_0^{-1}(p(\pi_0(a)))$ is a primitive recursive isomoprhism from $\mathcal{A}_i$ to $\mathcal{A}_j$. Similarly for $a \in \mathcal{A}_j$, $\pi_0^{-1}(p^{-1}(\pi_0(a)))$ is a primitive recursive isomorphism from $\mathcal{A}_j$ to $\mathcal{A}_i$. But $\mathcal{A}_i$ and $\mathcal{A}_j$ are not punctually isomorphic by assumption, so we obtain a contradiction. Therefore $\mathcal{A} \sqcup \mathcal{B}$ has punctual dimension ∞.

Case 2. Suppose $\mathcal{A}$ and $\mathcal{B}$ are finitely generated. Then $\mathcal{A} \sqcup \mathcal{B}$ is also finitely generated; hence by Lemma 3 $\mathcal{A} \sqcup \mathcal{B}$ has punctual dimension 1 or ∞.

Case 3. Now we are left with the case that $\mathcal{A}$ and $\mathcal{B}$ have finite punctual dimension and at least one of $\mathcal{A}$ or $\mathcal{B}$ is not finitely generated. In this case we prove that $\mathcal{A} \sqcup \mathcal{B}$ has punctual dimension ∞. Without loss of generality, we assume $\mathcal{A}$ is not finitely generated. Fix some punctual presentations of $\mathcal{A}$ and $\mathcal{B}$ that we shall also denote as $\mathcal{A}$ and $\mathcal{B}$ respectively.

For each i, we build punctual presentations $\mathcal{M}_i$ of $\mathcal{A} \sqcup \mathcal{B}$ such that for all $i \neq j$, $\mathcal{M}_i$ and $\mathcal{M}_j$ are not punctually isomorphic. To do this, for each i, we build primitive recursive presentations of $\mathcal{A}$, which we denote $\mathcal{A}_i$. Since $\mathcal{B}$ is punctual, $(\mathcal{A}_i, \mathcal{B})$ is a punctual pair. To build $\mathcal{A}_i$, we construct a primitive recursive subset of ω to be the domain of $\mathcal{A}_i$ and we also define an isomorphism $f_i : \mathcal{A}_i \to \mathcal{A}$ which will be primitive recursive on $\operatorname{dom} \mathcal{A}_i$. We define $\operatorname{dom} \mathcal{A}_i$ by deciding whether s is in the domain or not at stage s. Let $\langle f_i(\mathcal{A}_i[s]) \rangle$ denote the part of the substructure in $\mathcal{A}$ generated by $f_i(\mathcal{A}_i[s])$ at stage s.

Construction. Let (p_e, q_e) for $e \in \omega$ list all pairs of primitive recursive functions. We wish to meet the following requirements for each e, k, m where $k < m$:

$$P_{e,k,m} : p_e : \mathcal{M}_k \to \mathcal{M}_m \text{ is not an isomorphism or } q_e \neq p_e^{-1}$$

We will meet each requirement one at a time. We move on when (p_e, q_e) does not look like an isomorphism, by this we mean that there is x, y such that $p_e(x) = y$ and $q_e(y) \neq x$ (i.e. $q_e \neq p_e^{-1}$), or if p_e or q_e are not injective, finally if either p_e or q_e do not preserve the functions or relations including U. Order requirements in some effective list. At every stage of the construction we define $\mathcal{A}_i$ and f_i as described above; hence $(\mathcal{A}_i, \mathcal{B})$ is a punctual pair. We use Lemma 2 to uniformly produce $\mathcal{M}_i = \mathcal{M}(\mathcal{A}_i, \mathcal{B})$.

At stage 0, for all $i \in \omega$ declare $0 \in \operatorname{dom} \mathcal{A}_i$ and define $f_i(0) = 0$. Go to the next stage, and consider the first requirement on the list.

At stage s, let $P_{e,k,m}$ be the current requirement. For all $i \neq m$ declare $s \in \operatorname{dom} \mathcal{A}_i$ and do the first of the following that applies:

- if $(p_e, q_e)[s]$ witnesses that it is not a punctual isomorphism from $\mathcal{M}_k[s]$ to $\mathcal{M}_m[s]$ then declare $s \in \operatorname{dom} \mathcal{A}_m$. Move to the next requirement on the list,
- if $\langle f_m(\mathcal{A}_m[s]) \rangle \neq \langle f_m(\mathcal{A}_m[s-1]) \rangle$ then declare $s \in \operatorname{dom} \mathcal{A}_m$,
- otherwise, declare $s \notin \operatorname{dom} \mathcal{A}_m$.

In all cases for all i, if $s \in \operatorname{dom} \mathcal{A}_i$ then define $f_i(s) = n$ where n is least such that it is not in the range of f_i at stage s. Halt the stage.

Verification. We need to prove every requirement is met. Suppose not, then let $P_{e,k,m}$ be the least requirement on the list that is never met. By construction, this means that at every stage the pair p_e is a partial isomorphism and q_e is the inverse of p_e, hence p_e is an isomorphism. Now p_e restricted to domain $\mathcal{M}_k \restriction_U$ ranges over $\mathcal{M}_m \restriction_U$, similarly q_e restricted to domain $\mathcal{M}_m \restriction_U$ ranges over $\mathcal{M}_k \restriction_U$. Let t be the stage where we first start considering $P_{e,k,m}$. Now $\mathcal{A}_k \cong \mathcal{A}$ and $\mathcal{A}_m \cong \langle f_m(\mathcal{A}_m[t]) \rangle$. By assumption $\mathcal{A}$ is not finitely generated so $\mathcal{A}_k \not\cong \mathcal{A}_m$; hence (p_e, q_e) cannot represent a punctual isomorphism, a contradiction. Therefore every requirement is met, so $\mathcal{M}_i$ for each $i \in \omega$ witnesses that $\mathcal{A} \sqcup \mathcal{B}$ has punctual dimension ∞.

Remark 1. In fact, in the case that $\mathcal{A}$ and $\mathcal{B}$ both have finite punctual dimension and are finitely generated, $\mathcal{A} \sqcup \mathcal{B}$ has punctual dimension 1. This follows from the fact that we can non-uniformly fix the stage where all generators have shown up in $\mathcal{A} \sqcup \mathcal{B}$ since it in finitely generated. Now each side of $\mathcal{A} \sqcup \mathcal{B}$ induces punctual presentations of $\mathcal{A}$ and $\mathcal{B}$ after this stage. Note that $\mathcal{A}$ and $\mathcal{B}$ both have punctual dimension 1 by Lemma 3. We can then use this to show that any presentations of $\mathcal{A} \sqcup \mathcal{B}$ are pairwise punctually isomorphic.

2.2 Unordered Join

We begin by giving a formal definition of the unordered join. In contrast to the ordered join, each 'side' is no longer distinguishable.

Definition 8. *Let $\mathcal{K}$ be a class of countable structures in a finite language. The unordered join of $\mathcal{A}, \mathcal{B} \in \mathcal{K}$ is the structure $\mathcal{A} \tilde{\sqcup} \mathcal{B}$ in the language of $\mathcal{K}$ augmented with a binary predicate E such that the following holds:*

- E is a equivalence relation with exactly two equivalence classes. Let $[x]$ and $[y]$ be the two equivalence classes,
- $\mathcal{A} \tilde{\sqcup} \mathcal{B} \upharpoonright_{[x]} \cong \mathcal{A}$ and $\mathcal{A} \tilde{\sqcup} \mathcal{B} \upharpoonright_{[y]} \cong \mathcal{B}$.

Let $\mathcal{C}$ be a structure of computable dimension 2. Notice that with the above definition $\mathcal{C} \tilde{\sqcup} \mathcal{C}$ has computable dimension 3. We show that in the punctual case this no longer works, in a very similar way as in the ordered case. We use the same framework to do this. First we define how to obtain a primitive recursive presentation of the unordered join of $\mathcal{A}$ and $\mathcal{B}$, where $\mathcal{A}$ and $\mathcal{B}$ are primitive recursive presentations.

Definition 9. *Let* $\mathcal{A}, \mathcal{B} \in \mathcal{K}$ *be infinite primitive recursive structures. Let* $\Psi(\mathcal{A}, \mathcal{B})$ *be the primitive recursive presentation of* $\mathcal{A} \tilde{\sqcup} \mathcal{B}$ *such that:*

1. *for* $x, y \in \operatorname{dom} \Psi(\mathcal{A}, \mathcal{B})$, $x E y$ *if and only if* x *and* y *have the same parity,*
2. *the map* $\pi_0 : \mathcal{A} \to \{n \in \omega : n \text{ is even}\}$ *where* $\pi_0(x) = 2x$ *induces an isomorphism of* $\mathcal{A}$ *and* $\Psi(\mathcal{A}, \mathcal{B}) \upharpoonright_{[0]}$,
3. *the map* $\pi_1 : \mathcal{B} \to \{n \in \omega : n \text{ is odd}\}$ *where* $\pi_1(x) = 2x + 1$ *induces an isomorphism of* $\mathcal{B}$ *and* $\Psi(\mathcal{A}, \mathcal{B}) \upharpoonright_{[1]}$.

Now we finish the proof of Theorem 2 by completing the unordered case.

If $\mathcal{A} \not\cong \mathcal{B}$ then we can apply the same proof as we did in the ordered case by replacing $\Phi(\mathcal{A}, \mathcal{B})$ with $\Psi(\mathcal{A}, \mathcal{B})$. So let's consider the case when $\mathcal{A} \cong \mathcal{B}$. Then we are looking at the punctual dimension of $\mathcal{A} \tilde{\sqcup} \mathcal{A}$. We explain the modifications required to the proof for the ordered case. In the case that $\mathcal{A}$ has punctual dimension ∞, modify by defining $\mathcal{M}_i$ as $\Psi(\mathcal{A}_i, \mathcal{A}_{i+1})$. In the case that $\mathcal{A}$ is finitely generated then the exact same argument as the ordered case applies. Finally we have the case that $\mathcal{A}$ has finite punctual dimension and is not finitely generated, then apply the same construction of $\mathcal{M}_i$ as in the ordered case with Ψ replacing Φ. The only difference is that now we have two equivalence classes instead of a unary relation. If we suppose there is some requirement we got stuck on, then the pair (p_e, q_e) is an isomoprhism between some $\mathcal{M}_k$ and $\mathcal{M}_m$. Recall that in the construction, while we work on requirement $P_{e,k,m}$, $\mathcal{M}_k$ stops adding new generators to one of its equivalence classes. Call this equivalence class $[x]$. Now p_e restricted to domain $\mathcal{M}_k \upharpoonright_{[x]}$ must map to $\mathcal{M}_m \upharpoonright_{[\hat{x}]}$ for some $\hat{x}$, similarly q_e restricted to domain $\mathcal{M}_m \upharpoonright_{[\hat{x}]}$ maps to $\mathcal{M}_k \upharpoonright_{[x]}$. By construction $\mathcal{M}_m \upharpoonright_{[\hat{x}]} \cong \mathcal{A}$ but since $\mathcal{A}$ is not finitely generated $\mathcal{M}_k \upharpoonright_{[x]} \not\cong \mathcal{A}$; hence (p_e, q_e) is not an isomorphism between $\mathcal{M}_k$ and $\mathcal{M}_m$.

It is seen in the above proof, that only minor modifications are needed, so we strongly conjecture that the exact choice of the definition of the join will not affect the proof of Theorem 2.

3   A Structure of Finite Punctual Dimension n > 2

In this section we prove Theorem 3 by extending the techniques used in [18]. Given the space constraints, we provide a somewhat compressed version of the proof. A more detailed proof will appear in the author's PhD thesis.

For each n, we will construct a structure $\mathcal{A}$ with punctual dimension n. To do this, we construction n presentations of $\mathcal{A}$, denoted $\mathcal{A}_1, \cdots, \mathcal{A}_n$. We require that any pair of these presentations are not punctually isomorphic, hence we have requirements:

$R_e : p_e : \mathcal{A}_i \to \mathcal{A}_j$ is not an isomorphism for all $j \neq i$

where p_e is the eth primitive recursive function on some computable list. Our second type of requirements ensure that any other punctual presentation that is isomorphic to $\mathcal{A}$ is punctually isomorphic to an $\mathcal{A}_i$ for some $i \leq n$. Let $\langle \mathcal{P}_e \rangle_{e \in \omega}$ denote this list of all punctual structures. This gives use the following requirements to meet:

$N_e :$ if $\mathcal{P}_e \cong \mathcal{A}$ then for some $i \leq n$ there is a punctual isomorphism $q : \mathcal{P}_e \to \mathcal{A}_i$

In the next subsection we will briefly discuss the strategy to meet these requirements, refer to [18] and [9] for more details of the techniques and strategies mentioned.

3.1   Discussion

The structure we build, $\mathcal{A}$, has the following symbols in its language: unary functions s, c, r, p and a binary relation K. The structure with punctual dimension n has n 'chains of chains'. This naturally extends that the structure with punctual dimension 2 in [18] has 2 chains of chains. See Fig. 1 of an example of two chains chained together, showing how s, c, r, p are used. Note that K is not shown in this diagram, this is because it is determined by the construction and used for a technical reason, we discuss this later.

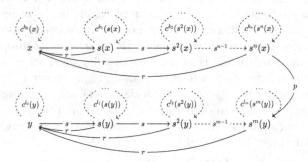

Fig. 1. Two chains 'chained together' by p. One of length n and the other of length m. k_i and l_i each represent some natural number given by the construction, this is the length of the ith loop in each chain, which is given by the least number of times required to apply c to the same element in this loop.

The construction has 2 different phases. One phase is the diagonalisation phase where an R-requirement is met. The other phase is the recovery phase where we work towards ensuring all $\mathcal{A}_i$ are isomorphic. We use the pressing strategy described in [18], first introduced in [16]. The pressing strategy uses the unary functions s, c and r to build a chain with loops that follow a particular pattern. The pressing strategy ensures that we can diagonalise by having chains of different patterns in each structure while the structures remain punctually isomorphic to any other isomorphic punctual presentations. In the construction we allocate positions in each chain for each punctual presentation $\mathcal{P}_e$ we are currently monitoring, this is part of the pressing strategy. See [16, 18] for a discussion of this.

In the diagonalisation phase we work to meet an R-requirement. In this phase each $\mathcal{A}_i$ will extend its ith chain of chains with a chain of a unique pattern. Once we see this diagonalisation, the construction will move into a recovery phase which has n recovery stages. Note that in the punctual dimension 2 case, only one step of recovery was needed since each structure only needs to recover the chain used in diagonalisation in the other structure. Now that we have n structures to recover, we use n steps to recover each chain used in diagonalisation in all $\mathcal{A}_i$. Note that at each step it is important that each $\mathcal{A}_i$ is recovering a different chain. At each step of recovery we build a new chain in each structure and wait for responses before using p to map it to the chain that each structure is currently recovery. This sort of procedure is carefully explained in [9].

At every stage each $\mathcal{A}_i$ looks different from all other $\mathcal{A}_j$. For $\mathcal{P}_e$ to be isomorphic to $\mathcal{A}$ it will need to choose an $\mathcal{A}_i$ to follow. If $\mathcal{P}_e$ does not follow us it will be diagonalised using the general machinery established in [9, 18]. Once $\mathcal{P}_e$ chooses an $\mathcal{A}_i$ to follow, it will have to continue to follow $\mathcal{A}_i$ for the rest of the construction as otherwise it will be diagonalised against (as discussed below). The techniques used in [9, 18] guarantee that $\mathcal{P}_e$ and $\mathcal{A}_i$ are punctually isomorphic.

We will use the same notation as in [18] for chains and chains of chains. We will list all finite strings of $\mathbb{N} \setminus \{0\}$ which will act as the pattern for the chains. We use x_m to denote a chain with pattern m which is open and $\underline{x_m}$ to denote that this chain is closed.

Suppose $\mathcal{A}_i$ is currently building chain x_i and $\mathcal{P}_7$ is following $\mathcal{A}_3$. If $\mathcal{P}_e$ introduces x_8 before we are ready to introduce this chain into $\mathcal{A}_3$, then we need to diagonalise against $\mathcal{P}_e$. We do this by noticing that x_8 and x_3 have never appeared together in any of $\mathcal{A}_i$. We can compute K on elements in x_3 and x_8 in $\mathcal{P}_e$. Then we promise that K differs on these elements in $\mathcal{A}$. This is the same technique as in [18]. It is notable that the arity of K does not depend on n. Whenever it is needed, there is always a new chain in $\mathcal{A}_i$ that has not appeared in any other $\mathcal{A}_j$. A difference is that we will need to ensure there are elements in each chain not only for each $\mathcal{P}_e$ we are monitoring but also for each chain that appears in every other structure so far.

3.2   Construction

We now detail the formal construction. Effectively list all finite strings of natural numbers (without zero), these will represent the possible patterns. We let M_t denote the collection of indices e such that we are monitoring $\mathcal{P}_e$ at stage t.

In the construction we will say, *build chain x_m in $\mathcal{A}_i$ at stage t* this means that we add a new element a to the end of the chain connected using the unary function s. In addition we will then add k many elements and create a loop of length k where k is determined by pattern m and the position in the chain by defining c^i for $i \leq k$. The pattern m will be chosen from our effective list of finite strings of natural numbers. When we open this chain we will allocate positions in the chain to each $\mathcal{P}_e$ with $e \in M_s$. Once we have seen that $\mathcal{P}_e$ is following the pattern in its corresponding positions, we will replace the future positions for $\mathcal{P}_e$ in this chain with 2^e. We also note that when we say *declare* $K^{\mathcal{A}_k}(x_l, x_j) \neq K^{\mathcal{P}_e}(x_l, x_j)$, we mean the $\langle e, j \rangle$th element in chain x_l and the $\langle e, l \rangle$th element in chain x_j.

We will compute s and c on elements in $\mathcal{P}_e$ and we observe the length of the loops in a chain in $\mathcal{P}_e$ and this will make some pattern m. Note that we have a bound on the length of loops that we are currently using as well as the length of current patterns. We say $\mathcal{P}_e$ has *responded* once it reveals the pattern of the open chain in $\mathcal{A}_i$ for some i in the positions allocated to $\mathcal{P}_e$. Note that at every stage there is exactly one 'open' chain in each $\mathcal{A}_i$. The open chain is the one that is currently being built, its length is based on the construction and waiting on responses from requirements.

Diagonalisation. Build chains $x_{k+1}, ..., x_{k+n}$ in $\mathcal{A}_1, \cdots, \mathcal{A}_n$ respectively, where k is the largest pattern used in the construction so far. At every stage we are in this phase continue making each chain longer, while monitoring p_e on these chains. Wait for p_e to show it is not an isomorphism between any pair of our presentations. This eventually happens by computing p_e on the chain we are currently building in every structure. Chains of this pattern do not exist in the other structures and hence eventually each chain is mapped to a chain with the incorrect pattern.

Recovery m. Continue building the open chains while waiting for $\mathcal{P}_i$ to respond for $i \in M_t$. If no chains are open then start building new chains $x_{l+1}, ..., x_{l+n}$ in $\mathcal{A}_1, \cdots, \mathcal{A}_n$ respectively, where l is the largest pattern currently used in the construction. Otherwise let $x_{l+1}, ..., x_{l+n}$ be the chains currently open in $\mathcal{A}_1, \cdots, \mathcal{A}_n$ respectively. Let $j = (i + m) \mod n$. Starting with $i = 1$, close the chains x_{l+i} in $\mathcal{A}_i$ and immediately extend the jth chain of chains in $\mathcal{A}_i$ to be isomorphic to the jth chain of chains in $\mathcal{A}_{i+1}$, map the last element of $\underline{x_{l+i}}$ to the end of this chain of chains. Repeat for the next i, ending with $i = n$.

Stage 0. Begin in the diagonalisation phase with requirement R_0, and let $M_0 = 0$

Stage t. If $\mathcal{P}_i$ reveals that it is not in fact a structure with n chain of chains that remove i from M_t. If $\mathcal{P}_i$ has revealed a pattern not yet used by us then remove this pattern from our listing of patterns and remove i from M_t. If $\mathcal{P}_i$ has revealed a pattern $\underline{x_l}$ that we have used but does not yet exist in the presentation $\mathcal{A}_k$ that $\mathcal{P}_i$ is following, then declare $K^{\mathcal{A}}(x_l, x_j) \neq K^{\mathcal{P}_e}(x_l, x_j)$ where $\underline{x_j}$ is the next chain that will be used to recover $\underline{x_l}$ in $\mathcal{A}_k$. Note that since these chains don't yet both exist in $\mathcal{A}_k$ this will be defined as soon as they exist together. Remove i from M_t.

If we are waiting for responses in the current phase then keep waiting while continuing to build the currently open chain and go to the next stage. Otherwise do the case that applies:

1. if we are in the diagonalisation phase, move to recovery with $m = 0$;
2. if we are in recovery phase with $m < n-1$ then move to recovery phase $m+1$;
3. if we are in recovery phase with $m = n-1$ then let R_e be the last requirement diagonalised against in the diagonalisation stage that we have just recovered from. Move to the diagonalisation phase with requirement R_{e+1}. Let i be least such that there exists $\hat{t} \leq t$ such that $\mathcal{P}_i \in M_{\hat{t}}$. Define $M_{t+1} = M_t \cup \{i+1\}$.

3.3   Verification

We verify that we meet all requirements. By construction, when in the diagonalisation phase there is a stage where we successfully diagonalise against p_e. At all phases, we are waiting for $\mathcal{P}_i$ to respond for $i \in M_t$. M_t is finite at all stages, and we do not grow M_t until we start a new diagonalisation phase. Since each $\mathcal{P}_i$ is punctual, it must reveal a chain that is currently open or shows it is not isomorphic to $\mathcal{A}$. This is true because we know the length of all closed chains. Hence $\mathcal{P}_i$ must eventually respond. M_t is finite, therefore we eventually finish every phase of the construction. Then there are infinitely many recovery phases and infinitely many diagonalisation phases. It follows that we meet to all R requirements; hence $\mathcal{A}_i$ and $\mathcal{A}_j$ not punctually isomorphic for all i, j.

We verify that the isomorphism type of $\mathcal{A}$ (without relation K) is:

$$
\begin{aligned}
&\underline{x_1} \leftarrow \underline{x_{2n}} \leftarrow \underline{x_{3n-1}} \leftarrow \underline{x_{4n-2}} \leftarrow \cdots \leftarrow \underline{x_{n^2+1}} \cdots \\
&\underline{x_2} \leftarrow \underline{x_{n+1}} \leftarrow \underline{x_{3n}} \leftarrow \underline{x_{4n-1}} \leftarrow \cdots \leftarrow \underline{x_{n^2+2}} \cdots \\
&\vdots \\
&\underline{x_n} \leftarrow \underline{x_{2n-1}} \leftarrow \underline{x_{3n-2}} \leftarrow \underline{x_{4n-3}} \leftarrow \cdots \leftarrow \underline{x_{n^2+n}} \cdots
\end{aligned}
$$

The part of $\mathcal{A}$ shown is the n chains of chains after one diagonalisation phase and full recovery. After each diagonalisation and full recovery, every chain of chain has been extended in all $\mathcal{A}_i$ and contain the chain $\underline{x_k}$ for all k used in the previous diagonalisation stage. It follows that $\mathcal{A}_i$ are pairwise isomorphic. The value of K is determined by construction between pairs of elements that are not yet in any $\mathcal{A}_i$ and when we choose its value, this is the value these elements will take in all structures.

If $\mathcal{P}_e$ is diagonalised against at some stage, then it is not isomorphic to $\mathcal{A}$. Suppose $\mathcal{P}_e$ is never diagonalised against, then $e \in M_t$ for all $t \geq \hat{t}$, where $\hat{t}$ is the first stage we begin considering $\mathcal{P}_e$. From stage $\hat{t}$ we will force $\mathcal{P}_e$ to choose which $\mathcal{A}_i$ to follow, by leaving chains open until this occurs. Let $\mathcal{A}_k$ be the structure $\mathcal{P}_e$ begins to follow. By construction, K is used to ensure that $\mathcal{P}_e$ always follows $\mathcal{A}_k$. Now at every phase, we will always leave the chain in $\mathcal{A}_k$ open repeating the pattern in the positions allocated to $\mathcal{P}_e$. We have a primitive recursive bound on the time it will take for $\mathcal{P}_e$ to reveal this new chain, because $\mathcal{P}_e$ is punctual. Hence we have a primitive recursive bound on when elements in $\mathcal{A}_k$ of this new open chain can be mapped into $\mathcal{P}_e$. Once $\mathcal{P}_e$ responds, we immediately stop copying the pattern in the open chain of $\mathcal{A}_k$ and hence we have a primitive recursive bound on the time to apply r, s and c in order to find where the segment $\mathcal{P}_e$ has revealed exists within the chain. Hence we can define the punctual isomorphism between $\mathcal{P}_e$ and $\mathcal{A}_k$ on this new chain. Then we can continue to define this isomorphism naturally on the chain once closed and we repeat this process on the next chain $\mathcal{A}_k$ opens. Therefore there is a punctual isomorphism between $\mathcal{P}_e$ and $\mathcal{A}_k$ and requirement N_e is met.

Therefore we are done. We have constructed n presentations of a structure which are not punctually isomorphic and any for other punctual structure, if it is isomorphic to this structure we have built then it is in fact punctually isomorphic to one of our n presentations. Therefore we have a structure of punctual dimension n.

References

1. Alaev, P.E.: Categoricity for primitively recursive and polynomial Boolean algebras. Algebra Logika **57**(4), 389–426 (2018)
2. Ash, C.J., Knight, J.: Computable Structures and the Hyperarithmetical Hierarchy. Studies in Logic and the Foundations of Mathematics, vol. 144. North-Holland Publishing Co., Amsterdam (2000)
3. Bazhenov, N., Downey, R., Kalimullin, I., Melnikov, A.: Foundations of online structure theory. Bull. Symb. Log. **25**(2), 141–181 (2019)
4. Bazhenov, N., Fiori-Carones, M., Liu, L., Melnikov, A.: Primitive recursive reverse mathematics. Ann. Pure Appl. Logic **175**(1), 103354 (2024)
5. Bazhenov, N., Harrison-Trainor, M., Kalimullin, I.S., Melnikov, A.G., Ng, K.M.: Automatic and polynomial-time algebraic structures. J. Symb. Log. **84**(4), 1630–1669 (2019)
6. Bazhenov, N., Kalimullin, I., Melnikov, A., Ng, K.M.: Online presentations of finitely generated structures. Theor. Comput. Sci. **844**, 195–216 (2020)
7. Csima, B.F., Stephenson, J.: Finite computable dimension and degrees of categoricity. Ann. Pure Appl. Logic **170**(1), 58–94 (2019)
8. Dorzhieva, M., Downey, R., Hammatt, E., Melnikov, A., Ng, K.M.: Punctually Presented Structures II: Comparing presentations Preprint
9. Downey, R., Greenberg, N., Melnikov, A., Ng, K.M., Turetsky, D.: Punctual categoricity and universality. J. Symb. Log. **85**(4), 1427–1466 (2020)
10. Downey, R., Melnikov, A., Ng, K.M.: Foundations of online structure theory II: the operator approach. Log. Methods Comput. Sci. **17**(3), Paper No. 6, 35 (2021)
11. Ershov, Y., Goncharov, S.: Constructive models. Siberian School of Algebra and Logic, Consultants Bureau, New York (2000)
12. Goncharov, S.: Autostability of models and abelian groups. Algebra i Logika **19**(1), 23–44, 132 (1980)
13. Goncharov, S.: The problem of the number of nonautoequivalent constructivizations. Algebra i Logika **19**(6), 621–639, 745 (1980)
14. Goncharov, S.S., Molokov, A.V., Romanovskii, N.S.: Nilpotent groups of finite algorithmic dimension. Sib. Math. J. **30**(1), 63–68 (1989)
15. Hirschfeldt, D., Khoussainov, B., Shore, R., Slinko, A.: Degree spectra and computable dimensions in algebraic structures. Ann. Pure Appl. Logic **115**(1–3), 71–113 (2002)

16. Kalimullin, I., Melnikov, A., Ng, K.M.: Algebraic structures computable without delay. Theor. Comput. Sci. **674**, 73–98 (2017)
17. Mal'cev, A.I.: Constructive algebras. I. Uspehi Mat. Nauk **16**(3(99)), 3–60 (1961)
18. Melnikov, A., Ng, K.M.: A structure of punctual dimension two. Proc. Am. Math. Soc. **148**(7), 3113–3128 (2020)
19. Montalbán, A.: Computable Structure Theory: Within the Arithmetic. Perspectives in Logic. Cambridge University Press (2021)
20. Rabin, M.O.: Computable algebra, general theory and theory of computable fields. Trans. Am. Math. Soc. **95**(2), 341–360 (1960)
21. Turetsky, D.: Coding in the automorphism group of a computably categorical structure (2020)

Counting Simple Rules
in Semi-conditional Grammars is not
Simple

Henning Fernau[1] , Lakshmanan Kuppusamy[2] ,
and Indhumathi Raman[3(✉)]

[1] Abteilung Informatikwissenschaften, Fachbereich 4, Universität Trier, 54286 Trier,
Germany
[2] School of Computer Science and Engineering, VIT University, Vellore 632 014,
India
[3] Department of Computing Technologies, SRM Institute of Science and Technology,
Kattankulathur, Chennai 603203, India
indhumar2@srmist.edu.in

Abstract. A semi-conditional grammar is a form of regulated rewriting system. Each rule consists of a context-free core rule $A \to w$ and (possibly) two strings w_+, w_-; the rule is applicable if w_+ (the permitting string) occurs as a substring of the current sentential form, but w_- (the forbidden string) does not. The maximum lengths i, j of the permitting or forbidden strings, respectively, give a natural measure of descriptional complexity, known as the *degree* of such grammars. Such a grammar is called *simple* if for each rule, either the permitting or the forbidden string is missing. As the simplicity requirement turns out to be a severe restriction and causes other descriptional complexity parameters to grow, we refine the study by introducing, as an additional parameter, the number of non-simple rules. Employing several normal form results on phrase-structure grammars as derived by Geffert (1991) and Masopust and Meduna (2007), we prove several new computational completeness results that interpolate between what was known so far on general and simple semi-conditional grammars.

1 Introduction

One of the key areas in formal language theory is descriptional complexity. In a nutshell, this area investigates how succinct can a grammar or automaton represent a formal language class (with respect to a certain collection of measures of descriptional complexity). In this paper, we focus on the descriptional complexity of semi-conditional grammars so that they still achieve computational completeness, i.e., they still characterize the class RE of recursively enumerable languages. To arrive at such results, it is often helpful to make use of other similar results and to simulate the corresponding devices. Among the most often used ones are the normal forms for type-0 grammars provided by Geffert in [6],

Table 1. Survey on descriptional complexity results for semi-conditional grammars.

Degree (i,j)	# Nonterminals	# Conditional Rules	# Non-Simple Rules	Reference
(2,1)	8	7	2	[10]
(2,1)	7	6	4	[14]
(2,1)	6	$7 + |P_{cf}|$	4	[3]
(2,2)	6	6	5	[3]
(3,1)	5	$9 + 2(|T| + 1) + |P_{cf}|$	$8 + 2(|T| + 1)$	[3]
(3,1)	6	13	10	[3]
(1,1)	?	?	0	[8]
(2,1)	9	8	0	[4]
(3,1)	7	7	0	[4]
(4,1)	7	6	0	[4]
(4,1)	6	8	0	[4]
(6,3)	4	18	15	Theorem 1
(3,2)	5	6	4	Theorem 2
(3,1)	6	6	4	Theorem 3
(2,1)	7	6	3	Theorem 4
(3,2)	6	6	3	Theorem 5

because they also use very few nonterminals to characterize RE. In addition, we will make use of a normal form derived by Meduna and Masopust in [9].

What are typical measures of descriptional complexity? For all grammatical mechanisms, typically in the context of regulated rewriting, bounding the number of nonterminals is a goal, leading to the notion of *nonterminal complexity*, we refer to [1,2,16] for its general history. In this paper, continuing earlier studies [3,4], we focus on semi-conditional grammars, as they offer a particularly rich selection of descriptional complexity measures. We refer to Table 1 for a survey on such results, listing bounds on several descriptional complexity measures such that, still, computational completeness can be achieved.

A semi-conditional grammar (SCG) is an extension of context-free grammar (introduced by Păun in [15]) in which each (context-free) rule is associated with two strings called the permitting and forbidden string. The formal definitions are presented below; here we only describe what is needed to understand the descriptional complexity measures mentioned in Table 1. The maximal length of the permitting string (say i) and the forbidden string (say j) constitutes the *degree* of the grammar, denoted by (i,j). A semi-conditional grammar is termed *simple* (or SSCG) if for each rule at most either the permitting string or the forbidden string is present; refer to [12]. If both these control strings are absent in a rule, then the rule is said to be an unconditional. Otherwise the rule is termed *conditional*. Important contributions to the theory of (S)SCG can be found in [7,8,10,14,16]. It is known that even simple semi-conditional grammars of degree $(1,1)$ are computationally complete, i.e., they characterize the family RE of recursively enumerable languages; see [8]. Nothing can be said on bounding other aspects of descriptional complexity in that case, though, as these parameters are language-dependent, which is indicated by question marks in the corresponding columns of Table 1, as this relies on a construction of Mayer [11]. The fact that we can get simple rules is due to another construction of Masopust [8]. In Table 1, T refers to the terminal alphabet and P_{cf} to a subset of the context-free rules of the original type-0 grammar that is simulated; see our discussions on Geffert normal form grammars below. The first part of the table lists bounds on descriptional complexity measures for general SCG. Besides the degree and the nonterminal complexity, also the number of conditional rules has been studied as a parameter.

In this paper, we commence the study of a new parameter, the *number of non-simple rules*, resulting in an additional column in our table. The listed numbers for results from the literature are obtained by a straightfoward analysis of the constructions that we cite. The second part collects results on simple semi-conditional grammars; hence, the count on non-simple rules always shows zero. The last part of the table collects our new results in this paper, which are always trade-off results between various parameters and the new parameter that we introduce here. However, we also want to highlight our first theorem, as it gives the best known bound on the nonterminal complexity of semi-conditional grammars, admittedly at the cost of larger numbers for the other measures of descriptional complexity. Notice that all these results stand in a line of results; we only list some of the predecessor papers here: [7,13,14,16]. In the light of this substantial previous research, it is also worth mentioning that even if we disregard the newly introduced parameter, all our constructions presented in this paper are record-holders if we consider the task to minimize the nonterminal and conditional rule complexity for fixed degree. For instance, no construction was known that proves that already SCG of degree $(3,1)$ with at most six nonterminals and at most six conditional rules characterize RE (see Theorem 3).

Summarizing, we can view this paper as working on the Pareto front of recursive enumerability for semiconditional grammars, refining earlier results by introducing and discussing a new measure of descriptional complexity that was, so far, considered only in an extreme case by SSCG.

2   Preliminaries and Definitions

It is assumed in this paper that the reader is familiar with the fundamentals of language theory and mathematics in general. Let $\mathbb{N}$ denote the set of non-negative integers. Let Σ^* denote the free monoid generated by a finite set Σ called alphabet under an operation termed concatenation, where λ denotes the unit of Σ^*, also called the empty string. Any element of Σ^* is called a word or string (over Σ). Any subset of Σ^* is called a language. A word v is a subword of $x \in \Sigma^*$ if there are words u, w such that $x = uvw$. Let $sub(x) \subseteq \Sigma^*$ denote the set of all subwords of $x \in \Sigma^*$. Clearly, $sub(x)$ is a finite language.

2.1 Semi-conditional Grammars

A *semi-conditional grammar* is a quadruple $G = (N, T, P, S)$, where N is the set of nonterminals, T is the terminal alphabet with $N \cap T = \emptyset$, $S \in N$ is the starting symbol, P is a finite set of rules of the form $(A \to x, \alpha, \beta)$ with $A \in N$, $x \in (N \cup T)^*$, $\alpha, \beta \in (N \cup T)^+ \cup \{\emptyset\}$, where $\emptyset \notin \{N \cup T\}$ is a special symbol, intuitively meaning that the condition is missing. The rule $l : (A \to x, \alpha, \beta) \in P$ (with label l) is said to be *non-simple* if $\alpha \neq \emptyset$ and $\beta \neq \emptyset$; it is *conditional* if $\alpha \neq \emptyset$ or $\beta \neq \emptyset$; it is *simple* if $\alpha = \emptyset$ or $\beta = \emptyset$; it is *unconditional* if $\alpha = \emptyset$ and $\beta = \emptyset$. String α is permitting, while β is forbidden, as formally explained now. The rule labeled l can be applied on a string $u \in (N \cup T)^* N (N \cup T)^*$ if and only if $A \in sub(u)$ and ($\alpha \in sub(u)$ or $\alpha = \emptyset$) and ($\beta \notin sub(u)$ or $\beta = \emptyset$).[1] Under these conditions, $u = u_1 A u_2$ will be transformed into $v = u_1 x u_2$, which is denoted by $u \Rightarrow_l v$. When no confusion exists on the rule being applied, we avoid mentioning the label and we simply write $u \Rightarrow v$. The language of G is defined as $L(G) = \{w \in T^* \mid S \Rightarrow^* w\}$, where $\Rightarrow^* = \bigcup_{i \geq 0} \Rightarrow^i$, with $\Rightarrow_l^i$ referring to i applications of rule l, while $\Rightarrow^i$ means i applications of any rules.

G is said to be of *degree* (i, j), where $i, j \in \mathbb{N}$, if in every rule $(A \to x, \alpha, \beta)$ of P we have $|\alpha| \leq i$ and $|\beta| \leq j$ whenever $\alpha, \beta \neq \emptyset$.

Let n denote an upper bound on the number of nonterminals, c denote an upper bound on the number of conditional rules and $\bar{s}$ denote an upper bound on the number of non-simple conditional rules. Then we refer to the family of semi-conditional grammars or languages of degree at most (i, j) as $SC(i, j, n, c, \bar{s})$. We refer to [12, 15] for some examples of semi-conditional grammars and their languages.

2.2 Useful Normal Forms for Type-0 Grammars

In [6], quite a number of normal forms for type-0 grammars have been derived. They all differ by the number of nonterminals that are used and also by the number of non-context-free rules. We will hence speak of (n, r)-GNF to refer to a Geffert normal form with n nonterminals and r non-context-free rules. However, all these normal forms characterize the class RE. The well-known such normal form is the $(5, 2)$-GNF with nonterminals S (the start symbol) and A, B, C, D that uses context-free rules with S as its left-hand side in phase one; in a second phase, non-context-free erasing rules $AB \to \lambda$ and $CD \to \lambda$ are applied to finally derive a terminal string. In [6], it was also proved that every RE language is generated by a type-0 grammar $G = (N, T, P, S)$ with three nonterminals only, i.e., $N = \{S, A, B\}$ is the set of non-terminals, T is the set of terminal symbols, S is the start symbol and P contains the context-free rules of the form $S \to w$

---

[1] Concerning terminology, forbidden strings are sometimes called forbidding in the literature, starting from [15]. We think that both strings play a different role: The presence of a permitting string enables a derivation step that is not allowed when this string is not a substring of the current string, while the presence of a forbidden string as a substring in the current string interdicts the application of the rule to which this forbidden string is attached.

(these types of rules are addressed when writing P_{cf} in Table 1) and the only non-context-free rule of the form $ABBBA \to \lambda$ calling as $(3,1)$-GNF.

Let us recall a few properties of this normal form.

1. The derivation of any terminal word in the $(3,1)$-GNF grammar G splits into two phases: in phase one, only rules of the form $S \to uSv$, $S \to uSa$ or $S \to uv$ are applied, where $u \in \{AB, ABB\}^*$, $v \in \{BA, BBA\}^*$ and $a \in T$; in the subsequent phase two, $ABBBA \to \lambda$ is applied exclusively.
2. Let w be a word that is derivable in G, i.e., $S \Rightarrow^* w$. Then, either $w \in (\{AB, ABB\} \cup T)^* \cup (\{BA, BBA\} \cup T)^*$, or w has a unique *center* $\zeta \in \{S\} \cup \{AB, ABB\}T^*\{BA, BBA\}$. Here, $\zeta = S$ happens iff w is derived in phase one. Then, $w = \alpha\zeta\beta$, where $\alpha \in \{AB, ABB\}^*$ and $\beta \in (\{BA, BBA\} \cup T)^*$. In the following, we collect some further combinatorial properties of w. (a) AA, AS and SA are not substrings of w. (b) If BBB or $BBBB$ is a subword of w, then this string will be a substring of ζ. (c) Whenever A occurs in α or β or ζ, then B also occurs in α or β or ζ, respectively. (d) If $w \Rightarrow^* t$ is possible for some $t \in T^*$, then indeed $w = \alpha\zeta\beta't$, with $\beta' \in \{BA, BBA\}^*$.

Similar structural properties can be stated for type-0 grammars in $(4,1)$-GNF which contain four nonterminals $\{S, A, B, C\}$. Rules are either context-free of the form $S \to w$ or non-context-free: $ABC \to \lambda$.

Masopust and Meduna [9] suggested the following modification of $(5,2)$-GNF (that we suggested calling MMNF in [5]) which is less popular than GNF itself. Let L be a recursively enumerable language with $L = L(\tilde{G})$, where $\tilde{G} = (\tilde{N}, T, \tilde{P}, \tilde{S})$ is a grammar in $(5,2)$-GNF with $\tilde{N} = \{S, A, B, C, D\}$. Then, there is a grammar $G = (\{S, 0, 1, \$\}, T, P_{\text{unc}} \cup \{0\$0 \to \$, 1\$1 \to \$, \$ \to \lambda\}, S)$, with P_{unc} containing only unconditional rules of the form

- $S \to h(u)Sa$ if $S \to uSa \in \tilde{P}$,
- $S \to h(u)Sh(v)$ if $S \to uSv \in \tilde{P}$,
- $S \to h(u)\$h(v)$ if $S \to uv \in \tilde{P}$,

where $h : \{A, B, C, D\}^* \to \{0, 1\}^*$ is a homomorphism defined by $h(A) = h(B) = 00$, $h(C) = 01$, and $h(D) = 10$, such that $L(G) = L(\tilde{G})$. Again, structural properties similar to GNFs can be observed.

3   New Computational Completeness Results

We will now present the five computational completeness results mentioned in the introduction and sketch a further complementing extension result that is however not delimiting the number of conditional rules.

The first result sticks out for at least two further reasons: (1) No previous construction yielded that four nonterminals are sufficient for SC grammars to arrive at computational completeness. (2) Such large degree constraints have not been used before.

1. $(B \to \$, ABBBA, \$)$
2. $(B \to \$\$, AB\$BA, \$\$)$
3. $(\$ \to \lambda, AB\$^3 A, AA)$
4. $(B \to \$^3, AB\$\$A, \$^3)$
5. $(\$ \to \lambda, A\$^5, \emptyset)$
6. $(\$ \to \lambda, A\$^4 A, \emptyset)$
7. $(\$ \to \lambda, A\$^3 A, B\$)$
8. $(\$ \to \lambda, A\$^2 A, B\$)$
9. $(\$ \to \lambda, A\$A, BBB)$
10. $(A \to \$, AA, \$)$
11. $(A \to \lambda, \emptyset, B)$
12. $(A \to \$\$, AB\$ABB, \$\$)$
13. $(A \to \$\$, BB\$ABA, \$\$)$
14. $(\$ \to \lambda, B\$^3 B, BBB)$
15. $(\$ \to \lambda, AB\$^2 BB, \$A)$
16. $(\$ \to \lambda, BB\$^2 BA, \$A)$
17. $(\$ \to \lambda, AB\$BBA, AA)$
18. $(\$ \to \lambda, ABB\$BA, AA)$

Fig. 1. Rules of complexity $(6, 3, 4, 18, 15)$ that simulate $ABBBA \to \lambda$

Theorem 1. $\mathrm{RE} = \mathrm{SC}(6, 3, 4, 18, 15)$.

Proof. The idea of the construction is to use the $(3,1)$-GNF with only non-context-free erasing rule $ABBBA \to \lambda$. More precisely, starting from such a grammar G with nonterminal alphabet $N = \{S, A, B\}$ and context-free rules with S as left-hand side, we take over all context-free rules, plus the conditional rules from Fig. 1 that are designed to simulate $ABBBA \to \lambda$. Notice that these rules satisfy the claimed parameters of the such-defined simulating semi-conditional grammar $G' = (N \cup T, T, P', S)$. We expect the derivation shown in Fig. 2 for the good case. For clarity, we underline the nonterminal on which the next action is happening. By a trivial induction, this shows that each string that is derivable in G can also be derived by G'.

$$\alpha AB\underline{B}BA\beta t \Rightarrow_1 \alpha AB\$\underline{B}A\beta t \Rightarrow_2 \alpha AB\$\$\$A\beta t \Rightarrow_3 \alpha A\underline{B}\$\$A\beta t$$
$$\Rightarrow_4 \alpha A\$^3\$\$\underline{A}\beta t \Rightarrow_5 \alpha A\$^4\underline{A}\beta t \Rightarrow_6 \alpha A\$^3\underline{A}\beta t \Rightarrow_7 \alpha A\$^2\underline{A}\beta t$$
$$\Rightarrow_8 \alpha A\$\underline{A}\beta t \Rightarrow_9 \alpha\underline{A}A\beta t \begin{cases} \Rightarrow_{11}^2 t & \text{if } \alpha = \beta = \lambda \text{ or} \\ \Rightarrow_{10} \alpha\$\underline{A}\beta t \text{ else, continuing like:} \end{cases}$$
$$\Rightarrow_{12/13} \alpha\$\$\$\beta t \Rightarrow_{14} \alpha\$\$\beta t \Rightarrow_{15/16} \alpha\$\beta t \Rightarrow_{17/18} \alpha\beta t$$

Fig. 2. Simulation of one application of $ABBBA \to \lambda$.

Now, consider a string w_0 (which is also expected to derive a terminal string in G') that is derivable both in G and in G', stemming from the second phase in the derivation of G, to avoid trivialities. We are discussing possible derivation steps in G' and how they correspond to derivations in G. In a string without $\$$, only the Rules 1, 10, or 11 will be applicable. However, as w_0 is also derivable in G, AA is not a substring of w_0, disabling Rule 10. Moreover, Rule 11 can only be applied if A is present, but this implies (as w_0 is also derivable in G) that B is present, rendering Rule 11 inapplicable. Hence, we must apply Rule 1 on w_0; there, we already check that only the good substring $ABBBA$ was present. In particular, this also rules out terminal symbols present in the center. According to the structure of encodings, we can assume that we started with a word $w_0 = \alpha ABBBA\beta t$, with $\alpha \in \{AB, ABB\}^*$, $\beta \in \{BA, BBA\}^*$ and $t \in T^*$. (This is a slight simplification of our discussion, as terminal symbols might occur in any place to the right of the center, but only in this situation, we can arrive at a terminal string finally, which will also follow by induction within G'.)

We can then obtain $w_1 = \alpha AB\$B\beta t$. We shall discuss what happens if at any other place B is changed to $\$$ (including other than the intended middle B in the center). Then there are no valid permitting contexts in the rules (or B is present, blocking Rule 11) and the derivation is stuck, with two exceptions. (1) If we replace an occurrence of B in the substring ABA that might occur in α or in β, then we might want to apply Rule 9 to this case. However, as we did not touch the central part so far, the substring BBB is still there and is forbidden in Rule 9. (2) If we replace the second occurrence of B by a $\$$ in the substring $ABBABB$ that might occur in α or in β, then we end up with a context permitted in Rule 12. Hence, it is possible to apply Rule 12 ($A \rightarrow \$\$$) to any occurrence of a A. But the introduction of $\$\$$ blocks applying Rule 2, so that we must delete the (now) three occurrences of $\$$ in another way. As all other rules dealing with deleting dollars are clearly inapplicable, we are left with Rule 14, but now the substring BBB is still present in the string, which is prohibited in Rule 14. A similar discussion applies to Rule 13. Notice that in order to get to a situation as described in the permitting context of Rule 13, we must have applied $B \rightarrow \$$ to the last occurrence of B in the central part when using Rule 1. We will defer the discussion of possible applications of Rules 12 or 13 in unintended places below.

Also, after applying Rule 1, it cannot be re-applied again until $\$$ is deleted. Now, with the obtained string w_1, Rule 2 is the only possible one to apply and on applying it, we can get either $\alpha A\$\$\$B A\beta t$ or $w_2 = \alpha AB\$\$\$A\beta t$. If any other B in α or in β is changed, then there are no valid permitting contexts, as can be seen from the rules (or B is present in forbidding context, blocking Rule 11), again with the exception of replacing an occurrence of B in the substring ABA. We might want to apply Rule 8 to delete some $\$$ again, but now the necessarily present substring $B\$$ (which was untouched in the center part on assuming the wrong B is touched) blocks any such attempt. Also, from the permitting contexts of Rule 3, we can see that the last B in the center only to be changed, leading to w_2. With $\alpha AB\$^3 A\beta t$, the only applicable rule is Rule 3 which results to $w_3 = \alpha AB\$^2 A\beta t$. There is again one subtle situation we need to check, though. Namely, it could be that $B \rightarrow \$^3$ is applied to some substring ABA with the intention to then erase the $\$^3$ using, in order, Rules 7, 8, 9. This is blocked by the substring $B\$$ whose presence is tested in both cases.

Now, the only applicable rule for w_3 is Rule 4 which changes a B to $\$\$\$$, as can be easily verified. If any other B but the one left over in the central part is replaced, then (as before) the only potentially applicable rule would be Rule 4, but its re-application is blocked by the substring $\$\$\$$. Therefore, we must derive in the next step $w_4 = \alpha A\$^5 A\beta t$. As the (central) contexts $A\$^5$, $A\$^4A$, $A\$^3A$, $A\$\$A$ and even $A\$A$ are unique, the next derivation steps are enforced, leading to $w_5 = \alpha A\$^4 A\beta t$, $w_6 = \alpha A\$^3 A\beta t$, $w_7 = \alpha A\$^2 A\beta t$, $w_8 = \alpha A\$A\beta t$ and finally $w_9 = \alpha AA\beta t$, using Rules 5 through 9.

Now, we have to distinguish three cases: If $\alpha = \beta = \lambda$ (this must happen eventually at least when a correct terminating derivation happens), then Rule 11 can be applied twice, deriving a terminal string as intended. If exactly one of

α or β is empty, then Rule 11 cannot be applied (as observed in the list of properties concerning w_0 that is also derivable in G: namely, if A occurs in α or β, then B occurs there, as well), but neither can we apply any other rule, so that the derivation is stuck. But looking at the original GNF grammar G, one also sees that there is no continuation in this case.

Hence, we are left with the case when $\alpha \neq \lambda$ and $\beta \neq \lambda$. In any possibly successful derivation of the original GNF grammar concerning w_0, this means that either $\alpha = \alpha' ABB$ and $\beta = BA\beta'$ or $\alpha = \alpha' AB$ and $\beta = BBA\beta'$. This explains the cases that are considered in the permitting contexts of Rules 12 through 17. Recall that we had $w_9 = \alpha AA\beta t$, enabling the application of Rule 10. One of the two occurrences of A in the central part (or any other occurrence of A) is hence turned into \$. As occurrences of A outside the central part are surrounded by B's, it might be possible to apply Rule 18 or Rule 19. But as AA is still present, this is in fact impossible. Another alternative is to apply Rule 2, assuming that we replaced the central B within the substring $ABABA$ of w_9. Similarly as analyzed above, we should then apply Rule 3. However, the AA in the forbidden context is present in the current string and hence we cannot apply Rule 3. If we replace the rightmost A in the central part of w_9, then the resulting string contains the substring $A\$BBA$, a situation already encountered and analyzed with a possible wrong application of Rule 1 above. Therefore, $w_{10} = \alpha\$A\beta t$ is enforced, enabling either Rule 12 or Rule 13 to be applied. In either case, it is intended to replace the other occurrence of A in the central part by \$\$. If another occurrence of A was replaced, we might find the permitting context of Rule 15 or of Rule 16 satisfied. However, the forbidden context \$$A$ is indeed present in the current string, thus enforcing applying Rule 12 or Rule 13 as intended, because any other rule is clearly inapplicable. This leads us to $w_{11} = \alpha\$\$\$\beta t$. Considering the two possibilities for suffix and prefix combinations for α and β as discussed above, we see that only Rule 14 is applicable, leading to $w_{12} = \alpha\$\$\beta t$. Similar considerations will now lead us to $w_{13} = \alpha\$\beta t$ and finally to $w_{13} = \alpha\beta t$ as intended.

This shows that no malicious derivations may occur during a derivation of the semi-conditional grammar G'. Hence by induction, $L(G) = L(G')$.   □

Remark 1. We can even take this one step further if we are willing to accept an arbitrary number of unconditional rules and bigger permitting and forbidden contexts, getting down to only three nonterminals. Namely, we will replace \$ consequently by the start symbol S and then put conditions like $(S \to uSa, \emptyset, SS)$ or $(S \to uSv, \emptyset, SS)$ or $(S \to uv, \emptyset, SS)$ for every rule of the form $S \to uSa$ or $S \to uSv$ or $S \to uv$, respectively. Moreover, we must put larger contexts. Namely, in particular, we have to start with $(B \to SS, ABBBA, S)$ as the first rule, so that the second rule is then $(B \to SSS, ABSSBA, SSS)$, because otherwise the derivation could produce a string of the form $\alpha ABSBA\beta t$ (only simulating the context-free rules) and then directly jump to the second rule. Notice that this would possibly correspond to an invalid computation, as AB does not match BA, while the S in the middle is now (mistakenly) interpreted as a placeholder for B. We leave most of the details to the reader.

We now turn to two results for SCG with permitting string length of three, both based on a simulation idea using MMNF. These simulations are far easier to grasp than the first one.

1. $(0 \to \#, 0\$0, \#)$ 3. $(1 \to \#, 1\$1, \#)$ 5. $(\# \to \$, \$\$\#, \emptyset)$
2. $(0 \to \$\#, \#\$0, \$\#)$ 4. $(1 \to \$\#, \#\$1, \$\#)$ 6. $(\$ \to \lambda, \emptyset, \#)$

Fig. 3. Simulating the non-context-free rules $0\$0 \to \$$ and $1\$1 \to \$$.

Theorem 2. $\mathrm{RE} = \mathrm{SC}(3, 2, 5, 6, 4)$.

Proof. The proof is based on simulating a type-0 grammar G in MMNF, with a nonterminal alphabet $N = \{S, 0, 1, \$\}$. The simulating grammar G' will use one further nonterminal, which is $\#$. It will have all the context-free rules of G as unconditional rules, plus the conditional rules listed in Fig. 3 to simulate the non-context-free rules $0\$0 \to \$$ and $1\$1 \to \$$. Out of these six rules, two are simple. We expect the following simulation of the rule $0\$0 \to \$$:

$$\alpha 0\$0\beta t \Rightarrow_1 \alpha\#\$0\beta t \Rightarrow_2 \alpha\#\$\$\#\beta t \Rightarrow_5^2 \alpha\$^4\beta t \Rightarrow_6^3 \alpha\$\beta t,$$

with appropriately chosen nonterminal strings α, β and terminal strings t. Similarly, the non-context-free erasing rule $1\$1 \to \$$ is simulated, using Rules 3 and 4 instead of Rules 1 and 2.

For the inductive step in the proof of the correctness of the proposed simulation, we discuss a sentential form $\alpha\$\beta t$ that is supposed to be derivable both in G and in G', which means that $\alpha \in \{00, 01\}^*$ and $\beta \in \{00, 10\}^*$ or $\alpha \in \{00, 01\}^*\{0\}$ and $\beta \in \{0\}\{00, 10\}^*$. As only in the first case, a mismatch is possible, we focus on that situation. So, let $\alpha \in \{00, 01\}^*$ and $\beta \in \{00, 10\}^*$. If α ends with 0 and β starts with 1 or vice versa, then no further derivation steps are possible in G. But as it can be easily checked with the proposed simulating rules in Fig. 3, in G', the only applicable rule would be the last one which deletes $\$$. Then, no other rule is applicable, and as α is not empty, also the derivation of G' is stuck. Therefore, we can assume that either $\alpha = \alpha'0$ and $\beta = 0\beta'$ or $\alpha = \alpha'1$ and $\beta = 1\beta'$. As the simulating rules are completely symmetric in both cases, we will assume that $\alpha = \alpha'0$ and $\beta = 0\beta'$ in the following discussion.

As can be seen by checking the permitting contexts, only Rule 1 and Rule 6 are applicable in such a situation. As the deletion of $\$$ in this situation will lead to a string with nonterminals $0, 1$ only (apart from terminal symbols), this branch of a derivation would see no continuation. Hence, we assume that Rule 1 is applied, turning any occurrence of a 0 into a $\#$. Due to its forbidden context $\#$, Rule 1 can only be applied once, and Rule 6 is also blocked now. Thereafter, checking the permitting contexts of the remaining rules, only Rule 2 might have become applicable, in the case when we actually chose to derive $w_0 := \alpha'0\$0\beta't \Rightarrow_1 \alpha'\#\$0\beta't =: w_1$ (as intended). This would turn any occurrence of 0 in w_1 into

1. $(0 \to \#, 0\$0, \#)$ 3. $(1 \to \#, 1\$1, \#)$ 5. $(\# \to \dagger, \$\dagger, \emptyset)$

2. $(0 \to \dagger, \#\$0, \dagger)$ 4. $(1 \to \dagger, \#\$1, \dagger)$ 6. $(\dagger \to \lambda, \emptyset, \#)$

Fig. 4. Simulating the non-context-free rules $0\$0 \to \$$ and $1\$1 \to \$$.

1. $(B \to B', \emptyset, B')$ 3. $(C \to C', A'B', C')$ 5. $(A' \to \lambda, A'C', B')$

2. $(A \to A', B'C, A')$ 4. $(B' \to A', A'B', \emptyset)$ 6. $(C' \to \lambda, \emptyset, A')$

Fig. 5. Simulating $ABC \to \lambda$ with only three non-simple rules.

$\$\#$, resulting in a string w_2. Due to the presence of the substring $\$\#$ within w_2, all rules but possibly Rule 5 are blocked. Rule 5 requires the substring $\$\$\#$, which enforces that in fact $w_2 = \alpha'\#\$\$\#\beta't$, as intended. On applying Rule 5 once, we either obtain $w_3 = \alpha'\$\$\$\#\beta't$ or $w_3' = \alpha'\#\$\$\$\beta't$. However, again checking forbidden contexts, it becomes clear the no further derivation steps are possible with string w_3' but Rules 2 or 4; however, both rules require (by their permitting contexts) not to see $\$$ following the (unique) substring $\#\$$, so that in fact any derivation attempt on w_3' is blocked. Therefore, we have to continue with w_3, applying Rule 4 again. This leads us to $w_4 = \alpha'\$\$\$\$\beta't$ as intended. None of the permitting contexts of Rules 1 through 5 will trigger, and this continues to be the case also for the strings $w_5 = \alpha'\$\$\$\beta't$, $w_6 = \alpha'\$\$\beta't$, forcing us to apply Rule 6 thrice. Now, $w_7 = \alpha'\$\beta't$ is of the intended form, allowing us to start another simulation cycle.   □

The next result is a typical trade-off result; its simulation is based on the very same idea as the previous one, but we have one more nonterminal and get a smaller degree in exchange. When comparing with the rules in Fig. 4, note that the deletion of $\$$ is now done unconditionally. Even disregarding the new parameter, we get a new record result for SCG of degree $(3, 1)$, improving on [3].

Theorem 3. $RE = SC(3, 1, 6, 6, 4)$.

Being very similar to the previous proof, we omit the correctness argument here. In our next result, we consider a degree of $(2, 1)$. We reduce the number of non-simple rules to 3 at the cost of one more nonterminal compared to [14].

Theorem 4. $RE = SC(2, 1, 7, 6, 3)$.

Proof. Our proof is based on the known computational completeness of type-0 grammars in $(4, 1)$-GNF. In particular, we explain how to simulate the non-context-free deletion rule $ABC \to \lambda$ by the rules presented in Fig. 5.

Invariants and Properties:

The next list of properties can be observed by analyzing the given six rules:

(i) If w contains no primed symbols, then only Rule $R1$ is applicable.

(ii) If w contains A', then (only) Rules $R1, R3, R4, R5$ may apply.

(iii) If w contains A' as the only primed symbol, possibly twice, then (only) Rule $R1$ may apply.

1. $(B \rightarrow B', ABC, B')$ 3. $(C \rightarrow B'A', A'B', B'A')$ 5. $(B' \rightarrow \lambda, A'B'A', \emptyset)$
2. $(A \rightarrow A', B'C, A')$ 4. $(B' \rightarrow \lambda, B'B', \emptyset)$ 6. $(A' \rightarrow \lambda, \emptyset, B')$

Fig. 6. Simulating $ABC \rightarrow \lambda$ with only three non-simple rules.

(iv) If w contains B', then (only) Rules $R2, R3, R4, R5, R6$ may apply.
 (v) If w contains B' as the only primed symbol, then (only) Rule $R2$ may apply.
(vi) If w contains C', then (only) Rules $R1, R2, R4, R5, R6$ may apply.
(vii) If w contains C' as the only primed symbol, then (only) Rules $R1, R6$ may apply.
(viii) If w contains A' and B', then (only) Rules $R3, R4, R5$ may apply.
(ix) If w contains A' and B' but not C', then (only) Rules $R3, R4$ may apply, both requiring the presence of the substring $A'B'$.
 (x) If w contains A' and C' but not B', then (only) Rules $R1, R5$ may apply.
(xi) If w contains A', B' and C', then (only) Rule $R4$ may apply.
(xii) If w contains B' and C' but not A', then (only) Rules $R2, R6$ may apply.

Our inductive argument sketched below will also prove the following invariants, which are clearly fulfilled in a string that contains no primed symbols at all:

(1) Any derivable sentential form can contain at most two occurrences of each of A', B', C', but never more than three primed symbols in total. If it contains two occurrences of some primed symbol, then this primed symbol must be A'.
(2) Any derivable sentential form that contains A' also contains B' or C'.
(3) Any derivable sentential form that contains both B' and C' also contains A', or if not, the derivation is immediately blocked.

In the first phase, context-free rules of the form $S \rightarrow \xi$ are used to finally produce a string of the form $\alpha \zeta \beta$, where $\alpha \in \{A, B\}^*$ is some nonterminal prefix, $\beta \in (\{B, C\} \cup T)^*$, and ζ is the center of the string, i.e., $\zeta \in \{ABC, AC, ABBC\}$, where the first possibility $\zeta = ABC$ is the situation that should be continued, while the other situations should be blocked. The intended derivation is then:

$$\alpha \zeta \beta \Rightarrow_1 \alpha AB'C\beta \Rightarrow_2 \alpha A'B'C\beta \Rightarrow_3 \alpha A'B'C'\beta \Rightarrow_4 \alpha(A')^2 C'\beta \Rightarrow_5^2 \alpha C'\beta \Rightarrow_6 \alpha\beta$$

The main work is to prove that (basically) no other derivation is possible.

As with previous proofs, also this proof is based on a number of case distinctions. It makes heavy use of the mentioned properties and invariants that we stated above, also to guide the reader in filling in the details of this proof.   □

Remark 2. The forbidden context B' in Rule $R5$ is needed. Otherwise, we could simulate $AAABCBC \rightarrow \lambda$ as follows which should not actually happen.

$$AAABCBC \Rightarrow^* AAC'BC \Rightarrow_1 AAC'B'C \Rightarrow_{2,5} AC'B'C \Rightarrow_6 AB'C \Rightarrow^* \lambda$$

With similar ideas, we can offer another trade-off result to Theorems 2 and 3.

Theorem 5. $RE = SC(3, 2, 6, 6, 3)$.

The simulation of the non-context-free deletion rule $ABC \to \lambda$ by a SCG grammar G' whose rules are given in Fig. 6. The intended derivation simulating $ABC \to \lambda$ is:

$$ABC \Rightarrow_1 AB'C \Rightarrow_2 A'B'C \Rightarrow_3 A'B'B'A' \Rightarrow_4 A'B'A' \Rightarrow_5 A'A' \Rightarrow_6^2 \lambda$$

Instead of a full proof, we mention some important properties of this simulation:

1. Early restarts, the main problem addressed in Remark 2, are avoided by checking for the permitting context ABC in the first rule.
2. We check whether the correct C is replaced (by Rule 3) or not in Rule 4, as the context $B'B'$ is not producible by any other way.
3. The permitting string $A'B'A'$ of Rule 5 guarantees that all previous rules must have been executed in the correct order.

We hope this gives sufficient information to the reader to verify the correctness of our construction.

4   Summary and Future Work

We initiated the study of the refining descriptional complexity parameter 'number of non-simple rules' in semi-conditional grammars in order to better understand the role of simple rules in SCG and to refine the analysis of the Pareto front of descriptional complexity for these grammars. We obtained a number of trade-off results, also compared with earlier results from the literature. For instance, the complexity vectors $(3, 1, 7, 7, 0)$, $(3, 1, 6, 6, 4)$, $(3, 2, 6, 6, 3)$ and $(3, 2, 5, 6, 4)$ are pairwise incomparable. Other similar parameter refinements can be also investigated. For instance, to interpolate between the degrees $(1, 1)$ and $(2, 1)$, one could quantify (within SCG of degree $(2, 1)$) the number of rules that actually have permitting strings of length two. We leave these and similar questions for future research.

References

1. Dassow, J., Păun, Gh.: Regulated Rewriting in Formal Language Theory. EATCS Monographs in Theoretical Computer Science, vol. 18. Springer, Cham (1989)
2. Fernau, H., Freund, R., Oswald, M., Reinhardt, K.: Refining the nonterminal complexity of graph-controlled, programmed, and matrix grammars. J. Autom. Lang. Comb. **12**(1/2), 117–138 (2007)
3. Fernau, H., Kuppusamy, L., Oladele, R.O.: New nonterminal complexity results for semi-conditional grammars. In: Manea, F., Miller, R.G., Nowotka, D. (eds.) CiE 2018. LNCS, vol. 10936, pp. 172–182. Springer, Cham (2018). https://doi.org/10.1007/978-3-319-94418-0_18
4. Fernau, H., Kuppusamy, L., Oladele, R.O., Raman, I.: Improved descriptional complexity results for simple semi-conditional grammars. Fund. Inform. **181**, 189–211 (2021)

5. Fernau, H., Kuppusamy, L., Oladele, R.O., Raman, I.: Improved descriptional complexity results on generalized forbidding grammars. Discret. Appl. Math. **319**, 2–18 (2022)
6. Geffert, V.: Normal forms for phrase-structure grammars. RAIRO Informatique théorique et Applications/Theor. Inform. Appl. **25**, 473–498 (1991)
7. Masopust, T.: Formal models: regulation and reduction. Ph.D. thesis, Faculty of Information Technology, Brno University of Technology, Brno, Czech Republic (2007)
8. Masopust, T.: A note on the generative power of some simple variants of context-free grammars regulated by context conditions. In: Dediu, A.H., Ionescu, A.M., Martín-Vide, C. (eds.) LATA 2009. LNCS, vol. 5457, pp. 554–565. Springer, Heidelberg (2009). https://doi.org/10.1007/978-3-642-00982-2_47
9. Masopust, T., Meduna, A.: Descriptional complexity of generalized forbidding grammars. In: Geffert, V., Pighizzini, G. (eds.) DCFS, pp. 170–177. University of Kosice, Slovakia (2007)
10. Masopust, T., Meduna, A.: Descriptional complexity of semi-conditional grammars. Inf. Process. Lett. **104**(1), 29–31 (2007)
11. Mayer, O.: Some restrictive devices for context-free languages. Inf. Control (now Inf. Comput.) **20**, 69–92 (1972)
12. Meduna, A., Gopalaratnam, M.: On semi-conditional grammars with productions having either forbidding or permitting conditions. Acta Cybernet. **11**, 309–323 (1994)
13. Meduna, A., Svec, M.: Reduction of simple semi-conditional grammars with respect to the number of conditional productions. Acta Cybernet. **15**(3), 353–360 (2002)
14. Okubo, F.: A note on the descriptional complexity of semi-conditional grammars. Inf. Process. Lett. **110**(1), 36–40 (2009)
15. Păun, Gh.: A variant of random context grammars: semi-conditional grammars. Theor. Comput. Sci. **41**, 1–17 (1985)
16. Vaszil, Gy.: On the descriptional complexity of some rewriting mechanisms regulated by context conditions. Theor. Comput. Sci. **330**, 361–373 (2005)

Universal Boolean Algebras
with Applications to Semantic Classes
of Models

Mikhail Peretyat'kin[1](✉) and Victor Selivanov[2,3]

[1] Institute of Mathematics and Mathematical Modeling, 050010 Almaty, Kazakhstan
peretyatkin@math.kz
[2] Department of Mathematics and Computer Science, St. Petersburg University,
199178 St. Petersburg, Russia
[3] A.P. Ershov Institute of Informatics Systems, 630090 Novosibirsk, Russia
vseliv@iis.nsk.su

Abstract. We explore numbered Boolean algebras over levels Ξ of arithmetical and analytical hierarchies. We show the existence and uniqueness (up to computable isomorphism) of universal Boolean Ξ-algebras, determine the levels in which such algebras exist, and classify the universal algebras up to isomorphism. We apply these results to the semantic class of all countable saturated models having decidable ω-stable theories in a fixed finite rich signature. It turns out that the Tarski-Lindenbaum algebra of this class equipped with a Gödel numbering of the sentences is a Boolean Σ_1^1-algebra whose computable ultrafilters form a dense subset in the set of all ultrafilters; moreover, this algebra is universal with respect to the class of Boolean Σ_1^1-algebras. This determines uniquely the isomorphism type of this Boolean algebra.

Keywords: Turing computability · class of a hierarchy · numbered Boolean algebra · Tarski-Lindenbaum algebra · computable isomorphism · semantic class of models · decidable theory · countable saturated model · ω-stable theory

1 Introduction

Tarski-Lindenbaum algebras are of central importance for model theory, and their computational aspects are very interesting for computability theory. Building on fundamental results of W. Hanf, [4] (in particular, his discovery of the universality property of the Tarski-Lindenbaum algebra of sentences of any finite rich signature), the first author of this paper made a comprehensive investigation of Tarski-Lindenbaum algebras of finitely axiomatizable theories and found

Peretyat'kin's research is funded by the Science Committee of the Ministry of Science and Higher Education of the Republic of Kazakhstan, grant number BR20281002. Selivanov's research is funded by the Russian Science Foundation, project number 19-71-30002.

many applications of the corresponding general construction to computable models (see monograph [12] and references therein).

The second author of this paper has noticed [19] that the Hanf universality property, considered for arbitrary positive (c.e.) Boolean algebras, characterizes a unique (up to computable isomorphism) universal c.e. Boolean algebra (BA). Later he has shown [20] that similar universal structures exist in any computably axiomatizable quasivariety. Moreover, the universal c.e. BA (and its relativizations) naturally appear in other branches of computability theory which leads to interesting applications [18, 21] (see also the survey paper [22]).

In this paper, we extend the notion of universal BA to classes of analytical hierarchy, complementing earlier results of Odintsov and Selivanov on the arithmetical hierarchy of BAs. We show the existence and uniqueness (up to computable isomorphism) of universal BAs in levels of the arithmetical and analytical hierarchy, determine the levels in which such algebras exist, and show that most of these universal algebras are not isomorphic to each other.

We show that such generalized universal BAs also naturally appear in computable model theory. Namely, we explore the semantic class of all countable saturated models having decidable theories in a fixed finite rich signature, continuing a series of Peretyat'kin's results on semantic classes. We show that the Tarski-Lindenbaum algebra of this class equipped with a Gödel numbering of the sentences is a Boolean Σ_1^1-algebra whose computable ultrafilters form a dense subset in the set of all ultrafilters; moreover, this algebra is universal with respect to the class of Boolean Σ_1^1-algebras. We also give detailed proofs of some facts which were only announced or sketched in earlier publications, e.g. [19].

2   Preliminaries

We consider theories in first-order predicate logic *with equality* and use general concepts of model theory, computability theory, BAs and constructive models found in [3, 7, 17, 23], and [5]. We consider signatures admitting Gödel's numberings of formulas. Generally, *incomplete theories* are considered.

A finite signature is called *rich*, if it contains at least one n-ary predicate or function symbol for $n > 1$, or two unary function symbols. A theory F is called *finitely axiomatizable* if it is defined by a finite set of axioms, and its signature is finite. By $SL(\sigma)$, we denote the set of all σ-sentences (i.e., closed formulas). In this work, we use a finite rich signature σ, and consider a fixed Gödel numbering Φ_i, $i \in \mathbb{N}$, of the set $SL(\sigma)$. The set of all Gödel numbers of formulas from a set $\Sigma \subseteq SL(\sigma)$ is denoted by $\mathrm{Nom}(\Sigma)$. We use notation $\mathcal{P}(A)$ for the power-set of A, and $|A|$ or $\mathrm{Card}(A)$ for cardinality of a set A. The sign $\cong$ means (depending on context) either *isomorphism* of models, or *computable isomorphism* of numbered models. The set of all finite binary sequences $\alpha = \langle \alpha_0, \alpha_1, \ldots, \alpha_n \rangle$, $\alpha_i \in \{0, 1\}$, is denoted by $2^{<\omega}$. The empty string is denoted by $\varnothing$. The *canonical (Gödel) index* of a binary string $\varepsilon = \langle \varepsilon_0, \varepsilon_1, \ldots, \varepsilon_{n-1} \rangle$, $\varepsilon_i \in \{0, 1\}$, is the number $\mathrm{Nom}(\varepsilon) = 2^n + \varepsilon_0 2^{n-1} + \varepsilon_1 2^{n-2} + \ldots + \varepsilon_{n-1} - 1$. We often write shortly $\langle \varepsilon \rangle$ instead of $\mathrm{Nom}(\varepsilon)$. By $\mathcal{L}(T)$, we denote the Tarski-Lindenbaum algebra of theory T over formulas without free variables, while $\mathcal{L}_n(T)$ is the Tarski-Lindenbaum algebra of formulas of T with n free variables $x_0, x_1, ..., x_{n-1}$, $n \geq 0$ (algebra $\mathcal{L}_n(T)$ is often considered in the case when theory T is complete).

We consider BAs in the signature $\sigma_{BA} = \{\cup, \cap, -, \mathbf{0}, \mathbf{1}\}$. Let $\mathcal{B}$ be a BA, and $a \in \mathcal{B}$. By $\mathcal{B}[a]$, we denote the restriction of the BA $\mathcal{B}$ to the set of all subelements of the element a counting that $\mathbf{1} = a$ and $-x$ is defined as $a \smallsetminus x$ in $\mathcal{B}[a]$. If b is an element in a BA and $\alpha \in \{0,1\}$, then b^α means b for $\alpha = 1$ and $-b$ for $\alpha = 0$. Similarly, if Φ is a formula and $\alpha \in \{0,1\}$, then Φ^α means Φ for $\alpha = 1$ and $\neg\Phi$ for $\alpha = 0$. A BA $\mathcal{B}$ is said to be *superatomic* if any its quotient-algebra $\mathfrak{B}/\mathcal{F}$ is atomic, [23, p. 35]. Any countable superatomic BA $\mathcal{B}$ is characterized by a pair (α, n), where α is an ordinal (called the *ordinal type* of $\mathcal{B}$), while n is a number in $\mathbb{N} \smallsetminus \{0\}$ (called the *degree* of $\mathcal{B}$); the pair (α, n) itself is said to be *full superatomic type* of $\mathcal{B}$, [2]. The parameter α indicates a step where the quotient algebra modulo iterated Fréchet ideal becomes finite (this is a non-limit ordinal), while $n > 0$ denotes the number of atoms in this finite BA. It is proved in [2, Th. 2] that a countable superatomic BA $\mathcal{B}$ is constructivizable if and only if its ordinal type α is a constructive ordinal.

Following Rogers [17, Sec. 5.2], we use the notation W_n for nth computably enumerable set in Post's numbering of the family of all c.e. sets. We denote by W_n^X the computably enumerable set with c.e. index n relative to an oracle $X \subseteq \mathbb{N}$, [17, Sec. 9.3]. Definition of the concept of a binary tree can be found in [12, Sec. 2.1] as well as in Preliminaries [14]. In this work, we use a more specialized term *compact binary trees* for these trees in order to distinguish them from *natural binary trees* represented by ω-tuples $\langle \alpha_i \mid i < \omega \rangle$, $\alpha_i \in \{0,1\}$. If $\mathcal{D}$ is a compact binary tree, we denote by $\Pi(\mathcal{D})$ the set of all its maximal chains. The tree $\mathcal{D}$ is said to be *superatomic* if the set $\Pi(\mathcal{D})$ is at most countable. We also use the following technical notations: $\mathfrak{P}_n$, is the table condition with the Gödel number n, $n \in \mathbb{N}$; $A \models \mathfrak{P}_i$, means that the table condition is satisfied in the set A, $A \subseteq \mathbb{N}$; $\Omega(m) = \{A \subseteq \mathbb{N} \mid (\forall i \in W_m) A \models \mathfrak{P}_i\}$, is parametric Stone space with index m; $\mathcal{D}_n^X$ is the closure of the set W_n^X up to a compact binary tree.

Main statement on the *canonical construction* of finitely axiomatizable theories can be found in [12, Th. 3.1.1]. Its part involved in construction of this work states the following:

Theorem 2.1. *Effectively in a pair of integers (m, s) and a finite rich signature σ, it is possible to construct a finitely axiomatizable theory $F = \mathbb{F}c(m, s, \sigma)$ of signature σ together with an effective sequence θ_n, $n \in \mathbb{N}$, of sentences of the signature σ such that the family of extensions of F defined by*

$$F[A] = F \cup \{\theta_i \mid i \in A\} \cup \{\neg\theta_j \mid j \in \mathbb{N} \smallsetminus A\}, \quad A \subseteq \mathbb{N}, \tag{2.1}$$

satisfies the following properties:

(A) *for any $A \subseteq \mathbb{N}$, the theory $F[A]$ is either complete or contradictory;*

(B) *the theory $F[A]$, $A \subseteq \mathbb{N}$, is consistent if and only if $A \in \Omega(m)$;*

(C) *for an arbitrary $A \in \Omega(m)$, the following statements are satisfied:*

(a) *theory $F[A]$ has a countable saturated model if and only if the tree $\mathcal{D}_s^A$ is superatomic,*

(b) *theory $F[A]$ is ω-stable if and only if the tree $\mathcal{D}_s^A$ is superatomic.*

We recall a technical statement.

Lemma 2.2. *There is an effective operator mapping an arbitrary constructive linear ordering $(\mathcal{L}, \nu)$ into a tree $\mathcal{D}(\mathcal{L}, \nu)$ with the following properties:*

(a) *the tree $\mathcal{D}(\mathcal{L}, \nu)$ is computable,*

(b) *the tree $\mathcal{D}(\mathcal{L}, \nu)$ is superatomic if and only if $\mathcal{L}$ is well ordered,*

(c) *if $\mathcal{L}$ is well ordered then the family of chains $\Pi(\mathcal{D}(\mathcal{L}, \nu))$ is computable.*

PROOF. See [12, Lem. 2.2.1]. □

We give a well-known example of a complete set in the hierarchy class Π_1^1.

Lemma 2.3. *There is a computable sequence $(\mathcal{L}_i, \nu_i)$, $i < \omega$, of constructive linear orderings such that $\mathcal{W} = \{ n \mid \mathcal{L}_n \text{ is a well-ordered set } \}$ is an m-complete in the class Π_1^1 set.*

PROOF. See e.g. a construction in [12, p. 44]. □

A *semantic class of models* is defined by a condition in terms of model-theoretic properties, [13, Sec. 6]. We consider the following semantic classes of models of a fixed finite rich signature σ: $P(\sigma)$ is the class of all prime models, $S(\sigma)$ is the class of all countable saturated models, $W(\sigma)$ is the class of all models with ω-stable theories, M_{dec} is the class of models with decidable theories, $M_{s.c.}$ is the class of all strongly constructivizable models. Additionally, we use notations $M_{s.c.}^1$ and $M_{s.c.}^\omega$ for subclasses of $M_{s.c.}$ including models with algorithmic dimensions 1 and ω, respectively, see [16]. We also consider some combinations of these classes.

3   Boolean Algebras over Classes of Hierarchies

Let Ξ be a complexity class, eg. Σ_n^0, Δ_n^0, Π_n^0, Σ_n^1, or Π_n^1 with $0 < n < \omega$ (actually, we do not concern other classes of hierarchies in this paper). A numbered BA $(\mathcal{B}, \nu)$ is called a Ξ-*algebra*, if all its signature operations are uniformly presentable by computable functions on ν-numbers, while the equality predicate in $\mathcal{B}$ is a Ξ-relation in the numbering ν; i.e., there exist computable functions $u(x, y)$, $v(x, y)$, $w(x)$, and a relation $E(x, y)$ which represent the BA as follows, for any $x, y \in \mathbb{N}$:

$$\nu(x) \cup \nu(y) = \nu(u(x, y)), \ \ \nu(x) \cap \nu(y) = \nu(v(x, y)), \ \ -\nu(x) = \nu(w(x)), \quad (3.1)$$
$$\nu(x) = \nu(y) \Leftrightarrow E(x, y), \ \ E \in \Xi.$$

A BA $\mathcal{B}$ is said to be a Ξ-*algebra*, if there is a numbering ν s.t. $(\mathcal{B}, \nu)$ is a Ξ-BA.

A BA $\mathcal{B}$ is Ξ-universal if for any Boolean Ξ-algebra $\mathcal{B}'$, there is an element a in $\mathcal{B}$ such that $\mathcal{B}' \cong \mathcal{B}[a]$. A numbered BA $(\mathcal{B}, \nu)$ is Ξ-universal if for any numbered Boolean Ξ-algebra $(\mathcal{B}', \nu')$ there is an element a in $\mathcal{B}$ such that $(\mathcal{B}', \nu') \cong (\mathcal{B}, \nu)[a]$. A BA $\mathcal{B}$ (numbered BA $(\mathcal{B}, \nu)$) which itself is a Ξ-algebra and is universal over the class of Boolean Ξ-algebras is said to be Ξ-universal Ξ-algebra, written $\mathcal{B} \approx \Xi$ (respectively, $(\mathcal{B}, \nu) \approx \Xi$). Such BAs of main interest in this paper.

Lemma 3.1. *Let Ξ be a complexity class, M be a class of models in an enumerable or finite signature. Then, $\mathrm{Th}(M) \in \Xi$ if and only if the Tarski-Lindenbaum algebra $(\mathcal{L}(\mathrm{Th}(M)), \gamma)$ with a Gödel numbering γ is a Ξ-BA.*

PROOF. Obviously, $\Phi \in \mathrm{Th}(M)$ if and only if $\Phi \sim 1$ in $\mathcal{L}(\mathrm{Th}(M))$. On the other hand, $\Phi \sim \Psi$ in $\mathcal{L}(\mathrm{Th}(M))$ if and only if we have $\Phi \leftrightarrow \Psi \in \mathrm{Th}(M)$. □

We turn to alternative versions of the notions.

Below, a set $X \subseteq \mathbb{N}$ is considered as an oracle. A numbered BA $(\mathcal{B}, \nu)$ is said to be X-*enumerable* if all operations in $(\mathcal{B}, \nu)$ are presented by computable functions, while the equality relation is X-enumerable in the numbering ν. A BA $\mathcal{B}$ is said to be an X-*enumerable* algebra if there is a numbering ν such that $(\mathcal{B}, \nu)$ is an X-enumerable BA. A numbered BA $(\mathcal{B}, \nu)$ is said to be X-*universal* if for any X-enumerable BA $(\mathcal{B}', \nu')$, there is an element a in $\mathcal{B}$ such that $(\mathcal{B}', \nu') \cong (\mathcal{B}[a], \nu[a]) = (\mathcal{B}, \nu)[a]$. A *numbered* BA $(\mathcal{B}, \nu)$ is said to be X-*universal* X-*enumerable* if it is both X-universal and X-enumerable. A Boolean algebra $\mathcal{B}$ is said to be X-*enumerable* X-*universal* if there is a numbering ν such that $(\mathcal{B}, \nu)$ is an X-enumerable X-universal BA.

As it is accepted, cf. [17, Sec. 14.1], the class of all relations on $\mathbb{N}$ expressible by Σ_n^X-forms is denoted by Σ_n^X, while the class of all relations expressible by Π_n^X-forms is denoted by Π_n^X, and we denote $\Delta_n^X = \Sigma_n^X \cap \Pi_n^X$. We also use notations $\Sigma_n^{1,X}$, $\Pi_n^{1,X}$, and $\Delta_n^{1,X}$ for analytical modes of these classes, cf. [17, Sec. 16.6].

Lemma 3.2. *A numbered BA $(\mathcal{B}, \nu)$ is X-enumerable if and only if $(\mathcal{B}, \nu)$ is a Σ_1^X-algebra, and $(\mathcal{B}, \nu)$ is X-universal if and only if $(\mathcal{B}, \nu)$ is Σ_1^X-universal.*

PROOF. Follows immediately. □

Lemma 3.3. *Any Boolean Π_1^X-algebra is a Boolean Δ_1^X-algebra.*

PROOF. Cf. [9, Sec. 2, Th. 1]. □

Lemma 3.4. *Any Boolean Δ_2^X-algebra is a Boolean Σ_1^X-algebra.*

PROOF. Cf. [9, Sec. 2, Th. 2]. □

Lemma 3.5. *For an arbitrary numbered Boolean Σ_1^X-algebra $(\mathcal{B}, \nu)$, there is a numbering υ of $\mathcal{B}$ such that $(\mathcal{B}, \upsilon)$ is a Boolean Σ_1^X-algebra whose computable ultrafilters form a dense set in the set of all ultrafilters of the algebra $(\mathcal{B}, \upsilon)$.*

PROOF. Cf. [15, Lem. 2].   □

Lemma 3.6. *A countable superatomic BA $\mathcal{B}$ is a Δ_1^X-BA if and only if its ordinal type α is a Δ_1^X-ordinal.*

PROOF. If α is a Δ_1^X-ordinal, BA $\mathcal{B}$ generated by intervals in the order $\omega^\alpha \cdot n$ is a superatomic BA of ordinal type (α, n), [2, Lem. 1.4]. Thus, it is a Δ_1^X-BA.

Now, let $(\mathcal{B}, \nu)$ be a countable superatomic Δ_1^X-BA of an ordinal type α. For an element $a \in \mathcal{B}$, we denote by $\mathrm{typ}(a)$ the full superatomic type of the BA $\mathcal{B}[a]$. Let us introduce the following ordering on the set of natural numbers:

$$k \preceq n \Leftrightarrow_{dfn} \mathrm{typ}(\nu(k)) < \mathrm{typ}(\nu(n)) \vee \left(\mathrm{typ}(\nu(k)) = \mathrm{typ}(\nu(n)) \wedge k \leq n \right), \quad (3.2)$$

where $<$ is the lexicographical ordering on the set $\mathrm{Ord} \times \mathbb{N}$. By construction, the system $(\mathbb{N}, \preceq)$ is a linear ordering; moreover, this is a well ordering of an ordinal type $\beta \geq \alpha$. We are going to show that the relation (3.2) is $\Sigma_1^{1,X}$. Since $(\mathcal{B}, \nu)$ is a countable superatomic Δ_1^X-BA, the equality $\mathrm{typ}(\nu(k)) = \mathrm{typ}(\nu(n))$ is satisfied iff $\mathcal{B}[\nu(k)]$ is isomorphic to $\mathcal{B}[\nu(n)]$. Furthermore, $\mathrm{typ}(\nu(k)) < \mathrm{typ}(\nu(n))$ iff either (a) there is an element $b \subset \nu(n)$ such that $\mathcal{B}[\nu(k)]$ is isomorphic to $\mathcal{B}[b]$, and $\mathcal{B}[\nu(n) \setminus b]$ is isomorphic to $\mathcal{B}[\nu(n)]$; or (b) there are elements $a_1, ..., a_p, b_1, ..., b_q$, $0 < p < q < \omega$, such that $a_i \cap a_j = \mathbf{0}$, for all i, j with $0 < i < j \leq p$, and $b_r \cap b_s = \mathbf{0}$, for all r, s with $0 < r < s \leq q$; moreover, $\nu(k) = a_1 \cup a_2 \cup ... \cup a_p$, $\nu(n) = b_1 \cup b_2 \cup ... \cup b_q$, and all BAs in the sequence $\mathcal{B}[a_1], \ldots, \mathcal{B}[a_p], \mathcal{B}[b_1], \ldots, \mathcal{B}[b_q]$ are isomorphic. Thus, $\preceq$ is indeed $\Sigma_1^{1,X}$ ensuring that β is $\Sigma_1^{1,X}$. Moreover, β is $\Delta_1^{1,X}$ because this is an ordinal. From $\alpha \leq \beta$, we obtain that α is also $\Delta_1^{1,X}$. By Spector's theorem [17, Sec. 16.6, Th. XXXVI], the ordinal α is a Δ_1^X-ordinal.   □

4   Universal Boolean Algebras

Hereafter, we denote by $(\mathfrak{B}, \delta)$ a fixed constructive countable atomless BA.

Lemma 4.1. *Let Ξ be a complexity class. A numbered BA $(\mathcal{B}, \nu)$ is a Ξ-algebra if and only if there is a filter (or ideal) $\mathfrak{F} \subseteq \mathfrak{B}$ in a constructive countable atomless BA $(\mathfrak{B}, \delta)$ such that $\delta^{-1}(\mathfrak{F}) \in \Xi$ and $(\mathcal{B}, \nu)$ is computably isomorphic to the quotient algebra $(\mathfrak{B}/\mathfrak{F}, \delta/\mathfrak{F})$.*

PROOF. By standard methods of freely generated algebras.   □

We are going to introduce indices for X-enumerable BAs. By $\mathcal{F}[Z]$, we denote a filter generated by the set Z in a BA. We introduce the following block of notations concerning the numbered atomless algebra $(\mathfrak{B}, \delta)$:

(a) $\mathfrak{F}_n^X = \mathcal{F}[\{\delta(k) \mid k \in W_n^X\}], \quad n \in \mathbb{N}$,   (4.1)

(b) $(\mathfrak{B}_n^X, \delta_n^X) = (\mathfrak{B}/\mathfrak{F}_n^X, \delta/\mathfrak{F}_n^X), \quad n \in \mathbb{N}$,

(c) $(\mathfrak{B}^X, \delta^X) = \bigotimes_{n \in \mathbb{N}} (\mathfrak{B}_n^X, \delta_n^X)$.

The number n in (4.1)(b) is called an X-*enumerable index* for algebra $(\mathfrak{B}_n^X, \delta_n^X)$. It represents an X-relativized version of the notion of a c.e. index for a c.e. BA.

Lemma 4.2. *For each X-enumerable BA $(\mathcal{B}, \nu)$ there exists an X-enumerable index $n \in \mathbb{N}$; i.e., an integer n such that $(\mathcal{B}, \nu) \cong (\mathfrak{B}_n^X, \delta_n^X)$.*

PROOF. From the fact that $(\mathfrak{B}, \delta)$ is a freely generated constructive BA.   □

Lemma 4.3. *Let $(\mathfrak{B}^*, \delta^*)$ be an X-universal BA. Effectively in an X-index n of an X-enumerable BA $(\mathcal{B}, \nu)$, it is possible to find a number m with $(\mathcal{B}, \nu) \cong (\mathfrak{B}', \delta')[\nu(m)]$ together with a computable function realizing this isomorphism.*

PROOF. This is a simple corollary of the fact that $(\mathfrak{B}^*, \delta^*)$ must contain an interval $(\mathfrak{B}^*, \delta^*)[a]$ that is computably isomorphic to the algebra $(4.1)(c)$.   □

Lemma 4.4. *Let $(\mathscr{B}^*, \lambda^*)$ be an X-enumerable X-universal BA, and $(\mathcal{B}', \nu')$ be an arbitrary X-enumerable BA. Then, there is a computable isomorphism between $(\mathcal{B}', \nu') \otimes (\mathscr{B}^*, \lambda^*)$ and $(\mathscr{B}^*, \lambda^*)$.*

PROOF. By $(\mathscr{B}, \lambda)$, we denote a BA which is the direct product of ω copies of the algebra $(\mathfrak{B}^X, \delta^X)$. Namely we put

$$(\mathscr{B}, \lambda) = \bigotimes_{0 < i < \omega} (\mathcal{B}_i, \nu_i), \quad \text{where } (\mathcal{B}_i, \nu_i) \cong (\mathfrak{B}^X, \delta^X), \text{ for all } i \in \mathbb{N} \setminus \{0\}. \quad (4.2)$$

Obviously, $(\mathscr{B}, \lambda)$ is an X-universal X-enumerable algebra. First, we prove the following technical statement:

$$\text{For any } X\text{-enumerable algebra } (\mathcal{B}_0, \nu_0), \ (\mathcal{B}_0, \nu_0) \otimes (\mathscr{B}, \lambda) \cong (\mathscr{B}, \lambda). \quad (4.3)$$

We are going to compare the following direct products of BAs

(a) $(\mathscr{B}', \lambda') = (\mathcal{B}_0, \nu_0) \otimes (\check{\mathcal{B}}_1, \check{\nu}_1) \otimes (\check{\mathcal{B}}_2, \check{\nu}_2) \otimes \ldots \otimes (\check{\mathcal{B}}_k, \check{\nu}_k) \otimes \ldots \quad (4.4)$

(b) $(\mathscr{B}, \lambda) = \hspace{3.5cm} (\hat{\mathcal{B}}_1, \hat{\nu}_1) \otimes (\hat{\mathcal{B}}_2, \hat{\nu}_2) \otimes \ldots \otimes (\hat{\mathcal{B}}_k, \hat{\nu}_k) \otimes \ldots$

where each algebra $(\check{\mathcal{B}}_i, \check{\nu}_i)$, as well as each algebra $(\hat{\mathcal{B}}_i, \hat{\nu}_i)$, $0 < i < \omega$, is isomorphic to $(\mathfrak{B}^X, \delta^X)$, while $(\mathcal{B}_0, \nu_0)$ is the mentioned in (4.3) X-enumerable BA. Since $\hat{\mathcal{B}}_1 \cong \mathfrak{B}^X$, it is possible to find an element $b_1 \in \hat{\mathcal{B}}_1$ such that $\mathcal{B}_0 \cong \hat{\mathcal{B}}_1[b_1]$. Consider the decomposition $\hat{\mathcal{B}}_1 \cong \hat{\mathcal{B}}_1[b_1] \otimes \hat{\mathcal{B}}_1[-b_1]$. Now, we have to link algebra $\hat{\mathcal{B}}_1[-b_1]$ to a member in $(4.4)(a)$. Based on the fact that $\check{\mathcal{B}}_1 \cong \mathfrak{B}^X$, we can find an element $a_1 \in \check{\mathcal{B}}_1$ such that $\hat{\mathcal{B}}_1[-b_1] \cong \check{\mathcal{B}}_1[a_1]$. Consider the decomposition $\check{\mathcal{B}}_1 \cong \check{\mathcal{B}}_1[a_1] \otimes \check{\mathcal{B}}_1[-a_1]$. Then, we link the interval $\check{\mathcal{B}}_1[-a_1]$ with $\hat{\mathcal{B}}_2[b_2]$ for a suitable element b_2 in $\hat{\mathcal{B}}_2$ and so on. Separate steps of the construction are performed efficiently in the numbers of elements in corresponding numberings. Therefore, the summary mapping μ from $(\mathscr{B}', \lambda')$ to $(\mathscr{B}, \lambda)$ obtained in ω steps is the required computable isomorphism. Thus, assertion (4.3) is proved.

We turn to the proof of Lemma 4.4. Since the BA $(\mathscr{B}, \lambda)$ is X-enumerable by construction while the algebra $(\mathscr{B}^*, \lambda^*)$ is X-universal, there exists an element $c \in \mathscr{B}^*$ such that $(\mathscr{B}, \lambda) \cong (\mathscr{B}^*, \lambda^*)[c]$. We have a decomposition $(\mathscr{B}^*, \lambda^*) \cong (\mathscr{B}^*, \lambda^*)[-c] \otimes (\mathscr{B}^*, \lambda^*)[c] \cong (\mathscr{B}^*, \lambda^*)[-c] \otimes (\mathscr{B}, \lambda)$. By assertion (4.3), we obtain $(\mathscr{B}^*, \lambda^*) \cong (\mathscr{B}, \lambda)$. Applying (4.3) again, we obtain the required isomorphism $(\mathscr{B}', \lambda') \otimes (\mathscr{B}^*, \lambda^*) \cong (\mathscr{B}^*, \lambda^*)$.   □

Notice that, the proof in Lemma 4.4 represents an X-relativized version of the method used in [10, Th. 5.1] and [11, Th. 6.5]. There is an alternative method of proof of Lemma 4.4 suggested in [19]. This method of proof is based on presentation (4.1)(c) for the X-universal X-enumerable BA together with Pudding Lemma, cf. [17, Sec. 1.8, Th. III], and [24, Ch. I, Sec. 3].   □

Now, we outline some natural hierarchies of BAs.

Theorem 4.5. *The following assertions hold:*

(a) *For each $\Xi \in \{\Sigma_n^0, \Sigma_n^1, \Pi_n^1 \mid 1 \le n < \omega\}$, there is a Ξ-BA $(\mathcal{B}, \nu)$ that is Ξ-universal.*

(b) *For each $\Xi \in \{\Sigma_n^0, \Sigma_n^1, \Pi_n^1 \mid 1 \le n < \omega\}$, any two Ξ-universal Ξ-BAs $(\mathcal{B}', \nu')$ and $(\mathcal{B}'', \nu'')$ are computably isomorphic.*

(c) *Let $\Xi', \Xi'' \in \{\Sigma_n^0 \mid 1 \le n < \omega\} \cup \{\Sigma_n^1 \mid 1 \le n < \omega\} \cup \{\Pi_n^1 \mid 1 \le n < \omega\}$ be two different classes of hierarchies, excepting the case $\{\Xi', \Xi''\} = \{\Pi_1^1, \Pi_2^1\}$. If $(\mathcal{B}', \nu')$ is a Ξ'-universal Ξ'-BA, and $(\mathcal{B}'', \nu'')$ is a Ξ''-universal Ξ''-BA, then $\mathcal{B}'$ is not isomorphic to $\mathcal{B}''$. This is provable in $ZF + (V = L)$ for $\{\Xi', \Xi''\} = \{\Sigma_n^1, \Pi_n^1\}$, $n \ge 3$, and in ZFC otherwise.*

PROOF. (a) In the arithmetical case $\Xi = \Sigma_n^0$, $0 < n < \omega$, the rule (4.1)(c) with $X = \varnothing^{(n-1)}$ defines a numerated Ξ-universal Ξ-BA. As for the cases $\Xi = \Sigma_n^1$ or $\Xi = \Pi_n^1$, $0 < n < \omega$, we obtain a numbered Ξ-universal Ξ-BA by the same rule (4.1)(c) applied to a set $X \subseteq \mathbb{N}$ that is m-complete in Ξ.

(b) Let $(\mathcal{B}', \nu')$ and $(\mathcal{B}'', \nu'')$ be Ξ-universal Ξ-BAs. Depending on the case for Ξ, we fix a set $X \subseteq \mathbb{N}$ with $\Sigma_1^X = \Xi$ as it is explained in Part (a). By Lemma 4.4, we have $(\mathcal{B}, \nu) \cong (\mathcal{B}', \nu') \otimes (\mathcal{B}, \nu)$. On the other hand, again by Lemma 4.4, we have $(\mathcal{B}', \nu') \cong (\mathcal{B}, \nu) \otimes (\mathcal{B}', \nu') \cong (\mathcal{B}', \nu') \otimes (\mathcal{B}, \nu)$. As a result, we have constructed the required isomorphism $(\mathcal{B}, \nu) \cong (\mathcal{B}', \nu')$.

(c) Let $\Xi' = \Sigma_n^0$, $\Xi'' = \Sigma_m^0$, $0 < n < m < \omega$, and $X = \varnothing^{(m-1)}$. In this case, $\mathcal{B}'$ is X-constructivizable. On the other hand, $\mathcal{B}''$ is not X-constructivizable because every X-enumerable BA is isomorphic to an interval $\mathcal{B}''[a]$; moreover, by the Feiner theorem, [1], [8, Th. 3.5], among such BAs there is a non-X-constructivizable BA presented as the quotient $\mathfrak{B}/\mathfrak{F}$ modulo an X-enumerable ideal $\mathfrak{F}$ in the atomless algebra $(\mathfrak{B}, \delta)$. Now, let Ξ' be Σ_n^0 and Ξ'' be either Σ_m^1 or Π_m^1, $0 < n < \omega$, $0 < m < \omega$. Let also $X = \varnothing^{(n)}$. We have $\Xi' = \Sigma_n^0 \subset \Sigma_{n+1}^0 \subset \Xi''$. Thus, $\mathcal{B}'$ is X-constructivizable, while $\mathcal{B}''$ is not X-constructivizable because, by the Feiner theorem [1], it must include an interval $\mathcal{B}''[a]$ that is a non-X-constructivizable BA. Thereby, in both cases $\mathcal{B}'$ is not isomorphic to $\mathcal{B}''$.

We turn to the case of analytical classes with $\omega(\Xi') \ne \omega(\Xi'')$. For definiteness, we suppose that $\alpha = \omega(\Xi') < \omega(\Xi'')$. Let $\mathcal{B}$ be a countable superatomic BA of ordinal type $(\alpha, 1)$. Then algebra $\mathcal{B}''$ has an interval $\mathcal{B}''[c]$ isomorphic to $\mathcal{B}$ because $\mathcal{B}''$ is Ξ''-universal BA. On the other hand, $\mathcal{B}'$ does not have such an interval because otherwise α would be Ξ'-constructivizable by Lemma 3.6. Thereby, $\mathcal{B}'$ is not isomorphic to $\mathcal{B}''$. As for the case $\omega(\Xi') = \omega(\Xi'')$, by [25], this equality occurs just for the pair $\{\Pi_1^1, \Pi_2^1\}$ excluded within Part (c) of Theorem 4.5.   □

Hypothesis 4.6. *Boolean algebras $\mathcal{B}'$ and $\mathcal{B}''$ that are Ξ-universal Ξ-algebras for $\Xi = \Pi_1^1$ and $\Xi = \Pi_2^1$, respectively, are isomorphic.*

Remark 4.7. *The proof shows that there is a Π_1^1-BA not isomorphic to a Σ_1^1-BA and, for each $n \geq 2$, there is a Σ_n^1-BA not isomorphic to a Π_n^1-BA. Currently, we do not know whether there is a Σ_1^1-BA not isomorphic to a Π_1^1-BA and for which $n \geq 2$ there is a Π_n^1-BA not isomorphic to a Σ_n^1-BA.*

Remark 4.8. *There are many natural refinements of the analytical hierarchy (see e.g. [6] and references therein) which may be used to classify BAs similarly to their classifications in arithmetical and analytical hierarchies. To our knowledge, this direction was not explored so far.*

5   Characterization of the Tarski-Lindenbaum Algebra

In this section, we give a characterization to the Tarski-Lindenbaum algebra of the class of models indicated in the title of the work. Namely, we explore the Tarski-Lindenbaum algebra of the class

$$SW_{dec} = SW_{dec}(\sigma) = S(\sigma) \cap W(\sigma) \cap M_{dec}(\sigma)$$

of all countable saturated models with ω-stable decidable theories in a finite rich signature σ.

We use a fixed Gödel numbering Φ_i, $i \in \mathbb{N}$, for the set of all σ-sentences.

Theorem 5.1. *The following assertions hold:*

(a) *$(\mathcal{L}(SW_{dec}), \gamma)$ is a Boolean Σ_1^1-algebra, where γ is a Gödel numbering of the set of σ-sentences,*

(b) *computable ultrafilters of $(\mathcal{L}(SW_{dec}), \gamma)$ form a dense set among arbitrary ultrafilters in the algebra,*

(c) *for an arbitrary numbered Boolean Σ_1^1-algebra $(\mathcal{B}, \nu)$ whose computable ultrafilters form a dense set among arbitrary ultrafilters, there is a σ-sentence Θ such that $(\mathcal{B}, \nu) \cong (\mathcal{L}(\mathrm{Th}(\mathrm{Mod}(\Theta) \cap SW_{dec})), \gamma)$.*

(d) *for an arbitrary Boolean Σ_1^1-algebra $\mathcal{B}$, there is a σ-sentence Θ such that $\mathcal{B} \cong \mathcal{L}(\mathrm{Th}(\mathrm{Mod}(\Theta) \cap SW_{dec}))$.*

PROOF. (a) A σ-sentence Ψ of signature σ has a countable saturated model with a decidable ω-stable theory iff there exist integers m and n satisfying:

1. $W_m \cap W_n = \varnothing \wedge W_m \cup W_n = \mathbb{N}$, $\forall \wedge \forall \exists$
2. $T = \{\Phi_i \mid i \in W_m\}$ is a complete theory, $\forall \exists$
3. $\Psi \in T$, $\exists$
4. $(\forall n < \omega)[\mathcal{L}_n(T)$ is a superatomic algebra$]$. $\forall^1$
5. $(\forall$ countable $\mathfrak{N} \in \mathrm{Mod}(T))(\forall n < \omega)[\mathcal{L}_n(\mathrm{Th}(\mathfrak{N}, |\mathfrak{N}|))$ is superatomic$]$. $\forall^1$

Thus, we obtain a prefix $\forall^1$ for this condition. Finally, sentences Φ and Ψ are equivalent on the class SW_{dec} if and only if $(\Phi \wedge \neg \Psi) \vee (\Psi \wedge \neg \Phi)$ does not have a model in this class. This gives the required prefix $\exists^1$ for (a).

(b) Let T be an arbitrary complete theory extending $\mathrm{Th}(SW_{dec})$, and $\Psi \in T$. Obviously, Ψ has a model $\mathfrak{M} \in SW_{dec}$. From this we have that complete decidable theory $T' = \mathrm{Th}(\mathfrak{M})$ presenting a computable ultrafilter in $\mathrm{St}(\mathrm{Th}(SW_{dec}))$, is found in the neighborhood Ψ of the given ultrafilter T in this Stone space.

The proof of Part (c) is given in the forthcoming text. As for Part (d), it is a consequence of Part (c) and Lemma 3.5 with an m-complete Σ_1^1 set X.

Let us begin the proof of Part (c) of Theorem 5.1.

We use the following m-complete in the class Π_1^1 set

$$A^1 = \{n \in \mathbb{N} \mid \mathcal{L}_n \text{ is a well ordering}\}, \tag{5.1}$$

where $\mathcal{L}_n = (L_n, \nu_n)$, $n \in \mathbb{N}$, is an effective sequence of constructive linear orderings, cf. Lemma 2.3. Therefore, $E^1 = \mathbb{N} \smallsetminus A^1$ is an m-complete Σ_1^1 set.

Given a numbered Boolean Σ_1^1-algebra $(\mathcal{B}, \nu)$ that satisfies

$$\text{Computable ultrafilters of } (\mathcal{B}, \nu) \text{ form a dense set in } \mathrm{St}(\mathcal{B}). \tag{5.2}$$

It is possible to assume, that $\mathcal{B}$ is a nontrivial algebra. By definition, signature operations $\cup$, $\cap$ and $-$ in $\mathcal{B}$ are presentable by computable functions on ν-numbers, while the equality is a Σ_1^1-relation in the numbering ν, i.e., $\nu(x) = \nu(y) \Leftrightarrow H(x, y)$ is satisfied for a binary relation $H \in \Sigma_1^1$. Respectively, the inequality relation $H'(x, y) =_{dfn} (\nu(x) \neq \nu(y))$ is Π_1^1. Therefore, there is a unary relation H^* in Π_1^1 such that, for any binary string $\alpha = \langle \alpha_0, \alpha_1, \ldots, \alpha_n \rangle$, we have

$$\nu(0)^{\alpha_0} \cap \nu(1)^{\alpha_1} \cap \ldots \cap \nu(n)^{\alpha_n} \neq \mathbf{0} \; \Leftrightarrow \; \langle \alpha_0, \alpha_1, \ldots, \alpha_n \rangle \in H^*, \quad H^* \in \Pi_1^1.$$

Since H^* is Π_1^1, it is m-reducible to A^1, i.e., there is a general computable function $f(x)$ such that for arbitrary tuples $\alpha \in 2^{<\omega}$, $\alpha = \langle \alpha_0, \ldots, \alpha_n \rangle$, we have

$$\nu(0)^{\alpha_0} \cap \nu(1)^{\alpha_1} \cap \ldots \cap \nu(n)^{\alpha_n} \neq \mathbf{0} \; \Leftrightarrow \; \mathcal{L}_{f(\langle \alpha_0, \alpha_1, \ldots, \alpha_n \rangle)} \text{ is well ordering.} \tag{5.3}$$

Now, our goal is to choose a pair (m, s) of integer parameters to be considered with the canonical construction, cf. Theorem 2.1.

Choice of m. We choose m such that $\Omega(m) = \mathcal{P}(\mathbb{N})$. For this, it is enough to get m such that $W_m = \varnothing$.

Choice of s. For this purpose, we describe a computable functional $\mathcal{F}$ from $\mathcal{P}(\mathbb{N})$ to $\mathcal{P}(\mathbb{N})$, actually, yielding compact binary trees. For an arbitrary $A \subseteq \mathbb{N}$, witness of $\mathcal{F}$ with input A is found via the function $f(x)$ in (5.3) by scheme

$$\mathcal{F} : A \mapsto \mathrm{Tree}(L^*, \nu^*) = \mathcal{F}(A) = \mathcal{D}_s^A, \quad \text{where} \tag{5.4}$$

(a) $(L^*, \nu^*) = \mathcal{L}_{f(\varnothing)} + \mathcal{L}_{f(\langle \alpha_0 \rangle)} + \ldots + \mathcal{L}_{f(\langle \alpha_0, \ldots, \alpha_n \rangle)} + \ldots$;

(b) $\alpha_k = \begin{cases} 1, & \text{if } k \in A, \\ 0, & \text{if } k \notin A, \end{cases} \quad \text{for all } k \in \mathbb{N}$;

(c) s is an index of the algorithm $A \mapsto \mathcal{F}(A)$ with an oracle A.

Here, $(L, \nu) \mapsto \text{Tree}(L, \nu)$ is an effective transformation from linear orderings to binary trees, cf. Lemma 2.2. The transformation $A \mapsto \mathscr{F}(A)$, $A \subseteq \mathbb{N}$, is realized via Turing's computation by an algorithm $\mathcal{M}$ with an oracle A. We put s to be a Gödel number of the algorithm $\mathcal{M}$ as it is stated (5.4)(c).

Choice of the pair of parameters (m, s) is finished.

Let us study main properties of the transformation $\mathscr{F} : A \mapsto \mathcal{D}_s^A$.

Lemma 5.2. *The following assertions hold:*

(a) *For any $A \subseteq \mathbb{N}$, $\mathcal{D}_s^A$ is a tree.*
(b) *For any computable set $A \subseteq \mathbb{N}$, $\mathcal{D}_s^A$ is a computable tree.*
(c) *For any computable set $A \subseteq \mathbb{N}$, the tree $\mathcal{D}_s^A$ is superatomic $\Leftrightarrow$ the linear order $L^\star$ in (5.4)(a) is well ordering.*

PROOF. By Lemma 2.2 for the passage $(L^\star, \nu^\star) \mapsto \text{Tree}(L^\star, \nu^\star)$. $\qquad\square$

Now we turn to the final part of the proof. To establish Part (c) of Theorem 5.1, we have to point out a sentence Θ of the given finite rich signature σ. For this, we use the canonical construction, cf. Theorem 2.1. Let us apply Theorem 2.1 to the pair (m, s) specifying also signature σ for the target theory. As a result, we obtain an effective sequence θ_i, $i \in \mathbb{N}$, of σ-sentences together with a finitely axiomatizable theory $F = \mathbb{F}\text{c}(m, s, \sigma)$ of signature σ. We put Θ to be the a conjunction of axioms of the theory $F = \mathbb{F}\text{c}(m, s, \sigma)$.

Notice that, Part (A) together with Part (B) of Theorem 2.1 ensure that, for an arbitrary set $A \in \Omega(m)$ and corresponding sequence $\alpha \in 2^{<\omega}$ linked with A via the rule (5.4)(b), it is satisfied

$$F[A] \vdash \theta_k^{\alpha_k}, \text{ for all } k \in \mathbb{N}. \tag{5.5}$$

Now, we are going to check that Θ satisfies requirements in Theorem 5.1(c).

Consider an arbitrary binary string $\alpha = \langle \alpha_0, ..., \alpha_k \rangle$ of a finite length. Let us construct an intersection of elements in $\mathcal{B}$ by the rule

$$b_\alpha = \nu(0)^{\alpha_0} \cap \nu(1)^{\alpha_1} \cap ... \cap \nu(k)^{\alpha_k}. \tag{5.6}$$

We also define a conjunction of sentences by the rule

$$\beta_\alpha = \theta_0^{\alpha_0} \wedge \theta_1^{\alpha_1} \wedge ... \wedge \theta_k^{\alpha_k}. \tag{5.7}$$

The main idea behind the construction is to obtain the following relation:

Lemma 5.3. *For any $\alpha \in 2^{<\omega}$ we have: $b_\alpha \neq \mathbf{0}$ if and only if $\Theta \wedge \beta_\alpha$ is satisfied in a model $\mathfrak{M} \in SW_{dec}$.*

PROOF. First, we assume that $b_\alpha \neq \mathbf{0}$. Since computable ultrafilters form a dense set among arbitrary ultrafilters in the BA $(\mathcal{B}, \nu)$, cf. (5.2), there is an infinite sequence $\alpha^* = \langle \alpha_i \mid i < \omega \rangle$ extending α such that the set A linked with α^* by rule (5.4)(b) is computable, and

$$\nu(0)^{\alpha_0} \cap ... \cap \nu(i)^{\alpha_i} \neq \mathbf{0}, \text{ for all } i \in \mathbb{N}. \tag{5.8}$$

By (5.3), we obtain that $\mathcal{L}_{f(\langle \alpha_0,...,\alpha_i \rangle)}$ is a well ordered set for all $i \in \mathbb{N}$; thus, the sequence of orders in (5.4)(a) consists of well orderings only. Therefore, their sum $(L^\star, \nu^\star)$ is also a well ordering. By Lemma 5.2(c), the tree $\mathcal{D}_s^A$ is superatomic. Moreover, $A \in \Omega(m)$ because $\Omega(m) = \mathcal{P}(\mathbb{N})$ by the choice of m. By Parts (A), (B), and (C) of Theorem 2.1, the theory $F[A]$ is consistent, complete, ω-stable and has a countable saturated model $\mathfrak{M}$. By Janiczak's theorem, the theory of $\mathfrak{M}$ is decidable because it is computably axiomatizable and complete. By virtue of (5.5), we have $F[A] \vdash \theta_i^{\alpha_i}$ for all $i \in \mathbb{N}$. From this, we obtain $\mathfrak{M} \models \beta_\alpha$. Thereby, the formula $\Theta \wedge \beta_\alpha$ is satisfied in the model $\mathfrak{M} \in SW_{dec}$.

Now, we assume that sentence $\Theta \wedge \beta_\alpha$ is satisfied in a model $\mathfrak{M} \in SW_{dec}$. Consider the set of integers

$$A = \{i \in \mathbb{N} \mid \mathfrak{M} \models \theta_i\}, \tag{5.9}$$

which is obviously computable. Build an infinite sequence $\alpha^* = \langle \alpha_i \mid i < \omega \rangle$ linked with A by the rule (5.4)(b). Since $A \in \Omega(m) = \mathcal{P}(\mathbb{N})$, the theory $F[A]$ is consistent and complete. By (5.9), all axioms of the theory $F[A]$ are satisfied in $\mathfrak{M}$. By Janiczak's Theorem, the theory $F[A]$ is decidable because it is computably axiomatizable and complete. We showed that the theory $F[A]$ is satisfied in a countable saturated model $\mathfrak{M}$ with ω-stable decidable theory. By Part (C) of Theorem 2.1, the tree $\mathcal{D}_s^A$ is superatomic. By Lemma 5.2(c), linear order $\mathcal{L}^\star$ in (5.4)(a) is well ordering. In view of (5.3), we obtain that $\mathcal{L}_{f(\langle \alpha_0,...,\alpha_s \rangle)}$ is a well ordered set for all $s \in \mathbb{N}$. Applying relation (5.3) to α, we finally obtain $b_\alpha \neq \mathbf{0}$.   □

Let us map elements $\nu(i)$, $i \in \mathbb{N}$, of BA $\mathcal{B}$ to σ-sentences θ_i, $i \in \mathbb{N}$, by the rule $\lambda^*(\nu(k)) = \theta_k$, $k \in \mathbb{N}$. By Lemma 5.3 together with the criterion [23, 12.3], we can extend this mapping up to an isomorphism $\lambda : (\mathcal{B}, \nu) \to (\mathcal{L}(\text{Th}(\text{Mod}(F) \cap M_{nfa})), \gamma)$. By construction, this isomorphism is computable.

Thereby, Part (c) of Theorem 5.1 is proved.   □

The results of Sects. 3 and 4 provide powerful tools for comparing Tarski-Lindenbaum algebras of different semantic classes of models. For instance, the following estimates are available: (a) $\mathcal{L}(P \cap M_{s.c.}) \approx \Sigma_3^0$, [14, Th. 1] together with Lemma 3.3 and Lemma 3.4; (b) $\mathcal{L}(S \cap M_{s.c.}) \approx \Sigma_1^1$, [15, Th. 1]; (c) $\mathcal{L}(P \cap M_{s.c.}^1) \approx \Sigma_2^0$, [16, Th. 1.1]. By Theorem 4.5, these three Tarski-Lindenbaum algebras are pairwise non-isomorphic. On the other hand, both algebra $\mathcal{L}(SW_{des})$, considered in Theorem 5.1 and the algebra $\mathcal{L}(S_{s.c.})$ in [15] are Σ_1^1-universal Σ_1^1-BA. By Theorem 4.5(b), these two algebras are isomorphic.

References

1. Feiner, L.: Hierarchies of Boolean algebras. J. Symb. Logic **35**(3), 365–373 (1970)
2. Goncharov, S.S.: Constructivizability of superatomic Boolean algebras. Algebra Logic **12**(1), 31–40 (1973)
3. Goncharov, S.S., Ershov, Y.L.: Constructive Models. Consultants Bureau XII, New York (2000)

4. Hanf, W.: The Boolean algebra of logic. Bull. AMS **31**, 587–589 (1975)
5. Harizanov, V.S.: Pure computable model theory, chap. 1. In: Ershov, Yu.L., Goncharov, S.S., Nerode, A., Remmel, J.B. (eds.) Handbook of Recursive Mathematics, pp. 1–114. North-Holland Publishing Company (1998)
6. Hinman, P.G.: Recursion-Theoretic Hierarchies. Cambridge (2017)
7. Hodges, W.: A Shorter Model Theory. Cambridge University Press, Cambridge (1997)
8. Odintsov S.P.: Generally constructive Boolean algebras, chap. 20. In: Ershov, Yu.L., Goncharov, S.S., Nerode, A., Remmel, J.B. (eds.) Handbook of Recursive Mathematics, pp. 1319–1354. North-Holland Publ. Co. (1998)
9. Odintsov, S.P., Selivanov, V.L.: Arithmetical hierarchy and ideals of numerated Boolean algebras. Siberian Math. J. **30**(6), 140–149 (1989)
10. Peretyat'kin, M.G.: Semantic universal classes of models. Algebra Logic **30**(4), 414–434 (1991)
11. Peretyat'kin, M.G.: Semantic universality of theories over superlist. Algebra Logic **30**(5), 517–539 (1992)
12. Peretyat'kin, M.G.: Finitely Axiomatizable Theories. Plenum, New York (1997)
13. Peretyat'kin, M.G.: Constructive models of finitely axiomatizable theories, chap. 9. In: Ershov, Yu.L., Goncharov, S.S., Nerode, A., Remmel, J.B. (eds.) Handbook of Recursive Mathematics, pp. 347–379. North-Holland Publ. Co. (1998)
14. Peretyat'kin, M.G.: On the Tarski-Lindenbaum algebra of the class of all strongly constructivizable prime models. In: Cooper, S.B., Dawar, A., Löwe, B. (eds.) CiE 2012. LNCS, vol. 7318, pp. 589–598. Springer, Heidelberg (2012). https://doi.org/10.1007/978-3-642-30870-3_59
15. Peretyat'kin, M.G.: The Tarski-Lindenbaum algebra of the class of all strongly constructivizable countable saturated models. In: Bonizzoni, P., Brattka, V., Löwe, B. (eds.) CiE 2013. LNCS, vol. 7921, pp. 342–352. Springer, Heidelberg (2013). https://doi.org/10.1007/978-3-642-39053-1_41
16. Peretyat'kin, M.G.: The Tarski-Lindenbaum algebra of the class of all strongly constructivizable prime models of algorithmic dimension one. Siberian Electron. Math. Rep. **17**, 913–922 (2020)
17. Rogers, H.J.: Theory of Recursive Functions and Effective Computability. Mc. Graw-Hill Book Co., New York (1967)
18. Selivanov, V.L.: Fine hierarchies and definable index sets. Algebra Logic **30**(6), 463–475 (1991)
19. Selivanov, V.L.: Universal Boolean algebras with applications. In: International Conference on Algebra (abstracts), Russia, Barnaul, 20–25 August 1991, vol. 127 (1991)
20. Selivanov, V.L.: On recursively enumerable structures. Ann. Pure Appl. Logic **78**, 243–258 (1996)
21. Selivanov, V.L.: Fine hierarchy and definability in the Lindenbaum algebra. In: Logic: From Foundations to Applications, Proceedings of the Logic Colloquium 93 in Keele, Oxford, pp. 425–452 (1996)
22. Selivanov, V.L.: Positive structures. In: Barry Cooper, S., Goncharov, S.S. (eds.) Computability and Models, Perspectives East and West, pp. 321–350. Kluwer Academic/Plenum Publishers, New York (2003)
23. Sikorski, R.: Boolean Algebras, 3rd edn. Springer, New York (1969)
24. Soare, R.I.: Recursively Enumerable Sets and Degrees. A Study of Computable Functions and Computably Generated Sets. Perspectives in Mathematical Logic. Springer, Heidelberg (1987)
25. Tanaka, H.: On analytic well-orderings. J. Symb. Log. **35**(2), 198–204 (1970)

Existential Definability of Unary Predicates in Büchi Arithmetic

Mikhail R. Starchak$^{(\boxtimes)}$

St. Petersburg State University, St. Petersburg, Russia
m.starchak@spbu.ru

Abstract. The paper provides a complete characterisation of the sets $S \subseteq \mathbb{N}$ that are *existentially* definable in the structure $\langle \mathbb{N}; 0, 1, +, V_k, \leq \rangle$ (existential k-Büchi arithmetic), where for a fixed integer base $k \geq 2$ the predicate $V_k(x, y)$ is true whenever y is the greatest power of k dividing x. A quantifier elimination approach enables us to describe such sets in terms of regular expressions with a special language $\Sigma_{l,m,c}$. For every triple of positive integers l, m, c, this language is defined as the set of all k-ary representations of non-negative integers congruent to c modulo m with bit-length divisible by l. For a pair of integers $l, m > 0$, let the class $\mathscr{C}_{l,m}$ comprise the languages $\{w\}$ and w^* for every word $w \in \{0, ..., k-1\}^*$ of length at most l, and the languages $\Sigma_{l',m',c'}$ for every triple l', m', c' satisfying $l' \leq l$, $m' \leq m$, $c' \in [1..m']$. Then a set $S \subseteq \mathbb{N}$ is *existentially* definable in k-Büchi arithmetic if and only if there exist positive integers l and m such that S can be obtained by a finite number of applications of concatenation and union to languages in $\mathscr{C}_{l,m}$.

Keywords: Existential definability · Quantifier elimination · Arithmetic theories · Büchi arithmetic · Regular languages

1 Introduction

Büchi-Bruyère's theorem [1,3] that links arithmetic theories and finite automata is one of the most fundamental results in logic and computer science. For a fixed integer base $k \geq 2$ and the alphabet $\Sigma_k = \{0, 1, ..., k-1\}$, the k-ary representations of vectors of a set $S \subseteq \mathbb{N}^n$ define a language $L_S \subseteq (\Sigma_k^n)^*$ in a natural way [2]. This set is called k-*regular* if there exists a finite automaton $\mathcal{A}$ over Σ_k^n that recognizes the language L_S. The theorem provides a first-order characterisation of k-regular sets: they coincide with the sets first-order (FO-)definable in the structure $\langle \mathbb{N}; 0, 1, +, V_k, \leq \rangle$, where the predicate $V_k(x, y)$ is true whenever y is the greatest power of k dividing x. The FO-theory of this structure is called k-*Büchi arithmetic*, and its decidability follows from the decidability of the emptiness problem for finite automata. This result gave rise to various theoretical and practical investigations: from the general study of automatic structures [5] to implementations of the automata-arithmetic correspondence in theorem provers [12].

L. Levy Patey et al. (Eds.): CiE 2024, LNCS 14773, pp. 218–232, 2024.
https://doi.org/10.1007/978-3-031-64309-5_18

Regarding this theorem, a very natural question is the quantifier alternation complexity of the FO-descriptions of k-regular sets by the formulas of k-Büchi arithmetic. It was shown by Villemaire [14] that $\exists\forall\exists$-formulas are expressive enough to define every k-regular set, and Haase and Różycki [7] have improved this result by showing that the $\exists\forall$-formulas have the same expressive power. However, there are k-regular languages, which cannot be defined by existential ($\exists$-)formulas of k-Büchi arithmetic. In particular, the set of all natural numbers with k-ary representations from the language $\{10, 01\}^*$ is not $\exists$-definable [7]. Notice that an existential FO-characterisation of k-regular sets was constructed in a recent work by Starchak [11, Theorem 1]. These sets coincide with the sets $\exists$-definable in the structure $\langle \mathbb{N}; 0, 1, +, \&_k, \leq \rangle$, where $\&_k$ is the bitwise minimum operation of base k.

To prove their undefinability result, Haase and Różycki provide necessary conditions for $\exists$-definability in k-Büchi arithmetic, which are formulated in terms of densities of regular languages. Moreover, they show that every subset of $\mathbb{N}$ of polynomial density *is* $\exists$-definable [7, Theorem 3]. The latter theorem is based on the description of such sets obtained by Szilard, Yu, Zhang, and Shallit [13] via a finite union of regular expressions of the form $v_0 w_1^* v_1 w_2^* v_2 ... w_n^* v_n$ for fixed words v_i and w_i. However, the paper [7] does not provide a complete characterisation of the sets $\exists$-definable in the structure $\langle \mathbb{N}; 0, 1, +, V_k, \leq \rangle$.

In order to study the expressiveness of the existential fragment of k-Büchi arithmetic, it is worth considering a less expressive structure where V_k is replaced with the set of powers of k, denoted by P_k. It is clear that $P_k(x) \Leftrightarrow V_k(x, x)$. A remarkable theorem of Semënov [10, Theorem 5] states that a set $S \subseteq \mathbb{N}$ is $\exists$-definable in $\langle \mathbb{N}; 0, 1, +, P_k, \leq \rangle$ if and only if S can be represented as a finite union of sets definable via expressions of the form $v_0 w_1^* v_1 w_2^* v_2 ... w_n^* v_n \Sigma_{l,m,c}$, where for every fixed $l, m, c \in \mathbb{N}$, the language $\Sigma_{l,m,c}$ specifies the set of all k-ary expansions of non-negative integers congruent to c modulo m with bit-length divisible by l. In combination with the fact that every set that is definable in $\langle \mathbb{N}; 0, 1, +, P_k, \leq \rangle$ is also $\exists$-definable in this structure [10, Theorem 4], the aforementioned description enabled Semënov to prove that definability in $\langle \mathbb{N}; 0, 1, +, P_k, \leq \rangle$ does not cover the whole concept of k-regularity.

The main obstacle in attempts to extend this description to the sets $\exists$-definable in $\langle \mathbb{N}; 0, 1, +, V_k, \leq \rangle$ lies in the approaches that are used for studying properties of these two structures. In contrast to the automata-theoretic tools applied by Haase and Różycki, the results obtained by Semënov are based on quantifier elimination. After a splitting of variables into *ordinary* for non-negative integers and *special* for powers of k, his proof operates with formulas in which only special variables are $\exists$-quantified because all ordinary ones are eliminated in the same way as in Presburger arithmetic [10]. The purpose of this paper is to develop quantifier-elimination techniques to generalize Semënov's theorem and thus to better understand the $\exists$-fragment of k-Büchi arithmetic.

Main Technique and Results. Let us now discuss the elimination technique and explain the organisation of the paper.

To simplify reasoning about $\exists$-definability in the structure $\langle \mathbb{N}; 0, 1, +, V_k, \leq \rangle$, we introduce a function rem_k. For a pair of non-negative integers x and y, this function computes the remainder of the division of x by y when y is a power of k, and evaluates to 0 otherwise. In Sect. 2, we show that the replacement of V_k with rem_k does not change the expressive power of the $\exists$-formulas. This section also provides some basic definitions from logic and introduces a language (which will be called $\mathcal{B}_k$) to deal with ordinary and special variables.

Section 3 is devoted to eliminating the ordinary variables for the case of the structure $\langle \mathbb{N}; 0, 1, +, \mathsf{rem}_k, \leq \rangle$. The main algorithm is based on a combination of the standard quantifier-elimination procedure for Presburger arithmetic [6] and simple manipulations with the remainders of ordinary variables modulo special variables. The key idea of the algorithm can be described as follows. Suppose we are given a formula with m special variables $k^{\alpha_1}, ..., k^{\alpha_m}$, and we are going to eliminate an ordinary variable x. Without any loss of generality, we may assume that there is a total order on the special variables $1 < k^{\alpha_1} < ... < k^{\alpha_m}$. The variable x is represented as a sum $x' \cdot k^{\alpha_m} + z$, where x' and z are new variables and $\mathsf{rem}_k(x, k^{\alpha_m}) = z$. After the replacement of x with this sum, the variable x' is eliminated similarly to the case of Presburger arithmetic, whereas z will already be out of the scope of the remainders modulo k^{α_m}. Repeating this step m times, we obtain an equivalent formula, where it remains to eliminate a variable that corresponds to $\mathsf{rem}_k(x, k^{\alpha_1})$. This variable is now out of the scope of the rem_k function, and the standard procedure for Presburger arithmetic concludes the elimination process.

This technique leads to a complete characterisation of the sets $S \subseteq \mathbb{N}$ that are $\exists$-definable in k-Büchi arithmetic. We prove in Sect. 4 that every such set S can be described by means of a parametric regular expression of the form

$$x_m \cdot 0^* x_{m-1} \cdot ... \cdot 0^* x_1 \cdot 0^* x_0, \tag{1}$$

where $x_0, x_1, ..., x_m$ are the k-ary expansions of $(m+1)$ auxiliary variables. The (non-negative integer) values of these variables, in turn, can be described by $\exists$-formulas of Presburger arithmetic with P_k. Thus, Semënov's theorem gives the desired characterisation of the set S. Informally speaking, the language $\Sigma_{l,m,c}$ can now appear everywhere in our representations.

In Sect. 5, it is shown that the definability results by Haase and Różycki are natural consequences of the main result (Theorem 1). We then consider an example and conclude the paper with a discussion of future research directions.

2   Two Sorts of Variables

To state the main result of the paper, we first recall some basic definitions and notations concerning the first-order (FO-)languages.

By L_σ we denote the FO-language of a signature σ, and the formulas of this language are called L_σ-formulas. An L_σ-formula is *existential* if it has the form $\exists \boldsymbol{y} \varphi(\boldsymbol{y}, \boldsymbol{z})$, where φ is a quantifier-free L_σ-formula. In this paper, the domain of the structures of a signature σ is the set of non-negative integers $\mathbb{N} = \{0, 1, 2, ...\}$

and the symbols from σ are interpreted in a natural way. Next, for any structure $\langle \mathbb{N}; \sigma \rangle$ and a subclass of L_σ-formulas $\mathcal{C}$, we say that a set $S \subseteq \mathbb{N}^n$ is $\mathcal{C}$-definable in $\langle \mathbb{N}; \sigma \rangle$ if there exists a formula $\varphi(\boldsymbol{x})$ from $\mathcal{C}$ such that for all $\boldsymbol{a} \in \mathbb{N}^n$ we have: $\boldsymbol{a} \in S$ if and only if $\exists \boldsymbol{y} \varphi(\boldsymbol{y}, \boldsymbol{a})$ is true in the structure $\langle \mathbb{N}; \sigma \rangle$. If we consider the class of existential L_σ-formulas, then we say that a set is *existentially* ($\exists$)-*definable* in the structure $\langle \mathbb{N}; \sigma \rangle$.

We are going to focus on existential definability in extensions of the structure $\langle \mathbb{N}; 0, 1, +, \leq \rangle$. Here, 0 and 1 are constants, $+$ is a binary function symbol, and $\leq$ is a binary predicate symbol. These symbols are interpreted over $\mathbb{N}$ in the usual way, and the FO-theory of this structure is known as Presburger arithmetic. The predicates of equality $=$ and strict inequality $<$ can be trivially defined: $x = y \Leftrightarrow (x \leq y) \wedge (y \leq x)$ and $(x < y) \Leftrightarrow (x + 1 \leq y)$, and these definitions are implicitly used in every extension of $\langle \mathbb{N}; 0, 1, +, \leq \rangle$. We fix some integer base $k \geq 2$ and consider extensions with the (already defined in Sect. 1) predicates P_k and V_k, and function rem_k. The FO-theory of the structure $\langle \mathbb{N}; 0, 1, +, V_k \leq \rangle$ is called k-*Büchi arithmetic*.

To study $\exists$-definability in k-Büchi arithmetic, we rely on the function rem_k instead of the predicate V_k and also follow the approach of Semënov [10], where the variables are divided into two sorts. Define a *language* $\mathcal{B}_k$, which uses *ordinary* variables $x_1, ..., x_n$ that take their values from $\mathbb{N}$ and *special* variables $k^{\alpha_1}, ..., k^{\alpha_m}$ that range over the set of non-negative integer powers of k. We will write $\boldsymbol{x}$ and $\boldsymbol{k^\alpha}$ for lists of variables of these two sorts.

The *terms* of the language $\mathcal{B}_k$ (called $\mathcal{B}_k$-terms) are expressions of the form

$$\sum_{i=1}^{n} a_i \cdot x_i + \sum_{i=1}^{n} \sum_{j=1}^{m} b_{i,j} \cdot \mathsf{rem}_k(x_i, k^{\alpha_j}) + \sum_{j=1}^{m} c_j \cdot k^{\alpha_j} + c_0, \qquad (2)$$

where the coefficients $a_i, b_{i,j}, c_j$ and the constant c_0 are from $\mathbb{Z}$. *Quantifier-free $\mathcal{B}_k$-formulas* have the form $\exists \boldsymbol{k^\alpha} \varphi(\boldsymbol{x}, \boldsymbol{k^\alpha})$, where φ is a disjunction of conjunctions of non-strict inequalities $(t_1 \leq t_2)$ and divisibilities $(d \mid t_3)$, where t_1, t_2, t_3 are terms of the form (2) and d is a positive integer constant. In this definition, all special variables occurring in φ are existentially quantified. For this reason, when we say that $\psi(\boldsymbol{x})$ is a quantifier-free $\mathcal{B}_k$-formula, this means that $\boldsymbol{x}$ comprises all ordinary variables occurring in ψ, but this formula may contain any number of special variables. Finally, $\mathcal{B}_k$-*formulas* have the form $\exists \boldsymbol{y} \psi(\boldsymbol{y}, \boldsymbol{z})$, where $\psi(\boldsymbol{y}, \boldsymbol{z})$ is a quantifier-free $\mathcal{B}_k$-formula for some lists of ordinary variables $\boldsymbol{y}$ and $\boldsymbol{z}$.

Since each quantifier over a special variable $\exists k^\alpha \varphi$ can be replaced with the formula $\exists z (P_k(z) \wedge \varphi[z \mathbin{/} k^\alpha])$, where $P_k(z) \Leftrightarrow (z = 1 \vee \mathsf{rem}_k(1, z) = 1)$, we can view the language $\mathcal{B}_k$ as a subclass of $\exists$-formulas of the FO-language of the signature $\langle 0, 1, +, \mathsf{rem}_k, \leq \rangle$. The following lemma establishes a close connection between $\mathcal{B}_k$-formulas and $\exists$-formulas of k-Büchi arithmetic.

Lemma 1. *A set $S \subseteq \mathbb{N}^n$ is $\exists$-definable in the structure $\langle \mathbb{N}; 0, 1, +, V_k \leq \rangle$ if and only if it is $\mathcal{B}_k$-definable in the structure $\langle \mathbb{N}; 0, 1, +, \mathsf{rem}_k, \leq \rangle$.*

M. Starchak

Proof. The "if" direction follows from the $\exists$-definability of the graph of the function rem_k in the structure $\langle \mathbb{N}; 0, 1, +, V_k \leq \rangle$. We see that

$$z = \mathsf{rem}_k(x, y) \Leftrightarrow (z = 0 \land \neg P_k(y)) \lor (P_k(y) \land (0 \leq z) \land (z < y) \land \tag{3}$$
$$\exists u \exists v(y \leq u \land V_k(v, u) \land x = v + z)),$$

where we only recall that the set of powers of k is definable by the formula $P_k(x) \Leftrightarrow V_k(x, x)$. Divisibilities by positive integer constants are definable in the same way as in Presburger arithmetic: $d \mid x \Leftrightarrow \exists y(d \cdot y = x)$.

For the converse, in a given $\exists$-formula of k-Büchi arithmetic $\exists \boldsymbol{y} \varphi(\boldsymbol{y}, \boldsymbol{z})$, we first transform φ into DNF. Since $\neg V_k(x, y) \Leftrightarrow \exists z(V_k(x, z) \land (z < y \lor y < z))$, it is sufficient to construct a $\mathcal{B}_k$-formula for the predicate V_k.

$$V_k(x, y) \Leftrightarrow \exists k^\alpha \bigvee_{a \in [1..k-1]} (\mathsf{rem}_k(x, k^\alpha) = a \cdot y \land k^\alpha = k \cdot y). \tag{4}$$

For atomic formulas $V_k(t_1, t_2)$, where t_1, t_2 have the form $a_1 \cdot x_1 + \ldots + a_n \cdot x_n + b$, we introduce new $\exists$-quantified ordinary variables u_1, u_2 and rewrite $V_k(t_1, t_2)$ as the conjunction of $(t_1 = u_1) \land (t_2 = u_2)$ and (4) applied to $V_k(u_1, u_2)$. □

In the next section, we prove the main property of the language $\mathcal{B}_k$ that we use in the sequel. Namely, that $\exists$-quantified *ordinary* variables can be eliminated in every $\mathcal{B}_k$-formula. Combining this with Lemma 1, we obtain a representation of a set $S \subseteq \mathbb{N}$ that is $\exists$-definable in $\langle \mathbb{N}; 0, 1, +, V_k, \leq \rangle$ via a quantifier-free $\mathcal{B}_k$-formula.

3 Elimination of Ordinary Variables

The elimination of ordinary variables in $\mathcal{B}_k$-formulas in some sense generalizes the quantifier-elimination algorithm for Presburger arithmetic, which we assume to be well-known to the reader. If an ordinary variable x does not occur in a given $\mathcal{B}_k$-formula in the scope of rem_k, then x can be eliminated by using this standard procedure for the structure $\langle \mathbb{N}; 0, 1, +, \leq, \{d \mid \cdot\}_{d \geq 2} \rangle$. This simple case will complete the inductive proof of Lemma 3.

This proof relies on a slightly more general kind of $\mathcal{B}_k$-terms. *Generalized $\mathcal{B}_k$-terms* are defined recursively: 1) every $\mathcal{B}_k$-term is generalized; 2) every term of the form $\sum_{i=1}^{n} \sum_{j=1}^{m} g_{i,j} \cdot \mathsf{rem}_k(t_i, k^{\alpha_j}) + t$ for generalized $\mathcal{B}_k$-terms t_i, t and integers $g_{i,j}$ is also a generalized $\mathcal{B}_k$-term. By replacing $\mathcal{B}_k$-terms with generalized $\mathcal{B}_k$-terms, we define the *generalized quantifier-free $\mathcal{B}_k$-formulas*. It is easy to prove the following lemma (the proof is given in Appendix A). After its formulation, we immediately proceed to the main lemma.

Lemma 2. *For every generalized quantifier-free $\mathcal{B}_k$-formula $\varphi(\boldsymbol{x})$, we can construct an equivalent in $\langle \mathbb{N}; 0, 1, +, \mathsf{rem}_k, \leq \rangle$ quantifier-free $\mathcal{B}_k$-formula $\psi(\boldsymbol{x})$.*

Lemma 3. *For every quantifier-free $\mathcal{B}_k$-formula $\varphi(x, \boldsymbol{y})$, we can construct a quantifier-free $\mathcal{B}_k$-formula $\psi(\boldsymbol{y})$ that is equivalent in $\langle \mathbb{N}; 0, 1, +, \mathsf{rem}_k, \leq \rangle$ to the $\mathcal{B}_k$-formula $\exists x \varphi(x, \boldsymbol{y})$.*

Proof. Let $\varphi(x, \boldsymbol{y})$ be a quantifier-free $\mathcal{B}_k$-formula, and let $\boldsymbol{k}^\alpha = k^{\alpha_1}, ..., k^{\alpha_m}$ comprise all special variables occurring in our formula. We begin by rewriting φ using a disjunction over all total orderings on special variables $\boldsymbol{k}^\alpha$.

Assume that $1 \prec_1 k^{\alpha_1} \prec_2 k^{\alpha_2} \prec_3 ... \prec_m k^{\alpha_m}$, where for all $i \in [1..m]$, the symbol $\prec_i$ is either $=$ or $<$. If $\prec_i$ is the equality symbol, then k^{α_i} is replaced with $k^{\alpha_{i-1}}$, assuming that $k^{\alpha_0} = 1$, and the special variable k^{α_i} is excluded from the list $\boldsymbol{k}^\alpha$. Without loss of generality, we can now consider quantifier-free $\mathcal{B}_k$-formula $\varphi(x, \boldsymbol{y})$ of the form

$$\exists \boldsymbol{k}^\alpha \, \exists \boldsymbol{k}^\beta \left(\theta(\boldsymbol{k}^\alpha) \wedge \varphi'(x, \boldsymbol{y}, \boldsymbol{k}^\alpha, \boldsymbol{k}^\beta) \right), \tag{5}$$

where θ is the formula $(1 < k^{\alpha_1} < ... < k^{\alpha_m})$, which is called an *ordering on* $\boldsymbol{k}^\alpha$, and φ' is a conjunction of inequalities $(t_1 \leq t_2)$ and divisibilities $(d \mid t_3)$ with $\mathcal{B}_k$-terms t_1, t_2, t_3 of the form

$$a \cdot x + \sum_{j=1}^{m} b_j \cdot \mathsf{rem}_k(x, k^{\alpha_j}) + t(\boldsymbol{y}, \boldsymbol{k}^\alpha, \boldsymbol{k}^\beta) \tag{6}$$

for integer coefficients $a, b_1, ..., b_m$ and for a $\mathcal{B}_k$-term $t(\boldsymbol{y}, \boldsymbol{k}^\alpha, \boldsymbol{k}^\beta)$. The list of special variables $\boldsymbol{k}^\beta$ is empty at the beginning of the elimination process. To emphasize the presence of the ordering θ inside the formula $\varphi(x, \boldsymbol{y})$, we call such formula *quantifier-free $\mathcal{B}_k$-formula equipped with the ordering θ*.

Our aim is to construct a quantifier-free $\mathcal{B}_k$-formula $\psi(z, \boldsymbol{y})$, which is equipped with the ordering θ and has the following properties. First of all, the formula $\exists z \psi(z, \boldsymbol{y})$ is equivalent to $\exists x \varphi(x, \boldsymbol{y})$ in the structure $\langle \mathbb{N}; 0, 1, +, \mathsf{rem}_k, \leq \rangle$. The second requirement concerns the remainders of z in $\psi(z, \boldsymbol{y})$: this formula may contain only remainders modulo $k^{\alpha_1}, ..., k^{\alpha_{m-1}}$, but not modulo k^{α_m} or any other special variables from $\psi(z, \boldsymbol{y})$. This process can be continued until we obtain a formula $\xi(u, \boldsymbol{y})$ such that $\exists u \xi(u, \boldsymbol{y})$ is equivalent to $\exists x \varphi(x, \boldsymbol{y})$ and ξ does not contain any remainders modulo special variables. To complete the proof of the lemma, it remains to apply the standard quantifier-elimination procedure for Presburger arithmetic. Let us now construct the formula $\psi(z, \boldsymbol{y})$.

In the formula φ, the variable x is replaced with the sum $(x' \cdot k^{\alpha_m} + z)$, and we add the inequalities $(0 \leq z < k^{\alpha_m})$. We have divided x by k^{α_m}, and z is the remainder of x modulo k^{α_m}. The term $\mathsf{rem}_k(x, k^{\alpha_m})$ is then replaced with z. Since k^{α_m} is the leading special variable with respect to the ordering θ, each remainder $\mathsf{rem}_k(x, k^{\alpha_i})$ is equal to $\mathsf{rem}_k(z, k^{\alpha_i})$ for all $i \in [1..m-1]$. After these replacements, the terms (6) of the formula φ have evolved into

$$a \cdot x' \cdot k^{\alpha_m} + \boxed{(a + b_m) \cdot z + \sum_{j=1}^{m-1} b_j \cdot \mathsf{rem}_k(z, k^{\alpha_j}) + t(\boldsymbol{y}, \boldsymbol{k}^\alpha, \boldsymbol{k}^\beta).} \tag{7}$$

Terms of the same form as the $\mathcal{B}_k$-term in the dashed box will be denoted by τ. We are now going to eliminate the variable x' from systems of inequalities and divisibilities with terms of the form (7). To this end, we construct an equivalent disjunction of systems, where x' occurs only linearly and inequalities of these systems feature fractions of the form $\frac{\tau'}{k^{\alpha_m}}$, where τ' are *generalized* $\mathcal{B}_k$-terms, which are divisible by k^{α_m}.

Handling of divisibilities is easy. For each formula $(d \mid a \cdot x' \cdot k^{\alpha_m} + \tau)$, we consider a disjunction over all possible remainders $r \in [0..d-1]$ of x' modulo d and replace our divisibility with the conjunction $(d \mid x' - r) \wedge (d \mid a \cdot r \cdot k^{\alpha_m} + \tau)$.

The inequalities are of the forms $(a \cdot x' \cdot k^{\alpha_m} \leq \tau)$ or $(a \cdot x' \cdot k^{\alpha_m} \geq \tau)$ for a positive integer a. Since left-hand-sides are divisible by k^{α_m}, we replace τ with the term $(\tau - \mathsf{rem}_k(\tau, k^{\alpha_m}))$ in the first case, and use the disjunction

$$\big((\mathsf{rem}_k(\tau, k^{\alpha_m}) = 0) \wedge (a \cdot x' \cdot k^{\alpha_m} \geq \tau)\big) \vee \big(a \cdot x' \cdot k^{\alpha_m} \geq \tau - \mathsf{rem}_k(\tau, k^{\alpha_m}) + k^{\alpha_m}\big)$$

in the second case. Now the terms from each inequality are divisible by k^{α_m}.

After division by k^{α_m}, we obtain a disjunction of systems, where the subsystem containing x' has the form

$$\bigwedge_{i \in I_1} (d_i \mid x' - r_i) \wedge \bigwedge_{i \in I_2} \left(a_i \cdot x' \geq \frac{\tau'_i}{k^{\alpha_m}}\right) \wedge \bigwedge_{i \in I_3} \left(a_i \cdot x' \leq \frac{\tau'_i}{k^{\alpha_m}}\right), \tag{8}$$

where I_1, I_2, I_3 are some finite sets of indices, all d_i and a_i are positive integers, τ'_i are *generalized* $\mathcal{B}_k$-terms of the form $\tau - \mathsf{rem}_k(\tau, k^{\alpha_m}) + c \cdot k^{\alpha_m}$ for $c \in \{0, 1\}$. Applying the Presburger quantifier-elimination algorithm [6] to (8), we rewrite the existence of an integer x' satisfying this formula. This yields a disjunction of systems of inequalities $(a_1 \cdot f_1 + b \leq a_2 \cdot f_2)$ and divisibilities $(d \mid f_3 - r)$, where the terms f_1, f_2, f_3 are fractions from (8), and $a_1, a_2, b, d, r \in \mathbb{Z}$, where $d \geq 2$. To remove fractions, we multiply every such atomic formula by k^{α_m}. Let us consider independently every system $\psi'(z, \boldsymbol{y}, \boldsymbol{k}^\alpha, \boldsymbol{k}^\beta)$ of the resulting disjunction.

In ψ', we have inequalities of the form $(a_1 \cdot \tau'_1 + b' \cdot k^{\alpha_m} \leq a_2 \cdot \tau'_2)$ and divisibilities of the form $(d \cdot k^{\alpha_m} \mid \tau' - r \cdot k^{\alpha_m})$. This formula is not a generalized $\mathcal{B}_k$-formula because of the modules of the divisibilities. To overcome this problem, for each divisibility we compute the integers d' and c' such that d' is the greatest divisor of d which is coprime with k, and c' is the smallest integer such that $d \cdot c' = d' \cdot k^p$ for some non-negative integer p. For example, if $k = 6$ and $d = 20$, then $d' = 5$ and $c' = 9$ such that $20 \cdot 9 = 5 \cdot 6^2$. By multiplying this divisibility relation by c', we see that it is equivalent to the conjunction

$$d' \mid c' \cdot (\tau' - r \cdot k^{\alpha_m}) \wedge \mathsf{rem}_k\big(c' \cdot (\tau' - r \cdot k^{\alpha_m}), k^\gamma\big) = 0 \wedge (k^\gamma = k^p \cdot k^{\alpha_m}),$$

where k^γ is a fresh special variable. These replacements are performed for each divisibility of ψ'. As a result, we obtain an equivalent generalized $\mathcal{B}_k$-formula, and Lemma 2 then yields an equivalent $\mathcal{B}_k$-formula $\psi''(z, \boldsymbol{y})$. Recall that k^{α_m} is the greatest special variable with respect to the ordering θ, all *new* variables k^γ are greater than k^{α_m}, and z is equal to $\mathsf{rem}_k(z, k^{\alpha_m})$. The transformations performed by Lemma 2 thus do not introduce new remainders with z. Putting all the pieces of the construction together, we obtain the desired $\mathcal{B}_k$-formula $\psi(z, \boldsymbol{y})$. □

4   The Main Theorem

Everything is now prepared to give a complete characterisation of the sets $S \subseteq \mathbb{N}$ that are existentially definable in k-Büchi arithmetic. We first introduce some useful notations.

For a word $w = a_m...a_0 \in \Sigma_k^*$, denote by $[\![w]\!]_k$ the integer $a_m k^m + ... + a_1 k + a_0$, and define $[\![\epsilon]\!]_k := 0$. For a language $L \subseteq \Sigma_k^*$, we define $[\![L]\!]_k := \{[\![w]\!]_k : w \in L\}$. A language $L \subseteq \Sigma_k^*$ is called k-*regular* if L is recognizable by some deterministic finite automaton over Σ_k (Σ_k-DFA). The function $[\![\cdot]\!]_k$ is bijective if it is defined over $N_k = \{0\} \cup (\Sigma_k \setminus \{0\}) \cdot \Sigma_k^*$; we identify $S \subseteq \mathbb{N}$ with the language $N_k \cap [\![S]\!]_k^{-1}$. For a triple of positive integers l, m, c, we define a language $\Sigma_{l,m,c}$ as the set of words $w \in N_k$ of length divisible by l such that $m \mid [\![w]\!]_k - c$. For every fixed l, m, c, the set $[\![\Sigma_{l,m,c}]\!]_k$ is $\exists$-definable in the structure $\langle \mathbb{N}; 0, 1, +, P_k, \leq \rangle$ by the formula

$$x \in [\![\Sigma_{l,m,c}]\!]_k \Leftrightarrow k^l - 1 \mid k \cdot \lambda_k(x) - 1 \wedge m \mid x - c, \tag{9}$$

where $\lambda_k(x)$ is the greatest power of k not exceeding x, and 1 otherwise. It is clear that $y = \lambda_k(x) \Leftrightarrow (y = 1 \wedge x = 0) \vee (P_k(y) \wedge y \leq x \wedge x + 1 \leq k \cdot y)$. For convenience, we assume that $\Sigma_{0,m,c} = \Sigma_{l,0,c} = \{\epsilon\}$ for every $l, m, c \in \mathbb{N}$.

Our characterisation of $\exists$-definable sets is based on the ordinary variable elimination from Sect. 3 and on the following result by Semënov [10, Theorem 5].

Lemma 4 (Semënov [10]). *A k-regular set $S \subseteq \mathbb{N}$ is existentially definable in the structure $\langle \mathbb{N}; 0, 1, +, P_k, \leq \rangle$ if and only if S can be represented as a finite union of expressions of the form $u_1 v_1^* ... u_n v_n^* \Sigma_{l,m,c}$, where $u_1, v_1, ..., u_n, v_n \in \Sigma_k^*$, and $l, m, c \in \mathbb{N}$.*

The formulation of the main theorem involves the notation of Hashiguchi [8]. Let $\mathcal{C}$ be a finite set of k-regular languages. Then we say that a k-regular language L has a $\{\cdot, \cup\}$-representation over $\mathcal{C}$ if L can be obtained by a finite number of applications of the operators of concatenation and union to $\mathcal{C}$. For a pair of positive integers l and m, we define a set of k-regular languages $\mathcal{C}_{l,m}$ as follows. This class contains the languages $\{w\}$ and w^* for every word $w \in \Sigma_k$ of length at most l, and the languages $\Sigma_{l',m',c'}$ for every $l' \leq l$, $m' \leq m$, $c' \in [0..m' - 1]$. Now we are going to prove the following theorem.

Theorem 1. *A k-regular set $S \subseteq \mathbb{N}$ is existentially definable in the structure $\langle \mathbb{N}; 0, 1, +, V_k, \leq \rangle$ if and only if there exist positive integers l and m such that S has $\{\cdot, \cup\}$-representation over $\mathcal{C}_{l,m}$.*

Proof (of necessity in Theorem 1). Applying Lemmas 1 and 3 to a given existential formula of k-Büchi arithmetic that defines S, we obtain a quantifier-free $\mathcal{B}_k$-formula $\varphi(x)$. Let $k^\alpha = k^{\alpha_1}, ..., k^{\alpha_m}$ comprise all special variables occurring in this formula. The terms of $\varphi(x)$ are $\mathcal{B}_k$-terms of the form

$$a \cdot x + \sum_{j=1}^{m} b_j \cdot \text{rem}_k(x, k^{\alpha_j}) + \sum_{j=1}^{m} c_j \cdot k^{\alpha_j} + c_0, \tag{10}$$

where all the coefficients are integers. The proof is by induction on the number of distinct remainders of x modulo special variables occurring in the formula. It is clear that if $\varphi(x)$ does not contain terms $\mathsf{rem}_k(x, k^{\alpha_j})$, then Lemma 4 gives the desired representation. Let us now provide the induction step.

As in the proof of Lemma 3, we introduce a disjunction over the orderings on $\boldsymbol{k}^\alpha$ and further assume that $\varphi(x)$ is a quantifier-free $\mathcal{B}_k$-formula equipped with the ordering $\theta(\boldsymbol{k}^\alpha)$ defined as $(1 < k^{\alpha_1} < ... < k^{\alpha_m})$. Let for some $p \in [1..m]$, the special variable k^{α_p} be the greatest one with respect to θ such that $\mathsf{rem}_k(x, k^{\alpha_p})$ occurs in $\varphi(x)$. This means that $\varphi(x)$ contains at most p distinct remainders of x modulo special variables, namely, modulo $k^{\alpha_1}, ..., k^{\alpha_p}$. By the induction hypothesis, the statement is proved for the case when a given quantifier-free $\mathcal{B}_k$-formula has *at most* $(p-1)$ distinct remainders.

To apply the hypothesis, we represent the variable x as a sum $y \cdot k^{\alpha_p} + z$ and add the inequalities $(0 \le z < k^{\alpha_p})$ to our formula. Observe that the k-ary expansion of x can now be represented via the regular expression $(y \cdot 0^{d_p} z)$, where $d_p \in \mathbb{N}$ is such that the bit-length of $0^{d_p} z$ is equal to α_p. Continuing our transformations, the remainder $\mathsf{rem}_k(x, k^{\alpha_p})$ becomes z, and for each $j \in [1..p-1]$, we replace $\mathsf{rem}_k(x, k^{\alpha_j})$ with $\mathsf{rem}_k(z, k^{\alpha_j})$. The atomic formulas are now $(t_1 \le t_2)$ and $(d \mid t_3)$ for positive integer constants d and terms t_1, t_2, t_3 of the form

$$\left(a \cdot y \cdot k^{\alpha_p} + \sum_{j=p}^{m} c_j \cdot k^{\alpha_j}\right) + \left((a+b_p) \cdot z + \sum_{j=1}^{p-1} \left(b_j \cdot \mathsf{rem}_k(z, k^{\alpha_j}) + c_j \cdot k^{\alpha_j}\right) + c_0\right). \quad (11)$$

To complete our preparatory steps, we replace the special variables $k^{\alpha_{p+1}}, ..., k^{\alpha_m}$ with $(k^{\beta_{p+1}} \cdot k^{\alpha_p}), ..., (k^{\beta_m} \cdot k^{\alpha_p})$. Since $\varphi(x)$ is equipped with the ordering $\theta(\boldsymbol{k}^\alpha)$, we split this ordering into θ_β defined as $(1 < k^{\beta_{p+1}} < ... < k^{\beta_m})$ and θ_α, which is $(1 < k^{\alpha_1} < ... < k^{\alpha_p})$. The list of variables $k^{\beta_{p+1}}, ..., k^{\beta_m}$ will be denoted by $\boldsymbol{k}^\beta$ and the list $k^{\alpha_1}, ..., k^{\alpha_{p-1}}$ by $\boldsymbol{k}^{\alpha'}$. With these new variables, each term (11) can be rewritten in a compact form

$$q(y, \boldsymbol{k}^\beta) \cdot k^{\alpha_p} + r(z, \boldsymbol{k}^{\alpha'}), \quad (12)$$

where $q(y, \boldsymbol{k}^\beta)$ and $r(z, \boldsymbol{k}^{\alpha'})$ are $\mathcal{B}_k$-terms such that the former does not contain any remainders of y, and the latter may have remainders of z modulo special variables from $\boldsymbol{k}^{\alpha'}$. Denote by $\psi(y, z)$ the result of all these transformations.

It is clear that for each $x \in \mathbb{N}$ satisfying φ, there is a unique pair $(y, z) \in \mathbb{N}^2$ satisfying ψ, and vice versa. However, $\psi(y, z)$ is not a $\mathcal{B}_k$-formula, and we are now going to construct a finite set of pairs $\{(\chi_i(y), \rho_i(z))\}_{i \in I}$ such that

- $\psi(y, z)$ is equivalent to the disjunction $\bigvee_{i \in I} \chi_i(y) \wedge \rho_i(z)$ in $\mathbb{N}$;
- for every $i \in I$, $\chi_i(y)$ is a $\mathcal{B}_k$-formula equipped with the ordering θ_β and does not contain remainders modulo special variables from $\boldsymbol{k}^\beta$;
- for every $i \in I$, $\rho_i(z)$ is a $\mathcal{B}_k$-formula equipped with the ordering θ_α and may only have remainders of z modulo special variables from $\boldsymbol{k}^{\alpha'}$, that is, at most $(p-1)$ distinct remainders of z.

In order to construct the desired set of pairs, each atomic formula of $\psi(y, z)$ is considered independently.

We first consider inequalities $t \leq 0$ of $\psi(y, z)$ with terms t of the form (12). Observe that $r(z, \boldsymbol{k}^{\boldsymbol{\alpha}'})$ is a linear term over the ordinary variable z, special variables from $\boldsymbol{k}^{\boldsymbol{\alpha}'}$, and remainders of z modulo these special variables. Since formula $\psi(z, y)$ implies $\theta_\alpha(\boldsymbol{k}^{\boldsymbol{\alpha}'}) \wedge (0 \leq z < k^{\alpha_p})$, we have that $\psi(z, y)$ implies that $|r(z, \boldsymbol{k}^{\boldsymbol{\alpha}'})| \leq C \cdot k^{\alpha_p}$, where C is the sum of the absolute values of coefficients of $r(z, \boldsymbol{k}^{\boldsymbol{\alpha}'})$. Then, the inequality $q(y, \boldsymbol{k}^{\boldsymbol{\beta}}) \cdot k^{\alpha_p} + r(z, \boldsymbol{k}^{\boldsymbol{\alpha}'}) \leq 0$ is equivalent to the disjunction

$$\bigvee_{c \in [-C..C]} (q(y, \boldsymbol{k}^{\boldsymbol{\beta}}) + c \leq 0) \wedge ((c-1) \cdot k^{\alpha_p} < r(z, \boldsymbol{k}^{\boldsymbol{\alpha}'}) \leq c \cdot k^{\alpha_p}). \quad (13)$$

Here, we have "divided with remainder" this inequality by k^{α_p}, and c is the smallest integer greater than or equal to $r(z, \boldsymbol{k}^{\boldsymbol{\alpha}'})/k^{\alpha_p}$.

The case of divisibility $d \mid q(y, \boldsymbol{k}^{\boldsymbol{\beta}}) \cdot k^{\alpha_p} + r(z, \boldsymbol{k}^{\boldsymbol{\alpha}'})$ is simple. We consider two remainders modulo d: for the special variable k^{α_p}, and for the term $r(z, \boldsymbol{k}^{\boldsymbol{\alpha}'})$:

$$\bigvee_{r_1 \in [1..d]} \bigvee_{r_2 \in [1..d]} (d \mid q(y, \boldsymbol{k}^{\boldsymbol{\beta}}) \cdot r_1 + r_2) \wedge (d \mid k^{\alpha_p} - r_1) \wedge (d \mid r(z, \boldsymbol{k}^{\boldsymbol{\alpha}'}) - r_2). \quad (14)$$

After replacing each atomic formula of $\psi(y, z)$ with disjunctions (13) and (14), we transform the resulting formula into DNF and obtain the desired set of pairs of formulas $\{\chi_i(y), \rho_i(z)\}_{i \in I}$. These formulas give us the definition

$$x \in S \Leftrightarrow \bigvee_{i \in I} \exists y \exists z \Big(x \in y \cdot 0^* z \wedge \chi_i(y) \wedge \rho_i(z) \Big). \quad (15)$$

Applying Lemma 4 to each formula $\chi_i(y)$, we rewrite (15) as

$$x \in S \Leftrightarrow \bigvee_{i \in I} \bigvee_{j \in J_i} \exists z \Big(x \in u_{1,j} v_{1,j}^* ... u_{n_j,j} v_{n_j,j}^* \Sigma_{l_j, m_j, c_j} 0^* z \wedge \rho_i(z) \Big). \quad (16)$$

To complete the proof, it remains to apply the induction hypothesis to each formula $\rho_i(z)$ of this disjunction. $\square$

Let us now prove Theorem 1 in the converse direction. By the distributivity of concatenation over union, it is sufficient to prove by induction on n that for every $L_1, ..., L_n \in \mathscr{C}_{l,m}$, the set $[\![L_1 \cdot L_2 \cdot ... \cdot L_n]\!]_k$ is $\exists$-definable in the structure $\langle \mathbb{N}; 0, 1, +, V_k, \leq \rangle$. This can be performed similarly to the proof of a simpler case [7, Proposition 2].

We begin with an analogue to [7, Lemma 8], and first give a $\exists$-definition of the set $[\![\Sigma_{l,m,c} \cdot 1 \cdot 0^U]\!]_k$ for non-negative integers l, m, c and an ultimately periodic set U. Recall that a set $S \subseteq \mathbb{N}$ is *ultimately periodic* if there is a four-tuple (t, s, B, R), where $t \geq 0$, $s > 0$, $B \subseteq \{0, ..., t-1\}$, and $R \subseteq \{0, ..., l-1\}$, such that

$$U = B \cup \bigcup_{n \geq 0} \{t + r + s \cdot n : r \in R\}.$$

Ultimately periodic sets are semi-linear sets in dimension one, and by a result of Ginsburg and Spanier [4], the semi-linear sets are exactly the sets definable in

Presburger arithmetic. In our proof, we use the predicate $S_U(x, y)$, which for an ultimately periodic set U specifies that $x = k^\alpha$ and $y = k^{\alpha+\beta}$ such that $\beta \in U$. The existential definition of the predicate S_U in the structure $\langle \mathbb{N}; 0, 1, +, V_k, \leq \rangle$ (see [7, Lemma 6]) is very similar to the formula (9). The proof of the lemma below is in Appendix B. It will be used to "reserve" a sufficient number of zeros for the definition of the language $\Sigma_{l,m,c} \cdot L$ when the set of lengths of words from L is ultimately periodic.

Lemma 5. *If l, m, c are non-negative integers and U is an ultimately periodic set, then $[\![\Sigma_{l,m,c} \cdot 1 \cdot 0^U]\!]_k$ is $\exists$-definable in the structure $\langle \mathbb{N}; 0, 1, +, V_k, \leq \rangle$.*

Proof (of sufficiency in Theorem 1). Denote by $\Sigma^+_{l,m,c}$ the language $\Sigma_{l,m,c} \setminus \{0\}$, and let $\mathscr{C}^+_{l,m}$ be the class constructed from $\mathscr{C}_{l,m}$ by replacing of languages w^* and $\Sigma_{l,m,c}$ with w^+ and $\Sigma^+_{l,m,c}$, respectively. Clearly, every set $S \subseteq \mathbb{N}$ has $\{\cdot, \cup\}$-representation over $\mathscr{C}_{l,m}$ if and only if it has $\{\cdot, \cup\}$-representation over $\mathscr{C}^+_{l,m}$.

Consider the languages $M = L_2 \cdot \ldots \cdot L_n$ and $N = L_1 \cdot M$ for some $L_1, \ldots, L_n$ from $\mathscr{C}^+_{l,m}$. Suppose that the predicate $x \in [\![M]\!]_k$ is $\exists$-definable in $\langle \mathbb{N}; 0, 1, +, V_k, \leq \rangle$. We are going to construct an existential definition of $x \in [\![N]\!]_k$ for the case when $L_1 = \Sigma^+_{l,m,c}$. As the statement is already proved in [7, Proposition 2] for the other languages from $\mathscr{C}^+_{l,m}$, the proof will thus be completed.

We follow along similar lines as [7, Proposition 2]. Because all words from languages $\Sigma^+_{l',m',c'}$ begin with a letter from $\Sigma_k \setminus \{0\}$, looking at the language $M = L_2 \cdot \ldots \cdot L_n$, we can easily represent it as $M_0 \cdot M'$ for $M_0 \subseteq 0^*$ and $M' \subseteq (\Sigma_k \setminus \{0\}) \cdot \Sigma^*_k$. The sets $Z = \{ |w| : w \in M_0 \}$ and $U = \{ |w| : w \in M \}$ are definable in Presburger arithmetic in the obvious way, and thus are ultimately periodic. Now we have

$$x \in [\![N]\!]_k \Leftrightarrow \exists y \exists z \exists s \big(y \in [\![\Sigma_{l,m,c} \cdot 1 \cdot 0^U]\!]_k \wedge z \in [\![M]\!]_k \wedge S_Z(k \cdot \lambda_k(z), s) \wedge$$
$$V_k(y, s) \wedge s < y \wedge k \cdot (x - z) = (y - s) \big).$$

Here, $S_Z(k \cdot \lambda_k(z), s)$ says that the k-ary expansion of s has the form $1 \cdot 0^c \cdot 0^{|z|}$ for some $c \in Z$. That is, s is a power of k that corresponds to the "1" that delimits $\Sigma^+_{l,m,c}$-part from the $M_0 \cdot M'$-part. In the final equality, this auxiliary bit is excluded: we obtain $(x - z)$ as a result of the right shift of $(y - s)$ by one bit. $\square$

5   Applications and Future Directions

Let us demonstrate that Theorem 1 gives an alternative approach for showing the separation result by Haase and Różycki [7, Corollary 1]. Here, for a set $S \subseteq \mathbb{N}$ and every integer $n > 0$, we define $d_S(n) = \#(S \cap [k^{n-1}..k^n - 1])$, where for a finite set A, its cardinality is denoted by $\#(A)$.

Corollary 1 (Haase and Różycki [7]). *Let the set $S \subseteq \mathbb{N}$ be existentially definable in the structure $\langle \mathbb{N}; 0, 1, +, V_k, \leq \rangle$, then there is a fixed constant $c > 0$ such that either*

(i) $d_S(n) \geq c \cdot k^n$ for infinitely many $n \in \mathbb{N}$; or
(ii) $d_S(n) = O(n^c)$ for every $n \in \mathbb{N}$.

Proof. Suppose first that Theorem 1 yields a $\{\cdot, \cup\}$-representation of the set S which involves the language $\Sigma_{l,m,c}$ for some triple of positive integers l, m, c. This implies the existence of a set $S' \subseteq S$ such that

$$[\![x]\!]_k \in S' \Leftrightarrow x \in w_1 \Sigma_{l,m,c} w_2$$

for some fixed words $w_1, w_2 \in \Sigma_k^*$. Let r be the length of $w_1 \cdot w_2$. Now consider the non-negative integers x with k-ary representations of length $lz + r$ for every $z \in \mathbb{Z}_{>0}$. It is obvious that $d_S(lz+r) \geq d_{S'}(lz+r) = \frac{1}{m}k^{lz}$, and thus condition (i) is satisfied for the constant $c = \frac{1}{mk^r}$ and every n of the form $lz + r$.

Otherwise, the set S can be represented without any occurrences of $\Sigma_{l,m,c}$ (observe that the cases $\Sigma_{0,m,c} = \Sigma_{l,0,c} = \{\epsilon\}$ can easily be excluded from the representation). In this case, by the main theorem of Szilard, Yu, Zhang, and Shallit [13, Theorem 2], S has polynomial density.   □

In this corollary, we see that the density of the set S depends solely on the occurrence of $\Sigma_{l,m,c}$ for $l, m \geq 1$ in the $\{\cdot, \cup\}$-representation of S. Since the density of the set $[\![\{10, 01\}^*]\!]_2$ does not satisfy the conditions of the corollary, it is not $\exists$-definable in $\langle \mathbb{N}; 0, 1, +, V_2, \leq \rangle$. However, the language $L := \{10, 01\}^*$ provides an interesting example.

Example 1. Let L^{C} denote the complement of the language L. It is easy to see that $[\![L^{\mathsf{C}}]\!]_2$ is definable by the expression

$$x \in (\epsilon \cup \Sigma_{1,1,0})11\big(\epsilon \cup \Sigma_{2,1,0} \cup 0\Sigma_{2,1,0}(1 \cup 0)\big) \cup \Sigma_{1,1,0}00\big(\Sigma_{2,1,0} \cup 0\Sigma_{2,1,0}(1 \cup 0)\big).$$

Here, we specify that the binary representation of x can be split into three parts u, v and w, which satisfy the following conditions. The word v is either "11" or "00", and in the first case u can be arbitrary, whereas in the second case, it is required that $[\![u]\!]_2 > 0$. The length of w is even, and if $w \neq \epsilon$, this word begins either with "1" or "01".

Notice that, since every set that is definable in $\langle \mathbb{N}; 0, 1, +, P_2, \leq \rangle$ is $\exists$-definable in this structure [10, Theorem 4], the set $[\![L^{\mathsf{C}}]\!]_2$ cannot be defined here.

Let us conclude this paper with the following observation concerning the open problem raised by Haase and Różycki [7, Conclusion]. The question was: *whether the property of $\exists$-definability in k-Büchi arithmetic is decidable for k-regular sets.* In the light of Theorem 1, this question is reduced to the following one. In order to apply the $\{\cdot, \cup\}$-representation theorem by Hashiguchi [8, Theorem 6.1], we need to construct an upper bound on the integers l and m depending on the number of states of a given Σ_k-DFA. Together with this question, now it is natural to ask whether $\exists$-definability in $\langle \mathbb{N}; 0, 1, +, P_k, \leq \rangle$ is decidable for the sets that are $\exists$-definable in k-Büchi arithmetic. More generally, given a pair of classes $\mathscr{R}_1$ and $\mathscr{R}_2$ of k-regular predicates, whether the property of $\exists$-definability in the structure $\langle \mathbb{N}; 0, 1, +, \mathscr{R}_1, \leq \rangle$ is decidable in the sets $\exists$-definable in $\langle \mathbb{N}; 0, 1, +, \mathscr{R}_2, \leq \rangle$. Note that by Muchnik's theorem [9], this problem is decidable when $\mathscr{R}_1 = \emptyset$. This is an interesting direction for future research.

Acknowledgments. The author thanks the anonymous reviewers for their comments and suggestions. This work was supported by the Russian Science Foundation, project 23-71-01041.

Disclosure of Interests. The author have no competing interests to declare that are relevant to the content of this article.

A   Proof of Lemma 2

Proof. Let $\varphi(x)$ be a generalized quantifier-free $\mathcal{B}_k$-formula. Our aim is to modify this formula by successively decreasing the depth of remainders.

First consider the term $\mathsf{rem}_k(g \cdot \mathsf{rem}_k(t_1, k^\beta) + t_2, k^\alpha)$, where $g \in \mathbb{Z}$ and t_1, t_2 are generalized $\mathcal{B}_k$-terms. We introduce a disjunction over $r \in \left[-|g|..|g|\right]$, and either add to our formula the inequality $(k^\beta < k^\alpha)$ and rewrite the remainder as

$$g \cdot \mathsf{rem}_k(t_1, k^\beta) + \mathsf{rem}_k(t_2, k^\alpha) + r \cdot k^\alpha,$$

or add the inequality $(k^\alpha \le k^\beta)$ and replace the remainder with

$$g \cdot \mathsf{rem}_k(t_1, k^\alpha) + \mathsf{rem}_k(t_2, k^\alpha) + r \cdot k^\alpha.$$

In both cases, we add to our formula the inequalities $(0 \le \tau < k^\alpha)$, where τ denotes the corresponding sum.

In the case of the term $\mathsf{rem}_k(a \cdot x + t_1, k^\alpha)$, where x is an ordinary variable, the coefficient a is an integer, and t_1 is a generalized $\mathcal{B}_k$-term, we use a disjunction over $r \in \left[-|a|..|a|\right]$. Now the remainder is replaced with the sum

$$a \cdot \mathsf{rem}_k(x, k^\alpha) + \mathsf{rem}_k(t_1, k^\alpha) + r \cdot k^\alpha.$$

Again, to express that this term (denote it by τ) is a remainder modulo k^α, we add to our formula the inequalities $(0 \le \tau < k^\alpha)$.

Finally, when dealing with the remainder $\mathsf{rem}_k(c \cdot k^\beta + t_1, k^\alpha)$, the case of $(k^\alpha \le k^\beta)$ yields the term $\mathsf{rem}_k(t_1, k^\alpha)$. When we have the inequality $(k^\beta < k^\alpha)$, the transformations are similar to the other cases.   □

B   Proof of Lemma 5

Proof. Our goal is to construct a $\exists$-formula that defines the set $[\![\Sigma_{l,m,c} \cdot 1 \cdot 0^U]\!]_k$ in the structure $\langle \mathbb{N}; 0, 1, +, V_k, \le \rangle$. Here, U is an ultimately periodic set, and for positive integers l, m, c such that $c \in [0..m-1]$, the language $\Sigma_{l,m,c}$ is defined as the set of all k-ary representations of non-negative integers congruent to c modulo m with bit-length divisible by l. Formula (9) provides an existential definition of the set $[\![\Sigma_{l,m,c}]\!]_k$. In this definition, $\lambda_k(x)$ is the greatest power of k not exceeding x if $x \ge 1$ and 1 in the case $x = 0$.

In our proof, we use two predicates defined in [7, Lemma 6]. These predicates are $S_l(x, y)$ and $S_U(x, y)$, which for a positive integer l and ultimately periodic set U specify that $x = k^\alpha$ and $y = k^{\alpha+\beta}$, such that, respectively, $l \mid \beta$ and $\beta \in U$. The formulas for S_l and S_U in [7] are similar to the definition (9).

Let m', d, and a be the positive integers such that $m = m' \cdot d$, where m' is the greatest integer divisor of m coprime with k, and $d \mid k^a \wedge d \nmid k^{a-1}$. For example, if $k = 6$ and $m = 20$, then $m' = 5$, $d = 4$, and $a = 2$.

Using the representation $x = k^a \cdot y + r$ for a remainder $r \in [0, k^a)$, we see that the divisibility $m \mid x - c$ is equivalent to

$$m \mid x - c \Leftrightarrow (m' \mid k^a \cdot y + r - c) \wedge (d \mid k^a \cdot y + r - c)$$
$$\Leftrightarrow (m' \mid y + (r - c) \cdot (k^a)^{-1}) \wedge (d \mid r - c),$$

where $(k^a)^{-1}$ is the multiplicative inverse of k^a modulo m'. We are now going to slightly reformulate the definition of the set $[\![\Sigma_{l,m,c}]\!]_k$. To do this, for the non-negative integers a and r we define a formula

$$\varphi_{a,r}(y) := (k^l - 1 \mid k^{a+1} \cdot \lambda_k(y) - 1) \wedge (m' \mid y + (r - c) \cdot (k^a)^{-1}).$$

The first divisibility specifies that $(l \mid |y| + a)$, where $|y|$ is the length of the k-ary expansion of y. This formula is used in the following variation of the definition (9):

$$[\![\Sigma_{l,m,c}]\!]_k = \bigcup_{r \in [0..k^a) \wedge d \mid r - c} \{k^a \cdot y + r \; : \; (0 \le y) \wedge \varphi_{a,r}(y)\}.$$

Let δ be the multiplicative order of k modulo m', and let t be the least common multiple of δ and l. Then, for every non-negative integer j we have

$$\varphi_{a,r}(k^{j \cdot t} \cdot y) \Leftrightarrow (l \mid j \cdot t + |y| + a) \wedge (m' \mid k^{j \cdot t} \cdot y + (r - c) \cdot (k^a)^{-1})$$
$$\Leftrightarrow (l \mid |y| + a) \wedge (m' \mid y + (r - c) \cdot (k^a)^{-1})$$
$$\Leftrightarrow \varphi_{a,r}(y).$$

The predicate $x \in [\![\Sigma_{l,m,c} \cdot 1 \cdot (0^t)^*]\!]_k$ can now be defined by the formula

$$\exists s \exists y \Big(S_t(k, s) \wedge \bigvee_{r \in [0..k^a) \wedge d \mid r - c} (\varphi_{a,r}(y) \wedge \mathrm{rem}_k(y, s) = 0 \wedge x = k^{a+1} \cdot y + r \cdot k \cdot s + s) \Big).$$

In this formula, s is equal to $k^{j \cdot t + 1}$ for some non-negative integer j. Therefore, the k-ary expansion of x ends with "$1 \cdot (0^{j \cdot t})$", and its prefix is $(k^a \cdot y + r)$ for an integer y that satisfies $\varphi_{a,r}(y)$.

We are now able to construct the desired definition.

$$x \in [\![\Sigma_{l,m,c} \cdot 1 \cdot 0^U]\!]_k \Leftrightarrow \bigvee_{q=0..t-1} k^q \cdot x \in [\![\Sigma_{l,m,c} \cdot 1 \cdot (0^t)^*]\!]_k \wedge \exists s (S_U(k, s) \wedge V_k(x, s)).$$

Here, we first specify that $x \in [\![\Sigma_{l,m,c} \cdot 1 \cdot 0^*]\!]_k$, and then require the number of trailing zeros to be from the ultimately periodic set U. $\square$

References

1. Bruyère, V.: Entiers et automates finis. Mémoire de fin d'études, University of Mons, Belgium (1985)
2. Bruyère, V., Hansel, G., Michaux, C., Villemaire, R.: Logic and p-recognizable sets of integers. Bull. Belgian Math. Soc. Simon Stevin $\mathbf{1}$(2), 191–238 (1994). https://doi.org/10.36045/bbms/1103408547
3. Büchi, R.J.: Weak second-order arithmetic and finite automata. Math. Log. Q. $\mathbf{6}$(1–6), 66–92 (1960). https://doi.org/10.1002/malq.19600060105
4. Ginsburg, S., Spanier, E.: Semigroups, Presburger formulas, and languages. Pac. J. Math $\mathbf{16}$(2), 285–296 (1966). https://doi.org/10.2140/pjm.1966.16.285
5. Grädel, E.: Automatic structures: twenty years later. In: Proceedings of the 35th Annual ACM/IEEE Symposium on Logic in Computer Science (LICS 2020), pp. 21–34. Association for Computing Machinery, New York (2020). https://doi.org/10.1145/3373718.3394734
6. Haase, C.: A survival guide to Presburger arithmetic. ACM SIGLOG News $\mathbf{5}$(3), 67–82 (2018). https://doi.org/10.1145/3242953.3242964
7. Haase, C., Różycki, J.: On the expressiveness of Büchi arithmetic. In: Kiefer, S., Tasson, C. (eds.) FOSSACS 2021. LNCS, vol. 12650, pp. 310–323. Springer, Cham (2021). https://doi.org/10.1007/978-3-030-71995-1_16
8. Hashiguchi, K.: Representation theorems on regular languages. J. Comput. Syst. Sci. $\mathbf{27}$(1), 101–115 (1983). https://doi.org/10.1016/0022-0000(83)90031-4
9. Muchnik, A.: The definable criterion for definability in Presburger arithmetic and its applications. Theor. Comput. Sci. $\mathbf{290}$(3), 1433–1444 (2003). https://doi.org/10.1016/s0304-3975(02)00047-6
10. Semënov, A.: On certain extensions of the arithmetic of addition of natural numbers. Math. USSR-Izvestiya $\mathbf{15}$(2), 401–418 (1980). https://doi.org/10.1070/im1980v015n02abeh001252
11. Starchak, M.: On the existential arithmetics with addition and bitwise minimum. In: Kupferman, O., Sobocinski, P. (eds.) FOSSACS 2023. LNCS, vol. 13992, pp. 176–195. Springer, Cham (2023). https://doi.org/10.1007/978-3-031-30829-1_9
12. Shallit, J.: The Logical Approach to Automatic Sequences: Exploring Combinatorics on Words with WALNUT, 1st edn. Cambridge University Press (2022). https://doi.org/10.1017/9781108775267
13. Szilard, A., Yu, S., Zhang, K., Shallit, J.: Characterizing regular languages with polynomial densities. In: Havel, I.M., Koubek, V. (eds.) MFCS 1992. LNCS, vol. 629, pp. 494–503. Springer, Heidelberg (1992). https://doi.org/10.1007/3-540-55808-X_48
14. Villemaire, R.: The theory of $\langle \mathbb{N}; +, V_k, V_l \rangle$ is undecidable. Theor. Comput. Sci. $\mathbf{106}$(2), 337–349 (1992). https://doi.org/10.1016/0304-3975(92)90256-f

Graph Homomorphism, Monotone Classes and Bounded Pathwidth

Tala Eagling-Vose[1]($\boxtimes$)(iD), Barnaby Martin[1](iD), Daniël Paulusma[1](iD), and Siani Smith[2](iD)

[1] Durham University, Durham, UK
{tala.j.eagling-vose,barnaby.d.martin,daniel.paulusma}@durham.ac.uk
[2] University of Bristol and Heilbronn Institute for Mathematical Research, Bristol, UK
siani.smith@bristol.ac.uk

Abstract. Monotone graph classes are those described by some set of forbidden subgraphs, i.e. *$\mathcal{H}$-subgraph-free* for some set of graphs $\mathcal{H}$. In recent work a framework was described for the study of such graph classes, if a problem falls into the framework then its computational complexity can be described, for all graph classes defined by a finite set of omitted subgraphs. This allows a dichotomy to be specified between those classes for which the problem is hard and easy.

Here we consider several variants of the homomorphism problem in relation to this framework. It is known that certain homomorphism problems, e.g. C_5-COLOURING, do not sit in the framework. By contrast, we show that the more general problem of GRAPH HOMOMORPHISM does sit in the framework. We also give the first example of a problem in the framework such that hardness is in the polynomial hierarchy above NP. This comes from a list colouring game, where we show that with the restriction of bounded alternation, this problem is contained in the framework. The hard cases are Π_{2k}^{P}-complete and the easy cases are in P. Finally we consider several locally constrained variants of the homomorphism problem, namely the locally bijective, surjective and injective variants. Like C_5-COLOURING, none of these is in the framework. However, where a bounded-degree restrictions are considered, we prove that each of these problems is in our framework.

Keywords: Monotone Classes · Sequential Colouring Construction Game · Quantified Constraint Satisfaction Problem · Vertex Separation Number · Pathwidth · Treedepth

1 Introduction

Let G and H be two graphs. If H can be obtained from G by a sequence of vertex deletions only, then H is *an induced* subgraph of G; else G is *H-free*. The induced subgraph relation has been well studied in the literature for many classical graph problems, such as COLOURING [23], FEEDBACK VERTEX SET [27], INDEPENDENT SET [18], and so on.

Here we focus on the subgraph relation. A graph G is said to contain a graph H as a *subgraph* if H can be obtained from G by a sequence of vertex deletions and edge deletions; else G is said to be *H-subgraph-free*. For a set of graphs $\mathcal{H}$, a graph G is *$\mathcal{H}$-subgraph-free* if G is H-subgraph-free for every $H \in \mathcal{H}$; we also write that G is $(H_1, \ldots, H_p)$-subgraph-free, if $\mathcal{H} = \{H_1, \ldots, H_p\}$. Graph classes closed under edge deletion are also called *monotone* [1,6]. Monotone classes that are specified by a finite set of omitted subgraphs are called *finitely-bounded*.

When compared to those for H-free graphs there are relatively few complexity classifications for H-subgraph-free graphs. Despite this; see [2] for complexity classifications of INDEPENDENT SET, DOMINATING SET and LONGEST PATH; and [15,21] for classifications of LIST COLOURING and MAX CUT, respectively. All of these classifications hold even for $\mathcal{H}$-subgraph-free graphs, where $\mathcal{H}$ is any finite set of graphs. In general, such classifications might be hard to obtain; see, for example, [16] for a partial classification of COLOURING for H-subgraph-free graphs.

Therefore, in [20] a more systematic approach was followed, namely by introducing a new framework for $\mathcal{H}$-subgraph-free graph classes (finite $\mathcal{H}$) adapting the approach of [21]. To explain the framework of [20] we need to introduce some additional terminology. *Treewidth* and *pathwdith* are two widly studied width parameters broadly capturing likeness to a tree or path respectivly. A class of graphs has bounded *treewidth* or *pathwdith* if there exists a constant c such that every graph in it has treewidth or pathwidh, respectively, at most c. Now let $G = (V, E)$ be a graph. Then G is *subcubic* if every vertex of G has degree at most 3. The *subdivision* of an edge $e = uv$ of G replaces e by a new vertex w with edges uw and wv. For an integer $k \geq 1$, the *k-subdivision* of G is the graph G^k obtained from G by subdividing each edge of G exactly k times. For a class of graphs $\mathcal{G}$ and an integer k, $\mathcal{G}^k$ consists of the k-subdivisions of the graphs in $\mathcal{G}$.

We say that a graph problem Π is computationally hard *under edge subdivision of subcubic graphs* if for every integer $j \geq 1$ there is an integer $\ell \geq j$ such that: if Π is computationally hard for the class $\mathcal{G}$ of subcubic graphs, then Π is computationally hard for $\mathcal{G}^\ell$. The framework of [20] makes a distinction between "efficiently solvable" and "computationally hard", which could for example mean a distinction between P and NP-complete.

Commonly, we can prove the condition holds by showing that computational hardness is maintained under k-subdivision for a small integer k (e.g. $k = 1, 2, 3, 4$) and then repeatedly apply the k-subdivision operation. We can therefore say a graph problem Π is a *C123-problem* (belongs to the framework) if it satisfies the three conditions:

C1. Π is efficiently solvable for every graph class of bounded pathwidth[1];

---

[1] In the original framework paper [20], pathwidth and treewidth are interchangeable in this position.

C2. Π is computationally hard for the class of subcubic graphs; and
C3. Π is computationally hard under edge subdivision of subcubic graphs.

To describe the impact of these conditions, we need some notation. The *claw* is the 4-vertex star. A *subdivided* claw is a graph obtained from a claw after subdividing each of its edges zero or more times. The *disjoint union* of two vertex-disjoint graphs G_1 and G_2 has vertex set $V(G_1) \cup V(G_2)$ and edge set $E(G_1) \cup E(G_2)$. The set S consists of the graphs that are disjoint unions of subdivided claws and paths. As shown in [20], C123-problems allow for full complexity classifications for $\mathcal{H}$-subgraph-free graphs (as long as $\mathcal{H}$ has finite size).

Theorem 1 ([20]). *Let Π be a C123-problem. For a finite set $\mathcal{H}$, the problem Π on $\mathcal{H}$-subgraph-free graphs is efficiently solvable if $\mathcal{H}$ contains a graph from S and computationally hard otherwise.*

Examples of C123-problems include INDEPENDENT SET, DOMINATING SET, LIST COLOURING, ODD CYCLE TRANSVERSAL, MAX CUT, STEINER TREE and VERTEX COVER; see [20]. However, there are still many graph problems that are not C123-problems, such as COLOURING (whose classification is still open even for H-subgraph-free graphs). Hence, it is a natural question if those problems can still be classified for graph classes defined by some set of forbidden subgraphs.

This paper considers the GRAPH HOMOMORPHISM problem alongside two variants: a graph colouring game, and locally constrained homomorphism problems. Here, we will define the first of these, while details of the latter two will be addressed in greater detail in their respective sections.

The problem H-COLOURING takes an input graph G and asks whether there is a homomorphism from G to H i.e. a function $h : V(G) \to V(H)$ such that $xy \in E(G)$ then $h(x)h(y) \in E(H)$. If there is, we write $G \to H$. The more general problem GRAPH HOMOMORPHISM takes both G and H as input, with the same question, whether $G \to H$. In general, H-COLOURING is not a C123-problem, for example, C_5-COLOURING does not satisfy C3 (as it satisfies C1 and C2, we label it a *C12-problem*). The topic of such C12-problems is elaborated in [25]. By contrast, we show that GRAPH HOMOMORPHISM is a C123-problem (where C3 is applied uniformly to both G and H). Grohe has argued in [17] that, assuming FPT $\neq$ W[1] (an assumption widely believed in Parameterized Complexity), GRAPH HOMOMORPHISM is in P on a restricted class of graphs if, and only if that class has bounded treewidth. Bearing in mind the interchangeability of treewidth and pathwidth in our framework, we are improving "not in P" to "NP-complete" for finitely-bounded monotone classes.

We continue by considering locally constrained variants of the GRAPH HOMOMORPHISM problem. These problems, LOCALLY BIJECTIVE HOMOMORPHISM, LOCALLY SURJECTIVE HOMOMORPHISM and LOCALLY INJECTIVE HOMOMORPHISM, denoted LBHOM, LSHOM and LIHOM respectively, have all been intensively studied in the literature [12]. When either G or H has bounded (vertex) degree, we prove that each of these three problems is a C123-problem, just like GRAPH HOMOMORPHISM, with a dichotomy between P and NP-complete on finitely-bounded monotone classes. Whereas without such a degree bound they are C23-problems, i.e. satisfy only C2 and C3 and are elaborated further in [5].

The graph colouring game we consider is a variant of that proposed by Bodlaender in [4], SEQUENTIAL COLOURING CONSTRUCTION GAME. Here two players alternate in colouring vertices of a graph with one of k colours, with the first player winning when a proper colouring is obtained. In particular, fixing $k = 3$, this problem closely relates to the *quantified constraint satisfaction problem* QCSP(K_3). Both of these problems are PSPACE-complete [4,7].

Bodlaender proves that SEQUENTIAL 3-COLOURING CONSTRUCTION GAME is in P on any class of bounded vertex separation number. It is well-known that classes of bounded vertex separation number and classes of bounded pathwidth coincide [22]. However here the vertex separation number is with respect to the order in which the vertices are played. A naïve reading of [4] risks a fundamental misinterpretation, as we prove that SEQUENTIAL 3-COLOURING CONSTRUCTION GAME is PSPACE-complete on some class of bounded pathwidth. We do this by mediating through the closely related problem QCSP(K_3) using a celebrated result of Atserias and Oliva [3]. In that paper, they prove that QUANTIFIED BOOLEAN FORMULAS (QBF) is PSPACE-complete on some class of bounded pathwidth, even when the input is restricted to conjunctive normal form (CNF).

Within the framework, just as LIST COLOURING was considered, we can extend our attention to a list colouring game. Adjoining some unary relations to QCSP(K_3), is analogous to moving from 3-COLOURING to LIST 3-COLOURING. Using only two of these lists we arrive at the problem QCSP($K_3, \{1,2\}, \{1,3\}$). Owing to the aforementioned hardness for bounded pathwidth, and unlike LIST COLOURING, QCSP($K_3, \{1,2\}, \{1,3\}$) is not a C123-problem, but is a C23-problem.

However, considering the bounded alternation restriction of this, we prove that Π_{2k}-QCSP($K_3, \{1,2\}, \{1,3\}$) is a C123-problem, for which the hard cases are Π_{2k}^{P}-complete while the easy cases are in P.

Finally, we consider our framework in relation to bounded pathwidth, which coincides (on finitely-bounded monotone classes) with essentially omitting some subdivided claw as a subgraph [28]. If we instead omit some path, we essentially get the graphs of bounded treedepth [26]. For LBHOM, LSHOM and LIHOM, there exists some bounded treedepth class on which they are NP-complete [8]. We will describe a C23-problem, namely LONG EDGE DISJOINT PATHS that is easy on graphs of bounded treedepth but hard on certain classes of bounded pathwidth. Within previous work on C23-problems an example with this behaviour has not yet been discussed. The complexity of QBF on bounded treedepth is a famous open problem (see e.g. [13], where it is proved to be in P under some further restrictions). The complexity of QCSP(K_3) on bounded treedepth may be similarly elusive to classify, and it is on this note that we conclude.

Owing to reasons of space, some proofs are omitted. Synoptic theorems, which sum up what has preceded them, may be given without proof.

2   Preliminaries

A *tree decomposition* for a graph $G = (V, E)$ is a pair (T, X) where T is a tree and X consists of subsets of vertices from V which we call bags. Each node of T corresponds to a single bag of X. For each vertex $v \in V$ the nodes of T containing v must induce a non-empty connected subgraph of T and for each edge $uv \in E$, there must be at least one bag containing both u and v. Similarly, we can define a *path decomposition* where T must instead be a path. We can then define the *width* of (T, X) to be one less than the size of the largest bag. From this, the *treewidth* of a graph, $tw(G)$, is the minimum width of any *tree decomposition* and the *pathwidth* $pw(G)$, is the minimum width of any *path decomposition*. As every path decomposition is also a tree decomposition $tw(G) \leq pw(G)$.

In the following, G and H are graphs, and f is a *homomorphism* from G to H, that is, $f(u)f(v)$ is an edge in H whenever uv is an edge in G. We denote the (open) neighbours of a vertex u in G by $N_G(u) = \{v \mid uv \in E(G)\}$. We say that f is *locally injective, locally bijective* or *locally surjective for a vertex* $u \in V(G)$ if the restriction $f_u : N_G(u) \to N_H(f(u))$ of f is injective, bijective or surjective, respectively. Now, f is said to be *locally injective, locally bijective* or *locally surjective* if f is locally injective, locally bijective or locally surjective for every $u \in V(G)$.

$QCSP(\mathcal{B})$, is defined for some relational structure $\mathcal{B}$ which for us will always be a graph. The problem takes as input a sentence $\phi = Q_1 x_1 Q_2 x_2 \cdots Q_n x_n \Phi$ such that $Q_i \in \{\exists, \forall\}$ and Φ is a conjunction of atomic formulas, *constraints*. The primal graph of a formula Φ contains a vertex for each $x_i \in \Phi$ and an edge if and only if the two variables occur together in a constraint. Let $\Pi_{2k}\text{-}QCSP(\mathcal{B})$ be the restriction of this problem to sentences in Π_{2k}-form, i.e. with quantifier prefix leading with universal quantifiers, alternating $2k - 1$ times, concluding with existential quantifiers.

3   Graph Homomorphism

In this section we will prove that GRAPH HOMOMORPHISM is a C123-problem.

GRAPH HOMOMORPHISM
   Instance: A graph G and a graph H
   Question: Is there a homomorphism from G to H?

Let us recall that we apply C1, C2 and C3 to both graphs. In particular, the subdivision of C3 uniformly applies to both inputs G and H. For a graph G, recall that G^r is G with each edge replaced by a path of length $r + 1$ (an r-subdivision). For example, $K_3{}^5 = C_{15}$.

Lemma 1 ([11]). GRAPH HOMOMORPHISM *satisfies C1.*

Lemma 2 ([14]). GRAPH HOMOMORPHISM *satisfies C2.*

Let us recall that we apply the subdivision of C3 uniformly to both inputs G and H.

Lemma 3. GRAPH HOMOMORPHISM *satisfies the variant of C3 that does not restrict to subcubic.*

Proof. Let $r \geq 1$ be fixed. Let G be connected and have the additional property that every edge is in a triangle. It is clear that this subset remains NP-complete (one can add a new triangle to each edge if necessary). We claim that:

$$G \to K_3 \text{ if and only if } G^{5^r-1} \to C_{3 \cdot 5^r}.$$

The forward direction is trivial. Let us address the backward direction and let h be a homomorphism from G^{5^r-1} to $C_{3 \cdot 5^r}$. Let X be the set of vertices of G^{5^r} that appear already in G. We claim that $h(X) \subseteq \{i, i + 5^r, i + 2 \cdot 5^r\}$ for some $i \in [3 \cdot 5^r]$ where addition is mod $3 \cdot 5^r$. Suppose otherwise, then there is an edge xy in G, so that the distance between $h(x)$ and $h(y)$ in $C_{3 \cdot 5^r}$ is $0 < i < 5^r$ (this is why we assumed G to be connected). But this is impossible since we may consider there exists z so that xyz is a triangle in G and this triangle must have been mapped to line in $C_{3 \cdot 5^r}$. Now, once we calculate i and subtract it, we can divide by 5^r to use h restricted to X to give a homomorphism from G to K_3. □

Note that Lemmas 1 and 3 are enough to guarantee a dichotomy for H-subgraph-free graphs where H is a single graph and not a finite set of graphs [20]. However, as C_3-COLOURING (or equivalently, 3-COLOURING) does not satisfy C2 due to Brooks' Theorem, we need to do more work to accomplish the following.

Lemma 4 GRAPH HOMOMORPHISM *satisfies C3.*

Theorem 2 GRAPH HOMOMORPHISM *is a C123-problem.*

4   Locally Constrained Homomorphisms

In this section we consider three locally constrained homomorphism problems and show that all three of them are C23-problems, which become C123-problems after imposing a degree bound.

LOCALLY BIJECTIVE HOMOMORPHISM
   Instance: A graph G and a graph H
   Question: Is there a locally bijective homomorphism from G to H?

LOCALLY INJECTIVE HOMOMORPHISM
   Instance: A graph G and a graph H
   Question: Is there a locally injective homomorphism from G to H?

> LOCALLY SURJECTIVE HOMOMORPHISM
> *Instance:* A graph G and a graph H
> *Question:* Is there a locally surjective homomorphism from G to H?

We will often use the abbreviations LBHOM, LSHOM and LIHOM for the three problems. We would also like to consider the bounded-degree versions of these problems, which we refer to as DEGREE-d-LBHOM, DEGREE-d-LSHOM and DEGREE-d-LIHOM, here we restrict the maximum degree of either G or H to be d; note that we require only one of these two graphs to have bounded degree.

Lemma 5 ([9]). *For each d, the three problems* DEGREE-d-LBHOM, DEGREE-d-LSHOM *and* DEGREE-d-LIHOM *satisfy C1.*

Lemma 6 ([9]). *The three problems* DEGREE-3-LBHOM, DEGREE-3-LSHOM, DEGREE-3-LIHOM *satisfy C2.*

In particular LBHOM, LSHOM and LIHOM remain NP-complete where G is subcubic and H is K_4 [9].

Lemma 7. LOCALLY BIJECTIVE HOMOMORPHISM *satisfies C3.*

Proof. We claim LBHOM is NP-complete for r-subdivisions of subcubic graphs for any integer r. Let X be the set of vertices of G^r that also appear in G and let Z be the vertices of K_4^r that also appear in K_4. We claim:

$$G \xrightarrow{\text{B}} K_4 \text{ if and only if } G^r \xrightarrow{\text{B}} K_4^r.$$

The forward direction is trivial. Let us consider the backward direction, let h_b be a locally bijective homomorphism from G^r to K_4^r, we claim $h_b(v) \in Z$ if, and only if $v \in X$. As h_b is locally bijective, degree must be preserved, meaning $h_b(v) \in Z$ if, and only if v has degree 3 therefore by showing all vertices in X must have degree 3 our claim is proven.

We may assume there exists at least one degree 3 vertex $v \in G^r$, let $P = (v, p_1, p_2, \ldots, p_{r-1}, p_r)$ be an arbitrary path of length r from v. Both v and p_r must be in X with all intermediate vertices having degree 2. Similarly for any path of length r from $h_b(v)$ as $h_b(v) \in Z$ all intermediate vertices must have degree 2 with that at distance r in Z. As p_1 must be mapped to some neighbour of $h_b(v)$, both p_1 and $h_b(p_1)$ have degree 2. Now as p_2 cannot map to $h_b(v)$ it must map to the next vertex on a path away from $h_b(v)$. As both p_{i-1} and $h_b(p_{i-1})$ have degree 2 it follows that $h_b(p_i)$ must have distance i from $h_b(v)$. Inductively it follows that $h_b(p_r)$ must have distance r from $h_b(v)$ implying $h_b(p_r) \in Z$ and therefore p_r has degree 3. As this holds for all vertices distance r from a degree 3 vertex it follows that all vertices in X must have degree 3 meaning h_b can be used restricted to X to give a homomorphism from G to K_4. □

Lemma 8. LOCALLY INJECTIVE HOMOMORPHISM *satisfies C3.*

Lemma 9. LOCALLY SURJECTIVE HOMOMORPHISM *satisfies C3.*

Theorem 3. LOCALLY BIJECTIVE HOMOMORPHISM, LOCALLY SURJECTIVE HOMOMORPHISM *and* LOCALLY INJECTIVE HOMOMORPHISM *are C23-problems.*

Theorem 4. DEGREE-3-LBHOM, DEGREE-3-LSHOM *and* DEGREE-3-LIHOM *are C123-problems.*

5   Sequential 3-Colouring Construction Game, QCSP(K_3)

We prove that QCSP(K_3) remains PSPACE-complete for graphs of bounded pathwidth. Afterwards, we do the same for the SEQUENTIAL 3-COLOURING CONSTRUCTION GAME. We first formally define the former problem.

QCSP(K_3)

   Instance: A sentence ϕ of the form $Q_1x_1Q_2x_2\ldots Q_nx_n\ \Phi$, where $Q_i \in \{\forall, \exists\}$ and Φ is a conjunction of atoms involving the edge relation E.

   Question: Is ϕ true on K_3?

QCSP(K_3) is sometimes known as *Quantified 3-Colouring* and as highlighted previously closely relates to the SEQUENTIAL 3-COLOURING CONSTRUCTION GAME proposed by Bodlaender in [4]. The two key differences between the problems lie in the requirement of strict alternation in players and each player must assign a colour not previously assigned to a neighbour, in particular, we will show the hardness on bounded pathwidth is preserved between problems.

Theorem 5. QCSP(K_3) *is PSPACE-complete for graphs of bounded pathwidth.*

We remind the reader that the path-width of a formula is equal to the path-width of the primal graph of its quantifier-free part.

Theorem 6. SEQUENTIAL 3-COLOURING CONSTRUCTION GAME *is PSPACE-complete for graphs of bounded pathwidth.*

Proof. We now consider the two additional restrictions of the SEQUENTIAL 3-COLOURING CONSTRUCTION GAME. Where the Universal player is unable to colour a vertex the same as a previously coloured neighbour the problem is identical to that of QCSP(K_3) and strict alternation can be overcome using dummy variables while preserving yes and no instances.

We will therefore use this to show the reduction used to prove Theorem 5 also holds for both problems. In ϕ'' all universally quantified variables are in the form z_i with a single neighbour y_i, as z_i comes before y_i in the linear ordering of vertices. This means the problems of SEQUENTIAL 3-COLOURING CONSTRUCTION GAME and QCSP(K_3) are equivalent on ϕ'' thus both problems remain hard for graphs of bounded path-width.   □

6 Π_{2k}-QCSP$(K_3, \{1,2\}, \{1,3\})$

In this section, we prove that QCSP$(K_3, \{1,2\}, \{1,3\})$ is a C23-problem, but the main result in this section is that its restriction Π_{2k}-QCSP$(K_3, \{1,2\}, \{1,3\})$ is a C123-problem. We obtain QCSP$(K_3, \{1,2\}, \{1,3\})$ by augmenting QCSP(K_3) with some unary relations that allow us to restrict existential variables to some subset of the domain.

QCSP$(K_3, \{1,2\}, \{1,3\})$

    Instance: A sentence ϕ of the form $Q_1 x_1 Q_2 x_2 \ldots Q_n x_n \; \Phi$, where $Q_i \in \{\forall, \exists\}$ and Φ is a conjunction of atoms involving the edge relation E and the unary relations $\{1,2\}, \{1,3\}$.

    Question: Is ϕ true on K_3?

Another variant, QCSP$(K_3, \{1,2\}, \{1,3\}, \{2,3\}, \{1\}, \{2\}, \{3\})$ is also known as *Quantified List* 3-*Colouring*. We consider a slight simplification of this problem as we show not all lists are necessary to ensure hardness, however, the hardness extends to the more general case.

In order to occupy our framework, we will consider bounded alternation versions of our problems. The problem Π_{2k}-QCSP$(K_3, \{1,2\}, \{1,3\})$ is the restriction of QCSP$(K_3, \{1,2\}, \{1,3\})$ to inputs in Π_{2k}-form. While it may lead to a less natural variant of SEQUENTIAL LIST 3-COLOURING CONSTRUCTION GAME as the original game insists on a strict alternation between the two players. In this case, bounding the number of alternations between the two players would make the game trivial, we instead allow each player to colour multiple vertices in their turn.

Lemma 10. Π_{2k}-QCSP$(K_3, \{1,2\}, \{1,3\})$ *is* $\Pi_{2k}^{\mathbf{P}}$-*complete for 2r-subdivisions of subcubic graphs.*

The proof of Lemma 10 also furnishes the following, which we note in passing.

Lemma 11. QCSP$(K_3, \{1,2\}, \{1,3\})$ *is PSPACE-complete for 2r-subdivisions of subcubic graphs.*

Lemma 12 ([10]). Π_{2k}-QCSP$(K_3, \{1,2\}, \{1,3\})$ *satisfies C1.*

Theorem 7. Π_{2k}-QCSP$(K_3, \{1,2\}, \{1,3\})$ *is a C123-problem.*

Unlike the bounded alternation case, QCSP$(K_3, \{1,2\}, \{1,3\})$ does not satisfy C1 with the hardness under bounded path-width following directly from QCSP(K_3).

Theorem 8. QCSP$(K_3, \{1,2\}, \{1,3\})$ *is a C23-problem.*

7 Long Edge Disjoint Paths

The *treedepth* of a graph G as the minimum height of a forest F such that for any pair of adjacent vertices in G one must be an ancestor of the other in F. In this section, we prove that LONG EDGE DISJOINT PATHS is a C23-problem that is polynomial-time solvable for graphs of bounded treedepth but NP-complete for certain classes of bounded path-width.

The EDGE DISJOINT PATHS problem takes as input a graph and k terminal pairs (s_i, t_i). The problem asks if there exists k edge-disjoint (but not necessarily vertex-disjoint) paths connecting each of (s_1, t_1), ..., (s_k, t_k). The EDGE DISJOINT PATHS problem is known to be a C23-problem [5]. Consider its variant LONG EDGE DISJOINT PATHS whose input is as EDGE DISJOINT PATHS but we require the yes-instances to be paths of length at least k.

Theorem 9. LONG EDGE DISJOINT PATHS *is a C23-problem which is in* P *on all classes of bounded treedepth.*

Proof. To prove that it satisfies C2 we reduce from EDGE DISJOINT PATHS where we first k-subdivide each edge (noting k is part of the input of this problem). This ensures that any edge-disjoint paths that connect the terminal pairs are of sufficient length.

The proof that it satisfies C3 is then exactly the same as that for EDGE DISJOINT PATHS, except that we should start with instances in the form of the previous paragraph, built from EDGE DISJOINT PATHS by performing a k-subdivision at the start. These obtained instances are yes-instances of LONG EDGE DISJOINT PATHS if, and only if their subdivisions are yes-instances. Note that if we started from arbitrary instances of LONG EDGE DISJOINT PATHS, we might map no-instances to yes-instances after subdivision.

Finally, on classes of bounded treedepth, which do not contain the m-vertex path P_m as a subgraph for some integer m, we may assume that $k \leq m$. Now a brute force approach to exploring for the paths may be undertaken.   □

Lemma 13. *Let $\mathcal{G}$ be a class of graphs of pathwidth at most p. For each k, $\mathcal{G}^k$ has pathwidth at most $p + 2$.*

Proof. Let G be an arbitrary graph in $\mathcal{G}$ and B be a path decomposition for G such that the largest bag has size at most $p+1$. From this, a path decomposition B' can be constructed for G^k such that the largest bag has size at most $p + 3$. Every edge $(u, v) \in G$ is replaced by a path $u, p_1, p_2, \cdots, p_k, v$ in G^k. Consider the first bag $b \in B$ such that u and v appear together, b can be replaced by a path of $k - 1$ bags, $b_1, b_2, \cdots, b_{k-1}$ in B'. Each bag contains all the vertices of b, and for each pair of adjacent vertices in the path $p_1, p_2, \cdots, p_k$ there will be a bag containing both. In particular $b_i = b \cup \{p_i, p_{i+1}\}$ where $1 \leq i \leq k - 1$ as p_i will only be adjacent to u, v, p_{i-1}, p_{i+1} thus making this a valid path decomposition. In addition, where multiple edges first appear in b we can apply this procedure for each path in series.   □

Theorem 10. LONG EDGE DISJOINT PATHS *is* NP-*complete for graphs of bounded pathwidth and so does not satisfy C1.*

Proof. We use the same trick that we used in the proof of Lemma 9 where we reduce from EDGE DISJOINT PATHS by first k-subdividing each edge (recall k is part of the input of this problem). This is now a correct reduction from EDGE DISJOINT PATHS to LONG EDGE DISJOINT PATHS. Finally, we need that the pathwidth remains bounded and this follows from the previous lemma. □

8 Conclusions

In this paper we identified for the first time C123-problems that distinguish between being polynomial-time solvable and hard in the polynomial hierarchy. We also identified several C23-problems, which are hard on bounded path-width, including LBHOM, LSHOM and LIHOM. Moreover, we proved hardness for bounded path-width for QCSP(K_3) and SEQUENTIAL 3-COLOURING CON-STRUCTION GAME. We do not know if the latter two problems satisfy C2 and C3. We leave this for future work.

We also gave an example of a problem (LONG EDGE DISJOINT PATHS) that is a C23-problem that is NP-complete for some class of graphs of bounded path-width but becomes polynomial-time solvable on all classes of bounded treedepth. Whether QCSP(K_3) is another such example is an open question. That is, we do not know if QCSP(K_3) is polynomial-time for graph classes of bounded treedepth. This is the major open problem arising from our work.

Acknowledgement. We are grateful to Mark Siggers for discussions around Theorem 2. We thank several anonymous reviewers for useful comments for the final version. The second author is supported by EPSRC grant EP/X03190X/1. The third author is supported by EPSRC Grant EP/X01357X/1.

Appendix

Lemma 4. GRAPH HOMOMORPHISM satisfies C3.

Proof. Let us recall the self-reduction from C_5-COLOURING to (subcubic) C_5-COLOURING in Theorem 3.1 from [14]. Each vertex with degree d becomes a chain of d C_5s, the $i + 1$th connected to the ith by identifying edge 1 on the former with edge 4 on the latter (one may take any cyclic ordering of the edges). Then the ith occurrence of the vertex is taken to be the top vertex of the ith C_5 in the chain (where edge 2 meets edge 3). Now, one can simply join the ith occurrence of vertex x to the jth occurrence of vertex y if the edge xy is the ith edge of x and the jth edge of y. This is exactly the reduction of Theorem 3.1 from [14]. We amend if by pretending each edge xy is in fact three edges and must be joined from the chain of C_5s representing x to the chain of C_5s representing y three times (this can at most result in a tripling of the degree). We assume that these joins are consecutive on each chain.

Let Y be the set of instances of C_5-COLOURING that can be obtained by this self-reduction. For $G \in Y$, all edges are in a C_5 except perhaps the edges that came from the edges in the original graph, which are now represented in G in triplicate. Let $r \geq 1$ be fixed. Let $G \in Y$. We claim that:

$$G \to C_5 \text{ if and only if } G^{5^r - 1} \to C_{5^{r+1}}.$$

The forward direction is trivial. Let us address the backward direction and let h be a homomorphism from G^{5^r} to $C_{5^{r+1}}$. Let X be the set of vertices of G^{5^r} that appear already in G. We claim that $h(X) \subseteq \{i, i+5^r, i+2 \cdot 5^r, i+3 \cdot 5^r, i+4 \cdot 5^r\}$ for some $i \in [5^{r+1}]$ where addition is mod 5^{r+1}. Suppose otherwise, then there is an edge xy in G so that the distance between $h(x)$ and $h(y)$ in $C_{5^{r+1}}$ is $0 < i < 5^r$. But this is impossible for the edges in G that were in a C_5 since we may consider there exists z_1, z_2, z_3 so that $xyz_1z_2z_3$ is a C_5 in G and this C_5 must have been mapped to line in $C_{5^{r+1}}$. Suppose now it happens for an edge that is not in a C_5 and remember these edges come in triplicate. If xy were the edge in the original graph, then consider that they became edges $x'y'$, $x''y''$, $x'''y'''$ in G. Now, w.l.o.g., if $h(x')$ and $h(y')$ are mapped at distance $0 < c < 5^r$ in $C_{5^{r+1}}$, then both $h(x'')$ and $h(y'')$, and $h(x''')$ and $h(y''')$ must be mapped to distance $5^r - c \mod 5^r$ since there are even cycles involving $x'y'$ and $x''y''$, and $x'y'$ and $x'''y'''$, where all other edges were in a C_5. But now we consider that there is an even cycle involving $x''y''$ and $x'''y'''$, where all other edges were in a C_5, and derive a contradiction.

Now, once we calculate i and subtract it, we can divide by 5^r to use h restricted to X to give a homomorphism from G to C_5.   □

Theorem 9. LOCALLY SURJECTIVE HOMOMORPHISM satisfies C3.

Proof. As with the bijective case let X be the set of vertices of G^r that also appear in G and let Z be the vertices of K_4^r that also appear in K_4. Now we claim:

$G \xrightarrow{\text{S}} K_4$ if and only if $G^r \xrightarrow{\text{S}} K_4^r$.

Again the forward direction is trivial and let us consider the backward direction, let h_s be a locally surjective homomorphism from G^r to K_4^r, we claim $h_s(v) \in Z$ if and only if $v \in X$. In the surjective case, the degree of a vertex of $v \in G^r$ can be greater than that of $h_s(v)$, although the inverse cannot be true thus implying that only vertices in X, specifically those with degree 3, can be mapped to a vertex in Z.

Now consider the other direction showing if $v \in X$ then $h_b(v) \in Z$, assume for contradiction, v were mapped to some vertex not in Z. As all vertices in G^r with degree 3 must be in X, the length of the shortest path from v to the closest degree 3 vertex must be $\geq r$. Let x be this degree 3 vertex and $P = (v, p_1, p_2, \ldots, x)$ be the path from v to x. In addition, as $h_s(v) \notin Z$ there must be exactly two vertices, $z, z' \in Z$, with distance $< r$ from $h_s(v)$ with every path of length r from $h_s(v)$ containing one of these. We claim the shortest path from v to x must map to a path from $h_s(v)$ via z or z', note this leads to a contradiction as a degree 2 vertex cannot be mapped to a vertex with degree 3.

First consider the vertex p_2, necessarily $h_s(p_2)$ is some neighbour of $h_s(v)$. If p_2 maps to either z or z' our claim is proven, else, $h_b(p_2)$ must have degree 2. Each neighbour of $h_s(p_2)$ must be mapped to at least one neighbour of p_2, as p_2 has degree 2, p_3 must map to a vertex distance 2 from v given it cannot map to $h_b(v)$. It then follows inductively that while $i < r$ and $h_s(p_i) \notin \{z, z'\}$, both p_i and $h_b(p_i)$ have degree 2, meaning $h_s(p_{i+1})$ must have distance i from $h_s(v)$. As every path of length r from $h_s(v)$ must go via either v or v' we once again have a contradiction. As $h_s(v) \in Z$ if and only if $v \in X$ we can again use h_s restricted to X to give a homomorphism from G to K_4. $\square$

Lemma 8. LOCALLY INJECTIVE HOMOMORPHISM satisfies C3.

Proof. Similarly to LBHOM and LSHOM, we claim:

$G \xrightarrow{\text{I}} K_4$ if and only if $G^r \xrightarrow{\text{I}} K_4^r$.

Again, the forward direction is trivial. For the backward direction, let h_i be a locally injective homomorphism from G^r to K_4^r, this means the degree of v can be less than that of $h_i(v)$ but the inverse cannot be true. We will again show that $h_i(v) \in Z$ if and only if $v \in X$. To aid in this we make a second claim, given two vertices distance r from each other, call these v and v^r, then v^r maps to some vertex in Z if and only if v maps to a vertex in Z.

Let $P = (v, p_1, p_2, \ldots, p_{r-1}, v^r)$ be the shortest path between v and v^r. First consider where $h_i(v) \in Z$, given any path of length r from $h_i(v)$, all intermediate vertices must have degree 2 and the vertex at distance r must also be in Z. Showing P must map to a path of length r from $h_i(v)$ therefore implies $h_i(v^r) \in Z$.

p_2 must map to some neighbour of $h_i(v)$, as all neighbours of $h_i(v)$ have degree 2, p_2 must have degree ≤ 2 and as it lies on a path it must have degree 2. Then as no two neighbours of p_2 can map to the same neighbour of $h_i(p_2)$, the vertex p_3 must map to a vertex distance 2 from v. Inductively it follows, where $i < r$, if $h_i(p_i)$ has distance $i - 1$ from $h_i(v)$, given $h_i(p_i)$ and therefore also p_i must have degree 2, $h_i(p_{i+1})$ has distance i from $h_i(v)$. Thus P maps to a path of length r from $h_i(v)$, implying $h_i(v^r) \in Z$.

Similarly, if $h_i(v) \notin Z$ a path of length r from $h_i(v)$, is made up of two paths with length $< r$. One from $h_i(v)$ to some vertex $z_j \in Z$ and one away from z_j, thus any vertex at distance r cannot be in Z. Given that both paths contain only degree 2 vertices, the reasoning from the previous case holds. Say z_j has distance l from $h_i(v)$, the first l vertices of our path must map a path of length l from $h_i(v)$ with the remaining path of length $r - l$ mapping to a path of length $r - l$ from v_j. This therefore proves our claim.

Given this holds for any two vertices in G^r distance r from one another, this must also hold for any multiple of r. If two vertices v, w have distance $k \cdot r$ from each other, for some integer k, then $h_i(v) \in Z$ if, and only if $h_i(w) \in Z$. We can now prove our main claim, $h_i(v) \in Z$ if and only if $v \in Z$.

Say some vertex $v \in X$ were mapped to some $h_i(v) \notin Z$, we may assume v has degree ≤ 2 as it is mapped to a vertex with degree 2. As we assume there exists at least one degree 3 vertex in G^r, let x be that closest to v. As both v and x are in X they must have distance some multiple of r. This implies $h_i(x) \notin Z$, however, this leads to a contradiction as a degree 3 vertex cannot be mapped to a vertex with degree 2.

In the other direction, assume some vertex $v \notin X$ were mapped to some vertex in Z, again let x be the closest degree 3 vertex to v. In addition, on the shortest path from v to x, let v' be the vertex closest to x such that its distance from v is some multiple of r. As $h_i(v') \in Z$ and the distance from v' to x is less than r, $h_i(x)$ must lay on the path between two vertices in Z. As previously this path from v' to x must map to a path of the same length from $h_i(v')$ to $h_i(x)$. This means x cannot map to a vertex in Z which again leads to a contradiction as x has degree 3 and $h_i(x)$ has degree 2.   □

Theorem 5. $QCSP(K_3)$ is PSPACE-complete for graphs of bounded pathwidth.

Proof. We will reduce from the PSPACE-complete problem Quantified Boolean Formulas (QBF) which was shown by Atserias et al. [3] to remain hard where the input is in CNF and the path-width of the primal constraint graph is constant.

Let $\phi = Q_1 x_1 Q_2 x_2 \ldots Q_n x_n \Phi$ be an instance of QBF where Φ is a CNF formula. The *primal graph* of Φ, $G(\Phi)$, contains a vertex for each variable of Φ and an edge where two variables appear in a clause together. Let the pathwidth of $G(\Phi)$ be a constant w. Each clause may then have length at most $w + 1$, as every clause must be contained as a clique in some bag.

To reduce from QBF to $QCSP(K_3)$ we will construct an intermediate instance of QUANTIFIED NOT-ALL-EQUAL 3-SATISFIABILITY (QNAE3SAT), ϕ'. Each clause C_i of Φ is replaced by a set of *NAE* relations C' in Φ. Introducing a constant False it is clear that $NAE(C_i, F)$ is satisfied if, and only if C_i is satisfied. Now it remains to ensure that there are three variables in each clause. Given C_i of Φ contains literals $l_1, \ldots, l_k$, $k \leq w$ we create $k - 2$ new existentially quantified variables $q_{i,j}$, $1 \leq j \leq k - 2$. We can now define C' as follows, if $k = 1$ let $C' = NAE(l_1, F, F)$, where $k = 2$ let $C' = NAE(l_1, l_2, F)$, otherwise where $k \geq 3$, $C' = NAE(l_1, l_2, q_1), NAE(\overline{q_1}, l_3, q_2), \ldots, NAE(\overline{q_{k-3}}, l_{k-1}, q_{k-2}), NAE(\overline{q_{k-2}}, l_k, F)$.

We now claim C'_i is satisfied by an assignment of variables if, and only if C_i is satisfied by this same assignment, thus given a winning strategy for Existential in ϕ which satisfies C_i, this also gives a winning strategy for Existential in ϕ' satisfying all clauses in C'_i. Take some winning strategy for Existential in ϕ, at least one literal in C_i must be evaluated as True. If l_j is the first such literal, $l_q \forall 1 \leq q < j$ are evaluated as False. If $j \in \{1, 2\}$, variables $q_1 \ldots q_{k-2}$ can be assigned False which satisfies all later clauses as each clause contains a positive and negative appearance of a variable. If $j \geq 3$ we can assign $q_1, \ldots, q_{j-2}$ True and $q_{j-1}, \ldots, q_{k-2}$ False, $C'_{i,1}$ is satisfied as neither l_1 nor l_2 are assigned True and all other clauses contain either F or a q variable and a negated q variable. If $j < k$ then $C'_{i,j-1}$ is satisfied as l_j is assigned True with $\overline{q_{j-2}}$ and q_{j-1} evaluated to 0. $C'_{i,k-1}$ is satisfied as $\overline{q_{k-2}}$ is assigned True and F must be evaluated to False.

Now assuming all variables clauses in C' are satisfied we claim at least one literal must be assigned True. Assume otherwise, q_1 must be assigned True to satisfy $C'_{i,1}$, now q_2 must be assigned True to satisfy $C'_{i,2}$, it follows that all q variables must be assigned True. However, this means $C'_{i,k-1}$ cannot be satisfied, thus leading to a contradiction.

From ϕ' we construct an instance of $\mathrm{QCSP}(K_3)$, ϕ''. We refer to the variable of ϕ'' as vertices and the vertices of K_3 as $\{1, 2, 3\}$. With the exception of F every variable x_i in ϕ' is replaced by a path of vertices x_i, y_i, z_i in ϕ''. We introduce a new vertex W which is made adjacent to F alongside all x and y variables. For each clause $C'_p \in \Phi'$ we also introduce a K_3 with each vertex corresponding to a literal of the clause. Consider where the first literal of C'_p is a positive appearance of $v_i \in \phi'$ then the first vertex of K_3 will be adjacent to $x_i \in \phi''$. If this literal were $\overline{x_i}$ then the same vertex in K_3 would be adjacent to y_i.

All variables in ϕ'' are existentially quantified except for z_i which follows the quantification of $v_i\phi'$ and the linear ordering of the vertices begins with W and F, followed by z vertices which follow the ordering of $x_i \in \phi$, the ordering of the remaining variables does not matter as they share the same quantification. The quantifier prefix is therefore $\exists\exists Q_1 Q_2 \ldots Q_n \exists^*$.

$(\phi' \to \phi'')$. Suppose ϕ' is a positive instance, that is we can define a winning strategy for Existential that wins over any strategy of Universal, we can map this to a winning strategy for Existential in ϕ''. Without loss of generality, W can be coloured 3 and F coloured 1, x and y variables must therefore be coloured either 1 or 2. We can now map assignments in ϕ' to a colouring ϕ''. If a universal variable z_i of ϕ'' is coloured 3, y_i can be coloured 1 and x_i coloured 2; otherwise, x_i can be coloured the same as z_i with y_i assigned the single remaining colour available to it. This allows us to map a colouring of the variables x_i, y_j, z_i associated with a universal vertex z_i to a strategy played by Universal in ϕ'.

If Universal assigns x_i the colour 1 in ϕ'' we map this to a strategy such that x_i is assigned False in ϕ by Universal, similarly if x_i coloured 2 in ϕ'' we map to a strategy where x_i is assigned True. Given this assignment of universal variables, we colour the remaining existential variables according to the winning existential strategy in ϕ' mapping the strategy to colours as done with the universal variables. Finally, we need to show we can colour each of the K_3s. As the colouring of variables maps to a winning strategy of QNAE3SAT, at most two literals in a clause can have the same assignment meaning at most two vertices in the triangle have a neighbour with the same colour. Thus using all three colours we can colour the triangle.

$(\phi'' \to \phi'.)$ Now suppose we have a winning strategy for Existential in ϕ'', we will again translate this into a winning strategy for Existential in ϕ'. We can assume W and F are coloured 3 and 1, respectively, meaning variables x and y variables must be coloured 1 or 2. For any assignment of universal variables in ϕ' we can map this to a strategy in ϕ''. We can now as before read off the existential variables, in particular our values of x. For each clause, all vertices of the K_3 must be coloured differently, meaning at most two of the vertices adjacent to the

K_3 may have the same colour. This means each clause in ϕ' must be satisfied giving us a winning strategy. $\qquad\square$

Lemma 14. *The path-width of Φ'' is at most $9w + 2$.*

Proof. Given the path-width of Φ is w we claim the path-width of Φ'' is w' where $w' \leq 9w + 2$. Let B be a path decomposition for Φ such that the size of the largest bag is $w + 1$. As each clause C_i of Φ appears as a clique in the primal graph all variables in C_i must be contained in at least one bag together. We say a clause is associated with a given bag if it is the first bag such that all variables in the clause appear together. Where a bag is associated with multiple clauses it can be replaced with a path of duplicates, thus a bag is associated with at most one clause. Notice this increases the number of bags by at most the number of clauses.

We now define a path decomposition B' for Φ'' with a bag $b_i' \in B'$ for each $b_i \in B$. Where b_i contains a variable $v_j \in \Phi$, then b_j contains $x, y, z \in \Phi''$. In addition, W and F are contained in each bag of B' meaning $|b_i'| = 3|B_i| + 2$. For a clause $c_i \in \phi$ of size k we have $k - 2$ new variables in Φ' $q_{i,j}$ for $1 \leq j \leq k - 2$ thus $3(k - 2)$ new vertices in Φ''. As c_i was replaced by $k - 1$ clauses in Φ', we also have $3(k - 1)$ new vertices for the K_3 dedicated to each clause. This leads to a total of $3(k - 2) + 3(k - 1) = 6k - 9$ new vertices for clause C_i. If we call these new vertices S_{C_i}, as $N[S_{C_i}] = S_{c_i} \cup C_i$, S_i can also be contained in the bag associated with C_i with this remaining a path decomposition. Thus if bag B_j is associated with clause C_i, $|B_j'| = 3|B_i| + 6k - 7$ and as $|B_p|, k \leq w + 1$ for all $B_p \in B$, $|B_p'| \leq 9w + 2$ for all $B_p' \in B$. $\qquad\square$

Lemma 10. Π_{2k}-QCSP$(K_3, \{1,2\}, \{1,3\})$ *is Π_{2k}^P-complete for $2r$-subdivisions of subcubic graphs.*

Proof. We will reduce from the Π_k^P-complete problem Π_k-QUANTIFIED-NOT-ALL-EQUAL-3-SAT (Π_k-QNAE-3-SAT) [19,24]. Let $\phi = Q_1 x_1 Q_2 x_2 \ldots Q_n x_n \Phi$ be an instance of Π_k-QNAE-3-SAT where $x_i \in \{0,1\}$, $\Phi = NAE_3(C_1) \vee NAE_3(C_2) \vee \ldots \vee NAE_3(C_m)$ where $C_i = (x_h, x_i, x_j)$ and $x_h, x_i, x_j \in \{x_1, x_2, \ldots, x_n\}$.

For each variable x_i in ϕ there are three variables $\exists x_i$, $Q_i z_i$ in ϕ' with $L(x_i) = \{1,2\}$ and $L(z_i) = \{1,2,3\}$. Paths of length $2p+1$ are introduced between z_i and x_i with each inner vertex having the list $\{1,2\}$. In addition for each clause C_p we use the three literal clause gadget from [15] introducing variables C_p, C_p', C_p'' where $L(C_p) = \{1,2\}$ and $L(C_p') = L(C_p'')\{1,2,3\}$. We add the paths of length $2p + 1$ between the vertices x_h C_p, x_i C_p', x_j C_p'', C_p C_p', C_p C_p'' with all inner vertices assigned the list $\{1,2\}$. Notice this forces the path to alternate between colours and enforces that given a single endpoint is coloured 1 or 2 the other endpoint cannot be coloured the same. There is also a path between C_p' and C_p'' with inner vertices assigned the list $\{1,3\}$, which has the same impact where a vertex is coloured 1 or 3 (Fig. 1).

The ordering of ϕ' follows that of ϕ for variables z_i. It is then followed by all remaining vertices, as these are all existentially quantified their ordering does not matter. This leads to a prefix $Q_1 z_1 Q_2 z_2 \ldots Q_n z_n \exists^*$.

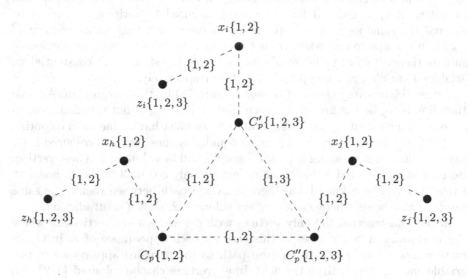

Fig. 1. Construction for clause C_p. Dashed lines denote paths of length $2p+1$ with the label corresponding to the list of internal vertices.

Suppose ϕ is a positive instance, that is we can define a winning strategy for the existential player, we can then also define a winning strategy for Existential in ϕ'. Given the colouring of universal variables in ϕ' we can map this to a strategy for the universal player in ϕ. Where z_i is coloured 1 or 2, x_i must take the other available colour not used by z_i, whereas if z_i is coloured 3 without loss of generality we can assign x_i 1. Given x_i is coloured 1 in ϕ' we can map this to a strategy where universal assigns 0 to x_i in ϕ similarly given a colouring of 2 in ϕ we can map this to an assignment of 1 in ϕ. We can now evaluate the existential vertices x_i in ϕ' according to the strategy of existential for variables x_i in ϕ, again mapping 0, 1 to 1, 2 respectively.

Given this strategy for colouring variables x_i in ϕ' we claim we can colour the remaining existential variables therefore showing there is a winning strategy for existential. First note all existential variables z_i can be coloured 3, next as the colouring of variables x_i equates to a winning strategy for existential in ϕ for all clauses $C_i = (x_h, x_i, x_j)$ in ϕ at most 2 of the variables can be assigned the same value meaning of C_p, C_p', C_p'' at most 2 of their respective x's can be given the same colour. The colour of x_h fixes that of C_p such that they are different which also forces both C_p' and C_p'' to be coloured differently to C_p. At least one variable of x_i, x_j must be coloured differently to x_h, say x_i, this means C_p must be coloured the same as x_i. We can then colour C_p' 1 or 2 whichever is not used by x_i leaving C_p'' to be coloured 3.

Now given Existential has a winning strategy in ϕ' we will construct a winning strategy for her in ϕ. Now given an assignment of universal variables in ϕ we can map this to a colouring of the universal vertices in ϕ', given a variable x_i is assigned 0 in ϕ we can map this to a strategy of Universal such that z_i is coloured 2, similarly if x_i is assigned 1 we map to z_i coloured 1. Notice as x_i cannot be coloured the same as z_i, this is the same strategy such that an assignment of x_i to 0 in ϕ maps to one where x_i is coloured 1 ϕ'. We can now, as previously, evaluate the existential variables of ϕ according to the strategy of Existential for variables x_i in ϕ', again mapping 1, 2 to 0, 1 respectively.

We now claim every clause of ϕ must be satisfied by this assignment. Assume otherwise, let c_p be the first clause such that $NAE_3(C_p)$ is not satisfied, note as this is a winning strategy for Existential in ϕ' we must have some valid colouring for C_p, C_p', C_p'' such that x_h, x_i, x_j are all equal. Say these were all coloured 1, C_p must be coloured 2, meaning neither C_p' nor C_p'' can be coloured 2. These vertices also cannot be coloured 1 due to x_i, x_j leaving only colour 3 for both, however, at most one can be coloured 3 as there is an odd path between them. The same reasoning also holds where x_h, x_i, x_j are coloured 2, thus a contradiction.

In this construction the only vertices with degree > 3 are vertices x_i where $x_i \in \phi$ appears in > 2 clauses in this case for each appearance of x_i in C_j we create a new vertex $x_{i,j}$ with an even path to the previous appearance of this variable and an even path to the next. Inner vertices can be coloured $\{1,2\}$ and as this is an even path $x_{i,j} = x_i$ for all j.   □

References

1. Alekseev, V.E., Boliac, R., Korobitsyn, D.V., Lozin, V.V.: NP-hard graph problems and boundary classes of graphs. Theor. Comput. Sci. **389**, 219–236 (2007)
2. Alekseev, V.E., Korobitsyn, D.V.: Complexity of some problems on hereditary graph classes. Diskret. Mat. **2**, 90–96 (1990)
3. Atserias, A., Oliva, S.: Bounded-width QBF is pspace-complete. J. Comput. Syst. Sci. **80**(7), 1415–1429 (2014)
4. Bodlaender, H.L.: On the complexity of some coloring games. Int. J. Found. Comput. Sci. **2**, 133–147 (1991)
5. Bodlaender, H.L., et al.: Complexity framework for forbidden subgraphs IV: the steiner forest problem. *CoRR*, abs/2305.01613, 2023
6. Boliac, R., Lozin, V.: On the clique-width of graphs in hereditary classes. In: Bose, P., Morin, P. (eds.) ISAAC 2002. LNCS, vol. 2518, pp. 44–54. Springer, Heidelberg (2002). https://doi.org/10.1007/3-540-36136-7_5
7. Börner, F., Bulatov, A.A., Chen, H., Jeavons, P., Krokhin, A.A.: The complexity of constraint satisfaction games and QCSP. Inf. Comput. **207**(9), 923–944 (2009)
8. Bulteau, L., Dabrowski, K.K., Köhler, N., Ordyniak, S., Paulusma, D.: An algorithmic framework for locally constrained homomorphisms. In: Bekos, M.A., Kaufmann, M. (eds.) Graph-Theoretic Concepts in Computer Science. WG 2022. LNCS, vol. 13453, pp. 114–128. Springer, Cham (2022). https://doi.org/10.1007/978-3-031-15914-5_9
9. Chaplick, S., Fiala, J., van't Hof, P., Paulusma, D., Tesar, M.: Locally constrained homomorphisms on graphs of bounded treewidth and bounded degree. Theor. Comput. Sci. **590**, 86–95 (2015)

10. Chen, H.: Quantified constraint satisfaction and bounded treewidth. In: De Mantaras, R.L., Saitta, L. (eds.), Proceedings of the 16th Eureopean Conference on Artificial Intelligence, ECAI'2004, including Prestigious Applicants of Intelligent Systems, PAIS 2004, Valencia, Spain, 22–27 August 2004, pp. 161–165. IOS Press (2004)
11. Dechter, R., Pearl, J.: Tree clustering for constraint networks. Artif. Intell. **38**(3), 353–366 (1989)
12. Fiala, J., Kratochvíl, J.: Locally constrained graph homomorphisms - structure, complexity, and applications. Comput. Sci. Rev. **2**(2), 97–111 (2008)
13. Fichte, J.K., Ganian, R., Hecher, M., Slivovsky, F., Ordyniak, S.: Structure-aware lower bounds and broadening the horizon of tractability for QBF. In: LICS, pp. 1–14 (2023)
14. Galluccio, A., Hell, P., Nešetřil, J.: The complexity of H-colouring of bounded degree graphs. Discret. Math. **222**, 101–109 (2000)
15. Golovach, P.A., Paulusma, D.: List coloring in the absence of two subgraphs. Discret. Appl. Math. **166**, 123–130 (2014)
16. Golovach, P.A., Paulusma, D., Ries, B.: Coloring graphs characterized by a forbidden subgraph. Discret. Appl. Math. **180**, 101–110 (2015)
17. Grohe, M.: The complexity of homomorphism and constraint satisfaction problems seen from the other side. J. ACM **54**, 1:1–1:24 (2007)
18. Grzesik, A., Klimošová, T., Pilipczuk, M., Pilipczuk, M.: Polynomial-time algorithm for Maximum Weight Independent set on P_6-free graphs. ACM Trans. Algorithms **18**, 4:1–4:57 (2022)
19. Hemaspaandra, E.: Dichotomy theorems for alternation-bounded quantified boolean formulas. *CoRR*, cs.CC/0406006 (2004)
20. Johnson, M., et al.: Complexity framework for forbidden subgraphs I: the framework. *CoRR*, 2211.12887, 2022
21. Kamiński, M.: Max-cut and containment relations in graphs. Theor. Comput. Sci. **438**, 89–95 (2012)
22. Kinnersley, N.G.: The vertex separation number of a graph equals its pathwidth. Inf. Process. Lett. **42**(6), 345–350 (1992). https://doi.org/10.1016/0020-0190(92)90234-M
23. Král', D., Kratochvíl, J., Tuza, Z., Woeginger, G.J.: Complexity of coloring graphs without forbidden induced subgraphs. In: Brandstädt, A., Le, V.B. (eds.) WG 2001. LNCS, vol. 2204, pp. 254–262. Springer, Heidelberg (2001). https://doi.org/10.1007/3-540-45477-2_23
24. Martin, B.: Logic, computation and constraint satisfaction. PhD thesis, University of Leicester, UK, 2005
25. Martin, B., Pandey, S., Paulusma, D., Siggers, M., Smith, S., van Leeuwen, E.J.: Complexity framework for forbidden subgraphs II: when hardness is not preserved under edge subdivision (2023). http://arxiv.org/abs/2211.14214arXiv:2211.14214
26. Nešetřil, J., Ossona de Mendez, P.: Sparsity. AC, vol. 28. Springer, Heidelberg (2012). https://doi.org/10.1007/978-3-642-27875-4
27. Paesani, G., Paulusma, D., Rzazewski, P.: Feedback vertex set and even cycle transversal for H-free graphs: finding large block graphs. SIAM J. Discret. Math. **36**, 2453–2472 (2022)
28. Robertson, N., Seymour, P.D.: Graph minors. III. Planar tree-width. J. Comb. Theory Ser. B **36**, 49–64 (1984)

Recursion-Theoretic Alternation

Eduardo Skapinakis[1,2]($\boxtimes$) (iD)

[1] Center for Mathematics and Applications (NOVA Math), NOVA School of Science and Technology (NOVA FCT), Setúbal, Portugal
e.scapinakis@campus.fct.unl.pt
[2] Carl Friedrich von Weizsäcker Zentrum, Universität Tübingen, Tübingen, Germany
eduardo.skapinakis@uni-tuebingen.de

Abstract. We introduce four recursion schemes, which, operating on a tree-like data structure, capture different models of computation based on alternating bounded quantifiers. By encoding inputs as *paths*, we recover and expand characterizations of complexity classes between deterministic linear time and polynomial space; by encoding them as *balanced trees*, we recover characterizations of *alternating* logarithmic time and polylogarithmic space.

We propose recursion-theoretic characterizations of *logarithmic* and *polylogarithmic time*, as defined via Turing machines with random access to the input, and show that the classes of functions obtained capture, at least, the desired classes, and, at most, their alternating versions.

Should the proposed characterizations be precise, we show that characterizations of linear and polynomially bounded alternating classes can be adapted to alternating classes with logarithmic and polylogarithmic resource bounds, simply by changing the way in which inputs are encoded. We discuss how, from these characterizations, some open problems in complexity theory can be obtained from known results by making alterations to recursion schemes.

Keywords: Alternation · Implicit complexity · Logarithmic resources · Tree recursion

1 Introduction

Recursion-theoretic approaches to complexity seek to characterize the problems that can be solved by some computational model, under some resource bound, in a purely syntactical way: as the closure of a set of functions under a set of operators (or schemes). Our interest in this approach follows part of the interest in the more general area of *implicit complexity*, which is to transport problems of complexity theory to different areas of mathematics, where they can be stated and treated with different proof methods. To this end, we present in this paper four operators, which capture complexity classes with logarithmic, polylogarithmic, linear and polynomial resource bounds. See Table 1 in Sect. 3 for a summary of the results.

© The Author(s), under exclusive license to Springer Nature Switzerland AG 2024
L. Levy Patey et al. (Eds.): CiE 2024, LNCS 14773, pp. 252–264, 2024.
https://doi.org/10.1007/978-3-031-64309-5_20

The paper is divided as follows: in Sect. 2 we introduce and motivate the necessary recursion schemes; in Sect. 3 we characterize complexity classes between LIN and PSPACE and propose candidates for similar characterizations of classes between LOG and POLYLOGSPACE, by altering the way in which inputs are encoded; in Sect. 4 we discuss how known results involving these classes turn into open problems in complexity theory when changes are made to one of the operators or to how inputs are encoded.

2 Background

Clote [12] contains all the required material from computational models and recursion-theoretic characterizations. We will rely on two variations of the multi-tape Turing machine: the *Alternating Turing Machine* (ATM) [9] and the *Random Access Turing Machine* (RATM) [22]. Informally, an ATM is a non-deterministic Turing machine that can "guess" solutions (with an OR state – existential quantifier) and "test" if every word is a solution (with an AND state – universal quantifier). A RATM is a Turing machine that is supplied with the size of the input in an auxiliary tape and has an extra *index tape*, where it can write a position p, in binary, and receive the pth digit of the input in one step. This allows any digit to be read by a logarithmically time bounded machine, which is not the case in the usual Turing machine model.

We denote by LIN, P, PSPACE and POLYLOGSPACE the class of problems that can be solved in linear time, polynomial time, polynomial space and polyloga-rithmic space, respectively, on a multitape Turing machine. We denote by LOG and POLYLOG the class of problems that can be solved in time $\mathcal{O}(\log(n))$ and $\mathcal{O}(\log^k(n))$, for some $k \in \mathbb{N}$, respectively, on a RATM. Given a complexity class $\mathcal{C}$, we denote by A$\mathcal{C}$ the class of problems that can be solved by an ATM under the bounds of $\mathcal{C}$. We denote by $\mathcal{C}$H the class of problems that can be solved by an ATM under the bounds of $\mathcal{C}$, with a fixed number of alternations between universal and existential states.

For $\mathcal{I}$ a class of functions and $\mathcal{O}$ a set of operators, we denote by $[\mathcal{I}; \mathcal{O}]$ the smallest class of functions containing the functions in $\mathcal{I}$ and closed under the operators in $\mathcal{O}$. To relate function classes with complexity classes we interpret the output 0 of a function as rejection and anything else as acceptance. We say that $[\mathcal{I}; \mathcal{O}]$ characterizes a class $\mathcal{C}$ if, under this interpretation, a set is in $\mathcal{C}$ if and only if its characteristic function is in $[\mathcal{I}; \mathcal{O}]$.

2.1 The Data Structure

We consider a tree-like data structure to encode binary inputs as in [4,17]. This choice has two important consequences: first, it allows us to relate polynomial and logarithmic resource classes, using the same operators and changing only how inputs are encoded; secondly, the presence of pairing and unpairing as initial functions allows us to unify characterizations for polynomial and linear time under the same operators, which allows us to better develop the analogy for the purposed characterization of (poly)logarithmic time.

Denote by $\mathbb{T}$ the algebra with two constants, 0 and 1, and a constructor $*$, of arity 2. The elements of $\mathbb{T}$ can be interpreted as trees. For example, using infix notation, $(0 * 1) * (0 * 0)$ and $((0 * 1) * 0) * 0$ can be interpreted, respectively, as the following trees:

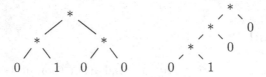

By default, $*$ is left associative, i.e. $0 * 1 * 0$ stands for $(0 * 1) * 0$, not $0 * (1 * 0)$. The length $|x|$ of a tree x is its number of leaves. The height $\lceil x \rceil$ is the maximal nesting depth of $*$. For example, while both trees $(0 * 1) * (0 * 0)$ and $((0 * 1) * 0) * 0$ have length 4, the first has height 2 and the second 3. We abbreviate multiple inputs $x_1, \ldots, x_n$ as $\bar{x}$ and denote by $|\bar{x}|$ and $\lceil \bar{x} \rceil$ the arrays $|x_1|, \ldots, |x_n|$ and $\lceil x_1 \rceil, \ldots, \lceil x_n \rceil$, respectively.

We encode binary inputs in one of two ways: either directly as a path, where all nodes labeled $*$ have at most one child labeled $*$ (example on the right, which represents the input 0100), or as a balanced tree, where all root-to-leaf paths have the same length (example on the left). In the later case, we may have to add 0's to the input until its size is a power of 2.

2.2   The Operators

We follow the input sorting discipline of Bellantoni and Cook [3] (see also Simmons [23] and Leivant [16]), sorting the input into normal positions (to the left of a semicolon) and safe positions (to the right). With a rule on composition that does not allow normal variables to be moved to the safe side, and a rule on recursion that places the previous iterations of the function on the safe side (see Definition 2), where the size of the inputs has a small effect on the size of the output[1], one avoids, in a purely *syntactical* way, a size explosion through recursion, which is manifested in the Bounding Lemmas 1 and 2 (see [3] for more details).

We introduce a new set of operators, inspired in [4], to deal with the tree-like data structure we are working on. They are quite artificial, but intuitively represent computations over trees and nondeterministic computations. Their constructions pays of in Sect. 3, where we show that, if a certain class of functions characterizes LOG, small alterations to these schemes allow us to capture a great variety of complexity classes, for some of which separation results are known.

---

[1] See Lemmas 1 and 2.

Definition 1 (Initial functions). *We denote by* $\mathcal{I}$ *the following class of functions:*

$$0, 1$$
$$* (; u, v) = u * v$$
$$\pi_j^{n,m}(x_1, \ldots, x_n; x_{n+1}, \ldots, x_m) = x_j, \ 1 \le j \le n + m$$
$$\mathsf{L}(; i) = i, \ i \in \{0, 1\} \quad \mathsf{L}(; u * v) = u$$
$$\mathsf{R}(; i) = i, \ i \in \{0, 1\} \quad \mathsf{R}(; u * v) = v$$
$$\mathsf{C}(; i, x_0, x_1, y) = x_i, \ i \in \{0, 1\} \quad \mathsf{C}(; u * v, x_0, x_1, y) = y$$

Essentially, the constructor $*$ works as a pairing function, with left and right unpairing L and R. The conditional function C distinguishes between 0, 1 and words constructed as $u * v$, which allows us to define functions with case distinction.

In the operators below, the last two have the particularity that the value of a function can depend on two of its possibly different previous iterations, which allows us to mimic the behaviour of a nondeterministic Turing machine. Recall that we interpret 0 as rejection and anything else as acceptance. Thus, we define $x \vee y$ as 0, whenever both x and y are 0, and 1 otherwise, and $x \wedge y$ as 0 if either x or y are 0, and 1 otherwise.

Definition 2 (Operators). *We use the following operators:*
SC *(input-sorted composition)*

$$f(\overline{x}; \overline{y}) = h(\overline{r}(\overline{x};); \overline{t}(\overline{x}; \overline{y}))$$

pSR *(input-sorted path recursion)*

$$f(p, i, \overline{x}; \overline{y}) = g(p, i, \overline{x}; \overline{y}), \ i \in \{0, 1\}$$

$$f(p, u * v, \overline{x}; \overline{y}) = \begin{cases} h(p, u * v, \overline{x}; \overline{y}, f(\mathsf{L}(; p), u, \overline{x}; \overline{y})) & \text{if } \mathsf{R}(; p) = 0 \\ h(p, u * v, \overline{x}; \overline{y}, f(\mathsf{L}(; p), v, \overline{x}; \overline{y})) & \text{otherwise} \end{cases}$$

vpSR *(very safe input-sorted path recursion) is defined as* pSR, *but* h *receives all inputs on the safe side (to the right of the semicolon).*
DR *(disjunction recursion)*

$$f(p, i, x;) = g(p, i, x;), \ i \in \{0, 1\}$$
$$f(p, u * v, x;) = f(p * 0, u, x;) \vee f(p * 1, v, x;)$$

AR *(alternating recursion)*

$$f(p, i, x;) = g(p, i, x;), \ i \in \{0, 1\}$$

$$f(p, u * v, x;) = \begin{cases} f(p * 0, u, x;) \wedge f(p * 1, v, x;) & \text{if } h(p, u * v, x;) = 0 \\ f(p * 0, u, x;) \vee f(p * 1, v, x;) & \text{otherwise} \end{cases}$$

The schemes pSR and vpSR are similar to *recursion on notation* from [3] and *very safe recursion on notation* from [6], but adapted to the tree-like data structure we consider – instead of the step case removing the last bit of the input word, it removes its left or right "branch". They differ from the tree recursion scheme used in [4], as, here, the value of f on input $u * v$ depends either on the value of f at u, or v, not on both (as, for example, in the schemes DR and AR). In [4], a rank measure is also used to restrict the values that can be recursed on, which gives rise to a characterization of (log-space) uniform NC, instead of POLYLOGSPACE (see Table 1 in Sect. 3).

The first input of a function defined with pSR is called the *path* parameter. When inputs are encoded as *balanced trees*, it allows a function to choose which path on the tree to navigate. For example, if f is defined by pSR with step function h and $x = (0 * 1) * (0 * 0)$, then, omitting some variables,

$$f(1 * 0, \boldsymbol{x};) = h(\ldots; f(1, \mathbf{0} * \mathbf{1};)) = h(\ldots; h(\ldots; f(1, \mathbf{1};)))$$

The path $1 * 0$ thus makes it so that f starts by looking at the left half of x (as $R(; 1 * 0) = 0$) and then the right half of x (as $R(; 1) = 1$). This allow us to use pSR to obtain any digit of the input, thus capturing the essence of a RATM. When inputs are encoded as *paths*, the path parameter is irrelevant and we just recover the original scheme of recursion on notation.

The schemes DR and AR represent a non-deterministic Turing machine as in [18–20], where the non-deterministically generated bits are captured by the path parameter p. For example, if we take a base function g, which, receiving a path p and a formula x, interprets the bits in p as assignments for the formula represented in x, then DR can be used to construct a function that decides SAT, as it will output 1 if and only if some assignment (path) satisfies the input formula. The scheme AR generalizes DR, allowing the function created to have an acceptance criteria that is a boolean function of its base case on every possible path. We call the function h in the scheme AR the *test* function, as it is responsible for testing whether the computation is supposed to continue with an AND or an OR state.

2.3   Bounds

In the recursion-theoretic setting, where functions are defined by equations, the *time* of computing $f(x)$ can be defined as the number of equalities that have to be invoked until $f(x)$ is rewritten to a natural number.[2] This means that the *time complexity* introduced by a recursion scheme is related to the number of recursive calls that need to be made until it reaches the base case.

In the recursion schemes from Definition 2, this number depends, not on the *length* of the input, but on the *height* of the tree that represents it.[3] This observation motivates the two ways of encoding integers in $\mathbb{T}$: either as *paths*,

---

[2] This idea can be formalized quite elegantly through term rewriting systems.

[3] For example, recursion over $(0 * 1) * (0 * 0)$ will take two recursive steps, whereas over $0 * 1 * 0 * 0$ it will take three, even though both inputs have the same length.

or as *balanced trees*. In the second case, while the number of available recursive steps is smaller than if the input was encoded as a path, since the *height* of a balanced tree is logarithmic in its number of leafs, each bit can be read *faster* than if the input was encoded as a path, which introduces an interesting trade-off between these two ways of encoding inputs: with balanced trees, one has *less* time to compute, but can reach parts of the input *faster*.

Note that the presence of $*$ as an initial function is problematic. For example, ignoring the path parameter, we can define an exponentially growing function:

$$\times (i; x) = x \qquad \times (u * v; x) = *(; x, \times(u; x)) \tag{1}$$
$$exp(i, x;) = x \qquad exp(u * v, x;) = \times(x; exp(u, x;))$$

However, even though the outputs of $f(x;) = exp(x, x;)$ have an exponential size, they have only a polynomial height, which is a propagation of the fact that $\lceil u * v \rceil = 1 + \max\{\lceil u \rceil, \lceil v \rceil\}$.

Similarly to [3,6], we have some form of "bounding lemmas", which we now apply to the height of the tree representing an input, instead of to its length. Recall that DR and AR only produce outputs with one bit, so we only require the bounds for the other two forms of recursion we introduced.

Lemma 1 ([6]). *For any $f \in [\mathcal{I}; \mathsf{SC}, \mathsf{vpSR}]$, there is a constant $k_f \in \mathbb{N}$ such that $\lceil f(\overline{x}; \overline{y}) \rceil \leq k_f \max \lceil \overline{x} \rceil + \max \lceil \overline{y} \rceil$.*

Note that the product defined in Equation (1) cannot be used as a step function in vpSR, since the step function is required to only take safe inputs.

Lemma 2 ([3]). *For any $f \in [\mathcal{I}; \mathsf{SC}, \mathsf{pSR}]$, there is a polynomial q_f with natural coefficients such that $\lceil f(\overline{x}; \overline{y}) \rceil \leq q_f(\lceil \overline{x} \rceil) + \max \lceil \overline{y} \rceil$.*

These lemmas tell us that, even when we use a scheme to produce exponentially large outputs, these cannot be used to "gain more time" by being given as input to a recursion scheme, as their heights, which determine the number of recursive steps, will still respect the class's bound.

3   The Characterizations

The results from this section are summarized in Table 1. The entries with the symbol "$\supseteq$" indicate that the respective operators capture at least the decision problems of the stated class, but that the other inclusion is unknown. The fact that for ALOG and POLYLOGSPACE the characterization are precise is due to Bloch [7], who characterizes these classes with schemes that can simulate ours, thus solving our unknown inclusion (see the Appendix). For the logarithmic classes, the equalities we state with circuit complexity hold under uniformity conditions on the function $1^n \mapsto C_n$, which, given a number n, generates a circuit with n input gates. The uniformity conditions are: for NC^1 and AC^0, log-time [2], and, for qAC^0, polylog-time [1].[4]

---

[4] qAC^0 is the class of languages recognizable by circuit families of constant depth and (quasi-polynomial) size $2^{\log(n)^{\mathcal{O}(1)}}$.

The classes POLYLOG and POLYLOGSPACE are characterized by logical means in Ferrarotti et al. [15] and POLYLOGH in Mix Barrington [1] and Ferrarotti et al. [14]. The class ALIN is characterized by Clote [11], AC^0 by Clote [10] and LINH by Bel'tyukov [5], although their formulations differ substantially from ours.[5] The citations in the table are for characterizations that are similar to the ones found in the respective reference. The top row represents how inputs are encoded.

Table 1. Summary of results

	Paths	Balanced trees
$[\mathcal{I}; \mathsf{SC}, \mathsf{vpSR}]$	LIN [6]	$\supseteq$ LOG
$[\mathcal{I}; \mathsf{SC}, \mathsf{vpSR}, \mathsf{DR}]$	LINH	$\supseteq$ LOGH $=$ AC^0
$[\mathcal{I}; \mathsf{SC}, \mathsf{vpSR}, \mathsf{AR}]$	ALIN	ALOG $=$ NC^1 [7]
$[\mathcal{I}; \mathsf{SC}, \mathsf{pSR}]$	P [3]	$\supseteq$ POLYLOG
$[\mathcal{I}; \mathsf{SC}, \mathsf{pSR}, \mathsf{DR}]$	PH [20]	$\supseteq$ POLYLOGH $= q$AC^0
$[\mathcal{I}; \mathsf{SC}, \mathsf{pSR}, \mathsf{AR}]$	PSPACE [18]	POLYLOGSPACE [7]

3.1 The Base Classes

Theorem 1. *When inputs are encoded as paths,* $[\mathcal{I}; \mathsf{SC}, \mathsf{vpSR}] = $ LIN.

Proof. "$\Leftarrow$"
From Theorem 10 of Bloch [6], LIN is characterized by the closure of functions that are included in Definition 1, under the schemes SC and *simultaneous very safe input sorted recursion on notation* (Definitions 6 and 7 of [6]). Since we have $*$ and L and R as initial functions, we have a recursion-free way of encoding and decoding, whence the *simultaneous recursion* of Bloch can be simulated by our vpSR. The inclusion thus follows.
    "$\Rightarrow$"

The only function in Definition 1 that is not in Definition 7 of [6] is our concatenation $*$, which can be used as a step function in vpSR. However, by Lemma 1, even if $*$ is used as a step function to define f through vpSR, the height of the outputs of f remain linear. If f just outputs the generated word, then a Turing machine can ignore the recursion process and output "accept", since the generated word is necessarily different from 0. Otherwise, suppose that the word is used by another function f'. To use the tree generated by f, f' will have to specify a path to navigate, *a priori*, so a linear time machine just has to generate a linear sized part of the output of f.

---

[5] Bel'tyukov characterizes the rudimentary predicates [25], which coincide with LINH [26].

From the above characterization and the remarks made in the beginning of Sect. 2.3 regarding the notion of *time* in recursion theory, we conjecture that changing the encoding of the inputs from paths to balanced trees yields a characterization of LOG. We show that at least one of the inclusions holds.

Theorem 2. *When inputs are encoded as balanced trees,* LOG $\subseteq$ [$\mathcal{I}$; SC, vpSR].

Proof. First, we discuss how to simulate the querying process of a RATM. Recall that RATMs are assumed to be supplied with the size of the input in an auxiliary tape. We do not need such an assumption as, when an input x is a balanced tree, of size 2^k, we can use vpSR to write a word of size k, by concatenating 1 with itself until x is 0 or 1. This takes a logarithmic number of steps in the size of x. Then, when a position m is queried (in binary) and has size k (otherwise we can padd it with 0s to the left) we can read it from left to right, interpreting each 0 as applying L to x and each 1 as applying R. This will lead vpSR to the mth position of x (starting the count at 0).[6]

Now, similarly to Lemma 17 of [6], we can construct a function in [$\mathcal{I}$; SC, vpSR] that simulates the evolution of a k-tape LOG machine M. We use a $2k+1$ tuple $\langle l_1, r_1, \ldots, l_k, r_k, q \rangle$ to represent the content of each tape to the left and right of the reading head and the state of the machine and use the recursion-free pairing and unpairing to simulate simultaneous recursion of $2k+1$ functions, each outputting the next value of the respective entry in the tuple, as a single function F. When the computation ends, we just output 0 or 1, depending on the state of the machine.

The converse inclusion is unknown. One of the issues that emerges is that, while in the recursion-theoretic setting, the operation $f(x;) = h(x, x;)$ can be done in one step, for models as Turing machines, copying the input to a new tape or duplicating the input requires linear time, which exceeds the bounds of the desired class.

Likewise, adapting from [3] to our tree-like data structure, and owing to Lemma 2, we have that [$\mathcal{I}$; SC, pSR] = P, when inputs are encoded as paths. Similarly, we also conjecture that [$\mathcal{I}$; SC, pSR] = POLYLOG when inputs are encoded as balanced trees.

3.2 Bounded Alternation

We consider the effect of the operator DR using the ideas from the characterization of NP and PH from Oitavem [19, 20].

Theorem 3. *Let* [$\mathcal{I}$; $\mathcal{O}$] *characterize a time complexity class* $\mathcal{C}$, *with outputs whose height respects the class's bounds. Then,* [$\mathcal{I}$; $\mathcal{O}$, DR] *characterizes* $\mathcal{C}$H.

---

[6] For example, suppose that 01 is written on the query tape to recover the 1st digit in the word 0100 (recall that we start the count at 0). The 0 indicates that the symbol is on the left half of the word and the 1 that it is on the right half of the subtree obtained.

Proof. "⇒"
The proof proceeds by induction. Consider the only complicated case, which is when $f \in [\mathcal{I}; \mathcal{O}, \text{DR}]$ is defined with DR from base function g, which, by induction hypothesis, can be implemented by an ATM M' in a bounded number of alternations k. Consider the ATM M that starts by "guessing" as many nondeterministic bits as those generated by f through DR and then implements M'. As M' performs k alternation, M performs at most $k+1$. Regarding time, since functions in $[\mathcal{I}; \mathcal{O}]$ only output trees with a height that respects the time bound of $\mathcal{C}$, the depth of the computation tree generated by DR also respects that same bound, whence the inclusion follows.
    "⇐"

Consider an ATM M that runs in the desired time bound, making a fixed number of alternations and then running a deterministic function respecting the time bound of $\mathcal{C}$, which can be expressed as function in $[\mathcal{I}; \mathcal{O}]$. Since M must have some fixed criteria for its fixed alternation, which we can assume happen in the beginning of the computation, we just need to use composition and DR to represent its alternations. The scheme DR represents an OR, and composing DR with a negation function represents an AND. This creates a function with a fixed number of nested DR schemes, which represent the maximum number of alternations made by M.

If $[\mathcal{I}; \mathcal{O}]$ is only known to contain a complexity class $\mathcal{C}$, then the second part of the proof still holds, so we get that $[\mathcal{I}; \mathcal{O}, \text{DR}]$ contains $\mathcal{C}\text{H}$.

3.3 Unbounded Alternation

We consider the effect of the operator AR using the ideas from the characterization of FPSPACE given in Oitavem [18]. As we will see, the presence of AR yields alternating classes, in our case ALIN, ALOG, AP and APOLYLOG, of which the latter two, from [9], equal PSPACE and POLYLOGSPACE, respectively.

Theorem 4. *Let $[\mathcal{I}; \mathcal{O}]$ characterize a time complexity class $\mathcal{C}$, with outputs whose height respects the class's bounds. Then, $[\mathcal{I}; \mathcal{O}, \text{AR}]$ characterizes AC.*

Proof. "⇒"
The only relevant case is when AR is used. Suppose that f is define by AR from base function g and test function h, both of which can be simulated by an ATM in the desired time bound. Then, f can be simulated by the ATM which, every time a recursive step of AR is made, "guesses" the answer of h and continues the simulation of f with an OR or AND state, depending on the guessed answer, until it reaches the base case. Here, it simulates h to remove the wrong "guesses" and simulates g to compute the output of f.
    "⇐"

Consider an ATM that runs in the time bound of $\mathcal{C}$ and suppose that the computation in the leaves, when there are no more alternations, can be represented as a function in $[\mathcal{I}; \mathcal{O}]$. Since the ATM respects the bounds of $\mathcal{C}$, it can be simulated for a specific path (choice of non-deterministic bits) with a function in $[\mathcal{I}; \mathcal{O}]$, so we consider the test function h, which, receiving a path p, simulates the ATM for that path, returning a value that determines the type of state of the ATM, which is then implemented through AR.

Analogously to the remark after the proof of Theorem 3, if $[\mathcal{I}; \mathcal{O}]$ contains a complexity class $\mathcal{C}$, then $[\mathcal{I}; \mathcal{O}, \mathsf{AR}]$ contains $A\mathcal{C}$.

4   Conclusion and Future Research

We conclude with a discussion on results involving some of the complexity classes we presented and directions for future research involving the effect of "small" perturbation to the operators that define them.

First, it is known that, in the multi-tape Turing machine model, LIN $\subsetneq$ LINH and LIN $\subsetneq$ ALIN [21]. Recovering these results in the recursion-theoretic setting would raise the following question: what happens when we replace vpSR with pSR (allowing normal inputs in recursion to be received on the normal side), thus comparing P with PH and PSPACE, instead of LIN with LINH and ALIN?

For the logarithmic classes, one of the inclusions in most of our characterizations is still unknown to hold, which is due to the difficulty in manipulating inputs on logarithmically bounded RATMs. Take the example of the proposed characterization of LOG. We believe that it is precise because, due to Bloch [7], the class obtained characterizes, at most, *alternating* logarithmic time, and yet there seems to be no need for alternation to compute the constructed schemes. In particular, there is no need for alternation in its linear counterpart, where the only difference is the way in which inputs are encoded.

Should our proposed characterizations be correct, there are two further interesting questions to explore. First, it is known that LOGH and POLYLOGH are proper hierarchies [13,24]. Recovering these results in the recursion-theoretic setting would raise the following question: what happens when we change the encoding of inputs as balanced trees to paths? This recovers the open questions of whether LINH and PH are proper hierarchies. Secondly, it is known that LOGH is strictly contained in ALOG [8]. Recovering this result in the recursion-theoretic setting would raise the following question: what happens when we change the encoding of inputs as balanced trees to paths? This recovers the open question of whether LINH is strictly contained in ALIN.

We thus propose an open problem and a research program. First, the converse inclusion in the characterization of LOG and POLYLOG is still unknown. Proving it holds would imply tight bounds on all result stated in Table 1. The research program is divided in two parts: first, study the possibility of recovering the above mentioned known results in the recursion-theoretic setting; then, explore the effects that modification on the operators, or to how inputs are encoded, have on the proofs.

This program is aimed at understanding the limitations of proof methods in recursion theory. Each operator of a class defines its own axis (called the δ axis in [4]), when one considers functions that are constructed by successive nestings of the operator. Bellantoni and Oitavem [4] gave an example where this δ axis forms a proper hierarchy, so a natural question is to explore the classes where one can show that this is the case. Moreover, their diagonalization argument does not seem to depend on how inputs are encoded, which draws interest to the connections between the logarithmic and polynomial setting.

We have emphasised the characterization of classes for which separation results are known, because they give us examples where we already know that a separation can, in theory, be proven. And if the proof no longer holds under the changes we mentioned, can we explain why? Is there a specific point where the proof breaks down, which reveals, e.g., the contradictory relativizations underlying these classes? To understand this is the goal of future research.

Acknowledgments. This work was funded by national funds through the FCT – Fundação para a Ciência e a Tecnologia, I.P., under the scope of the projects UIDB/00297/2020 (https://doi.org/10.54499/UIDB/00297/2020) and UIDP/00297/2020 (https://doi.org/10.54499/UIDP/00297/2020) (Center for Mathematics and Applications) and the FCT scholarship, reference 2022.10596.BD.

I am grateful to Isabel Oitavem for many helpful comments and to the anonymous referees for their suggestions.

Disclosure of Interests. The author has no competing interests to declare that are relevant to the content of this article.

Appendix

We have used the work of Bloch, in [6], to justify the lower bound for our characterization of LIN (Theorem 1), and in [7], to justify the upper bound for our characterization of ALOG and POLYLOGSPACE. In this Appendix, we discuss the relationship between our setting and his, to facilitate the comparison between the two perspectives.

Regarding LIN, all the base functions in Definition 7 of [6] have a corresponding function in our Definition 1, when inputs are encoded as paths. For example, the function $Half(;x) = \lfloor \frac{x}{2} \rfloor$ there corresponds to our L, when inputs are encoded as paths. The difference then is that Bloch uses *simultaneous recursion* instead of our regular recursion scheme. However, since we have $*$, L and R as initial functions, we can replace a system of equations defining $f_1, \ldots, f_k$ by a single recursion scheme, defining $f = f_1 * \cdots * f_k$ with a step function which uses L and R to extract each f_i from $f_1 * \cdots * f_k$, applies to it its respective step function, and encodes the result again.

Regarding ALOG and POLYLOGSPACE, rewriting from our tree-like data structure to binary inputs, all the functions from our Definition 1 are in the base class of [7] (Definition 1 there). For example, when inputs are encoded as balanced trees, our $*$ corresponds to the concatenation function and our L and R to the "front half" and "back half" functions. Definitions 6 and 7 of [7] contain the schemes of safe and very safe *divide and conquer* recursion, which allow a function to call itself on the back and front halves of the input word. In our data structure, this corresponds to, without a path parameter, allowing a function on input $u * v$ to call itself on input u and v, which generalizes our path-recursion schemes, where the function has to choose which path to follow. This means that, when inputs are encoded as balanced trees, our schemes pSR and vpSR can be simulated by the respective safe and very safe forms of *divide and conquer* recursion. Thus, our classes $[\mathcal{I}; \mathsf{SC}, \mathsf{vpSR}]$ and $[\mathcal{I}; \mathsf{SC}, \mathsf{pSR}]$ characterize, at most, ALOG and APOLYLOG, respectively (Theorems 14 and 24 of [7]). As AR introduces only the power of *alternation* in a class (see Theorem 4), and ALOG and APOLYLOG are already alternating classes, we get that $[\mathcal{I}; \mathsf{SC}, \mathsf{vpSR}, \mathsf{AR}]$ and $[\mathcal{I}; \mathsf{SC}, \mathsf{pSR}, \mathsf{AR}]$ also characterize, at most, ALOG and APOLYLOG, respectively, which is the desired upper bound.

References

1. Barrington, D.A.M.: Quasipolynomial size circuit classes. In: 1992 Seventh Annual Structure in Complexity Theory Conference, pp. 86–87. IEEE Computer Society (1992)
2. Barrington, D.A.M., Immerman, N., Straubing, H.: On uniformity within NC^1. J. Comput. Syst. Sci. **41**(3), 274–306 (1990)
3. Bellantoni, S., Cook, S.: A new recursion-theoretic characterization of the poly-time functions. In: Proceedings of the Twenty-Fourth Annual ACM Symposium on Theory of Computing, pp. 283–293 (1992)
4. Bellantoni, S., Oitavem, I.: Separating NC along the δ axis. Theor. Comput. Sci. **318**(1–2), 57–78 (2004)
5. Bel'tyukov, A.P.: A machine description and the hierarchy of initial Grzegorczyk classes. J. Sov. Math. **20**, 2280–2289 (1982)
6. Bloch, S.: Alternating function classes within P. Technical report, University of Manitoba Computer Science Department (1992)
7. Bloch, S.: Functional characterizations of uniform log-depth and polylog-depth circuit families. In: Computational Complexity Conference, pp. 193–206. Citeseer (1992)
8. Buss, S.R.: The graph of multiplication is equivalent to counting. Inf. Process. Lett. **41**(4), 199–201 (1992)
9. Chandra, A.K., Kozen, D.C., Stockmeyer, L.J.: Alternation. J. ACM **28**(1), 114–133 (1981)
10. Clote, P.: Sequential, machine-independent characterizations of the parallel complexity classes AlogTIME, AC^k, NC^k and NC, pp. 49–69. Birkhäuser Boston, Boston, MA (1990)
11. Clote, P.: Nondeterministic stack register machines. Theor. Comput. Sci. **178**(1–2), 37–76 (1997)
12. Clote, P.: Computation models and function algebras. In: Studies in Logic and the Foundations of Mathematics, vol. 140, pp. 589–681. Elsevier (1999)
13. Ferrarotti, F., González, S., Schewe, K.-D., Turull-Torres, J.M.: Proper hierarchies in polylogarithmic time and absence of complete problems. In: Herzig, A., Kontinen, J. (eds.) FoIKS 2020. LNCS, vol. 12012, pp. 90–105. Springer, Cham (2020). https://doi.org/10.1007/978-3-030-39951-1_6

14. Ferrarotti, F., González, S., Schewe, K.D., Turull-Torres, J.M.: The polylog-time hierarchy captured by restricted second-order logic. In: 2018 20th International Symposium on Symbolic and Numeric Algorithms for Scientific Computing (SYNASC), pp. 133–140. IEEE (2018)

15. Ferrarotti, F., González, S., Torres, J.M.T., Van den Bussche, J., Virtema, J.: Descriptive complexity of deterministic polylogarithmic time and space. J. Comput. Syst. Sci. **119**, 145–163 (2021)

16. Leivant, D.: A foundational delineation of computational feasibility. In: Proceedings 1991 Sixth Annual IEEE Symposium on Logic in Computer Science, pp. 2–11. IEEE Computer Society (1991)

17. Leivant, D.: A characterization of NC by tree recurrence. In: Proceedings 39th Annual Symposium on Foundations of Computer Science, pp. 716–724. IEEE (1998)

18. Oitavem, I.: Characterizing PSPACE with pointers. Math. Log. Q. **54**(3), 323–329 (2008)

19. Oitavem, I.: A recursion-theoretic approach to NP. Ann. Pure Appl. Log. **162**(8), 661–666 (2011)

20. Oitavem, I.: The polynomial hierarchy of functions and its levels. Theor. Comput. Sci. **900**, 25–34 (2022)

21. Paul, W.J., Pippenger, N., Szemeredi, E., Trotter, W.T.: On determinism versus non-determinism and related problems. In: 24th Annual Symposium on Foundations of Computer Science (SFCS 1983), pp. 429–438 (1983)

22. Regan, K.W., Vollmer, H.: Gap-languages and log-time complexity classes. Theor. Comput. Sci. **188**(1), 101–116 (1997)

23. Simmons, H.: The realm of primitive recursion. Arch. Math. Log. **27**(2), 177–188 (1988)

24. Sipser, M.: Borel sets and circuit complexity. In: Proceedings of the Fifteenth Annual ACM Symposium on Theory of Computing, pp. 61–69 (1983)

25. Smullyan, R.M.: Theory of Formal Systems. Princeton University Press, Princeton (1961)

26. Wrathall, C.: Rudimentary predicates and relative computation. SIAM J. Comput. **7**(2), 194–209 (1978)

Computable Structure Theory of Partial Combinatory Algebras

Ekaterina B. Fokina[1]([⊠])[iD] and Sebastiaan A. Terwijn[2][iD]

[1] Institute of Discrete Mathematics and Geometry, Technische Universität Wien,
Vienna, Austria
ekaterina.fokina@tuwien.ac.at
[2] Department of Mathematics, Radboud University Nijmegen,
Nijmegen, The Netherlands
terwijn@math.ru.nl

Abstract. We discuss the complexity of the class of countable partial combinatory algebras, coded as c.e. sets. We prove a completeness result, and also discuss the complexity of the isomorphism problem.

Keywords: partial structures · partial combinatory algebra · computably enumerable structures · index set · isomorphism problem

1 Introduction

In this paper we study the computability-theoretic properties of partial combinatory algebras (pcas). These are abstract models of computation with a partial application operator. In Sect. 2 we define and discuss pcas, including their use in constructive mathematics. The standard approach to measure the algorithmic complexity of structures is to identify a structure with its atomic diagram viewed as a subset of the natural numbers through a fixed Gödel numbering. We then call a structure *computable* (possibly, relatively to an oracle A) if its atomic diagram is a computable (relative to A) subset of ω. The main body of work in computable structure theory has been done using this framework, see e.g. the overview [17]. In particular, the definition implies that the structures under consideration are total. Moreover, functions are often simply identified with their graphs and the vocabulary is, thus, often restricted to contain only relational symbols.

Partial structures, that is, structures with partial operations, have received relatively little attention. In this paper we study one example of such partial structures, namely, partial combinatory algebras (pcas), and we discuss their complexity as a class of structures, as well as the isomorphism problem for pcas. The main definition we are concerned with is that of a computably enumerable (c.e.) structure. Notice that in the literature there are two independent

The work of Fokina was supported by the Austrian Science Fund FWF through the project P 36781.

approaches to define such structures. One of them is motivated by problems in algebra, in particular by word problems for groups and semigroups since the times of the Novikov-Boone theorem [9,35]. For an overview of earlier results with the focus on algebra see [26] and on the computability-theoretic aspects see [43]. In this setting c.e. structures are also called *positive*. The modern machinery has been developed in papers by Khoussainov and co-authors [24,27,28] by looking at the word problems as equivalence relations. Since recently, the research on the topic is being embedded into the active area of study of computably enumerable equivalence relations (ceers), e.g., in [12,13,34]. Notice that this approach still requires all the structures to be total and is, therefore, unsuitable for our needs.

In this paper we follow a different approach, as described in [10,11]. We still measure the complexity of the structure using its atomic diagram, but now we require the set to be not computable but computably enumerable. Notice that in the standard case of computable structures it makes no difference if we consider atomic or quantifier-free diagrams, and the notions are often used interchangeably. In our case it is essential that we only use atomic sentences, in particular, no negations are allowed in the atomic diagram. In this setting, it is not necessary for the functions to be total any more. Therefore, it provides a suitable way to develop computable structure theory for partial structures.

Our notation from computability theory is mostly standard. For unexplained notions we refer to Odifreddi [36] or Soare [45]. In particular ω denotes the natural numbers, φ_e the e-th partial computable (p.c.) function, and $W_e = \mathrm{dom}(\varphi_e)$ the e-th computably enumerable (c.e.) set. We let $\langle \cdot, \cdot \rangle$ denote an effective pairing function. Our notation for partial combinatory algebra follows van Oosten [40].

2   Partial Combinatory Algebras

We start with a quick review of the basic definitions from partial combinatory algebra. A *partial applicative structure* is a set $\mathcal{A}$ together with a partial map $\cdot$ from $\mathcal{A} \times \mathcal{A}$ to $\mathcal{A}$. We usually write ab instead of $a \cdot b$, and think of this as 'a applied to b'. If this is defined we denote this by $ab\downarrow$. By convention, application associates to the left, so we write abc instead of $(ab)c$. *Terms* over $\mathcal{A}$ are built from elements of $\mathcal{A}$, variables, and application. If t_1 and t_2 are terms then so is $t_1 t_2$. If $t(x_1, \ldots, x_n)$ is a term with variables x_i, and $a_1, \ldots, a_n \in \mathcal{A}$, then $t(a_1, \ldots, a_n)$ is the term obtained by substituting the a_i for the x_i. For closed terms (i.e. terms without variables) t and s, we write $t \simeq s$ if either both are undefined, or both are defined and equal. Here application is *strict* in the sense that for $t_1 t_2$ to be defined, it is required that both t_1, t_2 are defined. We say that an element $f \in \mathcal{A}$ is *total* if $fa\downarrow$ for every $a \in \mathcal{A}$.

Definition 2.1. *A partial applicative structure $\mathcal{A}$ is called combinatory complete if for any term $t(x_1, \ldots, x_n, x)$, $n \geqslant 0$, with free variables $x_1, \ldots, x_n, x$, there exists $b \in \mathcal{A}$ such that for all $a_1, \ldots, a_n, a \in \mathcal{A}$,*

(i) $ba_1 \cdots a_n \downarrow$,
(ii) $ba_1 \cdots a_n a \simeq t(a_1, \ldots, a_n, a)$.

A partial applicative structure $\mathcal{A}$ is a partial combinatory algebra (pca) if it is combinatory complete.

The following theorem characterizes combinatory completeness in a convenient way by the existence of combinators k and s, precisely as in the lambda calculus and classical combinatory algebra (where all applications are total). In [40] it is stated that the theorem is "essentially due to Feferman [15]." (The cautious formulation is needed because the presentation in [15] is not completely precise.)

Theorem 2.2. (Feferman) *A partial applicative structure $\mathcal{A}$ is a pca if and only if it has elements k and s with the following properties for all $a, b, c \in \mathcal{A}$:*

– *k is total and $kab = a$,*
– *$sab\downarrow$ and $sabc \simeq ac(bc)$.*

In our discussion of pcas, we restrict attention to countable pcas. A pca can be trivial, that is, have only one element a, with application defined as $a \cdot a = a$. In this case $k = s = a$. All nontrivial pcas are infinite and necessarily have $k \neq s$. In the following, we assume that all our pcas are nontrivial.

The standard example of a pca is Kleene's first model $\mathcal{K}_1$, with application on the natural numbers defined by

$$n \cdot m = \varphi_n(m).$$

This is the setting of classical computability theory.

Another important example of a pca is defined on Baire space ω^ω. Without specifying the precise coding, application $\alpha \cdot \beta$ in this model can be informally described by applying the continuous functional with code α to the real β. This model, from Kleene and Vesley [29], is usually referred to as Kleene's second model $\mathcal{K}_2$. An interesting variant of $\mathcal{K}_2$, called the van Oosten model, is obtained by extending the domain to include partial functions, cf. [39]. Now $\mathcal{K}_2$ is uncountable, whereas in this paper we will only consider countable pcas. However, restricting attention to computable sequences gives a pca $\mathcal{K}_2^{\text{eff}}$. Similarly, restricting to X-computable sequences gives a pca $\mathcal{K}_2^X$, and this is a countable pca for every X.

Many other examples of pcas, such as Scott's graph model from [42], can be found in the literature. Scott's model is closely related to the enumeration degrees in computability theory, cf. Odifreddi [37]. Not surprisingly, there is a close connection with lambda calculus and combinatory algebra, see Barendregt [4]. In fact, the lambda calculus itself is an example of a pca. For the connection with constructive mathematics, see e.g. Beeson [5], Troelstra and van Dalen [46], McCarty [32] (for constructive set theory), and Frittaion and Rathjen [18]. Many of the uncountable examples also have restrictions that yield interesting countable pcas.

Most commonly, in computable structure theory one considers computable representations of structures. We note, however, that a pca never has a computable representation, cf. Barendregt [4, 5.1.15]. We can however consider countable pcas that can be represented by c.e. sets, which is a more natural fit anyway given that we are dealing with partial structures.

Given a pca $\mathcal{A}$ on ω in which the relation $a \cdot b \downarrow = c$ is c.e., we can represent $\mathcal{A}$ by the c.e. set

$$W = \{\langle a, b, c \rangle \mid a \cdot b \downarrow = c\}.$$

The question then arises what the complexity is of the set of indices of c.e. sets that encode pcas in this way.

Definition 2.3. *The index set of c.e. pcas is defined as*

$$I(\mathrm{pca}) = \{e \mid W_e \text{ is a pca}\}.$$

Here, as well as in Sect. 4, we use the notation from Goncharov and Knight [21], who denoted by $I(\mathbb{K})$ the set of indices of computable structures in a class $\mathbb{K}$, and by $E(\mathbb{K})$ the corresponding isomorphism problem. Note that for classes $\mathbb{K}$ of total structures, the set $I(\mathbb{K})$ always has complexity at least Π_2^0, because to say that a partial computable function φ_e (such as the operations in the structure) is always defined already makes $I(\mathbb{K})$ Π_2^0-hard. For classes of partial structures, however, this is no longer the case.

3   The Complexity of the Class of Pcas

Using the definition of pcas as applicative structures that are combinatorially complete (Definition 2.1), we obtain Π_4^0 as an upper bound for the complexity of the index set $I(\mathrm{pca})$. Namely, for every term $t(x_1, \ldots, x_{n+1})$ there has to be an element $b \in \mathcal{A}$ such that for all $a_1, \ldots, a_{n+1} \in \mathcal{A}$, $ba_1 \cdots a_n \downarrow$ and $ba_1 \cdots a_{n+1} \simeq t(a_1, \ldots, a_{n+1})$. However, using Feferman's Theorem 2.2 about the existence of combinators yields a better definition, saving one quantifier.

Proposition 3.1. $I(\mathrm{pca}) \in \Sigma_3^0$.

Proof. This is a straightforward computation, using the existence of k and s from Theorem 2.2. Namely, W_e codes a pca if

$$\exists k, s \, \forall a, b, c \, (kab \downarrow = a \wedge sab \downarrow \wedge sabc \simeq ac(bc)).$$

Now $kab \downarrow = a$ and $sab \downarrow$ are easily seen to be Σ_1^0 statements, as by definition $xy \downarrow = z$ if $\langle x, y, z \rangle \in W_e$. Furthermore, $sabc \simeq ac(bc)$ is Π_2^0, because for all t both sides are undefined at stage t, or there is a stage t' that both become defined and are equal. Thus we see that the condition of Theorem 2.2 for a pca applied to W_e is a Σ_3^0 statement.

Theorem 3.2. $I(\mathrm{pca})$ *is* Σ_3^0-*complete.*

Proof. Fix an arbitrary Σ_3^0 set B, and let R be a computable predicate such that
$$x \in B \iff \exists i \forall y \exists z \, R(x, i, y, z)$$
for every x. For a given x, we call i *infinitary* if $\forall y \exists z R(x, i, y, z)$, and finitary otherwise. We construct for every x a c.e. partial applicative structure $\mathcal{A}$, depending on x in a computable way, such that if there is an infinitary i then $\mathcal{A}$ is a pca, and if all i are finitary then $\mathcal{A}$ is not a pca. The first infinitary row i, if there is any, will determine the structure of $\mathcal{A}$ as a pca. This will be some alternative coding of $\mathcal{K}_1$. The universe of $\mathcal{A}$ is ω, which we interpret as the set of all coded pairs $\{\langle i, a \rangle \mid i, a \in \omega\}$. For a fixed i, we refer to $\{\langle i, a \rangle \mid a \in \omega\}$ as the i-th row. Application in $\mathcal{A}$ is defined by $\langle i, a \rangle \cdot m = \varphi_e(m)$, where e is determined by i, a, and the construction. If i is the smallest infinitary row then we will have $\langle i, a+t \rangle \cdot m = \varphi_a(m)$ for some t and all a. Furthermore, in this case all $\langle j, b \rangle$ with $j \neq i$ will define only finite functions, i.e. $\langle j, b \rangle \cdot m \downarrow$ for only finitely many m.

During the construction, we will monitor which rows appear to be infinitary using a length function, defined as follows:
$$l(i, s) = \max_{y \leqslant s} (\forall y' < y)(\exists z \leqslant s) \, R(x, i, y', z).$$

In particular we have $l(i, 0) = 0$. Thus $l(i, s)$ measures how much progress has been made at stage s towards i being infinitary. Note that i is infinitary if and only if $\lim_s l(i, s) = \infty$. We call a row i *expansionary* at stage $s > 0$ if $l(i, s) > l(i, s-1)$.

If a row j is *initialized* at stage s of the construction, this means that all elements $\langle j, a \rangle$ with $a < s$ will remain finite functions, i.e. the application $\langle j, a \rangle \cdot m$ will remain undefined for all $m \geqslant s$.

Construction. At stage $s = 0$ all applications in $\mathcal{A}$ are undefined. At stage $s > 0$, let $i < s$ be the smallest expansionary row. (If no such i exists, do nothing and proceed to the next stage.) Initialize all rows $j > i$. Let t be the last stage at which i was initialized (and $t = 0$ if no such t exists). For all a with $a + t \leqslant s$ and all $m \leqslant s$, we let the definitions of $\langle i, a + t \rangle \cdot m$ progress, that is, we define
$$\langle i, a + t \rangle \cdot m = \varphi_{a,s}(m) \tag{1}$$
if the latter is defined. (If it is undefined, it may still become defined at a later stage.) Note that this definition is consistent with earlier stages of the construction, namely if $\langle i, a \rangle \cdot m$ was defined at some stage $s' < t$ then $a \leqslant s' < t$, and if $\langle i, a + t \rangle \cdot m$ was defined at stage s' with $t \leqslant s' < s$ then it is equal to $\varphi_{a,s'}(m)$, which equals $\varphi_{a,s}(m)$. This ends the construction.

If all rows i are finitary, then for each i, after some stage of the construction, the only expansionary rows are larger than i, and hence no further applications of the form $\langle i, a \rangle \cdot m$ are defined. Hence all elements $\langle i, a \rangle$ of $\mathcal{A}$ define only finite functions. This implies that $\mathcal{A}$ is not a pca, because the combinator k (which $\mathcal{A}$ needs to have by Theorem 2.2 in order to be a pca) is a total function.

If, on the other hand, there is at least one infinitary row i, we argue that $\mathcal{A}$ is a pca. Namely, let i be the smallest infinitary row. Then every row $j < i$

is expansionary at only finitely many stages, hence i is initialized only finitely often. Let t be the last stage at which i is initialized in the construction (and $t = 0$ if this never happened at all). Then there are infinitely many stages after t at which i is expansionary, and hence the definition (1) applies, so that we have for all $a, m \in \omega$,

$$\langle i, a + t \rangle \cdot m = \varphi_a(m). \tag{2}$$

We show that this implies that $\mathcal{A}$ is a pca. Instead of showing the existence of the combinators k and s, we prove the combinatory completeness from Definition 2.1 directly. Fix a term $t(x_1, \ldots, x_n, x)$. We have to show that an element $b \in \mathcal{A}$ as in Definition 2.1 exists. Note that since the construction is computable, the application in $\mathcal{A}$ is c.e. Hence the term $t(x_1, \ldots, x_n, x)$ defines a partial computable function, so that it suffices to prove the following claim:

Claim. For every partial computable function $\varphi_e(x_1, \ldots, x_n, x)$ there exists $b \in \mathcal{A}$ such that for all $a_1, \ldots, a_n, a \in \mathcal{A}$, $ba_1 \cdots a_n \downarrow$ and $ba_1 \cdots a_n a \simeq \varphi_e(a_1, \ldots, a_n, a)$.

We prove this claim by induction on n. For every a define $h(a) = \langle i, a + t \rangle$. By (2) we have $h(a) \cdot m = \varphi_a(m)$, so we may think of $h(a)$ as a code in $\mathcal{A}$ for φ_a.

For $n = 0$ we can take $b = h(e)$. Indeed we then have

$$ba = \langle i, e + t \rangle \cdot a = \varphi_e(a)$$

as required.

For $n > 0$ we can apply the usual s-m-n-theorem for the standard numbering of the p.c. functions φ_e to obtain:

$$\varphi_e(a_1, \ldots, a_n, a) = \varphi_{S_1^n(e, a_1, \ldots, a_n)}(a)$$
$$= h(S_1^n(e, a_1, \ldots, a_n)) \cdot a. \tag{3}$$

Since S_1^n is primitive recursive, $h(S_1^n(e, a_1, \ldots, a_n))$ is a total computable function of $a_1, \ldots, a_n$, so by the induction hypothesis there exists $b \in \mathcal{A}$ such that $ba_1 \cdots a_{n-1} \downarrow$ and $ba_1 \cdots a_n \simeq h(S_1^n(e, a_1, \ldots, a_n))$. Because the right-hand side is total, we also have $ba_1 \cdots a_n \downarrow$, and from (3) we see $ba_1 \cdots a_n a \simeq \varphi_e(a_1, \ldots, a_n, a)$.

This concludes the proof of the claim, and hence of the theorem.

Note that in the proof of Theorem 3.2, in the case that there is an infinitary row i, the applicative structure $\mathcal{A}$ is indeed a pca, and hence has combinators k and s. However, to know these elements we need the knowledge of the last stage t at which row i is initialized, and this is not known until after the construction.

4   The Isomorphism Problem for Pcas

The isomorphism problem for computable structures has been studied extensively in the literature. For example, one may consider the complexity of isomorphisms, as in Ash [2]. Or one can simply ask which pairs of indices represent classically computable structures. The paper by Goncharov and Knight [21] collects a number of such results, some of which are folklore and not properly recorded previously. We take this approach here for pcas.

There are several ways to define what it means that two pcas are isomorphic. Directly related to this, several notions of embeddability of pcas have been studied in the literature. For example, one can require that only the structure of applications is preserved, or that also the choice of the combinators k and s (that exist in any pca by Theorem 2.2) as special elements of the pca is preserved. The difference is in whether we want to consider k and s are part of the signature of pcas or not. For example, Zoethout [47, p33] explicitly says that k and s are not taken to be part of the structure of a pca. The weaker notion of embedding, without k and s, was studied in Bethke [7], Asperti and Ciabattoni [3], Shafer and Terwijn [44], and Golov and Terwijn [20]. The stronger notion, with k and s preserved, was studied in the context of completions of pcas, see e.g. Bethke, Klop, and de Vrijer [8]. An even weaker notion of embedding, using the notion of applicative morphism, was introduced in Longley [30], see also Longley and Normann [31].

Below we will use the weaker notion of isomorphism, where k and s are not part of the signature. Thus we have the following definition.

Definition 4.1. *For given pcas $\mathcal{A}$ and $\mathcal{B}$, an injection $f : \mathcal{A} \to \mathcal{B}$ is an embedding if for all $a, a' \in \mathcal{A}$, if $aa' \downarrow$ in $\mathcal{A}$ then $f(a)f(a') \downarrow = f(aa')$ in $\mathcal{B}$. If $\mathcal{A}$ embeds into $\mathcal{B}$ in this way we write $\mathcal{A} \hookrightarrow \mathcal{B}$.*

Two pcas $\mathcal{A}$ and $\mathcal{B}$ are isomorphic, denoted by $\mathcal{A} \cong \mathcal{B}$, if there exists a bijection $f : \mathcal{A} \to \mathcal{B}$ such that for all $a, b \in \mathcal{A}$, $ab \downarrow$ if and only if $f(a)f(b) \downarrow$, and in this case

$$f(a) \cdot f(b) = f(ab).$$

Definition 4.2. *The isomorphism problem for pcas is defined by the set*

$$E(\text{pca}) = \{(i, j) \mid i, j \in I(\text{pca}) \wedge W_i \cong W_j\}.$$

Here we are interested in the complexity of the set $E(\text{pca})$. Note that membership of a pair (i, j) in $E(\text{pca})$ asks for a, not necessarily computable, isomorphism $f : W_i \to W_j$ such that

$$\langle a, b, c \rangle \in W_i \iff \langle f(a), f(b), f(c) \rangle \in W_j.$$

Since this is a Σ^1_1 statement, Σ^1_1 is an obvious upper bound for the complexity of $E(\text{pca})$. The question of course is whether this is optimal or not. At the moment, we do not know the answer to this. In the next section we prove Σ^1_1-completeness for a bigger class generalizing pcas, called order-pcas.

5   Order-pcas

An interesting generalization of pcas called *order-pcas* was introduced in van Oosten [38], and further developed in Hofstra and van Oosten [23]. These order-pcas are also discussed in [40, section 1.8], and more recently in Zoethout [47].

In this section we show the Σ_1^1-completeness of the isomorphism problem for order-pcas.

The following definition extends the notion of partial applicative structure from Sect. 2.

Definition 5.1. *An order-pas is a set $\mathcal{A}$ equipped with a partial order $\leqslant$ and a partial application operation $\cdot$ (just as for pcas we write ab instead of $a \cdot b$), such that if $ab\downarrow$, $a' \leqslant a$, and $b' \leqslant b$, then $a'b'\downarrow$ and $a'b' \leqslant ab$.*

Now an order-pca is an order-pas that satisfies a weaker version of combinatorial completeness (Definition 2.1). A version of Theorem 2.2 then holds again (cf. [40, 1.8.4]), which we take here as definition:

Definition 5.2. *An order-pas $\mathcal{A}$ is an order-pca if there exist elements $k, s \in \mathcal{A}$ such that for all $a, b, c \in \mathcal{A}$,*

- *$kab\downarrow \leqslant a$,*
- *$sab\downarrow$,*
- *if $ac(bc)\downarrow$ then $sabc\downarrow$ and $sabc \leqslant ac(bc)$.*

In [40] the reader can find examples of order-pcas. Any pca is an order-pca with the discrete order (where no two elements are related). An important example of an order-pca is the following: Given a pca $\mathcal{A}$, the power set $\mathcal{P}(\mathcal{A})$ with inclusion is an order-pca, with application $\alpha \cdot \beta = \{ab \mid a \in \alpha, b \in \beta\}$ if $ab\downarrow$ for all $a \in \alpha$ and $b \in \beta$, and $\alpha \cdot \beta$ undefined otherwise. If k and s are the combinators of $\mathcal{A}$, then $\{k\}$ and $\{s\}$ satisfy the conditions of Definition 5.2. In this case we do not have that $\{s\}\alpha\beta\gamma\downarrow$ implies that $\alpha\gamma(\beta\gamma)\downarrow$, as the choice of $c \in \gamma$ in the latter two copies of γ need not be the same, so in general $\mathcal{P}(\mathcal{A})$ need not be a pca. Indeed, it is not difficult to check that $\mathcal{P}(\mathcal{K}_1)$ is not a pca.

Note that in Zoethout [47], order-pcas are simply called pcas, which may potentially be confusing since some order-pcas have properties that are never shared by pcas. For example, in a nontrivial order-pca it is possible that $k = s$, and that the application $a \cdot b$ is associative and commutative (cf. [40, p42]), whereas none of this is possible in a pca ([40, 1.3.1]).

We can code order-pcas by c.e. sets in the same way as before: An order-pca $\mathcal{A}$ on ω in which the relation $a \cdot b\downarrow = c$ is c.e. can be represented by the c.e. set $\{\langle a, b, c\rangle \mid a \cdot b\downarrow = c\}$. We essentially omit the order in the coding for the reasons that will become clear in a moment. We now have the following analogues of Definitions 2.3 and 4.2 for order-pcas.

Definition 5.3. *The index set of c.e. order-pcas is*

$$I(\text{order-pca}) = \{e \mid W_e \text{ is an order-pca}\}.$$

We call two order-pcas $\mathcal{A}$ and $\mathcal{B}$ isomorphic, denoted by $\mathcal{A} \cong \mathcal{B}$, if there exists a bijection $f : \mathcal{A} \to \mathcal{B}$ such that for all $a, b \in \mathcal{A}$, $ab\downarrow$ if and only if $f(a)f(b)\downarrow$, and in this case

$$f(a) \cdot f(b) = f(ab).$$

The isomorphism problem for order-pcas is now defined by the set

$$E(\text{order-pca}) = \{(i,j) \mid i,j \in I(\text{order-pca}) \wedge W_i \cong W_j\}.$$

Note that the set $I(\text{order-pca})$ is Σ_3^0-complete, by the proof of Theorem 3.2.

In the definition of isomorphism of order-pcas, we do not require the isomorphism to preserve the order, as this is not needed below. (In fact, for the case that we use in the result below, it will *follow* from the application structure that the isomorphism preserves the order.) Just as in the case of pcas, we do not consider the combinators k and s as in Definition 5.2 to be part of the structure of an order-pca, so we do not require isomorphisms to preserve the choice of these special elements either. This choice, however, does not affect the truth of the following theorem.

Theorem 5.4. *$E(\text{order-pca})$ is Σ_1^1-complete.*

Proof. The theorem follows from the fact that any lower semilattice, with meet operation $\wedge$, is an order-pca, when we take $\wedge$ as application, cf. van Oosten [40, p42]. (As elements k and s we can take any elements in such a structure.) This example of order-pcas also shows that these form a much larger class than the pcas, as in the latter application is never associative or commutative. From this example it follows in particular that any linear order is an order-pca. A slight complication for the reduction below is that in Definition 5.3, isomorphisms are not required to preserve the order, only the structure of applications. For the reduction to work we need that isomorphisms automatically preserve the order in the case of linear orders. So before we proceed, we prove this first.

Let L_0 and L_1 be linear orders. We view these as order-pcas as above, with the meet operation $a \wedge b$ now simply being the minimum of a and b. Suppose that $f : L_0 \rightarrow L_1$ is an isomorphism of order-pcas. Then for all $a, b \in L_0$, $f(a) \wedge f(b) = f(a \wedge b)$. So if $a \leqslant b$ in L_0 then $f(a) \wedge f(b) = f(a)$, and hence $f(a) \leqslant f(b)$ in L_1, from which we see that f indeed preserves the order.

To prove the theorem, we use that the isomorphism problem for computable linear orders is Σ_1^1-complete. A proof of this can be found in Goncharov and Knight [21, Theorem 4.4]. We modify this proof a bit to obtain the desired result.

It is a well-known result of Kleene that the set of indices of computable non-wellfounded trees is Σ_1^1-complete, cf. Moschovakis [33, 4A.3]. So we can fix a sequence of uniformly computable trees $T_n \subseteq \omega^{<\omega}$ such that the set $\{n \mid T_n \text{ non-wellfounded}\}$ is Σ_1^1-complete.

Every tree T in $\omega^{<\omega}$ has an associated linear order $L(T)$, namely the Kleene-Brouwer order on $\omega^{<\omega}$ restricted to T, cf. Kechris [25, p12]. This order has the property that T is wellfounded if and only if $L(T)$ is a wellorder. Furthermore, if T is computable, then $L(T)$ is also computable, and we can effectively obtain an index of $L(T)$ from an index of T.

Now let T be a non-wellfounded computable tree without hyperarithmetical paths (the existence of which was also proven by Kleene). Harrison [22] proved that such trees have order type $\omega_1^{\text{CK}}(1+\eta) + \gamma$ for some computable ordinal γ.

(See also Sacks [41, p56].) This is an essential ingredient to the proof in [21]. The proof then effectively modifies the sequence T_n to a sequence T_n^* such that the following holds.

If T_n is non-wellfounded, then $L(T_n^*) \cong L(T)$ as linear orders, and hence also as order-pcas.

If T_n is wellfounded, then $L(T_n^*)$ is a wellorder, and hence $L(T_n^*) \not\cong L(T)$ as linear orders. Since isomorphisms of order-pcas preserve the order (as we showed above), it follows that also $L(T_n^*) \not\cong L(T)$ as order-pcas.

From this we conclude that the set is Σ_1^1-complete.

Using the above ideas we can show more. In recent years there has been a lot of work on *computable reducibility* of equivalence relations on ω. It has a long history as an independent notion [6,14,19], but can also be seen as a natural effective analog of Borel reducibility if we consider equivalence relations over the naturals [1]. Computable reducibility has been used to measure the complexity of isomorphism problems, seen as equivalence relation on (subsets of) ω, see [16]. There it was shown that the isomorphism of many natural classes of computable structures is Σ_1^1-complete among equivalence relations on ω under the computable reducibility. This is in particular true for linear orders.

Theorem 5.5. *[[16], Theorem 5] The isomorphism on computable linear orders is Σ_1^1-complete among equivalence relations on ω under computable reducibility.*

Corollary 5.6. *The isomorphism on c.e. order-pcas is Σ_1^1-complete among equivalence relations on ω under computable reducibility.*

References

1. Andrews, U., Belin, D., San Mauro, L.: On the structure of computable reducibility on equivalence relations of natural numbers. J. Symb. Log. **88**(3), 1038–63 (2023)
2. Ash, C.J.: Isomorphic recursive structures. In: Ershov et al. (eds.), Handbook of Recursive Mathematics, vol. 1, Studies in Logic, vol. 138, pp. 167–181. Elsevier (1998)
3. Asperti, A., Ciabattoni, A.: A sufficient condition for completability of partial combinatory algebras. J. Symb. Log. **64**(4), 1209–1214 (1997)
4. Barendregt, H.P.: The lambda calculus. In: Studies in Logic and the Foundations of Mathematics, vol. 103, 2nd edn. North-Holland, Amsterdam (1984)
5. Beeson, M.J.: Foundations of Constructive Mathematics. Springer-Verlag, Berlin, Heidelberg (1985). https://doi.org/10.1007/978-3-642-68952-9
6. Bernardi, C., Sorbi, A.: Classifying positive equivalence relations. J. Symb. Log. **48**(3), 529–538 (1983)
7. Bethke, I.: Notes on Partial Combinatory Algebras, PhD thesis, Universiteit van Amsterdam, 1988
8. Bethke, I., Klop, J.W., de Vrijer, R.: Completing partial combinatory algebras with unique head-normal forms, Technical report CS-R9544, Centrum Wiskunde & Informatica (CWI) (1995)
9. Boone, W.W.: The word problem. Ann. Math. **70**(2), 207–265 (1959)

10. Cenzer, D., Harizanov, V., Remmel, J.: Σ_1^0 and Π_1^0 equivalence structures. Ann. Pure Appl. Log. **162**, 490–503 (2011)
11. Cenzer, D., Harizanov, V., Remmel, J.: Computability-theoretic properties of injection structures. Algebra Log. **53**, 39–69 (2014)
12. Delle Rose, V., San Mauro, L., Sorbi, A.: Word problems and ceers. Math. Log. Q. **66**(3), 341–354 (2020)
13. Delle Rose, V., San Mauro, L., Sorbi, A.: Classifying word problems of finitely generated algebras via computable reducibility. Int. J. Algebra Comput. **33**(4), 751–768 (2023)
14. Ershov, Yu.: Theorie der Numerierungen I. Z. Math. Logik Grundlag. Math. **19**, 289–388 (1973)
15. Feferman, S.: A language and axioms for explicit mathematics. In: Crossley, J.N. (ed.) Algebra and Logic. LNM, vol. 450, pp. 87–139. Springer, Berlin, Heidelberg (1975). https://doi.org/10.1007/BFb0062852
16. Fokina, E., Friedman, S.D., Harizanov, V., Knight, J.F., McCoy, C., Montalbán, A.: Isomorphism relations on computable structures. J. Symb. Log. **77**(1), 122–132 (2012)
17. Fokina, E., Harizanov, V., Melnikov, A.: Computable model theory. In: Downey, R. (ed.) Turing's Legacy: Developments from Turing's Ideas in Logic, Lect. Notes Log., vol. 42, pp. 124–194 (2014)
18. Frittaion, E., Rathjen, M.: Extensional realizability for intuitionistic set theory. J. Log. Comput. **31**(2), 630–653 (2021)
19. Gao, S., Gerdes, P.: Computably enumerable equivalence relations. Stud. Log. **67**, 27–59 (2001)
20. Golov, A., Terwijn, S.A.: Embeddings between partial combinatory algebras. Notre Dame J. Form. Log. **64**(1), 129–158 (2023)
21. Goncharov, S.S., Knight, J.F.: Computable structure and non-structure theorems. Algebra Log. **41**(6), 351–373 (2002)
22. Harrison, J.: Recursive pseudo well-orderings. Trans. Am. Math. Soc. **131**(2), 526–543 (1968)
23. Hofstra, P.J.W., van Oosten, J.: Ordered partial combinatory algebras. Math. Proc. Camb. Philos. Soc. **134**, 445–463 (2003)
24. Kasymov, N.K., Khoussainov, B.M.: Finitely generated enumerable and absolutely locally finite algebras. Vychisl. Sistemy (116, Prikladn, Logika) **162**, 3–15 (1986)
25. Kechris, A.S.: Classical Descriptive Set Theory. Springer-Verlag, New York (1995). https://doi.org/10.1007/978-1-4612-4190-4
26. Kharlampovich, O., Sapir, M.: Algorithmic problems in varieties. Int. J. Algebra Comput. **5**(4–5), 379–602 (1995)
27. Khoussainov, B.: A journey to computably enumerable structures (tutorial lectures). In: Manea, F., Miller, R.G., Nowotka, D. (eds.) CiE 2018. LNCS, vol. 10936, pp. 1–19. Springer, Cham (2018). https://doi.org/10.1007/978-3-319-94418-0_1
28. Khoussainov, B., Miasnikov, A.: Finitely presented expansions of groups, semigroups. Trans. Am. Math. Soc. **366**(3), 1455–1474 (2014)
29. Kleene, S.C., Vesley, R.E.: The foundations of intuitionistic mathematics, North-Holland, 1965
30. Longley, J.: Realizability Toposes and Language Semantics, PhD thesis, University of Edinburgh, 1994
31. Longley, J., Normann, D.: Higher-Order Computability. Springer, Berlin, Heidelberg (2015). https://doi.org/10.1007/978-3-662-47992-6
32. McCarty, D.C.: Realizability and recursive set theory. Ann. Pure Appl. Log. **32**(2), 153–183 (1986)

33. Moschovakis, Y.N.: Descriptive set theory, North-Holland, 1980
34. Nies, A., Sorbi, A.: Calibrating word problems of groups via the complexity of equivalence relations. Math. Struct. Comput. Sci. **28**(3), 1–15 (2018)
35. Novikov, P.S.: On the algorithmic unsolvability of the word problem in group theory. Trudy Mat. Inst. Steklov. **44**, 143 (1955)
36. Odifreddi, P.G.: Classical recursion theory, vol. 1. In: Studies in Logic and the Foundations of Mathematics, vol. 125, North-Holland (1989)
37. Odifreddi, P.G.: Classical recursion theory, vol. 2. In: Studies in Logic and the Foundations of Mathematics, vol. 143, North-Holland, Amsterdam (1999)
38. van Oosten, J.: Extensional realizability. Ann. Pure Appl. Log. **84**, 317–349 (1997)
39. van Oosten, J.: A combinatory algebra for sequential functionals of finite type. In: Cooper, S.B., Truss, J.K. (eds.), Models and Computability, Cambridge University Press, pp. 389–406 (1999)
40. van Oosten, J.: Realizability: an introduction to its categorical side. In: Studies in Logic and the Foundations of Mathematics, vol. 152. Elsevier (2008)
41. Sacks, G.E.: Higher recursion theory. Springer-Verlag (1990)
42. Scott, D.: Lambda calculus and recursion theory (preliminary version). In: Kanger, S. (ed.), Proceedings of the Third Scandinavian Logic Symposium, Studies in Logic and the Foundations of Mathematics, vol. 82, pp. 154–193 (1975)
43. Selivanov, V.: Positive structures. In: Cooper, S.B., Goncharov, S.S. (eds.) Computability and Models, pp. 321–350. Springer, New York (2003). https://doi.org/10.1007/978-1-4615-0755-0_14
44. Shafer, P., Terwijn, S.A.: Ordinal analysis of partial combinatory algebras. J. Symb. Log. **86**(3), 1154–1188 (2021)
45. Soare, R.I.: Recursively enumerable sets and degrees, Springer-Verlag (1987)
46. Troelstra, A.S., van Dalen, D.: Constructivism in mathematics, vol. 2. In: Studies in Logic and the Foundations of Mathematics, vol. 123, North-Holland (1988)
47. Zoethout, J.: Computability models and realizability toposes, PhD thesis, Utrecht University (2022)

Hyperarithmetic Numerals

Caleb M. H. Camrud[1,2]($\boxtimes$) and Timothy H. McNicholl[1]

[1] Department of Mathematics, Iowa State University, Ames 50011, IA, USA
mcnichol@iastate.edu
[2] Philosophy Department, Brown University, Providence 02912, RI, USA
caleb_camrud@brown.edu

Abstract. Within the framework of computable infinitary continuous logic, we develop a system of hyperarithmetic numerals. These numerals are infinitary sentences in a metric language L that have the same truth value in every interpretation of L. We prove that every hyperarithmetic real can be represented by a hyperarithmetic numeral at the same level of complexity.

1 Introduction

A *numeral* is a symbolic representation of a number. The common notions which may come to mind are the Arabic digits "0" through "9", though also commonly used are the Roman "I", "V", "X", *etc.* A numeral for our purposes, however, is defined as the following.

Definition 1.1. A possibly infinitary L-sentence φ is a *numeral* for a number r if for every L-structure $\mathcal{M}$, $\varphi^{\mathcal{M}} = r$.

In classical logic, the space of truth values includes only two numbers, 0 and 1, with 0 normally interpreted as falsity and 1 as truth. As such, in classical logic, we can consider sentences yielding *contradictions* as numerals for 0 and those representing *tautologies* as numerals for 1. To give a pair of examples, for every first order structure $\mathcal{M}$,

$$(\exists x \ x \neq x)^{\mathcal{M}} = 0 \quad \text{and} \quad (\forall x \ x = x)^{\mathcal{M}} = 1.$$

But in the continuous logic of [3], the space of truth values is the full continuum $[0,1]$. A natural question arises: for which $r \in [0,1]$ is there a sentence φ such that for every L-structure $\mathcal{M}$, $\varphi^{\mathcal{M}} = r$? That is, which numbers have L-numerals?

In the original version of the continuous logic of [3], there is a connective u for every continuous mapping on $[0,1]$. Notably, such versions of continuous logic have trivial numerals: for every $r \in [0,1]$, there is a connective $\underline{u}_r$ corresponding to the constant map $u_r : [0,1] \to \{r\}$. Hence, for every structure $\mathcal{M}$ and sentence φ, $(\underline{u}_r\varphi)^{\mathcal{M}} = u_r(\varphi^{\mathcal{M}}) = r$. In subsequent formulations of this logic, however, a restricted set of connectives consisting only of $\neg$, $-$, and $\frac{1}{2}$ was used [2,4, 5]. This was done for two primary reasons. First, $\neg$ plays precisely the role of classical negation ($\neg$) and $-$ of reverse implication ($\leftarrow$), while the interpretation

L. Levy Patey et al. (Eds.): CiE 2024, LNCS 14773, pp. 277–284, 2024.
https://doi.org/10.1007/978-3-031-64309-5_22

of the $\frac{1}{2}$ operator is similarly intuitive, halving the truth-value of the formula it is attached to. Second, in [2], it was shown that after interpretation, $\neg$, $\frac{1}{2}$, and $\dot{-}$ are dense in the set of all continuous maps on $[0, 1]$. Thus finitary well-formed formulas in these connectives can approximate those in the wider set of connectives arbitrarily well. Such an approximation is, moreover, sufficient for completeness (as was shown in [5]). To avoid trivialities, this is the logic we will be investigating in this paper.

Unfortunately, with this reduced set of connectives, the set of reals with L-numerals may be very small. For example, if L is the language of metric spaces, then only the dyadic rational numbers in $[0, 1]$ have L-numerals. However, in order to expand the space of numerals, one *may* consider infinitary sentences of L in the continuous infinitary logic developed by Eagle [7]. With this expansion, it is not hard to see that every number in $[0, 1]$ has an L-numeral; in fact every such number has an infinitary Σ_1 numeral. So in order to sharpen the question, we assume L is computably numbered and focus only on *computable* infinitary formulas.

Notably, we confine our attention to the language of metric spaces L_M which consists only of a symbol $\underline{d}$ for the metric. Since L_M is a sub-language of all other metric languages (*i.e.*, signatures of metric structures as in [3]), our results apply to any computably numbered metric language. We then investigate which reals have computable infinitary L-numerals. We also investigate the relationship between the complexity of a real number and the complexity of its L-numerals. We measure the complexity of a real by the complexity of its right and left Dedekind cuts in the hyperarithmetic hierarchy.

Our main result is the following.

Theorem 1.2. *Suppose* $0 < \alpha < \omega_1^{\mathrm{CK}}$, *and let* $r \in [0, 1]$.

(1) If the right Dedekind cut of r is Σ_α^0, then r has a computable Σ_α L_M-numeral Φ. Furthermore, a code of Φ can be computed from a Σ_α^0 index of the right Dedekind cut of r.

(2) If the left Dedekind cut of r is Σ_α^0, then r has a computable Π_α L_M-numeral Φ. Furthermore, a code of Φ can be computed from a Σ_α^0 index of the left Dedekind cut of r.

By means of a straightforward transfinite induction, it follows that the converses of the statements in Theorem 1.2 hold. But before we move to the proof of Theorem 1.2, we present some background material and a few preliminary developments.

2   Background and Preliminaries

Let $\mathbb{D}$ denote the set of all dyadic rational numbers. When $s \in \mathbb{R}$, let $D^<(s)$ and $D^>(s)$ denote the left and right Dedekind cuts of s, and $D^\leq(s)$ and $D^\geq(s)$ denote the complements of the right and left Dedekind cuts of s, respectively.

2.1   Preliminaries from Continuous Logic

The connectives of continuous logic, $\neg$, $\dot{-}$, and $\frac{1}{2}$, are interpreted in a metric structure as $(\neg\varphi)^{\mathcal{M}} = 1 - \varphi^{\mathcal{M}}$, $(\varphi \dot{-} \psi)^{\mathcal{M}} = \max\{\varphi^{\mathcal{M}} - \psi^{\mathcal{M}}, 0\}$, and $(\frac{1}{2}\varphi)^{\mathcal{M}} = \frac{1}{2} \cdot \varphi^{\mathcal{M}}$. A metric structure includes, as its basic binary relation in place of $=$, a metric d. Note that $a = b$ if and only if $d(a,b) = 0$. For this and other reasons, a structure satisfies φ if and only if $\varphi^{\mathcal{M}} = 0$, rather than when $\varphi^{\mathcal{M}} = 1$ as in the classical case. Moreover, since the functions and relations of a metric structure are uniformly continuous on that structure, every function and relation symbol in continuous logic is paired with a *modulus of continuity*. In the place of the classical quantifiers $\forall$ and $\exists$, continuous logic includes sup and inf, respectively, interpreted in the natural way. The (finitary) formulas are then defined recursively, as in classical logic, and each inherits a modulus of continuity from its function and relation symbols.

We now construct two canonical sets of numerals for the dyadic rationals in $[0,1]$: $(\nu_r^{\exists})_{r\in\mathbb{D}\cap[0,1]}$ and $(\nu_r^{\forall})_{r\in\mathbb{D}\cap[0,1]}$. The latter will be universal, and the former existential. We make use of the fact that $\mathbb{D} \cap [0,1]$ is the smallest set of real numbers that contains 0 and 1 and is closed under $x \mapsto \frac{1}{2}x$ and $x \mapsto 1 - x$. Accordingly, $\nu_r^{\exists}$ and $\nu_r^{\forall}$ are defined by the following equations.

$$\nu_0^{\exists} = \inf_{x_0} \underline{d}(x_0, x_0)$$

$$\nu_0^{\forall} = \sup_{x_0} \underline{d}(x_0, x_0)$$

$$\nu_{1-r}^{\exists} = \neg\nu_r^{\forall}$$

$$\nu_{1-r}^{\forall} = \neg\nu_r^{\exists}$$

$$\nu_{r/2}^{Q} = \frac{1}{2}\nu_r^{Q}, \quad Q \in \{\forall, \exists\}$$

On a naïve reading, the construction of the infinitary formulas of continuous logic follows the classical construction. First begin with the Π_0 (resp., Σ_0) formulas as the finitary formulas, and then define, for every ordinal α, the $\Sigma_{\alpha+1}$ ($\Pi_{\alpha+1}$) formulas as all those which are a countable disjunction (conjunction) of Π_α (Σ_α) formulas, *i.e.*, all those of the form $\inf_n \varphi_n$ ($\sup_n \varphi_n$), when $(\varphi_n)_{n\in\mathbb{N}}$ is a sequence of Π_α (Σ_α) formulas. The limit cases are generalized in the standard way. However, recall that formulas require moduli of continuity. As such, the formulas constructed above are really only *candidates* for infinitary formulas. The genuine formulas are then those which were constructed from sequences of formulas which are uniformly equicontinuous, with the formula inheriting its modulus of continuity from the respective witness of equicontinuity. For our purposes, however, the distinction fails to be of any significance, since we only construct infinitary *sentences*, sequences of which are all trivially uniformly equicontinuous. The *computable* infinitary formulas are then those which, relative to an effective numbering of a language, are constructed up to the level ω_1^{CK} from computably enumerable sequences of formulas, just like in the classical case. A uniform treatment of computing the modulus of continuity when given only the sequence of formulas, rather than the sequence paired with an index for a computable modulus of uniform equicontinuity, has not yet been developed. Nonetheless, since we are only working with sentences, this may be ignored.

2.2 Background from Computability Theory

We presume familiarity with the hyperarithmetic hierarchy as constructed in Chap. 5 of [1] (see also Chapter II of [8]). In [6], continuous computable infinitary logic is developed in more detail based on the classical computable infinitary logic (see Chap. 7 of [1]) and the continuous infinitary logic developed by Eagle in [7].

Let $\langle \, , \rangle$ be a computable bijection of $\mathbb{N} \times \mathbb{N}$ onto $\mathbb{N}$, and let $(\ )_0$ and $(\ )_1$ denote its left and right inverses respectively so that $\langle (n)_0, (n)_1 \rangle = n$ for all $n \in \mathbb{N}$, and fix a computable enumeration $(q_n)_{n \in \mathbb{N}}$ of $\mathbb{Q}$.

Let m, n be positive integers. Suppose $R \subseteq \mathbb{N}^m$, and let $X \subseteq \mathbb{N}$. We say that $e \in \mathbb{N}$ is a $\Sigma_n^0(X)$ *index* of R if e is a Δ_1^0 index of an $S \subseteq \mathcal{P}(\mathbb{N}) \times \mathbb{N}^{n+m}$ so that for all $y_1, \ldots, y_m \in \mathbb{N}$,

$$R(y_1, \ldots, y_m) \Leftrightarrow \exists x_1 \forall x_2 \ldots Q x_n S(X; y_1, \ldots, y_m, x_1, \ldots, x_n)$$

where $Q \in \{\forall, \exists\}$ is $\forall$ just in case n is even. By a Σ_n^0 *index* of R we mean a $\Sigma_n^0(\varnothing)$ index of R.

Suppose $\alpha < \omega_1^{\mathrm{CK}}$ and $A \subseteq \mathbb{N}$. By $\mathcal{O}$, we mean *Kleene's O*, the standard system of ordinal notation for the computable ordinals. When $e \in \mathcal{O}$ is a notation for α, by $\mathcal{H}(e)$ we mean $\varnothing^{(\alpha)}$. We say that $e \in \mathbb{N}$ is a Σ_α^0 *index of* A if $(e)_1 \in \mathcal{O}$ and $A = W_{(e)_0}^{\mathcal{H}((e)_1)}$.

Suppose $h : \mathbb{N} \to \omega_1^{\mathrm{CK}}$. We say h is *computable* if there is an $\hat{h} : \mathbb{N} \to \mathcal{O}$ so that $h(n) = |\hat{h}(n)|_{\mathcal{O}}$ for all $n \in N$ and so that $\mathrm{ran}(\hat{h})$ is linearly ordered by $<_{\mathcal{O}}$. If h is computable, then an *index* of h is an index of a function $\hat{h}$ with these properties.

2.3 Preliminaries from Computable Analysis

Let $r \in \mathbb{R}$, and suppose $\alpha < \omega_1^{\mathrm{CK}}$. We say r is *left (right) Σ_α^0* if its left (right) Dedekind cut is Σ_α^0. If r is left (right) Σ_α^0, then a *left (right) Σ_α^0 index* of r is a Σ_α^0 index of its left (right) Dedekind cut.

Let $(r_n)_{n \in \mathbb{N}}$ be a sequence of real numbers, and suppose $h : \mathbb{N} \to \omega_1^{\mathrm{CK}}$. We say that $(r_n)_{n \in \mathbb{N}}$ is *left (right) Σ_h^0* if r_n is left (right) $\Sigma_{h(n)}^0$ for every $n \in \mathbb{N}$. Suppose h is computable and let e be an index of h. If $(r_n)_{n \in \mathbb{N}}$ is left (right) Σ_h^0, and i is the index of a computable function $g : \mathbb{N} \to \mathbb{N}$ such that $D^<(r_n) = W_{g(n)}^{\mathcal{H}(h(n))}$ ($D^>(r_n)$), then we say that the coded pair $\langle e, i \rangle$ is a *left (right) Σ_h^0 index* of $(r_n)_{n \in \mathbb{N}}$.

3   Proof of Main Theorem

We divide the main part of the proof of Theorem 1.2 into the following lemmas.

Lemma 3.1. *If $r \in [0,1]$ is right Σ_2^0, then there is a left Σ_1^0 nonincreasing sequence $(r_n)_{n \in \mathbb{N}}$ so that $r = \inf_n r_n$ and so that $r_n \in [0,1]$.*

Proof. Suppose $r \in [0,1]$ is right Σ_2^0. Then, there is a computable $R \subseteq \mathbb{N}^2 \times \mathbb{Q}$ so that for all $q \in \mathbb{Q}$,

$$q > r \iff \exists x_0 \forall x_1 R(x_0, x_1, q).$$

Let

$$R_1(x_0, x_1, q) \iff (q_{(x_0)_1} \le q \ \wedge \ R((x_0)_0, x_1, q_{(x_0)_1}).$$

Set:

$$S_n = (-\infty, 0) \cup \{q \in \mathbb{Q} \cap (-\infty, 1) : \exists x_1 \neg R_1(n, x_1, q)\}$$
$$s_n = \sup S_n$$
$$r_n = \min\{s_0, \dots, s_n\}$$

Thus, by construction, $(r_n)_{n \in \mathbb{N}}$ is non-increasing, and $r_n \in [0,1]$.

We now show $r = \inf_n r_n$. It suffices to show that $r = \inf_n s_n$. We first note that for every $q \in \mathbb{Q}$,

$$q > r \iff \exists x_0 \forall x_1 R_1(x_0, x_1, q).$$

We now observe that for all $q, q' \in \mathbb{Q}$,

$$q < q' \ \wedge \ R_1(x_0, x_1, q) \ \Rightarrow \ R_1(x_0, x_1, q').$$

Hence, each S_n is closed downward. It now follows that $D^<(r) \subseteq D^\le(\inf_n s_n)$ and that $D^<(\inf_n s_n) \subseteq \bigcap_n S_n = D^\le(r)$. Thus, $r = \inf_n s_n$.

By construction,

$$D^<(r_n) = \{q \in \mathbb{Q} : \forall k \le n \, \exists q' \in S_k \, q < q'\}.$$

Since S_n is Σ_1^0 uniformly in n, $(r_n)_{n \in \mathbb{N}}$ is left Σ_1^0. $\square$

We note that Lemma 3.1 uniformly relativizes in that the proof yields a computable $f : \mathbb{N} \to \mathbb{N}$ so that for every $e \in \mathbb{N}$ and $X \subseteq \mathbb{N}$, if e is a right $\Sigma_2^0(X)$ index of a number $s \in [0,1]$, then $f(e)$ is a left $\Sigma_1^0(X)$ index of a sequence $(r_n)_{n \in \mathbb{N}}$ so that $s = \inf_n r_n$ and so that $r_n \in [0,1]$. This uniformity will be heavily exploited later.

Lemma 3.2. *If $r \in [0,1]$ is left Σ_2^0, then there is a right Σ_1^0 nondecreasing sequence $(r_n)_{n \in \mathbb{N}}$ so that $r = \sup_n r_n$ and so that $r_n \in [0,1]$.*

Proof Sketch. Suppose $r \in [0,1]$ is left Σ_2^0, and let $R \subseteq \mathbb{N}^2 \times \mathbb{Q}$ be a computable relation so that

$$q < r \iff \exists x_0 \, \forall x_1 \, R(x_0, x_1, q)$$

for every $q \in \mathbb{Q}$. Let

$$R_1(x_0, x_1, q) \iff q \leq q_{(x_0)_1} \wedge R((x_0)_0, x_1, q_{(x_0)_1}).$$

Set:

$$S_n = (1, \infty) \cup \{q \in \mathbb{Q} \cap (0, \infty) : \exists x_1 \neg R_1(n, x_1, q)\}$$
$$s_n = \inf S_n$$
$$r_n = \max\{s_0, \ldots, s_n\}$$

Thus, by construction, $(r_n)_{n \in \mathbb{N}}$ is nondecreasing, and $r_n \in [0,1]$. The rest of the proof is a straightforward modification of the proof of Lemma 3.1. Namely, one flips the order of the inequalities, and exchanges inf and sup as well as 'upward' and 'downward'. □

Again, we note that Lemma 3.2 relativizes uniformly.

Lemma 3.3. *Let $\alpha < \omega_1^{\text{CK}}$. If $r \in [0,1]$ is right $\Sigma_{\alpha+1}^0$, then there is a non-increasing left Σ_α^0 sequence $(r_n)_{n \in \mathbb{N}}$ so that $r = \inf_n r_n$ and so that $r_n \in [0,1]$.*

Proof. We first consider the case $\alpha = 0$. Let $(s_m)_{m \in \mathbb{N}}$ be an effective enumeration of $D^>(r)$. Set $r_n = \min\{1, s_0, \ldots, s_n\}$. Then, $(r_n)_{n \in \mathbb{N}}$ is a computable sequence of rational numbers, and $r = \inf_n r_n$.

The case $\alpha = 1$ is handled by Lemma 3.1.

Suppose $2 \leq \alpha < \omega$. Let $k = \alpha - 2$. Then, since r is right $\Sigma_{\alpha+1}^0$, $D^>(r)$ is $\Sigma_2^0(\varnothing^{(k+1)})$. By the relativization of Lemma 3.1, there is a left $\Sigma_1^0(\varnothing^{(k+1)})$ nonincreasing sequence $(r_n)_{n \in \mathbb{N}}$ so that $r = \inf_n r_n$ and so that $r_n \in [0,1]$. Thus, $(r_n)_{n \in \mathbb{N}}$ is left Σ_α^0.

Finally, suppose α is infinite (limit or successor). Thus, $D^>(r)$ is $\Sigma_1^0(\varnothing^{(\alpha+1)}) = \Sigma_2^0(\varnothing^{(\alpha)})$. Again, by the relativization of Lemma 3.1, there is a left $\Sigma_1^0(\varnothing^{(\alpha)}) = \Sigma_\alpha^0$ nonincreasing sequence so that $r = \inf_n r_n$ and so that $r_n \in [0,1]$. □

Lemma 3.4. *Let $\alpha < \omega_1^{\text{CK}}$. Suppose $r \in [0,1]$ is left $\Sigma_{\alpha+1}^0$. Then, there is a right Σ_α^0 nondecreasing sequence $(r_n)_{n \in \mathbb{N}}$ so that $r = \sup_n r_n$ and so that $r_n \in [0,1]$.*

Proof Sketch: Similar to proof of Lemma 3.3. □

Again, we observe that the above lemmas all uniformly relativize.

Lemma 3.5. *Suppose $0 < \alpha < \omega_1^{\text{CK}}$ is a limit ordinal, and suppose $r \in [0,1]$ is right Σ_α^0. Then, there is a computable $h : \mathbb{N} \to \alpha$ and a right Σ_h^0 non-increasing sequence $(r_n)_{n \in \mathbb{N}}$ so that $r = \inf_n r_n$ and so that $r_n \in [0,1]$.*

Proof. By standard techniques, there is a sequence $(S_\beta)_{\beta<\alpha}$ so that $D^>(r) = \bigcup_{\beta<\alpha} S_\beta$ and so that S_β is Σ^0_β uniformly in β. Without loss of generality, we may assume that S_β is upwardly closed. Let $s_\beta = \inf S_\beta \cup (1,\infty)$. Thus, $s_\beta \in [0,1]$ is right Σ^0_β uniformly in β.

To see that $r = \inf_\beta s_\beta$, first suppose q is a rational number so that $q > r$. Then, $q \in S_\beta$ for some $\beta < \alpha$, and so $q \geq \inf S_\beta \geq s_\beta$. Thus, $q \geq \inf_{\beta<\alpha} s_\beta$. On the other hand, suppose $q > \inf_{\beta<\alpha} s_\beta$. Then, there exists $q' \in S_\beta \cup (1,\infty)$ so that $q > q'$. If $q' \in S_\beta$, then $q \in S_\beta$ and so $q > r$. If $q' > 1$, then since $r \leq 1$, $q > r$. Thus, $\inf_{\beta<\alpha} s_\beta \geq r$.

Finally, let $h : \mathbb{N} \to \alpha$ be computable, increasing, and cofinal with index computed from the notation of α, and set

$$r_n = \min\{s_{h(0)}, \ldots, s_{h(n)}\}.$$

It follows that $D^>(r_n) = \bigcup_{\beta<h(n)} S_\beta$ is $\Sigma^0_{h(n)}$, uniformly in n.   □

Lemma 3.6. *Suppose* $0 < \alpha < \omega_1^{CK}$ *is a limit ordinal, and suppose* $r \in [0,1]$ *is left* Σ^0_α. *Then, there is a computable* $h : \mathbb{N} \to \alpha$ *and a left* Σ^0_h *non-increasing sequence* $(r_n)_{n\in\mathbb{N}}$ *so that* $r = \sup_n r_n$ *and so that* $r_n \in [0,1]$.

Proof Sketch. Similar to proof of 3.5, exchanging inf and sup, $>$ and $<$, *etc.*   □

Proof of Theorem 1.2. We proceed by effective transfinite recursion. We begin with the case $\alpha = 1$. Suppose $D^<(r)$ is Σ^0_1. Let g be a computable surjection of $\mathbb{N}$ onto $(D^<(r) \cap \mathbb{D} \cap (0,1)) \cup \{0\}$. Set $\Phi = \sup_n \nu^{\exists}_{g(n)}$. Suppose $\mathcal{M}$ is an interpretation of L_M (*i.e.*, a metric space). Then, $\Phi^{\mathcal{M}} = \sup_n r_n = r$, by the density of the dyadics. If $D^>(r)$ is Σ^0_1, then we take $(r_n)_{n\in\mathbb{N}}$ to be an effective enumeration of $(D^>(r) \cap \mathbb{D} \cap (0,1)) \cup \{1\}$.

We now handle the recursive steps. Let $\alpha < \omega_1^{CK}$, and suppose r is left $\Sigma^0_{\alpha+1}$. By Lemma 3.4, there is a right Σ^0_α sequence $(r_n)_{n\in\mathbb{N}}$ so that $r = \sup_n r_n$, with $r_n \in [0,1]$. From $n \in \mathbb{N}$, it is possible to compute a code of a Σ^0_α sentence Φ_n of L_M so that $\Phi_n^{\mathcal{M}} = r$ for every interpretation $\mathcal{M}$ of L_M. We can then compute a code of $\Phi = \sup_n \Phi_n$. Hence, $\Phi^{\mathcal{M}} = r$ for every interpretation $\mathcal{M}$ of L_M. The case where r is right Σ^0_1 is handled similarly.

Suppose $\alpha > 0$ is a limit ordinal. We first consider the case where r is left Σ^0_α. By Lemma 3.6, there is a computable $g : \mathbb{N} \to \mathbb{N}$ and $h : \mathbb{N} \to \alpha$ such that $r = \sup_n r_n$ and each $D^<(r_n) = W^{\mathcal{H}(h(n))}_{g(n)}$. That is, the sequence $(r_n)_{n\in\mathbb{N}}$ is left Σ^0_h. For each $n \in \mathbb{N}$, let Φ_n be a computable $\Pi^0_{h(n)}$ (thus also $\Sigma^0_{h(n)+1}$) infinitary formula of L so that $\Phi_n^{\mathcal{M}} = \Phi_n$, and set $\Phi = \sup_n \Phi_n$.

The case where r is right Σ^0_α is handled similarly.   □

4   Conclusion

We conclude with some speculation about the complexity of theories in continuous logic.

Suppose $\mathcal{M}$ is an interpretation of L. By the *computable infinitary theory of* $\mathcal{M}$ we mean the *function* that maps each computable infinitary sentence Φ of L to $\Phi^{\mathcal{M}}$. We denote this function $\mathrm{Th}^C_{\omega_1\omega}(\mathcal{M})$. Let $X \subseteq \omega$. We say that X *computes* $\mathrm{Th}^C_{\omega_1\omega}(\mathcal{M})$ if X computes a partial function $f :\subseteq \mathbb{N}^2 \to \mathbb{Q}$ so that whenever e is a code of a computable infinitary sentence of L and $k \in \mathbb{N}$, $|f(e,k) - q| < 2^{-k}$.

Corollary 4.1. *Suppose $\mathcal{M}$ is an interpretation of L, and suppose X computes $\mathrm{Th}^C_{\omega_1\omega}(\mathcal{M})$. Then, X computes every hyperarithmetic set. Thus, no hyperarithmetic set computes $\mathrm{Th}^C_{\omega_1\omega}(\mathcal{M})$.*

Question 4.2. *If $\mathcal{M}$ is an interpretation of L, does it follow that there is a least Turing degree $\mathbf{d}$ so that every $X \in \mathbf{d}$ computes $\mathrm{Th}^C_{\omega_1\omega}(\mathcal{M})$?*

Acknowledgement. We are grateful to the CiE 2024 Program Committee, especially Elaine Pimentel and Ludovic Levy Patey, as well as three anonymous reviewers for their valuable feedback on the improvement of this paper.

References

1. Ash, C.J., Knight, J.: Computable structures and the hyperarithmetical hierarchy, Studies in Logic and the Foundations of Mathematics, vol. 144. North-Holland Publishing Co., Amsterdam (2000)
2. Ben Yaacov, I., Usvyatsov, A.: Continuous first-order logic and local stability. Trans. Am. Math. Soc. **362**, 5213–5259 (2010)
3. Yaacov, I.B., Berenstein, A, Ward Henson, C., Usvyatsov, A.: Model theory for metric structures. Lond. Math. Soc. Lect. Note Ser. **350**, 315–427. Cambridge Univ. Press, Cambridge (2008). Model theory with applications to algebra and analysis. Vol. 2
4. Ben Yaacov, I., Iovino, J.: Model theoretic forcing in analysis. Ann. Pure Appl. Logic **158**(3), 163–174 (2009)
5. Yaacov, I.B., Pedersen, A.P.: A proof of completeness for continuous first-order logic. J. Symb. Log. **75**(1), 168–190 (2010)
6. Camrud, C., Goldbring, I., McNicholl, T.H.: On the complexity of the theory of a computably presented metric structure. Arch. Math. Logic **62**(7), 1111–1129 (2023)
7. Eagle, C.J.: Expressive Power of Infinitary [0,1]-Logics, Beyond First Order Model Theory, pp. 3–22. CRC Press, Boca Raton, FL (2017)
8. Sacks, G.E.: Higher recursion theory, Perspectives in Mathematical Logic. Springer-Verlag, Berlin (1990). MR1080970 (92a:03062)

Lipschitz Determinacy and Arithmetic Transfinite Recursion

Andrés Cordón-Franco[1]($\boxtimes$), F. Félix Lara-Martín[1], and Manuel J. S. Loureiro[2]

[1] Dpto. Ciencias de la Computación e Inteligencia Artificial, Universidad de Sevilla, Seville, Spain
{acordon,fflara}@us.es
[2] Faculty of Engineering, Lusofona University, Lisbon, Portugal
mloureiro@ulusofona.pt

Abstract. We investigate the logical strength of Lipschitz determinacy, and the tightly related Semi-Linear Ordering principle, for the first levels of the Borel hierarchy in the Baire space. As a result, we obtain characterizations of ATR$_0$ in terms of these determinacy principles.

Keywords: Reverse mathematics · Determinacy · Lipschitz games · Semilinear Ordering principle

1 Introduction

Reverse mathematics is a well-established research program in Mathematical Logic motivated by the fundamental question: *Which set existence axioms are needed to prove the known theorems of mathematics?* As a contribution to this program, we study in the context of second order arithmetic the logical strength of the Lipschitz determinacy principle Det$_L$ and the Semi-Linear Ordering principle SLO$_L$ restricted to the first levels of the Borel hierarchy in the Baire space. In our main result we characterize ATR$_0$ (one of the "Big Five" theories widely studied in second order arithmetic) by using these determinacy principles.

Lipschitz games were first introduced in the setting of descriptive set theory by W.W. Wadge [12] as a tool for studying the relative complexity of subsets of the Baire space ω^ω. Given $A, B \subseteq \omega^\omega$, A is said to be Lipschitz reducible to B, in symbols $A \leq_L B$, if there is a Lipschitz function F such that $x \in A$ if, and only if, $F(x) \in B$ (note that $\leq_L$ is a natural analog of the many-one reducibility of computability theory). Wadge proved that $\leq_L$ can be studied in terms of *Lipschitz games*. The Lipschitz game $G_L(A, B)$ is the game on ω where players I and II alternatively play natural numbers a_i and b_i, and player II wins just in case $\langle a_0, a_1, a_2, \dots \rangle \in A \Leftrightarrow \langle b_0, b_1, b_2, \dots \rangle \in B$. By the so-called Wadge's lemma, a winning strategy for player II in $G_L(A, B)$ yields a Lipschitz function witnessing $A \leq_L B$, whereas a winning strategy for player I yields a Lipschitz function

A. Cordón-Franco and F. F. Lara-Martín—Were partially supported by grant PID2020-116773GB-I00, Ministerio de Ciencia e Innovación (Spanish Government).

witnessing $\omega^\omega \setminus B \leq_L A$. Wadge then assumed determinacy for Lipschitz games as a working hypothesis and he extensively studied the structure of the Lipschitz degrees (i.e. the equivalence classes generated by $\leq_L$) in the Baire space. In particular, assuming determinacy, he derived the following somewhat surprising comparability property, known as the *Semi-Linear Ordering principle*:

$$\text{SLO}_L = \text{"For all } A, B \subseteq \omega^\omega, \text{ either } A \leq_L B \text{ or } \omega^\omega \setminus B \leq_L A.\text{"}$$

In other words, $\leq_L$ is a linear order provided we identify the degree of a set with that of its complement.

Lipschitz determinacy and SLO_L can be naturally formalized in the language of second order arithmetic (see Sect. 2). To fix notation, given formula classes Γ_1 and Γ_2, let (Γ_1, Γ_2)-Det_L denote the principle of determinacy for Lipschitz games $G_L(A, B)$ in the Baire space where A is Γ_1-definable and B is Γ_2-definable. Likewise, let (Γ_1, Γ_2)-SLO_L denote the corresponding semi-linear ordering principle, i.e., the principle asserting that either player II has a winning strategy in $G_L(A, B)$ or player II has a winning strategy in $G_L(\neg B, A)$, where A is Γ_1-definable and B is Γ_2-definable. If $\Gamma_1 = \Gamma_2$, we will write Γ_1-Det_L or Γ_1-SLO_L.

Two remarkable results on the logical strength of Lipschitz determinacy are to be mentioned. Firstly, A. Louveau and J. Saint Raymond [7] showed that Borel Lipschitz determinacy is provable within second order arithmetic Z_2. Secondly, and very recently, A. Day et al. [2] have shown that the subsystem $\text{ATR}_0 + \Pi_1^1$-induction already proves Borel Lipschitz determinacy. These results evidence that, in the context of second order arithmetic Borel Lipschitz determinacy is a much weaker principle than Borel general determinacy, as Δ_4^0-determinacy for general infinite games is already not provable in Z_2 (see [8]). In the present paper we show that, however, this huge difference in strength does not occur at the initial levels of the Borel hierarchy. Namely,

Theorem 1. *1. Over* ACA_0, Δ_1^0-Det_L, Δ_1^0-SLO_L *and* ATR_0 *are pairwise equivalent.*
2. Over RCA_0, (Δ_1^0, Π_1^0)-Det_L, Π_1^0-Det_L, $(\Delta_1^0, \Sigma_1^0 \wedge \Pi_1^0)$-$\text{SLO}_L$ *and* ATR_0 *are pairwise equivalent.*

By a theorem of J. R. Steel [11], ATR_0 is equivalent to clopen and closed determinacy for general infinite games. Hence, for clopen and closed sets Lipschitz and general determinacy are equivalent principles.

Our proof methods have a certain topological flavor. The analysis of the complete sets with respect to the reducibility relation $\leq_L$ developed in [12] can be adapted to prove determinacy of Lipschitz games: roughly speaking, the player who plays in a set with a richer topological structure will win the game.

The paper is divided into five sections. Section 1 is introductory and Sect. 2 contains some preliminaries. In Sect. 3 we study Lipschitz determinacy and SLO_L for clopen sets and obtain a reversal for ATR_0 over the base theory ACA_0. In Sect. 4 we study Lipschitz determinacy and SLO_L for closed sets and obtain a reversal for ATR_0 over RCA_0. Section 5 contains some concluding remarks.

2   Preliminaries

We assume familiarity with subsystems of second order arithmetic RCA_0, ACA_0 and ATR_0, as presented in [10]. Our notation and terminology are standard and follow [10] (for details and full technical background the reader should consult that book). A formalization of general two-person infinite games within second order arithmetic is described in section V.8 of [10] as well as in Sect. 3 of [9]. (As usual, Γ-Det will denote the principle of general determinacy restricted to Γ games in the Baire space.) A formalization of Lipschitz determinacy and SLO_L in second order arithmetic can be found in [6] or in Sect. 2 of [1]. Here we restrict ourselves to presenting some basic notions and terminology that will be used extensively in this paper.

Within RCA_0, we define $\mathbb{N}$ to be the unique set X such that $\forall i\,(i \in X)$ and we define a numerical pairing function by letting $(i,j) = (i+j)^2 + i$. Using Δ_1^0 comprehension, we can prove that for all sets $X, Y \subseteq \mathbb{N}$, there exists a set $X \times Y \subseteq \mathbb{N}$ consisting of all (i,j) such that $i \in X$ and $j \in Y$. A function $f : X \to Y$ is defined to be a set $f \subseteq X \times Y$ such that for all $i \in X$ there is exactly one $j \in Y$ such that $(i,j) \in f$ (we will also write $f \in Y^X$). For $i \in X$, $f(i)$ is defined to be the unique j such that $(i,j) \in f$. Finite sequences of natural numbers can be encoded as a single natural number and this coding can be developed formally within RCA_0. The set of all (codes of) finite sequences from X is denoted $X^{<\mathbb{N}}$. The *empty sequence* is denoted $\langle\rangle$. Given any $s, t \in X^{<\mathbb{N}}$, $|s|$ denotes the length of s, $s(i)$ or $(s)_i$ denotes the $(i+1)$-th element of s for $i < |s|$, and, for each $j \leq |s|$, $s[j]$ is the j-th initial segment of s, i.e. $\langle s(0), \ldots, s(j-1)\rangle$. If $s = t[j]$ for some $j \leq |t|$, we write $s \subseteq t$ and say that s is an initial segment of t (or t is an extension of s). The concatenation of s and t, written $s * t$, is the sequence $\langle s(0), \ldots, s(|s|-1), t(0), \ldots, t(|t|-1)\rangle$. If $f \in X^{\mathbb{N}}$, $s * f$ denotes $\langle s(0), \ldots, s(|s|-1), f(0), f(1), \ldots\rangle$, and $f[j]$ denotes $\langle f(0), \ldots, f(j-1)\rangle$. If $s = f[|s|]$, we write $s \subset f$ and say that s is an initial segment of f (or f is an extension of s). If s and t are sequences with $|s| = |t|$, $s \otimes t$ denotes the sequence of length $2\,|s|$ where $(s \otimes t)_{2i} = (s)_i$ and $(s \otimes t)_{2i+1} = (t)_i$ if $0 \leq i < |s|$.

Consider formulas $A(f)$ and $B(g)$ with distinguished function variables $f, g \in \mathbb{N}^{\mathbb{N}}$. A *Lipschitz game in the Baire space*, denoted $G_L(A, B)$, is defined as follows: Two players, say player I (male) and player II (female), alternately choose an element x in $\mathbb{N}$ to form the resulting plays $f = \langle x_0, x_1, x_2, \ldots \rangle \in \mathbb{N}^{\mathbb{N}}$ and $g = \langle y_0, y_1, y_2, \ldots \rangle \in \mathbb{N}^{\mathbb{N}}$:

Player I	x_0		x_1		x_2	$\cdots$
Player II		y_0		y_1	y_2	$\cdots$

Player II wins just in case $A(f) \leftrightarrow B(g)$ holds. Put $\mathrm{Seq}_{\mathrm{even}} = \{s \in \mathbb{N}^{<\mathbb{N}} : |s| \text{ is even}\}$ and $\mathrm{Seq}_{\mathrm{odd}} = \{s \in \mathbb{N}^{<\mathbb{N}} : |s| \text{ is odd}\}$. A *strategy for player I* in the game $G_L(A, B)$ is a function $\sigma_{\mathrm{I}} : \mathrm{Seq}_{\mathrm{even}} \to \mathbb{N}$ and a *strategy for player II* is a function $\sigma_{\mathrm{II}} : \mathrm{Seq}_{\mathrm{odd}} \to \mathbb{N}$. If players I and II follow strategies σ_{I} and σ_{II}, respectively, the resulting plays are uniquely determined. We will write $\sigma_{\mathrm{I}} \otimes_L^{\mathrm{I}} \sigma_{\mathrm{II}}$ to denote player I's resulting play and write $\sigma_{\mathrm{I}} \otimes_L^{\mathrm{II}} \sigma_{\mathrm{II}}$ to denote player II's resulting play. A strategy for a player is a *winning strategy* if the player wins the game as long as he/she plays following it, no matter what his/her opponent plays. A game is *determined* if either player I or player II has a winning strategy. The following axiom, denoted $\mathsf{Det}_L(A, B)$, expresses that the Lipschitz game $G_L(A, B)$ is determined:

$$\exists \sigma_{\mathrm{I}} \forall \sigma_{\mathrm{II}} \neg (A(\sigma_{\mathrm{I}} \otimes_L^{\mathrm{I}} \sigma_{\mathrm{II}}) \leftrightarrow B(\sigma_{\mathrm{I}} \otimes_L^{\mathrm{II}} \sigma_{\mathrm{II}})) \vee \exists \sigma_{\mathrm{II}} \forall \sigma_{\mathrm{I}} (A(\sigma_{\mathrm{I}} \otimes_L^{\mathrm{I}} \sigma_{\mathrm{II}}) \leftrightarrow B(\sigma_{\mathrm{I}} \otimes_L^{\mathrm{II}} \sigma_{\mathrm{II}})),$$

where σ_{I} and σ_{II} range over strategies for player I and strategies for player II, respectively. Let Γ_1 and Γ_2 be formula classes with distinguished function variables $f, g \in \mathbb{N}^{\mathbb{N}}$, respectively. The scheme of (Γ_1, Γ_2)-*Lipschitz determinacy in the Baire space*, denoted (Γ_1, Γ_2)-Det_L, is given by the axioms $\mathsf{Det}_L(A, B)$, where $A(f) \in \Gamma_1$ and $B(g) \in \Gamma_2$ (if $\Gamma_1 = \Gamma_2$, we will simply write Γ_1-Det_L). The scheme of Δ_n^0-*Lipschitz determinacy in the Baire space*, denoted Δ_n^0-Det_L, is given by

$$\forall f \in \mathbb{N}^{\mathbb{N}}(A(f) \leftrightarrow C(f)) \wedge \forall g \in \mathbb{N}^{\mathbb{N}}(B(g) \leftrightarrow D(g)) \rightarrow \mathsf{Det}_L(A, B),$$

where $A, B \in \Sigma_n^0$ and $C, D \in \Pi_n^0$. The theories (Γ, Δ_n^0)-Det_L and (Δ_n^0, Γ)-Det_L are defined similarly.

Remark 1. It is easily verified that (Γ_1, Γ_2)-Det_L and $(\neg\Gamma_1, \neg\Gamma_2)$-$\mathsf{Det}_L$ are equivalent over RCA_0, for $G_L(A, B)$ and $G_L(\neg A, \neg B)$ are essentially the same game.

As for SLO_L, the axiom $\mathsf{Red}_L^{\bullet}(A, B) \equiv \exists \sigma_{\mathrm{II}} \forall \sigma_{\mathrm{I}} (A(\sigma_{\mathrm{I}} \otimes_L^{\mathrm{I}} \sigma_{\mathrm{II}}) \leftrightarrow B(\sigma_{\mathrm{I}} \otimes_L^{\mathrm{II}} \sigma_{\mathrm{II}}))$ expresses that *A is Lipschitz reducible to B* (i.e., player II has a winning strategy in the game $G_L(A, B)$). The scheme of (Γ_1, Γ_2)-*Lipschitz semilinear ordering principle in the Baire space*, denoted (Γ_1, Γ_2)-SLO_L, is given by the axiom scheme $\mathsf{Red}_L(A, B) \vee \mathsf{Red}_L(\neg B, A)$, where $A \in \Gamma_1$ and $B \in \Gamma_2$. The theories Δ_n^0-SLO_L, (Δ_n^0, Γ)-SLO_L, ... are defined similarly.

Lemma 1. *It is provable over RCA_0 that (Γ_1, Γ_2)-Det_L implies (Γ_1, Γ_2)-SLO_L, and the same holds for classes (Δ_n^0, Δ_m^0), (Γ, Δ_m^0) and (Δ_n^0, Γ).*

Proof. See Lemma 5.2 of [1]. $\qquad\qquad\qquad\qquad\qquad\qquad\qquad\qquad\qquad\qquad\qquad\square$

3 Lipschitz Determinacy for Clopen Sets

First of all we introduce the combinatorial tools we will need to analyse the determinacy of Lipschitz games in the Baire space. A set $T \subseteq X^{<\mathbb{N}}$ is called a *tree* over X if T is closed under initial segments, i.e. $s \in T$ and $t \subseteq s$ imply $t \in T$. We call the elements of T the *nodes* of T. A tree is *infinite* if, for any n, there exists $s \in T$ with $|s| = n$, i.e. if the set of nodes of T is infinite. If $S \subseteq X^{<\mathbb{N}}$ is a tree over X and $S \subseteq T$, then S is called a *subtree* of T.

Fix any tree $T \subseteq X^{<\mathbb{N}}$. A node $s \in T$ is called *terminal* if $\forall a \in X$ $(s * \langle a \rangle \notin T)$. A function $f \in X^{\mathbb{N}}$ is called a *path* of T if $\forall n \in \mathbb{N} (f[n] \in T)$. The set of all paths of T is denoted by $[T]$. A tree $T \subseteq X^{<\mathbb{N}}$ is *well-founded* if it has no path, i.e. $[T] = \emptyset$.

A key fact for the analysis of Lipschitz games is that closed sets in the Baire space correspond to the sets of paths of trees. This fact can be proved in RCA_0 and it is, indeed, an immediate consequence of the normal form theorem for Σ_1^0 formulas (Theorem II.2.7 of [10]).

Proposition 1 ([10], Lemma VI.1.5). *The following is provable in RCA_0. Suppose $X \subseteq \mathbb{N}$. Assume $\varphi(f) \in \Pi_1^0$, with $f \in X^{\mathbb{N}}$. Then, there is a tree $T \subseteq X^{<\mathbb{N}}$ satisfying that $[T] = \{f \in X^{\mathbb{N}} : \varphi(f)\}$.*

Thus, we identify points in the Baire space with functions $f \in \mathbb{N}^{\mathbb{N}}$, and we identify closed sets in the Baire space with Π_1^0 formulas containing a second order free variable f which ranges over $\mathbb{N}^{\mathbb{N}}$. Similarly, open sets will correspond to Σ_1^0 formulas and so on. We also identify a closed set with the set of paths of a tree, $[T]$, and, by abuse of language, use set theoretic notations to mean the arithmetic formula expressing the corresponding set. (For instance, an expression of the form $f \in [T] - [S]$ is to be understood as the $\Pi_1^0 \wedge \Sigma_1^0$ formula expressing that f is a path of T and is not a path of S.) The following definition is made in RCA_0.

Definition 1. *Given $X \subseteq \mathbb{N}$, we say that a tree $T \subseteq X^{<\mathbb{N}}$ defines a clopen set if there is a tree $T' \subseteq X^{<\mathbb{N}}$ such that $\forall f \in X^{\mathbb{N}} (f \notin [T] \leftrightarrow f \in [T'])$.*

The goal of this section is to prove the following reversal for ATR_0 in terms of Lipschitz determinacy and semilinear ordering principle for clopen sets. This result was also obtained in [6] (unpublished).

Theorem 2. *The following are equivalent over ACA_0:*

1. ATR_0.
2. $\Delta_1^0\text{-Det}_L$.
3. $\Delta_1^0\text{-SLO}_L$.

The remainder of this section is devoted to providing a proof of this result. Our analysis of clopen Lipschitz determinacy rests on basic properties of well-founded trees and ordinal rank functions associated with them. Thus, we shall begin by providing in the next subsection a survey of some basic facts on countable well orderings and well-founded trees that are provable in ATR_0 and that will be needed in the proof of Theorem 2.

3.1   Well-Founded Trees and Ranks

As we mentioned earlier, we identify $\mathbb{N} \times \mathbb{N}$ with a subset of $\mathbb{N}$ using the pairing function $(i, j) = (i + j)^2 + i$. Thus, a binary relation X on $\mathbb{N}$ is identified with a subset of $\mathbb{N} \times \mathbb{N}$. Working over RCA_0 we cannot assume the existence (as sets) of the domain or the range of X. To deal with this difficulty, in RCA_0 an ordering is defined to be a *reflexive* relation (of course, satisfying other additional properties). In RCA_0 we say that the relation $X \subseteq \mathbb{N} \times \mathbb{N}$ is *reflexive* if

$\forall i \forall j ((i,j) \in X \to ((i,i) \in X \wedge (j,j) \in X))$. If X is reflexive then, by Δ_0^0-comprehension, there exists the set field$(X) = \{i : (i,i) \in X\}$. We also write $i \leq_X j$ for $(i,j) \in X$, and $i <_X j$ for $(i,j) \in X \wedge (j,i) \notin X$.

Within RCA$_0$, given a reflexive binary relation X, we say that X is *well founded* if there is no $f : \mathbb{N} \to \text{field}(X)$ such that $f(n+1) <_X f(n)$ for all $n \in \mathbb{N}$. We say that X is a *countable linear ordering* if it is a reflexive, antisymmetric, transitive, and total relation on its field. We say that X is a *countable well ordering* if it is both well founded and a countable linear ordering.

There is an arithmetical formula LO(X) expressing that X is a countable linear ordering, and it can be easily checked that there exist Π_1^1 formulas WF(X) and WO(X) (with a single free variable X) expressing, respectively, that X is a well founded (reflexive) relation and X is a countable well ordering.

We shall use Greek letters α, β, γ, ... to denote countable well orderings. If α is a well ordering then $\alpha + 1$ denotes a well ordering obtained from α by adding an upper bound as follows:

$$\alpha + 1 = \{(2m, 2n) : (m,n) \in \alpha\} \cup \{(1,1)\} \cup \{(2m, 1) : m \in \text{field}(\alpha)\}.$$

Let us now consider a natural comparability notion between countable well orderings that turns out to be equivalent to Arithmetic Transfinite Recursion.

Definition 2. *Let α and β be countable well orderings. We say that α is weakly less than or equal to β, $\alpha \leq_w \beta$, if there is an injection $f : \text{field}(\alpha) \to \text{field}(\beta)$ such that $\forall i, j \in \text{field}(\alpha) \, (i \leq_\alpha j \leftrightarrow f(i) \leq_\beta f(j))$.*
We write $\alpha <_w \beta$ if $\alpha + 1 \leq_w \beta$.

Theorem 3 ([5], Theorem 4). *Over RCA$_0$, ATR$_0$ is equivalent to the comparability principle: $\forall \alpha, \beta \, (\alpha \leq_w \beta \vee \beta \leq_w \alpha)$.*

The following definitions are made in RCA$_0$. We follow [5] and Sect. 3 of [3]. Note that for each tree T, the reverse inclusion $\supseteq$ defines a reflexive binary relation on T and T is well-founded if and only if $\supseteq$ is a well-founded relation.

Definition 3. *Let $S, T \subseteq X^{<\mathbb{N}}$ be trees. We shall write $S \preceq T$ if there is a function $f : S \to T$ such that $\forall s_1, s_2 \in S \, (s_1 \subset s_2 \to f(s_1) \subset f(s_2))$.*

Definition 4. *Let $T \subseteq X^{<\mathbb{N}}$ be a tree. A rank function for T is a pair (rk, α) where α is a countable well ordering and rk $: T \to \text{field}(\alpha)$ satisfies $\alpha = \text{rk}(\langle \rangle) + 1$ and $\text{rk}(t) = \sup\{\text{rk}(s) + 1 : t \subset s \wedge |s| = |t| + 1\}$, for every $t \in T$, with $\sup \emptyset = 0$. We say that T is a ranked tree if there exists some rank function for T.*

The following basic properties of rank functions can be proved in RCA$_0$. In particular, from part 2 in the next proposition we see that RCA$_0$ essentially proves uniqueness of rank functions (see Proposition 3.4 in [3]).

Proposition 2. *The following is provable in RCA$_0$. Let $T \subseteq X^{<\mathbb{N}}$ be a tree and let (rk, α) be a rank function for T. Then*

1. $\forall t_1, t_2 \in T \, (t_1 \subset t_2 \to \text{rk}(t_2) <_\alpha \text{rk}(t_1))$.

2. If (rk', β) is a rank function for T, then there is an order preserving bijection $h : \mathrm{field}(\alpha) \to \mathrm{field}(\beta)$ such that for all $t \in T$, $\mathrm{rk}(t) = h(\mathrm{rk}'(t))$.

It can be easily checked that (in RCA_0) every ranked tree is well-founded. The converse can be derived in ATR_0 (this is, essentially, Theorem 7 of [4]):

Theorem 4. *Over* RCA_0, ATR_0 *is equivalent to the statement "Every well-founded tree is ranked."*

Rank functions provide a powerful tool in the study of immersions between well-founded trees. The following lemma will be a key ingredient in our proof of Theorem 2.

Lemma 2. *The following is provable in* ACA_0. *Let* $S, T \subseteq \mathbb{N}^{<\mathbb{N}}$ *be ranked trees with rank functions* (rk_1, α) *and* (rk_2, β), *resp., such that* $S \preceq T$. *Then* $\alpha \leq_w \beta$.

Proof. See Lemma 3.7 in [3].

Theorem 2 is obtained over the base theory ACA_0 due to the use of the above lemma (whether Theorem 2 holds over RCA_0 is left as a pending question).

3.2   Proof of Theorem 2

By Theorem V.8.7 in [10] we know that $\Delta_1^0\text{-Det}$ can be proved in ATR_0 (as a matter of fact, both principles are equivalent over RCA_0). As a consequence, ATR_0 is strong enough to prove determinacy of clopen Lipschitz games, for a Lipschitz game for clopen sets can be effectively reduced to a clopen (general) infinite game. Thus (1) implies (2) and, by Lemma 1, $\Delta_1^0\text{-Det}_L$ implies $\Delta_1^0\text{-SLO}_L$ (that is, (2) implies (3)). Therefore, we only must show how to derive ATR_0 from $\Delta_1^0\text{-SLO}_L$ (working over ACA_0). Let α and β be countable well orderings. We shall prove that $\alpha \leq_w \beta \vee \beta \leq_w \alpha$. By Theorem 3 this suffices to derive ATR_0.

Let $S(\alpha)$ be the tree of decreasing sequences (w.r.t. $<_\alpha$) of elements of $\mathrm{field}(\alpha)$

$$S(\alpha) = \{s \in \mathrm{field}(\alpha)^{<\mathbb{N}} : \ \forall i, j < |s| \ (i < j \to (s)_j <_\alpha (s)_i)\}.$$

Then RCA_0 can prove that $S(\alpha)$ is ranked. Indeed a rank function for $S(\alpha)$ is $\mathrm{rk} : S(\alpha) \to \alpha + 1$, defined by (let us note that according to the formal definition of $\alpha + 1$, $1 \in \mathrm{field}(\alpha + 1)$ corresponds to the "ordinal" α)

$$\mathrm{rk}(s) = \begin{cases} 1 & \text{if } s = \langle\rangle \\ (s)_l & \text{if } |s| = l + 1 \end{cases}$$

A similar tree $T(\beta)$ can be defined using β accordingly. Let us define the following trees

$$S = S(\alpha) \cup \{s : \exists t \in S(\alpha) \, \exists t' \in \mathbb{N}^{<\mathbb{N}} \, \exists j \, (t * \langle 2j \rangle \notin S(\alpha) \wedge s = t * \langle 2j \rangle * t')\},$$

$$S' = S(\alpha) \cup \{s : \exists t \in S(\alpha) \, \exists t' \in \mathbb{N}^{<\mathbb{N}} \, \exists j \, (t * \langle 2j+1 \rangle \notin S(\alpha) \wedge s = t * \langle 2j+1 \rangle * t')\}.$$

Then S and S' are pruned trees (recall that a tree T is said to be pruned if every sequence of T lies on a path of T). In addition, $[S]$ is a clopen set (since $[S']$ corresponds to its complement in the Baire space) and $S \cap S' = S(\alpha)$. In a similar way we define

$$T = T(\beta) \cup \{s : \exists t \in T(\beta) \, \exists t' \in \mathbb{N}^{<\mathbb{N}} \, \exists j \, (t * \langle 2j \rangle \notin T(\beta) \wedge s = t * \langle 2j \rangle * t')\},$$

$$T' = T(\beta) \cup \{s : \exists t \in T(\beta) \, \exists t' \in \mathbb{N}^{<\mathbb{N}} \, \exists j \, (t * \langle 2j+1 \rangle \notin T(\beta) \wedge s = t * \langle 2j+1 \rangle * t')\}.$$

Once again T and T' are pruned trees, $[T]$ and $[T']$ are clopen sets and $T(\beta) = T \cap T'$.

By Δ_1^0-SLO$_L$ we have $\mathsf{Red}_L([S],[T])$ or $\mathsf{Red}_L([T'],[S])$, since $[T']$ coincides with the complement of $[T]$. If $\mathsf{Red}_L([S],[T])$ holds then player II has a winning strategy σ_{II} in the Lipschitz game $G_L([S],[T])$. In such a case, we define by primitive recursion a function $F : \mathbb{N}^{<\mathbb{N}} \to \mathbb{N}^{<\mathbb{N}}$ putting $F(\langle \rangle) = \langle \rangle$ and

$$F(s * \langle k \rangle) = F(s) * \langle \sigma_{\mathrm{II}}((s \otimes F(s)) * \langle k \rangle) \rangle.$$

Recall that if s and t are sequences with $|s| = |t|$, $s \otimes t$ denotes the sequence of length $2|s|$ where $(s \otimes t)_{2i} = (s)_i$ and $(s \otimes t)_{2i+1} = (t)_i$ if $0 \leq i < |s|$. Obviously, if $s_1 \subset s_2$ then $F(s_1) \subset F(s_2)$ and it can be easily checked that

$$\forall s \, (s \in S(\alpha) \to F(s) \in T(\beta)).$$

Indeed, if $s_0 \in S(\alpha)$ but $F(s_0) \notin T(\beta)$ then $F(s_0) \in T - T'$ or $F(s_0) \in T' - T$. Assume $F(s_0) \in T - T'$ (the other case is similar). Then there exists $s' \in S(\alpha)$ such that $s_0 \subseteq s'$ and $s' * \langle 1 \rangle \in S' - S(\alpha)$. Define a strategy σ_{I} for player I as follows:

$$\sigma_{\mathrm{I}}(s \otimes t) = \begin{cases} (s')_i & \text{if } |s| = i < |s'| \\ 1 & \text{otherwise} \end{cases}$$

Then $\sigma_{\mathrm{I}} \otimes_L^{\mathrm{I}} \sigma_{\mathrm{II}} \in [S']$ but $\sigma_{\mathrm{I}} \otimes_L^{\mathrm{II}} \sigma_{\mathrm{II}} \in [T]$. This is a contradiction since σ_{II} is a winning strategy for player II in $G_L([S],[T])$. Thus, using F we show that $S(\alpha) \preceq T(\beta)$ and, by Lemma 2, $\alpha + 1 \leq_w \beta + 1$. It easily follows that $\alpha \leq_w \beta$.

If $\mathsf{Red}_L([T'],[S])$ holds then there exists a winning strategy for player II in the Lipschitz game $G_L([T'],[S])$, and we can prove reasoning as in the previous case that $T(\beta) \preceq S(\alpha)$ and, as a consequence, $\beta \leq_w \alpha$.   □

4   Lipschitz Determinacy for Closed Sets

In this section we shall prove new reversals for ATR$_0$ over the weaker base theory RCA$_0$. The following definition isolates a notion that will play a key role in our proofs of determinacy within ATR$_0$.

Definition 5. *We say that a tree $T \subseteq \mathbb{N}^{<\mathbb{N}}$ defines a true closed set if*

$$TrueClosed(T) \equiv \exists f \in \mathbb{N}^{\mathbb{N}} \, [f \in [T] \wedge \forall k \, \exists s \, (f[k] \subseteq s \wedge s \notin T)].$$

Lemma 3. ACA_0 *proves that if* $T \subseteq \mathbb{N}^{<\mathbb{N}}$ *is a tree then either* $TrueClosed(T)$ *holds or* T *defines a clopen set.*

Proof. We work in ACA_0. Suppose that $TrueClosed(T)$ does not hold and define $S = \{s \in \mathbb{N}^{<\mathbb{N}} : \exists t\,(s \subseteq t \wedge t \notin T)\}$. The set S exists by Σ_1^0–comprehension, and it is clear that S is a tree. It is easy to check that $\forall f \in \mathbb{N}^{\mathbb{N}}\,(f \notin [T] \leftrightarrow f \in [S])$ and hence T defines a clopen set. $\qquad\square$

Proposition 3. ATR_0 *proves* Π_1^0-Det_L *and* $(\Delta_1^0, \Sigma_1^0 \wedge \Pi_1^0)$-$\mathrm{Det}_L$.

Proof. First we show that ATR_0 proves Π_1^0-Det_L. Consider $A(f), B(g) \in \Pi_1^0$. By Proposition 1 there are trees $S, T \subseteq \mathbb{N}^{<\mathbb{N}}$ satisfying that $[S] = \{f \in \mathbb{N}^{\mathbb{N}} : A(f)\}$ and $[T] = \{g \in \mathbb{N}^{\mathbb{N}} : B(g)\}$. We must show that the Lipschitz game $G_L([S], [T])$ is determined.

<u>Case 1</u>: $TrueClosed(T)$ holds, i.e., there exists $g_0 \in [T]$ such that $\forall k\,\exists s\,(g_0[k] \subseteq s \wedge s \notin T)$. In this case, there is a winning strategy for player II, σ_{II}, defined as follows: For all $s, t \in \mathbb{N}^{<\mathbb{N}}$ with $|s| = j$ and $|t| = j$, put

$$
\sigma_{II}((s \otimes t) * \langle n \rangle) = \begin{cases} g_0(j) & \text{if } s * \langle n \rangle \in S \\ \min\{k : t * \langle k \rangle \notin T\} & \text{if } s * \langle n \rangle \notin S \wedge \exists k\,(t * \langle k \rangle \notin T) \\ g_0(j) & \text{if } s * \langle n \rangle \notin S \wedge \forall k\,(t * \langle k \rangle \in T) \end{cases}
$$

(In words, player II plays using the boundary point g_0 while player I has played inside S and if player I leaves S at some round then player II will eventually leave T too.) The existence of σ_{II} is granted by ACA_0 and it is straightforward to check that σ_{II} is a winning strategy for player II.

<u>Case 2</u>: Case 1 does not hold but $TrueClosed(S)$ does, i.e., there exists $f_0 \in [S]$ such that $\forall k\,\exists s\,(f_0[k] \subseteq s \wedge s \notin S)$. Put $T' = \{t \in T : \exists t'\,(t \subseteq t' \wedge t' \notin T)\}$. Then, T' exists by arithmetical comprehension, and T' is a well-founded tree since Case 1 fails. Note that if $t_0 \in T - T'$ then we have $\forall t'\,(t_0 \subseteq t' \to t' \in T)$. Thus, a winning strategy for player I, σ_I, can be defined as follows: Let $\sigma_I(\langle\rangle) = f_0(0)$ and for all $s, t \in \mathbb{N}^{<\mathbb{N}}$ with $|s| = |t| = j \geq 1$, put

$$
\sigma_I(s \otimes t) = \begin{cases} f_0(j) & \text{if } t \notin T \vee t \in T' \\ \min\{k : s * \langle k \rangle \notin S\} & \text{if } t \in T - T' \wedge \exists k\,(s * \langle k \rangle \notin S) \\ f_0(j) & \text{if } t \in T - T' \wedge \forall k\,(s * \langle k \rangle \in S) \end{cases}
$$

Again, σ_I exists by ACA_0 and, having in mind that player II must eventually play outside T' since T' is well–founded, it is easy to check that σ_I is a winning strategy for player I.

<u>Case 3</u>: Both $TrueClosed(T)$ and $TrueClosed(S)$ fail. By Lemma 3 $[T]$ and $[S]$ are clopen sets and hence $G_L([S], [T])$ is determined by Theorem 2.

We conclude by showing that ATR_0 proves $(\Delta_1^0, \Sigma_1^0 \wedge \Pi_1^0)$-$\mathrm{Det}_L$. Given $A(f) \in \Delta_1^0$ and $B_0(g), B_1(g) \in \Pi_1^0$ we show that the Lipschitz game $G_L(A, B_0 \wedge \neg B_1)$ is determined. By Proposition 1 there are trees $S, S', T_0, T_1 \subseteq \mathbb{N}^{<\mathbb{N}}$ satisfying that

$[S] = \{f \in \mathbb{N}^{\mathbb{N}} : A(f)\}$, $[S'] = \{f \in \mathbb{N}^{\mathbb{N}} : \neg A(f)\}$ and $[T_i] = \{g \in \mathbb{N}^{\mathbb{N}} : B_i(g)\}$, for $i = 0, 1$. It is easily seen that $S \cap S'$ is a well-founded tree and, without loss of generality, we can assume that $T_1 \subseteq T_0$. We must show that the game $G_L([S], [T_0] - [T_1])$ is determined. Again we distinguish several cases:

Case A: $TrueClosed(T_0)$ does not hold. Then by Lemma 3, T_0 defines a clopen set and there exists a tree T_0' such that $\forall g \in \mathbb{N}^{\mathbb{N}} (g \notin [T_0] \leftrightarrow g \in [T_0'])$. Then the game $G_L([S], [T_0] - [T_1])$ is equivalent to a game $G_L(A, C)$ for a formula $C(g) \in \Sigma_1^0$, since

$$g \in [T_0] - [T_1] \leftrightarrow g \notin [T_0'] \wedge g \notin [T_1] \leftrightarrow \exists k \, (g[k] \notin T_0' \wedge g[k] \notin T_1)$$

But let us note that, by Remark 1, Σ_1^0-Det_L is equivalent to Π_1^0-Det_L and so it follows that $G_L([S], [T_0] - [T_1])$ is determined.

Case B: $TrueClosed(T_0)$ holds and there exists some function $g_0 \in [T_0] - [T_1]$ such that $\forall k \exists s \, (g_0[k] \subseteq s \wedge s \notin T_0)$. In this case, there is a winning strategy for player II, σ_{II}, defined essentially as in Case 1. Bearing in mind that $S \cap S'$ is well-founded, player II plays using the boundary point g_0 as follows: while player I has played inside $S \cap S'$ player II plays using g_0 and if player I leaves $S \cap S'$ at some round then player II will eventually leave T_0 if player I plays in $S' - (S \cap S')$ or will remain inside $T_0 - T_1$ if player I plays in $S - (S \cap S')$.

Case C: $TrueClosed(T_0)$ holds, but Case B fails. That is, every $g_0 \in [T_0]$ such that $\forall k \exists s \, (g_0[k] \subseteq s \wedge s \notin T_0)$ satisfies $g_0 \in [T_1]$. Then, by Arithmetical Comprehension there exists $C = \{t : \forall s \, (t \subseteq s \rightarrow s \in T_0)\}$, and, for every $g \in \mathbb{N}^{\mathbb{N}}$,

$$g \in [T_0] - [T_1] \leftrightarrow \exists k \, (g[k] \in C \wedge g[k] \notin T_1)$$

As a consequence, the game $G_L([S], [T_0] - [T_1])$ is again equivalent to a game $G_L(A, D)$, for a formula $D(g) \in \Sigma_1^0$ and, as noted in Case A, is determined. $\square$

Theorem 5. *The following principles are pairwise equivalent over* RCA$_0$:

1. ATR$_0$.
2. Π_1^0-Det_L.
3. (Δ_1^0, Π_1^0)-Det_L.
4. $(\Delta_1^0, \Sigma_1^0 \wedge \Pi_1^0)$-SLO$_L$

Proof. Let us observe that, by Proposition 3, (1) implies (2) and (4). On the other hand, obviously, (2) implies (3) and so we only have to show that both (3) and (4) imply (1).

(3)$\Rightarrow$(1): By Theorem 2 it is sufficient to show that RCA$_0$ + (Δ_1^0, Π_1^0)-Det_L implies ACA$_0$. Assume RCA$_0$ + (Δ_1^0, Π_1^0)-Det_L and consider $\varphi(x) \in \Sigma_1^0$ (we disregard parameters). We must show that the set $\{x : \varphi(x)\}$ exists. Write $\varphi(x) \equiv \exists y \, \varphi_0(x, y)$ with $\varphi_0 \in \Delta_0^0$. Define $A(f)$ to be $\forall i \le f(0) \, (f(i) = f(0) - i)$ and $B(g)$ to be

$$\forall l [l = g(0) \rightarrow \forall i \le l \, (g(i) = l - i) \wedge \forall i \le l \, (\exists y \, \varphi_0(i, y) \rightarrow \exists y \le g(l+1) \, \varphi_0(i, y))]$$

That is to say, a play for player I is in A if it is of the form

$$\langle k, (k-1), (k-2), \ldots, 0 \rangle * f'$$

for some $k \in \mathbb{N}$ and $f' \in \mathbb{N}^{\mathbb{N}}$. A play for player II is in B if it is of the form

$$\langle l, (l-1), \ (l-2), \ \ldots, \ 0 \rangle * \langle m \rangle * g'$$

for some $l, m \in \mathbb{N}$ and $g' \in \mathbb{N}^{\mathbb{N}}$ and, in addition, for each $i \le l$, if $\varphi(i)$ holds then $\exists y \le m \, \varphi_0(i, y)$ holds too. Note that $A(f) \in \Delta_1^0$ and $B(g) \in \Pi_1^0$.

Claim. Player I cannot have a winning strategy in the game $G_L(A, B)$.

Proof. Towards a contradiction, assume that σ is a winning strategy for player I and fix $k_0 = \sigma(\langle\rangle)$. By the strong Σ_1^0 bounding scheme (which is available in RCA$_0$), there exists m_0 satisfying that $\forall i \le k_0 \, (\exists y \, \varphi_0(i, y) \to \exists y \le m_0 \, \varphi_0(i, y))$. Now consider a strategy for player II, τ, defined as follows: Player II mimics player I's first $k_0 + 1$ moves and in her $(k_0 + 2)$-th move, player II picks m_0. Clearly, we have $(A(\sigma \otimes^{\mathrm{I}} \tau) \leftrightarrow B(\sigma \otimes^{\mathrm{II}} \tau))$, which contradicts the fact that σ is a winning strategy for player I. $\qquad\square$

In view of the previous claim, it follows from (Δ_1^0, Π_1^0)-Det$_L$ that player II has a winning strategy, say σ_0, in $G_L(A, B)$. For each $k \in \mathbb{N}$, let σ_{I}^k denote the strategy for player I according to which player I plays as follows:

$$\langle k+1, k, (k-1), (k-2), \ \ldots, 0 \rangle * \langle 0, 0, 0, \ldots \rangle$$

It is clear that $A(\sigma_{\mathrm{I}}^k \otimes^{\mathrm{I}} \sigma_0)$ holds and hence $B(\sigma_{\mathrm{I}}^k \otimes^{\mathrm{II}} \sigma_0)$ holds as well, for σ_0 is a winning strategy for player II. Put $g = \sigma_{\mathrm{I}}^k \otimes^{\mathrm{II}} \sigma_0$, $l = g(0)$ and $m = g(l+1)$. Then, we have $\forall i \le l \, (\exists y \, \varphi_0(i, y) \to \exists y \le m \, \varphi_0(i, y))$. But observe that $k \le l$ (for otherwise it is easy to construct a strategy for player I that would allow player I to beat player II's strategy σ_0). As a result, we have $\varphi(k) \leftrightarrow \exists y \le m \, \varphi_0(k, y)$. By Δ_1^0-comprehension, there exists $S \subseteq \mathrm{Seq}_{\mathrm{even}} \times \mathbb{N} \times \mathbb{N}$ such that $(S)_k = \sigma_{\mathrm{I}}^k$ for each k, where $(S)_k = \{(s, n) \in \mathrm{Seq}_{\mathrm{even}} \times \mathbb{N} : (s, n, k) \in S\}$. Then, for each $k \in \mathbb{N}$

$$\varphi(k) \leftrightarrow \exists l, m \, (l = ((S)_k \otimes^{\mathrm{II}} \sigma_0)(0) \wedge m = ((S)_k \otimes^{\mathrm{II}} \sigma_0)(l+1) \wedge \exists y \le m \, \varphi_0(k, y))$$

and

$$\varphi(k) \leftrightarrow \forall l, m \, (l = ((S)_k \otimes^{\mathrm{II}} \sigma_0)(0) \wedge m = ((S)_k \otimes^{\mathrm{II}} \sigma_0)(l+1) \to \exists y \le m \, \varphi_0(k, y))$$

Thus, the set $\{x : \varphi(x)\}$ exists by Δ_1^0-comprehension.

(4)$\Rightarrow$(1): By Theorem 2 it suffices to show that RCA$_0$ + $(\Delta_1^0, \Sigma_1^0 \wedge \Pi_1^0)$-SLO$_L$ implies ACA$_0$. To this end, we will adapt the proof of (3)$\Rightarrow$(1). Assume RCA$_0$ + $(\Delta_1^0, \Sigma_1^0 \wedge \Pi_1^0)$-SLO$_L$ and consider $\varphi(x) \in \Sigma_1^0$. Write $\varphi(x) \equiv \exists y \, \varphi_0(x, y)$ with $\varphi_0 \in \Delta_0^0$. Define $A(f)$ to be $\forall i \le f(0) \, (f(i) = f(0) - i)$ and $B'(g)$ to be

$$\exists l \, [g(l) = 1 \wedge \forall l' < l \, (g(l') = 0)] \wedge \forall l \, [g(l) = 1 \wedge \forall l' < l \, (g(l') = 0) \to \forall i \le l \, (\exists y \, \varphi_0(i, y) \to \exists y \le g(l+1) \, \varphi_0(i, y))]$$

That is to say, a play for player I is in A if it is of the form

$$\langle k, (k-1), (k-2), \ldots, 0 \rangle * f'$$

for some $k \in \mathbb{N}$ and $f' \in \mathbb{N}^{\mathbb{N}}$. A play for player II is in B' if it is of the form

$$\overbrace{\langle 0, \ldots, 0 \rangle}^{l-1 \text{ times}} * \langle 1 \rangle * \langle m \rangle * g'$$

for some $l, m \in \mathbb{N}$ and $g' \in \mathbb{N}^{\mathbb{N}}$ and, in addition, for each $i \leq l$, if $\varphi(i)$ holds then $\exists y \leq m \, \varphi_0(i, y)$ holds too. Note that $A(f) \in \Delta_1^0$ and $B'(g) \in \Sigma_1^0 \wedge \Pi_1^0$.

Reasoning as in the proof of $(3) \Rightarrow (1)$, one can show that player II cannot have a winning strategy in the game $G_L(\neg B', A)$. Hence, by $(\Delta_1^0, \Sigma_1^0 \wedge \Pi_1^0)$-SLO$_L$ player II has a winning strategy in the game $G_L(A, B')$, say σ_0. Again reasoning as in the proof of $(3) \Rightarrow (1)$, one can show that $\{x : \varphi(x)\}$ exists by Δ_1^0-comprehension using σ_0 as a parameter. $\qquad \square$

We leave as a pending question whether (Δ_1^0, Π_1^0)-SLO$_L$ implies ACA$_0$ over RCA$_0$. A positive answer would improve Theorem 5.

5   Concluding Remarks

This paper studies the logical strength of Lipschitz determinacy for the first levels of the Borel hierarchy in the Baire space in terms of subsystems of second order arithmetic. Two natural questions for future research arise in this context. We know from [2] that full Borel Lipschitz determinacy is provable within the subsystem ATR$_0$ + Π_1^1-induction, while we have shown here that ATR$_0$ suffices for proving $(\Delta_1^0, \Sigma_1^0 \wedge \Pi_1^0)$-Det$_L$. But, (*Q1*) what is the highest level (Γ_1, Γ_2) for which (Γ_1, Γ_2)-Det$_L$ remains provable in ATR$_0$? (*Q2*) What is the smallest level (Γ_2, Γ_3), if any, for which (Γ_2, Γ_3)-Det$_L$ implies ATR$_0$ + Π_1^1-induction over an appropriate base theory?

In [12], Wadge also introduced the so-called *Wadge games* (a variation of Lipschitz games where player II is allowed to pass) to analyze reducibility via continuous functions in the Baire space. A natural line for future work would involve calibrating the logical strength of Wadge determinacy and Wadge SLO for different levels of the Borel hierarchy in the Baire space. Some progress in this direction has already been made in [6], and [1] provides an analysis of both Lipschitz and Wadge determinacy for the initial levels of the Borel hierarchy in the Cantor space.

References

1. Cordón-Franco, A., Lara-Martín, F.F., Loureiro, M.J.S.: Lipschitz and Wadge binary games in second order arithmetic. Ann. Pure Appl. Log. **174**(9) (2023). paper 103301
2. Day, A., Greenberg, N., Harrison-Trainor, M., Turetsky, D.: An effective classification of Borel Wadge classes. Submitted
3. Greenberg, N., Montalbán, A.: Ranked structures and arithmetic transfinite recursion. Trans. Am. Math. Soc. **360**(3), 1265–1307 (2008)
4. Hirst, J.L.: Reverse mathematics and rank functions for directed graphs. Arch. Math. Logic **39**, 569–579 (2000)
5. Hirst, J.L.: A survey of the reverse mathematics of ordinal arithmetic. In: Simpson, S.G. (ed.) Reverse Mathematics 2001, Lecture Notes in Logic, vol. 21, pp. 222–234 (2001)

6. Loureiro, M.J.S.: Semilinear order property and infinite games, Ph.D. thesis, University of Seville, Spain, 2016
7. Louveau, A., Saint Raymond, J.: Borel classes and closed games: Wadge-type and Hurewitcz-type results. Trans. Am. Math. Soc. **304**, 431–467 (1987)
8. Montalbán, A., Shore, R.A.: The limits of determinacy in second order arithmetic. Proc. Lond. Math. Soc. **104**, 223–252 (2012)
9. Nemoto, T., MedSalem, M.O., Tanaka, K.: Infinite games in the Cantor space and subsystems of second order arithmetic. Math. Log. Quart. **53**, 226–236 (2007)
10. Simpson, S.G.: Subsystems of Second Order Arithmetic. Perspectives in Mathematical Logic, 2nd edn. Cambridge University Press, Cambridge (2009)
11. Steel, J.R.: Determinateness and subsystems of analysis, Ph.D. thesis, University of California, Berkeley, 1977
12. Wadge, W.W.: Reducibility and Determinateness on the Baire Space, Ph.D. thesis, University of California, Berkeley, 1983

Higher-Order Feedback Computation

Juan P. Aguilera[1], Robert S. Lubarsky[2], and Leonardo Pacheco[1(✉)] (iD)

[1] TU Wien, Vienna, Austria
aguilera@logic.at, leonardo.pacheco@tuwien.ac.at
[2] Florida Atlantic University, Boca Raton, USA
rlubarsk@fau.edu

Abstract. Feedback Turing machines are Turing machines which can query a halting oracle which has information on the convergence or divergence of *feedback* computations. To avoid a contradiction by diagonalization, feedback Turing machines have two ways of not converging: they can diverge as standard Turing machines, or they can freeze. A natural question to ask is: what about feedback Turing machines which can ask if computations of the same type converge, diverge, or freeze? We define αth order feedback Turing machines for each computable ordinal α. We also describe feedback computable and semi-computable sets using inductive definitions and Gale–Stewart games.

Keywords: Turing computation · Feedback computation · Fixed-point operators

1 Introduction

Feedback Turing machines are Turing machines which can query a halting oracle $h :\subseteq \omega \times \omega \to \{\downarrow, \uparrow\}$, which has information on the convergence or divergence of *feedback* computations. That is, given the code e for a feedback Turing machine and an input n the oracle answers if the computation $\{e\}^h(n)$ converges or diverges. To avoid a contradiction by diagonalization, feedback Turing machines have two ways of not converging: they can diverge as standard Turing machines, or they can freeze. A feedback Turing machine freezes when it asks the halting oracle h about a pair $\langle e, n \rangle$ not in the domain of h.

Feedback Turing machines were first studied by Ackerman, Freer and Lubarsky [2,3]. They proved that the feedback computable sets are the Δ_1^1 sets and the feedback semi-computable sets are the Π_1^1 sets. We can also show that the feedback semi-computable sets are the winning regions of Gale–Stewart games with Σ_1^0 payoff [14]. It is quite curious that some of the key results of [2] were announced in Rogers' textbook on recursion theory [15], almost 50 years before proofs were published.

Lubarsky [11] defined feedback infinite time Turing machines and their subcomputation trees. He showed that feedback writable, feedback eventually writable, and feedback accidentally writable reals coincide; this does not happen for standard infinite time Turing machines. By a result of Welch [16], the feedback infinite time Turing machine semi-computable sets are the winning regions of Σ_3^0 Gale–Stewart games. On the other hand, one can also add feedback to weaker notions of computability. Ackerman *et al.* [2,3] studied feedback primitive recursion. Feedback primitive recursive sets coincide with the computable sets. That is, computability via Turing machines itself is a kind of feedback computation. Ackerman *et al.* also lifted the results of feedback computability over ω to feedback computability over 2^ω in [1].

A natural question to ask is: what about feedback Turing machines which can ask if computations of the same type converge, diverge, or freeze? These new machines are second-order feedback machines. Note that we must now have a new and stronger notion of freezing to avoid a contradiction by diagonalization. Having defined second-order feedback computation, it is now natural to ask: what about third-, fourth-, and higher-order feedback?

We define αth order feedback Turing machines for each computable ordinal α using inductive definitions. We also give an alternative definition of αth order feedback Turing computability using subcomputation trees. We describe feedback computable and semi-computable sets using inductive definitions and Gale–Stewart games. Specifically, we prove the following level-by-level correspondence:

Theorem 1. *For all $\alpha < \omega_1^{\mathrm{ck}}$, the following classes of sets of integers coincide:*

1. *the $(\alpha+1)$-feedback semi-computable sets;*
2. *the $\Sigma_{\alpha+1}^\mu$-definable sets; and*
3. *the $\partial(\Sigma_2^0)_\alpha$ sets.*

Proof. Items 1 and 2 are equivalent by Theorems 2 and 3. Items 2 and 3 are equivalent by [8,9]. □

We now turn our attention to μ-arithmetic. μ-arithmetic is obtained by adding least and greatest fixed-point operators to first-order arithmetic. It was inspired by Kozen's [10] modal μ-calculus, an extension of modal logic by fixed-point operators. Lubarsky [12] characterized the μ-definable sets using n-reflecting ordinals. This characterization was later used by Bradfield [7] to show the strictness of the modal μ-calculus' alternation hierarchy, a problem which stayed open for almost a decade. We should note that we are restricted to taking fixed points of positive formulas in the μ-arithmetic; a closely related system is Möllerfeld's σ-arithmetic [13], which lifts this restriction. As the μ- and the σ-arithmetics define the same sets of natural numbers, we restrict ourselves to the μ-arithmetic.

Gale–Stewart games are strong and flexible tools in descriptive set theory. In a Gale–Stewart game $G(A)$ with payoff $A \subseteq \omega^\omega$, two players alternate picking natural numbers to for a sequence α. The first player wins the game $G(A)$ iff they have a strategy which guarantees the generated sequences are inside A, no matter what the second player does. Given a set $A \subseteq \omega^\omega$, the set $\partial A \subseteq \omega^{<\omega}$ is the set of finite sequence $s \in \omega^{<\omega}$ such that the first player has a winning strategy for $G(A)$ starting from s. In other words, ∂A is the set of winning positions for the first player in $G(A)$. Bradfield [6] proved that the μ-definable sets are the winning positions of games whose payoff sets are finite boolean combinations of Σ_2^0 sets. This was later extended by Bradfield, Duparc, and Quickert [8,9] to transfinite μ-formulas and transfinite boolean combinations.

Closely related to higher-order feedback computability are the feedback hyperjump studied by Aguilera and Lubarsky [4] and feedback ^2E-computability studied by Aguilera and Soto [5]. These concepts have two variations: a strict one and a loose one. These refer to how the subcomputation trees are defined: in the loose variations, ill-founded subcomputation trees can be witnesses to non-freezing computations. We will see a similar phenomenon in subcomputation trees for higher-order feedback computations.

Corollary 1. *The following are equivalent:*

1. *2-feedback semi-computability;*
2. *loose feedback ^2E-semi-computability; and*
3. *computable reducibility to the loose feedback hyperjump $\mathcal{LO}$.*

Proof. By [5] and [4].

Outline. In Sect. 2, we define α-feedback computability. In Sect. 3, we define subcomputation trees for α-feedback computations. In Sect. 4, we define the transfinite μ-arithmetic and its alternation hierarchy. In Sects. 5 and 6, we prove the equivalence between feedback computability and μ-definability.

2   Higher-Order Feedback Computability

Fix $\alpha < \omega_1^{ck}$ and a computable notation for α. We define αth order feedback Turing machines. We omit the reference to the ordinal when not ambiguous and abbreviate "αth order feedback Turing machines" by "feedback machines". Write $-1 \le \beta < \alpha$ to mean $\beta = -1$ or $\beta < \alpha$. We will use symbols $\uparrow_\beta$ as notation for the outputs of the freezing oracles. Note that $\uparrow_{-1}$ will be used to indicate convergent computations; we also write $\uparrow_{-1}$ as $\downarrow$. Similarly, $\uparrow_0$ will indicate divergent (and non-freezing) computations.

We can extend any standard encoding of Turing machines as natural numbers to α-feedback Turing machines. We use the fixed encoding of α as a computable ordering to add commands to query the freezing oracles. The encoding of freezing queries are no different from encodings of oracle queries in a relativized computation. Kleene's Recursion Theorem also holds for α-feedback Turing machines by the standard proof, which will be useful for us later.

Intuitively, an α-feedback machine can query freezing oracles

$$f_\beta : F_\beta \to \{\uparrow_{\beta'} |\, -1 \le \beta' \le \beta\},$$

with $F_\beta \subseteq \omega \times \omega$ and $\beta < \alpha$. We call f_β the β-freezing oracle. The domain F_β of f_β contains the indices and inputs of computations which $\le \beta$-freeze. Given the code

$e \in \omega$ of a feedback machine and some input $n \in \omega$, we denote the computation $\{e\}^{\{f_\beta\}_{\beta<\alpha}}(n)$ by $\langle e \rangle^\alpha(n)$. The oracle f_β returns $\uparrow_\gamma \in \{\uparrow_{\beta'} \mid -1 \leq \beta' < \beta\}$ iff $\langle e \rangle^\alpha(n)$ γ-freezes.

A computation $(\beta+1)$-freezes iff it queries f_β about some pair not in F_β. If λ is a limit, a computation λ-freezes iff it makes a query about $\langle e, n \rangle \notin \bigcup_{\alpha < \lambda} F_\alpha$.[1] We also say that a computation 0-freezes when it is divergent and that it -1-freezes when it is convergent. We write $\langle e \rangle^\alpha(n) \uparrow_\beta$ iff $\langle e \rangle^\alpha(n)$ β-freezes.

Formally, we define:

Definition 1. *Let* $\alpha < \omega_1^{ck}$. *For all* $\beta < \alpha$, *let* $F_\beta \subseteq \omega \times \omega$ *be the least relation such that the function* $f_\beta : F_\beta \to \{\uparrow_{\beta'} \mid -1 \leq \beta' < \beta\}$ *is such that* $\langle e, n \rangle \in F_\beta$ *and* $f_\beta(e, n) = \uparrow_\gamma$ *iff* $\langle e \rangle^\alpha(n)$ *makes no* β'-*freezing query outside of* $F_{\beta'}$ *and* γ-*freezes.*

A set $A \subseteq \omega$ *is* α-*feedback computable iff there is an* α-*feedback machine with index* e *such that:*

$$\langle e \rangle^\alpha(n) = \begin{cases} 1, & \text{if } n \in A \\ 0, & \text{if } n \notin A \end{cases}$$

A set $A \subseteq \omega$ *is* α-*feedback semi-computable iff there is an* α-*feedback machine with index* e *such that*

$$\langle e \rangle^\alpha(n) \downarrow \text{ iff } n \in A.$$

Using Theorem 1, we can show that $A \subseteq \omega$ is α-feedback computable iff A and $\omega \setminus A$ are α-feedback semi-computable.

One should be careful that the freezing oracles depend on the fixed α. For a more precise notation, we could write f_β as f_β^α. We do not do so as we always work with a fixed α. To see why the freezing oracles depend on α, consider the 0-freezing oracle f_0^1 for 1-feedback machines and the 0-freezing oracle f_0^2 for 2-feedback machines are different partial functions. f_0^2 has information about halting computations which have freezing subcomputations via queries to f_1^2.

Note that our 1-feedback machines are equivalent to the feedback machines in Ackerman *et al.* [3]. Furthermore, our 0-freezing oracle f_0 for 1-feedback machines is equivalent to their halting oracle. We could also call f_0 the halting oracle, but we prefer not to do so for uniformity of notation. Note also that 0-feedback machines are just standard Turing machines.

Before proceeding, we show that the freezing oracles $\{f_\beta\}_{\beta<\alpha}$ are well-defined using simultaneous inductive definitions. We will come back to this proposition when we show that feedback semi-computable sets are definable in μ-arithmetic.

Proposition 1. *Fix* $\alpha < \omega_1^{ck}$. *For all* $\beta < \alpha$, *there is a smallest relation* $F_\beta \subseteq \omega \times \omega$ *and a function* $f_\beta : F_\beta \to \{\uparrow_{\beta'} \mid -1 \leq \beta' < \beta\}$ *such that* $\langle e, n \rangle \in F_\beta$ *and* $f_\beta(e, n) = \uparrow_\gamma$ *iff* $\langle e \rangle^\alpha(n)$ *makes no* β'-*freezing query outside of* $F_{\beta'}$ *and* γ-*freezes.*

Proof. We define the F_β and f_β by simultaneous inductive definitions.

Given $\beta < \alpha$, Γ_β is an auxiliary function taking sequences $\{g_{\beta'}\}_{\beta' < \alpha}$ of freezing oracles to the set of indices and inputs which β-freeze:

$$\Gamma_\beta(\{g_{\beta'}\}_{\beta'<\alpha}) = \{\langle e, n \rangle \mid \{e\}^{\{g_{\beta'}\}_{\beta'<\alpha}}(n)\beta - \text{freezes}\}.$$

---

[1] See the definition of *subcomputation trees* below.

We define operators $h_{(\beta,\cdot)}$ using the $\Gamma_{\beta'}$ with $\beta' \leq \beta$:

$$h^{-1}_{(\beta,\{g_\gamma\}_{\gamma<\alpha})}(\uparrow_{\beta'}) = \Gamma_{\beta'}(\{g_\gamma\}_{\beta'<\alpha}) \text{ for } \beta' \leq \beta.$$

Each $h_{(\beta,\cdot)}$ can be seen as an operator on sequences of partial functions from ω to ω. Furthermore, $h_{(\beta,\cdot)}$ is monotone: given sequences of partial functions $\{g_\gamma\}_{\gamma<\alpha}$ and $\{g'_\gamma\}_{\gamma<\alpha}$ such that $g_\gamma \subseteq g'_\gamma$ for all $\gamma < \alpha$, then $h_{(\beta,\{g_\gamma\}_{\gamma<\alpha})} \subseteq h_{(\beta,\{g'_\gamma\}_{\gamma<\alpha})}$. Let $\{f_\beta\}_{\beta<\alpha}$ be the sequence of the smallest partial functions such that of $h_{(\beta,\{f_\beta\}_{\beta<\alpha})} = f_\beta$. That is, if $h_{(\beta,\{f'_\beta\}_{\beta<\alpha})} = f'_\beta$, then $f_\beta \subseteq f'_\beta$ for all $\beta < \alpha$.

3   Subcomputation Trees

Fix $e, n \in \omega$ and $\alpha < \omega_1^{\mathrm{ck}}$. We define a subcomputation tree $T_{e,n}$ to witness the convergence, divergence, or freezing of the α-feedback computation $\langle e \rangle^\alpha(n)$. Our trees are similar to the subcomputation trees for 1-feedback Turing computation found in [3].

We will also consider a trimmed version $T_{e,n}^{\mathrm{trim}}$ of the subcomputation trees. As the subtrees for 1-feedback computation, $T_{e,n}^{\mathrm{trim}}$ will be wellfounded iff $\langle e \rangle^\alpha(n)$ is convergent or divergent, and $T_{e,n}^{\mathrm{trim}}$ will be non-wellfounded iff $\langle e \rangle^\alpha(n)$ is β-freezing for some $\beta \geq 1$. We will trim $T_{e,n}$ because higher-order queries allow non-wellfounded trees to witness converging and diverging feedback computations.

After we finish the construction of $T_{e,n}$ and $T_{e,n}^{\mathrm{trim}}$, we will have:

Proposition 2. *Let $e, n \in \omega$ and $T_{e,n}^{\mathrm{trim}}$ be the trimmed subcomputation tree of $\langle e \rangle^\alpha(n)$. Then:*

1. *The computation $\langle e \rangle^\alpha(n)$ is non-freezing iff $T_{e,n}^{\mathrm{trim}}$ is well-founded.*
2. *The computation $\langle e \rangle^\alpha(n)$ is β-freezing iff $T_{e,n}^{\mathrm{trim}}$ has an infinite path $\rho = \{\langle e_i, n_i \rangle\}_{i\in\omega}$ such that*

$$\beta = \limsup\{\beta_i + 1 \mid \text{the edge between } \langle e_i, n_i \rangle \text{ and } \langle e_{i+1}, n_{i+1} \rangle \text{ is labeled } \beta_i\}.$$

Furthermore, the path ρ is the rightmost infinite path in the tree $T_{e,n}^{\mathrm{trim}}$.

Fix an index e and an input n, we build the subcomputation tree of $\langle e \rangle^\alpha(n)$ by stages. The subcomputation tree $T_{e,n}$ will be a labeled subtree of $\omega^{<\omega}$. We label each node of $T_{e,n}$ with a pair $\langle e', n' \rangle$ consisting of an index e' for a feedback Turing machine and an input n'. At each node $\langle e', n' \rangle$, we simulate a feedback machine with index e' starting on input n'. At all times there is a node of $T_{e,n}$ that is in control of the computation. On successor stages, we will run one instruction in the computation being simulated at the control node. When querying the freezing oracle f_β about $\langle e'', n'' \rangle$, we pass the control to a new child node labeled $\langle e'', n'' \rangle$. We label the edge between $\langle e', n' \rangle$ and $\langle e'', n'' \rangle$ with the ordinal $\beta < \alpha$ (Fig. 1).

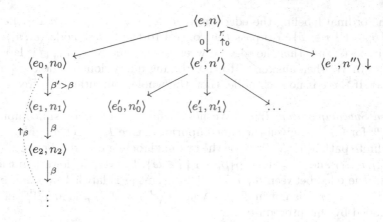

Fig. 1. The tree $T_{\langle e,n\rangle}$ of a converging computation $\langle e,n\rangle$ with diverging and freezing subcomputations.

First Stage. We add root node to $T_{e,n}$. Label the root node by $\langle e,n\rangle$; it is initially in control of the computation. Go to the next construction stage.

Successor Stages. Suppose the control is currently at the node $\langle e',n'\rangle$ of $T_{e,n}$. What we do in this stage of the construction depends on what is the next instruction on the computation being simulated at $\langle e',n'\rangle$.

Suppose the next instruction is not a query to a freezing oracle. Run the instruction. If the computation does not converge, we go to the next stage; the control stays at the same node. If the computation converges, there are two possibilities. If the control node is the root node, the whole computation halts. If the control node is not the root node, we pass control to its parent node; the parent then gets the answer $\downarrow$ to its freezing query and we go to the next stage.

Suppose the next instruction is a query to a freezing oracle h_β about a computation $\langle e'',n''\rangle$. We create a new child node to the right of all existing children. We label the child node by $\langle e'',n''\rangle$ and the path between parent and child by β. The child node now controls the computation. Go to the next stage.

Limit Stages. Suppose that we are on a limit stage of the construction of $T_{e,n}$. In this stage, we decide if some subcomputation of $\langle e\rangle^\alpha(n)$ diverged or froze.

Suppose that the control goes back to a node $\langle e',n'\rangle$ infinitely many times in a final segment of our construction (or that the control stays at a same node $\langle e',n'\rangle$). In this case, the computation at the node $\langle e',n'\rangle$ diverges. If $\langle e',n'\rangle$ is the root node, then the whole computation diverges. If $\langle e',n'\rangle$ is not the root node, pass the control to its parent and answer the parent's freezing query with $\uparrow_0$; we then go to the next stage.

Suppose there is no node $\langle e',n'\rangle$ such that the control goes back to $\langle e',n'\rangle$ infinitely many times in a final segment of the construction up to this point. Let $\rho = \{\langle e_i,n_i\rangle\}_{i\in\omega}$ be the rightmost infinite path in the tree. The control of the computation will have been in nodes of ρ on infinitely many stages. Let

β_i be the ordinal labeling the edge between $\langle e_i, n_i \rangle$ and $\langle e_{i+1}, n_{i+1} \rangle$. Let $\beta :=$ $\limsup\{\beta_i + 1 \mid i \in \omega\}$. We pass the control to the lowest node $\langle e_i, n_i \rangle$ in the path, if it exists, such that the edge between $\langle e_i, n_i \rangle$ and $\langle e_{i+1}, n_{i+1} \rangle$ is labeled by some $\beta' \geq \beta$. We then answer $\uparrow^\beta$ to the freezing query done in the computation at $\langle e_i, n_i \rangle$. If there is no such node, then the whole computation β-freezes.

Trimmed Subcomputation Trees. We now define the trimmed subcomputation tree $T_{e,n}^{\mathrm{trim}}$ for $\langle e \rangle^\alpha(n)$, given the subcomputation tree $T_{e,n}$. Let $\rho = \{\langle e_i, n_i \rangle\}_{i \in \omega}$ be an infinite path in $T_{e,n}$. Let β_i be the ordinal labeling the edge between $\langle e_i, n_i \rangle$ and $\langle e_{i+1}, n_{i+1} \rangle$ and $\beta := \limsup\{\beta_i + 1 \mid i \in \omega\}$. Let $\langle e_i, n_i \rangle$ lowest in the path such that the edge between $\langle e_i, n_i \rangle$ and $\langle e_{i+1}, n_{i+1} \rangle$ is labeled by some $\beta' \geq \beta$. For all $j > i$, $\langle e_j, n_j \rangle$ is not in $T_{e,n}^{\mathrm{trim}}$. A node $\langle e', n' \rangle$ of $T_{e,n}$ is in $T_{e,n}^{\mathrm{trim}}$ iff it was not excluded by this procedure.

4   The μ-Arithmetic

The language $\mathcal{L}_\mu$ of μ-arithmetic is obtained by adding countably many set variables and the fixed-point operators μ and ν to the language $\mathcal{L}_1$ of first-order arithmetic. Therefore, the μ-arithmetic has two types of terms: number and set terms.

Number terms are build up from constants 0 and 1, number variables, addition, and multiplication:

$$t := 0 \mid 1 \mid x \mid t + t \mid t \times t.$$

We define μ-formulas and μ-terms by simultaneous induction. Set terms are set variables or fixed-points:

$$T := X \mid \mu x X.\varphi \mid \nu x X.\varphi,$$

Atomic formulas are of the form $t = t'$ and $t \in T$, where t, t are number terms and T is a set term. Formulas are defined as follows:

$$\varphi := t = t \mid t \in T \mid \neg\varphi \mid \varphi \vee \varphi \mid \varphi \wedge \varphi \mid \exists x.\varphi \mid \forall x.\varphi \mid \bigvee_{i<\omega} \varphi_i \mid \bigwedge_{i<\omega} \varphi_i.$$

The set terms $\mu x X.\varphi$ and $\nu x X.\varphi$ are well-formed iff X is positive in φ. That is, each occurrence of X in φ is in the scope of an even number of negations (possibly none). The formulas $\bigvee_{i<\omega} \varphi_i$ and $\bigwedge_{i<\omega} \varphi_i$ are only defined if there is a computable enumeration of the formulas φ_i and there is a finite collection $\mathcal{X}$ of number and set variables such that the free variables of each φ_i are in $\mathcal{X}$. This restriction allows us to, given a transfinite formula with only positive occurrences of variables, obtain a closed set term with finitely many applications of fixed-point operators.

We use η to denote either μ or ν. Note that the fixed-point operator $\eta x X$ in a set term $\eta x X.\varphi$ binds both the occurrences of the number variable x and the occurrences of the set variable X. We usually denote the variables in a fixed point operator $\eta x X$ by lowercase and uppercase versions of the same letter.

We can encode the μ-formulas as usual. We only need to take care when encoding transfinite disjunctions and conjunctions. As we only to consider conjunctions and disjunctions of recursively enumerable many formulas, we can code this with indexes for programs enumerating codes for the formulas in these conjunctions and disjunctions. A note of caution: a number may encode some non-well-formed formula with non-wellfounded syntax tree, but this will not be a problem since we will never quantify over all the codes.

We interpret the μ-formulas over the set of natural numbers, where the first-order objects and set membership have their standard interpretations. We only need to define the interpretation of the fixed-point operators. If X is positive in $\varphi(x, X)$, define the operator $\Gamma_\varphi : \mathcal{P}(\omega) \to \mathcal{P}(\omega)$ by:

$$\Gamma_\varphi(A) := \{n \in \omega \mid \varphi(n, A)\}.$$

We can show by induction on the structure of φ that, if X is positive in φ, then Γ_φ is monotone: if $A \subseteq B$, then $\Gamma_\varphi(A) \subseteq \Gamma_\varphi(B)$. By the Knaster–Tarski Theorem, Γ_φ has least and greatest fixed-points. Denote by $\mu x X.\varphi$ the least fixed-point of Γ_φ and by $\nu x X.\varphi$ the greatest fixed-point of Γ_φ.

We can use games to define a different but equivalent alternative for the μ-arithmetic's semantics. We sketch it here at is is quite useful to understand the meaning of μ-formulas. Given a μ-formula φ and interpretations for its free set variables, Verifier and Refuter play a game to decide whether φ hold. When discussing formula ψ, one of the players will have to propose a new formula to discuss. For example, when discussing $\exists x.\psi(x)$, Verifier has to choose some $\psi(n)$; similarly, when discussing $\bigwedge_{i \in \omega} \psi_i$, Refuter has to choose some ψ_i. If discussing $\neg\psi$, the players switch roles and discuss ψ. When discussing $\tau \in \eta x X.\psi$, the players discuss $\psi(\tau, \eta x X.\psi)$. When discussing $\tau \in X$, the players go to $\tau \in \eta x X.\psi$, where $\eta x X.\psi$ the smallest formula where X is bound; in this case, we say that X was regenerated. We summarize the possible plays in Table 1 below.

At a position of the form $t = s$, Verifier wins iff the equality is true. Let ρ be an infinite play and $X_0, \ldots, X_n$ be the variables regenerated infinitely often and $\eta_0.\psi_0, \ldots \eta_n.\psi_n$ be the associated formulas. Let η_i be the fixed-point operator with biggest scope. Verifier wins ρ iff η_i is a ν.

For context, the evaluation game for any transfinite μ-formula is determined because it can be written as a Δ_3^0 Gale–Stewart game; and so it is determined by Borel determinacy. See [9] for a proof that Verifier wins the evaluation game for φ iff φ is true.

The alternation hierarchy classifies the μ-formulas according to the alternation of least and greatest fixed-point operators. For all computable α, the αth level of the alternation hierarchy is defined by:

- $\Sigma_0^\mu = \Pi_0^\mu :=$ all first-order formulas (with set variables);
- $\Sigma_{\alpha+1}^\mu :=$ the closure of $\Sigma_\alpha^\mu \cup \Pi_\alpha^\mu$ under $\wedge, \vee, \exists, \forall$ and $\tau \in \mu x X.\varphi$;
- $\Pi_{\alpha+1}^\mu :=$ the closure of $\Sigma_\alpha^\mu \cup \Pi_\alpha^\mu$ under $\wedge, \vee, \exists, \forall$ and $\tau \in \nu x X.\varphi$;

Table 1. The rules of evaluation game for μ-arithmetic.

Verifier		Refuter	
Position	Admissible moves	Position	Admissible moves
$\psi_1 \vee \psi_2$	$\{\psi_1, \psi_2\}$	$\psi_1 \wedge \psi_2$	$\{\psi_1, \psi_2\}$
$\exists x.\psi(x)$	$\{\psi(n) \mid n \in \omega\}$	$\forall x.\psi(n)$	$\{\psi(n) \mid n \in \omega\}$
$\bigvee_{i \in \omega} \psi_i$	$\{\psi_i \mid i \in \omega\}$	$\bigwedge_{i \in \omega} \psi_i$	$\{\psi_i, \mid i \in \omega\}$
$\tau \in \mu x X.\psi(x, X)$	$\{\psi(\tau, \mu x X.\psi)\}$	$\tau \in \nu x X.\psi(x, X)$	$\{\psi(\tau, \nu x X.\psi)\}$

- $\Sigma^\mu_\lambda :=$ the closure of $\bigcup_{\alpha < \lambda} \Sigma^\mu_\alpha$ under recursive enumerable disjunctions $\bigvee_{i < \omega}$, when λ is a limit;
- $\Pi^\mu_\lambda :=$ the closure of $\bigcup_{\alpha < \lambda} \Sigma^\mu_\alpha$ under recursive enumerable conjunctions $\bigwedge_{i < \omega}$, when λ is a limit.

We say that $A \subseteq \omega$ is $\Sigma^\mu_{\alpha+1}$-definable iff there is a $\Sigma^\mu_{\alpha+1}$-formula $n \in \mu x X.\varphi$ such that $A = \{n \in \omega \mid n \in \mu x X.\varphi\}$. If λ is a limit ordinal, $A \subseteq \omega$ is Σ^μ_λ-definable iff there is a Σ^μ_λ-formula $\bigvee_{i \in \omega} n \in \mu x X.\psi_i$ such that $A = \{n \in \omega \mid \bigvee_{i \in \omega} n \in \mu x X.\psi_i\}$.

It will also be useful to consider formulas in a kind of prenex normal form. Lubarsky [12] showed that all finite μ-formulas can be put in the form:

$$\tau_n \in \mu x_n X_n.\tau_{n-1} \in \nu x_{n-1} X_{n-1}.\tau_{n-2} \in \mu x_{n-2} X_{n-2}. \ldots \tau_1 \in \eta x_1 X_1.\varphi,$$

with φ first-order formula.

Bradfield *et al.* [8,9] extended Lubarsky's normal form to transfinite formulas. A transfinite μ-formula is in normal form iff it is:

- a finite μ-formula in normal form;
- an infinite disjunction or conjunction of μ-formulas in normal form; or
- a formula of the form $\tau \in \eta x X.\varphi$ where φ is in normal form.

Bradfield *et al.* show that all transfinite μ-formulas are equivalent to one in normal form by induction of the construction of formulas and Lubarsky's result.

5 μ-Definability Implies Feedback Computability

In this section, we define an evaluation function eval for Σ^μ_α-formulas using α-feedback machines. The function eval receives the code of a formula φ (along with some auxiliary input) and outputs 1 iff φ is true. To evaluate a given formula we will decompose it and check it by parts.

Feedback will be used in two places. First, to check quantifiers, infinite disjunctions, and infinite conjunctions. For example, we can imagine a program which evaluates $\varphi(n)$ for all $n \in \omega$ and stops when it finds some n such that $\varphi(n)$ fails; the formula $\forall x.\varphi(x)$ is true iff this program does not stop. We can verify this with a 0-freezing query. Second, to evaluate fixed-point formulas. eval

β-freezing on input φ will be (roughly) equivalent to φ being false; a $(\beta + 1)$-freezing query tells us if φ is true.

We will make heavy use of Kleene's Recursion Theorem in the proof. It holds for α-feedback computability, by the standard proof.

Theorem 2. *Let $A \subseteq \omega$ and $\alpha < \omega_1^{ck}$. If A is Σ_α^μ-definable then A is α-feedback semi-computable.*

See Appendix A for a proof of Theorem 2.

6   Feedback Computability Implies μ-Definability

In this section, we show that α-feedback semi-computable sets are Σ_α^μ-definable. To do so, we show that the graph of the freezing oracle f_α is Σ_α^μ-definable. The heart of this proof is Proposition 1, but we need to take care when stating the inductive definitions: μ-formulas can only have finitely many free set variables. We show how we can overcome this technicality using an encoding for α and only two set variables.

Theorem 3. *Let $A \subseteq \omega$ and $\alpha < \omega_1^{ck}$. If A is αth-order feedback semi-computable then A is Σ_α^μ-definable.*

Proof. Fix $\alpha < \omega_1^{ck}$. We prove that the graph of f_α is Σ_α^μ-definable for α a successor ordinal. The case for limit ordinals is similar; we will indicate the changes in the appropriate place.

We use computation histories for computations $\langle e \rangle^\alpha(n)$. A computation history encodes a finite initial segment of a computation. Such encoding is possible because at each step, the computation only needs a finite amount of memory. Any such encoding is good as long that we can decide if some natural number encodes a computation history or not. We also require that, from a computation history h, we can recover the index e, the initial input n and the step-by-step computation of $\langle e \rangle^\alpha(n)$ up to a finite time. Note that a freezing oracle query counts as only one step here. A computation will be halting iff it has a finite computation history which halts (this history will have no extension). A computation diverges iff there are computation histories of unbounded length. For $\beta \leq \alpha$, a computation β-freezes iff there is a sequence of histories $\{h_i\}_{i \in \omega}$ such that: $e_0 = e$ and $n_0 = n$; h_i is a computation history for $\langle e_i \rangle^\alpha(n_i)$ ending in a query to f_{β_i} about $\langle e_{i+1} \rangle^\alpha(n_{i+1})$; and $\beta = \limsup\{\beta_i + 1 \mid i \in \omega\}$.

We will first give a wrong proof: we define the graph of the freezing oracle f_β by a $\Sigma_{\beta+1}^\mu$-formula χ_β with free variables $X_{\beta+1}, X_{\beta+2}, \ldots, X_\alpha$. For $\beta \geq \omega \cdot 2$, $\chi_\beta(x)$ is not a well-formed μ-formula. We explain later how to modify the χ_β and obtain proper μ-formulas.

The graph of the freezing oracle f_0 is defined by the formula $\chi_0(x)$ defined as follows. $\chi_0(x)$ is of the form $x \in \mu x_0 X_0 . \varphi_0(x_0)$. $\varphi_0(x_0)$ is true if $x_0 = \langle e, n, \downarrow \rangle$ and there is a computation history witnessing that $\langle e \rangle^\alpha(n)$ halts; or if $x_0 = \langle e, n, \uparrow_0 \rangle$ and for all k there is a computation history of length k for $\langle e \rangle^\alpha(n)$ which is non-halting. Note that X_β is free in χ_0 for all $0 < \beta \leq \alpha$, since the only fixed-point operator in χ_0 is $\mu x_0 X_0$.

Suppose the formula χ_β defines the graph of f_β. We now define the graph of the freezing oracle $f_{\beta+1}$ with a formula $\chi_{\beta+1}$. The formula $\chi_{\beta+1}(x)$ is of the form $x \in \mu x_{\beta+1} X_{\beta+1}.\varphi_{\beta+1}(x_{\beta+1})$. Here, $\varphi_{\beta+1}(x_{\beta+1})$ is true if either $\chi_\beta(x_{\beta+1})$ holds, or $x_{\beta+1} = \langle e, n, \uparrow_{\{}\beta+1\} \rangle$ and there is a sequence of histories $\{h_i\}_{i \in \omega}$ witnessing that $\langle e \rangle^\alpha(n)$ β'-freezes for β' with $\beta \le \beta' < \alpha$. The last disjunct can be computed by a greatest fixed-point: start with the set of all finite sequences of histories and trim off the sequences which cannot be the initial segments of such an witnessing history $\{h_i\}_{i \in \omega}$; the resulting tree is non-empty only if such sequence of histories exist.

If we have defined χ_β for all $\beta < \lambda$, we define $\chi_\lambda(x)$ by $\bigvee_{\beta < \lambda} \chi_\beta(x)$. When proving that λ-feedback computable are Σ_λ^μ-definable, we define χ_λ similarly, but omit the references for $\beta' > \beta$ in each χ_β.

We use α's encoding on ω to substitute references for X_β with references to X_α. We can do so because a query to f_β is a query to f_α where we ignore the output if it is $\uparrow_{\beta'}$ for some $\beta' > \beta$. The corrected formula is a well-formed μ-formula equivalent to the non-well-formed formula. This finishes the definition of the freezing oracle f_α.

Now, suppose A is αth order feedback semi-computable via a machine with index e. For all $\beta < \alpha$, we can recover f_β from f_α using the computable encoding of α. Thus $n \in A$ iff there is a computation history for e starting with input n where the computation halts; here, the computation histories can consult the freezing oracles $\{f_\beta\}_{\beta \le \alpha}$.

Acknowledgments. This study was funded by FWF project TAI-797.

Disclosure of Interests. The authors have no competing interests to declare that are relevant to the content of this article.

A   Proof of Theorem 2

Let $A \subseteq \omega$ and $\alpha < \omega_1^{\text{ck}}$. We show that, if A is Σ_α^μ-definable, then A is α-feedback semi-computable.

We begin by defining an evaluation function eval for Σ_α^μ-formulas. We then prove by induction on $\beta \le \alpha$ that the Σ_β^μ-definable sets are α-feedback semi-computable.

For this proof, we work with a fixed set of set variables $\{X_i \mid i \in \omega\}$. We also assume that the μ-formulas are in normal form. We do not consider formulas with free *number* variables. eval is defined by recursion on the structure of the Σ_α^μ-formulas: we begin at the first order formulas and go up level-by-level.

The function $\text{eval}(\varphi, s)$ takes as input a formula φ, and a sequence s of natural numbers. The sequence s is a sequence of indices of (possibly partial) characteristic function of sets. If $i < \text{length}(s)$ then s_i denotes the index in the ith position of s. If $i \ge \text{length}(s)$, then s_i is the index for the characteristic function of the empty set. s will be useful when evaluating the fixed-point operators.

We define `eval` for first-order formulas, along with auxiliary functions `exists` and `forall`:

- $\text{eval}(t = t', s) := \begin{cases} 1, \text{ if } t = t' \\ 0, \text{ otherwise} \end{cases}$

- $\text{eval}(t \in X_i, s) := \begin{cases} 1, \text{ if } \langle s_i \rangle^{\alpha}(t) = 1 \\ 0, \text{ otherwise} \end{cases}$

- $\text{eval}(\neg\psi, s) := \begin{cases} 1, \text{ if } \text{eval}(\psi, s) = 0 \\ 0, \text{ otherwise} \end{cases}$

- $\text{eval}(\psi \wedge \theta, s) := \begin{cases} 1, \text{ if } \text{eval}(\psi, s) = \text{eval}(\theta, s) = 1 \\ 0, \text{ otherwise} \end{cases}$

- $\text{eval}(\psi \vee \theta, s) := \begin{cases} 1, \text{ if } \text{eval}(\psi, s) = 1 \text{ or } \text{eval}(\theta, s) = 1 \\ 0, \text{ otherwise} \end{cases}$

- $\text{forall}(\psi(x), s, i) := \begin{cases} 0, & \text{if } \text{eval}(\psi(i), s) = 0 \\ \text{forall}(\psi(x), s, i+1), & \text{otherwise} \end{cases}$

- $\text{eval}(\forall x.\psi, s) := \begin{cases} 1, \text{ if } \text{forall}(\psi(x), s, 0) \text{ diverges} \\ 0, \text{ otherwise} \end{cases}$

- $\text{exists}(\psi(x), s, i) := \begin{cases} 1, & \text{if } \text{eval}(\psi(i), s) = 1 \\ \text{exists}(\psi(x), s, i+1), & \text{otherwise} \end{cases}$

- $\text{eval}(\exists x.\psi, s) := \begin{cases} 1, \text{ if } \text{exists}(\psi(x), s, 0) \text{ converges} \\ 0, \text{ otherwise} \end{cases}$

On `forall` and `exists`, $\psi(i)$ is obtained by substituting the indicated number variable x by i.

We similarly define `eval` on infinitary formulas using auxiliary functions `conjunction` and `disjunction`:

- $\text{disjunction}(\bigvee_{i \in \omega} \psi_i, s, i) := \begin{cases} 1, & \text{if } \text{eval}(\psi_i, s) = 1 \\ \text{disjunction}(\bigvee_{i \in \omega} \psi_i, s, i+1), & \text{otherwise} \end{cases}$

- $\text{eval}(\bigvee_{i \in \omega} \psi_i, s) := \begin{cases} 1, \text{ if } \text{disjunction}(\bigvee_{i \in \omega} \psi_i, s, 0) \text{converges} \\ 0, \text{ otherwise} \end{cases}$

- $\text{conjunction}(\bigwedge_{i \in \omega} \psi_i, s, i) := \begin{cases} 0, & \text{if } \text{eval}(\psi(i), s) = 0 \\ \text{conjunction}(\bigwedge_{i \in \omega}, s, i+1), & \text{otherwise} \end{cases}$

- $\text{eval}(\bigwedge_{i \in \omega} \psi_i, s) := \begin{cases} 0, \text{ if } \text{conjunction}(\bigwedge_{i \in \omega} \psi_i, s, 0) \text{converges} \\ 1, \text{ otherwise} \end{cases}$

Remember that as we only allow recursively enumerable conjunctions and disjunctions, we can recover ψ_i from a code of $\bigwedge_{i \in \omega} \psi_i$ or $\bigvee_{i \in \omega} \psi_i$.

We now extend `eval` to formulas with fixed-points. Suppose $t \in \mu x X.\psi$ is a $\Sigma^{\mu}_{\beta+1}$-formula, define:

$$\text{eval}(t \in \mu x_i X_i.\psi, s) := \begin{cases} 1, & \text{if } \text{eval}(\psi(t), s[X_i := \emptyset]) = 1 \\ & \text{or } \text{eval}(\psi(t), s[X_i := \mu x_i X_i.\psi]) = 1 \\ \uparrow_{\beta}, & \text{otherwise} \end{cases}$$

Where $s[X := \emptyset]$ is obtained by putting an index for the empty set in the ith position of s, and $s[X_i := \mu x X.\psi]$ is obtained by putting an index for

$\lambda n.\mathtt{eval}(n \in \mu x_i X_i.\psi)$ in the ith position of s. If s becomes a longer sequence by this procedure, fill the unused positions of s with indexes for the empty set.

If we have extended $\mathtt{eval}$ to Σ^μ_β-formulas, extend it to Π^μ_β-formulas by:

$$\mathtt{eval}(t \in \nu x X.\psi, s) := \begin{cases} 1, \text{ if } \mathtt{eval}(t \in \mu x X.\neg\psi(\neg X), s)\beta - \text{freezes} \\ 0, \text{ otherwise} \end{cases}$$

This finishes the definition of $\mathtt{eval}$.

We prove by bounded induction on $\beta \le \alpha$ that the Σ^μ_β-definable sets are α-feedback semi-computable. We slightly strengthen the induction hypothesis to show that, for $\beta < \alpha$, Π^μ_β-definable sets are α-feedback computable.

References

1. Ackerman, N.L., Freer, C.E., Lubarsky, R.S.: Feedback computability on cantor space **15**(2), 7:1–7:18
2. Ackerman, N.L., Freer, C.E., Lubarsky, R.S.: Feedback turing computability, and turing computability as feedback. In: 30th Annual ACM/IEEE Symposium on Logic in Computer Science, pp. 523–534 (2015). https://doi.org/10.1109/LICS.2015.55
3. Ackerman, N.L., Freer, C.E., Lubarsky, R.S.: An introduction to feedback turing computability **30**(1), 27–6. https://doi.org/10.1093/logcom/exaa002
4. Aguilera, J.P., Lubarsky, R.S.: Feedback hyperjump **31**(1), 20–39.https://doi.org/10.1093/logcom/exaa085
5. Aguilera, J.P., Soto, M.: Type-2 feedback computability
6. Bradfield, J.C.: Fixpoints, games and the difference hierarchy **37**(1), 1. https://doi.org/10.1051/ita:2003011
7. Bradfield, J.C.: The modal mu-calculus alternation hierarchy is strict **195**(2), 133–15. https://doi.org/10.1016/S0304-3975(97)00217-X
8. Bradfield, J.C., Duparc, J., Quickert, S.: Fixpoint alternation and the Wadge hierarchy. https://www.julianbradfield.org/Research/fixwadge.pdf
9. Bradfield, J., Duparc, J., Quickert, S.: Transfinite extension of the Mu-calculus. In: Ong, L. (ed.) CSL 2005. LNCS, vol. 3634, pp. 384–396. Springer, Heidelberg (2005). https://doi.org/10.1007/11538363_27
10. Kozen, D.: Results on the propositional μ-calculus **27**(3), 333–3. https://doi.org/10.1016/0304-3975(82)90125-6
11. Lubarsky, R.S.: ITTMs with feedback. In: Schlinder, R. (ed.) Ways of Proof Theory, pp. 341–354
12. Lubarsky, R.S.: μ-definable sets of integers **58**(1), 291–313.https://doi.org/10.2307/2275338
13. Möllerfeld, M.: Generalized inductive definitions: the μ-calculus and Π^1_2-comprehension
14. Moschovakis, Y.: Descriptive Set Theory, Mathematical Surveys and Monographs, vol. 155. American Mathematical Society. https://doi.org/10.1090/surv/155
15. Rogers, H.: Theory of Recursive Functions and Effective Computability
16. Welch, P.: $G_{\delta\sigma}$-games and generalized computation. https://arxiv.org/abs/1509.09135

Quantum First-Order Logics that Capture Logarithmic-Time/Space Quantum Computability

Tomoyuki Yamakami[✉]

Faculty of Engineering, University of Fukui, 3-9-1 Bunkyo, Fukui 910-8507, Japan
TomoyukiYamakami@gmail.com

Abstract. We introduce a quantum analogue of classical first-order logic (FO) and develop a theory of quantum first-order logic (QFO) as a basis of the productive discussions on the power of logical expressiveness of QFO toward quantum computing. The purpose of this work is to logically express "quantum computation" by introducing specially-featured quantum connectives and quantum quantifiers that quantify fixed-dimensional pure quantum states. Our approach is founded on the schematic definitions of time-bounded quantum functions [J. Symb. Log. 85, 1546–1587] and quantum quantifiers for Quantum NP [Proc. IFIP TCS 2002, 323–336]. We demonstrate that quantum first-order logics possess an ability of expressing quantum logarithmic-time computability by the use of new "tabular" quantum variables. In contrast, an extra use of quantum transitive closure operators also helps us characterize quantum logarithmic-space computability.

1 Background, Motivations, and Challenges

A physical realization of quantum mechanical computing device has been sought for decades. A theoretical framework of such quantum computing was formulated in the 1980s by Benioff and Deutsch as a quantum extension of classical computing. Refer to the textbooks, e.g., [12] for the references. Following Deutsch's early model, *quantum Turing machines* (QTMs) were fully developed by Bernstein and Vazirani [3]. Subsequently, a multiple-tape variant of QTMs was studied in [14,16]. A more generic approach toward quantum computability was taken by *quantum functions*[1] [17] whose inputs are quantum states of finite-dimensional Hilbert spaces and by *Quantum NP* [15], in which such quantum states are quantified by quantum quantifiers. In this line of study, Yamakami [17,19] lately proposed the "schematic definitions" to capture the polynomial- and (poly)logarithmic-time computable quantum functions.

From a quite different perspective, nonetheless, a large volume of work has been dedicated to "express" various aspects of quantum physics in numerous logical frameworks from an early introduction of quantum logic by Birkhoff and von

---

[1] This notion is slightly different from the same name used in [16].

© The Author(s), under exclusive license to Springer Nature Switzerland AG 2024
L. Levy Patey et al. (Eds.): CiE 2024, LNCS 14773, pp. 311–323, 2024.
https://doi.org/10.1007/978-3-031-64309-5_25

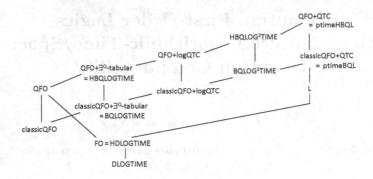

Fig. 1. Inclusion relationships among the complexity classes discussed in this work.

Neumann [2] to recent notions of quantum dynamic logic [4], quantum predicate logic [13], quantum Hoare logic [20,21], etc. In such a vast landscape of quantum logics, there is still an urgent need of logically (or syntactically) expressing time/space-bounded quantum computing. What kinds of quantum logics precisely capture such quantum computability?

When we look into classical logic, there is a long history of expressing classical time/space-bounded computability using only (classical) *logical terms* and *logical formulas*. Fagin [5], for example, gave a logical characterization of languages in NP. Afterwards, Gurevich and Lewis [6] explored a close connection between uniform AC^0 and the (classical) first-order logic (FO), and Immerman [9–11] then used FO as a basis to capture other complexity classes, such as P and NL. Barrington, Immerman, and Straubing [1] demonstrated that FO precisely captures the family of all languages recognized by constant-depth alternating logtime Turing machines, denoted HDLOGTIME.

The classical first-order logic (FO) has proven to be a quite useful means of logically expressing the complexity classes of combinatorial decision problems (or equivalently, languages). It is therefore natural to look for a quantum analogue of FO, dubbed as *QFO*, in hopes of capturing time/space-bounded quantum computability, in particular, the complexity classes BQLOGTIME and BQL (see Sect. 4.1 for their definitions). This work intends to explore the spectacular features of QFO. For this purpose, we wish to adopt a quantum schematic definition approach of [17,19] for a novel formulation of QFO because a schematic definition looks closer to a "logical" system[2] than the existing machine models, such as QTMs and quantum circuits.

Our major results of this work are illustrated in Fig. 1. A more explanatory version of this work will be available shortly at arXiv.org for the reader's reference.

---

[2] Lately, the schematic definition of [17] was implemented as a quantum programming language [7].

2   Basic Definitions

Given the set $\mathbb{N}$ of all *natural numbers* (including 0), the notation $\mathbb{N}^+$ is meant for $\mathbb{N} - \{0\}$. Given integers m and n with $m \leq n$, the integer interval $[m, n]_{\mathbb{Z}}$ is the set $\{m, m+1, m+2, \ldots, n\}$ and $[n]$ abbreviates $[1, n]_{\mathbb{Z}}$ if $n \in \mathbb{N}^+$. The symbol $\imath$ expresses $\sqrt{-1}$ and e stands for the base of the natural logarithms. All *logarithms* in this work are taken to the base 2 and, in particular, we define $\mathrm{ilog}(n)$ and $\mathrm{iloglog}(n)$ to be $\lceil \log n \rceil$ for $n \geq 1$ and $\lceil \log \log n \rceil$ for $n \geq 2$, respectively. For convenience, we set $\mathrm{ilog}(0) = \mathrm{iloglog}(0) = 0$. We mostly use the binary alphabet $\{0, 1\}$ and binary strings over it. The notation $s_i^{(n)}$ denotes the ith string in $\{0, 1\}^n$ *in the lexicographic order*. Later, we freely identify i with $s_i^{(\mathrm{ilog}(n))}$ as long as n is clear with $i \in [\hat{n}]$, where $\hat{n} = 2^{\mathrm{ilog}(n)}$. Given a finite sequence γ on $\mathbb{N}$ and any index $i \in \mathbb{N}^+$, $|\gamma|$ denotes the size of γ and $(\gamma)_{(i)}$ denotes the ith entry of γ if $i \leq |\gamma|$. A *promise (decision) problem* $\mathcal{L}$ over the binary alphabet $\{0, 1\}$ is a pair (A, B) of disjoint subsets of $\{0, 1\}^*$.

A vector in a finite-dimensional Hilbert space is expressed using the *ket notation* $|\cdot\rangle$ as in $|\phi\rangle$, while an element of its dual space is denoted $\langle\phi|$ using the *bra notation*. Let $\mathrm{tr}_i(|\phi\rangle)$ denote the quantum state obtained from $|\phi\rangle$ by *tracing out* all qubit locations of $|\phi\rangle$ except for the ith qubit.

The notation $\mathcal{H}_{2^n}$ expresses a 2^n-dimensional Hilbert space. A *qubit* is a unit-norm vector in $\mathcal{H}_2$ and both $|0\rangle$ and $|1\rangle$ express the normalized basis of $\mathcal{H}_2$. Notice that the set $\{|s\rangle \mid s \in \{0, 1\}^n\}$ *spans* the entire space $\mathcal{H}_{2^n}$. A *quantum string* (or a *qustring*, for short) $|\phi\rangle$ of n qubits refers to a unit-norm quantum state of n qubits and n is the *length* of $|\phi\rangle$, expressed as $\ell(|\phi\rangle)$. The notation Φ_{2^n} denotes the collection of all qustrings of length n. As a special case, we make the set Φ_0 composed only of the *null vector*. Let $\Phi_\infty = \bigcup_{n \geq 0} \Phi_{2^n}$. See, e.g., [14, 16, 17, 19] for more detail.

We expand the scope of promise problems (A, B) from classical strings to qustrings in Φ_∞ by resetting (A, B) to satisfy $A, B \subseteq \Phi_\infty$ and $A \cap B = \varnothing$. As a concrete example, consider the promise problem (A, B) defined by $A = \{|\phi\rangle \in \Phi_\infty \mid \|\langle 0|\phi\rangle\|^2 \geq 2/3\}$ and $B = \{|\phi\rangle \in \Phi_\infty \mid \|\langle 1|\phi\rangle\|^2 \geq 2/3\}$.

We reserve the notations $\forall x$ and $\exists x$ for the quantifiers whose bound variable x ranges over predetermined classical objects (such as strings, numbers, and graph vertices). In contrast, $\forall|\phi\rangle$ and $\exists|\phi\rangle$ express quantum quantifiers that quantify qustrings $|\phi\rangle$. For example, the notation $(\forall|\phi\rangle \in \Phi_{2^{\mathrm{ilog}(n)}}) P(|\phi\rangle)$ expresses that a statement $P(|\phi\rangle)$ holds for "all qustrings $|\phi\rangle$ in $\Phi_{2^{\mathrm{ilog}(n)}}$"; in comparison, $(\exists|\phi\rangle \in \Phi_{2^{\mathrm{ilog}(n)}}) P(|\phi\rangle)$ indicates that $P(|\phi\rangle)$ holds for "some of the qustrings $|\phi\rangle$ in $\Phi_{2^{\mathrm{ilog}(n)}}$". See [15, 17, 19].

3   Definition of Quantum First-Order Logic

3.1   Syntax of QFO

A *vocabulary* (or an *alphabet*) T is a set of quantum predicate symbols of fixed arities, quantum function symbols of fixed arities, and constant symbols (which are actually quantum function symbols of arity 0). We begin with an explanation of classical terms and quantum terms.

[**Variables**]. We use two types of variables: *classical variables* and *pure-state quantum variables*.[3] Each pure-state quantum variable y has *qubit size* $|y|$, which indicates a positive integer. This y is intended to refer to a qustring of length $|y|$. Classical variables $i, j, k, \ldots$ are *classical terms* and pure-state quantum variables $x, y, z, \ldots$ are *quantum terms*.

[**Function Symbols**]. *Classical function symbols* of arity 0, also called *(classical) constant symbols*, are composed of 0, 1, ilog(n), and n. A classical function symbol of arity 1 is the successor function suc, where $suc(i)$ means $i + 1$ and they form classical terms. We inductively define $suc^{(0)}(i) = i$, $suc^{(j+1)}(i) = suc(suc^{(j)}(i))$ for any $j \in \mathbb{N}$ and we informally write $i + e$ for $suc^{(e)}(i)$ for a constant $e \in \mathbb{N}^+$. *Quantum function symbols* of arity 2 are $QBIT$ and $\otimes$ (tenser product). If i is a classical term and y is a quantum term, then $QBIT(i, y)$ is a quantum term of qubit size 1. For readability, we abbreviate $QBIT(i, y)$ as $y[i]$, which is called the *ith qubit* of y or the *ith component* of y. If s and t are respectively quantum terms of qubit sizes l_1 and l_2, then $s \otimes t$ is a quantum term of qubit size $l_1 + l_2$. The *instance function symbol* X is a special function symbol of arity 1, which is distinguished from all other symbols. Inputs to X are assumed to be a binary string of length n. If s is a quantum term of qubit size ilog(n) or a classical term of size at most n, then $X(s)$ is a quantum term of qubit size 1. Notice that, in the classical setting, $X(\cdot)$ is treated as a predicate symbol instead of a function symbol.

Given a quantum term t, the notation $Var(t)$ denotes the set of all pure-state quantum variables that appear during a construction process of t.

We then explain the notion of quantum formulas. Given a quantum formula R, let $Var(R)$ denote the set of all quantum variables that appear in R.

[**Predicate Symbols**]. *Classical predicate symbols* of arity 2 are $=$, $\leq$, and $<$. If s and t are classical terms, then $s = t$, $s \leq t$, and $s < t$ are called *classical formulas*. A unitary transformation of a given quantum state made by an application of a fixed unitary matrix is expressed in this work as a set of input-output pairs. *Quantum predicate symbols* of arity 2 include $\mathcal{P}_I$ (identity) and $\mathcal{P}_{ROT_\theta}$ (rotation at x-axis) for any $\theta \in \mathbb{R}$. Here, we do not introduce $\mathcal{P}_{CNOT}$ (controlled-NOT) because, as we will see later, $\mathcal{P}_{CNOT}$ is "definable" within our logical system. If s, t are quantum terms with $Var(s) \cap Var(t) = \varnothing$, the expression $\mathcal{P}_F(s : t)$ for any $F \in \{I, ROT_\theta \mid \theta \in \mathbb{R}\}$ and any $\theta \in \mathbb{R}$ is an *atomic quantum formula*. Another quantum predicate symbol of arity 2 is $\simeq_\varepsilon$, which is called the *(quantum) measurement predicate*. If s is a quantum term and b is either 0 or 1, then the expression $\simeq_\varepsilon (s : b)$ is an *atomic quantum formula*, where ε is a real number in $[0, 1]$. For readability, we write $s \simeq_\varepsilon b$ instead of formally writing $\simeq_\varepsilon (s : b)$ for a constant $b \in \{0, 1\}$.

---

[3] This notion comes from the formulation of Quantum NP [15], in which quantum states in a finite-dimensional Hilbert space are quantified by "quantum" quantifiers.

For any quantum predicate symbol R, we use the expression of the form $R(s : t)$ with a colon (:) used as a separator. Terms s and t in $R(s : t)$ are respectively called the *first argument* and the *second argument* of R. When a pure-state quantum variable y or its component $y[i]$ appears in the first argument place of a quantum predicate, it is said to be *processed*.

[**Quantum Logical Connectives**]. Quantum logical connectives include $\wedge$ (quantum AND), $\|$ (quantum OR), and $\neg^Q$ (quantum negation). In our formulation, we interpret $\wedge$ to represent the successive execution of two separate independent "computations". Concerning the standard connective $\vee$, the expression $P \vee R$ indicates that we need to choose the correct formula between P and R but this process is not a "reversible" computation. We thus replace $\vee$ by the branching scheme of [17,19] with the new symbol "$\|$". If $z[i]$ does not appear in the second argument places of R_1 and R_2, then $(z[i])[R_1 \| R_2]$ is a quantum formula, where $z[i]$ is called an *antecedent component*.

The classical negation is supported by de Morgan's law but, since this law does not hold in the quantum setting, we should abandon the use of the classical negation and, in contrast, we provide a distinctive role to the quantum negation $\neg^Q$ in our formalism. In a QTM computation, the "negation" of its final outcome is made at the very end of the computation by exchanging between accepting inner states and rejecting inner states. The use of our $\neg^Q$ reflects this computational "negation".

[**Quantifiers**]. If s is of the form $|y|$ or any constant symbol in $\{0, 1, \mathrm{ilog}(n)\}$, then $(\exists i \leq s)R(i)$ and $(\forall i \leq s)R(i)$ are both quantum formulas. If y is a pure-state quantum variable and s is a quantum term, then $(\forall^Q y, |y| = s)R(y)$ and $(\exists^Q y, |y| = s)R(y)$ are both quantum formulas. Variables appearing within the scope of quantifiers are said to be *bound* and other variables are *free*.

A quantum formula ϕ is said to be *query-free* if it does not include the instance function symbol X. We say that ϕ is *measurement-free* if ϕ contains no subformulas of the form $t \simeq_\varepsilon 0$ and $t \simeq_\varepsilon 1$ for any quantum terms t. Moreover, ϕ is called a *sentence* if there is no free variable in ϕ.

Unfortunately, not all quantum formulas are in a proper "admissible" form. Let us take a quick look at a few simple cases, which should be avoided because of the violation of the rules of quantum physics.

(1) Unlike classical computation, the duplicate use of the same variable is in general impossible due to the *no-cloning theorem* of quantum mechanics. Hence, in general, we cannot keep a copy of the same quantum states. For example, in the expression $\mathcal{P}_F(x[i] : y[i]) \wedge \mathcal{P}_G(x[i] : z[i])$, the component $x[i]$ appears twice in the first argument places of $\mathcal{P}_F$ and $\mathcal{P}_G$ as if $x[i]$ is duplicated. Thus, we cannot use it for two different quantum predicates. To describe this situation, we introduce a graph that expresses a transformation sequence of quantum variables. Given a quantum formula R, we define a directed graph $G_R = (V, E)$, which is called the *variable connection graph* of R, as follows. Let $V = Var(R)$ and let E consist of all edges (y, z) for two quantum variables y and z such that there exists a quantum predicate symbol of the form $\mathcal{P}_F$ for which either y or its component $y[i]$ is the first argument of R and either z or $z[j]$ is the second argument of R.

The variable connection graph of R must be topologically ordered.[4] In this case, we succinctly say that the quantum formula R is *order-consistent*.

(2) Since each quantum predicate realizes a quantum transform, its second argument is uniquely determined by its first argument. Therefore, the second argument place cannot contain constants or the instance function symbol X.

(3) Similarly to (2), the expression like $\mathcal{P}_F(x[i] : z[i]) \wedge \mathcal{P}_G(y[i] : z[i])$ must be avoided because $z[i]$ could have two different values in $\mathcal{P}_F$ and $\mathcal{P}_G$. Neither a pure-state quantum variable z nor its component $z[i]$ appears in the first argument place (as well as the second argument place) of two different quantum predicates.

(4) Consider the expression $(\forall i \leq s)[\mathcal{P}_F(x[i] : z[i])] \wedge (\forall j \leq t)[\mathcal{P}_G(y[j] : z[j])]$, which does not fall into (1)–(2). However, if the scopes of two classical quantifiers $(\forall i \leq s)$ and $(\forall j \leq t)$ overlap, then two distinct components $z[i]$ and $z[j]$ coincide whenever i equals j. We thus need to avoid such an expression.

A quantum formula R is called *well formed* if it fulfills all the above conditions. As a simple example of well-formed quantum formula, we set $\mathcal{P}_{CNOT}(y : z)$ to be $(|y| = |z| = 2) \wedge \mathcal{P}_I(y[1] : z[1]) \wedge (z[1])[\mathcal{P}_I(y[2] : z[2]) \| \mathcal{P}_{ROT_\pi}(y[2] : z[2])]$. In this way, we can express $CNOT$ (controlled NOT) in our quantum logical system. This is the reason why we do not include $\mathcal{P}_{CNOT}$ as our predicate symbol. Since we are interested only in well-formed quantum formulas, for readability, all quantum formulas are implicitly assumed to be well-formed and we often drop the term "well-formed" from "well-formed quantum formulas."

Given a quantum formula ϕ, a quantum variable y as well as its component $y[i]$ in ϕ is called *predecessor-dependent* in ϕ if it appears in the second argument place of a certain quantum predicate symbol of ϕ; otherwise, we call it *predecessor-independent* in ϕ. When all quantum variables used in ϕ are predecessor-dependent in ϕ, we call this ϕ *predecessor-dependent*.

Given a quantum formula ϕ of the form $(\exists^Q y, |y| = s) R(y)$, if y is predecessor-dependent in ϕ, then $\exists^Q y$ is called *consequential quantum existential quantifier*. Otherwise, we call it an *introductory quantum existential quantifier*. With this respect, quantum universal quantifiers are always treated as introductory quantum quantifiers. Therefore, introductory quantum existential quantifiers together with quantum universal quantifiers are collectively called *introductory quantum quantifiers*. We say that a quantum formula ϕ is *introductory quantum quantifier-free* (or iqq-free, for short) if all quantum quantifiers used in ϕ are only consequential.

Given a constant $\varepsilon_0 \in [0, 1/2)$, a quantum formula ϕ is said to be ε_0-*error bounded* if all measurement predicate symbols appearing in ϕ have the form $t \simeq_\varepsilon 0$ and $t \simeq_{\varepsilon'} 1$ with $\varepsilon, \varepsilon' \leq \varepsilon_0$ for certain quantum terms t.

3.2   Semantics of QFO

A *structure* (or a *model*) $\mathcal{M}$ with vocabulary T is a set consisting of a universe $\mathcal{U}$, relations of fixed arities, functions of fixed arities, and constants from $\mathcal{U}$.

---

[4] A directed graph $G = (V, E)$ with $V = \{v_1, v_2, \ldots, v_n\}$ is said to be *topologically ordered* if, for any $i, j \in [n]$, $(v_i, v_j) \in E$ and $i \neq j$ imply $i < j$.

Each relation, each function, and each constant respectively correspond to their associated predicate symbol, functions symbol, and constant symbol.

[I.] An *interpretation* ξ is a function that assigns numbers and quantum states to classical and quantum terms, respectively. This ξ assigns natural numbers $\hat{i}$ to classical variables i and $\hat{i}+1$ to $suc(i)$. To a free pure-state quantum variable y, ξ assigns a qustring $|\phi_y\rangle \in \Phi_{|y|}$ together with $\xi(|y|) = \ell(|\phi_y\rangle)$. For the symbols $QBIT$ and $\otimes$, we use the following interpretation: $\xi(s \otimes t) = |\phi_s\rangle|\phi_t\rangle|\phi_y\rangle$ if $\xi(s) = |\phi_s\rangle|\phi_y\rangle$ and $\xi(t) = |\phi_t\rangle|\phi_y\rangle$ with $Var(s) = Var(t) = \{y\}$. The value $\xi(QBIT(s,y)) = \xi(y[s])$ is defined as follows. If $|\phi_y\rangle = \sum_{u:|u|=|y|} \beta_u|u\rangle$ and $\xi(i) = \hat{i}$, then $\xi(y[i]) = \sum_{u:|u|=|y|} \beta_u|\hat{i}\rangle|(u)_{(\hat{i})}\rangle|u\rangle|\phi_y\rangle$. Moreover, X is interpreted as an n-bit string x, namely, $\xi(X) = |x\rangle$. If $\xi(i) = \hat{i}$, then $\xi(X(i)) = |\hat{i}\rangle|(x)_{(\hat{i})}\rangle|x\rangle$. If $\xi(s) = \sum_{z:|z|=|s|} \alpha_z|z\rangle|\phi\rangle$, then $\xi(X(s)) = \sum_{z:|z|=|s|} \alpha_z|z\rangle|(x)_{(z)}\rangle|x\rangle|\phi\rangle$, where each string z is viewed as an integer.

[II.] Let us define the evaluation $eval[R](\mathcal{M})$ of a quantum formula R by $\mathcal{M}$.

(1) Let s,t,u,v denote four quantum terms. For any transform $C \in \{I, ROT_\theta \mid \theta \in \mathbb{R}\}$ and for any two quantum states $\rho, \tau \in \mathcal{H}_2$, we set $eval[\mathcal{P}_C(y[i] : z[j])](|\phi_y\rangle, |\phi_z\rangle, \mathcal{M})$ to be 1 if there exist a permutation p and indices $\hat{i}, \hat{j}$ for which $\xi(y[i])$ and $\xi(z[j])$ are as above, $p(\hat{i}) = \hat{j}$, and $SWAP_p((I^{\hat{i}-1} \otimes C \otimes I^{|y|-\hat{i}})|\phi_y\rangle) = |\phi_z\rangle$. Otherwise, we set it to be 0.

(2) For a classical formula of the form $s = t$, we set $eval[s = t](\hat{s}, \hat{t}, \mathcal{M}) = 1$ iff $\xi(s) = \hat{s}$ and $\xi(t) = \hat{t}$ for classical numbers $\hat{s}$ and $\hat{t}$ and they are equal. The cases of $s \leq t$ and $s < t$ are similarly treated. For any bit $b \in \{0,1\}$, we define $eval[y[i] \simeq_\varepsilon b](|\phi_y\rangle, b, \mathcal{M})$ to be 1 if $\xi(i) = \hat{i}$ and $\xi(y[i])$ is observed to be b with error probability at most ε, i.e., $\||\phi_{y,\hat{i}}(b)\rangle\|^2 \geq 1 - \varepsilon$, where $|\phi_{y,\hat{i}}(b)\rangle = \sum_{v_1,v_2} |\hat{i}\rangle|b\rangle|v_1 b v_2\rangle|\phi_y\rangle$ with $|v_1| = \hat{i} - 1$ and $|v_1 v_2| = |y| - 1$. Otherwise, it is set to be 0.

(3) For $\wedge$, we set $eval[P \wedge Q](\mathcal{M}_{P \wedge Q})$ to be 1 if both $eval[P](\mathcal{M}_P) = 1$ and $eval[Q](\mathcal{M}_Q) = 1$ hold for appropriate structures $\mathcal{M}_P$ and $\mathcal{M}_Q$ and $\mathcal{M}_{P \wedge Q}$ is the union of $\mathcal{M}_P$ and $\mathcal{M}_Q$. Otherwise, we set it to be 0. For $\|$, we set $eval[(y[i])[P_1 \| P_2]](|\phi_y\rangle, \mathcal{M})$ to be 1 both $eval[P_1](|\phi_{y,\hat{i}}(0)\rangle, |\phi_y\rangle, \mathcal{M}) = 1$ and $eval[P_2](|\phi_{y,\hat{i}}(1)\rangle, |\phi_y\rangle, \mathcal{M}) = 1$ hold when $\xi(y[i]) = \sum_{u:|u|=|y|} \beta_u|\hat{i}\rangle|(u)_{(\hat{i})}\rangle|u\rangle|\phi_y\rangle$. Otherwise, we set it to be 0.

(4) We set $eval[(\exists^Q y)R(y)](\mathcal{M})$ to be 1 if there exists a qustring $|\phi\rangle$ of length $|y|$ such that $eval[R(y)](|\phi_y\rangle, \mathcal{M}) = 1$. Otherwise, we set it to be 0. Moreover, we set $eval[(\forall^Q y)R(y)](\mathcal{M})$ to be 1 if $eval[R(y)](|\phi_y\rangle, \mathcal{M}) = 1$ for all qustrings $|\phi_y\rangle$ of length $|y|$. Otherwise, it is 0.

(5) We define the value of $eval[(\neg^Q)P](\mathcal{M})$ inductively as follows.

(i) For any classical formula and any quantum predicate symbol $\mathcal{P}_G$, $eval[(\neg^Q)(s = t)](\mathcal{M})$ and $eval[(\neg^Q)\mathcal{P}_G(s : t)](\mathcal{M})$ respectively equal $eval[s = t](\mathcal{M})$ and $eval[\mathcal{P}_G(s : t)](\mathcal{M})$. In contrast, we set $eval[(\neg^Q)(s \simeq_\varepsilon b)](\mathcal{M}) = eval[s \simeq_\varepsilon \bar{b}](\mathcal{M})$, where b is in $\{0,1\}$ and $\bar{b} = 1 - b$.

(ii) The double quantum negation makes $eval[(\neg^Q)(\neg^Q)P](\mathcal{M}) = eval[P](\mathcal{M})$. Moreover, we set $eval[(\neg^Q)(P \wedge Q)](\mathcal{M}) = eval[(\neg^Q)P \wedge (\neg^Q)Q](\mathcal{M})$ and $eval[(\neg^Q)(y[i])[P_1 \| P_2]](\mathcal{M}) = eval[(y[i])[(\neg^Q)P_1 \| (\neg^Q)P_2]](\mathcal{M})$.

(iii) We set $eval[(\neg^Q)(\forall i)P(i)](\mathcal{M})$ to equal $eval[(\forall i)(\neg^Q)P(i)](\mathcal{M})$.

(iv) If y is a predecessor-independent variable, then we set $eval[(\neg^Q)(\exists^Q y)$ $P(y)](\mathcal{M})$ to be $eval[(\forall^Q y)(\neg^Q)P(y)](\mathcal{M})$ and $eval[(\neg^Q)(\forall^Q y)P(y)](\mathcal{M})$ to be $eval[(\exists^Q y)(\neg^Q)P(y)](\mathcal{M})$. For a predecessor-dependent variable y, on the contrary, we set $eval[(\neg^Q)(\exists^Q y)P(y)](\mathcal{M})$ to be $eval[(\exists^Q y)(\neg^Q)P(y)](\mathcal{M})$.

A structure $\mathcal{M}$ is said to *satisfy* a quantum formula ϕ if ϕ is evaluated to be 1 by $\mathcal{M}$ (i.e., $eval[\phi](\mathcal{M}) = 1$). A quantum sentence is said to be *satisfiable* if there is a structure $\mathcal{M}$ that satisfies ϕ. Given two quantum formulas ϕ_1 and ϕ_2 including the same set of variables, we say that ϕ_1 and ϕ_2 are *semantically equivalent* if, for any structure $\mathcal{M}$ for ϕ_1 and ϕ_2, it holds that $eval[\phi_1](\mathcal{M}) = 1$ iff $eval[\phi_2](\mathcal{M}) = 1$.

3.3 Quantum First-Order Logic (or QFO)

Given a quantum formula ϕ with quantum terms t, $Mes(\phi)$ indicates the sum of all ε's appearing in the collection of all subformulas of the form $t \simeq_\varepsilon 0$ and $t \simeq_\varepsilon 1$. Such subformulas correspond to the actions of observing quantum states in the computational basis.

A promise problem $(L^{(+)}, L^{(-)})$ over the binary alphabet $\{0,1\}$ is said to be *(syntactically) expressible* by a quantum sentence ϕ if there exists a fixed constant $\varepsilon_0 \in [0, 1/2)$ such that, for any given string $x \in \{0,1\}^*$, (1) $Mes(\phi) \leq \varepsilon_0$ holds, and (2) assuming that x is evaluated as the instance function symbol X and its length $|x|$ is evaluated as the constant symbol n, if $x \in L^{(+)}$, then these values make ϕ true, and if $x \in L^{(-)}$, then they make $\neg^Q \phi$ true. We write QFO to denote the class of all promise problems that are expressible by quantum sentences of quantum first-order logic. As a subclass of QFO, classicQFO further requires that all problems are expressible by iqq-free quantum sentences.

4 Complexity Classes Characterized by QFO

4.1 Logtime/Logspace Quantum Turing Machines

Let us seek for a few useful applications of QFO and classicQFO to the characterization of certain types of quantum computing. To explain how to express quantum computing, we first define two complexity classes BQL and BQLOGTIME of *promise problems* over the binary alphabet[5] $\{0,1\}$.

Similar to a logtime deterministic Turing machine (DTM) [1], a model of (poly)logtime quantum Turing machine (QTM) was considered in [19] and was characterized in terms of a finite set of elementary quantum (recursion) schemes, which are variations of a recursive schematic definition initiated in [17]. To handle such a restricted model, we first recall a QTM of [18], which is equipped with multiple rewritable work tapes and *random-access mechanism* that operates a

---

[5] In quantum complexity theory, underlying alphabets of QTMs are not necessarily limited to $\{0,1\}$. Here, the restriction onto $\{0,1\}$ is only meant to be in accordance with the definition of QFO and also to simplify the subsequent argument.

tape head along a rewritable index tape to access a read-only input tape. To access the ith input qubit, e.g., the machine must write $s_i^{(\mathrm{ilog}(n))}$ on the index tape and enters the designated query state. In a single step, the input-tape head jumps to the ith cell so that the machine can read the content of this cell.

The notation BQL stands for the of all set of all promise problems solvable with bounded-error probability (say, $\geq 2/3$) by QTMs using logarithmic space but with no runtime bound. When QTMs are further required to run in expected polynomial time, we use the notation "ptime-BQL". See [18] for more detail. Similarly, we define BQLOGTIME to be the collection of all promise problems solvable by QTMs that run in $O(\log n)$ steps (called logtime QTMs) with bounded-error probability (see [19]). We further expand BQLOGTIME to HBQLOGTIME by allowing a finite number of applications of "limited" quantum quantifiers as follows. A promise problem $(L^{(+)}, L^{(-)})$ is in $\Sigma_k^Q \mathrm{BQLOGTIME}$ if there exist k constants $c_1, c_2, \ldots, c_k$, another constant $\varepsilon \in [0, 1/2)$, and a logtime QTM M such that (i) for any string $x \in L^{(+)}$, $(\exists |\phi_1\rangle \in \Phi_{2^{m_1}})(\forall |\phi_2\rangle \in \Phi_{2^{m_2}}) \cdots (Q_k |\phi_k\rangle \in \Phi_{2^{m_k}})\mathrm{Prob}[M(|x\rangle, |\phi_1\rangle, |\phi_2\rangle, \ldots, |\phi_k\rangle) = 1] \geq 1 - \varepsilon$ and (ii) for any string $x \in L^{(-)}$, $(\forall |\phi_1\rangle \in \Phi_{2^{m_1}})(\exists |\phi_2\rangle \in \Phi_{2^{m_2}}) \cdots (\bar{Q}_k |\phi_k\rangle \in \Phi_{2^{m_k}})\mathrm{Prob}[M(|x\rangle, |\phi_1\rangle, |\phi_2\rangle, \ldots, |\phi_k\rangle) = 0] \geq 1 - \varepsilon$, where $m_i = c_i \mathrm{ilog}(|x|)$ for all $i \in [k]$, Q_k is $\exists$ (resp., $\forall$) if k is odd (resp., even), and $\bar{Q}_k$ is $\exists$ (resp., $\forall$) if $Q_k = \forall$ (resp., $\exists$). The desired class HBQLOGTIME is the union $\bigcup_{k \in \mathbb{N}^+} \Sigma_k^Q \mathrm{BQLOGTIME}$. Similarly, we can expand BQL to HBQL. See also [19].

4.2   Complexity of QFO and ClassicQFO

We discuss the descriptive complexity of QFO and classicQFO in comparison with time-bounded complexity classes.

Lemma 1. classicQFO $\subseteq$ BQLOGTIME.

Proof Idea.   Letting $\mathcal{L}$ denote any promise problem in classicQFO expressed by a certain iqq-free quantum sentence $\phi(X)$, we intend to show that $\mathcal{L} \in$ BQLOGTIME. This is achieved by demonstrating how to simulate on appropriate logtime QTMs the evaluation process (explained in Sect. 3.2) of quantum logical connectives and classical/quantum quantifiers. All quantum predicate symbols $\mathcal{P}_F$ can be easily simulated by an appropriate QTM. The quantum AND ($\wedge$) can be simulated by a sequence of two quantum computations and the quantum OR ($\|$) can be simulated by the branching scheme of [17] for quantum functions. Consequential quantifiers can be eliminated by replacing their bound variables with outcomes of their corresponding part of M's computation. $\square$

Since QFO is obtained by applying $\exists^Q$ and $\forall^Q$ to underlying quantum formulas used in classicQFO, we thus obtain the following from Lemma 1.

Theorem 2. QFO $\subseteq$ HBQLOGTIME.

We further claim that the quantum first-order logic naturally extends the classical first-order logic.

Theorem 3. FO ⊆ QFO.

Proof Idea.   We first identify natural numbers with binary strings and then interpret these binary strings to corresponding quantum strings. In the case where ϕ is quantifier-free, we inductively build a new quantum formula ϕ^Q to satisfy that $\mathcal{S}_w \models \phi$ iff $\mathcal{S}_w \models \phi^Q$. We then express classical quantifiers that are applied to a quantifier-free formula as appropriate quantum quantifiers.   □

4.3   Quantum Transitive Closure

Since FO is quite weak in expressing power, several supplementary operators have been sought in the past literature to significantly enhance its expressibility. One of such effective operators is a *transitive closure operator* (TC), which intuitively works as a restricted type of recursion scheme. See, e.g., [8] for its usage.

As for QFO, we wish to seek out a "feasible" quantum analogue of such a transitive closure operator. We conveniently call it the *quantum transitive closure operator* (QTC) and we make it apply to a *quantum bare relation* R of arity $k + m + 2$, which is a measurement-free, iqq-free quantum formula of the form $R(i, x_1, x_2, \ldots, x_k : j, y_1, y_2, \ldots, y_m)$ with $k + m + 2$ free variables, where i, j are classical variables, $x_1, x_2, \ldots, x_k$ are predecessor-independent quantum variables, and $y_1, y_2, \ldots, y_m$ are predecessor-dependent quantum variables. Intuitively, we inductively apply R by decrementing a counter from i by one until reaching j. We may require $i \geq j$ for the proper termination of such a recursive procedure.

We then write classicQFO + QTC (resp., QFO + QTC) to refer to the set of promise problems expressible by classicQFO (resp., QFO) together with the free use of the QTC operator for quantum bare relations. If QTC satisfies that the start value of i is upper-bounded by ilog(n), then we write $logQTC$.

To describe our first result, we expand BQLOGTIME to BQLOG^{2}TIME by allowing $O(\log^2 n)$ runtime of underlying QTMs.

Proposition 4. BQLOGTIME ⊆ classicQFO + $logQTC$ ⊆ BQLOG^{2}TIME.

Proof Idea.   Since classicQFO ⊆ BQLOGTIME by Lemma 1, it suffices to simulate the behavior of the $logQTC$-operator on an appropriate $O(\log^2 n)$-time QTM. Consider a quantum formula of the form $QTC[\phi](i, s : j, t)$ for a quantum bare relation ϕ. Since ϕ is measurement-free and iqq-free, by Lemma 1, $\phi(i, s : j, t)$ can be simulatable by running the following procedure. Initially, we set k to be i and we inductively simulate ϕ by decrementing k down to j. Notice that the simulation can be conducted at most i times since $i \leq O(\log n)$. Thus, this procedure clearly takes $O(\log^2 n)$ steps. To simulate a logtime QTM M, by contrast, we define a quantum formula $NEXT(i, y : j, z)$ to express within the logical system of classicQFO a transition of M at time cilog(n) $- i$ using M's surface configurations.   □

Corollary 5. HBQLOGTIME ⊆ QFO + $logQTC$ ⊆ HBQLOG^{2}TIME.

A similar idea of the proof of Proposition 4 works to obtain the following precise characterization.

Theorem 6. classicQFO + QTC = ptime-BQL.

Corollary 7. QFO + QTC = ptime-HBQL.

5   Tabular Quantum Variables and Their Quantification

To describe a series of $O(\log n)$ quantum operations, we need a series of $O(\log n)$ consequential quantum variables. However, in our logical framework, we cannot prepare such a number of variables nor operate them sequentially. An easy solution to this difficulty is to expand the use of consequential quantum variables by simply introducing a new type of variables, each of which embodies multiple "standard" variables. These new variables are called *tabular quantum variables*, denoted by Y, Z, W, ..., which indicate functions mapping $[\mathrm{ilog}(n)] \times [c_2] \times \cdots \times [c_k]$ to $\Phi_{2^{\mathrm{ilog}(n)}}$ with fixed constants $k \in \mathbb{N}^+$ and $c_2, c_3, \ldots, c_k \in \mathbb{N}^+$. The word "tabular" reflects the fact that a function f can be viewed as a "table" whose entries are of the form $(x, f(x))$. Given a tabular quantum variable Y, $Y(i_1, i_2, \ldots, i_k)$ expresses the output qustring $|\phi_{i_1,i_2,\ldots,i_k}\rangle$ of Y on input $(i_1, i_2, \ldots, i_k)$ and is treated as a pure-state variable. To avoid any unwanted usage of such tabular quantum variables, we explicitly demand that $Y(i_1, i_2, \ldots, i_k)$ is *predecessor-dependent* for all choices of tuples $(i_1, i_2, \ldots, i_k)$. As for the well-formedness condition, since we treat $Y(i_1, \ldots, i_k)$ for each tuple $(i_1, \ldots, i_k)$ as a different pure-state quantum variable, it suffices to require the same condition imposed on quantum formulas in Sect. 3.1.

The term "$\exists^Q$-tabular" indicates the use of tabular quantum variables and second-order consequential existential quantifiers that quantify these newly introduced variables.

Theorem 8. classicQFO + $\exists^Q$-*tabular* = BQLOGTIME.

Proof Idea.   (goal: classicQFO + $\exists^Q$-tabular $\subseteq$ BQLOGTIME) By Lemma 1, classicQFO $\subseteq$ BQLOGTIME follows. We then show that an appropriate logtime QTM can simulate quantum existential quantifiers over tabular quantum variables.

(goal: BQLOGTIME $\subseteq$ classicQFO + $\exists^Q$-tabular) Consider any QTM M running in $ci\log(n)$ steps ($c \in \mathbb{N}^+$) with error probability at most $\varepsilon \in [0, 1/2)$. It suffices to simulate the changes of tape contents of M step by step. This can be done by introducing two groups of c tabular quantum variables, $Y_1, Y_2, \ldots, Y_c$ and $W_1, W_2, \ldots, W_c$, each of which maps $[\mathrm{ilog}(n)] \times [3]$ to $\Phi_{2^{\mathrm{ilog}(n)}}$. We express the content of tape cell i of M at time t by two qubits $Y(t, 1)[i] \otimes W(t, 1)[i]$ for $i, t \in [\mathrm{ilog}(n)]$. At time t, if the tape head rests at tape cell i, then $Y(t, 1)[i]$ is set to be 1. Otherwise, $Y(t, 1)[i]$ is 0. The desired simulation utilizes the fact that, since the tape head moves only one cell per step, it suffices to focus on only three consecutive cells at each step because all the other cells are not altered.‘   □

Corollary 9. QFO ⊆ HQBLOGTIME.

References

1. Barrington, D.A.M., Immerman, N., Straubing, H.: On uniformity within NC^1. J. Comput. System Sci. **41**, 274–306 (1990)
2. Birkhoff, G., von Neumann, J.: The logic of quantum mechanics. Ann. Math. **37**, 823–843 (1936)
3. Bernstein, E., Vazirani, U.: Quantum complexity theory. SIAM J. Comput. **26**, 1411–1473 (1997)
4. Brunet, O., Jorrand, P.: Dynamic quantum logic for quantum programs. Int. J. Quantum Inf. **2**, 45–54 (2004)
5. Fagin, R.: Gneralized first-order spectra and polynomial-time recognizable sets. In: Complexity of Computation (ed. R. Karp), SIAM-AMS Proc. 7, pp. 27–41 (1974)
6. Gurevich, Y., Lewis, H.R.: A logic for constant-depth circuits. Inform. Control **61**, 65–74 (1984)
7. Hainry, E., Péchoux, R., Silva, M.: A programmming language characterizing quantum polynomial time. In: Kupferman, O., Sobocinski, P. (eds.) FoSSaCS 2023. LNCS, vol. 13992, pp. 156–175. Springer, Cham (2023). https://doi.org/10.1007/978-3-031-30829-1_8
8. Immerman, N.: Relational queries computable in polynomial time. Inform. Control **68**, 86–104 (1986)
9. Immerman, N.: Languages that capture complexity classes. SIAM J. Comput. **16**, 760–778 (1987)
10. Immerman, N.: Expressiblity as a compelxity measure: results and directions. In: SICT 1987, pp. 194–202 (1987)
11. Immerman, N.: Expressibility and parallel complexity. SIAM J. Comput. **18**, 625–638 (1989)
12. Kitaev, A.Y. , Shen, A.H., Vyalyi, M.N.: Classical and Quantumn Computation (Graduate Studies in Mathematics). Am. Math. Soc. (2002)
13. Kornell, A.: Discrete quantum structures. arXiv:2004.04377v6 (2022)
14. Yamakami, T.: A foundation of programming a multi-tape quantum Turing machine. In: Kutyłowski, M., Pacholski, L., Wierzbicki, T. (eds.) MFCS 1999. LNCS, vol. 1672, pp. 430–441. Springer, Heidelberg (1999). https://doi.org/10.1007/3-540-48340-3_39
15. Yamakami, T.: Quantum NP and a quantum hierarchy. In: IFIP TCS 2002, The International Federation for Information Processing, vol. 96(Track 1), pp. 323–336 (2002)
16. Yamakami, T.: Analysis of quantum functions. Int. J. Fund. Comput. Sci. **14**, 815–852 (2003)
17. Yamakami, T.: A schematic definition of quantum polynomial time computability. J. Symbolic Logic **85**, 1546–1587 (2020)
18. Yamakami, T.: Nonuniform families of polynomial-size quantum finite automata and quantum logarithmic-space computation with polynomial-size advice. Inf. Comput. **286**, 104783 (2022)
19. Yamakami, T.: Expressing power of elementary quantum recursion schemes for quantum logarithmic-time computability. In: WoLLIC 2022, LNCS, vol. 13468, pp. 88–104, Springer (2022). A corrected and expanded version under a slightly different title is available at arXiv:2311.15884

20. Ying, M.: Toward automatic verification of quantum programs. Form. Asp. Comput. **31**, 3–25 (2019)
21. Ying, M.: Birkhoff-von Newmann quantum logic as an assertion language for quantum programs. Available at arXiv: 2205.01955v1 (2022)

Fundamental Sequences Based on Localization

Gunnar Wilken[✉][iD]

Okinawa Institute of Science and Technology Graduate University,
Okinawa 904-0495, Japan
wilken@oist.jp

Abstract. We introduce systems of fundamental sequences for relativized ϑ-function-based notation systems of strength Π_1^1-CA_0 and prove the Bachmann property for these systems, which is essential for monotonicity properties of fast growing hierarchies defined on the basis of fundamental sequences. The central notion of our construction is the notion of *localization*, which was introduced in [9]. Our assignment extends Buchholz' assignment for ordinals below Bachmann-Howard ordinal, see [1]. The specific system of ϑ-functions over ordinal addition as basic function fits the framework of the ordinal arithmetical toolkit developed in [9] and enables the investigation of fundamental sequences and independence phenomena also in the context of patterns of resemblance, an approach to ordinal notations that is both semantic and combinatorial and was first introduced by Carlson in [3] and further analyzed in [4,8,10,11]. Our exposition is put into the context of the abstract approach to fundamental sequences developed by Buchholz, Cichon, and Weiermann in [2]. An extended version of this article containing complete proofs will be published elsewhere.

Keywords: Proof theory · Ordinal notations · Fundamental sequences

1 Systems of Fundamental Sequences for $\mathbf{T}^\tau$

In this section we revisit, independently re-establish, and extend well known results originally due to W. Buchholz regarding fundamental sequences for ordinal notations up to the Bachmann-Howard ordinal, cf. [1]. For independent work also building on Buchholz' results, but in a different direction, see [6].

The strength of our extension characterizes theories like Π_1^1-CA_0, $\mathrm{ID}_{<\omega}$, and $\mathrm{KP}\ell_0$. We develop these results for notations used in the analysis of patterns of resemblance of orders 1 and 2. This further extends the theory of ordinal arithmetic developed as a byproduct when analyzing patterns of resemblance that was layed out in [9], applied in [10] and [11], slightly extended in [4], and put to full usage in [12,14]. For an overview and gentle introduction, see [8] and [13]. The present article also sets the stage for a theory of *pattern related fundamental sequences* that gives rise to independence phenomena related to patterns.

© The Author(s), under exclusive license to Springer Nature Switzerland AG 2024
L. Levy Patey et al. (Eds.): CiE 2024, LNCS 14773, pp. 324–338, 2024.
https://doi.org/10.1007/978-3-031-64309-5_26

1.1 Preliminaries: Relativized Notation Systems T^τ, Fixed Point Conditions for ϑ-Functions, Localization

For $\tau \in \mathbb{E}_1$, i.e. τ is either equal to 1 or any epsilon number (epsilon numbers are ordinals closed under ω-exponentiation, where ω denotes the least infinite ordinal), we defined the relativized notation system T^τ in Subsect. 2.1.2 of [14]. T^τ is built up over a sequence $\tau = \Omega_0 = \vartheta_0(0), \Omega_1 = \vartheta_1(0), \Omega_2 = \vartheta_2(0), \ldots$, where $\Omega_1, \Omega_2, \ldots$ is a strictly increasing sequence of regular ordinals such that $\Omega_1 > \tau$. Terms in systems T^τ are composed of parameters below τ, ordinal summation, and ϑ_j-functions for $j < \omega$, where ϑ_0 is also written as ϑ^τ. ϑ_j-functions uniquely denote ordinals closed under ordinal addition in the segment (Ω_j, Ω_{j+1}). The only restriction for the application of a ϑ_j-function to a term in the system is that the argument be strictly below Ω_{j+2}. The operation $\cdot^{*j}$, cf. Definition 2.24 of [14] searches a T^τ-term for its ϑ_j-subterm of largest ordinal value, but under the restriction to treat ϑ_i-subterms for $i < j$ as atomic. If such largest ϑ_j-subterm does not exist, $\cdot^{*j}$ returns 0, rather than any value from the interval $(0, \Omega_j)$. We also write $*^\tau$ instead of $*^0$ if $\Omega_0 = \tau$.

By slight abuse of notation we can consider notation systems $T^{\Omega_{i+1}}$ to be systems relativized to the initial segment Ω_{i+1} of ordinals and built up over $\Omega_{i+1} = \vartheta_{i+1}(0), \Omega_{i+2} = \vartheta_{i+2}(0), \ldots$, i.e. without renaming the indices of ϑ-functions. Results on T^τ from [14] then directly carry over to such systems $T^{\Omega_{i+1}}$ and the corresponding ϑ-functions. For convenience, we cite a well-known useful proposition regarding ϑ-functions, where we make use of a convention also used throughout [14], namely that when writing the argument of a ϑ_j-function, $j < \omega$, as $\Delta + \eta$, more generally, using a sum of a capital Greek letter and a lower case Greek letter, we automatically mean that Δ is a (possibly 0) multiple of Ω_{j+1}, while $\eta < \Omega_{j+1}$. Moreover, we can use this proposition as an alternative definition of ϑ-functions in order to shortcut the definition process lined out in Subsect. 2.1 of [14] and fully carried out in [9].

Proposition 1. *For $\alpha = \vartheta_j(\Delta + \eta)$ we have*

$$\alpha = \min\{\theta \geq \Omega_j \mid (\Delta + \eta)^{*j} < \theta \text{ and}$$
$$\forall \Gamma + \rho < \Delta + \eta \, ((\Gamma + \rho)^{*j} < \theta \to \vartheta_j(\Gamma + \rho) < \theta).\}$$

For convenience we cite Lemma 2.26 of [14] regarding the well-known comparison of ϑ-terms, which is rooted in the pivotal property $\beta^* < \vartheta(\beta)$ of ϑ-functions.

Proposition 2. *For $\alpha, \beta, \gamma \in T^\tau \cap \Omega_{j+2}$ we have $\beta^{*j} < \vartheta_j(\beta)$ and*

$$\vartheta_j(\alpha) < \vartheta_j(\gamma) \quad \Leftrightarrow \quad (\alpha < \gamma \wedge \alpha^{*j} < \vartheta_j(\gamma)) \vee \vartheta_j(\alpha) \leq \gamma^{*j}.$$

Some Basic Terminology. We denote the class of additive principal numbers, i.e. ordinals greater than 0 that are closed under ordinal addition, by $\mathbb{P}$. Likewise, we denote the class $\mathrm{Lim}(\mathbb{P})$ of limits of additive principal numbers by $\mathbb{L}$, and the class of epsilon numbers by $\mathbb{E}$.

Any ordinal $\alpha \notin \mathbb{P} \cup \{0\}$ is called *additively decomposable*, and any α can be written in *additive normal form* $\alpha =_{\mathrm{ANF}} \alpha_1 + \ldots + \alpha_n$ where $\alpha_1, \ldots, \alpha_n$ is a weakly decreasing sequence of additive principal numbers. We will often use the notation $\alpha =_{\mathrm{NF}} \beta + \gamma$ for additively decomposable α, which means that $\beta, \gamma > 0$, γ is additively indecomposable (additive principal), and β is minimal such that $\alpha = \beta + \gamma$, hence $\beta = \alpha_1 + \ldots + \alpha_{n-1}$ and $\gamma = \alpha_n$. We will also use the notation $\mathrm{end}(\alpha)$ for γ, and clearly $\mathrm{end}(\alpha) = \alpha$ if $\alpha \in \mathbb{P} \cup \{0\}$. We write $\mathrm{mc}(\alpha) := \alpha_1$ for the maximal (additive) component of α and set $\mathrm{mc}(0) := 0$. For ordinals α, β such that $\alpha \leq \beta$ we write $-\alpha + \beta$ for the unique γ such that $\alpha + \gamma = \beta$. And for $k < \omega$ we write $\alpha \dot{-} k$ for the least ordinal α' such that α can be written as $\alpha = \alpha' + l$ where $l \leq k$.

For $\alpha \notin \mathbb{E} \cup \{0\}$ the *Cantor normal form* representation of α is useful and indicated as $\alpha =_{\mathrm{CNF}} \omega^{\alpha_1} + \ldots + \omega^{\alpha_n}$ where $\alpha > \alpha_1 \geq \ldots \geq \alpha_n$. For completeness, in the case $\alpha = 0$ we have $n = 0$, and clearly $\alpha = \omega^\alpha$ for $\alpha \in \mathbb{E}$.

Informally, for an ordinal $\alpha = \vartheta^\tau(\Delta + \eta)$ the term Δ indicates the *fixed point level* of α, in arithmetized form. This mechanism creates the strength of ordinal notations using functions like ϑ, as e.g. opposed to the various versions of Veblen functions φ of increasing arity. An easy observation into this direction is given by the following lemma.

Lemma 3 (2.29 of [14], 4.3 of [9]). *For $\alpha = \vartheta^\tau(\Delta + \eta) \in T^\tau$ we have $\alpha \in \mathbb{E}^{>\tau}$ if and only if $\Delta > 0$.*

Note also that the function $\sigma \mapsto \vartheta_j(\Delta + \sigma)$ is strictly increasing for $\sigma < \Omega_{j+1}$, hence $\eta \leq \sup_{\sigma < \eta} \vartheta_j(\Delta + \sigma)$, and let the condition $F_j(\Delta, \eta)$ be defined as

$$F_j(\Delta, \eta) \quad :\Leftrightarrow \quad \eta = \sup_{\sigma < \eta}{}^+ \vartheta_j(\Delta + \sigma),$$

where the usage of proper supremum excludes the unintended equality $1 = \sup_{\sigma < 1} \vartheta_0(\sigma) = \vartheta_0(0)$ (for $\tau = 1$). [1]

An easy application of the above proposition is to see that for $\alpha = \vartheta_j(\Delta + \eta)$ such that $\eta \in \mathrm{Lim}$ and $\neg F_j(\Delta, \eta)$ we have the continuous, strictly monotonically increasing approximation

$$\alpha = \sup_{\sigma < \eta} \vartheta_j(\Delta + \sigma). \tag{1}$$

Another very useful lemma in this context is Lemma 2.30 of [14], stating that

Proposition 4. *For $\alpha = \vartheta_j(\Delta + \eta)$ we have*

$$F_j(\Delta, \eta) \Leftrightarrow \eta \text{ is of a form } \eta = \vartheta_j(\Gamma + \rho) \text{ such that } \Gamma > \Delta \text{ and } \eta > \Delta^{*j}. \tag{2}$$

The notion of *localization* was introduced in Sect. 4 of [9], see also [14] for a summary in Subsect. 2.2. We give a version of the definition of localization (cf. Definition 4.6 of [9] and Definition 2.32 of [14]) for segments $[\Omega_i, \Omega_{i+1})$, $i < \omega$,

---

[1] An acknowledgement to Samuel Alexander for pointing out this flaw in earlier publications like [14].

called Ω_i-localization, which is completely analogous to τ-localization for the lowest level $[\Omega_0, \Omega_1)$ in the setting $\Omega_0 = \tau$. By $P_i(\alpha)$ we denote the set of all ϑ_i-subterms of a term $\alpha \in T^\tau$ that are not in the scope of a ϑ_j-subterm of α for any $j < i$, cf. 2.23–2.27 of [14]. Thus, for any ϑ_i-term $\alpha = \vartheta_i(\xi)$, where $\xi \in T^\tau \cap \Omega_{i+2}$, we have $\xi^{*i} = \max(P_i(\xi)) = \max(P_i(\alpha)\backslash\{\alpha\})$.

Definition 5. *Let $\alpha = \vartheta_i(\Delta + \eta) \in T^\tau$ where $i < \omega$. We define a finite sequence of ordinals as follows: Set $\alpha_0 := \Omega_i$. Suppose α_n is already defined and $\alpha_n < \alpha$. Let $\alpha_{n+1} := \vartheta_i(\xi) \in P_i(\alpha)\backslash(\alpha_n + 1)$ where ξ is maximal. This yields a finite sequence $\Omega_i = \alpha_0 < \ldots < \alpha_n = \alpha$ for some $n < \omega$ which we call the Ω_i-localization of α.*

Note that we could as well regard α in the above definition as a term of T^{Ω_j} for any $j \leq i$. For convenience we also include the corresponding reformulation of lemmas stating key properties and structural importance of localization.

Lemma 6 (cf. 2.33 of [14] and 4.7, 4.8, 4.9 of [9]). *Let $\alpha = \vartheta_i(\Delta + \eta) \in T^\tau$, $\alpha > \Omega_i$, and denote the Ω_i-localization of α by $(\Omega_i = \alpha_0, \ldots, \alpha_n = \alpha)$ where $\alpha_j = \vartheta_i(\Delta_j + \eta_j)$ for $j = 1, \ldots, n$. Then*

1. *For $j < n$ and any $\beta = \vartheta_i(\Gamma + \rho) \in (\alpha_j, \alpha_{j+1})$ we have $\Gamma + \rho < \Delta_{j+1} + \eta_{j+1}$.*
2. *$(\Delta_j)_{1 \leq j \leq n}$ forms a strictly descending sequence of multiples of Ω_{i+1}.*
3. *For $j < n$ the sequence $(\alpha_0, \ldots, \alpha_j)$ is the Ω_i-localization of α_j.*

*The **guiding picture** for localizations is, setting $\alpha_j^+ := \vartheta_i(\Delta_j + \eta_j + 1)$ for $j = 1, \ldots, n$,*

$$\Omega_i < \alpha_1 < \ldots < \alpha_n = \alpha < \alpha^+ = \alpha_n^+ < \ldots < \alpha_1^+.$$

Lemma 7 (2.31 of [14], 4.5 of [9]). *For $\alpha = \vartheta^\tau(\Delta + \eta) \in T^\tau$ and $\vartheta^\tau(\Gamma + \rho) \in (\alpha, \alpha^+)$ we have $\Gamma < \Delta$.*

Lemma 8 (2.35 of [14], 5.2 of [4]). *Let $\alpha, \beta \in T^\tau \cap (\Omega_i, \Omega_{i+1}) \cap \mathbb{P}$ with $\alpha < \beta$, $i < \omega$. For the Ω_i-localizations $\Omega_i = \alpha_0, \ldots, \alpha_n = \alpha$ and $\Omega_i = \beta_0, \ldots, \beta_m = \beta$ we have*

$$\alpha := (\alpha_1, \ldots, \alpha_n) <_{\text{lex}} (\beta_1, \ldots, \beta_m) =: \beta.$$

Lemma 9 (2.36 of [14], 5.3 of [4]). *Let $\alpha = \vartheta_i(\xi) \in T^\tau$ with Ω_i-localization $\alpha := (\alpha_0, \ldots, \alpha_n)$ and $\beta \in P_i(\xi)$. If there is $\alpha_j \in P_i(\beta)$ where $0 \leq j \leq n$ then $(\alpha_0, \ldots, \alpha_j)$ is an initial sequence of the Ω_i-localization of any $\gamma \in T^\tau \cap [\beta, \alpha]$.*

A noteworthy consequence of Lemma 8 is that for $\alpha = \vartheta_i(\xi)$ with Ω_i-localization $\Omega_i = \alpha_0, \ldots, \alpha_n = \alpha$ the sequence $\alpha_0, \ldots, \alpha_{n-1}$ is an initial sequence of the Ω_i-localization of ξ^{*i}, provided that $\xi^{*i} \geq \Omega_i$, since in that case $\alpha_{n-1} \leq \xi^{*i} < \alpha$.

As a simple example consider the ordinal α denoted by $\vartheta_0(\vartheta_1(0) + \tau)$ where $\tau := \vartheta_0(\vartheta_1(\vartheta_2(0)))$ is the Bachmann-Howard ordinal. The (Ω_0-)localization of α is (τ, α). α is the least epsilon number strictly above τ. In order to describe where the successor-epsilon number α, the fixed point level of which is $\Omega_1 = \vartheta_1(0)$, is located, it is essential to specify the greatest ordinal below α of higher fixed point level, namely τ, the fixed point level of which is $\vartheta_1(\Omega_2) = \varepsilon_{\Omega+1}$.

1.2   Systems of Fundamental Sequences

We now fix concrete instances of well-known notions of systems of fundamental sequences and Bachmann systems, and refer the reader to the seminal paper by Buchholz, Cichon, and Weiermann [2] for more background and an abstract approach.

Definition 10. *We define the notion of* (Cantorian) *system of fundamental sequences on a set S of ordinals. A mapping $\cdot\{\cdot\} : S \times \mathbb{N} \to \sup S$ is called a system of fundamental sequences if the following conditions hold:*

1. *$0\{n\} = 0$ if $0 \in S$.*
2. *$\zeta\{n\} = \zeta'$ if $\zeta = \zeta' + 1$ and $\zeta \in S$.*
3. *For $\lambda \in S \cap \mathrm{Lim}$, the sequence $(\lambda\{n\})_{n \in \mathbb{N}} \subseteq \sup S$ is strictly increasing such that $\lambda = \sup_{n \in \mathbb{N}} \lambda\{n\}$.*

A system $\cdot\{\cdot\} : S \times \mathbb{N} \to \sup S$ of fundamental sequences is called Cantorian *if the following conditions hold:*

4. *For $\alpha =_{\mathrm{NF}} \xi + \eta \in S$ we have $\eta \in S$ and $\alpha\{n\} = \xi + \eta\{n\}$ for $n < \omega$.*
5. *For $\alpha = \omega^{\zeta} \in S$ such that $\zeta = \zeta' + 1$ we have $\alpha\{n\} = \omega^{\zeta} \cdot (n+1)$.*

A system $\cdot\{\cdot\} : S \times \mathbb{N} \to \sup S$ of fundamental sequences is said to have the Bachmann property *(see Schmidt [7]), if for all $\alpha, \beta \in S$ and $n < \omega$ we have $\alpha\{n\} \leq \beta\{0\}$ whenever $\alpha\{n\} < \beta < \alpha$. Such systems are called* Bachmann *systems.*

For convenience we introduce the notion of *base system* for the set of parameters. The intention is that we want to allow $\alpha[0] = 0$ only for $\alpha = 0, 1, \Omega_i$ where $i \in (0, \omega)$.

Definition 11. *For $\tau \in \mathbb{E}_1 \cap \aleph_1$ (for countable τ) suppose $\cdot\{\cdot\} : (\tau+1) \times \mathbb{N} \to \tau$ is a Cantorian system of fundamental sequences with the following additional property:*

6. *For $\alpha \in (\tau + 1) \cap \mathbb{P}^{>1}$, i.e. for additive principal limits $\alpha \leq \tau$, we have $\alpha\{0\} \in \mathbb{P}$.*

We call such a system a base system.

We want to extend a mapping as in the above definition to a mapping $\cdot\{\cdot\} : \mathring{\mathrm{T}}^{\tau} \times \mathbb{N} \to \mathring{\mathrm{T}}^{\tau}$ where $\mathring{\mathrm{T}}^{\tau}$ is the maximal subset of T^{τ} such that $(\mathring{\mathrm{T}}^{\tau}, \cdot\{\cdot\})$ is a Cantorian system of fundamental sequences. It will be shown that the set

$$\mathring{\mathrm{T}}^{\tau} := \{\alpha \in \mathrm{T}^{\tau} \mid \mathrm{d}(\alpha) = 0\},$$

where the domain function d is defined below, yields a system of fundamental sequences with the desired properties. Note that for simplicity we have suppressed a superscript notation d^{τ} and written simply d instead, assuming that the corresponding τ is understood from the context.

Before we can define d, we need to define a crucial function already introduced as essential tool in the analysis of pure patterns of order 2 in [5]. It can be seen as a characteristic function for uncountable "moduli" in ordinal terms.

Definition 12 (cf. Definition 3.3 of [14]). *We define a characteristic function* $\chi^{\Omega_{i+1}} : T^{\Omega_{i+1}} \to \{0,1\}$, *where* $i < \omega$, *by recursion on the build-up of* $T^{\Omega_{i+1}}$:

1. $\chi^{\Omega_{i+1}}(\alpha) := \begin{cases} 0 & \text{if } \alpha < \Omega_{i+1} \\ 1 & \text{if } \alpha = \Omega_{i+1}, \end{cases}$

2. $\chi^{\Omega_{i+1}}(\alpha) := \chi^{\Omega_{i+1}}(\eta) \text{ if } \alpha =_{\mathrm{NF}} \xi + \eta,$

3. $\chi^{\Omega_{i+1}}(\alpha) := \begin{cases} \chi^{\Omega_{i+1}}(\Delta) & \text{if } \eta \notin \mathrm{Lim} \text{ or } F_j(\Delta, \eta) \\ \chi^{\Omega_{i+1}}(\eta) & \text{otherwise}, \end{cases}$

   if $\alpha = \vartheta_j(\Delta + \eta) > \Omega_{i+1}$ *and hence* $j \geq i + 1$.

Remark 13. Recall the first paragraphs of Subsect. 1.1 and note that the mapping $\chi^{\Omega_{i+1}}$ remains well defined if restricted to notations from T^{Ω_j} for $j \leq i$. For $j = 0$ and suitable $\Omega_0 = \tau \in \mathbb{E}_1$ this holds with $T^0 = T^\tau$. We will tacitly make use of the canonical embeddings from T^{Ω_i} into T^{Ω_j} for $i < j$.

Definition 14. *We define a domain indicator function* $\mathrm{d} : T^\tau \to \omega$ *recursively in the term build-up.*

1. $\mathrm{d}(\alpha) := 0 \text{ if } \alpha < \tau,$

2. $\mathrm{d}(\alpha) := \mathrm{d}(\eta) \text{ if } \alpha =_{\mathrm{NF}} \xi + \eta > \tau,$

3. *for* $\alpha = \vartheta_i(\Delta + \eta)$,

   3.1. $\mathrm{d}(\alpha) := \mathrm{d}(\eta)$, *if* $\eta \in \mathrm{Lim}$ *and* $F_i(\Delta, \eta)$ *does not hold*,

   3.2. *if* $\eta \notin \mathrm{Lim}$ *or* $F_i(\Delta, \eta)$:

   3.2.1. $\mathrm{d}(\alpha) := \begin{cases} i & \text{if } \eta = 0 \\ 0 & \text{otherwise} \end{cases}$ *in case of* $\Delta = 0$,

   3.2.2. $\mathrm{d}(\alpha) := 0$ *in case of* $\chi^{\Omega_{i+1}}(\Delta) = 1$,

   3.2.3. $\mathrm{d}(\alpha) := \mathrm{d}(\Delta)$ *otherwise*.

The following lemma shows the partitioning of T^τ into terms of equal cofinality, using the just introduced auxiliary functions χ and d.

Lemma 15. T^τ *is partitioned into the union of disjoint sets*

$$T^\tau = \mathring{T}^\tau \,\dot{\cup}\, \sum_{i<\omega} \{\alpha \in T^\tau \mid \chi^{\Omega_{i+1}}(\alpha) = 1\}.$$

Proof. The proof is given in full detail in the extended version of this article.

We are now prepared to define for each $\alpha \in T^\tau$, $\tau < \alpha \in \mathrm{Lim}$, a strictly increasing sequence $\alpha[\cdot]$ with supremum α, given a base system for all parameters $\leq \tau$ according to Definition 11. The extended system $\cdot[\cdot]$ inherits the properties $0[n] = 0$ and $(\alpha + 1)[\zeta] = \alpha$ for all $\alpha \in T^\tau$ as well as the property that for $\alpha \in \mathbb{P}^{>1}$ we have $\alpha[0] \in \mathbb{P}$, *provided that $\alpha \neq \Omega_i$ for all $i \in (0, \omega)$.*

Definition 16. *For $\tau \in \mathbb{E}_1 \cap \aleph_1$ let $\cdot\{\cdot\} : (\tau + 1) \times \mathbb{N} \to \tau$ be a base system according to Definition 11. Fix the canonical assignment $\Omega_0 := \tau$ and $\Omega_{i+1} := \aleph_{i+1}$ for $i < \omega$. Let $\alpha \in T^\tau$. By recursion on the build-up of α we define the function $\alpha[\cdot] : \aleph_d \to T^{\Omega_d}$ where $d := \mathrm{d}(\alpha)$. Let ζ range over $\aleph_d$.*

1. $\alpha[\zeta] := \alpha\{\zeta\}$ *if $\alpha \leq \tau$.*
2. $\alpha[\zeta] := \xi + \eta[\zeta]$ *if $\alpha =_{\mathrm{NF}} \xi + \eta > \tau$.*
3. *For $\alpha = \vartheta_i(\Delta + \eta)$ where $i < \omega$, $\vartheta_0 = \vartheta^\tau$, note that $d \leq i$, and denote the Ω_i-localization of α by $\Omega_i = \alpha_0, \ldots, \alpha_m = \alpha$. We define a support term $\underline{\alpha}$ by*

$$
\underline{\alpha} := \begin{cases} \alpha_{m-1} & \text{if either } F_i(\Delta, \eta), \\ & \text{or: } \eta = 0 \text{ and } \Delta[0]^{\star i} < \alpha_{m-1} = \Delta^{\star i} \text{ where } m > 1 \\ \vartheta_i(\Delta + \eta') & \text{if } \eta = \eta' + 1 \\ 0 & \text{otherwise.} \end{cases}
$$

For $\alpha > \tau$ the definition then proceeds as follows.

3.1. *If $\eta \in \mathrm{Lim}$ and $\neg F_i(\Delta, \eta)$, that is, $\eta \in \mathrm{Lim} \cap \sup_{\sigma < \eta} \vartheta_i(\Delta + \sigma)$, we have $d = \mathrm{d}(\eta)$ and define*
$$
\alpha[\zeta] := \vartheta_i(\Delta + \eta[\zeta]).
$$

3.2. *If otherwise $\eta \notin \mathrm{Lim}$ or $F_i(\Delta, \eta)$, we distinguish between the following 3 subcases.*

3.2.1. *If $\Delta = 0$, define*
$$
\alpha[\zeta] := \begin{cases} \underline{\alpha} \cdot (\zeta + 1) & \text{if } \eta > 0 \text{ (and hence } d = 0) \\ \zeta & \text{otherwise.} \end{cases}
$$

3.2.2. *$\chi^{\Omega_{i+1}}(\Delta) = 1$. This implies that $d = 0$, and we define recursively in $n < \omega$*
$$
\alpha[0] := \vartheta_i(\Delta[\underline{\alpha}]) \quad \text{and} \quad \alpha[n+1] := \vartheta_i(\Delta[\alpha[n]]).
$$

3.2.3. *Otherwise. Then $d = \mathrm{d}(\Delta)$ and*
$$
\alpha[\zeta] := \vartheta_i(\Delta[\zeta] + \underline{\alpha}).
$$

Recalling that
$$
\mathring{T}^\tau = \mathrm{d}^{-1}(0),
$$

we call the system $(\mathring{T}^\tau, \cdot\{\cdot\})$ (more sloppily also simply the entire mapping $\cdot\{\cdot\}$), where the mapping $\cdot\{\cdot\}$ is simply the restriction of $\cdot[\cdot]$ to $\mathring{T}^\tau$, a Buchholz system over τ. Note that this system is determined uniquely modulo the choice of $\cdot\{\cdot\} : (\tau + 1) \times \mathbb{N} \to \tau$, which in turn is trivially determined if $\tau = 1$.

Remark 17. 1. Any $\alpha \in T^\tau$ gives rise to a unique function

$$\alpha[\cdot] : \aleph_{d(\alpha)} \to 1 + \alpha$$

such that $\sup_{\zeta < \aleph_{d(\alpha)}} \alpha[\zeta] = \sup \alpha$ and which is strictly increasing for $\alpha \in \mathrm{Lim}$ and constant otherwise, as will be confirmed shortly.
2. Recall the first paragraphs of Subsect. 1.1 and Remark 13, and note that restricting parameters ζ to T^{Ω_k} for some $k < d(\alpha)$ yields a function $\alpha[\cdot]$: $T^{\Omega_k} \cap \aleph_d \to T^{\Omega_k}$, so that the application of $*^i$ for $i \geq k$ becomes meaningful.

The following remark contains helpful observations regarding the support term $\underline{\alpha}$. Before discussing this in technical detail, we should mention that localizing an ordinal α in terms of fixed point levels can be refined to the notion of *fine-localization*, which was introduced in Sect. 5 of [4] and takes the level of *limit point thinning* into account. In the context of Definition 16, in particular in view of clause 3.1, we only need to refine from taking the predecessor α_{m-1} to taking $\underline{\alpha}$, which is a simple case of fine-localization. Other cases of fine-localization are *automatically* taken care of by clause 3.1.

Remark 18. If $\eta = \eta' + 1$ for some η we have $\alpha = \underline{\alpha}^+$, so the next ordinal of fixed point level Δ is built up above $\underline{\alpha}$. In case of $F_j(\Delta, \eta)$ we have $\eta = (\Delta + \eta)^{*j} = \alpha_{m-1} = \underline{\alpha}$ with $m > 1$ by (2), so that the next ordinal of fixed point level Δ is built up above the predecessor of α in its localization, which has fixed point level strictly greater than Δ.

As mentioned above, in clause 3.1 of Definition 16 of $\alpha[\zeta]$ the support issue is automatically taken care of by $\eta[\zeta]$ as we do not have $\eta = \alpha_{m-1}$ and can therefore rely on continuity of $\eta_0 \mapsto \vartheta_i(\Delta + \eta_0)$ at η, cf. (1).

In clause 3.2.1 we either have $\eta > 0$ to the effect that $\alpha = \underline{\alpha} \cdot \omega$ is a successor-additive principal number that must be approximated by finite multiples of $\underline{\alpha}$. If $\eta = 0$, we must have $\alpha = \Omega_i$ with $i > 0$, so that α is of uncountable cofinality and hence is approximated by parameters $\zeta < \Omega_i$.

In clause 3.2.2 the ordinal α is approximated by approximation of its fixed point level Δ via term nesting starting from the support term $\underline{\alpha}$, which as just described takes care of the possible contribution of η, taking into account the collapsing that takes place when ϑ_i is applied to $\Delta + \eta$, where Δ is of cofinality Ω_{i+1} before collapsing.

In clause 3.2.3, if $\eta = 0$, we need the support term to be $\underline{\alpha} = \alpha_{m-1}$ if $\Delta[0]^{*i} < \alpha_{m-1} = \Delta^{*i}$, since otherwise we would have $\alpha[\zeta] < \alpha_{m-1}$ for all ζ, and the sequence for α would fall short. The need for the support term is seen by examples like $\alpha = \vartheta_1(\vartheta_2(\nu))$ where $\nu = \vartheta_1(\vartheta_2(\vartheta_2(\Omega_1)))$, the Ω_1-localization of which is (Ω_1, ν, α), and for which we have $\vartheta_1(\vartheta_2(\nu[\zeta])) < \nu$ for every $\zeta < \Omega_1$.

If on the other hand $\eta = 0 = \underline{\alpha}$ in clause 3.2.3, it will follow from parts 5 and 6 of Lemma 19 that the situation $\Delta[0]^{*i} < \alpha_{m-1} < \Delta^{*i}$ can not occur, in other words: if $\eta = 0$, $m > 1$, and $\Delta[0]^{*i} < \Delta^{*i}$, it follows that $\alpha_{m-1} \leq \Delta[0]^{*i}$. Thus, if we need a support term $\underline{\alpha} > 0$, α_{m-1} suffices and is equal to Δ^{*i}.

Note that this *minimal* choice of support term $\underline{\alpha}$ to guarantee convergence of the sequence to α is crucial for the assignment of fundamental sequences to satisfy Bachmann property. A simple example illustrates this. Consider in clause 3.2.3 for $\alpha = \vartheta_i(\Delta)$ (assuming that $\eta = 0$) the alternative definition $\alpha_\zeta := \vartheta_i(\Delta[\zeta] + \Delta^{*i})$, which still converges to α. Now consider, writing ω instead of $\vartheta_0(\vartheta_0(0))$, $\alpha := \vartheta_0(\vartheta_1(\omega)) = \varphi_{\omega^\omega}(0)$. We then have $\alpha[n] = \vartheta_0(\vartheta_1(n+1)) = \varphi_{\omega^{n+1}}(0)$ and $\alpha_n = \vartheta_0(\vartheta_1(n+1) + \omega) = \varphi_{\omega^{n+1}}(\omega)$. For $\beta := \alpha[n+1] = \varphi_{\omega^{n+2}}(0)$ we have $\beta[0] = \varphi_{\omega^{n+1}}(0)$ and $\beta_0 = \varphi_{\omega^{n+1}}(1)$, and we observe that $\alpha[n], \alpha_n < \beta < \alpha$ and $\alpha[n] = \beta[0] < \beta_0 < \alpha_n$, demonstrating that the alternative definition using the *-operation instead of localization only where necessary does not satisfy Bachmann property.

We turn to the main technical lemma for Buchholz systems over τ.

Lemma 19. *In the setting of Definition 16, let $\alpha \in T^\tau \setminus \tau$ be a limit number, and let ζ range over $\aleph_d$ where $d := d(\alpha)$.*

1. *For $\alpha = \vartheta_j(\Delta + \eta)$ such that $\underline{\alpha} > 0$ and $\chi^{\Omega_{j+1}}(\Delta) = 0$ we have*

$$\Delta[\zeta]^{*j} < \underline{\alpha}.$$

2. *The mapping $\zeta \mapsto \alpha[\zeta]$ is strictly increasing with proper supremum α.*
3. *The mapping $\zeta \mapsto \alpha[\zeta]^{*k}$ is weakly increasing with upper bound α^{*k} for $d \le k$.*
4. *If $d = i + 1 > 0$, we have*

$$\zeta^{*k} \le \alpha[\zeta]^{*k} \le \max\{\alpha^{*k}, \zeta^{*k}\} \quad and \quad \alpha^{*k} \le \max\{\alpha[\zeta]^{*k}, 1\}$$

for any $k \le i$.

5. *For $\alpha = \vartheta_j(\Delta + \eta) > \Omega_j$ with Ω_j-localization $\Omega_j = \alpha_0, \ldots, \alpha_m = \alpha$ we have*

$$\alpha_{m-1} \le \alpha[0].$$

6. *If $\alpha = \vartheta_j(\Delta + \eta)$ and i is such that $d \le i \le j$ and $\alpha[0]^{*i} < \alpha^{*i}$ where $\alpha^{*i} > \Omega_i$, then we have $d(\alpha^{*i}) = d$, and one of the following two cases applies.*
   (a) *α^{*i} is of the form $\nu \cdot \omega$ for some additive principal $\nu \ge \Omega_i$, where we have $d = 0$, $\alpha[n]^{*i} = \nu$, and $\alpha^{*i}[n] = \nu \cdot (n+1)$ for $n < \omega$.*
   (b) *Otherwise. Then $\alpha^{*i}[\zeta] \le \alpha[\zeta]^{*i}$ for all $\zeta < \aleph_d$, and there exists $\zeta_0 < \aleph_d$ such that $\alpha^{*i}[\zeta] = \alpha[\zeta]^{*i}$ for all $\zeta \in (\zeta_0, \aleph_d)$.*
7. *For any β such that $\alpha[\zeta] \le \beta < \alpha$ we have*

$$\beta^{*k} \ge \alpha[\zeta]^{*k}$$

for all k if $\zeta = 0$, and for all $\zeta < \aleph_d$ and all k such that $k + 1 \ge d$.

Proof. The proof of this main lemma is given in full detail in the extended version of this article.

Corollary 20. *Any Buchholz system $\mathring{T}^\tau$ is indeed a Cantorian system of fundamental sequences on $\mathring{T}^\tau$ provided that its restriction to $\tau + 1$ is a Cantorian system of fundamental sequences.*

We now take a closer look at Ω_i-localizations of elements of fundamental sequences. This plays a crucial role in proving Bachmann property.

Lemma 21. *Let* $\alpha = \vartheta_i(\Delta + \eta) > \Omega_i$ *with* Ω_i-*localization* $(\Omega_i = \alpha_0, \ldots, \alpha_m = \alpha)$ *and* $\zeta < \aleph_{d(\alpha)}$. *We display the* Ω_i-*localization of* $\alpha[\zeta]$, *distinguishing between the cases of definition.*

1. $\eta \in \mathrm{Lim}$ *such that* $F_i(\Delta, \eta)$ *does not hold. Then the* Ω_i-*localization of* $\alpha[\zeta]$ *is* $(\alpha_0, \ldots, \alpha_{m-1}, \alpha[\zeta])$, *unless* $\zeta = 0$ *and* $\alpha = \vartheta_i(\Omega_k)$ *with* $0 < k \leq i$, *in which case the* Ω_i-*localization of* $\alpha[0]$ *is* (Ω_i).
2. $\eta \notin \mathrm{Lim}$ *or* $F_i(\Delta, \eta)$ *holds.*
   (a) $\Delta = 0$. *Here* $\alpha[\zeta] \in \mathbb{P}$ *if and only if* $\zeta = 0$. *The* Ω_i-*localization of* $\alpha[0]$ *then is* $(\alpha_0, \ldots, \alpha_{m-1})$, *unless* $\eta = \eta' + 1$ *for some* $\eta' > 0$, *in which case it is* $(\alpha_0, \ldots, \alpha_{m-1}, \underline{\alpha})$ *where* $\underline{\alpha} = \vartheta_i(\eta')$.
   (b) $\chi^{\Omega_{i+1}}(\Delta) = 1$. *The* Ω_i-*localization of* $\alpha[\zeta]$ *then is* $(\alpha_0, \ldots, \alpha_{m-1}, \underline{\alpha}, \alpha[\zeta])$ *if* $\eta = \eta' + 1$ *for some* η' *where* $\underline{\alpha} = \vartheta_i(\Delta + \eta')$, *otherwise it is* $(\alpha_0, \ldots, \alpha_{m-1}, \alpha[\zeta])$, *unless* $\zeta = 0$, $\Delta = \Omega_{i+1}$, *and* $\eta = 0$, *in which case it simply is* (Ω_i).
   (c) $\Delta > 0$ *and* $\chi^{\Omega_{i+1}}(\Delta) = 0$. *Then the* Ω_i-*localization of* $\alpha[\zeta]$ *is* $(\alpha_0, \ldots, \alpha_{m-1}, \alpha[\zeta])$, *unless* $\eta = \eta' + 1$ *for some* η', *in which case it is* $(\alpha_0, \ldots, \alpha_{m-1}, \underline{\alpha}, \alpha[\zeta])$ *where* $\underline{\alpha} = \vartheta_i(\Delta + \eta')$.

Proof. The proof is given in full detail in the extended version of this article.

Examples

We list a few instructive examples of fundamental sequences, writing Ω for Ω_1 and * for $*_0$.

1. $\alpha := \varphi_\omega(0) = \vartheta_0(\Omega \cdot \omega) = \vartheta_0(\vartheta_1(1))$, for which $\alpha\{n\} = \varphi_{n+1}(0)$.
2. $\beta := \vartheta_0(\Omega^\omega) = \vartheta_0(\vartheta_1(\vartheta_1(1)))$, the so-called small Veblen number, for which $\beta\{n\} = \varphi(1, 0_{n+2})$ where 0_k is a 0-vector of length k, cf. Lemma 4.11 and subsequent remark of [8]. [2]
3. $\gamma := \varphi_{\Gamma_0}(1) = \vartheta_0(\vartheta_1(\Gamma_0)) = \vartheta_0(\vartheta_1(\vartheta_0(\vartheta_1(\vartheta_1(0)))))$, for which $\gamma\{n\} = \vartheta_0(\vartheta_1(\Gamma_0\{n\}) + \Gamma_0)$ with $\Gamma_0\{0\} = \vartheta_0(\vartheta_1(0)) = \varepsilon_0$ and $\Gamma_0\{n+1\} = \vartheta_0(\vartheta_1(\Gamma_0\{n\}))$, that is, $\Gamma_0\{n\} = (\vartheta_0 \circ \vartheta_1)^{(n+1)}(0)$.
4. $\delta := \varphi_{\varepsilon_{\Gamma_0+1}}(0) = \vartheta_0(\vartheta_1(\vartheta_0(\Omega_1 + \Gamma_0)))$, for which $\delta\{n\} = \vartheta_0(\Delta\{n\})$, as $\underline{\Delta} = 0$ because $\Delta\{0\}^* = \Gamma_0 \cdot \omega > \Gamma_0$, where $\Delta := \vartheta_1(\vartheta_0(\Omega_1 + \Gamma_0))$. $\Delta\{n\} = \vartheta_1(\varepsilon_{\Gamma_0+1}\{n\})$, where $\varepsilon_{\Gamma_0+1}\{0\} = \Gamma_0 \cdot \omega$ and $\varepsilon_{\Gamma_0+1}\{n\}$ consists of a tower of height $n + 1$ for $n > 0$:

$$\varepsilon_{\Gamma_0+1}\{n\} = \Gamma_0^{\cdot^{\cdot^{\Gamma_0^\omega}}}.$$

5. $\eta := \vartheta_0(\vartheta_1(\vartheta_2(\Omega_1)))$. Then $\eta\{0\}$ is the Bachmann-Howard ordinal, and in general we have

$$\eta\{n\} = (\vartheta_0 \circ \vartheta_1 \circ \vartheta_2)^{(n+1)}(0).$$

Note that we have $\vartheta_2(\Omega_1) = \Omega_2 \cdot \Omega_1$ and $\chi^{\Omega_1}(\Delta) = 1$ for $\Delta := \vartheta_1(\vartheta_2(\Omega_1)) = \varphi_{\Omega_1}(1)$, and for $\zeta < \Omega_1$ we have $\Delta[\zeta] = \vartheta_1(\vartheta_2(\zeta)) = \varphi_{\omega^\zeta}(\Omega_1 + 1)$.

---

[2] Note that ϑ-functions in [8] are defined over $+$ and ω-exponentiation as basic functions, which however does not change the equality at this level.

1.3 Bachmann Property

We turn to the *Bachmann property*, assuming that the restriction of our system to $\tau + 1$ has got this property. We first provide a lemma that comes in handy in order to modularize the proof of Bachmann property and is useful itself, e.g. in proving Lemma 30.

Lemma 22. *For* $\Gamma = \vartheta_{j+1}(\Sigma + \sigma)$ *and* $\Delta = \vartheta_{j+1}(\Xi + \xi)$ *such that* $\chi^{\Omega_{i+1}}(\Delta) = 1$ *and* $\Delta[\zeta] < \Gamma < \Delta$ *we have*
$$\Delta[\zeta] \leq \Gamma[0].$$

Proof. The proof is given in full detail in the extended version of this article.

Theorem 23. *Any Buchholz system over some* τ *satisfies Bachmann property and hence is a Cantorian Bachmann system, provided that its restriction to* $\tau + 1$ *is a Cantorian system of fundamental sequences satisfying Bachmann property.*

Proof. The proof is given in full detail in the extended version of this article.

2 Norms, Regularity, and the Hardy Hierarchy

Assuming that all additively decomposable terms in T^τ, including possible parameters $< \tau$ in the case $\tau \in \mathbb{E}$, are automatically given in additive normal form, every ordinal represented in T^τ has a *unique* term representation composed of the constant 0, constants $\xi \in \mathbb{P} \cap \tau$, the binary function $+$ for ordinal addition, and the unary functions ϑ_i for each $i < \omega$, since the ordinals $\tau = \Omega_0, \Omega_1, \Omega_2, \ldots$ are represented as $\vartheta_0(0), \vartheta_1(0), \vartheta_2(0), \ldots$. Counting the number of function symbols 0, ξ for $\xi \in \mathbb{P} \cap \tau$, $+$, and ϑ_i for each $i < \omega$ that occur in such unique term representation of an ordinal α in T^τ provides us with a measure of term length of the unique representation of α.

Unless parameters $\xi \in \mathbb{P} \cap \tau$ for some $\tau \in \mathbb{E}$ are represented using a suitable notation system (say, T^σ for some $\sigma < \tau$, allowing for a finite iteration of this process) and the measure of term length is accordingly modified, sets of ordinals $\beta \in \mathrm{T}^\tau \cap \alpha$ of term length bounded by some $n < \omega$ for given $\alpha \in \mathrm{T}^\tau$ are in general not finite. We therefore restrict ourselves to $\tau = 1$ when using the notion of term length. The measure of term length is then called the *canonical norm* and gives rise to the notion of *regularity* of a Bachmann system. Note however that, as just mentioned, there is a straightforward way to extend term length and canonical norm to relativized systems T^τ after replacing additively indecomposable parameters below τ by suitable term notations.

For more background on the origins of using norms of ordinals and an abstract treatment of fundamental sequences, normed Bachmann systems, and Hardy hierarchies we again refer to [2].

Definition 24 (cf. [2]).

1. *For any ordinal* α *in* T^τ *where* $\tau = 1$ *the canonical norm* $\|\alpha\|$ *of* α *is defined as total the number of functions 0, $+$, and ϑ_i for each $i < \omega$ that occur in the unique term representation of* α.

2. *A Buchholz system* $(\overset{\circ}{\mathrm{T}}{}^\tau, \cdot\{\cdot\})$ *is called* regular, *if (assuming $\tau = 1$) for any ordinal $\alpha \in \overset{\circ}{\mathrm{T}}{}^\tau \cap \mathrm{Lim}$ and any $\beta \in \mathrm{T}^\tau \cap \alpha$ we have*

$$\beta \leq \alpha\{\|\beta\|\}.$$

For a given mapping $N : \mathrm{T}^\tau \to \omega$ we call $(\overset{\circ}{\mathrm{T}}{}^\tau, \cdot\{\cdot\}, N)$ regular *with respect to N, if for any ordinal $\alpha \in \overset{\circ}{\mathrm{T}}{}^\tau \cap \mathrm{Lim}$ and any $\beta \in \mathrm{T}^\tau \cap \alpha$ we have*

$$\beta \leq \alpha\{N(\beta)\}.$$

3. *A system $(\overset{\circ}{\mathrm{T}}{}^\tau, \cdot\{\cdot\}, N)$ where $(\overset{\circ}{\mathrm{T}}{}^\tau, \cdot\{\cdot\})$ is a Buchholz system and N is a mapping $N : \mathrm{T}^\tau \to \omega$ is called a* normed Bachmann system *if*
   (a) *for all $\alpha \in \overset{\circ}{\mathrm{T}}{}^\tau$, $\beta \in \mathrm{T}^\tau$, and $n < \omega$ such that $\alpha\{n\} < \beta < \alpha$ we have $N(\alpha\{n\}) < N(\beta)$, and*
   (b) *for all $\alpha \in \overset{\circ}{\mathrm{T}}{}^\tau \cap \mathrm{Lim}$ we have $N(\alpha) \leq N(\alpha\{0\}) + 1$.*
4. *We call a mapping $N : \mathrm{T}^\tau \to \omega$ a* norm *on T^τ if for all $\alpha \in \mathrm{T}^\tau$ and all $n < \omega$ the set*

$$\{\beta \in \mathrm{T}^\tau \cap \alpha \mid N(\beta) \leq n\}$$

is finite.

We will also continue to use the more convenient notation $\alpha[n]$ and write $N\beta$ instead of $N(\beta)$.

Remark 25. 1. Note that for any $\alpha \in \mathrm{T}^\tau$ where $\tau = 1$ and $n < \omega$ the set

$$\{\beta \in \mathrm{T}^\tau \cap \alpha \mid \|\beta\| \leq n\}$$

is finite, since the occurrence of any ϑ_k with large k in a term $\beta < \alpha$ must come with stepwise collapsing eventually down below α and hence must have a correspondingly large term length and thus canonical norm.
2. In [2], instead of $\overset{\circ}{\mathrm{T}}{}^\tau$, countable initial segments of ordinals are considered as domains of systems of fundamental sequences and Bachmann systems. In our context this would mean to consider $\overset{\circ}{\mathrm{T}}{}^\tau \cap \Omega_1$ instead of $\overset{\circ}{\mathrm{T}}{}^\tau$. However, as we have seen, we need the entire set $\overset{\circ}{\mathrm{T}}{}^\tau$, or even T^τ, for inductive proofs to work. See the following remark for the abstract setting of [2].

Remark 26. In [2] it is shown that for a system $(\tau, \cdot[\cdot], N)$ where τ is a countable ordinal with mappings $\cdot[\cdot] : \tau \times \omega \to \tau$ and $N : \tau \to \omega$ such that

(B1) $(\forall \alpha < \tau, n < \omega)\ [0[n] = 0\ \&\ (\alpha + 1)[n] = \alpha\ \&$
$[\alpha \in \mathrm{Lim} \Rightarrow \alpha[n] < \alpha[n + 1] < \alpha]],$

(B3) $(\forall \alpha, \beta < \tau, n < \omega)\ [\alpha[n] < \beta < \alpha \Rightarrow N\alpha[n] < N\beta],$ and

(B4) $(\forall \alpha \in \mathrm{Lim} \cap \tau)\ [N\alpha \leq N\alpha[0] + 1],$

which is called a *normed Bachmann system* in [2], it *follows* that (see Lemma 1 of [2] and cf. Lemma 30 below):

1. The system $(\tau, \cdot[\cdot], N)$ is a Bachmann system, i.e. property

(B2) $(\forall \alpha, \beta < \tau, n < \omega)$ $[\alpha[n] < \beta < \alpha \Rightarrow \alpha[n] \leq \beta[0]]$ holds, since the assumption $\alpha[n] < \beta < \alpha$ & $\beta[0] < \alpha[n]$ would imply
$N\alpha[n] < N\beta \leq N\beta[0] + 1 \leq N\alpha[n]$,

2. N is a norm, and
3. $(\tau, \cdot[\cdot], N)$ is a regular Bachmann system, i.e. we have
   $(\forall \beta < \alpha < \tau)$ $[\beta \leq \alpha[N\beta]]$.

Furthermore, for any $(\tau, \cdot[\cdot])$ satisfying $(B1)$ and $(B2)$, it *follows* that

4. $(\forall \alpha \in \mathrm{Lim} \cap \tau)$ $\alpha = \sup\{\alpha[n] \mid n < \omega\}$, cf. Lemma 3 of [2].

Before turning to another norm of interest, we prove regularity of $\mathring{\mathrm{T}}^\tau$ regarding the canonical norm, where for simplicity we restrict ourselves to $\tau = 1$.

Theorem 27. *The Buchholz system $\mathring{\mathrm{T}}^\tau$ for $\tau = 1$ is regular: for any limit ordinal $\alpha \in \mathring{\mathrm{T}}^\tau$ and $\beta \in \mathrm{T}^\tau \cap \alpha$ we have*

$$\beta \leq \alpha\{\|\beta\|\}.$$

Proof. The proof is given in full detail in the extended version of this article.

We now turn to the definition of the norm of iterated application of $\cdot[0]$ to terms of T^τ for systems T^τ as in Definition 16.

Definition 28. *In the setting of Definition 16, for $\alpha \in \mathrm{T}^\tau$ let $\alpha[0]^0 := \alpha$ and $\alpha[0]^{i+1} := (\alpha[0]^i)[0]$. Define $G : \mathrm{T}^\tau \to \omega$ by $G\alpha := \min\{i \mid \alpha[0]^i = 0\}$ as in Lemma 2 of [2].*

Lemma 29. *(cf. Lemmas 1 and 2 of [2]) In the setting of Definition 28, the system $(\mathring{\mathrm{T}}^\tau, \cdot[\cdot], G)$ is a normed and regular Bachmann system.*

Proof. The proof is given in full detail in the extended version of this article.

Lemma 30. *Suppose $\tau = 1$. For terms in T^τ we have*

1. $G\alpha = G\beta + G\gamma$ if $\alpha =_{\mathrm{NF}} \beta + \gamma$.
2. For $\alpha \in \mathrm{T}^\tau$ such that $\mathrm{d} := \mathrm{d}(\alpha) > 0$ we have $G\alpha[\gamma] \geq G\alpha[0] + G\gamma$ for all $\gamma \in \mathrm{T}^\tau \cap \aleph_{\mathrm{d}}$.
3. $G\vartheta_i(\Delta + \eta) \geq G\Delta + G\eta + 1$.

Proof. The proof is given in full detail in the extended version of this article.

The above lemma allows us to straightforwardly prove the following generous upper bound of $\|\alpha\|$ in terms of $G\alpha$.

Lemma 31. *Suppose $\tau = 1$. For any $\alpha \in \mathrm{T}^\tau$ we have*

$$\|\alpha\| \leq (G\alpha + 1)^2.$$

Proof. The proof is given in full detail in the extended version of this article.

Corollary 32. *G is a norm on T^τ if $\tau = 1$.*

Proof. The proof is given in full detail in the extended version of this article.

Definition 33 (cf. [2]). *For a Buchholz system $(\overset{\circ}{T}{}^\tau, \cdot[\cdot])$ as in Definition 16, set $\tau^\infty := T^\tau \cap \Omega_1$ and define the* Hardy hierarchy $(H_\alpha)_{\alpha < \tau^\infty}$ *by*

$$H_0(n) := n \quad and \quad H_\alpha(n) := H_{\alpha[n]}(n+1) \text{ for } \alpha > 0.$$

By Lemma 29 we know that the system $(\overset{\circ}{T}{}^\tau, \cdot[\cdot], G)$ is a normed and regular Bachmann system, hence also the restriction $(\tau^\infty, \cdot[\cdot], G)$ is such a system, and setting $\tau = 1$ for simplicity, also $(\overset{\circ}{T}{}^\tau, \cdot[\cdot], \|\cdot\|)$ and $(1^\infty, \cdot[\cdot], \|\cdot\|)$ are regular Bachmann systems, where 1^∞ is the proof theoretic ordinal of $\Pi_1^1\text{-CA}_0$. [2] provides lemmas of basic properties of the Hardy hierarchy (when based on a regular Bachmann system), which we include here for convenience as they illuminate the interplay of the notions involved.

Lemma 34 (Lemma 3 of [2]). *Let $(\tau^\infty, \cdot[\cdot], N)$ be a regular Bachmann system.*

1. $H_\alpha(n) < H_\alpha(n+1)$.
2. $\beta[m] < \alpha < \beta \Rightarrow H_{\beta[m]}(n) \leq H_\alpha(n)$.
3. $0 < \alpha \,\&\, m \leq n \Rightarrow H_{\alpha[m]}(n+1) \leq H_\alpha(n)$.
4. $(\forall \beta < \alpha)\,[N\beta \leq n \Rightarrow H_\beta(n+1) \leq H_\alpha(n)]$.
5. $H_\alpha(n) = \min\{k \geq n \mid \alpha[n][n+1]\ldots[k-1] = 0\} = \min\{k \mid \alpha[n : k] = 0\}$, *where $\alpha[n : k] := \alpha + (n \overset{.}{-} k)$ for $k \leq n$, and $\alpha[n : k+1] := (\alpha[n : k])[k]$ for $k \geq n$.*

Let $NF(\alpha, \beta)$ abbreviate the expression stating that $\alpha, \beta > 0$ with Cantor normal forms $\alpha =_{\mathrm{CNF}} \omega^{\alpha_0} + \ldots, \omega^{\alpha_m}$ and $\beta =_{\mathrm{CNF}} \omega^{\beta_0} + \ldots + \omega^{\beta_n}$ satisfying $\alpha_m \geq \beta_0$. Since the Buchholz systems considered here satisfy the properties

$(B5')$ $(\forall \alpha, \beta, n)\,[NF(\alpha, \beta) \Rightarrow (\alpha + \beta)[n] = \alpha + \beta[n]]$ and

$(B6')$ $(\forall m, n < \omega)\,[\omega^{m+1}[n] = \omega^m \cdot (n+1)]$,

i.e. are Cantorian in the sense of Definition 10, we have the following lemma, also cited from [2].

Lemma 35 (Lemma 4 of [2]). *In the same setting as in the previous lemma, we have*

1. $NF(\alpha, \beta) \Rightarrow H_\alpha(H_\beta(n)) \leq H_{\alpha+\beta}(n)$.
2. $(H_{\omega^m})^{(n+1)}(n+1) \leq H_{\omega^{m+1}}(n)$.
3. *For each primitive recursive function f there exists m such that*

$$(\forall x)\,[f(x) < H_{\omega^m}(\max\{x\})].$$

It is well-known and it also follows from [2] that for any function f that is provably total in $\Pi_1^1\text{-CA}_0$ there is an $\alpha < 1^\infty$ such that $f(x) < H_\alpha(\max\{x\})$.

3 Conclusion

We have established systems of fundamental sequences in the context of relativized notation systems T^τ used in the analysis of patterns of resemblance of orders 1 and 2 [4,10–12,14], and investigated ways to relate them to the uniform approach to fundamental sequences and hierarchies of fast growing number theoretic functions (Hardy hierarchies) as set out in [2]. Work in progress will rely on the framework established here to develop a theory of pattern related fundamental sequences, to elaborate their connection to hierarchies of fast-growing functions, and to derive independence phenomena.

Acknowledgements. I would like to express my gratitude for very helpful comments and advice to an anonymous referee.

References

1. Buchholz, W.: Ordinal notations and fundamental sequences. Preprint (2003). https://www.mathematik.uni-muenchen.de/~buchholz/articles/ordfunc.pdf
2. Buchholz, W., Cichon, A., Weiermann, A.: A uniform approach to fundamental sequences and hierarchies. Math. Log. Q. **40**, 273–286 (1994)
3. Carlson, T.J.: Elementary patterns of resemblance. Ann. Pure Appl. Logic **108**, 19–77 (2001)
4. Carlson, T.J., Wilken, G.: Normal forms for elementary patterns. J. Symbolic Logic **77**, 174–194 (2012)
5. Carlson, T.J., Wilken, G.: Tracking chains of Σ_2-elementarity. Ann. Pure Appl. Logic **163**, 23–67 (2012)
6. Fernàndez-Duque, D., Weiermann, A.: Fundamental sequences and fast-growing hierarchies for the Bachmann-Howard ordinal. Preprint (2024). https://arxiv.org/pdf/2203.07758.pdf
7. Schmidt, D.: Built-up systems of fundamental sequences and hierarchies of number-theoretic functions. Archiv für Mathematische Logik und Grundlagenforschung **18**, 47–53 (1976)
8. Wilken, G.: The Bachmann-Howard structure in terms of Σ_1-elementarity. Arch. Math. Logic **45**, 807–829 (2006)
9. Wilken, G.: Ordinal arithmetic based on Skolem hulling. Ann. Pure Appl. Logic **145**, 130–161 (2007)
10. Wilken, G.: Σ_1-elementarity and Skolem hull operators. Ann. Pure Appl. Logic **145**, 162–175 (2007)
11. Wilken, G.: Assignment of ordinals to elementary patterns of resemblance. J. Symbolic Logic **72**, 704–720 (2007)
12. Wilken, G.: Pure patterns of order 2. Ann. Pure Appl. Logic **169**, 54–82 (2018)
13. Wilken, G.: A glimpse of Σ_3-elementarity. In: The Legacy of Kurt Schütte, pp. 415–441. Springer, Cham (2020). https://doi.org/10.1007/978-3-030-49424-7_21
14. Wilken, G.: Pure Σ_2-elementarity beyond the core. Ann. Pure Appl. Logic **172**, 1–93 (2021)

The Weakness of Finding Descending Sequences in Ill-Founded Linear Orders

Jun Le Goh[1] , Arno Pauly[2] , and Manlio Valenti[2(✉)]

[1] National University of Singapore, Singapore 119076, Singapore
[2] Swansea University, Swansea SA1 8EN, UK
manlio.valenti@swansea.ac.uk

Abstract. We prove that the Weihrauch degree of the problem of finding a bad sequence in a non-well quasi order (BS) is strictly above that of finding a descending sequence in an ill-founded linear order (DS). This corrects our mistaken claim in [8], which stated that they are Weihrauch equivalent. We prove that König's lemma KL and the problem $\mathsf{wList}_{2^\mathbb{N}, \leq \omega}$ of enumerating a given non-empty countable closed subset of $2^\mathbb{N}$ are not Weihrauch reducible to DS either, resolving two main open questions raised in [8].

Keywords: Weihrauch reducibility · well quasi-orders · first-order part

1 Introduction and Background

A quasi-order $(Q, \preceq)$ is called *well quasi-order* (abbreviated wqo) if, for every infinite sequence $(q_n)_{n \in \mathbb{N}}$ of elements of Q, there are i, j with $i < j$ such that $q_i \preceq_Q q_j$. This can be restated by saying that a quasi-order is a wqo if it contains no infinite bad sequences, where a sequence $(q_n)_{n<\alpha}$ is called bad if $q_i \not\preceq_Q q_j$ for every $i < j < \alpha$. Equivalently, wqo's can be defined as quasi-orders that contain no infinite descending sequence and no infinite antichain. There is an extensive literature on the theory of wqo's. For an overview, we refer the reader to [10].

We study the difficulty of solving the following computational problems:

- given a countable ill-founded linear order, find an infinite Descending Sequence in it (DS), and
- given a countable non-well quasi-order, find a Bad Sequence in it (BS).

A suitable framework for this is the Weihrauch lattice (see [2] for a self-contained introduction). Several results on DS were proved in our previous paper [8]; however, [8, Proposition 4.5] falsely claims that DS and BS are Weihrauch equivalent. In Theorem 1 we refute our claim by proving that the first-order part of BS is not Weihrauch reducible to DS. On the other hand, the deterministic part and the k-finitary parts of BS are Weihrauch equivalent to the corresponding parts of DS (Theorem 3, Corollary 5).

© The Author(s), under exclusive license to Springer Nature Switzerland AG 2024
L. Levy Patey et al. (Eds.): CiE 2024, LNCS 14773, pp. 339–350, 2024.
https://doi.org/10.1007/978-3-031-64309-5_27

We will also resolve (negatively) two main open questions raised in [8, Questions 6.1 and 6.2], namely whether KL and wList$_{2^{\mathbb{N}}, \leq \omega}$ are Weihrauch reducible to DS (Corollaries 2, 3). The core of our proof (Theorem 2) is

$$\mathsf{lim} \equiv_{\mathrm{W}} \max_{\leq_{\mathrm{W}}} \{f \mid \widehat{\mathsf{ACC_N}} \times f \leq_{\mathrm{W}} \mathsf{DS}\}.$$

That is, even though $\widehat{\mathsf{ACC_N}}$ is fairly weak (in particular it is below lim, KL and DS), DS cannot even compute $\widehat{\mathsf{ACC_N}} \times f$ if $f \not\leq_{\mathrm{W}} \mathsf{lim}$. The existence of the maximum above provides an example of a "parallel quotient" [5, Remark 1].

In the rest of this section we briefly introduce relevant notions in Weihrauch complexity, followed with a note that BS is equivalent to its restriction to partial orders (Proposition 2).

A *represented space* $\mathbf{X} = (X, \delta_{\mathbf{X}})$ consists of a set X and a (possibly partial) surjection $\delta_{\mathbf{X}} :\subseteq \mathbb{N}^{\mathbb{N}} \to X$. Many mathematical objects of interest can be represented in standard ways which we do not spell out here (see e.g. [2, Definition 2.5]), such as: $\mathbb{N}^{\mathbb{N}}, \mathbb{N}, \mathbb{N}^{<\mathbb{N}}$, initial segments of $\mathbb{N}$, the set of binary relations on $\mathbb{N}$, the set of Γ-definable subsets of $\mathbb{N}$ where Γ is a pointclass in the projective hierarchy, countable Cartesian products and countable disjoint unions of represented spaces.

A *problem* f is a (possibly partial) multivalued function between represented spaces $\mathbf{X}$ and $\mathbf{Y}$, denoted $f :\subseteq \mathbf{X} \rightrightarrows \mathbf{Y}$. For each $x \in X$, $f(x)$ denotes the set of possible outputs (i.e., *f-solutions*) corresponding to the input x. The *domain* $\mathrm{dom}(f)$ is the set of all $x \in X$ such that $f(x)$ is non-empty. Such x is called an *f-instance*. If $f(x)$ is a singleton for all $x \in \mathrm{dom}(f)$, we say f is *single-valued* and write $f :\subseteq \mathbf{X} \to \mathbf{Y}$. In this case, if y is the f-solution to x, we write $f(x) = y$ instead of (the formally correct) $f(x) = \{y\}$. We say a problem is *computable* (resp. *continuous*) if there is some computable (resp. continuous) $F :\subseteq \mathbb{N}^{\mathbb{N}} \to \mathbb{N}^{\mathbb{N}}$ such that if p is a name for some $x \in \mathrm{dom}(f)$, then $F(p)$ is a name for an f-solution to x.

A problem f is *Weihrauch reducible* to a problem g, written $f \leq_{\mathrm{W}} g$, if there are computable maps $\Phi, \Psi :\subseteq \mathbb{N}^{\mathbb{N}} \to \mathbb{N}^{\mathbb{N}}$ such that if p is a name for some $x \in \mathrm{dom}(f)$, then

1. $\Phi(p)$ is a name for some $y \in \mathrm{dom}(g)$, and
2. if q is a name for some g-solution of y, then $\Psi(p, q)$ is a name for some f-solution of x.

If Φ and Ψ satisfy the above, we say that $f \leq_{\mathrm{W}} g$ *via* Φ, Ψ.

Weihrauch reducibility forms a preorder on problems. We say f and g are *Weihrauch equivalent*, written $f \equiv_{\mathrm{W}} g$, if $f \leq_{\mathrm{W}} g$ and $g \leq_{\mathrm{W}} f$. The $\equiv_{\mathrm{W}}$-equivalence classes (*Weihrauch degrees*) are partially ordered by $\leq_{\mathrm{W}}$. Among the numerous algebraic operations in the Weihrauch degrees, we consider:

– for problems $f_i :\subseteq \mathbf{X}_i \rightrightarrows \mathbf{Y}_i$, the *parallel product*

$$f_0 \times f_1 :\subseteq \mathbf{X}_0 \times \mathbf{X}_1 \rightrightarrows \mathbf{Y}_0 \times \mathbf{Y}_1 \text{ defined by } (x_0, x_1) \mapsto f_0(x_0) \times f_1(x_1),$$

i.e., given an f_0-instance and an f_1-instance, solve both,

– for a problem $f :\subseteq \mathbf{X} \rightrightarrows \mathbf{Y}$, the *(infinite) parallelization*

$$\widehat{f} :\subseteq \mathbf{X}^{\mathbb{N}} \rightrightarrows \mathbf{Y}^{\mathbb{N}} \text{ defined by } (x_i)_i \mapsto \prod_i f(x_i),$$

i.e., given a countable sequence of f-instances, solve all of them.

These operations are defined on problems, but they all lift to the Weihrauch degrees. Parallelization even forms a closure operator, i.e., $f \leq_W \widehat{f}$, $f \leq_W g$ implies $\widehat{f} \leq_W \widehat{g}$, and $\widehat{\widehat{f}} \equiv_W \widehat{f}$.

The Weihrauch degrees also support a number of interior operators, which have been used to separate degrees of interest (see e.g. [13, Sect. 3.1]). For any problem f and any represented space $\mathbf{X}$,

$$\mathrm{Det}_{\mathbf{X}}(f) := \max_{\leq_W}\{g \leq_W f \mid g \text{ has codomain } \mathbf{X} \text{ and is single-valued}\}$$

exists [8, Theorem 3.2]. We call $\mathrm{Det}_{\mathbb{N}^{\mathbb{N}}}(f)$ the *deterministic part of* f and denote it by $\mathrm{Det}(f)$ for short. Observe that [8, Proposition 3.6] can be generalized slightly:

Proposition 1. $\mathrm{Det}(f) \leq_W \widehat{\mathrm{Det}_2(f)}$.

Proof. Suppose g is single-valued, has codomain $\mathbb{N}^{\mathbb{N}}$, and $g \leq_W f$. Define a single-valued problem h as follows: Given $n, m \in \mathbb{N}$ and a g-instance x, produce 1 if $g(x)(n) \geq m$, otherwise produce 0. It is easy to see that $g \leq_W \widehat{h}$ and $h \leq_W f$. The latter implies $h \leq_W \mathrm{Det}_2(f)$ and so $g \leq_W \widehat{h} \leq_W \widehat{\mathrm{Det}_2(f)}$.

For any problem f and $\mathbf{X} = \mathbb{N}$ or $\mathbf{k}$, it is also known that

$$\max_{\leq_W}\{g \leq_W f \mid g \text{ has codomain } \mathbf{X}\}$$

exists. For $\mathbf{X} = \mathbb{N}$ we call it the *first-order part of* f [6, Theorem 2.2], denoted by $^1 f$, while for $\mathbf{X} = \mathbf{k}$ we call it the $\mathbf{k}$-*finitary part of* f [4, Proposition 2.9], denoted by $\mathrm{Fin}_{\mathbf{k}}(f)$. We have $\mathrm{Det}_{\mathbb{N}}(f) \leq_W {}^1 f$ and $\mathrm{Det}_{\mathbf{k}}(f) \leq_W \mathrm{Fin}_{\mathbf{k}}(f) \leq_W {}^1 f$.

To study the problems DS and BS from the point of view of Weihrauch reducibility, we need to introduce the represented spaces of linear orders and quasi-orders. We only work with countable linear orders/quasi-orders with domain contained in $\mathbb{N}$. We represent a linear order $(L, \leq_L)$ with the characteristic function of the set $\{\langle n, m \rangle : n \leq_L m\}$. Likewise, we represent a quasi-order $(Q, \preceq_Q)$ with the characteristic function of the set $\{\langle n, m \rangle : n \preceq_Q m\}$.

We conclude this section observing a fact about BS which was implicit in [8].

Proposition 2. BS *is Weihrauch equivalent to its restriction to partial orders.*

Proof. Given a non-well quasi-order $(Q, \preceq_Q)$ where $Q \subseteq \mathbb{N}$, compute the set $S = \{a \in Q \mid (\forall b <_{\mathbb{N}} a)(a \not\preceq_Q b \text{ or } b \not\preceq_Q a)\}$. The restriction $(S, \preceq_Q)$ is a non-well partial order because it is isomorphic to the partial order of $\preceq_Q$-equivalence classes.

Henceforth we will use Proposition 2 without mention.

2   Separating BS and DS

We shall separate BS and DS by separating their first-order parts.

Theorem 1. ^{1}BS $\not\leq_W$ ^{1}DS *and so* DS $<_W$ BS.

Recall from [8, Theorem 4.10] that ^{1}DS $\equiv_W$ $\mathbf{\Pi}_1^1$–Bound, which is the problem of producing an upper bound for a finite subset of $\mathbb{N}$ (given via a $\mathbf{\Pi}_1^1$ code). Observe that $\mathbf{\Pi}_1^1$–Bound is *upwards closed*, i.e., if $n \in g(x)$ then $m \in g(x)$ for all $m > n$.

Lemma 1. *Let f be a problem with codomain $\mathbb{N}$. The following are equivalent:*

1. *there exists an upwards closed problem g with codomain $\mathbb{N}$ such that $f \leq_W g$;*
2. *there is a computable procedure which takes as input any $x \in \mathrm{dom}(f)$ and produces a sequence $p_x \in \mathbb{N}^{\mathbb{N}}$ of guesses for f-solutions to x which is correct cofinitely often.*

Proof. For 1. $\Rightarrow$ 2., let g be upwards closed and assume $f \leq_W g$ via Φ and Ψ. Given $x \in \mathrm{dom}(f)$, run the computations $(\Psi(x,m))_{m \in \mathbb{N}}$ in parallel. Once some $\Psi(x,m)$ halts, we output its result and cancel $\Psi(x,n)$ for all $n < m$. This produces a sequence of numbers. The fact that g is upwards closed guarantees that cofinitely many elements of this sequence are elements of $f(x)$.

For the converse direction, for every $x \in \mathrm{dom}(f)$, let $p_x \in \mathbb{N}^{\mathbb{N}}$ be as in the hypothesis. Define $M_x := \max\{m \mid p_x(m) \notin f(x)\}$ and let $g(x) := \{n \mid n > M_x\}$. Clearly g is upwards closed. The fact that $f \leq_W g$ follows from the fact that $x \mapsto p_x$ is computable.

Given a non-well quasi-order $(Q, \preceq_Q)$, we say that a finite sequence σ is extendible to an infinite $\preceq_Q$-bad sequence (or, more compactly, σ is $\preceq_Q$-extendible) if there is a $\preceq_Q$-bad sequence $(q_n)_{n \in \mathbb{N}}$ such that $(\forall i < |\sigma|)(\sigma(i) = q_i)$. We omit the order whenever there is no ambiguity.

Observe that ^{1}BS can compute the problem "given a non-well partial order $(P, \leq_P)$, produce an element of P that is extendible to an infinite bad sequence". In light of Lemma 1, to prove Theorem 1 it suffices to show that one cannot computably "guess" solutions for BS. In other words, given a computable procedure which tries to guess extendible elements in a non-wqo, we want to construct a non-wqo P on which the procedure outputs a non-extendible element infinitely often. This would imply that ^{1}BS $\not\leq_W$ $\mathbf{\Pi}_1^1$–Bound. The non-wqos P we construct will be "tree-like" in the following sense:

Definition 1. *A tree decomposition of a partial order $(P, \leq_P)$ consists of a tree $T \subseteq 2^{<\mathbb{N}}$ and a function $\iota : T \to P$ such that:*

1. *If $w_1, w_2 \in T$ and w_1 is a proper prefix of w_2 (written $w_1 \sqsubset w_2$), then $\iota(w_1) <_P \iota(w_2)$.*

2. *P is partitioned into finite P-intervals, where each interval has the form*

$$(wb] = \{v \in P \mid \iota(w) <_P v \leq_P \iota(wb)\}$$

for some vertex $wb \in T$ (with final entry b), or $(\varepsilon] = \{\iota(\varepsilon)\}$ (where ε denotes the root of $2^{<\mathbb{N}}$). For $v \in P$ let $\lceil v \rceil \in T$ be uniquely defined by $v \in (\lceil v \rceil]$.
3. *If $w_1, w_2 \in T$ are incompatible, so are $\iota(w_1)$ and $\iota(w_2)$ (i.e. they have no common upper bound in P).*

The following lemma is straightforward.

Lemma 2. *If $\iota : T \to P$ is a tree decomposition, then P has no infinite descending sequences. Moreover, T is wqo (i.e. it has finite width) if and only if P is wqo. In other words, T has an infinite antichain iff so does P.*

Proof. The fact that every partial order that admits a tree decomposition does not have an infinite descending sequence follows from the fact that if $(v_n)_{n \in \mathbb{N}}$ is an infinite descending sequence in P, then since every interval $(\lceil v_n \rceil]$ is finite, up to removing duplicates, the sequence $(\lceil v_n \rceil)_{n \in \mathbb{N}}$ would be an infinite descending sequence in T.

If $(w_n)_{n \in \mathbb{N}}$ is an infinite antichain in T then, by definition of tree decomposition, $(\iota(w_n))_{n \in \mathbb{N}}$ is an infinite antichain in P. Conversely, if $(v_n)_{n \in \mathbb{N}}$ is an infinite antichain in P, then for every n, for all but finitely m, $\lceil v_n \rceil$ is $\sqsubseteq$-incomparable with $\lceil v_m \rceil$. In particular, we can obtain an infinite antichain in T by choosing a subsequence $(v_{n_i})_{i \in \mathbb{N}}$ such that, for every $i \neq j$, $\lceil v_{n_i} \rceil$ and $\lceil v_{n_j} \rceil$ are $\sqsubseteq$-incomparable.

Lemma 3. *There is no computable procedure that, given in input a partial order which admits a tree decomposition, outputs an infinite sequence of elements of that partial order such that if the input is not wqo, then cofinitely many elements in the output are extendible to a bad sequence.*

We point out a subtle yet important aspect regarding Lemma 3: The procedure only has access to the partial order, not to a tree decomposition of it.

Proof. Fix a computable "guessing" procedure g that receives as input a partial order (admitting a tree decomposition) and outputs an infinite sequence of elements in that partial order. We shall build a partial order P together with a tree decomposition $\iota : T \to P$ in stages such that, infinitely often, g outputs an element of P that does not extend to an infinite bad sequence.

Start with $T_0 = \{\varepsilon\}$ and P_0 having a single element v_ε, with $\iota_0(\varepsilon) = v_\varepsilon$. In stage s, we have built a finite tree decomposition $\iota_s : T_s \to P_s$ and wish to extend it to some $\iota_{s+1} : T_{s+1} \to P_{s+1}$. The tree T_{s+1} will always be obtained by giving each leaf in T_s a single successor, and then adding two successors to exactly one of the new leaves. To decide which leaf gets two successors, say a finite extension Q of P_s is *suitable* for $\iota_s : T_s \to P_s$ if for every $v \in Q \backslash P_s$, there is exactly one leaf $w \in T_s$ such that $\iota_s(w) <_Q v$. Pick the left-most leaf σ of T_s with the following property:

There is some suitable extension Q of P_s such that, when given Q, the guessing procedure g would guess an element of Q which is comparable with $\iota_s(\sigma)$.

To see that such σ must exist, consider extending P_s by adding an "infinite comb" (i.e. a copy of $\{0^n1^i \mid n \in \mathbb{N}, i \in \{0,1\}\}$) above the ι_s-image of a single leaf in T_s. The resulting partial order Q is non-wqo, admits a tree decomposition (obtained by extending T_s and ι_s in the obvious way), and its finite approximations (extending P_s) are suitable for ι_s. Hence, by hypothesis, g eventually guesses some element, which must be comparable with $\iota_s(\sigma)$, for some leaf $\sigma \in T_s$ (because all elements of Q are).

Having identified σ, we fix any corresponding suitable extension Q of P_s. In order to extend ι_s, we further extend Q to Q' by adding a new maximal element v_w to Q for each leaf $w \in T_s$ as follows: v_w lies above all $v \in Q \backslash P_s$ such that $\iota_s(w) <_P v$, and is incomparable with all other elements (including the other new maximal elements $v_{w'}$). To extend T_s, we add a new leaf $\tau \frown 0$ to T_s for each leaf τ, obtaining a tree T'. We extend ι_s to yield a tree decomposition $\iota' : T' \to Q'$ in the obvious way.

Finally, we add two successors to $\sigma \frown 0$ in T', i.e., define $T_{s+1} = T' \cup \{\sigma \frown 00, \sigma \frown 01\}$. We also add two successors v_1, v_2 to $\iota'(\sigma \frown 0)$ in Q' to obtain P_{s+1}, and extend ι' to ι_{s+1} by setting $\iota_{s+1}(\sigma \frown 0i) = v_i$. This concludes stage s.

It is clear from the construction that $\iota : T \to P$ is a tree decomposition. Let us discuss the shape of the tree T. In stage s, we introduced a bifurcation above a leaf σ_s of T_s. These are the only bifurcations in T. Observe that, whenever $s' < s$, σ_s is either above or to the right of $\sigma_{s'}$, because every suitable extension of P_s is also a suitable extension of $P_{s'}$ and, at stage s', the chosen leaf was the left-most. Therefore T has a unique non-isolated infinite path $p = \lim_s \sigma_s$, and a vertex w in T is extendible to an infinite antichain in T if and only if it does not belong to p.

We may now apply Lemma 2 to analyze P. First, since T is not wqo, neither is P. Second, we claim that if $v <_P \iota(\sigma)$ for some vertex σ on p, then v is not extendible to an infinite bad sequence. To prove this, suppose v is extendible. Then so is $\iota(\sigma)$. The proof of Lemma 2 implies that $\lceil \iota(\sigma) \rceil = \sigma$ is extendible to an infinite antichain in T. So σ cannot lie on p, proving our claim.

To complete the proof, observe that our construction of ι ensures that for each s, $g(P)$ eventually outputs a guess which is below $\iota(\sigma_s \frown 0)$. Whenever $\sigma_s \frown 0$ lies along p (which holds for infinitely many s), this guess is wrong by the above claim.

We may now complete the proof of Theorem 1.

Proof (Theorem 1). Suppose towards a contradiction that $^1\mathsf{BS} \leq_W \mathbf{\Pi}_1^1-\mathsf{Bound}$. Since the problem of finding an element in a non-wqo which extends to an infinite bad sequence is first-order, it is Weihrauch reducible to $\mathbf{\Pi}_1^1-\mathsf{Bound}$ as well. Now $\mathbf{\Pi}_1^1-\mathsf{Bound}$ is upwards closed, so there is a computable guessing procedure for this problem (Lemma 1). However such a procedure cannot exist, even for partial orders which admit a tree decomposition (Lemma 3).

3   Separating KL and DS

Recall the following problems [2, Sect. 6, Definition 7.4(7), Theorem 8.10]:

ACC_N: Given an enumeration of a set $A \subseteq \mathbb{N}$ of size at most 1, find a number not in A.
lim: Given a convergent sequence in $\mathbb{N}^{\mathbb{N}}$, find its limit.
KL: Given an infinite finitely branching subtree of $\mathbb{N}^{<\mathbb{N}}$, find an infinite path through it.

It is known that $\widehat{ACC_N} <_W$ lim $<_W$ KL (see [2]). For our separation of KL $\not\leq_W$ DS in Corollary 2, all we need to know about KL are the facts stated before the corollary. The core of our proof is the following.

Theorem 2. *Let f be a problem. The following are equivalent:*

1. $\widehat{ACC_N} \times f \leq_W$ DS
2. $f \leq_W$ lim.

Proof. The implication from 2. to 1. follows from lim $\leq_W$ DS (as shown in [8, Theorem 4.16]), as lim is closed under parallel product. For the other direction, we consider a name x for an input to f together with witnesses Φ, Ψ for the reduction. We show that, from them, we can uniformly compute an input q to $\widehat{ACC_N}$ together with an enumeration of a set W such that W is the well-founded part of the (ill-founded) linear order L built by Φ on (q, x). We can then use lim to obtain the characteristic function of W. Having access to this lets us find an infinite descending sequence in L greedily by avoiding ever choosing an element of W. From such a descending sequence Ψ then computes a solution to f for x.

It remains to construct $q = \langle q_0, q_1, \ldots \rangle$ and W to achieve the above. At the beginning, W is empty, and we extend each q_i in a way that removes no solution from its ACC_N-instance. As we do so, for each $i \notin W$ (in parallel), we monitor whether the following condition has occurred:

> L (as computed by the finite prefix of (q, x) built/observed thus far) contains i and some (finite) descending sequence ℓ such that
> 1. ℓ is L-above i (i.e. $i <_L \min_L \ell$);
> 2. the functional Ψ, upon reading the current prefix of (q, x) and ℓ, produces some output m for the i-th ACC_N-instance.

Once the above occurs for i (if ever), we remove m as a valid solution to q_i. This means that ℓ cannot be extendible to an infinite descending sequence in L, so i must be in the well-founded part of L. Hence we shall enumerate i into W. This completes our action for i, after which we return to monitoring the above condition for numbers not in W. This completes the construction.

It is clear that each q_i is an ACC_N-instance (with solution set $\mathbb{N}$ if the condition is never triggered, otherwise with solution set $\mathbb{N}\backslash\{m\}$). Hence $L = \Phi(q, x)$ is an ill-founded linear order. As argued above, W is contained in the well-founded part of L. Conversely, suppose i lies in the well-founded part of L. Fix an infinite descending sequence r which lies above i. Then Ψ has to produce all $\mathsf{ACC_N}$ answers upon receiving (q, x) and r, including an answer to q_i. This answer is determined by finite prefixes only, and after having constructed a sufficiently long prefix of q, some finite prefix ℓ of r will trigger the condition for i (unless something else triggered it previously), which ensures that i gets placed into W. This shows that W is exactly the well-founded part of L, thereby concluding the proof.

Corollary 1. *If f is a parallelizable problem (i.e., $f \equiv_W \widehat{f}$) with $\mathsf{ACC_N} \leq_W f \leq_W \mathsf{DS}$, then $f \leq_W \mathsf{lim}$.*

Proof. Since $\mathsf{ACC_N} \leq_W f \leq_W \mathsf{DS}$ and f is parallelizable, we have $\widehat{\mathsf{ACC_N}} \times f \leq_W f \leq_W \mathsf{DS}$. By the previous theorem, $f \leq_W \mathsf{lim}$.

Since KL is parallelizable, $\mathsf{ACC_N} \leq_W \mathsf{KL}$, yet $\mathsf{KL} \not\leq_W \mathsf{lim}$, we obtain a negative answer to [8, Question 6.1]:

Corollary 2. $\mathsf{KL} \not\leq_W \mathsf{DS}$.

Similarly, consider the problem $\mathsf{wList}_{2^N, \leq \omega}$ of enumerating all elements (possibly with repetition) of a given non-empty countable closed subset of 2^N. Since $\mathsf{wList}_{2^N, \leq \omega}$ is parallelizable, $\mathsf{ACC_N} \leq_W \mathsf{lim} \leq_W \mathsf{wList}_{2^N, \leq \omega}$, yet $\mathsf{wList}_{2^N, \leq \omega} \not\leq_W \mathsf{lim}$ [9, Proposition 6.12, 6.13, Corollary 6.16], we obtain a negative answer to [8, Question 6.2]:

Corollary 3. $\mathsf{wList}_{2^N, \leq \omega} \not\leq_W \mathsf{DS}$.

Note that KL is a parallelization of a first-order problem (such as RT^1_2). Using a recent result of Pauly and Soldà [12], we can characterize (up to *continuous* Weihrauch reducibility $\leq_W^*$) the parallelizations of first-order problems which are reducible to DS.

Corollary 4. *If $\widehat{f} \leq_W^* \mathsf{DS}$, then $^1f \leq_W^* \mathsf{C_N}$. Therefore, for any first-order f,*

$$\widehat{f} \leq_W^* \mathsf{DS} \qquad \text{if and only if} \qquad f \leq_W^* \mathsf{C_N}.$$

Proof. If ^1f is continuous, the conclusion of the first statement is satisfied. Otherwise, $\mathsf{ACC_N} \leq_W^* f$ by [12, Theorem 1]. The relativization of Theorem 2 then implies $\widehat{f} \leq_W^* \mathsf{lim}$. We conclude $^1f \leq_W^* {}^1\mathsf{lim} \equiv_W \mathsf{C_N}$. The second statement then follows from $\widehat{\mathsf{C_N}} \equiv_W \mathsf{lim} \leq_W \mathsf{DS}$.

4   The Finitary Part and Deterministic Part of BS

In this section, we show that BS and DS cannot be separated by looking at their respective finitary or deterministic parts. Recall from [8, Theorems. 4.16, 4.31] that $\mathsf{Det}(\mathsf{DS}) \equiv_W \mathsf{lim}$ and $\mathsf{Fin_k}(\mathsf{DS}) \equiv_W \mathsf{RT}^1_k$. Since both the deterministic and the finitary parts are monotone, this implies that $\mathsf{lim} \leq_W \mathsf{Det}(\mathsf{BS})$ and $\mathsf{RT}^1_k \leq_W \mathsf{Fin_k}(\mathsf{BS})$, so we only need to show that the converse reductions hold.

To this end, we first introduce a technical lemma. For a fixed partial order $(P, \leq_P)$, we can define the following quasi-order on the (finite or infinite) $\leq_P$-bad sequences:

$$\alpha \trianglelefteq^P \beta :\Longleftrightarrow \alpha = \beta \text{ or } (\exists i < |\alpha|)(\forall j < |\beta|)(\alpha(i) \leq_P \beta(j)).$$

We just write $\trianglelefteq$ when the partial order is clear from the context.

Lemma 4. *Let $(P, \leq_P)$ be a non-well partial order and let α, β be finite $\leq_P$-bad sequences. If $\alpha \trianglelefteq \beta$ and α is extendible to an infinite $\leq_P$-bad sequence, then so is β. If α is not extendible then there is an infinite $\leq_P$-bad sequence $B \in \mathbb{N}^{\mathbb{N}}$ such that $\alpha \trianglelefteq B$. (Hence $\alpha \trianglelefteq \beta$ for every initial segment β of B.)*

Proof. To prove the first part of the theorem, fix $\alpha \trianglelefteq \beta$ and let $A \in \mathbb{N}^{\mathbb{N}}$ be an infinite $\leq_P$-bad sequence extending α. Let also $i < |\alpha|$ be a witness for $\alpha \trianglelefteq \beta$. For every $j > i$ and every $k < |\beta|$, $\beta(k) \not\leq_P A(j)$ (otherwise $A(i) = \alpha(i) \leq_P \beta(k) \leq_P A(j)$ would contradict the fact that A is a $\leq_P$-bad sequence), which implies that β is extendible.

Assume now that α is non-extendible and let $F \in \mathbb{N}^{\mathbb{N}}$ be a $\leq_P$-bad sequence. We show that there is $i < |\alpha|$ and infinitely many k such that $\alpha(i) <_P F(k)$. This is enough to conclude the proof, as we could take B as any subsequence of F with $\alpha(i) <_P B(k)$ for every k (i.e. $\alpha \trianglelefteq B$).

Assume that, for every $i < |\alpha|$ there is k_i such that for every $k \geq k_i$, $\alpha(i) \not\leq_P F(k)$ (since P is a partial order, there can be at most one k such that $\alpha(i) = F(k)$). Since α is finite, we can take $k := \max_{i < |\alpha|} k_i$ and consider the sequence $\alpha \frown (F(k+1), F(k+2), \dots)$. We have now reached a contradiction as this is an infinite $\leq_P$-bad sequence extending α.

Let $(P, \leq_P)$ be a partial order. We call a $A \subseteq P$ *dense* if for every $w \in P$ there is some $u \geq_P w$ with $u \in A$. We call it *upwards-closed*, if $w \in A$ and $w \leq_P u$ implies $u \in A$. By $\mathbf{\Sigma}_1^1$–DUCC we denote the following problem: Given a partial order P and a dense upwards-closed subset $A \subseteq P$ (given via a $\mathbf{\Sigma}_1^1$ code), find some element of A. We can think of a $\mathbf{\Sigma}_1^1$ code for $(P, \leq_P)$ as a sequence $(T_n)_{n \in \mathbb{N}}$ of subtrees of $\mathbb{N}^{<\mathbb{N}}$ such that, for every $n, m \in \mathbb{N}$, $n \leq_P m$ iff $T_{\langle n, m \rangle}$ is ill-founded (and $n \in P$ iff $n \leq_P n$). We refer to [8] for a more detailed discussion on various presentations of orders.

Proposition 3. $^1\mathsf{BS} \leq_{\mathrm{W}} \mathbf{\Sigma}_1^1$–DUCC.

Proof. Let f be a problem with codomain $\mathbb{N}$ and assume $f \leq_{\mathrm{W}} \mathsf{BS}$ via Φ, Ψ. Fix $x \in \mathrm{dom}(f)$. Let $(P, \leq_P)$ denote the non-well partial order defined by $\Phi(x)$. We say that a finite $\leq_P$-bad sequence β is *sufficiently long* if $\Psi(x, \beta)$ returns a natural number in at most $|\beta|$ steps.

To show that $f \leq_{\mathrm{W}} \mathbf{\Sigma}_1^1$–DUCC, it is enough to notice that Lemma 4 implies that the set of sufficiently long finite extendible bad sequences is $\mathbf{\Sigma}_1^{1,x}$, non-empty, dense, and upwards-closed with respect to $\trianglelefteq^P$.

Lemma 5. $\mathbf{\Sigma}_1^1$–DUCC $\equiv_{\mathrm{W}} \mathbf{\Sigma}_1^1$–DUCC$(2^{<\mathbb{N}}, \cdot)$, *where the latter denotes the restriction of the former to $2^{<\mathbb{N}}$ with the prefix ordering $\sqsubseteq$.*

Proof. Clearly, we only need to show that $\mathbf{\Sigma}_1^1\text{--DUCC} \leq_W \mathbf{\Sigma}_1^1\text{--DUCC}(2^{<\mathbb{N}}, \cdot)$. Let the input be $((P, \leq_P), A)$ where A is a $\mathbf{\Sigma}_1^1$, non-empty, dense, and upwards-closed subset of the partial order $(P, \leq_P)$. We uniformly define a computable labelling $\lambda : 2^{<\mathbb{N}} \to P$ such that $\lambda^{-1}(A)$ is non-empty, dense, and upwards-closed. This suffices to prove the claimed reduction, as the preimage of A via λ is (uniformly) $\mathbf{\Sigma}_1^1$ and, given $\sigma \in \lambda^{-1}(A)$, we can simply compute $\lambda(\sigma) \in A$.

Let $(x_n)_{n \in \mathbb{N}}$ be an enumeration of P. We define an auxiliary computable function $\overline{\lambda} : P \times 2^{<\mathbb{N}} \to 2^{<\mathbb{N}}$ as follows: for every i, $\overline{\lambda}(x, 0^i) := \overline{\lambda}(x, 0^i 1) := x$. To define $\overline{\lambda}(x, 0^i 1 b \frown \sigma)$ we distinguish two cases:

$$\overline{\lambda}(x, 0^i 1 b \frown \sigma) := \begin{cases} \overline{\lambda}(x, \sigma) & \text{if } b = 0 \text{ or } x \not\leq_P x_i \\ \overline{\lambda}(x_i, \sigma) & \text{if } b = 1 \text{ and } x \leq_P x_i. \end{cases}$$

We then define $\lambda(\sigma) := \overline{\lambda}(x_0, \sigma)$. It is clear that λ is computable and total. Let us show that $\lambda^{-1}(A)$ is a valid input for $\mathbf{\Sigma}_1^1\text{--DUCC}(2^{<\mathbb{N}}, \cdot)$. Observe first that, for every $\sigma \sqsubseteq \tau$, $\lambda(\sigma) \leq_P \lambda(\tau)$, which implies that $\lambda^{-1}(A)$ is upwards-closed.

To prove the density, fix $\sigma \in 2^{<\mathbb{N}}$ and assume $\lambda(\sigma) \notin A$. Since A is dense, there is i such that $\lambda(\sigma) \leq_P x_i \in A$. Let $\tau \sqsupseteq \sigma$ be such that, for every ρ, $\lambda(\tau \frown \rho) = \lambda(\rho)$. Notice that such τ always exists: indeed, if $\overline{\sigma}$ is the longest tail of σ of the form 0^j or $0^j 1$ for some j, then $\tau := \sigma \frown d0$, where $d = 1$ if $\overline{\sigma} = 0^j$ and $d = \varepsilon$ otherwise, satisfies the above requirement. In particular, $\lambda(\tau \frown 0^i 11) = x_i$. This proves that $\lambda^{-1}(A)$ is dense and therefore concludes the proof.

Theorem 3. $\mathsf{Fin_k}(\mathsf{BS}) \equiv_W \mathsf{Fin_k}(\mathbf{\Sigma}_1^1\text{--DUCC}) \equiv_W \mathsf{Fin_k}(\mathsf{DS}) \equiv_W \mathsf{RT}_k^1$.

Proof. We have $\mathsf{RT}_k^1 \equiv_W \mathsf{Fin_k}(\mathsf{DS}) \leq_W \mathsf{Fin_k}(\mathsf{BS}) \leq_W \mathsf{Fin_k}(\mathbf{\Sigma}_1^1\text{--DUCC})$ by [8, Theorem 4.31] and Proposition 3. It remains to show that $\mathsf{Fin_k}(\mathbf{\Sigma}_1^1\text{--DUCC}) \leq_W \mathsf{RT}_k^1$. By Lemma 5, it is enough to show that $\mathsf{Fin_k}(\mathbf{\Sigma}_1^1\text{--DUCC}(2^{<\mathbb{N}}, \cdot)) \leq_W \mathsf{RT}_k^1$.

Let f be a problem with codomain k and assume $f \leq_W \mathbf{\Sigma}_1^1\text{--DUCC}(2^{<\mathbb{N}}, \cdot)$ via Φ, Ψ. Observe that every $x \in \mathrm{dom}(f)$ induces a coloring $c : 2^{<\mathbb{N}} \to k$ as follows: run $\Psi(x, \sigma)$ in parallel on every $\sigma \in 2^{<\mathbb{N}}$. Whenever we see that $\Psi(x, \sigma)$ returns a number less than k, we define $c(\tau) := \Psi(x, \sigma)$ for every $\tau \sqsubseteq \sigma$ such that $c(\tau)$ is not defined yet. By density of $\Phi(x)$, c is total.

By the Chubb-Hirst-McNicholl tree theorem [3], there is some $\sigma \in 2^{<\mathbb{N}}$ and some color $i < k$ such that i appears densely above σ. We claim that if i appears densely above σ then $i \in f(x)$. To prove this, recall $\Phi(x)$ codes a set which is dense and upwards-closed. By density of both this set and the color i, we may fix some $\tau \sqsupseteq \sigma$ which lies in the set coded by $\Phi(x)$ and has color i. Then fix $\rho \sqsupseteq \tau$ such that $c(\tau)$ was defined to be $\Psi(x, \rho)$. Now ρ lies in the set coded by $\Phi(x)$ as well, so $i = c(\tau) = \Psi(x, \rho)$ lies in $f(x)$.

Since a k-coloring of $2^{<\mathbb{N}}$ can be naturally turned into a k-coloring of $\mathbb{Q}$ (using a canonical computable order isomorphism between them), the problem "given a k-coloring of $2^{<\mathbb{N}}$, find σ and i such that i appears densely above σ" can be solved by RT_k^1, as shown in [11, Corollary 42].

It is immediate from the previous theorem that the finitary parts of BS and DS in the sense of Cipriani and Pauly [4, Definition 2.10] agree as well. Finally, we shall prove that the deterministic parts of BS and DS agree.

Lemma 6. *If* $\mathrm{Fin}_2(f) \leq_W \mathrm{RT}_2^1$, *then* $\mathrm{Det}(f) \leq_W \mathrm{lim}$.

Proof. By algebraic properties of Det and Fin_k, we have

$$\mathrm{Det}(f) \leq_W \widehat{\mathrm{Det}_2(f)} \leq_W \widehat{\mathrm{Fin}_2(f)} \leq_W \widehat{\mathrm{RT}_2^1} \equiv_W \mathrm{KL}.$$

So $\mathrm{Det}(f) \leq_W \mathrm{Det}(\mathrm{KL}) \equiv_W \mathrm{lim}$: Use the fact $\mathrm{KL} \equiv_W \mathrm{WKL} * \mathrm{lim}$ and the choice elimination principle [2, 11.7.25] (see also [8, Theorem 3.9]).

Since $\mathrm{Det}(\mathrm{BS}) \geq_W \mathrm{Det}(\mathrm{DS}) \equiv_W \mathrm{lim}$ [8, Theorem 4.16], we conclude that:

Corollary 5. $\mathrm{Det}(\mathrm{BS}) \equiv_W \mathrm{Det}(\mathrm{DS}) \equiv_W \mathrm{lim}$.

Corollary 6. $\mathrm{Det}_\mathbb{N}(\mathrm{BS}) \equiv_W \mathrm{C}_\mathbb{N}$.

Proof. Since $\mathbb{N}$ computably embeds in $\mathbb{N}^\mathbb{N}$, for every problem f we have $\mathrm{Det}_\mathbb{N}(f) \leq_W \mathrm{Det}(f)$. In particular, by Corollary 5, $\mathrm{Det}_\mathbb{N}(\mathrm{BS}) \leq_W \mathrm{Det}(\mathrm{BS}) \equiv_W \mathrm{lim}$. Since $^1\mathrm{lim} \equiv_W \mathrm{C}_\mathbb{N}$ ([1, Proposition 13.10], see also [13, Theorem 7.2]), this implies $\mathrm{Det}_\mathbb{N}(\mathrm{BS}) \leq_W \mathrm{C}_\mathbb{N}$. The converse reduction follows from the fact that $\mathrm{C}_\mathbb{N} \equiv_W \mathrm{Det}_\mathbb{N}(\mathrm{DS})$ [8, Proposition 4.14].

We remark that for establishing $\mathrm{Fin}_k(\Sigma_1^1\mathrm{-DUCC}) \leq_W \mathrm{RT}_k^1$ in Theorem 3 it was immaterial that the set of correct solutions was provided as a Σ_1^1-set. If we consider any other represented point class Γ which is effectively closed under taking preimages under computable functions, and define $\Gamma\mathrm{-DUCC}$ in the obvious way, we can obtain:

Corollary 7. $\mathrm{Fin}_k(\Gamma\mathrm{-DUCC}) \leq_W \mathrm{RT}_k^1$.

This observation could be useful e.g. for exploring the Weihrauch degree of finding bad arrays in non-better-quasi-orders (cf. [7]).

Acknowledgments. We are grateful to Takayuki Kihara for pointing out the mistake in our previous article. We thank also Cécilia Pradic for comments which greatly improved the presentation of the argument in Sect. 2.

References

1. Brattka, V., Gherardi, G., Marcone, A.: The Bolzano-Weierstrass theorem is the jump of weak König's Lemma. Ann. Pure Appl. Logic **163**(6), 623–655 (2012). https://doi.org/10.1016/j.apal.2011.10.006
2. Brattka, V., Gherardi, G., Pauly, A.: Weihrauch complexity in computable analysis. In: Handbook of Computability and Complexity in Analysis. TAC, pp. 367–417. Springer, Cham (2021). https://doi.org/10.1007/978-3-030-59234-9_11

3. Chubb, J., Hirst, J.L., McNicholl, T.H.: Reverse mathematics, computability, and partitions of trees. J. Symbolic Logic **74**(1), 201–215 (2009)
4. Cipriani, V., Pauly, A.: Embeddability of graphs and Weihrauch degrees (2023). https://doi.org/10.48550/arXiv.2305.00935
5. Dzhafarov, D.D., Goh, J.L., Hirschfeldt, D.R., Patey, L., Pauly, A.: Ramsey's theorem and products in the Weihrauch degrees. Computability **9**(2), 85–110 (2020). https://doi.org/10.3233/com-180203
6. Dzhafarov, D.D., Solomon, R., Yokoyama, K.: On the first-order parts of problems in the Weihrauch degrees. Computability (to appear). https://doi.org/10.48550/arXiv.2301.12733
7. Freund, A., Pakhomov, F., Soldà, G.: The logical strength of minimal bad arrays (2023). https://doi.org/10.48550/arXiv.2304.00278
8. Goh, J.L., Pauly, A., Valenti, M.: Finding descending sequences through ill-founded linear orders. J. Symbolic Logic **86**(2), 817–854 (2021). https://doi.org/10.1017/jsl.2021.15
9. Kihara, T., Marcone, A., Pauly, A.: Searching for an analogue of ATR_0 in the Weihrauch lattice. J. Symbolic Logic **85**(3), 1006–1043 (2020). https://doi.org/10.1017/jsl.2020.12
10. Marcone, A.: WQO and BQO Theory in Subsystems of Second Order Arithmetic, pp. 303–330. Lecture Notes in Logic, Cambridge University Press (2005). https://doi.org/10.1017/9781316755846.020
11. Pauly, A., Pradic, C., Soldà, G.: On the Weihrauch degree of the additive Ramsey theorem. Computability (to appear). https://doi.org/10.48550/arXiv.2301.02833
12. Pauly, A., Soldà, G.: Sequential discontinuity and first-order problems (2024). https://doi.org/10.48550/arXiv.2401.12641
13. Soldà, G., Valenti, M.: Algebraic properties of the first-order part of a problem. Ann. Pure Appl. Logic **174**(7), 103270 (2023). https://doi.org/10.1016/j.apal.2023.103270

Sequential Discontinuity and First-Order Problems

Arno Pauly[1] and Giovanni Soldà[2]([⊠])

[1] Swansea University, Swansea, UK
[2] Ghent University, Ghent, Belgium
Giovanni.A.solda@gmail.com

Abstract. We explore the low levels of the structure of the continuous Weihrauch degrees of first-order problems. In particular, we show that there exists a minimal discontinuous first-order degree, namely that of ACC_N, without any determinacy assumptions. The same degree is also revealed as the least sequentially discontinuous one, i.e. the least degree with a representative whose restriction to some sequence converging to a limit point is still discontinuous.

The study of games related to continuous Weihrauch reducibility constitutes an important ingredient in the proof of the main theorem. We present some initial additional results about the degrees of first-order problems that can be obtained using this approach.

1 Introduction

A well-known continuity notion is that convergent sequences get mapped to convergent sequences. As spaces of relevance for computable analysis are sequential, this notion adequately characterizes continuity for functions for us. Multivalued functions, on the other hand, can exhibit a very different behaviour. To one extreme, the multivalued function $NON : \{0,1\}^{\mathbb{N}} \rightrightarrows \{0,1\}^{\mathbb{N}}$ with $q \in NON(p)$ iff $q \not\leq_T p$ is discontinuous, yet whenever restricted to a subset of its domain of cardinality less than the continuum even has a constant realizer. It thus seems a natural question to ask when discontinuity of a multivalued function stems from its behaviour restricted to some convergent sequence.

The answer to this turns out to be related to the notion of first-order part of a Weihrauch degree, proposed by Dzafahrov, Solomon and Yokoyama [13]. It is defined as:

$$^1(f) := \max_{\leq_W}\{g :\subseteq \mathbb{N}^{\mathbb{N}} \rightrightarrows \mathbb{N} \mid g \leq_W f\}$$

It turns out that there is a weakest Weihrauch degree with non-trivial first-order part (up to continuous reductions), namely the degree of ACC_N (All or Co-unique Choice) which is the restriction of C_N to sets $A \subseteq \mathbb{N}$ with $|\mathbb{N}\backslash A| \leq 1$ studied in [7]. We show the following:

Theorem 1. *The following are equivalent for a multi-valued function* $f :\subseteq \mathbb{N}^{\mathbb{N}} \rightrightarrows \mathbb{N}^{\mathbb{N}}$:

L. Levy Patey et al. (Eds.): CiE 2024, LNCS 14773, pp. 351–365, 2024.
https://doi.org/10.1007/978-3-031-64309-5_28

1. $^1(f)$ is discontinuous.
2. There exists a convergent sequence $(a_n)_{n \in \mathbb{N}}$ with $\overline{\{a_n \mid n \in \mathbb{N}\}} \subseteq \operatorname{dom}(f)$ such that $f|_{\overline{\{a_n \mid n \in \mathbb{N}\}}}$ is discontinuous.
3. $\mathsf{ACC}_{\mathbb{N}} \leq_W^* f$

For the benefit of the reader, we recall that $\leq_W^*$ denotes continuous Weihrauch reducibility: see Sect. 2.2 for more on this.

We prove our main theorem in two separate parts. The equivalence between 2. and 3. follows by a direct analysis of how a multivalued function with domain $\omega +$ 1 can be discontinuous; it is given as Lemma 2 in Sect. 3. The equivalence between 1. and 3. is built on the generalization of Wadge-style games to multivalued functions proposed in [18]. We elucidate this in Sect. 4. The relevant half of Theorem 1 is summarized in Corollary 1, but we obtain additional results of independent interest.

2   Background

We assume that the reader is familiar with the basics of represented spaces and Weihrauch reducibility, and refer to [19] as reference for the former and [6] as reference for the latter.

2.1   Represented Spaces

Completions of a Represented Space. We use the notions of completions of represented spaces and multiretraceability discussed in [4,5,11], but we will introduce these concepts somewhat differently than those works. The reason is that *the completion* of a represented space as defined there is not compatible with computable isomorphisms, and we thus prefer to speak of *a completion* – in particular since for our purposes any completion in the sense we introduce below is equally good.

Definition 1 (cf. [5, Proposition 2.6]). *A represented space* $\mathbf{X}$ *is multiretraceable, if every computable partial function* $f :\subseteq \{0,1\}^{\mathbb{N}} \to \mathbf{X}$ *has a total computable extension* $F : \{0,1\}^{\mathbb{N}} \to \mathbf{X}$.

Clearly, not every represented space is multiretraceable: for instance, a characterization of the multiretraceable countably-based T_0-spaces is given in [17, Corollary 4.7].

Definition 2. *A completion of a represented space* $\mathbf{X}$ *consists of a computable embedding* $\iota : \mathbf{X} \hookrightarrow \mathbf{Y}$ *into a multitraceable space* $\mathbf{Y}$.

Proposition 1 ([11], cf. [5]). *Every represented space has a completion.*

Proposition 2. *If* $\iota_1 : \mathbf{X} \hookrightarrow \mathbf{Y}_1$ *and* $\iota_2 : \mathbf{X} \hookrightarrow \mathbf{Y}_2$ *are completions of* $\mathbf{X}$, *then there is a computable multivalued function* $T : \mathbf{Y}_1 \rightrightarrows \mathbf{Y}_2$ *such that* $\iota_2 = T \circ \iota_1$.

Proof. Let $\delta_1 :\subseteq \{0,1\}^{\mathbb{N}} \to \mathbf{Y}_1$ be the representation of $\mathbf{Y}_1$. We note that $\iota_2 \circ \iota_1^{-1} \circ \delta_1 :\subseteq \{0,1\}^{\mathbb{N}} \to \mathbf{Y}_2$ is a partial computable function, and thus has computable total extension $F : \{0,1\}^{\mathbb{N}} \to \mathbf{Y}_2$. Now $T := F \circ \delta_1^{-1}$ is the desired map.

We will use $\overline{\mathbf{X}}$ to denote some completion of $\mathbf{X}$ in the following, and will prove for each use that the specific choice of completion is irrelevant by invoking Proposition 2.

Layering of Spaces

Definition 3. *Given two represented spaces* $\mathbf{X}$, $\mathbf{Y}$ *we define the represented space* $\frac{\mathbf{X}}{\mathbf{Y}}$ *to have the underlying set* $\{\frac{x}{\cdot} \mid x \in \mathbf{X}\} \cup \{\frac{\cdot}{y} \mid y \in \mathbf{Y}\}$ *with the representation defined as follows: Let* $\delta_{\mathbf{X}} :\subseteq \{0,1\}^{\mathbb{N}} \to \mathbf{X}$, $\delta_{\mathbf{Y}} :\subseteq \{0,1\}^{\mathbb{N}} \to \mathbf{Y}$ *be the original representations. Then we introduce the representation* $\delta_{\mathrm{new}} :\subseteq \{0,1,2\}^{\mathbb{N}} \to \{\frac{x}{\cdot} \mid x \in \mathbf{X}\} \cup \{\frac{\cdot}{y} \mid y \in \mathbf{Y}\}$ *as* $\delta_{\mathrm{new}}(q) = \frac{\cdot}{\delta_{\mathbf{Y}}(q)}$ *for any* $q \in \mathrm{dom}(\delta_{\mathbf{Y}}) \subseteq \{0,1\}^{\mathbb{N}}$ *and* $\delta_{\mathrm{new}}(w2p) = \frac{\delta_{\mathbf{X}}(p)}{\cdot}$ *for* $w \in \{0,1\}^*$, $p \in \mathrm{dom}(\delta_{\mathbf{X}})$.

Informally spoken, a point in $\frac{\mathbf{X}}{\mathbf{Y}}$ starts off looking like a point in $\mathbf{Y}$, and it might indeed be a point in $\mathbf{Y}$. It can also, at any moment, change to be some arbitrary point in $\mathbf{X}$ instead. For example, we find that $\mathbb{S} \cong \frac{1}{1}$. For subsets $A \subseteq \mathbf{X}$, $B \subseteq \mathbf{Y}$ we shall write $\frac{A}{\cdot} = \{\frac{x}{\cdot} \mid x \in A\}$ and $\frac{\cdot}{B} = \{\frac{\cdot}{y} \mid y \in B\}$.

Observation 2. *We find that* $\mathcal{O}(\frac{\mathbf{X}}{\mathbf{Y}}) = \{\frac{U}{\cdot} \mid U \in \mathcal{O}(\mathbf{X})\} \cup \{\frac{X}{\cdot} \cup \frac{\cdot}{V} \mid V \in \mathcal{O}(\mathbf{Y})\}$.

We recall that a topological space X is *scattered* if every non-empty $A \subseteq X$ contains a point which is isolated in A.

Proposition 3. *The space* $\frac{\mathbf{X}}{\mathbf{Y}}$ *is scattered iff both* $\mathbf{X}$ *and* $\mathbf{Y}$ *are; and then furthermore:*

$$\mathrm{CBr}(\frac{\mathbf{X}}{\mathbf{Y}}) = \mathrm{CBr}(\mathbf{X}) + \mathrm{CBr}(\mathbf{Y})$$

Some Represented Spaces of Particular Interest

Definition 4. *The represented space* $(\omega + 1)$ *has the underlying set* $\mathbb{N} \cup \{\omega\}$ *and comes with the representation* $\delta_{\omega+1} : \{0,1\}^{\mathbb{N}} \to (\omega+1)$ *where* $\delta_{\omega+1}(0^n 1p) = n$ *for any* $p \in \{0,1\}^{\mathbb{N}}$ *and* $\delta_{\omega+1}(0^{\omega}) = \omega$.

For added clarity, we note that the represented space $\omega + 1$ as given above is *not* multiretraceable, and hence the obvious embedding $\mathbb{N} \to \omega + 1$ is not a completion in the sense of Definition 2: indeed, consider for instance the partial map $f :\subseteq 2^{\mathbb{N}} \to \omega + 1$ such that on input p it outputs 0 if the first 1 in p occurs in an even position and 1 if it occurs in an odd position.

2.2 Weihrauch Reducibility

We use $f \leq_{\mathrm{W}} g$ to denote that f is Weihrauch reducible to g. By $f \leq_{\mathrm{W}}^* g$ we denote that f is continuous Weihrauch reducible to g, meaning that the reduction witnesses are merely required to be continuous rather than computable functions. We can also view $f \leq_{\mathrm{W}}^* g$ to mean that f is Weihrauch reducible to g relative to some oracle, as continuity is just computability relative to an arbitrary oracle.

The First-Order Part of a Weihrauch Degree. As mentioned in the introduction, the first-order part of a Weihrauch degree f, denoted by ^1f, was proposed by Dzafahrov, Solomon and Yokoyama [13]. It is defined as:

$$^1(f) := \max_{\leq_W}\{g :\subseteq \mathbb{N}^{\mathbb{N}} \rightrightarrows \mathbb{N} \mid g \leq_W f\}$$

As the Weihrauch lattice is not complete [16], a proof is needed to show that the first-order part indeed exists. This is straight-forward, however. The first-order part was thoroughly studied in [23], and has turned out to be a convenient tool to obtain separations between Weihrauch degrees (e.g. [10,12,14]).

3   Discontinuity of Multivalued Functions on $\omega + 1$

One component of our main theorem is provided by an analysis of the possible Weihrauch degrees for multivalued functions with domain $\omega + 1$. We start by providing a multivalued function with domain $\omega + 1$ which is equivalent to $\mathsf{ACC}_{\mathbb{N}}$.

Definition 5. $\mathsf{SEQACC}_{\mathbb{N}}$: $\omega + 1 \rightrightarrows \mathbb{N}$ *is the problem defined as* $\mathsf{SEQACC}_{\mathbb{N}}(\langle n, m \rangle) = \mathbb{N}\backslash\{n\}$, *and* $\mathsf{SEQACC}_{\mathbb{N}}(\omega) = \mathbb{N}$.

Lemma 1. $\mathsf{ACC}_{\mathbb{N}} \equiv_{sW} \mathsf{SEQACC}_{\mathbb{N}}$

Lemma 2. *The following are equivalent for a partial multivalued function* $f :\subseteq \mathbb{N}^{\mathbb{N}} \rightrightarrows \mathbb{N}^{\mathbb{N}}$:

1. *there exists a converging sequence* $(a_n)_{n \in \omega} \to a$ *such that* $a_n \in \mathrm{dom}\, f$ *for every* $n \in \omega$, $a \in \mathrm{dom}\, f$, *and* $f|_{\overline{\{a_n : n \in \mathbb{N}\}}}$ *is discontinuous.*
2. $\mathsf{ACC}_{\mathbb{N}} \leq_W^* f$

Proof. We first prove $2 \to 1$: by Lemma 1, we can suppose that $\mathsf{SEQACC}_{\mathbb{N}} \leq_W^* f$. The image of $\omega + 1$ under the reduction yields the convergent sequence $(a_n)_{n \in \omega} \to a$; and the corresponding restriction $f|_{\overline{\{a_n : n \in \mathbb{N}\}}}$ still satisfies $\mathsf{SEQACC}_{\mathbb{N}} \leq_W^* f|_{\overline{\{a_n : n \in \mathbb{N}\}}}$, and thus is discontinuous.

Now on to $1 \to 2$: Let $(a_n)_{n \in \omega} \to a$ be a sequence as in the hypotheses. We claim that the following holds:

$$\forall p \in f(a)\, \exists k \in \mathbb{N}\, \forall N \in \mathbb{N}\, \exists j > N(f(a_j) \cap [p_{\leq k}] = \emptyset).$$

Suppose for a contradiction that this is false. Then, there is $p \in f(a)$ such that for every integer k there is an N_k with the property that for every a_j with $j > N_k$, $f(a_j) \cap [p_{\leq k}]$ is not empty, say that it contains a certain $q_{k,j}$. Then, we can define a realizer F for f that is continuous on $\overline{\{a_n : n \in \mathbb{N}\}}$ as follows: for every $i \in \mathbb{N}$ let $M_i = \sum_{j < i} N_j + 1$, and for every $j \in [M_i, M_{i+1} - 1]$ let $F(a_j) = q_{i,j}$ (notice that the $[M_i, M_{i+1} - 1]$ partition $\mathbb{N}$, hence F is defined on every a_j). Moreover, let $F(a) = p$, and let $F(x) \in f(x)$ for every other element $x \in \mathrm{dom}\, f$. It is immediately verified that this F is a realizer as we wanted it.

Notice that the $p_{\leq k}$ as above form a countable set, and assume we have an enumeration of it, say $(w_i : i \in \mathbb{N})$ (an element might be enumerated several times). Then, we can define the function $\lambda : \mathbb{N} \times \mathbb{N} \to \mathbb{N}$ as $\lambda(n, i) = j$, where j is minimal such that $d(a_j, a) < 1/2^n$ and $f(a_j) \cap [w_i] = \emptyset$ (it is easy to see that such a j exists). We will use the function λ and the set $\{w_i : i \in \mathbb{N}\}$ as oracles for the functionals witnessing that $\mathsf{ACC}_\mathbb{N} \leq^*_W f$.

Let $g \in \operatorname{dom} \mathsf{ACC}_\mathbb{N}$ be an enumeration of a set U that contains at most one point. We define the inner functional H in steps as follows: at step n, we check whether a number i is enumerated in U by g. If this is the case, the construction stops and we output $H(g) = a_{\lambda(n,i)}$, whereas if this is not the case we set $H(g)(n) = a(n)$. Our assumption that $a_j \to a$ guarantees that the construction works.

Finally, we define the outer functional K on input (q, g) (where $q \in f(H(g))$) as follows: for every $i \in \mathbb{N}$, we check simultaneously whether q extends w_i and whether i is enumerated in U by g. Notice that at least one of these searches gives a positive result, since if no i is enumerated in U by g, then $H(g) = a$. Suppose then that the search for a certain i gave positive result: then, if the search was successful because we found that i is enumerated in U by g, we set $K(q, g) = i + 1$, which is then clearly in $\mathsf{ACC}_\mathbb{N}(g)$. If instead the search was successful because q extends w_i, we set $K(q, g) = i$: by the fact that q extends w_i, we know that at no point, while determining $H(g)$, it was found that i is enumerated in U, and hence $i \in \mathsf{ACC}_\mathbb{N}(g)$.

4   Games for Weihrauch Reducibility

In this section we identify the least degree of discontinuity a multivalued function with a given codomain can attain. We begin by introducing a suitable representative of this degree.

Definition 6. *Let* $\neq_\mathbf{X} : \overline{\mathbf{X}} \rightrightarrows \mathbf{X}$ *by defined by* $y \in \neq_\mathbf{X}(x)$ *iff* $x \neq y$.

We can see that $\neq_\mathbf{X}$ does not have a continuous realizer by taking the "usual" completion of $\mathbf{X}$ (namely, extending the domain of the representation with a "skip" symbol and the codomain with a point $\perp$). Suppose a continuous realizer F existed: to diagonalize against it, notice that by continuity we can produce a $q \in \{0, 1, \text{skip}\}^\mathbb{N}$ such that $F(q) = p$, where p is q with the "skip"'s removed, by coping the output of F for initial segments of q. Given this, the more general case is taken care of by the following Proposition.

Proposition 4. *Let* $\iota_1 : \mathbf{X} \hookrightarrow \mathbf{Y}_1$, $\iota_2 : \mathbf{X} \hookrightarrow \mathbf{Y}_2$ *be two completions of* $\mathbf{X}$, *and let* $\neq^1_\mathbf{X}$ *and* $\neq^2_\mathbf{X}$ *be the maps defined using those. Then* $\neq^1_\mathbf{X} \equiv_{sW} \neq^2_\mathbf{X}$.

In the case that $\mathbf{X}$ is empty or consists of a single point the above definition does not entirely make sense. It will be convenient to assume that $\neq_\emptyset \equiv_W 0$, where 0 is the no-where defined function, and that for every singleton space $\mathbf{1}$ it holds that $\neq_\mathbf{1} \equiv_W \infty$ where ∞ is the (artificial) top element in the Weihrauch degrees (see the discussion in [8, Section 2.1]).

For discrete spaces $\mathbf{X}$, we find that the degree of $\neq_\mathbf{X}$ is a familiar principle:

Observation 3. $\neq_{\mathbb{N}} \equiv_{sW} ACC_{\mathbb{N}}$ *and* $\neq_{\mathbf{n}} \equiv_{sW} ACC_{\mathbf{n}}$.

We obtain our main result for this section by analysing a generalization of Wadge games for multivalued function between represented spaces. We are primarily following [18] for this, but similar ideas are present e.g. in [2,20].

Definition 7. *The Wadge game for a multivalued function* $f : \mathbf{X} \rightrightarrows \mathbf{Y}$ *is played by two players, I and II taking turns. Player I always plays a natural number, Player II can play a natural number or skip her turn. The game is zero-sum, and winning is determined by the following rules, with earlier rules taking precedence over later ones.*

1. *If Player I's moves do not form a name for an element* $x \in \mathbf{X}$, *Player I loses the game.*
2. *If Player II does not play a number infinitely often, or if the numbers she plays does not form a name for some* $y \in \mathbf{Y}$, *Player II loses.*
3. *Otherwise, Player II wins iff* $y \in f(x)$.

The motivation behind the definition of the Wadge game is the following rather straight-forward observation:

Observation 4. *Player II has a winning strategy for the Wadge game for* $f : \mathbf{X} \rightrightarrows \mathbf{Y}$ *iff* f *is continuous.*

If winning strategies for Player II witness continuity of the multivalued function f, it is very natural to ask what a winning strategy for Player I would do. If the game is determined, such an analysis gives rise to a dichotomy as follows:

Theorem 5 (ZF + DC + AD). *A multivalued function* $f : \mathbf{Z} \rightrightarrows \mathbf{X}$ *is either continuous or satisfies* $\neq_{\mathbf{X}} \leq^*_W f$.

Proof. By assumption, the Wadge game for $f : \mathbf{Z} \rightrightarrows \mathbf{X}$ is determined. By Observation 4, Player II wins the game iff f is continuous. Thus, Player I wins the game iff f is discontinuous.

A winning strategy for Player I can be described as a function $\lambda : (\mathbb{N} \cup \{\text{skip}\})^* \to \mathbb{N}$ which needs to satisfy that for any sequence $q \in (\mathbb{N} \cup \{\text{skip}\})^\omega$ the sequence

$$g(q) := \lambda(q_{<0})\lambda(q_{<1})\lambda(q_{<2})\lambda(q_{<3})\cdots$$

constitutes a name for some $x \in \mathbf{Z}$. Moreover, if removing all skip's from q produces a name for some $y \in \mathbf{X}$, then it must hold that $y \notin f(x)$.

We can obtain a completion $\overline{\mathbf{X}}$ of $\mathbf{X}$ by using $q \in (\mathbb{N} \cup \{\text{skip}\})^\omega$ as names (with some renumbering), and letting any sequence q where removing the skip's yields a name for some $y \in \mathbf{X}$ be a name for $y \in \overline{\mathbf{X}}$, and letting any other sequence be a name for a fresh element $\perp$. We find that the function g obtained from the winning strategy of Player I is a realizer of a continuous multivalued function $G : \overline{\mathbf{X}} \rightrightarrows \mathbf{Z}$. Moreover, we have that $f \circ G : \overline{\mathbf{X}} \rightrightarrows \mathbf{X}$ tightens $\neq_{\mathbf{X}} : \overline{\mathbf{X}} \rightrightarrows \mathbf{X}$, and thus witnesses that $\neq_{\mathbf{X}} \leq^*_W f$.

Notice that the theorem above admits a converse without the use of determinacy: namely, if we have access to the continuous functionals H, K witnessing that $\neq_{\mathbf{X}} \leq^*_W f$, we can compute a strategy for player I in the Wadge game for f, as we now describe. Player I waits for player II to output a point x of $\mathbf{X}$, playing "skips" in the meantime. As player II outputs more significant bits of x, player I outputs the result of $H(K(x))$. If, by contradiction, it was the case that $x \in f(H(K(x)))$, then $K(x) \in \neq_{\mathbf{X}}(K(x))$ should also hold, thus proving the claim.

Theorem 5 generalizes the approach used by Brattka in [2] to identify the "least discontinuous" problem, assuming enough determinacy. The discontinuity problem DIS studied by Brattka is essentially the same as $\neq_{\mathbb{N}^{\mathbb{N}}}$ (the problems have formally different domains, but the same realizers).

If we are considering multivalued functions with codomain $\mathbb{N}$ specifically, we do not need to appeal to the axiom of determinacy to render the corresponding games determined. Instead, we prove the following:

Lemma 3. *Let $f :\subseteq \mathbb{N}^{\mathbb{N}} \rightrightarrows \mathbb{N}$ be a partial multivalued function. Then, the Wadge game for f is determined.*

The main idea of the proof is to make explicit what it means for player I to have a winning strategy in the restricted setting given by the hypotheses of the lemma. After this is done, one sees that player I not having a winning strategy implies that player II has one.

Corollary 1. *The following are equivalent for a multifunction $f : \mathbf{Z} \rightrightarrows \mathbb{N}$:*

1. *f is discontinuous.*
2. *$\mathsf{ACC}_{\mathbb{N}} \leq^*_W f$*

Proof. This follows from Theorem 5, with Lemma 3 removing the need to invoke AD and Observation 3 letting us replace $\neq_{\mathbb{N}}$ by $\mathsf{ACC}_{\mathbb{N}}$.

In the very same way we also obtain the following:

Corollary 2. *The following are equivalent for a multivalued function $f : \mathbf{Z} \rightrightarrows \mathbf{n}$:*

1. *f is discontinuous.*
2. *$\mathsf{ACC}_{\mathbf{n}} \leq^*_W f$*

Similar to the first-order part, the k-finitary part of a Weihrauch degree g is the maximal degree of some $f : \mathbf{X} \rightrightarrows \mathbf{k}$ with $f \leq_W g$ [10]. We then see that, up to some oracle, the weakest non-trivial k-finitary part is just $\mathsf{ACC}_{\mathbf{n}}$.

4.1   On the Complexity of $\neq_{\mathbf{X}}$

Since $\neq_{\mathbf{X}}$ characterizes the least discontinuous degree of discontinuity possible for a multivalued function with codomain $\mathbf{X}$, we will briefly explore how the degree of $\neq_{\mathbf{X}}$ varies with the space $\mathbf{X}$. To roughly summarize our results, sufficiently complicated spaces all share the same degree (that of $\neq_{\mathbb{N}^{\mathbb{N}}}$), while for scattered spaces we see substantial variation.

Proposition 5. *Let* $\emptyset \neq \mathbf{X} \subseteq \mathbf{Y}$. *Then* $\neq_{\mathbf{Y}} \leq_{sW} \neq_{\mathbf{X}}$.

Proposition 6. *Let* $s : \mathbf{X} \to \mathbf{Y}$ *be a computable surjection, and let* $t : \mathbf{Y} \rightrightarrows \mathbf{X}$ *be computable with* $s \circ t = \mathrm{id}_{\mathbf{Y}}$. *Then* $\neq_{\mathbf{X}} \leq_{sW} \neq_{\mathbf{Y}}$.

Corollary 3. *Let* $\mathbf{X}$ *be an uncountable Polish space. Then* $\neq_{\mathbf{X}} \equiv_W^* \neq_{\mathbb{N}^{\mathbb{N}}}$.

Corollary 4. $\neq_{\mathcal{O}(\mathbb{N})} \equiv_{sW} \neq_{\mathbb{N}^{\mathbb{N}}}$

For Sierpiński space $\mathbb{S}$ we find that the least degree of discontinuity of a multivalued function with codomain $\mathbb{S}$ is actually no less than the least degree of a discontinuous *function* with codomain $\mathbb{S}$:

Proposition 7. $\neq_{\mathbb{S}} \equiv_{sW} (\neg : \mathbb{S} \to \mathbb{S}) \equiv_W LPO$

Corollary 5. *Let* $P : \mathbf{X} \rightrightarrows \mathbb{S}$ *be discontinuous. Then* $LPO \leq_W^* P$.

The following shows that two scattered spaces of Cantor-Bendixson rank 2 can yield different least degrees of discontinuity:

Proposition 8. $\neq_{\mathbb{N} \times (\omega+1)} <_W \neq_{\frac{\mathbb{N}}{\mathbb{N}}}$

4.2 More Dichotomies in the Continuous First-Order Weihrauch Degrees

As shown in [18], every lower cone in the Weihrauch degrees can be characterized by a Wadge-style game. We can thus use the core idea of Theorem 5 to identify further dichotomies. In principle, we can obtain a dual to any given Weihrauch degree (assuming enough determinacy) (i.e. pairs f, g such that any Weihrauch degree h satisfies exactly one of $f \leq_W^* h$ and $h \leq_W^* g$). However, in general the construction will be very cumbersome and come with rather strong determinacy requirements. If we restrict to first-order problems, we can actually obtain some insight, as we shall demonstrate next.

Definition 8. *The problem* $\Pi_2^0 \mathrm{ACC}_{\mathbb{N}}$ *receives as input a* Π_2^0-*subset* $A \subseteq \mathbb{N}$ *with* $|\mathbb{N} \setminus A| \leq 1$ *and returns some* $i \in A$.

It is often more convenient to think about $\Pi_2^0 \mathrm{ACC}_{\mathbb{N}}$ as the problem "Given some $p \in \mathbb{N}^{\mathbb{N}}$, find some $k \in \mathbb{N}$ such that $\lim_{n \to \infty} p(n) \neq k$", where the inequality is assumed to be satisfied if the limit does not exist. Our interest in $\Pi_2^0 \mathrm{ACC}_{\mathbb{N}}$ stems from the fact that for first-order problems, it forms a dichotomy with $C_{\mathbb{N}}$ as the following two theorems (which share a proof) show:

Theorem 6 (ZF + DC + AD). *For any problem* f *exactly one of the following holds:*

1. $^1(f) \leq_W^* C_{\mathbb{N}}$
2. $\Pi_2^0 \mathrm{ACC}_{\mathbb{N}} \leq_W^* f$

Theorem 7 (ZFC). *Let* $f :\subseteq \mathbb{N}^\mathbb{N} \rightrightarrows \mathbb{N}$ *be such that each* $f^{-1}(n)$ *is Borel (in* $\mathbb{N}^\mathbb{N}$*). Then exactly one of the following holds:*

1. $f \leq^*_W C_\mathbb{N}$
2. $\Pi^0_2 \text{ACC}_\mathbb{N} \leq^*_W f$

Proof. Recall that, as shown in [3, Theorem 7.11], a multivalued function f reduces to $C_\mathbb{N}$ if and only if it is computable with finitely many mind-changes. As noted in [18], these multifunctions admit a nice characterization in terms of games, as we now explain. We call the *backtrack game for* f (whose definition is implicit in [25]) the following: player I plays a natural number at every turn, whereas player II has three options, namely she either plays a natural number, or she skips, or she erases all of her previous moves, with the proviso that she can only use this third option finitely many times. Player II wins if either Player I fails to build a point x in the domain of f, or if she builds a point in $f(x)$ following the rules. It is clear that f is computable with finitely many mind changes if and only if Player II has a winning strategy in the backtrack game for f.

Suppose now that f has codomain $\mathbb{N}$, and consider the following game: at every turn, both Player I and Player II play a natural number, and

1. The numbers played by Player I need to form some $p \in \text{dom}(f)$, otherwise he loses.
2. From some time onwards, Player II needs to play a constant number n, otherwise she loses.
3. Finally, Player II wins iff her ultimately choice n satisfies $n \in f(p)$.

It is not difficult to see that Player II has a winning strategy in the game above if and only if it has a winning strategy in the backtrack game for f. Let us see the right-to-left implication, the other one being analogous: suppose Player I is playing according to strategy λ, and let p be the infinite string such that, for every i, $p(i)$ is equal to the last number played by Player II before turn i when she plays according to λ. This way, we forget about all her mind-changes and skips, an only keep the moves in which she played a number. Since playing in $\mathbb{N}$ means that she has only one meaningful move, at some point the sequence p stabilizes. It is clear that if λ was winning and Player I produced the point x, then $\lim p \in f(x)$.

Suppose now that f does not reduce to $C_\mathbb{N}$. By either AD or Borel determinacy, we can suppose that Player *I* has a winning strategy in the game described above. Using the formulation given above of $\Pi^0_2 \text{ACC}_\mathbb{N}$, we see that winning strategy λ of Player I for this game yields a witness for the reduction $\Pi^0_2 \text{ACC}_\mathbb{N} \leq^*_W f$: given $p \in \text{dom} \, \Pi^0_2 \text{ACC}_\mathbb{N}$, we produce a $g(p) \in \text{dom} \, f$ exactly as we did in Theorem 5, namely by putting $g(p) = \lambda(p_{<0})\lambda(p_{<1})\ldots$. The other half of the reduction is given by the identity functional.

Finally, it is enough to observe that $\Pi^0_2 \text{ACC}_\mathbb{N} \nleq^*_W C_\mathbb{N}$ to obtain both theorems.

5   Characterising Admissibility via Discontinuity of Functions

As a side note, we observe that the minimal degree of discontinuity for certain functions into a space can characterize the admissibly represented spaces (amongst the T_0-spaces). Admissibility of represented spaces fundamentally characterizes which represented spaces can be treated as topological spaces. More formally, the categories of admissibly represented spaces and of QCB_0 topological spaces coincide, and are full subcategories of the categories of represented spaces and of sequential topological spaces respectively. Much of the investigation of this notion is due to Schröder [21, 22].

Proposition 9. *The following are equivalent for a T_0 represented space* **X**:

1. **X** *is admissible.*
2. *Every function* $f : (\omega + 1) \to$ **X** *is either continuous (in the represented space sense) or satisfies* $LPO \equiv_W^* f$

Proof. $1 \Rightarrow 2$: Since **X** is admissible, for functions into **X** having a continuous realizer coincides with topological continuity. For a function of type $f : (\omega+1) \to$ **X** topological continuity can only fail if there is some $U \in \mathcal{O}(\mathbf{X})$ such that $\omega \in f^{-1}(U)$, but for infinitely many $n \in \omega$ it holds that $n \notin f^{-1}(U)$. Consider the continuous multivalued function $H : \mathbb{S} \to (\omega + 1)$ that maps $\top$ to any $n \in \omega$ with $n \notin f^{-1}(U)$ and $\bot$ to ω; and the continuous characteristic function $\chi_U : \mathbf{X} \to \mathbb{S}$. We find that $\chi_U \circ f \circ H = (\neg : \mathbb{S} \to \mathbb{S})$, hence $LPO \leq_W^* f$. The reduction $f \leq_W^* LPO$ holds for any function f with domain $\omega + 1$.

$2 \Rightarrow 1$: We have already established that the dichotomy in (2) ensures that for functions of type $f : (\omega+1) \to$ **X**, represented space continuity and realizer continuity coincide. We then note that this property suffices in place of admissibility in the proof of [22, Lemma 11] (establishing that admissibly represented spaces have countable pseudobasis). We conclude that **X** has a countable pseudobase. By [22, Theorem 12], as **X** is also T_0, it is admissible.

To see that we cannot drop the T_0 requirement from the preceding proposition, consider the space $\mathfrak{T}$ of Turing degrees. This is a non-trivial space with the indiscrete topology, so in particular not admissible. However, every function $f : (\omega + 1) \to \mathfrak{T}$ is continuous.

Example 1. Consider the decimal reals $\mathbb{R}_{10}$. As this space is T_0 but not admissible, we know that there must be a function $f : \omega + 1 \to \mathbb{R}_{10}$ with $1 <_W^* f <_W^* LPO$. We find one such example in $f(n) = (-1)^n 2^{-n}$, $f(\omega) = 0$. This function satisfies $f \equiv_W C_2$.

6   Outlook

We believe that our main result, Theorem 1 is the $n = 1$ case of a more general result, which we hope to provide in future work. There is further potential follow-up research. The possible directions include:

1. How does the Weihrauch degree of $\neq_{\mathbf{X}}$ vary with properties of the space $\mathbf{X}$? Of particular interest would be to classify $\neq_{\mathbb{Q}}$ (where $\mathbb{Q}$ is equipped with the Euclidean topology); compare the discussion regarding the degree of overt choice on $\mathbb{Q}$ in [9].
2. What are further interesting dichotomies in the continuous Weihrauch degrees (or substructures thereof), akin to the results in Subsect. 4.2?
3. Can we fully classify the continuous Weihrauch degrees of multivalued functions with domain $(\omega + 1)$? Besides our result in Sect. 3, also the notion of weak k-continuity and results thereabout from [24] seem relevant.

Acknowledgements. The authors are very grateful to Vittorio Cipriani, Eike Neumann, Cécilia Pradic and Manlio Valenti for many helpful discussions on several parts of the paper. Soldà's work was funded by an LMS Early Career Fellowship (ref. 2021-20), and by the FWO grant G0F8421N.

A   Proof of Proposition 3

Proposition 3. *The space $\frac{\mathbf{X}}{\mathbf{Y}}$ is scattered iff both $\mathbf{X}$ and $\mathbf{Y}$ are; and then furthermore:*

$$\mathrm{CBr}\left(\frac{\mathbf{X}}{\mathbf{Y}}\right) = \mathrm{CBr}(\mathbf{X}) + \mathrm{CBr}(\mathbf{Y})$$

Proof. We find that $\frac{x}{\cdot} \in \frac{\mathbf{X}}{\mathbf{Y}}$ is isolated iff $x \in \mathbf{X}$ is isolated. On the other hand, $\frac{\cdot}{y} \in \frac{\mathbf{X}}{\mathbf{Y}}$ is isolated only if $\mathbf{X}$ is the empty space and $y \in \mathbf{Y}$ is isolated. If $\mathbf{Z}'$ denotes the Cantor-Bendixson derivative, it follows that for $\mathbf{X} \neq \emptyset$, we have $\left(\frac{\mathbf{X}}{\mathbf{Y}}\right)' = \frac{\mathbf{X}'}{\mathbf{Y}}$. Together with the observation that $\frac{\emptyset}{\mathbf{Y}} \cong \mathbf{Y}$, the claim follows.

B   Proof of Lemma 1

Lemma 1. $\mathsf{ACC}_{\mathbb{N}} \equiv_{sW} \mathsf{SEQACC}_{\mathbb{N}}$

Proof. We start showing that $\mathsf{ACC}_{\mathbb{N}} \leq_{sW} \mathsf{SEQACC}_{\mathbb{N}}$. An instance of $\mathsf{ACC}_{\mathbb{N}}$ is an enumeration g of an open set U of $\mathbb{N}$ that contains at most one point. We define the inner functional H as follows: at every step s, if nothing was enumerated in U, we let $H(g)_{\leq s} = 0^s$. If instead at stage s g enumerated the number n in U, we set $H(g) = 0^{\langle n, s \rangle} ⌢ 1^{\mathbb{N}}$. After applying $\mathsf{SEQACC}_{\mathbb{N}}$, it is clear that we can take the identity as outer functional.

Next we show that $\mathsf{SEQACC}_{\mathbb{N}} \leq_{sW} \mathsf{ACC}_{\mathbb{N}}$. Again, we only need to define the inner functional H, and we will do it as follows: given a certain sequence $p \in 2^{\mathbb{N}}$, we enumerate nothing in the open set U unless, at step s, we see that $p = 0^s ⌢ 1 ⌢ q$, in which case we enumerate $\pi_1(s)$ in U.

C   Proof of Proposition 4

Proposition 4. *Let $\iota_1 : \mathbf{X} \hookrightarrow \mathbf{Y}_1$, $\iota_2 : \mathbf{X} \hookrightarrow \mathbf{Y}_2$ be two completions of $\mathbf{X}$, and let $\neq_{\mathbf{X}}^1$ and $\neq_{\mathbf{X}}^2$ be the maps defined using those. Then $\neq_{\mathbf{X}}^1 \equiv_{sW} \neq_{\mathbf{X}}^2$.*

Proof. Consider the computable multivalued function $T : \mathbf{Y}_1 \rightrightarrows \mathbf{Y}_2$ provided by Proposition 2. Then $\neq_{\mathbf{X}}^2 \circ T$ tightens $\neq_{\mathbf{X}}^1$, thus $\neq_{\mathbf{X}}^1 \leq_{\mathrm{W}} \neq_{\mathbf{X}}^2$. By symmetry, the claim follows.

D   Proof of Lemma 3

Lemma 3. *Let $f :\subseteq \mathbb{N}^{\mathbb{N}} \rightrightarrows \mathbb{N}$ be a partial multivalued function. Then, the Wadge game for f is determined.*

Proof. We show that if Player I does not have a strategy for the game, then Player II does. To do this, we spell out what it means for Player I to have a winning strategy: Player I has a winning strategy if and only if there is an $x \in \mathrm{dom}\, f$ such that there are infinitely many $t_0 \sqsubset t_1 \sqsubset t_2 \sqsubset \cdots \sqsubset x$ such that, for every $i, j \in \mathbb{N}$, there is an $x_j^i \in \mathrm{dom}\, f$ such that $t_j \sqsubseteq x_j^i$ and $i \notin f(x_j^i)$, as we now show.

Suppose that the condition above holds, then the strategy for Player I consists simply in playing t_j as long as Player II responds by playing $\emptyset$: if Player II ever commits to a certain value i, then by our assumption we have an available move for player I that proves that Player II's commitment is wrong. If Player II never commits, Player I wins since $x \in \mathrm{dom}\, f$.

On the other hand, if Player I has a strategy, we can build an x as above by supposing that Player II constantly skips her turn: it is easy to verify that this describes an x as we want.

Hence, suppose that no x as above exists: this means that for every $x \in \mathrm{dom}\, f$, there is $t_x \sqsubset x$ and an integer i_{t_x} such that every for every $y \in \mathrm{dom}\, f \cap [t_x]$ $i_{t_x} \in f(y)$. This gives rise to a strategy for player II: player II plays $\emptyset$ until player I plays some string in a t_x, for some x (if player I never does this, then it is not producing an element of $\mathrm{dom}\, f$, which guarantees that player II wins), and then responds i_{t_x}.

E   Proofs in Section 4.1

Proposition 5. *Let $\emptyset \neq \mathbf{X} \subseteq \mathbf{Y}$. Then $\neq_{\mathbf{Y}} \leq_{sW} \neq_{\mathbf{X}}$.*

Proof. By the defining properties of the completion, the computable partial map $\mathrm{id} :\subseteq \mathbf{Y} \rightarrow \mathbf{X}$ extends to a computable multivalued map $K : \overline{\mathbf{Y}} \rightrightarrows \overline{\mathbf{X}}$ satisfying $K(x) = x$ for all $x \in \mathbf{X}$. This serves as inner reduction witness, together with $\mathrm{id} : \mathbf{X} \rightarrow \mathbf{Y}$ as outer reduction witness.

Proposition 6. *Let $s : \mathbf{X} \rightarrow \mathbf{Y}$ be a computable surjection, and let $t : \mathbf{Y} \rightrightarrows \mathbf{X}$ be computable with $s \circ t = \mathrm{id}_{\mathbf{Y}}$. Then $\neq_{\mathbf{X}} \leq_{sW} \neq_{\mathbf{Y}}$.*

Proof. The reduction is witnessed by the lifting of s to $\bar{s} : \mathbf{X} \rightrightarrows \mathbf{Y}$ together with the map t.

Corollary 3. *Let* $\mathbf{X}$ *be an uncountable Polish space. Then* $\neq_{\mathbf{X}} \equiv_W^* \neq_{\mathbb{N}^{\mathbb{N}}}$.

Proof. An uncountable Polish space contains a perfect subset, i.e. a subset homeomorphic to Cantor space: if we call this subset $\mathbf{Y}$, Proposition 5 allows us to conclude that $\neq_{\mathbf{X}} \leq_{sW} \neq_{\mathbf{Y}}$, and by the assumption that $\mathbf{Y}$ is homeomorphic to Cantor space, we conclude that $\neq_{\mathbf{X}} \leq_W^* \neq_{\{0,1\}^{\mathbb{N}}}$.[1] Every Polish space has a total Baire space representation up to some oracle (e.g. [1, Corollary 4.4.12]), which via Proposition 6 shows $\neq_{\mathbb{N}^{\mathbb{N}}} \leq_W^* \neq_{\mathbf{X}}$. As $\{0,1\}^{\mathbb{N}}$ and $\mathbb{N}^{\mathbb{N}}$ are mutually embeddable, Proposition 5 also implies that $\neq_{\mathbb{N}^{\mathbb{N}}} \equiv_W \neq_{\{0,1\}^{\mathbb{N}}}$.

Corollary 4. $\neq_{\mathcal{O}(\mathbb{N})} \equiv_{sW} \neq_{\mathbb{N}^{\mathbb{N}}}$

Proof. On the one hand $\mathbb{N}^{\mathbb{N}}$ embeds into $\mathcal{O}(\mathbb{N})$ as a subspace, on the other hand $\mathcal{O}(\mathbb{N})$ has a representation with domain $\mathbb{N}^{\mathbb{N}}$. Thus the claim follows from Propositions 5, 6.

Proposition 7. $\neq_{\mathbb{S}} \equiv_{sW} (\neg : \mathbb{S} \to \mathbb{S}) \equiv_W LPO$

Proof. Notice that $\mathbb{S}$ is multiretraceable, so the first (strong) equivalence follows from Proposition 4. Moreover, it is obvious that $(\neg : \mathbb{S} \to \mathbb{S}) \leq_{sW} LPO$. Whereas it is easy to see that $LPO \leq_W (\neg : \mathbb{S} \to \mathbb{S})$, a straightforward continuity argument yields that this reduction cannot be made strong.

Corollary 5. *Let* $P : \mathbf{X} \rightrightarrows \mathbb{S}$ *be discontinuous. Then* $LPO \leq_W^* P$.

Proof. By combining Theorem 5 with Proposition 7, together with the straightforward observation that generalized Wadge games for multivalued functions with codomain $\mathbb{S}$ are always determined.

Proposition 8. $\neq_{\mathbb{N} \times (\omega+1)} <_W \neq_{\frac{\mathbb{N}}{\mathbb{N}}}$

Proof. The reduction follows via Proposition 6. To see that it is strict we assume for the sake of a contradiction that $\neq_{\frac{\mathbb{N}}{\mathbb{N}}} \leq_W^* \neq_{\mathbb{N} \times (\omega+1)}$ via K and H. We can readily verify that the inner reduction witness H needs to map the completely undefined name in the completion of $\frac{\mathbb{N}}{\mathbb{N}}$ to the completely undefined name in the completion of $\mathbb{N} \times (\omega+1)$. In particular, K will start outputting a name for some $\overline{f(n)}$ upon having read sufficiently long prefixes of the completely undefined name and of $(n, \omega) \in \mathbb{N} \times (\omega + 1)$. Now consider what happens if the original input is changing from being undefined to being $\overline{f(n)}$ after that prefix has passed. For the reduction to work, it needs to be the case that H is mapping this name for $\overline{f(n)}$ to (n, ω), and that K adjusts its output to some $\overline{g(m)}$ depending on which

---

[1] We remark that we cannot hope to do obtain a Weihrauch reduction in place of the continuous Weihrauch reduction: Gregoriades has constructed an uncountable computable Polish space where all computable points are isolated, and all other points are non-hyper-arithmetic [15].

(n, m) it receives from the oracle. However, we can again let a sufficiently long prefix pass, and now adjust the original input to be a name for $\frac{g(m)}{\cdot}$ for some m such that H has already forgone the opportunity to output (n, m) given the prefix already read. This constitutes the desired contradiction.

References

1. Brattka, V.: Recursive and computable operations over topological structures. Ph.D. thesis, FernUniversität Hagen (1999), informatik Berichte 255
2. Brattka, V.: The discontinuity problem. J. Symbolic Logic **88**(3), 1191–1212 (2023). https://doi.org/10.1017/jsl.2021.106
3. Brattka, V., de Brecht, M., Pauly, A.: Closed choice and a uniform low basis theorem. Ann. Pure Appl. Logic **163**(8), 986–1008 (2012). https://doi.org/10.1016/j.apal.2011.12.020
4. Brattka, V., Gherardi, G.: Weihrauch goes Brouwerian. J. Symbolic Logic **85**(4), 1614–1653 (2020). https://doi.org/10.1017/JSL.2020.76
5. Brattka, V., Gherardi, G.: Completion of choice. Ann. Pure Appl. Log. **172**(3), 102914 (2021). https://doi.org/10.1016/J.APAL.2020.102914
6. Brattka, V., Gherardi, G., Pauly, A.: Weihrauch complexity in computable analysis. In: Handbook of Computability and Complexity in Analysis. TAC, pp. 367–417. Springer, Cham (2021). https://doi.org/10.1007/978-3-030-59234-9_11
7. Brattka, V., Hendtlass, M., Kreuzer, A.: On the uniform computational content of computability theory. Theory Comput. Syst. **61**(4) (2017). https://doi.org/10.1007/s00224-017-9798-1
8. Brattka, V., Pauly, A.: On the algebraic structure of Weihrauch degrees. Logical Methods Comput. Sci. **14**(4) (2018). https://doi.org/10.23638/LMCS-14(4:4)2018
9. Brecht, M.d., Pauly, A., Schröder, M.: Overt choice. Computability **9**(3-4), 169–191 (2020). https://doi.org/10.3233/com-190253
10. Cipriani, V., Pauly, A.: Embeddability of graphs and Weihrauch degrees (2023). https://arxiv.org/abs/2305.00935
11. Dzhafarov, D.: Joins in the strong Weihrauch degrees (2017). https://arxiv.org/abs/1704.01494
12. Dzhafarov, D.D., Solomon, R., Valenti, M.: The tree pigeonhole principle in the Weihrauch degrees (2023). https://arxiv.org/abs/2312.10535
13. Dzhafarov, D.D., Solomon, R., Yokoyama, K.: On the first-order parts of problems in the Weihrauch degrees (2023). https:/arXiv:2301.12733
14. Goh, J.L., Pauly, A., Valenti, M.: Finding descending sequences through ill-founded linear orders. J. Symbolic Logic **86**(2) (2021). DOIurl-https://doi.org/10.1017/jsl.2021.15
15. Gregoriades, V.: Classes of Polish spaces under effective Borel isomorphism. Mem. Am. Math. Soc. (2016). https://doi.org/10.1090/memo/1135
16. Higuchi, K., Pauly, A.: The degree-structure of Weihrauch-reducibility. Logical Methods Comput. Sci. **9**(2) (2013). https://doi.org/10.2168/LMCS-9(2:2)2013
17. Hoyrup, M.: The fixed-point property for represented spaces. Ann. Pure Appl. Logic **173**(5) (2022)
18. Nobrega, H., Pauly, A.: Game characterizations and lower cones in the Weihrauch degrees. Logical Methods Comput. Sci. **15**(3), 11.1–11.29 (2019). https://doi.org/10.23638/LMCS-15(3:11)2019

19. Pauly, A.: On the topological aspects of the theory of represented spaces. Computability **5**(2), 159–180 (2016). https://doi.org/10.3233/COM-150049
20. Pequignot, Y.: A Wadge hierarchy for second countable spaces. Archive Math. Logic, 1–25 (2015). https://doi.org/10.1007/s00153-015-0434-y
21. Schröder, M.: Admissible Representations for Continuous Computations. Ph.D. thesis, FernUniversität Hagen (2002)
22. Schröder, M.: Extended admissibility. Theoret. Comput. Sci. **284**(2), 519–538 (2002). https://doi.org/10.1016/S0304-3975(01)00109-8
23. Soldà, G., Valenti, M.: Algebraic properties of the first-order part of a problem. Ann. Pure Appl. Log. **174**(7), 103270 (2023). https://doi.org/10.1016/j.apal.2023.103270
24. Uftring, P.: Weihrauch degrees without roots. Computability (202X). https://arxiv.org/abs/2308.01422
25. Wesep, R.: Wadge degrees and descriptive set theory. In: Kechris, A.S., Moschovakis, Y.N. (eds.) Cabal Seminar 76–77. LNM, vol. 689, pp. 151–170. Springer, Heidelberg (1978). https://doi.org/10.1007/BFb0069298

Complexities of Theories of Profinite Subgroups of S_ω via Tree Presentations

Jason Block[(✉)]

CUNY Graduate Center, New York, NY 10016, USA
jblock@gradcenter.cuny.edu

Abstract. Although S_ω (the group of all permutations of $\mathbb{N}$) is size continuum, both it and its closed subgroups can be presented as the set of paths through a countable tree. The subgroups of S_ω that can be presented this way with finite branching trees are exactly the profinite ones. We use these tree presentations to find upper bounds on the complexity of the existential theories of profinite subgroups of S_ω, as well as to prove sharpness for these bounds. These complexity results enable us to distinguish a simple subclass of profinite groups, those with *orbit independence*, for which we find an upper bound on the complexity of the entire first order theory.

Keywords: Computable structure theory · Permutation groups · Profinite groups · Tree presentations

1 Introduction

Traditional computable structure theory deals only with countable structures. As a result, it cannot be used to study most subgroups of S_ω (the group of all permutations of $\mathbb{N}$). However, as described in Sect. 2, a large class of these subgroups (specifically the *closed* subgroups) can be presented as the set of paths through a countable tree. We will focus our attention on the subgroups that can be presented as the paths through a finite branching tree (the *compact* subgroups), which are exactly the profinite ones. In [5] the author uses such a presentation to study the absolute Galois group of $\mathbb{Q}$, which is indeed a profinite group that can be viewed as a subgroup of S_ω after fixing an enumeration of the algebraic closure of $\mathbb{Q}$.

Much interest in profinite groups stems from their connection to Galois theory. As shown in [8], every profinite group is the Galois group of some field extension. However, the purpose of this paper is to examine profinite groups simply as groups in their own right. It can be difficult to get an effective handle on uncountable groups, but when such a group acts on $\mathbb{N}$ by permutations we are given the opportunity to do so. Thus, we restrict our attention to the profinite subgroups of S_ω.

Effective notions for profinite groups within the context of Galois theory were examined in [4] and further in [3]. Following this work, effective notions for

© The Author(s), under exclusive license to Springer Nature Switzerland AG 2024
L. Levy Patey et al. (Eds.): CiE 2024, LNCS 14773, pp. 366–376, 2024.
https://doi.org/10.1007/978-3-031-64309-5_29

profinite groups in general were studied in [7]. The authors of [3] and [7] define a profinite group to be *recursively profinite* if it is isomorphic to the inverse limit of a uniformly computable sequence of finite groups and surjective homomorphisms. As we will see in Proposition 4, a profinite group P is recursively profinite if and only if it is isomorphic to a subgroup G of S_ω such that T_G (the tree that represents G) is computable. More recently, effectively closed subgroups of S_ω were examined in [2].

In Sect. 3, we use tree presentations to determine bounds on the complexity of the existential theory of profinite subgroups of S_ω. Note that since all elements of S_ω are functions from $\mathbb{N} \to \mathbb{N}$, an existential sentence about a subgroup is a Σ_1^1 statement. However, we will see that the existential theory of any profinite subgroup G of S_ω is Σ_2^0 relative to the degree of T_G. Additionally, if G has *orbit independence*, then the existential theory is Σ_1^0 relative to the degree of T_G. We will also show that these bounds are sharp. Specifically, there exists a profinite G with orbit independence such that T_G is computable and the existential theory of G is Σ_1^0 complete, and such a G without orbit independence such that the existential theory is Σ_2^0 complete. Last, we show that the (entire) first order theory of a profinite G with orbit independence is Δ_2^0 relative to the degree of T_G.

2   Tree Presentations

Definition 1. *Let G be a subgroup of S_ω. We define the tree T_G to be the subtree of $\mathbb{N}^{<\omega}$ containing all initial segments of elements of G. That is,*

$$T_G := \{\tau \in \mathbb{N}^{<\omega} : (\exists g \in G, n \in \mathbb{N})[\tau = g(0)g(1) \cdots g(n)]\}$$

where $m \in \mathbb{N}$ is mapped to $g(m)$ under g. We define the ordering of T_G via initial segments and write $\tau \sqsubset \sigma$ if τ is an initial segment of σ.

It should be noted that T_G will have no terminal nodes. That is, every element of T_G is an initial segment of another.

Definition 2. *Let G be a subgroup of S_ω. We define the degree of T_G to be the join of the Turing degrees of*

- *The domain of T_G under some computable coding of $\mathbb{N}^{<\omega}$ in which $\sqsubset$ is decidable; and*
- *A branching function $Br : T_G \to \mathbb{N} \cup \{\infty\}$ such that $Br(\tau)$ is equal to the number of direct successors of τ in T_G.*

We denote the degree of T_G as $\deg(T_G)$.

We will focus on groups where T_G is finite branching, in which case the range of Br will be a subset of $\mathbb{N}$. It should be noted that $\deg(T_G)$ is not invariant under group isomorphism in that it is possible to have $G \cong G'$ with $\deg(T_G) \neq \deg(T_{G'})$.

Definition 3. *Given a tree* $T \subset \mathbb{N}^{<\omega}$, *we define* $[T]$ *to be the set of all paths through* T. *We endow* $[T]$ *with the standard product topology in which the basic clopen sets are those of the form* $\{f \in \mathbb{N}^\omega : \tau \sqsubset f\}$ *for some* $\tau \in T$.

It is clear that every element of G is represented as a path through T_G. In particular, the function $i : G \to [T_G]$ defined by

$$i(g) = g(0)g(1) \cdots$$

is an embedding. However, it is possible for there to be additional paths through T_G that do not correspond to any element of G in such a way. For example, consider the group G generated by $\{(0\,1), (2\,3), (4\,5), \dots\}$ where $(n\,m)$ denotes the permutation that swaps n and m and leaves everything else fixed. We see that G is countable but $[T_G]$ is size continuum. The following proposition gives a simple topological condition for when a group G corresponds nicely with $[T_G]$.

Proposition 1. *Let* G *be a subgroup of* S_ω. *The map* $i : G \to [T_G]$ *is a bijection if and only if* $i(G)$ *is a closed subset of* $[T_G]$. $\qquad\square$

We say that G is a *closed group* when $i(G)$ is closed. Thus, the subgroups of S_ω that can be represented as the paths through this type of tree are exactly the closed ones. Additionally, we say that G is a *compact group* if $i(G)$ is compact.

Definition 4. *A topological group is called profinite if it is isomorphic to the inverse limit of an inverse system of discrete finite groups.*

The following proposition yields a simple topological definition for profinite groups.

Proposition 2 (Folklore; see e.g. Theorem 3.7 from [6]). *A topological group is profinite if and only if it is Hausdorff, compact, and totally disconnected.* $\qquad\square$

Definition 5. *Given a subgroup* G *of* S_ω *and* $n \in \mathbb{N}$, *we define the orbit of* n *under* G *as*

$$\mathrm{orb}_G(n) := \{g(n) \in \mathbb{N} : g \in G\}.$$

The following proposition is also folklore, but we give a brief proof.

Proposition 3. *Let* G *be a subgroup of* S_ω. *The following are equivalent:*

(1) G is compact,
(2) G is closed and all orbits under G are finite,
(3) G is profinite.

Proof. Suppose that G is compact. Since our topology is Hausdorff, we have that G is closed. By Proposition 1, we have that $i(G) = [T_G]$. Assume towards a contradiction that there is some $n \in \mathbb{N}$ with $\mathrm{orb}_G(n)$ infinite. Let $\{\tau_i\}_{i\in\mathbb{N}}$ be the (infinite) collection of all elements of T_G of length $n + 1$. Note that

$\{\{f : \tau_i \sqsubset f\}\}_{i \in \mathbb{N}}$ is an open cover of $[T_G] = i(G)$ with no finite subcover, which contradicts that G is compact. Hence, (1) $\implies$ (2).

If G is closed and all orbits in G are finite, then it follows that G is compact as a consequence of König's lemma. Hence, (2) $\implies$ (1).

The topology we have defined is Hausdorff and totally disconnected. If G is compact, then G is also profinite by Proposition 2. Hence, (3) $\iff$ (1). $\qquad\square$

We have that all profinite subgroups of S_ω will have countably many orbits (all of which are finite). We fix an enumeration of these orbits as follows:

Definition 6. *Let G be a profinite subgroup of S_ω. Define $\{O_{G,i}\}_{i \in \mathbb{N}}$ so that $O_{G,0} = orb_G(0)$ and $O_{G,n+1}$ is the orbit of the least natural number not in any $O_{G,m}$ with $m \leq n$.*

We can use these orbits to define finite approximations of G up to the first $k \in \mathbb{N}$ many orbits.

Definition 7. *Let G be a profinite subgroup of S_ω. Given $g \in G$ and $k \in \mathbb{N}$, define $g_k = g \restriction \bigcup_{i \leq k} O_{G,i}$. Define*

$$G_k := \{g_k : g \in G\}.$$

We can also define the restriction of G to only the kth orbit.

Definition 8. *Let G be a profinite subgroup of S_ω. Define*

$$H_k := \{g \restriction O_{G,k} : g \in G\}.$$

Note that both G_k and H_k are finite groups for all $k \in \mathbb{N}$. Additionally, they are both uniformly computable given T_G.

Definition 9. *Let G be a profinite subgroup of S_ω. We say that G has orbit independence if it is isomorphic to the Cartesian product of all H_k. That is,*

$$G \cong \prod_{k \in \mathbb{N}} H_k.$$

For an example of a profinite subgroup that does not have orbit independence, consider

$$G = \{1_G, (0\,1)(2\,3)\}$$

where 1_G denotes the identity permutation. Note that $H_0 \cong H_1 \cong C_2$ (the cyclic group on 2 elements) and H_n is trivial for all $n > 1$. Thus, $\prod H_k \cong C_2 \times C_2$ but $G \cong C_2$. As we shall see, groups with orbit independence tend to be simpler to work with.

It should be noted that our definition for the degree of T_G is compatible with the notion of a recursively profinite group used by La Roche and Smith.

Definition 10 ([3,7]). *A profinite group P is called recursively profinite if there exists a uniformly computable sequence $\{P_n, \pi_n\}_{n \in \mathbb{N}}$ such that each P_n is a finite group, each π_n is a surjective homomorphism from P_{n+1} to P_n, and P is isomorphic to the inverse limit of the sequence.*

Proposition 4. *A profinite group P is recursively profinite if and only if it is isomorphic to a subgroup G of S_ω with T_G computable.*

Proof. Suppose that $P \cong G$ with T_G computable. Defining $\nu_n : G_{n+1} \to G_n$ (with G_n as in Definition 8) so that $\nu_n(g_{n+1}) = g_n$, we get that $\{G_n, \nu_n\}_{n \in \mathbb{N}}$ is a uniformly computable sequence as required in Definition 10 whose inverse limit is isomorphic to P.

For the other direction, suppose that $\{P_n, \pi_n\}_{n \in \mathbb{N}}$ is as in Definition 10. For each $n \in \mathbb{N}$, let N_n be a natural number such that P_n is isomorphic to a subgroup of S_{N_n} (the group of permutations of $\{0, ..., N_n - 1\}$). Define $f_0 : P_0 \to S_{N_0}$ such that f_0 is a group embedding. Given f_n, define $f_{n+1} : P_{n+1} \to S_{N_{n+1}}$ such that f_{n+1} is a group embedding and "respects" π_{n+1} in the sense that if $\pi_{n+1}(p_{n+1}) = p_n$, then $f_{n+1}(p_{n+1}) \upharpoonright N_n = f_n(p_n)$. Define G to be the set of $g \in S_\omega$ such that for all $n \in \mathbb{N}$, there exists a $p \in P_n$ with $f_n(p) = g \upharpoonright N_n$. We have that $G \cong P$ and that T_G is exactly the set

$$\{\tau \in \mathbb{N}^{<\omega} : (\exists n \in \mathbb{N}, p \in P_n, m < N_n) [\tau = f_n(p)(0) f_n(p)(1) \cdots f_n(p)(m)]\}.$$

It is clear that the domain and branching function of T_G are computable, hence we have that T_G is computable.   □

3   Complexity of Theories

We now consider the complexity of the existential theory of a profinite subgroup of S_ω. To do so, we must first establish a few lemmas.

Definition 11. *A positive formula is a first order formula that can be expressed without the use of any negation symbols. A negative formula is the negation of a positive formula.*

Lemma 1. *Let G be a profinite subgroup of S_ω and let α^+ be a positive formula in the language of groups. If $k < l$, then*

$$G_l \models \alpha^+(\bar{g}_l) \implies G_k \models \alpha^+(\bar{g}_k)$$

for any $\bar{g} \in G^{<\omega}$.

Proof. If α^+ is quantifier free, than it is expressible as a disjunction of conjunctions of atomic formulas. Recall that an atomic formula in the language of groups is equivalent to the statement that some word is equal to the identity. If $G_l \models \alpha^+(\bar{g}_l)$, then one of the disjuncts must hold which just means that some collection of words $W_1(\bar{g}_l), ..., W_n(\bar{g}_l)$ over the alphabet $\{x, x^{-1} : x \in \bar{g}_l\}$ are all equal to 1_{G_l}. Since each element of $\bar{g}_k$ is an initial segment of an element of $\bar{g}_l$, we must also have that $W_1(\bar{g}_k) = \cdots = W_n(\bar{g}_k) = 1_{G_k}$ and so $G_k \models \alpha^+(\bar{g}_k)$.

Now suppose that the result holds for all Σ_n and Π_n formulas. If α^+ is Σ_{n+1}, then we have $\alpha^+ \equiv \exists \bar{x} \beta^+$ where β^+ is a Π_n positive formula. If $G_l \models (\exists \bar{x}) \beta^+(\bar{g}_l, \bar{x})$ then there exists some $\bar{h} \in G^{<\omega}$ such that $G_l \models \beta^+(\bar{g}_l, \bar{h}_l)$. Since the result holds of Π_n formulas, we get that $G_k \models \beta^+(\bar{g}_k, \bar{h}_k)$ and so $G_k \models \alpha^+(\bar{g}_k)$.

If α^+ is Π_{n+1}, then we have $\alpha^+ \equiv \forall \bar{x} \beta^+$ where β^+ is Σ_n. If $G_l \models (\forall \bar{x}) \beta^+(\bar{g}_l, \bar{x})$ then $G_l \models \beta^+(\bar{g}_l, \bar{h}_l)$ for all $\bar{h} \in G^{<\omega}$. Again, since the result holds for all Σ_n formulas we have that $G_k \models \beta^+(\bar{g}_k, \bar{h}_k)$ and so $G_k \models \alpha^+(\bar{g}_k)$. $\square$

Corollary 1. *Let G, k and l be as in the previous Lemma. If α^- is a negative formula, then*

$$G_k \models \alpha^-(\bar{g}_k) \implies G_l \models \alpha^-(\bar{g}_l)$$

for any $\bar{g} \in G^{<\omega}$. $\square$

Lemma 2. *Let G be a profinite subgroup of S_ω. If α is quantifier free, then $G \models \alpha(\bar{g})$ if and only if $G_k \models \alpha(\bar{g}_k)$ for all sufficiently large $k \in \mathbb{N}$.*

Proof. For the base case, let α be atomic. We have that $\alpha(\bar{x}) \equiv W(\bar{x}) = 1$ where $W(\bar{x})$ is a word over $\{x, x^{-1} : x \in \bar{x}\}$ and 1 is the group identity symbol. Clearly, if $W(\bar{g}) = 1_G$ then $W(\bar{g}_k) = 1_{G_k}$ for all k. On the other hand, if $W(\bar{g}_k) = 1_{G_k}$ for sufficiently large k then we have by the previous lemma that $W(\bar{g}_k) = 1_{G_k}$ for all $k \in \mathbb{N}$. Thus given any $n \in \mathbb{N}$ and a large enough l such that $n \in \text{dom}(\bar{g}_l)$, we have that $W(\bar{g}_l)$ maps n to n. Hence, $W(\bar{g}) = 1_G$.

Negative Step: Let $\alpha \equiv \neg \beta$ with β atomic. Suppose $G \models \neg \beta(\bar{g})$. This gives that there is a k such that $G_k \models \neg \beta(\bar{g}_k)$. By the previous lemma, we must have that $G_l \models \neg \beta(\bar{g}_l)$ for all $l \geq k$ and thus for all sufficiently large l.

Now suppose that $G_k \models \neg \beta(\bar{g}_k)$ for sufficiently large k. There must only be finitely many k such that $G_k \models \beta(\bar{g}_k)$. Thus, from the base case, we have that $G \models \neg \beta(\bar{g})$.

Conjunctive/Disjunctive Step: If the statement holds for β_1 and β_2, then it is clear that it holds for $\beta_1 \& \beta_2$ as well. If the statement holds for β_1 or for β_2, then it is clear that it holds for $\beta_1 \vee \beta_2$ as well. $\square$

Lemma 3. *Every atomic sentence in the language of groups is true in every group.*

Proof. Every such sentence has the form

$$1^n = 1^m$$

with $n, m \in \mathbb{Z}$. $\square$

The following lemma gives an example of the power of orbit independence.

Lemma 4. *Let G be a profinite subgroup of S_ω with orbit independence. Let α be an existential sentence in the language of groups. We have that $G \models \alpha$ if and only if $G_k \models \alpha$ for some $k \in \mathbb{N}$.*

Proof. We have that $\alpha \equiv \exists \bar{x} \beta$ where β is a quantifier free formula. If $G \models \alpha$ then there is some $\bar{g} \in G^{<\omega}$ such that $G \models \beta(\bar{g})$. Thus, Lemma 2 gives that there is a k with $G_k \models \beta(\bar{g}_k)$ and so $G_k \models \alpha$.

Now suppose that $G_k \models \alpha$. We have that for some $\bar{\gamma} \in G_k^{<\omega}$, $G_k \models \beta(\bar{\gamma})$. Define an embedding $f : G_k \to G$ such that $f(\gamma) \restriction \mathrm{dom}(\gamma) = \gamma$ and $f(\gamma)$ is just the identity on all orbits $O_{G,l}$ with $l > k$. Note that since G has orbit independence, we will in fact have that $f(\gamma) \in G$.

Note that

$$\beta(\bar{x}) \equiv \bigvee_i \bigwedge_j \beta_{i,j}^+(\bar{x}) \,\&\, \beta_{i,j}^-(\bar{x})$$

where each β^+ is atomic and each β^- negated atomic. Since $G_k \models \beta(\bar{\gamma})$, there is some i such that $G_k \models \bigwedge_j \beta_{i,j}^+(\bar{\gamma}) \,\&\, \beta_{i,j}^-(\bar{\gamma})$. It is clear that any negated atomic formula that holds of $\bar{\gamma}$ in G_k will also hold of $f(\bar{\gamma})$ in G. Thus if $G \not\models \alpha$, there would have to be some j such that $G \not\models \beta_{i,j}^+(f(\bar{\gamma}))$. However since we are assuming $G_k \models \beta_{i,j}^+(\bar{\gamma})$, there would have to be some $l > k$ such that $H_l \models \neg\beta_{i,j}^+(f(\bar{\gamma}) \restriction O_{G,l})$. Since $\bar{\gamma}$ is just the identity on all orbits $O_{G,l}$ with $l > k$, we would have $H_l \models \neg\beta_{i,j}^+(\bar{1})$. The formula $\beta_{i,j}^+(\bar{1})$ is an atomic sentence in the language of groups, and so by Lemma 3 we get that $H_l \models \beta_{i,j}^+(\bar{1})$. Hence, we must have that $G \models \alpha$. $\square$

Theorem 1. *Let G be a profinite subgroup of S_ω with orbit independence. The existential theory of G is Σ_1^0 relative to $\deg(T_G)$.*

Proof. Let α be an existential sentence. By the previous lemma, $G \models \alpha$ if and only if

$$(\exists k)[G_k \models \alpha]$$

which is Σ_1^0 relative to $\deg(T_G)$. $\square$

The following proposition gives that the above theorem is sharp.

Proposition 5. *There exists a profinite subgroup G of S_ω with orbit independence such that T_G is computable and the existential theory of G is Σ_1^0 complete.*

Proof. By the previous theorem, we need only build a G with T_G computable such that the existential theory codes $\emptyset'$. Define the formula α_n for all $n \in \mathbb{N}$ by

$$\alpha_n := (\exists x)[x \neq 1 \,\&\, x^{p_n} = 1]$$

where 1 is the identity element and $\{p_n\}_{n \in \mathbb{N}}$ is the sequence of all primes. We build G such that $G \models \alpha_n$ if and only if $n \in \emptyset'$.

Construction.

Stage 0: Define $O_{G,0} = \{0\}$ and define H_0 to be the trivial group.

Stage s: Let $N_s \in \mathbb{N}$ be the least not in any $O_{G,i}$ with $i < s$. Find the least $e \leq s$ such that $\Phi_{e,s}(e) \downarrow$ and $G_{s-1} \models \neg\alpha_e$. If no such e exists, define $O_{G,s} = \{N_s\}$ and H_s to be the trivial group. If there is such an e, define $O_{G,s} = \{N_s, N_s + 1, ..., N_s + p_e - 1\}$ and define H_s to be cyclic on $O_{G,s}$.

Verification. Since each G_s is computable, it is clear that the tree T_G is computable. If $n \notin \emptyset'$, then no H_s will be of size p_n. Thus, no element has order p_n, which gives $G \models \neg\alpha_n$. If $n \in \emptyset'$, then there will come a stage t in which n is the least such that $\Phi_{n,t}(e) \downarrow$ and there is currently no H_s of size p_n. We will then make H_t cyclic and of size p_n which will assure that $G \models \alpha_n$. $\qquad\square$

Theorem 2. *Let G be any profinite subgroup of S_ω (not necessarily with orbit independence). The existential theory of G is Σ_2^0 relative to $\deg(T_G)$.*

Proof. Suppose $\alpha = \exists \bar{x} \beta$ with β quantifier free. By Lemma 2, given $\bar{g} \in G^{<\omega}$ we have that $G \models \beta(\bar{g})$ if and only if $G_k \models \beta(\bar{g}_k)$ for all but finitely many $k \in \mathbb{N}$. Let T_β be the subset of T_G defined by

$$T_\beta := \{\tau \in T_G : G_{l(\tau)} \models \beta(\tau))\}$$

where $l(\tau)$ is defined as the natural number such that $\tau \in G_{l(\tau)}$. Note that T_β is computable given T_G. We have that $G \models \alpha$ if and only if

$$(\exists \bar{\tau} \in T_G^{<\omega})(\forall k \geq l(\bar{\tau})) \left[\bigvee_{\bar{\sigma} \in G_k^{<\omega}} \left(\bar{\tau} \sqsubseteq \bar{\sigma} \;\&\; \bigwedge_{\bar{\tau} \sqsubseteq \bar{\rho} \sqsubseteq \bar{\sigma}} \bar{\rho} \in T_\beta \right) \right]$$

which is Σ_2^0 relative to $\deg(T_G)$ (recall that $\deg(T_G)$ computes the branching function T_G, and can thus compute the elements of each G_k). $\qquad\square$

The following proposition gives that the above theorem is sharp.

Proposition 6. *There exists a profinite subgroup G of S_ω (without orbit independence) with T_G computable such that the existential theory of G is Σ_2^0 complete.*

Proof. Recall that the set $\mathrm{Fin} = \{e \in \mathbb{N} : |W_e| < \infty\}$ (where W_e is the domain of Φ_e, the eth Turing program) is Σ_2^0 complete. Let $\{p_n\}_{n \in \mathbb{N}}$ be the sequence of all primes. Given $n \in \mathbb{N}$, define the formula

$$\alpha_n := (\exists x)[x \neq 1 \;\&\; x^{p_n} = 1].$$

We construct G so that

$$G \models \alpha_n \iff n \in \mathrm{Fin}.$$

This, along with Lemma 2, ensures that the existential theory of G is Σ_2^0 complete.

We construct G in stages, defining G_s at stage s of the construction. At stages of the form $s = \langle n, m \rangle$, we work toward making sure that G will model α_n just if W_n is finite. Specifically, if $|W_{n,m+1}| > |W_{n,m}|$ then we make sure that if $g \in G_{s-1}$ with $g \neq 1_{G_{s-1}}$, then any $g' \in G_s$ with $g \sqsubset g'$ has $g'^{p_n} \neq 1_{G_s}$. We also create a new element not equal to 1_{G_s} that is of order p_n. If $W_{n,m+1} = W_{n,m}$, then we define H_s to be the trivial group (thus if $g \sqsubset g'$ with $g \in G_{s-1}$ and $g' \in G_s$, then $g'^{p_n} = 1_{G_s}$ if and only if $g^{p_n} = 1_{G_{s-1}}$).

Construction. Define a bijection $\langle \rangle : \mathbb{N}^2 \to \mathbb{N}$ such that $0 = \langle 0, 0 \rangle$ and $\langle n, m \rangle < \langle n, m + 1 \rangle$ for all $n, m \in \mathbb{N}$. Define $l_0 = 0$. For all $s > 0$, define l_s to be the least natural number not in $O_{G,s-1}$.

Stage $0 = \langle 0, 0 \rangle$: Define $O_{G,0} = \{0, 1\}$ and $H_0 = G_0 = \{(0)(1), (0\,1)\}$.

Stage $s = \langle n, 0 \rangle$ with $n > 0$: Define $O_{G,s} = \{l_s, l_s + 1, ..., l_s + p_n - 1\}$. Define H_s to be the cyclic group on $O_{G,s}$. Define $G_s = \{g^{\frown} h : g \in G_{s-1}, h \in H_s\}$.

Stage $s = \langle n, m \rangle$ with $m > 0$: Check if $|W_{n,m}| > |W_{n,m-1}|$.

- If no, then define $O_{G,s} = \{l_s\}$ and $G_s = \{g^{\frown}(l_s) : g \in G_{s-1}\}$. Note, this gives that H_s is the trivial group.
- If yes, then take N so that this is the Nth time that $|W_{n,x}| > |W_{n,x-1}|$. That is, define

$$N = 1 + |\{x \in \mathbb{N} : 0 < x < m \,\&\, |W_{n,x}| > |W_{n,x-1}|\}|.$$

Define $O_{G,s} = \{l_s, l_s + 1, ..., l_s + p_n^{N+1} - 1\}$ and define H_s to be the cyclic group on $O_{G,s}$. Define t to be the stage that we had added an orbit of size p_n^N. We define

$$G_s = \{g_i^{\frown} h_i : 0 \leq i < p_n^N \,\&\, h_i \in H_s \,\&\, g_i \in G_{s-1} \text{ with } g_i(l_t) - l_t \equiv h_i(l_s) - l_s \mod p_n^N\}.$$

For example, suppose we are at stage $1 = \langle 0, 1 \rangle$. If $W_{0,1} = W_{0,0} = \emptyset$, then we will have

$$G_1 = \{(0)(1)(2), (0\,1)(2)\}.$$

If $W_{0,1} \neq \emptyset$, then we will have

$$G_1 = \{(0)(1)(2)(3)(4)(5), (0)(1)(2\,4)(3\,5), (0\,1)(2\,3\,4\,5), (0\,1)(2\,5\,4\,3)\}.$$

Verification. Since each G_s is computable, it is clear that the tree T_G is computable. Thus we need only show that $G \models \alpha_n$ if and only if $n \in \text{Fin}$.

Lemma 5. *Let* $s = \langle n, m \rangle$ *with* $|W_{n,m}| > |W_{n,m-1}|$. *If* $g \in G_s$ *with* $g^{p_n} = 1_{G_s}$, *then* $g \upharpoonright l_s = 1_{G_{s-1}}$.

Proof (of Lemma 5.) Let N and t be defined as they were at stage $s = \langle n, m \rangle$ of the construction. Note that $(g_i ^\frown h_i)^{p_n} = 1_{G_s}$ if and only if $h_i^{p_n} = 1_{H_s}$ and $g_i^{p_n} = 1_{G_{s-1}}$. Since $h_i^{p_n} = 1_{H_s}$, we must have that $h_i(l_s) \equiv 0 \mod p_n^N$. This gives that $g_i(l_t) = l_t$, and so g_i is the identity permutation when restricted to $O_{G,t}$. Similarly, we will get that g_i is the identity permutation on $O_{G,r}$ for all r of the form $r = \langle n, x \rangle$. In order for $g_i^{p_n} = 1_{G_{s-1}}$, we must also have that g_i is the identity permutation on $O_{G,r}$ for all r that are not of the form $\langle n, x \rangle$ as all of these $O_{G,r}$ will either be of size 1, or of a size not divisible by p_n. Hence, we get that $g_i = g \restriction l_s = 1_{G_{s-1}}$. □

If $n \notin \mathrm{Fin}$, then there will be infinitely many stages s of the form $s = \langle n, m \rangle$ with $|W_{n,m}| > |W_{n,m-1}|$. Let $g \in G$. If $g^{p_n} = 1$, then by Lemma 5 we have $g_{s-1} = g \restriction l_{s-1} = 1_{G_{s-1}}$ for each such s. However, if $g \in G$ was a witness to α_n then we would have by Lemma 2 that $G_k \models g_k \neq 1_{G_k}$ & $g_k^{p_n} = 1_{G_k}$ (where $g_k = g \restriction l_k$) for all but finitely many k, which is a contradiction. Hence, there is no witness to α_n in G and so $G \models \neg\alpha_n$.

Now suppose that $n \in \mathrm{Fin}$. We have that there is a least natural number m such that W_n gains no new elements after stage m. This gives that for $s = \langle n, m \rangle$, $|H_s|$ is a multiple of p_n, but no H_x with $x > s$ will have $|H_x|$ divisible by p_n. Note that by our instructions, there will be an element $g \in G_s$ that is not the identity, but is of order p_n. Since we will never have $|W_{n,x}| > W_{n,x-1}$ for any $x > s$, we will have that there is an element of G that is equal to g on G_s, and is equal to the identity on all orbits higher than that of G_s. This element will be a witness to α_n. □

So far we have only considered existential theories. We conclude by now expanding to entire first order theories for subgroups with orbit independence, which we show to be Δ_2^0 relative to $\deg(T_G)$ as a consequence of the following theorem of Feferman and Vaught.

Theorem 3 (Theorem 6.6 from [1]). *Given any first order $\mathcal{L}$-sentence ϕ, we can compute $n \in \mathbb{N}$ such that for every family $\{A_i : i \in I\}$ of $\mathcal{L}$-structures there exists $J \subseteq I$ with $|J| \leq n$ such that if $\prod_{i \in I} A_i \models \phi$, then $\prod_{i \in J'} A_i \models \phi$ for all J' with $J \subseteq J' \subseteq I$.* □

Corollary 2. *Let G be a profinite subgroup of S_ω with orbit independence. Let α be any first order sentence in the language of groups. We have $G \models \alpha$ if and only if $G_k \models \alpha$ for all sufficiently large $k \in \mathbb{N}$.*

Proof. Since G has orbit independence, we have that $G \cong \prod_{i \in \mathbb{N}} H_i$. If $G \models \alpha$, then Corollary 3 gives that there is some finite $J \subset \mathbb{N}$ such that if $J' \supseteq J$, then $\prod_{i \in J'} H_i \models \alpha$. Thus, for all $k \geq \max(J)$ we have $G_k \models \alpha$. For the other direction note that if $G \nvDash \alpha$, then $G \models \neg\alpha$ and so the same reasoning gives that $G_k \models \neg\alpha$ for sufficiently large k. □

Theorem 4. *Let G be a profinite subgroup of S_ω with orbit independence. The first order theory of G is Δ_2^0 relative to $\deg(T_G)$.*

Proof. Let $\mathrm{Th}(G)$ denote the first order theory of G. By Corollary 2 we have that $\alpha \in \mathrm{Th}(G)$ if and only if

$$(\exists l)(\forall k > l)[G_k \models \alpha]$$

which is Σ_2^0 relative to $\deg(T_G)$. On the other hand, we have $\alpha \notin \mathrm{Th}(G)$ if and only if

$$(\exists l)(\forall k > l)[G_k \models \neg\alpha]$$

which is Σ_2^0 relative to $\deg(T_G)$. Hence, both $\mathrm{Th}(G)$ and its complement are Σ_2^0 relative to $\deg(T_G)$ and so $\mathrm{Th}(G)$ is Δ_2^0 relative to $\deg(T_G)$. □

This draws a strong distinction between the complexity of theories of profinite groups with and without orbit independence. Note that by the proof of Proposition 6 it is possible for just the existential theory of G to be Σ_2^0 complete relative to $\deg(T_G)$ when G does not have orbit independence. However, the entire first order theory of G will be Δ_2^0 relative to $\deg(T_G)$ when G has orbit independence.

References

1. Feferman, S., Vaught, R.: The first order properties of products of algebraic systems. Fundam. Math. **47**(1), 57–103 (1959)
2. Greenberg, N., Melnikov, A., Nies, A., Turetsky, D.: Effectively closed subgroups of the infinite symmetric group. Proc. Am. Math. Soc. **146**(12), 5421–5435 (2018)
3. La Roche, P.: Effective Galois theory. J. Symbolic Logic **46**(2), 385–392 (1981)
4. Metakides, G., Nerode, A.: Effective content of field theory. Ann. Math. Logic **17**, 289–320 (1979)
5. Miller, R.: Computability for the absolute Galois group of ℚ. To appear, available at arXiv:2307.08935
6. Osserman, B.: Inverse limits and profinite groups. Electronic manuscript
7. Smith, R.: Effective aspects of profinite groups. J. Symbolic Logic **46**(4), 851–863 (1981)
8. Waterhouse, W.: Profinite groups are Galois groups. Proc. Am. Math. Soci. **42**(4), 639–640 (1974)

On the Existence of Infinite Monomial Division Chains with Finitely Many Indeterminates

Chris J. Conidis[✉]

College of Staten Island, New York, USA
chris.conidis@csi.cuny.edu

Abstract. Let R be a ring, and let $\overrightarrow{X} = \{X_0, X_1, \ldots, X_N\}$, $N \in \mathbb{N}$, finitely many indeterminate variables. We introduce a combinatorial principle in this context called MDC that produces, for any given infinite sequence of monomials

$$Z_0, Z_1, Z_2, \ldots, Z_k, \ldots \in R[\overrightarrow{X}], \ k \in \mathbb{N},$$

of strictly increasing degree, an infinite subsequence

$$Z_{k_0}, Z_{k_1}, \cdots, Z_{k_n}, \cdots, \ n \in \mathbb{N},$$

such that for each n we have that Z_{k_n} divides $Z_{k_{n+1}}$. We show that, in the context of Reverse Mathematics and Subsystems of Second-Order Arithmetic, MDC is an arithmetical principle equivalent to $B\Sigma_2 + WO(\mathbb{N}^{\mathbb{N}})$, where $B\Sigma_2$ is a bounding principle for Σ_2 formulas equivalent to the Infinite Pigeonhole Principle (over RCA_0), and $WO(\mathbb{N}^{\mathbb{N}})$ asserts that finite sequences of natural numbers $\mathbb{N}^{\mathbb{N}}$ are well-ordered via the length-lexicographic ordering.

1 Introduction

If $\mathbb{N} = \{0, 1, 2, \ldots\}$ denotes the set of natural numbers, then a well-known algebraic fact called the Hilbert Basis Theorem (HBT) says that, for any field F[1], the (finitely generated polynomial) ring $F[\overrightarrow{X}] = F[X_1, X_2, \ldots, X_n]$ is Noetherian (i.e. satisfies the ascending chain condition on its ideals) for any natural number n. This classic result was first established by Hilbert [7] via nonconstructive methods. Later on, Buchberger's Algorithm [6, Theorem 15.9] for computing Gröbner Bases in $F[\overrightarrow{X}]$ yielded a constructive (computable) argument for the Hilbert Basis Theorem using the well-foundedness of the ordinal $\mathbb{N}^{\mathbb{N}}$. After Buchberger's results, Simpson [12] showed that, in the context of Reverse Mathematics and subsystems of Second-Order Arithmetic (see [5,13] for more

---

[1] Recall that a field is essentially any "number system" with commutative addition and multiplication operations such that any nonzero element has a multiplicative inverse.

© The Author(s), under exclusive license to Springer Nature Switzerland AG 2024
L. Levy Patey et al. (Eds.): CiE 2024, LNCS 14773, pp. 377–389, 2024.
https://doi.org/10.1007/978-3-031-64309-5_30

details), the Hilbert Basis Theorem for $F[\vec{X}]$ is logically equivalent to the First-Order statement asserting the well-ordering of $\mathbb{N}^\mathbb{N}$. The main aim of this article is to:

1. introduce a combinatorial principle called MDC, that assserts the existence of infinite monomial division chains in any infinite sequence of monomials, and is employed in the standard proof of the Hilbert Basis Theorem for finitely generated polynomial rings with coefficients in a given Noetherian ring,
2. catalog the relationship between MDC and other combinatorial principles previously studied in the context of Reverse Mathematics, and finally
3. give two different proofs of MDC from two incomparable axiom systems in the context of Reverse Mathematics.

In particular, we will show that the strength of MDC is strictly stronger than the one for polynomial rings over fields characterized by Simpson in [12]. Moreover, in addition to classifying its strength in the context of Reverse Mathematics and subsystems of Second-Order Arithmetic, we will show (see Sect. 2.3 below for more details) exactly how this principle is related to (i.e. yields) the Hilbert Basis Theorem in the context of polynomial rings with coefficients in a given Noetherian ring R possessing a (generalized) division algorithm that effectively determines when a given ring element is in the ideal generated by finitely many elements. A final open question asks whether MDC is *necessary* to prove this version of the Hilbert Basis Theorem. Along the way we observe that, under the assumption that $\mathbb{N}^\mathbb{N}$ is well-ordered, monomials under the division relation form well-quasi-orderings. Moreover, a consequence of our main result characterizing MDC shows that it is equivalent to a combinatorial principle for well-quasi-orderings called wqo(set) introduced and studied by Cholak, Marcone, and Solomon in [2].

2   Preliminaries

To begin with, let $\mathbb{N} = \{0, 1, 2, \ldots\}$ denote a possibly nonstandard set of natural numbers, and for any $N \in \mathbb{N}$, define

$$\mathbb{N}^N = \underbrace{\mathbb{N} \times \mathbb{N} \times \cdots \times \mathbb{N}}_{N}.$$

We identify $N \in \mathbb{N}$ with the set of natural numbers preceding it

$$N = \{0, 1, \ldots, N-1\}.$$

Since we are working exclusively in the context of Second-Order Arithmetic, all of the structures that we will consider are countable.

For any $N \in \mathbb{N}$,
$$\vec{X} = \{X_0, X_1, \ldots, X_N\}$$

is a set of indeterminate variables, and we can speak of $\vec{X}$–monomials that are products of the form

$$\prod_{i=0}^{N} X_i^{\alpha_i}, \ \alpha_i \in \mathbb{N}.$$

We can identify a monomial m with its sequence of exponents

$$m \sim \langle \alpha_0, \alpha_1, \ldots, \alpha_N \rangle = \langle \alpha_i : i \in N+1 \rangle \in \mathbb{N}^{N+1}.$$

We say that a monomial $m_0 \sim \langle \alpha_{i,0} : i \in N+1 \rangle$ *divides* a monomial $m_1 \sim \langle \alpha_{i,1} : i \in N+1 \rangle$ whenever we have that

$$\alpha_{i,0} \leq \alpha_{i,1}, \ i = 0, 1, \ldots, N,$$

and this corresponds to division in polynomial rings (see [5] for basic definitions and facts about polynomial rings). We write $x \mid y$ to mean that x divides y. Recall that the *degree* of the monomial $m = \langle \alpha_i : i \in N+1 \rangle$ is

$$\deg(m) = \sum_{i=0}^{N} \alpha_i \in \mathbb{N}.$$

We assume a familiarity with basic Commutative Ring Theory, as found in [1,4,6,10]. For us, R will always refer to a countable commutative ring with identity element $1 = 1_R \in R$. Recall that an *ideal* of R (R–ideal) is a subset of R closed under addition, subtraction, and multiplication by all R–elements. For any finite sequence $a_0, a_1, \ldots, a_n \in R$, $n \in \mathbb{N}$, define

$$\langle a_0, a_1, a_2, \ldots, a_n \rangle_R = \left\{ \sum_{i=0}^{n} r_i \cdot a_i : r_i \in R \right\}.$$

Recall that R is *Noetherian* if it satisfies the ascending chain condition (ACC) on its ideals. This means that R is not Noetherian whenever it contains an infinite strictly ascending chain of ideals

$$I_0 \subsetneq I_1 \subsetneq I_2 \subsetneq \cdots \subsetneq I_k \subsetneq \cdots \subsetneq R, \ k \in \mathbb{N}.$$

If R is a ring, then its *division algorithm* is the relation

$$x \in \langle a_0, a_1, \ldots, a_N \rangle_R,$$

$N \in \mathbb{N}$, $x, a_0, a_1, \ldots, a_N \in R$. Finally, recall that the Hilbert Basis Theorem (HBT) says that, for each ring R and $n \in \mathbb{N}$, the polynomial ring

$$R[\vec{X}] = R[X_0, X_1, \ldots, X_n]$$

is Noetherian whenever R is Noetherian.

2.1   Reverse Mathematics

Induction over RCA$_0$. We assume familiarity with the arithmetical hierarchy consisting of the Σ_n and Π_n arithmetic formulas; more information on this topic can be found in either [14, Chapter 4] or [5, Section 5.2]. Throughout this article we will always assume a hypothesis denoted RCA$_0$ that, generally speaking, validates computable mathematical constructions via Δ_1^0−comprehension, along with a restricted induction scheme called IΣ_1 that grants induction for arithmetic formulas of complexity Σ_1 consisting of a Δ_1^0−predicate preceded by a single existential quantifier. It is well-known that, over RCA$_0$, the Σ_n−induction scheme is equivalent to the Π_n−induction scheme, and moreover the Σ_{n+1}−induction scheme is strictly stronger than the Σ_n−induction scheme. For more information on the formalism of Reverse Mathematics and RCA$_0$, we refer the reader to either [13, Chapter II] or [5, Chapter 5]. For us, Σ_1−induction is subsumed in RCA$_0$, and IΣ_2 will be the strongest arithmetical principle that we refer to throughout this article.

B$\Sigma_2$and the Infinite Pigeonhole Principle. There is another logical principle denoted BΣ_2 that is implied by IΣ_2 and says that for any Δ_1^0 formula ϕ with free variables A, x, y, $A \subseteq \mathbb{N}$, $x, y \in \mathbb{N}$, and corresponding Σ_2−predicate

$$\varphi = (\exists x)(\forall y > x)\phi,$$

for any given $N \in \mathbb{N}$ there exists $x_N \in \mathbb{N}$ such that

$$\varphi(a) \text{ if and only if } (\forall y > x_N)\phi(a), \text{ for all } a \in N + 1.$$

BΣ_2 is called the Σ_2−Bounding Principle, or simply Σ_2−Bounding. Moreover, a well-known result of Hirst says that, over RCA$_0$, BΣ_2 is equivalent to the Infinite Pigeonhole Principle that says for any $N \in \mathbb{N}$ and function $f : \mathbb{N} \to N$ there exists $n \in N$ such that the fiber $f^{-1}(n) \subseteq \mathbb{N}$ is infinite. In light of Hirst's result, we will use BΣ_2 to refer to the Infinite Pigeonhole Principle.

The Well-Ordering of $\mathbb{N}^\mathbb{N}$. Recall that a linearly ordered set is *well-ordered* if it does not contain any infinite strictly descending sequences. We use WO($\mathbb{N}^\mathbb{N}$) to denote the principle that says, for each $n \in \mathbb{N}$, the (standard) lexicographic ordering on set of length-n sequences of natural numbers $\mathbb{N}^n$ is a well-ordering. By [12, Proposition 2.6], this is equivalent to saying that the length-lexicographic ordering on finite sequences of natural numbers $\mathbb{N}^\mathbb{N}$ is a well-ordering. Moreover, Simpson has analyzed the reverse mathematical strength of HBT for polynomial rings of the form

$$K[\overrightarrow{X}] = K[X_0, X_1, \ldots, X_N], \ N \in \mathbb{N},$$

where K is a field, and found that, over RCA$_0$, WO($\mathbb{N}^\mathbb{N}$) is equivalent to the assertion that for any field K and $N \in \mathbb{N}$, $K[\overrightarrow{X}]$ is a Noetherian ring. The proof is essentially a formalization of Buchberger's Algorithm [6, Chapter 15] for computing Gröbner Bases via multivariate polynomial division in RCA$_0$. One consequence of Simpson's result is that, over RCA$_0$, WO($\mathbb{N}^\mathbb{N}$) proves that if

$$Z_0, Z_1, \ldots, Z_k, \ldots, \ k \in \mathbb{N},$$

is an infinite sequence of $\overrightarrow{X}$−monomials, then for some $k \neq \ell$, $k, \ell \in \mathbb{N}$, we have that Z_k divides Z_ℓ. We will use this fact later on to show that $\mathsf{WO}(\mathbb{N}^{\mathbb{N}})$ along with the Chain-Antichain Principle for infinite partial orders implies MDC over $\mathsf{RCA_0}$.

2.2 Preliminary Combinatorics Related to MDC

We begin this section by formally stating MDC, the combinatorial principle whose proof-theoretic strength the following section examines in detail.

Theorem 1 (MDC). *Fix a finite set of indeterminates $\overrightarrow{X} = \{X_0, X_1, \ldots, X_N\}$, $N \in \mathbb{N}$, and suppose that*

$$Z_0, Z_1, Z_2, \ldots, Z_k, \ldots, \quad k \in \mathbb{N},$$

is an infinite sequence of $\overrightarrow{X}$−monomials of strictly increasing degree. Then there is a subsequence of natural numbers

$$k_0 < k_1 < k_2 < \cdots < k_n < \cdots, \quad n, k_n \in \mathbb{N},$$

such that

$$Z_{k_n} \mid Z_{k_{n+1}}$$

for all $n \in \mathbb{N}$.
We call $\{Z_{n_k}\}_{n \in \mathbb{N}}$ a monomial division chain *(for $\{Z_k\}_{k \in \mathbb{N}}$).*

Monomials Under the Division Relation Form a Well-Partial-Order, Which is Also a Well-Quasi-Order

Definition 1. *A partial order is a pair $\mathcal{P} = (P, \leq_P)$ such that $P \subseteq \mathbb{N}$ and $\leq_P$ is a binary reflexive antisymmetric and transitive relation on P.*

Definition 2. *A quasi-order is a pair $\mathcal{Q} = (Q, \leq_Q)$ such that $Q \subseteq \mathbb{N}$ and $\leq_Q$ is a binary reflexive transitive relation on Q.*

It is trivial to see that every partial order is a quasi-order.

Definition 3. *A partial order $\mathcal{P} = (P, \leq_P)$ is a well partial order (WPO) if for each function $f : \mathbb{N} \to P$ we have that $f(n) \leq_P f(m)$ for some $n \leq_{\mathbb{N}} m$.*
A quasi-order $\mathcal{Q} = (Q, \leq_Q)$ is a well-quasi-order (WQO) if for each function $f : \mathbb{N} \to Q$ we have that $f(n) \leq_Q f(m)$ for some $n \leq_{\mathbb{N}} m$.

It is trivial to see that every well partial order is a well-quasi-order. Therefore, every claim about all well-quasi-orders is also true for all well partial orders.

Remark 1. Let $\overrightarrow{X} = \{X_0, X_1, \ldots, X_N\}$, $N \in \mathbb{N}$, be a finite set of indeterminates generating the monomial set M, and let $\leq_M$ denote the binary division relation such that for all $m_1, m_2 \in M$, we have that $m_1 \leq_M m_2$ if and only if m_1 divides m_2. Then it follows that

$$\mathcal{M} = (M, \leq_M)$$

is both a partial order and a quasi-order. Moreover, Simpson [12] has shown that, under the assumption of $\mathsf{WO}(\mathbb{N}^\mathbb{N})$, $\mathcal{M}$ is a WPO and WQO. Thus, any statement pertaining to all WQOs is also true of $\mathcal{M}$.

We now give two proofs of MDC that we will eventually make use of in the following section that proves our main results. The first proof of MDC is essentially [2, Lemma 3.4], which says that the Chain-Antichain Principle for infinite partial orders (CAC) implies that every infinite WQO has an infinite nondescending sequence of elements; the reader can consult [8] for more details on the computational aspects of this interesting combinatorial principle that is implied by the Ramsey's Theorem for pairs. Our second proof of MDC is more direct and follows from the relatively benign axiom that is $\mathsf{RCA}_0 + \mathsf{I}\Sigma_2$. More specifically, our second proof of MDC uses the Σ_2−induction axiom $\mathsf{I}\Sigma_2$ in its RCA_0−equivalent form of Π_2^0−comprehension for finite (i.e. bounded) sets.

Definition 4. *Let $\mathcal{P} = (P, \leq_P)$ be a parial order with universe P and order relation $\leq_P$, and let $X \subseteq P$. We call X a* chain *if for any $x, y \in P$ we have that either $x \leq_P y$ or $y <_P x$. On the other hand, we say that X is an* antichain *if for any $x, y \in X$, neither $x \leq_P y$ nor $y \leq_P x$ whenever $x \neq y$.*

Note that there is an infinite partial order that is neither a chain nor an antichain.

Theorem 2 (Chain-Antichain Theorem for Infinite Partial Orders (CAC). *Let $\mathcal{P} = (\mathbb{N}, \leq_P)$ be an infinite partial order. Then there is an infinite $X \subseteq \mathbb{N}$ such that the partial (sub)order $\mathcal{X} = (X, <_X)$, where $<_X$ is the restriction of $<_P$ to X, is either a chain or an antichain.*

Proof (First proof of Theorem 1; [2, Lemma 3.4]). Let $\overrightarrow{X} = \{X_0, X_1, \ldots, X_N\}$, $N \in \mathbb{N}$, be given, and let $\{Z_k\}_{k \in \mathbb{N}}$ be an infinite sequence of $\overrightarrow{X}$−monomials of strictly increasing degree. Define a partial order $\mathcal{P} = (\mathbb{N}, <_P)$ via

$$k <_P \ell, \quad \text{whenever} \quad Z_k \mid Z_\ell.$$

Now, CAC says that $\mathcal{P}$ contains an infinite suborder $\mathcal{X} = (X, <_X)$ that is either a chain or an antichain. However, Buchberger's Algorithm for computing Gröbner Bases [6, Chapter 15], which follows from $\mathsf{WO}(\mathbb{N}^\mathbb{N})$ (see [13, Section 3] for more details), implies that in any infinite sequence of monomials there exist two monomials one of which divides the other. This excludes the possibility that $\mathcal{X}$ is an antichain, and so $\mathcal{X}$ is a chain and (by our construction of $<_X$) we have that

$$Z_x \mid Z_y$$

for any $x, y \in X$, $x < y$. In other words X corresponds to an infinite monomial division chain of $\{Z_k\}_{k \in \mathbb{N}}$.

Proof (Second proof of Theorem 1). First note that, since $|\vec{X}| = N + 1$ it has 2^{N+1}−many subsets. We identify each indeterminate $X \in \vec{X}$ with its index, essentially identifying $\vec{X}$ with $N + 1 \subset \mathbb{N}$, and, as we previously discussed, every $\vec{X}$−monomial m can be identified with a finite sequence of natural numbers

$$Z_k \sim \langle \alpha_{0,k}, \alpha_{1,k}, \ldots, \alpha_{N,k} \rangle \in \mathbb{N}^N, \text{ where } Z_k = \prod_{i=0}^{N} X_i^{\alpha_{i,k}}.$$

Now (via $I\Sigma_2$ in the guise of Bounded Π_2−Comprehension) let $I \subseteq \mathcal{P}(N + 1)$ be defined as follows:

$$I = \{ S \subseteq N + 1 : (\forall n)(\exists k)(\forall i \in S)[\alpha_{i,k} \geq n] \}.$$

In other words I contains those subsets $S \subseteq \vec{X}$ for which there exist infinitely many numbers $k \in \mathbb{N}$ such that the coordinates (exponents) of those (indeterminate) indices in S strictly increase, uniformly in k. Moreover, since $\deg(Z_k) > k$, by the Infinite Pigeonhole Principle it follows that there exists an indeterminate index $i \in N + 1$ with a corresponding infinite strictly increasing sequence of natural numbers $\{k_n\}_{n \in \mathbb{N}}$ such that for each $n \in \mathbb{N}$ we have that

$$\alpha_{i,k_n} \geq n.$$

Thus, I contains some nonempty element $\{i\} \subseteq \vec{X}$.

Let $Y \in I$, $Y \subseteq N + 1$, be maximal with respect to inclusion. By our construction of I there is an infinite strictly increasing sequence $\{k_n\}_{n \in \mathbb{N}}$ such that for each n,

$$\alpha_{y,k_n} \geq n, \; y \in Y,$$

and by the maximality of $Y \in I$, for each $i \in (N + 1) \backslash Y$ there exists $\alpha_i \in \mathbb{N}$ such that

$$\alpha_{i,k_n} \leq \alpha_i, \; n \in \mathbb{N}.$$

Now, since $Y \subset N + 1$ is finite, by $B\Sigma_2$ there exists an exponent $\alpha \in \mathbb{N}$ such that for each $i \in (N + 1) \backslash Y$ and $n \in \mathbb{N}$ we have that

$$\alpha_{i,k_n} \leq \alpha.$$

Furthermore, via the Infinite Pigeonhole Principle applied to "monomial pigeons" Z_{k_n}, $n \in \mathbb{N}$, and pigeonholes made up of the finitely many α−bounded sequences of (natural numbers) exponents corresponding to indeterminate indices in $(N + 1) \backslash Y$ appearing in Z_{k_n}, we can assume that α_{i,k_n} is independent of $n \in \mathbb{N}$ (i.e. constant), for each $i \in (N + 1) \backslash Y$. Finally, it follows from our construction of I and the fact that $Y \in I$, that for each $n \in \mathbb{N}$ and $i \in N + 1$ we can refine $\{k_n\}_{n \in \mathbb{N}}$ by taking an infinite computable subsequence if required so that without any loss of generality the following two conditions are satisfied:

− $\alpha_{i,k_n} < \alpha_{i,k_{n+1}}$ when $i \in Y$, and
− $\alpha_{i,k_n} = \alpha_{i,k_{n+1}}$ when $i \notin Y$,

from which it follows that the $\{Z_{k_n}\}_{n \in \mathbb{N}}$ are an infinite monomial division chain.

384   C. J. Conidis

2.3   The Significance of Monomial Division Chains in the Context of the Hilbert Basis Theorem

We show the significance of MDC by revealing its role in the standard proof of the Hilbert Basis Theorem first espoused by Hilbert, and now found throughout the field. Recall that the Hilbert Basis Theorem [4, Section 9.6, Theorems 21 & 22] says that if R is a Noetherian ring, $N \in \mathbb{N}$, and $\overrightarrow{X} = \{X_0, X_1, \ldots, X_N\}$, then the polynomial ring

$$R[\overrightarrow{X}] = R[X_0, X_1, \ldots, X_N]$$

in the indeterminates $\overrightarrow{X}$ with coefficients in R is also Noetherian. This is equivalent to saying that R is not Noetherian whenever $R[\overrightarrow{X}]$ is not a Noetherian ring, or that R contains an infinite strictly ascending chain of ideals whenever $R[\overrightarrow{X}]$ contains such a chain. We prove this via MDC in the following paragraphs. Before that, however, recall that we can linearly (well) order the $\overrightarrow{X}$−monomials based on the lexicographic ordering on exponents, and this gives rise to the notion of the *leading monomial* and corresponding *leading coefficient* of any nonzero $R[\overrightarrow{X}]$−polynomial.

Let $\{I_k\}_{k \in \mathbb{N}}$ be an infinite strictly ascending chain of ideals in $R[\overrightarrow{X}]$, and for each $k \in \mathbb{N}$ let $x_k \in I_{k+1} \backslash I_k \subseteq R[\overrightarrow{X}]$. It follows that for each $k \in \mathbb{N}$,

$$x_k \notin \langle x_0, x_1, \ldots, x_{k-1} \rangle_{R[\overrightarrow{X}]} \subseteq I_k.$$

For each $k \in \mathbb{N}$, let $r_k \in R$ be the leading coefficient of x_k, and let m_k be its leading monomial, so that $r_k m_k$ is its *leading summand*. Under the assumption that R possesses a division algorithm we can take for granted that, for each $k \in \mathbb{N}$, we have that

$$r_k m_k \notin \langle r_0 m_0, r_1 m_1, \ldots, r_{k-1} m_{k-1} \rangle_{R[\overrightarrow{X}]}.$$

There are now two cases to consider.

The first case says that $\{\deg(m_k) : k \in \mathbb{N}\}$ is bounded (i.e. finite), then by the Infinite Pigeonhole Principle[2] there is an infinite set of natural numbers $\{k_n\}_{n \in \mathbb{N}}$ such that the monomial $m_{k_n} = m$ does not depend on n. Now, since

$$r_{k_{n+1}} m_{k_{n+1}} \notin \langle r_{k_0} m_{k_0}, r_{k_1} m_{k_1}, \ldots, r_{k_n} m_{k_n} \rangle_{R[\overrightarrow{X}]},$$

or in this case

$$r_{k_{n+1}} m \notin \langle r_{k_0} m, r_{k_1} m, \ldots, r_{k_n} m \rangle_{R[\overrightarrow{X}]},$$

it follows that

$$r_{k_{n+1}} \notin \langle r_{k_0}, r_{k_1}, \ldots, r_{k_n} \rangle_R,$$

for each $n \in \mathbb{N}$, and so the ideals

$$J_n = \langle r_{k_0}, r_{k_1}, \ldots, r_{k_n} \rangle_R, \ n \in \mathbb{N},$$

---

[2] Later on we will show that MDC implies BΣ_2 over RCA$_0$. Therefore, our use of the Infinite Pigeonhole Principle can be thought of as an implicit utilization of MDC.

form an infinite strictly ascending R–chain.

The second case says that $\{\deg(m_k) : k \in \mathbb{N}\}$ is unbounded. In this case there is an infinite subsequence of $\{m_k\}_{k \in \mathbb{N}}$ of strictly increasing degree. Furthermore we can apply MDC to this subsequence to obtain an infinite sequence of natural numbers $\{k_n\}_{n \in \mathbb{N}}$ such that $\{m_{k_n}\}_{n \in \mathbb{N}}$ is an infinite division chain of $\vec{X}$–monomials, i.e. we have that

$$m_{k_a} \mid m_{k_b}$$

for all $a, b \in \mathbb{N}$, $a < b$. Similar to the previous paragraph, since

$$r_{k_{n+1}} m_{k_{n+1}} \notin \langle r_{k_0} m_{k_0}, r_{k_1} m_{k_1}, \ldots, r_{k_n} m_{k_n} \rangle_{R[\vec{X}]},$$

and

$$m_{k_0}, m_{k_1}, \ldots, m_{k_n} \mid m_{k_{n+1}},$$

it follows that

$$r_{k_{n+1}} \notin \langle r_{k_0}, r_{k_1}, \ldots, r_{k_n} \rangle_R$$

for each $n \in \mathbb{N}$, and so

$$J_n = \langle r_{k_0}, r_{k_1}, \ldots, r_{k_n} \rangle_R$$

forms an infinite strictly ascending R–chain.

3 Our Main Results: Two Different Proofs of MDC over RCA$_0$ via Two Incomparable Subsystems of Second-Order Arithmetic

Theorem 3 (RCA$_0$ + IΣ_2). (MDC) *Fix a finite set of indeterminates* $\vec{X} = \{X_0, X_1, \ldots, X_N\}$, $N \in \mathbb{N}$, *and suppose that*

$$Z_0, Z_1, Z_2, \ldots, Z_k, \ldots, \quad k \in \mathbb{N},$$

is an infinite sequence of $\vec{X}$–*monomials of strictly increasing degree. Then there subsequence of natural numbers*

$$n_0 < n_1 < n_2 < \cdots < n_k < \cdots, \quad k, n_k \in \mathbb{N},$$

such that

$$Z_{n_k} \mid Z_{n_{k+1}}$$

for all $k \in \mathbb{N}$.

Proof. The reader can verify that our second proof of Theorem 1 in the previous section utilizes

- Bounded Π_2^0–Comprehension (equivalent to IΣ_2);
- BΣ_2 (which follows from IΣ_2); and
- the Infinite Pigeonhole Principle (equivalent to BΣ_2 which follows from IΣ_2);

386   C. J. Conidis

and is therefore valid in $\mathsf{RCA}_0 + \mathsf{I}\Sigma_2$.

The following theorem is a consequence of [2, Lemma 3.20], which is a more general statement regarding WQOs. The proof given there is essentially the same as the one that follows here.

Theorem 4 (RCA_0). MDC *implies* $\mathsf{B}\Sigma_2$.

Proof. Assume that $\mathsf{B}\Sigma_2$ fails via finitely many finite sets

$$A_0, A_1, A_2, \ldots, A_N, \ N \in \mathbb{N},$$

that partition $\mathbb{N}$. Let $R = \mathbb{Q}[\vec{X}] = \mathbb{Q}[X_0, X_1, \ldots, X_N]$, and define an infinite sequence of R−monomials $Z_0, Z_1, Z_2, \ldots, Z_n, \ldots, n \in \mathbb{N}$, via

$$Z_n = X_j^n$$

for the unique $j \in \mathbb{N}$, $0 \leq j \leq N$, such that $n \in A_j$. Since each Z_n is the power of some indeterminate X_j, it follows that

$$Z_k \mid Z_\ell$$

only if $k, \ell \in A_j$, and since A_j is finite there cannot exist an infinite monomial division chain.

A proof of the following theorem is also given in [2, Lemma 3.4] in the more general context of WQOs.

Theorem 5 ($\mathsf{RCA}_0 + \mathsf{WO}(\mathbb{N}^{\mathbb{N}})$). CAC *implies* MDC.

Proof. The reader can verify that our first proof of Theorem 1 in the previous section above is valid in $\mathsf{RCA}_0 + \mathsf{CAC} + \mathsf{WO}(\mathbb{N}^{\mathbb{N}})$. Recall that a consequence of [12, Lemma 3.4] is that $\mathsf{RCA}_0 + \mathsf{WO}(\mathbb{N}^{\mathbb{N}})$ can prove that in any infinite sequence of monomials there must exist a pair of monomials one of which divides the other.

The following corollaries summarize our work so far.

Corollary 1 (RCA_0). MDC *is implied by both the arithmetic axiom* $\mathsf{I}\Sigma_2$, *as well as the second-order axiom* $\mathsf{CAC} + \mathsf{WO}(\mathbb{N}^{\mathbb{N}})$.

Corollary 2 (RCA_0). MDC *implies* $\mathsf{B}\Sigma_2$ *and* $\mathsf{WO}(\mathbb{N}^{\mathbb{N}})$.

Now, since $\mathsf{I}\Sigma_2$ is an arithmetic axiom system, there are models of RCA_0 in which $\mathsf{I}\Sigma_2$ holds, but CAC does not. On the other hand an eventual consequence of the following theorem is that there exist models of Second-Order Arithmetic in which $\mathsf{CAC} + \mathsf{WO}(\mathbb{N}^{\mathbb{N}})$ is satisfied but $\mathsf{I}\Sigma_2$ is not. In summary, $\mathsf{I}\Sigma_2$ and CAC are incomparable subsystems of Second-Order Arithmetic in which (we have now seen that) MDC holds.

Corollary 3 (RCA$_0$). *Let* $\mathbb{N}$ *be a model of First-Order Arithemtic in which* $B\Sigma_2 + WO(\mathbb{N}^\mathbb{N})$ *holds. Then* $\mathbb{N}$ *is the first-order part of a model* $\mathcal{M}$ *of Second-Order Arithmetic in which* WQO *holds.*

Proof. Our second proof of Theorem 1 can be applied in the context of WQOs to show that WQO is implied by $I\Sigma_2$. Meanwhile, [2, Lemma 3.4] (similar to our first proof of Theorem 1) explains why WQO follows from CAC+WO($\mathbb{N}^\mathbb{N}$). Now, a result of Chong, Slaman, and Yang [3, Corollary 5.2] says that any model of $B\Sigma_2$ can be extended to a model of CAC without changing its first-order part, and hence without changing its arithmetical theory. Thus, if we begin with a model $\mathcal{M}_1$ of RCA$_0$ + $B\Sigma_2$ + WO($\mathbb{N}^\mathbb{N}$) with first-order part $\mathbb{N}$, then [3, Corollary 5.2] says that $\mathcal{M}_1$ can be extended to a model $\mathcal{M}_2$ of RCA$_0$ + $B\Sigma_2$ + WO($\mathbb{N}^\mathbb{N}$) + CAC with first-order part $\mathbb{N}$. Now, via our first proof of Theorem 1 in the previous section which also applies in the more general context of WQOs via [2, Lemma 3.4], it follows that WQO holds in $\mathcal{M}_2$.

Corollary 4 (RCA$_0$). MDC *and* WQO *are each strictly stronger than either* $B\Sigma_2$ *or* WO($\mathbb{N}^\mathbb{N}$), *and neither implies* $I\Sigma_2$.

Proof. In an unpublished manuscript [11] Simpson has shown that $B\Sigma_2$ and WO($\mathbb{N}^\mathbb{N}$) are incomparable over RCA$_0$, i.e. neither one implies the other and therefore the conjunction $B\Sigma_2 + WO(\mathbb{N}^\mathbb{N})$ is strictly stronger than either individual principle $B\Sigma_2$, WO($\mathbb{N}^\mathbb{N}$). In the same manuscript Simpson also shows that $B\Sigma_2 + WO(\mathbb{N}^\mathbb{N})$ is strictly weaker than (i.e. does not prove) $I\Sigma_2$.[3]

If we let $\mathbb{N}$ be a model of First-Order Arithmetic in which $B\Sigma_2 + WO(\mathbb{N}^\mathbb{N})$ holds but $I\Sigma_2$ does not, then Corollary 3 above says that $\mathbb{N}$ can be extended to a model of Second-Order Arithemtic $\mathcal{M}$ in which CAC $+ B\Sigma_2 + WO(\mathbb{N}^\mathbb{N}) + \neg I\Sigma_2$ holds, and Theorems 3 and 5 above say that WQO (and hence MDC) is valid in $\mathcal{M}$. Therefore, $\mathcal{M}$ witnesses the fact that WQO and MDC do not imply $I\Sigma_2$.

4 Avenues for Further Research

Our results here suggest the following two avenues of further research, one of which pertains to MDC, and another pertaining to HBT which we have not directly addressed here other than our remarks in Sect. 2.3 above that essentially show how HBT for rings that possess division algorithms follows from MDC over RCA$_0$.

4.1 Problem 1: Characterizing MDC over RCA$_0$

In general we desire characterizations of MDC and WQO over RCA$_0$.

Question 1 (RCA$_0$). Is MDC equivalent to WQO? Or are there models of MDC + $\neg$WQO?

---

[3] The results referred to in this paragraph were probably known prior to [11]; they are referred to diagrammatically in [9, page 69].

In the previous section we showed that our two proofs of Theorem 1 above are indeed different. More precisely our results show that WQO and MDC are each

- implied by $(\mathsf{CAC} + \mathsf{WO}(\mathbb{N}^{\mathbb{N}})) \wedge \mathsf{I}\Sigma_2$, and
- imply $\mathsf{B}\Sigma_2 + \mathsf{WO}(\mathbb{N}^{\mathbb{N}})$,

and thus raises the following question.

Question 2 (RCA$_0$). Characterize the strengths of WQO and MDC by showing, for each principle, that it is either

- equivalent to $(\mathsf{CAC} + \mathsf{WO}(\mathbb{N}^{\mathbb{N}})) \wedge \mathsf{I}\Sigma_2$, or
- equivalent to $\mathsf{B}\Sigma_2 + \mathsf{WO}(\mathbb{N}^{\mathbb{N}})$, or else
- strictly between these upper and lower bounds.

Remark 2. Establishing the first item would essentially involve a proof of CAC via $\mathsf{RCA}_0 + \mathsf{WQO} + \neg\mathsf{I}\Sigma_2$, which would be interesting to see.

4.2 Problem 2: Characterizing HBT over RCA$_0$

Recall that HBT denotes the Hilbert Basis Theorem which says that for each $n \in \mathbb{N}$ and Noetherian ring R with a division algorithm, the polynomial ring $R[\vec{X}] = R[X_0, X_1, \ldots, X_N]$ is Noetherian.

Our analysis of MDC here is motivated by HBT because MDC plays the key role in every known proof of HBT. However, we do not yet know the exact reverse mathematical strength of HBT over RCA$_0$, and therefore cannot say definitively whether or not MDC is an essential assumption in the proof of HBT. Simpson [12] has shows that HBT implies $\mathsf{WO}(\mathbb{N}^{\mathbb{N}})$, and our remarks in Subsect. 2.3 above can be formalized in Second-Order Arithmetic to show that HBT follows from MDC over RCA$_0$.

Theorem 6 (RCA$_0$). HBT *implies* $\mathsf{WO}(\mathbb{N}^{\mathbb{N}})$, *and is implied by* $\mathsf{CAC} + \mathsf{WO}(\mathbb{N}^{\mathbb{N}})$ (MDC).

However, Simpson [11] has shown that $\mathsf{WO}(\mathbb{N}^{\mathbb{N}})$ is not equivalent to $\mathsf{WO}(\mathbb{N}^{\mathbb{N}}) + \mathsf{B}\Sigma_2$, and thus the exact strength of HBT remains open.

Question 3. What is the exact strength of HBT over RCA$_0$? Is HBT equivalent to $\mathsf{WO}(\mathbb{N}^{\mathbb{N}})$? Is it equivalent to $\mathsf{B}\Sigma_2 + \mathsf{WO}(\mathbb{N}^{\mathbb{N}})$? Or is it strictly in between?

Remark 3. It is interesting to note that a proof of HBT via $\mathsf{WO}(\mathbb{N}^{\mathbb{N}})$ would require novel algebraic methods that do not filter through MDC. On the other hand, if HBT is equivalent to $\mathsf{WO}(\mathbb{N}^{\mathbb{N}}) + \mathsf{B}\Sigma_2$ that would imply that MDC is necessary to prove HBT (as suggested thus far by empirical evidence).

References

1. Atiyah, M.F., MacDonald, I.G.: Introduction to Commutative Algebra. Perseus (1969)
2. Cholak, P.A., Marcone, A., Solomon, D.R.: Reverse mathematics and the equivalence of definitions for well and better quasi-orders. J. Symbolic Logic **69**(3), 683–712 (2004)
3. Chong, C.T., Slaman, T.A., Yang, Y.: Π_1^1-conservation of combinatorial principles weaker than Ramsey's theorem for pairs. Adv. Math. **230**(3), 1060–1077 (2012)
4. Dummit, D.S., Foote, R.M.: Abstract Algebra. Wiley, Hoboken (1999)
5. Dzhafarov, D.D., Mummert, C.: Reverse Mathematics. Springer, Cham (2022)
6. Eisenbud, D.: Commutative Algebra with a View Toward Algebraic Geometry. Springer, New York (1995)
7. Hilbert, D.: Über die theorie der algebraischen formen. Math. Ann. **36**(4), 473–534 (1890)
8. Hirschfeldt, D.R., Shore, R.A.: Combinatorial principles weaker than Ramsey's theorem for pairs. J. Symb. Log. **71**, 171–206 (2007)
9. Hájek, P., Pudlák, P.: The Metamathematics of First-Order Arithmetic. Cambridge University Press, Cambridge (2016)
10. Matsumura, H.: Commutative Ring Theory. Cambridge University Press, Cambridge (2004)
11. Simpson, S.G.: Comparing WO(ω^ω) with Σ_2^0 induction. https://arxiv.org/abs/1508.02655
12. Simpson, S.G.: Ordinal numbers and the Hilbert basis theorem. J. Symbolic Logic **53**(3), 961–974 (1988)
13. Simpson, S.G.: Subsystems of Second Order Arithmetic, 2nd edn. Cambridge University Press, Cambridge (2009)
14. Soare, R.I.: Turing Computability. Springer, Heidelberg (2016)

A Weak First-Order Theory of Sequences

Lars Kristiansen[1,2]($\boxtimes$) and Juvenal Murwanashyaka[3]

[1] Department of Mathematics, University of Oslo, Oslo, Norway
larsk@math.uio.no
[2] Department of Informatics, University of Oslo, Oslo, Norway
[3] Institute of Mathematics of the Czech Academy of Sciences, Prague,
Czech Republic
murwanashyaka@math.cas.cz

Abstract. We introduce a first-order theory Seq which is mutually interpretable with Robinson's Q. The universe of a standard model for Seq consists of sequences. We prove that Seq directly interprets the adjunctive set theory AST, and we prove that Seq interprets the tree theory T and the set theory AST + EXT.

1 Introduction

First-order theories like Robinson's Q, Grzegorczyk's TC and adjunctive set theory AST serve as important metamathematical tools. These are natural theories given by a handful of transparent axioms. They are all mutually interpretable with each other and also with a number of other natural theories, e.g., tree theories studied in Kristiansen & Murwanashyaka [9], Damnjanovic [3,4] and Murwanashyaka [11], and concatenation theories studied in Murwanashyaka [10].

At a first glance all these theories might seem very weak, and they are indeed weak, but it turns out that they provide the building blocks needed to construct (interpret, encode, formalise, emulate, reconstruct, ... pick you choice) substantial mathematics. This (maybe somewhat unexpected) strength stems from the theories' ability to represent sequences. Intuitively, access to sequences seems to be both necessary and sufficient in order to construct substantial parts of mathematics. Now, it is rather tricky to deal with sequences in weak number theory (Q), see Nelson [6] and Chapter V of Hajek & Pudlak [8]; neither is it all that straightforward in concatenation theory (TC) as we encounter the growing comma problem, see Visser [13]. It might be easier in weak set theory (AST), but still it is far from trivial.

In this paper we introduce Seq which is designed to be a minimal first-order theory mutually interpretable with Q (we conjecture that Seq is minimal in the sense that it will not interpret Q if we remove any of its five axioms). Moreover, it is designed to provide, as directly as possible, the means needed to represent sequences. This implies that Seq in some respects may be a more natural starting point for a construction of mathematics than the theories discussed above. Seq provides directly the basic building blocks we need to represent sequences. In the

L. Levy Patey et al. (Eds.): CiE 2024, LNCS 14773, pp. 390–404, 2024.
https://doi.org/10.1007/978-3-031-64309-5_31

other theories we need to put effort into building these basic building blocks. Of course, when we work in Seq, we have to represent, let us say, natural numbers by sequences, but it is both easier and more natural to represent natural numbers by sequences than it is to represent sequences by natural numbers.

We do not claim that Seq is more natural than other theories in any absolute sense. A theory will of course have its own distinctive features, and e.g., Q is a very natural starting point for Nelson's investigations into predicative arithmetic [6], and TC is a very natural theory from Grzegorczyk's [7] point of view since he wants to "formulate the proof of undecidability not on the grounds of arithmetic but directly on a theory of text". We just claim that Seq is a natural theory from a certain point of view, and it is not on our agenda to discuss if this naturalness is a matter of taste or a matter of deeper (philosophical or mathematical) nature.

An Overview of the Paper. In Sect. 2 we introduce the theory Seq, together with a weaker variant called WSeq. We prove that the two theories have a certain strength, and moreover, we prove that Seq directly interprets AST, and thus, Seq is a sequential theory (a theory is *sequential* by definition if it directly interprets AST). In the two subsequent sections (3 and 4) we explain how the tree theory T, and how the adjunctive set theory AST + EXT, can be interpreted into Seq. In Sect. 5 we supplement these (admittedly somewhat sketchy) explanations with a number of technical details (and even more details are available in [1]). The techniques used towards the end of the paper might be of some independent interest: We represent finite binary trees and hereditarily finite sets by certain sequences of natural numbers which we call *snakes*.

We will not prove the theorem below in this paper.

Theorem 1. Q *interprets* Seq *(the axioms of* Seq *is given in Fig. 1).*

A full proof of the theorem will for sure be long and technical, but still, we think it should be clear that the theorem can be proved by using techniques described in Chapter V of Hajek & Pudlak [8].

Discussion of Some Related Work. Our work should be compared to some work of Damnjanovic [2] [3]. Prior to this work of Damnjanovic, it was known that AST interprets Q. In [2], Damnjanovic introduces the concatenation theory QT and proves that Q interprets QT and that QT interprets AST + EXT. Thus, since AST interprets Q, it follows from the results in [2] that AST interprets AST + EXT. By the same token, just replace QT with Seq, it follows from our results that AST interprets AST + EXT. Kristiansen & Murvanashyaka [9] introduces the tree theory T. They prove that T interprets Q and conjecture that Q interprets T. Damnjanovic [3] proves that Q indeed interprets T by proving that QT interprets T. We prove that Seq interprets T. Thus it also follows the results in this paper that Q interprets T.

These considerations show that there are certain similarities between our work and the work of Damnjanovic: when Damnjanovic resorts to QT, we resort to Seq. To the authors, these similarities have become apparent in hindsight, and they may reflect that QT and Seq share some salient features.

Seq_1 $\forall xy[\ x \vdash y \neq e\ ]$
Seq_2 $\forall x_1 x_2 y_1 y_2[\ x_1 \vdash x_2 = y_1 \vdash y_2\ \rightarrow\ (\ x_1 = y_1\ \wedge\ x_2 = y_2\ )\ ]$
Seq_3 $\forall x[\ x \circ e = x\ ]$
Seq_4 $\forall xyz[\ x \circ (y \vdash z) = (x \circ y) \vdash z\ ]$
Seq_5 $\forall x[\ x = e\ \vee\ \exists yz[\ x = y \vdash z\ ]\ ]$

Fig. 1. The axioms of Seq.

2   The Theories Seq and WSeq

Let $\mathcal{L}$ be the first-order language $\{e, \vdash, \circ\}$ where $\vdash$ and $\circ$ are binary function symbols and e is a constant symbol. The $\mathcal{L}$-theory Seq is given by the five axioms in Fig. 1.

We define the set of *sequences* inductively: the empty sequence () is a sequence; $(s_1, s_2, \ldots, s_n)$ is a sequence if $s_1, \ldots, s_n$ are sequences (for any $n > 0$).

We define the standard model $\mathfrak{S}$ for the theory Seq. The universe of $\mathfrak{S}$ is the set of all sequences (as defined above). Furhermore, $e^{\mathfrak{S}} = ()$; the operator $\vdash^{\mathfrak{S}}$ appends an element to a sequence, that is

$$(s_1, s_2, \ldots, s_n) \vdash^{\mathfrak{S}} (t_1, t_2, \ldots, t_m) = (s_1, s_2, \ldots, s_n, (t_1, t_2, \ldots, t_m))$$

for any sequence $(s_1, s_2, \ldots, s_n)$ and any sequence $(t_1, t_2, \ldots, t_m)$; the operator $\circ^{\mathfrak{S}}$ concatenates two sequences, that is

$$(s_1, s_2, \ldots, s_n) \circ^{\mathfrak{S}} (t_1, t_2, \ldots, t_m) = (s_1, s_2, \ldots, s_n, t_1, t_2, \ldots, t_m)$$

for any sequence $(s_1, s_2, \ldots, s_n)$ and any sequence $(t_1, t_2, \ldots, t_m)$.

For any $\mathcal{L}$-terms t_1, t_2 the formula $t_1 \sqsubseteq t_2$ is shorthand for $\exists y[t_1 \circ y = t_2]$, and the formula $t_1 \not\sqsubseteq t_2$ is shorthand for $\neg t_1 \sqsubseteq t_2$. The formula $\forall x \sqsubseteq t[\phi]$ is shorthand for $\forall x[x \sqsubseteq t \rightarrow \phi]$. We define the Σ-*formulas* inductively: ϕ and $\neg\phi$ are Σ-formulas if ϕ is an atomic $\mathcal{L}$-formula; $s \sqsubseteq t$ and $s \not\sqsubseteq t$ are Σ-formulas if s and t are $\mathcal{L}$-terms; $\alpha \wedge \beta$ and $\alpha \vee \beta$ are Σ-formulas if α and β are Σ-formulas; $\exists x[\phi]$ is a Σ-formula if ϕ is a Σ-formula and x is a variable; $\forall x \sqsubseteq t[\phi]$ is a Σ-formula if ϕ is a Σ-formula, x is a variable and t is an $\mathcal{L}$-term that does not contain x.

For any sequence s, we define $\bar{s}$ by $\overline{(s_1, \ldots, s_n)} = (\ldots ((e \vdash \overline{s_1}) \vdash \overline{s_2}) \ldots) \vdash \overline{s_n}$ and $\overline{()} = e$. The first-order theory WSeq is given by the axioms in Fig. 2 (we conjecture that WSeq is mutually interpretable with Robinson's R). A detailed proof of the next theorem can be found in [1].

Theorem 2 (Σ-completeness of WSeq). *For any Σ-sentence ϕ, we have*

$$\mathfrak{S} \models \phi\ \Rightarrow\ \text{WSeq} \vdash \phi.$$

Lemma 3. *For any sequence s, we have*

$$\text{Seq} \vdash \forall x\ [\ x \sqsubseteq \bar{s}\ \leftrightarrow\ \bigvee_{t \in \mathcal{I}(s)} x = \bar{t}\ ]$$

where $\mathcal{I}(s)$ is the set of all initial segments of s.

The non-logical axioms of WSeq are given by the three axioms schemes:

(WSeq$_1$) $$\bar{s} \neq \bar{t}$$

where s and t are distinct sequences.

(WSeq$_2$) $$\overline{(s_1, \ldots, s_n)} \circ \overline{(t_1, \ldots, t_m)} = \overline{(s_1, \ldots, s_n, t_1, \ldots, t_m)}$$

for any sequences $(s_1, \ldots, s_n)$ and $(t_1, \ldots, t_m)$.

(WSeq$_3$) $$\forall x [\, x \sqsubseteq \bar{s} \;\rightarrow\; \bigvee_{t \in \mathcal{I}(s)} x = \bar{t} \,]$$

where s is a sequence and $\mathcal{I}(s)$ is the set of all initial segments of s.

Fig. 2. The non-logical axioms of WSeq.

Proof. We prove the lemma by induction on the complexity of the sequence s.

Assume $s = ()$. Then, $\bar{s} = e$ and $\bigvee_{t \in \mathcal{I}(s)} x = \bar{t}$ will simply be the formula $x = e$. Thus, we have to prove that $\mathsf{Seq} \vdash x \sqsubseteq e \leftrightarrow x = e$. In order to prove the right-left implication, assume that $x = e$. Then we need to prove that $e \sqsubseteq e$. This holds since we have $e \circ e = e$ by Seq_3. In order to prove the left-right implication assume that $x \sqsubseteq e$. Then there exists w such that $e = x \circ w$. By Seq_5, we can split the proof into the case (i) $w = e$ and the case (ii) $w = v \vdash u$ for some v, u. In case (i), we have $x = e$ by Seq_3. In case (ii) we have a contradiction: By Seq_4 we have $e = x \circ (v \vdash u) = (x \circ v) \vdash u$ which contradicts Seq_1. Thus, $x \sqsubseteq e$ if and only if $x = e$.

Assume $s = (s_1, \ldots, s_{n+1})$. Let $s' = (s_1, \ldots, s_n)$. Observe that $\mathcal{I}(s) = \mathcal{I}(s') \cup \{s\}$ and $\bar{s} = \bar{s'} \vdash \overline{s_{n+1}}$. Clearly, $t \in \mathcal{I}(s)$ implies $\bar{t} \sqsubseteq \bar{s}$, and thus $\bigvee_{t \in \mathcal{I}(s)} x = \bar{t}$ implies $x \sqsubseteq \bar{s}$. In order to prove the left-right implication assume that $x \sqsubseteq \bar{s}$. Then there exists w such that $\bar{s} = x \circ w$. By Seq_5, we split the proof into the case (i) $w = e$ and the case (ii) $w = v \vdash u$ for some v, u. In case (i), we have $x = \bar{s}$ by Seq_3. In case (ii), we have $\bar{s'} = x \circ v$ by Seq_4 and Seq_2, which by the induction hypothesis, implies $x = \bar{t}$ for some $t \in \mathcal{I}(s)$. Thus, $x \sqsubseteq \bar{s}$ if and only if $x = \bar{t}$ for some $t \in \mathcal{I}(s)$. □

Theorem 4 (Σ-completeness of Seq). *The theory Seq is an extension of the theory WSeq, that is, we have*

$$\mathsf{WSeq} \vdash \phi \;\Rightarrow\; \mathsf{Seq} \vdash \phi$$

for any $\mathcal{L}$-formula ϕ (and thus, Seq is Σ-complete).

Proof. It is easy to see that Seq proves any instance of the axiom scheme WSeq$_1$ (use Seq_1 and Seq_2). We prove that Seq proves any instance of WSeq$_2$ by induction on the length of the sequence $(t_1, \ldots, t_m)$. Let $(t_1, \ldots, t_m)$ be the empty sequence $()$. Then $\overline{(t_1, \ldots, t_m)} = e$, and WSeq$_2$ holds by Seq_3. Let $m > 0$. Then we have $\overline{(s_1, \ldots, s_n)} \circ \overline{(t_1, \ldots, t_m)} = \overline{(s_1, \ldots, s_n, t_1, \ldots, t_m)}$ by Seq_4 and

$$\text{AST}_1 \quad \exists y \forall x [\, x \notin y \,] \qquad\qquad\qquad\qquad\qquad \text{(empty set)}$$
$$\text{AST}_2 \quad \forall xy \exists z \forall u [\, u \in z \leftrightarrow (\, u \in x \lor u = y \,) \,] \quad \text{(adjunction)}$$
$$\text{EXT} \quad \forall xy [\, \forall z [\, z \in x \leftrightarrow z \in y \,] \rightarrow x = y \,]. \quad \text{(extensionality)}$$

Fig. 3. The axioms of AST + EXT. The theory AST consists only of AST_1 and AST_2.

the induction hypothesis. Finally, Seq proves any instance of WSeq_3 by Lemma 3.   □

The theory AST is given by the axioms AST_1 and AST_2 in Fig. 3. We will prove that Seq directly interprets AST. From now on, we may skip the concatenation operator in first-order formulas and simply write st in place of $s \circ t$.

We define the direct translation $\cdot^\tau$. Let $(x \in y)^\tau = \exists v_1 v_2 [(v_1 \vdash x) v_2 = y]$. Then, $(\text{AST}_1)^\tau$ is $\exists y \forall x \neg \exists v_1 v_2 [\, (v_1 \vdash x) v_2 = y \,]$, and $(\text{AST}_2)^\tau$ is

$$\forall xy \exists z \forall u [\, \exists v_1 v_2 [(v_1 \vdash u) v_2 = z] \leftrightarrow (\, \exists v_1 v_2 [(v_1 \vdash u) v_2 = x] \lor u = y \,) \,].$$

Theorem 5. *We have (I)* $\text{Seq} \vdash (\text{AST}_1)^\tau$ *and (II)* $\text{Seq} \vdash (\text{AST}_2)^\tau$ *(and thus, AST is directly interpretable in* Seq*).*

Proof. We will prove $\text{Seq} \vdash \forall x v_1 v_2 [(v_1 \vdash x) v_2 \neq e]$ (then clause (I) follows by pure logic). Let v_1, x, v_2 be arbitrary. By Seq_5, we have *(i)* $v_2 = e$ or *(ii)* $v_2 = w_1 \vdash w_2$ for some w_1, w_2. *Case (i)*: By Seq_3, we have $(v_1 \vdash x) v_2 = v_1 \vdash x$, and by Seq_1, we have $(v_1 \vdash x) v_2 \neq e$. *Case (ii)*: By Seq_4, we have $(v_1 \vdash x) v_2 = (v_1 \vdash x)(w_1 \vdash w_2) = ((v_1 \vdash x) w_1) \vdash w_2$ and thus, by Seq_1, we have $(v_1 \vdash x) v_2 \neq e$. This proves (I). Clause (II) follows from

(†) $\text{Seq} \vdash \exists v_1 v_2 [\, (v_1 \vdash u) v_2 = x \vdash y \,] \rightarrow (\, \exists v_1 v_2 [\, (v_1 \vdash u) v_2 = x \,] \lor u = y \,)$
(‡) $\text{Seq} \vdash (\, \exists v_1 v_2 [\, (v_1 \vdash u) v_2 = x \,] \lor u = y \,) \rightarrow \exists v_1 v_2 [\, (v_1 \vdash u) v_2 = x \vdash y \,]$

by pure logic. First we prove (†). Assume that v_1, v_2 are such that $(v_1 \vdash u) v_2 = x \vdash y$. By Seq_5, we have *(i)* $v_2 = e$ or *(ii)* $v_2 = w_1 \vdash w_2$ for some w_1, w_2. *Case (i)*: By Seq_3, we have $x \vdash y = (v_1 \vdash u) v_2 = v_1 \vdash u$, and thus we have $u = y$ by Seq_2. *Case (ii)*: We have $x \vdash y = (v_1 \vdash u) v_2 = (v_1 \vdash u)(w_1 \vdash w_2) = ((v_1 \vdash u) w_1) \vdash w_2$ by Seq_4, and by Seq_2, we get $x = (v_1 \vdash u) w_1$. Hence we have $\exists v_1, v_2 [(v_1 \vdash u) v_2 = x]$. This proves (†).

We turn to the proof of (‡). Assume we have $(w_1 \vdash u) w_2 = x$ for some w_1, w_2. By Seq_4, we have $x \vdash y = (w_1 \vdash u) w_2 \vdash y = (w_1 \vdash u)(w_2 \vdash y)$, and hence, we have $\exists v_1 v_2 [(v_1 \vdash u) v_2 = x \vdash y]$. Assume that $u = y$. By Seq_3, we have $(x \vdash y) e = x \vdash y$, and hence, we have $\exists v_1 v_2 [(v_1 \vdash u) v_2 = x \vdash y]$. This proves (‡).   □

Mycielski et al. [5] have proved that AST interprets Q. Hence, AST is an essentially undecidable theory, moreover, any theory that interprets AST will also be essentially undecidable. The notion of a sequential theory is explained in

$$T_1 \quad \forall xy[\ \langle x,y \rangle \neq \bot\ ]$$
$$T_2 \quad \forall x_1 x_2 y_1 y_2[\ \langle x_1,x_2 \rangle = \langle y_1,y_2 \rangle\ \rightarrow\ (\ x_1 = y_1\ \wedge\ x_2 = y_2\ )\ ]$$
$$T_3 \quad \forall x[\ x \sqsubseteq \bot\ \leftrightarrow\ x = \bot\ ]$$
$$T_4 \quad \forall xyz[\ x \sqsubseteq \langle y,z \rangle\ \leftrightarrow\ (\ x = \langle y,z \rangle \vee x \sqsubseteq y \vee x \sqsubseteq z\ )\ ]\ .$$

Fig. 4. The axioms of T

Visser [12]. By definition, a theory is sequential iff it directly interprets AST. By Theorem 5, AST is directly interpretable in Seq. Hence, the following corollary holds.

Corollary 6. *(i)* Seq *is a sequential theory.* *(ii)* Seq *is an essentially undecidable theory.*

3   T is Interpretable in Seq (the Ideas)

In this section we explain the main ideas behind our interpretation of T in Seq.

Recall the theory T over the language $\mathcal{L}_T = \{\bot, \langle \cdot, \cdot \rangle, \sqsubseteq\}$ where $\bot$ is a constant symbol, $\langle \cdot, \cdot \rangle$ is a binary function symbol and $\sqsubseteq$ is a binary relation symbol. The axioms of T are given Fig. 4, and the intended model is a term model: The universe is the set of all variable-free $\mathcal{L}_T$-terms. Each term is interpreted as itself, and $\sqsubseteq$ is interpreted as the subterm relation (s is a subterm of t iff $s = t$ or $t = \langle t_1, t_2 \rangle$ and s is a subterm of t_1 or t_2). This term model is obviously isomorphic to a model where the universe consists of (finite) (full) binary trees and where $\sqsubseteq$ is interpreted as the subtree relation. Variable-free $\mathcal{L}_T$-terms will be called *finite binary trees* or *binary trees*, or just *trees*.

Let $\{a,b\}^*$ denote the set of all finite strings over the alphabet $\{a,b\}$. We define the set **Pol** $\subseteq \{a,b\}^*$ inductively: the string a is in **Pol**; the string $b\alpha\beta$ is in **Pol** if α and β are strings in **Pol**. Note that any string in **Pol** can be viewed as a finite binary trees written in Polish notation. For any $\alpha \in \{a,b\}^*$, let $(\#_a \alpha)$ and $(\#_b \alpha)$ denote, respectively, the number of occurrences of the alphabet symbols a and b in α. A proof of the next lemma can be found in Damnjanovic [3].

Lemma 7. $\alpha \in$ **Pol** *iff* $(\#_a \alpha) = (\#_b \alpha) + 1$ *and* $(\#_a \beta) \leq (\#_b \beta)$ *for any strict prefix* β *of* α.

The characterisation given by Lemma 7 can be used to prove unique readability of Polish notation for binary trees: If $\alpha \in$ **Pol**, then either $\alpha = a$, or there exist unique $\beta, \gamma \in$ **Pol** such that $\alpha = b\beta\gamma$.

Finite sequences over the natural numbers of a certain form will be called *snakes*. We will represent finite binary trees by snakes. Each tree will be represented by a unique snake, and each snake will represent some tree.

Definition 8. *The sequence* $(x_1, \ldots, x_n)$ *is a snake if* $n = 1$ *and* $x_1 = x_n = 0$. *The sequence* $(x_1, \ldots, x_n)$ *is a snake if (1)* $x_1 = 2$ *and* $x_n = 0$, *(2)* $x_i > 0$ *for* $i = 1, \ldots, n-1$ *and (3)* $|x_i - x_{i+1}| = 1$ *for* $i = 1, \ldots, n-1$.

*For any binary tree t, let $\widehat{t}$ denote the corresponding string in **Pol**, that is,
$\widehat{\bot} = a$ and $\widehat{\langle t_1, t_2 \rangle} = b\widehat{t_1}\widehat{t_2}$. The binary tree t will be represented by the snake $\tilde{t}$
given by*

- *if $\widehat{t} = a$, let $\tilde{t} = (0)$ (that is, $\tilde{t}$ is a sequence of length one, and 0 is the one
  and only element of the sequence)*
- *if $\widehat{t} = \alpha_1 \alpha_2 \ldots \alpha_n$ where $\alpha_i \in \{a, b\}$, let $\tilde{t} = (x_1, \ldots x_n)$ where*

$$x_1 = 2 \quad and \quad x_{i+1} = \begin{cases} x_i - 1 & if \ \alpha_{i+1} = a \\ x_i + 1 & if \ \alpha_{i+1} = b \end{cases} \quad for \ i = 1, \ldots, n-1. \quad (1)$$

Examples: The sequence $2, 1, 0$ is a snake. The sequence $2, 1, 2, 1, 2, 1, 0$ is a snake
and so is $2, 1, 2, 3, 4, 5, 4, 3, 2, 1, 2, 3, 4, 3, 2, 1, 0$.   □

Let us check that $\tilde{t} = (x_1, \ldots x_n)$ indeed is a snake: Let $\widehat{t} = \alpha_1 \alpha_2 \ldots \alpha_n$ where
$\alpha_i \in \{a, b\}$. By (1), we have $(\#_b \ \alpha_1 \ldots \alpha_i) + 1 - (\#_a \ \alpha_1 \ldots \alpha_i) = x_i$, and thus,
it follows from Lemma 7 that $\tilde{t}$ is a snake (for any tree t). It also follows from
Lemma 7 and our discussion above that the mapping $t \mapsto \tilde{t}$ is a bijection between
the finite binary trees and the snakes.

Examples: The tree $\langle \bot, \langle \bot, \bot \rangle \rangle$ is uniquely represented by the string $babaa$ which
again is uniquely represented by the snake $2, 1, 2, 1, 0$. The tree $\langle \langle \bot, \langle \bot, \bot \rangle \rangle, \bot \rangle$ is
uniquely represented by the string $bbabaaa$ which again is uniquely represented
by the snake $2, 3, 2, 3, 2, 1, 0$.   □

Definition 9. *For any snakes $(x_1, \ldots, x_n)$ and $(y_1, \ldots, y_m)$, let*

$$(x_1, \ldots, x_n) \oplus (y_1, \ldots, y_m) = (2, x_1 + 1, x_2 + 1, \ldots, x_n + 1, y_1, y_2, \ldots, y_m) .$$

Lemma 10. *For any trees t_1 and t_2, we have $\widetilde{\langle t_1, t_2 \rangle} = \tilde{t_1} \oplus \tilde{t_2}$.*

Proof. Let $\tilde{t_1} = (x_1, \ldots, x_n)$ and $\tilde{t_2} = (y_1, \ldots, y_m)$. Thus, we have $\alpha_1, \ldots, \alpha_n \in$
$\{a, b\}$ such that $\widehat{t_1} = \alpha_1 \ldots \alpha_n \in$ **Pol**, and moreover, $\beta_1, \ldots, \beta_m \in \{a, b\}$ such
that $\widehat{t_2} = \beta_1 \ldots \beta_m \in$ **Pol**. Observe that $\widehat{\langle t_1, t_2 \rangle} = b\alpha_1 \ldots \alpha_n \beta_1, \ldots, \beta_m$, and
thus, we have

$$\widetilde{\langle t_1, t_2 \rangle} = (2, x_1 + 1, x_2 + 1, \ldots, x_n + 1, y_1, y_2, \ldots, y_m)$$

by Definition 8. The lemma follows by Definition 9.   □

Definition 11. *A snake $(x_1, \ldots, x_n)$ is isomorphic with a strict part of the
snake $(y_1, \ldots, y_m)$ if there exists natural numbers k, ℓ such that $y_{k+1} = y_k + 1$
and $y_{k+i} = x_i + \ell$ (for $i = 1, \ldots, n$) and $y_{k+n} + 2 = y_{k+1}$.*

*The relation $(x_1, \ldots, x_n) \, R \, (y_1, \ldots, y_m)$ holds iff (i) $(x_1, \ldots, x_n) = (0)$ or (ii)
$(x_1, \ldots, x_n) = (y_1, \ldots, y_m)$ or (iii) $(x_1, \ldots, x_n)$ is isomorphic with a strict part
of $(y_1, \ldots, y_m)$.*

Lemma 12. *For any trees t_1 and t_2, we have $t_1 \sqsubseteq t_2$ iff $\tilde{t_1} R \tilde{t_2}$.*

Proof. Let $\tilde{t_1} = (x_1, \ldots, x_n)$ and $\tilde{t_2} = (y_1, \ldots, y_m)$. Thus, we have $\alpha_1, \ldots, \alpha_n \in \{a, b\}$ such that $\tilde{t_1} = \alpha_1 \ldots \alpha_n \in \mathbf{Pol}$, and moreover, $\beta_1, \ldots, \beta_m \in \{a, b\}$ such that $\tilde{t_2} = \beta_1 \ldots \beta_m \in \mathbf{Pol}$.

Assume $\tilde{t_1} = \tilde{t_2}$. Then t_1 and t_2 are the same tree. The relation $\tilde{t_1} R \tilde{t_2}$ holds by Definition 11. Moreover, we have $t_1 \sqsubseteq t_2$ as any tree is a subtree of itself.

Assume $\tilde{t_1} = (0)$. Then t_1 is the empty tree. The relation $\tilde{t_1} R \tilde{t_2}$ holds by Definition 11, and we also have $t_1 \sqsubseteq t_2$ as the empty tree is a subtree of any tree.

Assume $\tilde{t_1} \neq \tilde{t_2}$ and $\tilde{t_1} \neq (0)$. We need to prove that (i) $t_1 \sqsubseteq t_2$ implies $\tilde{t_1} R \tilde{t_2}$ and (ii) $\tilde{t_1} R \tilde{t_2}$ implies $t_1 \sqsubseteq t_2$. We will prove (i) and omit the proof of (ii).

Assume $t_1 \sqsubseteq t_2$. Then we have

$$\beta_1 \ldots \beta_m = \beta_1 \ldots \beta_k \alpha_1 \alpha_2 \ldots \alpha_n \beta_{k+n+1} \ldots \beta_m$$
$$= \beta_1 \ldots \beta_k b \alpha_2 \ldots \alpha_n \beta_{k+n+1} \ldots \beta_m \quad (2)$$

for some k such that $1 \leq k$ and $k + n \leq m$. Consider the snake $(y_1, \ldots, y_k, \ldots, y_m)$. We have $y_k > 0$. Hence, there exists $\ell \geq 0$ such that $y_k = \ell + 1$. By (2) and Definition 8, we have

$$(y_1, \ldots, y_m) = (y_1, \ldots, y_k, x_1 + \ell, x_2 + \ell, \ldots, x_n + \ell, y_{k+n+1}, \ldots, y_m)$$

and moreover, since $y_{k+n} = x_n + \ell$ and $x_n = 0$ and $x_1 = 2$, we have $y_{k+n} + 2 = x_n + \ell + 2 = x_1 + \ell = y_{k+1}$. This proves that there exist natural numbers k, ℓ such that $y_{k+1} = y_k + 1$ and $y_{k+i} = x_i + \ell$ (for $i = 1, \ldots, n$) and $y_{k+n} + 2 = y_{k+1}$. Thus, we have $\tilde{t_1} R \tilde{t_2}$ by Definition 11. $\qquad\square$

We can interpret T in Seq by representing trees as snakes. The function $\langle \cdot, \cdot \rangle$ is interpreted as $\oplus$, and the relation $\sqsubseteq$ is interpreted as R. More details are given in Sect. 5. Extensive proofs can be found in [1].

4   AST + EXT is Interpretable in Seq (the Ideas)

Our interpretation of AST + EXT in Seq builds on our interpretation of T in Seq. In this section we give a high-level explanation of how our interpretation works.

For convenience we will, in what follows, identify the strings in **Pol** with the snakes and regard, e.g., *babaa* as notation for the snake $2, 1, 2, 1, 0$ (it may be convenient to describe a snake by a giving a string in **Pol**).

We define the *finite trees* inductively: $\bot$ is a tree (the empty tree); $\langle T_1, \ldots, T_n \rangle$ is a tree if $T_1, \ldots, T_n$ are trees (for any $n > 0$). Let $F(\bot) = \bot$ and

$$F(\langle T_1, \ldots, T_n \rangle) = \langle \ldots \langle \langle \langle \bot, F(T_1) \rangle, F(T_2) \rangle, F(T_3) \rangle \ldots, F(T_n) \rangle.$$

Then F is a bijection between the finite trees and the binary trees (this bijection is also used in Damnjanovic [4]). Thus, we can represent the finite trees by snakes: every snake represents a finite tree, and every finite tree is represented by one, and only one, snake. A snake of the form $b^k a \beta_1 \beta_2 \ldots \beta_k$ (where $k > 0$) will represent by a tree of the form $\langle T_1, T_2, \ldots, T_k \rangle$ where the tree T_i is represented by the snake given by β_i (for $i = 1, \ldots, k$).

Examples: The snake $2, 3, 4, 3, 2, 1, 0$ (*bbbaaaa*) represent the tree $\langle 0, 0, 0 \rangle$. The snake $2, 1, 2, 1, 0$ (*babaa*) represents the tree $\langle \langle 0 \rangle \rangle$. The snake

$$2, 3, 2, 3, 4, 5, 4, 3, 2, 1, 2, 1, 2, 1, 0 \quad (bbabbbaaaaababaa)$$

represents the tree $\langle\, \langle 0, 0, 0 \rangle, \langle \langle 0 \rangle \rangle \,\rangle$. □

Observe that a tree of the form $\langle T_1, T_2, T_3, T_4 \rangle$ is represented by a snake of the form

$$2, 3, 4, 5, 4 \underbrace{\ldots 3}_{\text{rep. of } T_1}, \underbrace{\ldots 2}_{\text{rep. of } T_2}, \underbrace{\ldots, 1}_{\text{rep. of } T_3}, \underbrace{\ldots, 0}_{\text{rep. of } T_4}$$

and more generally, a tree of the form $\langle T_1, \ldots, T_k \rangle$ (where $k > 0$) is represented by a snake of the form

$$2, \ldots, k+1, k, \underbrace{\ldots k-1}_{\text{rep. of } T_1}, \underbrace{\ldots k-2}_{\text{rep. of } T_2}, \ldots 1, \underbrace{\ldots 0}_{\text{rep. of } T_k}$$

where every number preceeding $k - i$ in the sequence

$$\underbrace{\ldots k - i}_{\text{rep. of } T_i}$$

is strictly greater than $k - i$ (if T_i is the empty tree, the sequence will just consist of $k - i$).

This representation of finite trees by snakes indicates that it also should be possible to represent hereditarily finite sets by snakes. Let $\alpha, \beta \in \{a, b\}^*$. We write $\alpha \ll \beta$ if α strictly precedes β in the lexicographic ordering (any strict ordering of snakes can replace $\ll$ in the next definition).

Definition 13. *A snake* $(x_1, \ldots, x_n)$ *is an ordered snake if* $n = 1$ *and* $x_1 = 0$ *or if* $(x_1, \ldots, x_n)$ *is of the form* $b^k a \alpha_1 \ldots \alpha_k$ *with* $\alpha_i \ll \alpha_{i+1}$ *(for* $i = 1, \ldots, k - 1$*).*

We define a mapping between the hereditarily finite sets and the ordered snakes: (1) We map the empty set to the snake 0. *(2)* Let $S_1, \ldots S_k$ be hereditarily finite sets where S_i and S_j are different sets when $i \neq j$. Let $\beta_1, \ldots, \beta_k \in \{a, b\}^*$, respectively, denote the ordered snakes mapped to $S_1, \ldots S_k$. Let p be a permutation of $\{1, \ldots, k\}$ such that such that $\beta_{p(1)} \ll \beta_{p(2)} \ll \ldots \ll \beta_{p(k)}$ (such a permutation exists since the sets $S_1, \ldots S_k$ are all different). We map the set $\{S_1, \ldots S_k\}$ to the ordered snake given by $b^k a \beta_{p(1)} \ldots \beta_{p(k)}$.

This mapping is a bijection. Thus, we can represent each hereditarily finite set with a unique ordered snake, and moreover, every ordered snake represents a hereditarily finite set. We can interpret AST + EXT in Seq by interpreting sets as ordered snakes. More details are given in the next section and in [1].

5 More Details

Terminology and Notation. A *class* is a formula with a free variable. When K is a class, we may write $x \in K$ in place of $K(x)$ and use standard set-theoretic notation, e.g. we write $\exists x \in K[\phi]$ in place of $\exists x[K(x) \wedge \phi]$. We write ϕ^K for the *restriction of ϕ to the class K*: (i) $\phi^K = \phi$ if ϕ if ϕ is an atomic formula; (ii) $(\neg\phi)^K = \neg\phi^K$ and $(\phi \oslash \psi)^K = \phi^K \oslash \psi^K$ for $\oslash \in \{\vee, \wedge, \rightarrow, \leftrightarrow\}$; (iii) $(\forall x\, \phi)^K = \forall x\, [K(x) \rightarrow \phi^K]$; (iv) $(\exists x\, \phi)^K = \exists x\, [K(x) \wedge \phi^K]$.

Indexed Sequences. We introduce an extension Seq^+ of Seq which is convenient for developing indexed sequences (we have a number-like indexing domain and a function $(w)_i$ that picks the i-th element of w). First, we introduce a variant of Seq. Let Seq^* be the theory we obtain by taking Seq and replacing Seq_3 and Seq_5 with the axioms

Seq_3^* $\forall x[\, xe = x \, \wedge \, ex = x \,] \, \wedge \, \forall xy[\, x = xy \vee x = yx \rightarrow y = e\,]$
Seq_5^* $\forall xyzw[\, xy = zw \, \leftrightarrow \, \exists u[(z = xu \wedge uw = y) \vee (x = zu \wedge uy = w)]\,]$.

Observe that $\circ$ is left and right cancellative in Seq^*. We will refer to the left-right implication of Seq_5^* as the *editor axiom*, the right-left implication is logically equivalent to associativity of $\circ$. The next lemma implies that Seq and Seq^* are mutually interpretable. A detailed proof of the lemma can be found in [1]. (It is not clear to us whether Seq^* is a sequential theory, that is, whether it directly interprets AST.)

Lemma 14. *There exists a class $\mathcal{J}$ such that $\mathsf{Seq} \vdash \phi^{\mathcal{J}}$ for each theorem ϕ of Seq^*. Define $x \preceq y$ by $\exists z \in \mathcal{J}[y = xz]$. Then $\preceq$ is a reflexive and transitive relation such that $\forall y \in \mathcal{J}\forall x \preceq y[x \in \mathcal{J}]$, and moreover, we have $\forall w[e \vdash w \in \mathcal{J}]$.*

Proof. Let A denote the class of all z such that $ez = z$ and $\forall xy\,[x(yz) = (xy)z]$. It can be checked that A contains e and is closed under $\circ$ and $\vdash$. Furthermore, $e \vdash w \in A$ for any w and $z_0 \in A$ if $A \ni z_0 \vdash z_1$ for some z_1. Next, let $v \sqsubseteq_A w$ be shorthand for $\exists t \in A[w = vt]$. The relation $\sqsubseteq_A$ is reflexive and transitive. We let $\mathcal{J}$ consist of all w such that for any $v \sqsubseteq_A w$ we have: (i) $v \in A$; (ii) $\forall x \in A\, [v = vx \vee v = xv \rightarrow x = e]$; (iii) if $xy = zv$ and $y \in A$, then

$$\exists u \in A\,[\,(x = zu \wedge uy = v) \vee (z = xu \wedge uv = y\,)\,].$$

It can be checked that $\mathcal{J} \subseteq A$ contains e and is closed under $\circ$ and $\vdash$. Since $\sqsubseteq_A$ is transitive, $\mathcal{J}$ is downward closed under $\sqsubseteq_A$ (and hence also under $\preceq$), that is, $v \in \mathcal{J}$ if $v \sqsubseteq_A w$ and $w \in \mathcal{J}$. Downward closure under $\sqsubseteq_A$ ensures that Seq_5^* holds restricted to $\mathcal{J}$. The other axioms of Seq^* hold restricted to $\mathcal{J}$ since they are universal. □

The *indexing domain* is a totally ordered class N of number-like objects with a successor operation (S) and an addition operation (+) that provably in Seq satisfies the first five axioms of Robinson's Q: (1) S is one-to-one; (2) 0 is not in the range of S; (3) any non-zero element has a predecessor; (4)-(5) primitive recursive equations for $+$. Let $0 := e$, $Sx := e \vdash x$ and $x + y := xy$. By the right-left implication of Seq_5^*, $+$ is associative on $\mathcal{J}$. By Seq_2 and Seq_1, S is one-to-one and 0 is not in the range of S. By Seq_3 and Seq_4, the primitive recursive equations for $+$ hold. By the axioms of Seq and the closure properties of $\mathcal{J}$, we have $\forall x[x \preceq 0 \leftrightarrow x = 0]$ and $\forall x, y[x \preceq Sy \leftrightarrow (x = Sy \vee x \preceq y)]$. By the right-left implication of Seq_5^*, $\forall xyz [(x+y)+z = x+(y+z)]$ holds restricted to $\mathcal{J}$. Let $[0, x]$ denote the class of of all u such that $u \preceq x$. Observe that $\forall x[0 \preceq x]$ holds since e is an identity element with respect to $\circ$ on $\mathcal{J}$. We define a modified subtraction operation on $\mathcal{J}$. Given $x, y, z \in \mathcal{J}$, let $x \mathbin{\dot{-}} y = z$ be shorthand for: $x = yz$ or $z = e \wedge \forall u \in \mathcal{J}[x \neq yu]$. It follows from Seq_5^* and the second conjunct of Seq_3^* that $\dot{-}$ is a well-defined function on $\mathcal{J}$.

Let $[0, x]$ denote the class of of all u such that $u \preceq x$. Let I consist of all $w \in \mathcal{J}$ such that the following hold for all $x \leq w$: (1) $([0, x], \preceq)$ is a total order; (2) $x = 0$ or there exists y such that $x = Sy$; (3) if $u \prec x$, then $Su \preceq x$; (4) if $y \in \mathcal{J}$ and $\forall u \prec y[Su \preceq y]$, then $x \preceq y$ or $y \preceq x$; (5) for any $u \in \mathcal{J}$, we have $S(u + x) = Su + x$; (6) for any $u, v \in \mathcal{J}$, if $u + x = v + x$, then $u = v$. It can be checked that I is closed under 0 and S and downward closed under $\preceq$, that is, $v \in I$ if $v \preceq w$ and $w \in I$. Let J consist of all $w \in I$ such that for any $x \preceq w$ and any $u \in I$, we have $u + x = x + u$. It can be checked that J is closed under 0 and S and downward closed under $\preceq$. We restrict J to a subclass N that is also closed under addition (this uses associativity of $+$): N consist of all $x \in J$ such that $\forall y \in J[y + x \in J]$. It can be checked that J is closed under 0, S and $+$ and downward closed under $\preceq$. Let $x \leq y$ be shorthand for $\exists z \in \mathsf{N}[x + z = y]$. We write $x < y$ for $x \leq y \wedge x \neq y$.

Lemma 15 (Seq). *The first five axioms of* Q *hold restricted to* N, *and addition on* N *is associative, commutative and cancellative. Furthermore,* $(\mathsf{N}, \leq)$ *is a linear order with least element 0 such that* $\forall x, y \in \mathsf{N}[x \leq Sy \leftrightarrow (x = Sy \vee x \leq y)]$ *and* $\forall x \in \mathsf{N} \forall y \leq x[y \in \mathsf{N}]$.

To improve the readability, we will occasionally use (x, y) as alternative notation for $x \vdash y$ when $x \in \mathsf{N}$ and it is natural to regard x an index pointing to y. We will now define the class $\mathcal{S}_0$ of *indexed sequences*. Intuitively, an indexed sequence with (indexing) domain $[m, n]$, where $m \leq n$ are elements of N, is a sequence of the form $((m, x_m), (m + 1, x_{m+1}), \ldots, (n, x_n))$. Let $f \in \mathcal{S}_0$ iff $f \in \mathcal{J}$ and there exist $m, n \in \mathsf{N}$ such that

- (0) $m \leq n$
- (1) for each $m \leq k \leq n$ there exists $u \in \mathcal{J}$ such that $f = (s \vdash (k, u))t$ for some $s, t \in \mathcal{J}$
- (2) if $f = (s \vdash w)t$ for some $s, t, w \in \mathcal{J}$, then there exist $m \leq k \leq n$ and $u \in \mathcal{J}$ such that $w = (k, u)$
- (3) if $f = (s \vdash (k, u))t$ and $s \neq e$, then $m < k$ and there exist $\ell, v, s_0 \in \mathcal{J}$ such that $k = S\ell$ and $s = s_0 \vdash (\ell, v)$
- (4) if $f = (s \vdash (k, u))t$, then there is no $k \leq k' \in \mathsf{N}$ and $u', s_0, t_0 \in \mathcal{J}$ such that $s = (s_0 \vdash (k', u'))t_0$.

If $f \in \mathcal{J}$ and (0), (1), (2), (3), (4) hold, we will call $[m, n]$ the domain of f and use the suggestive notation $f : [m, n] \to \mathcal{J}$, furthermore, if $m \leq k \leq n$, we write $f(k)$ for the unique element $u \in \mathcal{J}$ such that $f = (s \vdash (k, u))t$ for some $s, t \in \mathcal{J}$. (uniqueness is proved using the fact that the editor axiom holds restricted to $\mathcal{J}$). An element of the class $\mathcal{S}_0$ will be called an *indexed sequence*. The next theorem, which is proved in [1], says that we can reason with indexed sequences in the usual way if we restrict the indexing domain N to a sufficiently small subdomain N*. It follows easily from the theorem that Seq interprets the extension Seq$^+$ given by the axioms of Seq and the axioms of Seq*. From now on, we will work in Seq$^+$ and simply express indexed sequences as $f : [0, n] \to \mathcal{V}$.

Theorem 16 (Seq). *There exists a subdomain* N* *of* N *such that*

- (I) *for any element* $x \in \mathcal{J}$ *and any* $n \in$ N* *there exists a unique indexed sequence* $\frac{x}{[0,n]} : [0, n] \to \mathcal{J}$ *such that* $\frac{x}{[0,n]}(j) = x$ *for all* $0 \leq j \leq n$
- (II) *for any* $k, n \in$ N* *and any indexed sequence* $f : [0, n] \to \mathcal{J}$, *there exists a unique indexed sequence* $f_k^0 : [k, k + n] \to \mathcal{J}$ *such that* $f_k^0(k + j) = f(j)$ *for all* $0 \leq j \leq n$
- (III) *for any* $n \in$ N* *and any two indexed sequences* $f, g : [0, n] \to \mathcal{J}$, *there exist two unique indexed sequences* $f \oplus g : [0, n] \to \mathcal{J}$ *and* $f \ominus g : [0, n] \to \mathcal{J}$ *such that* $f \oplus g(j) = f(j) + g(j)$ *and* $f \ominus g(j) = f(j) \dot{-} g(j)$ *for all* $0 \leq j \leq n$
- (IV) *for any* $n, m \in$ N* *and any two indexed sequences* $f : [0, n] \to \mathcal{J}$ *and* $g : [0, m] \to \mathcal{J}$ *there exists a unique indexed sequence* $f^\frown g : [0, n+m+1] \to \mathcal{J}$ *such that* $f^\frown g = f \circ g_{n+1}^0$ *and*

$$f^\frown g(j) = \begin{cases} f(j) & \text{if } 0 \leq j \leq n \\ g(j \dot{-} (n+1)) & \text{if } n+1 \leq j \leq n+m+1 \end{cases}$$

- (V) *for any* $n \in$ N*, *any* $0 \leq k < n$ *and any indexed sequence* $f : [0, n] \to \mathcal{J}$, *there exist unique indexed sequences* $g : [0, k] \to \mathcal{J}$ *and* $h : [0, n \dot{-} (k+1)] \to \mathcal{J}$ *such that* $f = g^\frown h$
- (VI) *for any* $n, m, k \in$ N* *and any three indexed sequences* $f : [0, n] \to \mathcal{J}$, $g : [0, m] \to \mathcal{J}$ *and* $h : [0, k] \to \mathcal{J}$ *we have* $(f^\frown g)^\frown h = f^\frown (g^\frown h)$
- (VII) *for any* $n, m, k, \ell \in$ N* *and any four indexed sequences* $f : [0, n] \to \mathcal{J}$, $g : [0, m] \to \mathcal{J}$, $p : [0, k] \to \mathcal{J}$ *and* $q : [0, \ell] \to \mathcal{J}$ *such that* $f^\frown g = p^\frown q$, *we have one of the following: (1)* $f = p$ *and* $g = q$; *(2) there exist a unique* $r \in$ N* *and a unique indexed sequence* $h : [0, r] \to \mathcal{J}$ *such that* $f = p^\frown h$ *and* $h^\frown g = q$; *(3) there exist a unique* $r \in$ N* *and a unique indexed sequence* $h : [0, r] \to \mathcal{J}$ *such that* $p = f^\frown h$ *and* $h^\frown q = g$
- (VIII) *for any* $n, m, k \in$ N* *and any three indexed sequences* $f : [0, n] \to \mathcal{J}$, $g : [0, m] \to \mathcal{J}$ *and* $h : [0, k] \to \mathcal{J}$ *we have* $f = g$ *if* $f^\frown h = g^\frown h$ *or* $h^\frown f = h^\frown g$.

Proof. Let K consist of all $n^* \in$ N such that (I)-(VIII) hold when we replace each occurrence of $i \in$ N* with $i \leq n^*$. Clearly, K is downward closed under $\leq$. It can be checked that K is closed under 0 and S. The verification uses the

following observation which can be proved using, in particular, the fact that the
editor axiom holds restricted to $\mathcal{J}$.

(Claim) Consider an indexed sequence $f : [m, n] \to \mathcal{J}$ and an index
$m \leqslant k < n$. Then, there exist two unique indexed sequences $g : [m, k] \to \mathcal{J}$
and $h : [k + 1, n] \to \mathcal{J}$ such that $f = g \circ h$. Furthermore, $g = s \vdash (k, f(k))$
and $h = t \vdash (n, f(n))$ for some $s, t \in \mathcal{J}$.

We obtain N^* by restricting K to a subclass which is also closed under addition:
N^* consist of all x such that $\forall y \in K [y + x \in K]$. It can be checked that N^* is
closed under $0, \mathsf{S}, +$ and is downward closed under $\leq$.   □

Interpretation of T *in* Seq. We start by defining the class of *snakes* denoted $\mathcal{S}$.
Let $\mathcal{S}$ consist of all indexed sequences $f : [0, n] \to \mathcal{V}$ such that $n \in \mathsf{N}^*$ and
$f(j) \in \mathsf{N}^*$ for all $j \leq n$, and moreover, one of the following holds

 – $n = 0$ and $f(0) = 0$
 – $f(0) = 2$, $f(n) = 0$, $f(j) \neq 0$ for all $j < n$ and for each $i < n$ we have
   $f(i) = f(i + 1) + 1$ or $f(i + 1) = f(i) + 1$.

We interpret T in Seq as follows: (A) The domain is $\mathcal{S}$ and $\perp := \frac{0}{[0,0]}$. (B) Assume
$f : [0, n] \to \mathcal{V}$ and $g : [0, m] \to \mathcal{V}$. Let $\langle f, g \rangle := \frac{2}{[0,0]} \frown (f \oplus \frac{1}{[0,n]}) \frown g$ (see Lemma
10 and recall the notation of Theorem 16, observe that $\mathcal{S}$ is closed under $\langle \cdot, \cdot \rangle$).
(C) Assume $f : [0, n] \to \mathcal{V}$ and $g : [0, m] \to \mathcal{V}$. By definition, the relation $f \sqsubseteq g$
holds iff one of the following holds: (i) $n = 0$; (ii) $f = g$; (iii) there exist $k, \ell \in \mathsf{N}^*$
such that $g(k + 1) = g(k) + 1$, $g(k + 1) = g(k + n) + 2$ and $g(k + i + 1) = f(i) + \ell$
for all $0 \leq i \leq n$ (see Lemma 12).

It is easy to check that $\perp$ is not in the range of $\langle \cdot, \cdot \rangle$ and $\forall x[x \sqsubseteq \perp \leftrightarrow x = \perp]$.
By using clause (VI) of Theorem 16, it can be verified that $\langle \cdot, \cdot \rangle$ is one-to-one. It
remains to show that $h \sqsubseteq \langle f, g \rangle \leftrightarrow (h = \langle f, g \rangle \lor h \sqsubseteq f \lor h \sqsubseteq g)$. It is easy to
see that the right-left implication holds. We show that the left-right implication
holds. Assume $h : [0, r] \to \mathcal{V}$ and $[0, n]$ and $[0, m]$ are the domains of f and g,
respectively. By Clause (VI) of Theorem 16, it suffices to show that we cannot
witness $h \sqsubseteq \langle f, g \rangle$ with $0 \leq k < n + 1 < n + r \leq n + m + 2$. Indeed, assume this
were the case. We have two cases: $\ell > 0$ and $\ell = 0$. We consider the case $\ell > 0$.
Now, there must exist $0 \leq j < r$ such that $1 = f(n) + 1 = \langle f, g \rangle (n + 1) = h(j) + \ell$.
This means that $\ell = 1$. Hence, $h(j) = 0$, which contradicts the assumption that
$h(i) \neq 0$ for all $i < r$ since $h \in \mathcal{S}$. Finally, we consider the case $\ell = 0$. We have
$2 = h(0) = \langle f, g \rangle (k + 1) = f(k + 1) + 1$. Hence, $f(k + 1) = 1$. But, we also know,
by clause (iii) in the definition of $\sqsubseteq$, that $\langle f, g \rangle (k) + 1 = \langle f, g \rangle (k + 1)$. Hence,
$f(k) = 0$. Since $f \in \mathcal{S}$, this contradicts the assumption that $f(j) \neq 0$ for all
$j < n$.

Interpretation of AST + EXT *in* Seq. Our interpretation of AST + EXT in Seq
builds on the interpretation of T in Seq. Assume $f : [0, n] \to \mathsf{N}^*$ and $g : [0, m] \to$
N^*. Let $f \ll g$ if and only if $n < m$ or $n = m$ and there is a least $k \leq n$ such that
$f(j) = g(j)$ for all $j < k$ and $f(k) < g(k)$. We restrict N^* to get a subclass of $\mathcal{S}$

linearly ordered by $\ll$. Let J_0 consist of all $n' \in \mathsf{N}^*$ such that for all $n \leq n'$ the class of all indexed sequences $f : [0, m] \to \mathsf{N}^*$, where $m \leq n$, is linearly ordered by $\ll$. It is easy to check that J_0 is closed under 0 and S and downward closed under $\leq$. We restrict J_0 to a subclass J that is also closed under $+$. Observe that J also is closed under the modified subtraction function $\dot{-}$.

Let $\mathcal{W}$ denote the class of all $f : [0, n] \to \mathsf{N}^*$ such that $f = \frac{0}{[0,0]}$ (i.e. $n = 0$ and $f(0) = 0$) or the following holds:

- (A) $f \in \mathcal{S}$ (f is a snake)
- (B) There exists a least $0 \leq k^* \leq n$ such that $f(k^*) = k^*$, $f(j+1) = f(j)+1$ for all $0 \leq j+1 < k^*$ and $f(k^* - 1) = f(k^*) + 1$
- (C) For each $0 \leq \ell < k^*$ there is a least $0 \leq j \leq n$ such that $f(j) = \ell$
- (D) Assume $0 \leq k^* \leq m_0 < m_1 \leq m_2 < m_3 \leq n$ are such that: (1) m_0 is the least index j such that $f(j) = \ell_0 + 1$ for $0 \leq \ell_0 := f(m_0) < k^*$ and m_1 is the least index j such that $f(j) = \ell_0$; (2) m_2 is the least index j such that $f(j) = \ell_1 + 1$ for $0 \leq \ell_1 := f(m_2) < k^*$ and m_3 is the least index j such that $f(j) = \ell_1$. Then, $\ell_0 < \ell_1$. Furthermore, let $g_0 : [0, m_1 - m_0] \to \mathsf{N}^*$ and $g_1 : [0, m_3 - m_2] \to \mathsf{N}^*$ be such that $f(m_0 + j + 1) = g_0(j) + \ell_0$ and $f(m_2 + j + 1) = g_1(j) + \ell_1$. Then, $g_0 \ll g_1$.

Intuitively, $\mathcal{W}$ is the restriction of the class $\mathcal{S}$ of snakes to the class of lexicographically ordered snakes (see Definition 13).

We refer to the unique index k^* as the *cardinality* of (the set encoded by) f. We define a membership relation on $\mathcal{W}$. Assume $f : [0, n] \to \mathsf{N}^*$ and $g : [0, m] \to \mathsf{N}^*$ are in $\mathcal{W}$. Let k^* be the cardinality of f. Let $g \in^* f$ if and only if there exist $0 \leq \ell < k^*$ and $k^* \leq m_0 < m_1 \leq n$ such that:

- (1) m_0 is the least $0 \leq j \leq n$ such that $f(j) = \ell + 1$
- (2) m_1 is the least $0 \leq j \leq n$ such that $f(j) = \ell$
- (3) $m_1 = m_0 + m + 1$ and $f(m_0 + j + 1) = g(j) + \ell$ for all $0 \leq j \leq m$.

Clearly, $\frac{0}{[0,0]}$ is the unique empty set with respect to $\in^*$. We restrict J in order to get adjunction and extensionality. Let K_0 consist of all $n' \in J$ such that for all $n \leq n'$:

- (1) for any $q : [0, n] \to \mathsf{N}^*$, $f : [0, k] \to \mathsf{N}^*$ and $g : [0, m] \to \mathsf{N}^*$ in $\mathcal{W}$ such that $f \sqsubseteq q$ and $g \notin^* f$, there exists $h : [0, k + m + 2] \to \mathsf{N}^*$ in $\mathcal{W}$ such that $p \in^* h$ if and only if $p \in^* f$ or $p = g$
- (2) if $f : [0, n] \to \mathsf{N}^*$ and $g : [0, m] \to \mathsf{N}^*$ are elements of $\mathcal{W}$ that contain the same elements with respect to $\in^*$, then $f = g$.

It is easy to check that K_0 contains 0 and is downward closed under $\leq$. It can also be checked that K_0 is closed under S, see [1] for more details. We restrict K_0 to a subclass K that is closed under $+$. Let $\mathcal{W}^*$ consist of all $f : [0, n] \to \mathsf{N}^*$ in $\mathcal{W}$ such that $n \in K$. In our interpretation of $\mathsf{AST} + \mathsf{EXT}$ in Seq we use the domain $\mathcal{W}^*$ and translate the membership relation as $\in^*$. It follows from the definition of K that this indeed defines an interpretation of $\mathsf{AST} + \mathsf{EXT}$ in Seq^+.

Observe that an element of $f \in \mathcal{W}^*$ is a subtree of f, and thus also an element of $\mathcal{W}^*$, since $\mathcal{W}^*$ is downward closed under the restriction of $\sqsubseteq$ to $\mathcal{W} \times \mathcal{W}$. More details can be found in [1].

References

1. Kristiansen, L., Murwanashyaka, J.: Notes on interpretability between weak first-order theories: theories of sequences. arXiv:2402.14286
2. Damnjanovic, Z.: Mutual interpretability of robinson arithmetic and adjunctive set with extensionality. Bull. Symbolic Logic **23**, 381–404 (2017)
3. Damnjanovic, Z.: Mutual interpretability of weak essentially undecidable theories. J. Symb. Log. **87**, 1374–1395 (2022)
4. Damnjanovic, Z.: Tree Theory: Interpretability Between Weak First-Order Theories of Trees. Bulletin of Symbolic Logic. Published online by Cambridge University Press, pp. 1–80, 10 February 2023
5. Mycielski, J., Pudlak, P., Stern, A.S.: A Lattice of Chapters of Mathematics (Interpretations Between Theorems). vol. 426 of Memoirs of the American Mathematical Society. AMS, Providence (1990)
6. Nelson, E.: Predicative Arithmetic. Princeton University Press, Princeton (1986)
7. Grzegorczyk, A.: Undecidability without arithmetization. Stud. Logica. **79**, 163–230 (2005)
8. Hájek, P., Pudlák, P.: Metamathematics of First-Order Arithmetic. Cambridge University Press, Cambridge (2017)
9. Kristiansen, L., Murwanashyaka, J.: On interpretability between some weak essentially undecidable theories. In: Anselmo, M., Della Vedova, G., Manea, F., Pauly, A. (eds.) CiE 2020. LNCS, vol. 12098, pp. 63–74. Springer, Cham (2020). https://doi.org/10.1007/978-3-030-51466-2_6
10. Murwanashyaka, J.: Weak essentially undecidable theories of concatenation. Arch. Math. Logic **61**, 939–976 (2022)
11. Murwanashyaka, J.: Weak sequential theories of finite full binary trees. In: Berger, U., Franklin, J.N.Y., Manea, F., Pauly, A. (eds.) Revolutions and Revelations in Computability. CiE 2022. Lecture Notes in Computer Science, vol. 13359, pp. 208–219. Springer, Cham (2022). https://doi.org/10.1007/978-3-031-08740-0_18
12. Visser, A.: Pairs, sets and sequences in first-order theories. Arch. Math. Logic **47**, 299–326 (2008)
13. Visser, A.: Growing commas. A study of sequentiality and concatenation. Notre Dame J. Formal Logic **50**, 61–85 (2009)

On the Group of Computable Automorphisms of the Linear Order of the Reals

Ruslan Kornev[✉]

Novosibirsk State University, 1 Pirogova Street, Novosibirsk 630090, Russia
kornevrus@gmail.com

Abstract. We study the group $\mathrm{Aut}_c(\mathbb{R})$ of computable automorphisms of the linear order of the reals. It is shown that this group shares several common properties with the group $\mathrm{Aut}_c(\mathbb{Q})$ of computable automorphisms of the rationals: they both are not divisible and each of them has exactly three nontrivial normal subgroups. Each of these groups contains an element that is not conjugate with its square. However, $\mathrm{Aut}_c(\mathbb{R})$ also possesses properties that are not present in $\mathrm{Aut}_c(\mathbb{Q})$: $\mathrm{Aut}_c(\mathbb{R})$ contains a bump that is not conjugate with its square and, for every c.e. real z, $\mathrm{Aut}_c(\mathbb{R})$ contains a bump with upper boundary point z.

Keywords: automorphism groups · ordered permutation groups · lattice-ordered groups · computability theory · computable analysis

1 Introduction

We study $\mathrm{Aut}_c(\mathbb{R})$, the group of computable automorphisms of $(\mathbb{R}, \leqslant)$, where $\leqslant$ is the usual linear order on $\mathbb{R}$. Our main interest will be in proving or disproving certain standard results of the theory of ordered permutation groups and investigating certain standard properties of such groups for $\mathrm{Aut}_c(\mathbb{R})$, such as divisibility, normal subgroups, conjugacy criterion for bumps and the general Holland's conjugacy criterion, etc.

Theory of automorphism groups of linear orders and their subgroups, called *ordered permutation groups,* emerged in 1960s in the works of Ch. Holland (see [1]). For a linear order A, $\mathrm{Aut}(A)$ denotes the automorphism group of A. Pointwise order on $\mathrm{Aut}(A)$ makes $\mathrm{Aut}(A)$ an ordered group. Moreover, $\mathrm{Aut}(A)$ is lattice-ordered, i.e., forms a lattice under the pointwise order. Holland's paper [1] contains the following result that highlights the importance of automorphism groups of linear orders for the study of lattice-ordered groups.

Theorem 1. (Holland [1]). *Every lattice-ordered group is isomorphically embeddable into* $\mathrm{Aut}(A)$ *for some linear order A.*

This result can be strengthened as follows.

© The Author(s), under exclusive license to Springer Nature Switzerland AG 2024
L. Levy Patey et al. (Eds.): CiE 2024, LNCS 14773, pp. 405–419, 2024.
https://doi.org/10.1007/978-3-031-64309-5_32

Theorem 2. (Holland [1], Weinberg [2]). *Every lattice-ordered group is isomorphically embeddable into a divisible group of the form* $\mathrm{Aut}(A)$.

Holland [1] also established a number of properties of the automorphism group $\mathrm{Aut}(\mathbb{R})$ of the order on the reals. Later it was shown that these properties hold more generally, in the case of groups $\mathrm{Aut}(A)$ acting 2-transitively on A; see Glass [3]. To state these results, we need the following definitions from [3].

Let A be a linear order, $f \in \mathrm{Aut}(A)$, $x \in A$. The *f-orbital* of x, written $\mathrm{orbital}_f(x)$, is the convexification of the set $\{f^n(x) \mid n \in \mathbb{Z}\}$. If $y \in \mathrm{orbital}_f(x)$, then $\mathrm{orbital}_f(x) = \mathrm{orbital}_f(y)$, i.e. we can speak simply of f-orbitals, or orbitals of f. Clearly, the set of f-orbitals forms a partition of A and is linearly ordered by the induced order: $\mathrm{orbital}_f(x) \leqslant \mathrm{orbital}_f(y)$ if $x \leqslant y$. Ordered set of orbitals of f is called the *orbital structure* of f.

$\mathrm{orbital}_f(x)$ is called *positive* if $f(x) > x$, *negative* if $f(x) < x$, and *neutral* if $f(x) = x$; in the respective cases we also say that it has positive, negative or neutral *parity*. Parity of an orbital does not depend on the choice of the point x above. Neutral orbital consists of a single point, and a nonneutral orbital I is a (possibly unbounded) open convex subset of A; $\sup I$ and $\inf I$ are, generally speaking, elements of the Dedekind completion $\bar{A}$ of A (see [3,4]). Note that for all nonzero $n \in \mathbb{Z}$ automorphisms f^n have the same orbitals as f, positive orbitals of f^n are precisely the positive orbitals of f for $n > 0$, and positive orbitals of f^{-1} are precisely the negative orbitals of f. Automorphism f is called a *bump* if it has exactly one nonneutral orbital.

The set $spf = \{x \in A \mid f(x) \neq x\}$ is called the *support* of f. We say that f is unbounded, bounded above, bounded below, or bounded, if so is spf. Define the following subgroups of $\mathrm{Aut}(A)$:

- $L(A) = \{f \in \mathrm{Aut}(A) \mid spf \text{ is bounded above}\}$,
- $R(A) = \{f \in \mathrm{Aut}(A) \mid spf \text{ is bounded below}\}$,
- $B(A) = L(A) \cap R(A)$.

Conjugation is closely related to orbital structures of automorphisms. We use the well-known notations $f^g = g^{-1}fg$ for the conjugate of f by g and $[f,g] = f^{-1}g^{-1}fg$ for the commutator of f and g. If $h = g^{-1}fg$, then $g(h(a)) = f(g(a))$ for all $a \in A$, in particular, for every fixed point a of h, $g(a)$ is a fixed point of f, and if $h(a) > a$, then $f(g(a)) > g(a)$; this fact is known as the Fundamental Triviality [3]. Moreover, for every orbital I of h, $g(I)$ is an orbital of f. In other words, g induces an ordermorphism between the orbital structures of h and f that preserves parity of orbitals. This implies that $L(A)$, $R(A)$ and $B(A)$ are normal subgroups of $\mathrm{Aut}(A)$.

Theorem 3. (Holland [1]). *The following properties hold of* $\mathrm{Aut}(\mathbb{R})$:

1. $\mathrm{Aut}(\mathbb{R})$ *is divisible,*
2. *(Holland's criterion)* $f, g \in \mathrm{Aut}(\mathbb{R})$ *are conjugate in* $\mathrm{Aut}(\mathbb{R})$ *if and only if there is a parity preserving ordermorphism between their orbital structures,*
3. *As a consequence, for every* $f \in \mathrm{Aut}(\mathbb{R})$, f *and* f^2 *are conjugate, or, equivalently,* $f = [f,g]$ *for some* $g \in \mathrm{Aut}(\mathbb{R})$,

4. $L(\mathbb{R})$, $R(\mathbb{R})$ and $B(\mathbb{R})$ are the only normal subgroups of Aut($\mathbb{R}$).

Holland's criterion follows from the fact that all bumps of the same sign and the same boundity (property to be bounded above, below, on both sides or unbounded) are pairwise conjugate in Aut($\mathbb{R}$). As noted before, Theorem 3 holds of every 2-transitive group Aut(A) (with some extra assumptions on A), in particular, it holds of Aut($\mathbb{Q}$). However, unlike Aut($\mathbb{R}$), group Aut($\mathbb{Q}$) has two conjugacy classes of positive bumps bounded above: clearly, bumps f and g such that $a = \sup(spf)$ is rational and $b = \sup(spg)$ is irrational, cannot be conjugate in Aut($\mathbb{Q}$) since the conjugating automorphism must map a to b.

Papers [4] and [5] studied the group of computable automorphisms of the rationals Aut$_c(\mathbb{Q})$. It was shown in [5] that most of the classical techniques used in the proof of the above result of Holland's do not work in the computable setting, however, some of the properties of Aut($\mathbb{R}$) still hold in Aut$_c(\mathbb{Q})$.

Theorem 4. ([5]).

1. Aut$_c(\mathbb{Q})$ is not divisible;
2. Every element of Aut$_c(\mathbb{Q})$ is a commutator;
3. There is an $f \in$ Aut$_c(\mathbb{Q})$ that is not conjugate with f^2;
4. $L_c(\mathbb{Q})$, $R_c(\mathbb{Q})$ and $B_c(\mathbb{Q})$ are the only nontrivial normal subgroups of Aut$_c(\mathbb{Q})$, where $L_c(\mathbb{Q}) = L(\mathbb{Q}) \cap$ Aut$_c(\mathbb{Q})$, and similarly for $R_c(\mathbb{Q})$ and $B_c(\mathbb{Q})$.

In the present paper, we continue studying computability aspects of the theory of ordered permutations groups by considering the group of computable automorphisms of real numbers. Our investigation is a part of a more general program aimed at extending results and techniques from effective algebra to computable analysis. We note that the TTE approach to computable analysis [6,7], which our work is based upon, is itself rooted in Ershov's numbering approach [8] to computable model theory, and a significant number of modern advances in computable analysis are inspired by notions, techniques and results in the field of computable algebra. For instance, line of research dedicated to computable categoricity of structures of uncountable cardinality (see e.g. [9,10]) is the computable-analytical analogue of the classical topic in computable structure theory [11–13]. We also mention recent results on effective versions of duality that show the connections between computable properties (e.g., computable presentability) of an algebraic structure and its analytical counterpart: Stone duality for Boolean albegras and Stone spaces [14,15], and Pontryagin duality for abelian groups and Polish groups [16].

As mentioned above, we use the well-known TTE approach to computability on $\mathbb{R}$ [7]. Fix a numbering $(q_n)_{n \in \omega}$ of $\mathbb{Q}$. A sequence $g \in \omega^\omega$ is called a *Cauchy name* of a real number x if $q_{g(n)} \to x$ and $|q_{g(n)} - q_{g(m)}| \leqslant 2^{-n}$ for all $n \in \omega$ and all $m > n$. Automorphism $f \in$ Aut($\mathbb{R}$) is called *computable* if there is a Turing functional Φ_e such that, for every real x and every Cauchy name g for x, $\Phi_e(g) = (\Phi_e^g(n))_{n \in \omega}$ is a Cauchy name for $f(x)$; in this case we say that Φ_e *realizes* f. Equivalently, f is computable if and only if there exists a computable function $F \colon \omega^2 \to \omega$ such that, for all n, $(F(n,k))_{k \in \omega}$ is a Cauchy name for $f(q_n)$.

It is well-known (see e.g. [17]) that the inverse of a computable automorphism is also computable, so computable automorphisms form a group, that we denote by $\text{Aut}_c(\mathbb{R})$.

We are ready to announce some of the results proved in the paper. We begin by noting that all of the techniques designed in [5] for the group $\text{Aut}_c(\mathbb{Q})$ can be transferred to the setting of $\text{Aut}_c(\mathbb{R})$ with no harm, namely, Theorem 4 holds in $\text{Aut}_c(\mathbb{R})$. In other words, the following properties hold of $\text{Aut}_c(\mathbb{R})$: it is not divisible (Theorem 5 below), there is an element $f \in \text{Aut}_c(\mathbb{R})$ that is not conjugate with f^2 (Theorem 6), every element of $\text{Aut}_c(\mathbb{R})$ is a commutator (Corollary 1), and $L_c(\mathbb{R})$, $R_c(\mathbb{R})$ and $B_c(\mathbb{R})$ are the only nontrivial normal subgroups of $\text{Aut}_c(\mathbb{R})$ (Theorem 7). Furthermore, we argue that proofs of these results even become easier in the new setting because of the approximative nature of computability on $\mathbb{R}$: instead of computing the value $f(q)$ exactly, where $q \in \mathbb{Q}$, we can just output an approximation of this value, keeping a possibility to vary it by a small amount later, if needed.

For every computable automorphism $f \in \text{Aut}_c(\mathbb{R})$ and every $x \in \mathbb{R}$, $f(x)$ has the same Turing degree as x; more precisely, f must preserve m-degrees of reals (see the paper [17]). This means that $\text{Aut}_c(\mathbb{R})$ is not transitive: there is no $f \in \text{Aut}_c(\mathbb{R})$ mapping a computable number to a noncomputable one. However, $\text{Aut}_c(\mathbb{R})$ acts m-transitively for all m on the set of computable real numbers, as follows from the next lemma, proof of which is not hard and will be omitted (see §2 of [4] where similar results are proved, note though that Lemma 1 does not hold in $\text{Aut}_c(\mathbb{Q})$).

Lemma 1. (cf. Lemmas 2.2 and 2.3 of [4]). *Let $(a_i)_{i \in \mathbb{Z}}$ and $(b_i)_{i \in \mathbb{Z}}$ be computable sequences of computable real numbers, both unbounded above and below, such that $a_i < a_j$ and $b_i < b_j$ when $i < j$. Then there is an $f \in \text{Aut}_c(\mathbb{R})$ such that $f(a_i) = b_i$ for all i.*

Every automorphism $f \in \text{Aut}(\mathbb{Q})$ can be uniquely extended by continuity to an automorphism $\bar{f} \in \text{Aut}(\mathbb{R})$. Under the continuation embedding $f \mapsto \bar{f}$, $\text{Aut}_c(\mathbb{Q})$ becomes a subgroup of $\text{Aut}_c(\mathbb{R})$. Note that $\text{Aut}_c(\mathbb{Q})$ is not an elementary subgroup of $\text{Aut}_c(\mathbb{R})$: to see this, construct positive bumps $f, g \in \text{Aut}_c(\mathbb{Q})$ such that $\sup(spf) = 0$ and $\sup(spg) = \sqrt{2}$. Clearly, f and g are not conjugate in $\text{Aut}_c(\mathbb{Q})$, but it is not hard to see that they are conjugate in $\text{Aut}_c(\mathbb{R})$. Because of the precise nature of classical first-order computability, boundary points of bumps in $\text{Aut}_c(\mathbb{Q})$ are always computable [4]. This is not the case in $\text{Aut}_c(\mathbb{R})$, but it is not hard to see that for every bump $f \in \text{Aut}_c(\mathbb{R})$, $\sup(spf)$ is c.e. (i.e., left-c.e.) and $\inf(spf)$ is co-c.e. (right-c.e.), if these bounds exist. In Theorem 8 for any given c.e. real z we construct a bounded above bump f whose upper boundary point is equal to z.

Theorem 8 means that, unlike in $\text{Aut}_c(\mathbb{Q})$, there are infinitely many conjugacy classes of bumps in $\text{Aut}_c(\mathbb{R})$. If bumps can be defined by the same first order group-theoretic formula in $\text{Aut}_c(\mathbb{R})$ and $\text{Aut}_c(\mathbb{Q})$, the previous fact will imply that these groups are not elementarily equivalent. Final result of the paper, Theorem 9, contributes towards the problem of definability in $\text{Aut}_c(\mathbb{R})$. Definability plays a major role in the study of ordered permutation groups (see Chap. 2 of Glass's book [3]). Classic results of McCleary [18] permit to define various properties of automorphisms in $\mathrm{Aut}(\mathbb{R})$ (comparability with the identity, being a bump, boundity, etc.) in the group-theoretic language. Morozov and Truss [4] studied definable properties of automorphisms in $\mathrm{Aut}_c(\mathbb{Q})$. They observed that the classical formula that defines bumps in $\mathrm{Aut}(\mathbb{R})$ does not work in $\mathrm{Aut}_c(\mathbb{Q})$, and came up with a new formula for bumps. This formula implies that for every bump $f \in \mathrm{Aut}_c(\mathbb{Q})$ and every automorphism $h \in \mathrm{Aut}_c(\mathbb{Q})$ the element ff^h must be conjugate with f, given that ff^h is a bump.

Theorem 9 shows that the formula of Morozov and Truss does not define bumps in $\mathrm{Aut}_c(\mathbb{R})$, for there exists a positive bounded above bump $f \in \mathrm{Aut}_c(\mathbb{R})$ that is not conjugate with f^2. This is also a strengthening of Theorem 6. Therefore, to prove that $\mathrm{Aut}_c(\mathbb{R})$ is not elementarily equivalent to $\mathrm{Aut}_c(\mathbb{Q})$, one should find another formula for bumps that works in both of these groups. We study definable properties in $\mathrm{Aut}_c(\mathbb{R})$ and the problem of elementary equivalence of $\mathrm{Aut}_c(\mathbb{R})$ and $\mathrm{Aut}_c(\mathbb{Q})$ in an upcoming journal paper.

We conclude the introduction with a limited version of Holland's criterion. Recall that all bumps of the same sign and the same boundity are pairwise conjugate in $\mathrm{Aut}(\mathbb{R})$.

Lemma 2. *Suppose that $f, g \in \mathrm{Aut}_c(\mathbb{R})$ are positive bounded above bumps such that $\sup(spf)$ and $\sup(spg)$ are computable. Then f and g are conjugate in $\mathrm{Aut}_c(\mathbb{R})$.*

Proof. See the proof of Lemma 2.12 of [4].

As a consequence, we obtain the following lemma.

Lemma 3. (Effective Holland's criterion). *Suppose that $f, g \in \mathrm{Aut}_c(\mathbb{R})$ are conjugate in $\mathrm{Aut}(\mathbb{R})$ and have finitely many nontrivial orbitals whose boundary points are computable. Then f and g are conjugate in $\mathrm{Aut}_c(\mathbb{R})$.*

2   Divisibility, Commutators and Normal Subgroups

Theorem 5. $\mathrm{Aut}_c(\mathbb{R})$ *is not divisible. More precisely, there is an $f \in \mathrm{Aut}_c(\mathbb{R})$ that does not have a computable kth root, for all $k \geqslant 2$.*

Proof. We follow the main lines of the proof of the similar result for $\mathrm{Aut}_c(\mathbb{Q})$ (Theorem 4.1 of [5]). Similarly to [5] (see e.g. Theorem 3.1 of the cited paper), we first outline the so called global properties of automorphism f that will be reused in future constructions. These are the following:

1. $f \geqslant e$,
2. $f(x) = x$ if $x \leqslant 0$ or $x = 4k$ for some $k \in \omega$,
3. $f(x) = x$ only if $x \leqslant 0$ or $x = 2k$ for some $k \in \omega$.

That is, nonnegative fixed points of f are endpoints of intervals $(4k, 4(k+1))$ and sometimes midpoints of these intervals. Intervals $(4k, 4(k+1))$ will be used in the construction for diagonalization. The following requirements have to be satisfied:

P_n: If Φ_n realizes a function $g \in \mathrm{Aut}_c(\mathbb{R})$, then $g^k \neq f$ for all $k \geqslant 2$.

The strategy for P_n will be the same as in [5]: if g looks like a root of f, then we make sure that g and f do not commute.

We work with requirement P_n on interval $(4n, 4(n+1))$. Each requirement will be handled independently with no injury, so we can restrict our attention just to the isolated requirement P_0 and describe the construction only on $(0, 4)$.

Define the initial approximation f_0 of f as follows: $f_0(0) = 0$, $f_0\left(\frac{1}{4}\right) = \frac{1}{2}$, $f_0\left(1\frac{1}{2}\right) = 1\frac{3}{4}$, $f_0(2) = 2$, $f_0\left(2\frac{1}{4}\right) = 2\frac{1}{2}$, $f_0\left(3\frac{1}{2}\right) = 3\frac{3}{4}$, $f_0(4) = 4$, and f_0 is linear elsewhere. Clearly, f_0 has the global properties of f. During the construction, we either might not change f_0 whatsoever (i.e. f will be equal to f_0 in the end) or change it once, collapsing the two positive orbitals $(0, 2)$ and $(2, 4)$ of f_0 into one positive orbital via a small variation of f_0 for diagonalization purposes. Thus, two possible options can occur: f has two positive orbitals $(0, 2)$ and $(2, 4)$ inside the interval $(0, 4)$, or the whole interval $(0, 4)$ is a positive orbital of f, which again complies with the global properties. The construction will run in stages, at stage s we must output a 2^{-s}-approximation of f. If P_0 hasn't required attention by stage s, then at the end of this stage we just agree that f can deviate from f_0 by no more than 2^{-s} in the future; and if P_0 does require attention at stage s, then we collapse the two orbitals of f_0 into one orbital by a variation not exceeding 2^{-s} which gives us the final form of f that never changes from now on.

Suppose that Φ_0 realizes a (total) function $g\colon \mathbb{R} \to \mathbb{R}$; if this is not the case, P_0 is satisfied automatically. If g is indeed a root of f, then $e < g < f$, in particular, $1 < g(1) < f(1)$ and $3 < g(3) < f(3)$. We check whether these inequalities hold, computing $g(1)$ and $g(3)$ with increasing precision. More formally, using Φ_0, we enumerate left and right Dedekind cuts of $g(1)$. If $g(1)$ really is between 1 and $f(1)$, then at some point 1 should appear in the left Dedekind cut of $g(1)$, and $f(1)$ should appear in the right cut. Moreover, Φ_0 should also give us rational numbers p and q such that $p > 1$ is in the left cut, $q < f(1)$ is in the right cut of $g(1)$. If this never happens, then $g(1) \notin (1, f(1))$, thus g cannot be a root of f, and P_0 is satisfied. Similar process runs for $g(3)$, with one difference that will be revealed shortly.

We keep enumerating left and right cuts of $g(1)$ and $g(3)$ until rational numbers p, q, u, v are found such that the following conditions hold:

1. $1 < p$ are in the left cut of $g(1)$,
2. $q < f_0(1)$ are in the right cut of $g(1)$,
3. 3 is in the left cut of $g(3)$,
4. $u < v < f_0(3)$ are in the right cut of $g(3)$.

If this process never halts, then g cannot be a root of f_0, and P_0 is satisfied by keeping $f = f_0$. If, however, the process halts and the numbers p, q, u, v are discovered at a stage s, then we say that P_0 *requires attention* at s, and we must actively diagonalize. We act as follows. Fix a $k > 1$ such that $f_0^{-k}(3) - f_0^k(1) \leqslant 2^{-s-1}$. Denote $\tilde{p} = f_0^k(p)$, $\tilde{q} = f_0^k(q)$, $\tilde{u} = f_0^{-k-1}(u)$, $\tilde{v} = f_0^{-k-1}(v)$. It is clear that $f_0^k(g(1)) \in (\tilde{p}, \tilde{q})$ and

$$f_0^k(1) < \tilde{p} < \tilde{q} < f_0^{k+1}(1) < f_0^{-k-1}(3) < \tilde{u} < \tilde{v} < f_0^{-k}(3).$$

Pick rational numbers b, c such that $f_0^{k+1}(1) < b < c < f_0^{-k-1}(3)$ and let

$$f(\tilde{p}) = b, f(\tilde{q}) = c, f(f_0^{k+1}(1)) = f_0^{-k-1}(3), f(b) = \tilde{u}, f(c) = \tilde{v}.$$

Also let $f(x) = f_0(x)$ for $x \in [0, f_0^k(1)] \cup [f_0^{-k-1}(3), 4]$ and let f be linear elsewhere on $[0, 4]$ (Fig. 1).

It follows from the above definitions that $f^{2k+3}(1) = 3$ (so 1 and 3 are now in the same f-orbital) and thus $g(f^{2k+3}(1)) = g(3)$. By the Patching Lemma it is easy to see that $f \in \text{Aut}(\mathbb{Q})$. Note also that $f^{2k+3}(p) = f^{k+3}(\tilde{p}) = f^{k+2}(b) = f^{k+1}(\tilde{u}) = u$ and $f^{2k+3}(q) = v$ which means $f^{2k+3}(g(1)) \in (u, v)$, but $g(3) < u$. Hence $g(f^{2k+3}(1)) \neq f^{2k+3}(g(1))$ meaning that g does not commute with f, and P_0 is satisfied. Formal construction runs as follows.

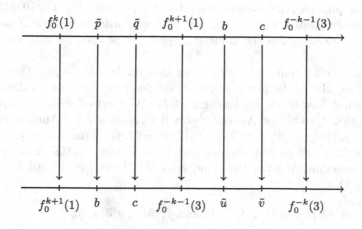

Fig. 1. Obtaining f by a variation of f_0.

Construction. Using Φ_0, enumerate Dedekind cuts of $g(1)$ and $g(3)$, occasionally ending stages and starting new ones. If P_0 requires attention at some stage, do as prescribed above to satisfy P_0.

It is clear that f is a computable automorphism, as long as we prove that if P_0 requires attention at stage s and f is obtained from f_0 by the procedure described above, then $\max_{x \in [0,4]} |f(x) - f_0(x)| \leqslant 2^{-s}$. By construction, since f and f_0 differ only on the interval $D = [f_0^k(1), f_0^{-k-1}(3)]$ and they both map D into the interval $[f_0^{k+1}(1), f_0^{-k}(3)]$, then

$$\max_{x \in [0,4]} |f(x) - f_0(x)| = \max_{x \in D} |f(x) - f_0(x)|$$

$$\leqslant \max_{x \in D} |f(x) - x| + \max_{x \in D} |x - f_0(x)|$$

$$\leqslant f_0^{-k}(3) - f_0^k(1) + f_0^{-k}(3) - f_0^k(1) \leqslant 2^{-s}.$$

Theorem 6. *There exists an automorphism* $f \in \text{Aut}_c(\mathbb{R})$ *such that, for all* $h \in \text{Aut}_c(\mathbb{R})$, $f \neq [f, h]$.

Proof. We need to meet the following list of requirements:

P_n: If Φ_n realizes a function $g \in \text{Aut}_c(\mathbb{R})$, then $f^2 \neq g^{-1}fg$.

The strategy for P_n will be to ensure that $f^k \neq g^{-1}f^kg$ for some $k \in \mathbb{Z}$. Automorphism f will possess the same global properties as the automorphism from the previous proof. First of all note that, as in the analogous result in [5] (Lemmas 5.6 and 5.7), these properties guarantee that if $f^2 = g^{-1}fg$ for $g \in \text{Aut}(\mathbb{R})$, then $g(I) = I$ for every nontrivial orbital I of f (and moreover $g(I) = I$ for every orbital I of f consisting of positive real numbers). This is because such a g induces a parity preserving ordermorphism between the orbital structures of f and f^2, but by the global properties the set $P = \{\text{orbital}(x) \mid x > 0\}$ of f-orbitals of positive reals contains a least element (either $(0, 2)$ or $(0, 4)$), so this ordermorphism maps P onto P. Finally, P is well-ordered by type ω because of the global properties, thus the induced mapping must coincide with the identity on P.

We work with requirement P_n on the interval $(4n, 4(n + 1))$. There will be no injury, so, like in the previous proof, we describe the construction only on $(0, 4)$ and show how to diagonalize against P_0. We start off with the same initial approximation f_0 as before. As seen above, if Φ_0 realizes a $g \in \text{Aut}_c(\mathbb{R})$ such that $f_0^2 = g^{-1}f_0g$, then $g(0, 2) = (0, 2)$ and $g(2, 4) = (2, 4)$, in particular, $g(1) \in (0, 2)$ and $g(3) \in (2, 4)$. So at first we just wait until g shows us this; more precisely, using Φ_0, we enumerate the Dedekind cuts of $g(1)$ and $g(3)$ until $i, j \in \mathbb{Z}$ are found such that

$$f_0^i(1) < g(1) < f_0^{i+2}(1) \text{ and } f_0^j(3) < g(3) < f_0^{j+2}(3). \tag{2.1}$$

If this never happens, then g cannot conjugate f_0^2 and f_0, and we win by keeping $f = f_0$. If, however, these i and j are found at a stage s, we say that P_0 *requires attention* at stage s. Now we want to collapse the two orbitals $(0, 2)$ and $(2, 4)$ into one by letting $f^{2k}(1) = 3$ for some k, which implies that $g(f^{2k}(1)) = g(3)$, and to satisfy P_0 we only need to make sure that $f^k(g(1)) \neq g(3)$. This can be achieved by a careful choice of a suitable k. From (2.1) it is quite easy to see that any $k \geqslant i - j + 2$ will do the job, details will be given later. Let us move on to the formal construction.

Construction. Using Φ_0, enumerate Dedekind cuts of $g(1)$ and $g(3)$, occasionally ending stages and starting new ones. If P_0 requires attention at stage s, react as follows. Pick a natural number $k \geqslant \max(i + 3, -j + 1, i - j + 2)$ such that $f_0^{-k+1}(3) - f_0^{k-1}(1) \leqslant 2^{-s-1}$. Let $f(f_0^k(1)) = f_0^{-k+1}(3)$, $f(x) = f_0(x)$ for $x \in [0, f_0^{k-1}(1)] \cup [f_0^{-k+1}(3), 4]$ and let f be linear elsewhere on $[0, 4]$.

Verification. Suppose that P_0 reqiures attention at stage s and f is obtained by a variation of f_0 as described above. The fact that f differs from f_0 only on the small interval $D = (f_0^{k-1}(1), f_0^{-k+1}(3))$, just like before, guarantees that $\max_{x \in [0,4]} |f(x) - f_0(x)| \leqslant 2^{-s}$. It is clear that $f^{2k}(1) = 3$. Property $k \geqslant \max(i + 3, -j + 1)$ implies that D does not intersect with $[f_0^i(1), f_0^{i+2}(1)]$ and $[f_0^j(3), f_0^{j+2}(3)]$, which ensures that the inequalities $f^i(1) < g(1) < f^{i+2}(1)$ and $f^j(3) < g(3) < f^{j+2}(3)$ are kept. Finally, inequality $k \geqslant i - j + 2$ can be rewritten as $-k + i + 2 \leqslant j$, which means that

$$f^k(g(1)) < f^{k+i+2}(1) = f^{-k+i+2}(f^{2k}(1)) \leqslant f^j(3) < g(3) = g(f^{2k}(1)),$$

and P_0 is satisfied.

In spite of the previous result, it is possible to prove that every element of $\mathrm{Aut}_c(\mathbb{R})$ is a commutator. The proof is completely identical to that of the rational case; it requires a simple lemma that permits to convert any given element of $\mathrm{Aut}_c(\mathbb{R})$ into an unbounded bump and then use Lemma 3, the effective Holland's criterion.

Lemma 4. (Lemma 5.3 of [5]). *For any $h \in \mathrm{Aut}_c(\mathbb{R})$ there exists a $p \in \mathrm{Aut}_c(\mathbb{R})$ such that both p and ph are unbounded positive bumps.*

Proof. Repeat the proof of the cited result. ∎

Corollary 1. (Theorem 5.4 of [5]). *Every element of $\mathrm{Aut}_c(\mathbb{R})$ is a commutator.*

Proof. Repeat the proof of the cited result and note that all unbounded bumps are conjugate in $\mathrm{Aut}_c(\mathbb{R})$ by the effective Holland's criterion. ∎

We move on to the next result stating that $B_c(\mathbb{R})$, $L_c(\mathbb{R})$ and $R_c(\mathbb{R})$ are the only nontrivial normal subgroups of $\mathrm{Aut}_c(\mathbb{R})$. Again, proof of this result will be based on the proof of the analogous fact for $\mathrm{Aut}_c(\mathbb{Q})$, and this time the old proof can be adapted to the new setting with almost no differences. We move the proof to the appendix.

Theorem 7. *$B_c(\mathbb{R})$, $L_c(\mathbb{R})$ and $R_c(\mathbb{R})$ are the only nontrivial normal subgroups of $\mathrm{Aut}_c(\mathbb{R})$.*

3 Conjugacy Classes of Bumps

Theorem 8. *Let z be a c.e. real number. Then there exists a bump $f \in \mathrm{Aut}_c(\mathbb{R})$ such that $z = \sup(spf)$.*

Proof. We assume that $z \in (0,1)$. Let $(q_n)_n$ be a computable increasing sequence of rational numbers converging to z. Without loss of generality we assume that $q_{n+2} - q_{n+1} \leqslant q_{n+1} - q_n$ for all n, i.e. distances between consecutive points do not increase (indeed, if $q_{n+2} - q_{n+1} > q_{n+1} - q_n$ for some n, we can just add finitely many new points between q_{n+2} and q_{n+1} splitting the distance). Automorphism f will be defined in stages. At stage s we output an approximation $f_s \in \text{Aut}_c(\mathbb{Q})$ for f, each f_s is piecewise linear with finitely many rational breakpoints. First of all we let $f_s(x) = x$ for all $s \in \omega$ and all $x \geqslant 2$.

Stage 0. Let $f_0(x) = x + q_1 - q_0$ for $x \leqslant 1$ and let f_0 be linear on $[1,2]$ (we assume that $q_1 - q_0 < 1$). Thus, 1 and 2 are the only breakpoints of f_0 and $f_0(q_0) = q_1$.

Stage $s + 1$. Define f_{s+1} as follows: $f_{s+1}(x) = f_s(x)$ for $x \leqslant q_s$, $f_{s+1}(x) = x + q_{s+2} - q_{s+1}$ for $x \in [q_{s+1}, 1]$, f_{s+1} is linear on $[q_s, q_{s+1}]$ and $[1,2]$. Thus, $f_{s+1}(q_{s+1}) = q_{s+2}$.

It follows from the construction that $f_{n+1}(x) = f_n(x)$ for $x \notin (q_n, 2)$, $n \in \omega$. Since $(q_{n+1} - q_n)_n$ monotonically converges to 0, we have $f_{n+1} \leqslant f_n$ for all n, i.e., $(f_n)_n$ is nonincreasing, and $f_n(x) \to x$ for $x \geqslant z$. We formally define f to be the pointwise limit of $(f_n)_n$. It is clear that f is a bump and $z = \sup(spf)$. To see that f is computable, note that, since $e \leqslant f \leqslant f_n$ (Fig. 2),

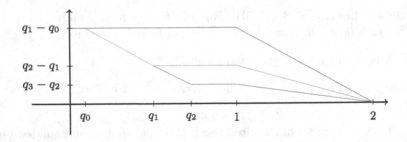

Fig. 2. Graphs of $g_n(x) = f_n(x) - x$ for several n.

$$\max_{x \in \mathbb{R}} |f_n(x) - f(x)| = \max_{x \in [q_n, 2]} |f_n(x) - f(x)| \leqslant \max_{x \in [q_n, 2]} |f_n(x) - x| = q_{n+1} - q_n,$$

i.e., $f_n \to f$ uniformly with a computable modulus of convergence.

Theorem 9. *There exists a positive bump $f \in L_c(\mathbb{R}) \setminus R_c(\mathbb{R})$ such that f and f^2 are not conjugate in $\text{Aut}_c(\mathbb{R})$.*

Proof. The construction is similar to that of Theorem 8. At each stage s we output an approximation f_s of f, where f_s is piecewise linear with finitely many rational breakpoints. First of all, for all s, we let $f_s(x) = x + 1$ for $x \leqslant 0$ and $f_s(x) = x$ for $x \geqslant 8$, so the entire construction will be carried out within the interval $(0,8)$. At every stage s there will be a rational number $r_s < 6$ such that $f_t(x) = f_s(x)$ for all $t \geqslant s$ and $x \leqslant r_s$, that is, after stage s we can only diagonalize inside $(r_s, 8)$. Moreover, to make sure that f is computable, we will guarantee that $|f_t(x) - x| \leqslant 2^{-s}$ for all $t \geqslant s$ and $x \in [r_s, 8]$; more precisely, we ensure that $f_s(x) = x + 2^{-s}$ for $x \in [r_s, 6]$, f_s linearly fades to the identity on $[6, 8]$, and $f_t(x) \leqslant f_s(x)$ on $[r_s, 8]$ from now on. These conditions imply that the upper boundary point of spf is a noncomputable real number between 0 and 6. We will also control that $r_s = f_s^k(0)$ for some k.

As usual, we need to diagonalize against every Turing functional, i.e., meet the following list of requirements:

P_e: If Φ_e realizes a function $g \in \mathrm{Aut}_c(\mathbb{R})$, then $f \neq g^{-1} f^2 g$.

The strategy for P_e proceeds as follows. Suppose that Φ_e realizes a function $g: \mathbb{R} \to \mathbb{R}$. We wait until the following events occur:

1. A rational number $a \in \{-1, -2, \dots\}$ and an integer i are found such that $f_0^i(a) < g(a) < f_0^{i+2}(a) \leqslant 0$,
2. $\mu(e)$ is computed, where μ is a modulus of continuity of g on the interval $[0, 6]$, i.e., for all $x, y \in [0, 6]$ and for all $n \in \omega$, $|x - y| \leqslant 2^{-\mu(n)}$ implies $|g(x) - g(y)| \leqslant 2^{-n}$.

It is clear that if Φ_e does indeed realize a total function g, then these conditions are met in finite time, since any real function defined on a closed interval computes its modulus of continuity (by compactness and the Use Principle); if at a stage s we observe that these conditions hold, we say that P_e *requires attention* at stage s. Now, if $f = g^{-1} f^2 g$, the first condition implies that $g(f^k(a)) \in (f^{2k+i}(a), f^{2k+i+2}(a))$ for all $k \in \mathbb{Z}$. Note also that $f^k(a) = 0$ for some positive k.

Suppose that P_e requires attention at stage $s + 1 > e$. Recall that we are allowed to work within the interval $(r_s, 8)$ and that $f_s(r_s) = r_s + 2^{-s}$. Let:

$$b_0 = r_s + 2^{-s}, \quad b_2 = b_1 + 2^{-\max(\mu(e), s+1)},$$
$$b_1 = b_0 + 2^{-s-1}, \; b_3 = b_2 + 2^{-e}.$$

Define a piecewise linear automorphism $\tilde{f}$ as follows:

- $\tilde{f}(x) = f_s(x)$ for $x \leqslant r_s$,
- $\tilde{f}(x) = x + 2^{-s-1}$ for $x \in [b_2, 6]$,
- $\tilde{f}(b_1) = b_1$, $\tilde{f}(8) = 8$,
- $\tilde{f}$ is linear on $[r_s, b_1]$, $[b_1, b_2]$ and $[6, 8]$.

$\tilde{f}$ has two nontrivial orbitals separated by the point b_1, we obtain the next approximation f_{s+1} by properly collapsing these orbitals into one. Fix $j > 0$ such that $r_s = f_s^j(a)$; such an integer exists, by the properties of a and r_s. Clearly, $b_0 = \tilde{f}^{j+1}(a)$ and $b_3 = \tilde{f}^l(b_2)$, where $l = 2^{s+1-e}$. Choose a natural number k_0 such that $k_1 = k_0 + j + i + 4 \geqslant l$. We are ready to define f_{s+1}:

- $f_{s+1}(x) = \tilde{f}(x)$ for all $x \leqslant \tilde{f}^{k_0-1}(b_0)$ and $x \geqslant \tilde{f}^{-k_1}(b_2)$,
- $f_{s+1}(\tilde{f}^{k_0}(b_0)) = \tilde{f}^{-k_1}(b_2)$,

– f_{s+1} is linear on $[\tilde{f}^{k_0-1}(b_0), \tilde{f}^{k_0}(b_0)]$.

It follows from this definition that $b_2 = f_{s+1}^{k_0+k_1+1}(b_0) = f_{s+1}^{k_0+k_1+j+2}(a)$. Let $c_0 = \tilde{f}^{-k_1}(b_2) = f_{s+1}^{k_0+j+2}(a)$ and $c_1 = f_{s+1}^{l}(c_0)$, then by the properties of the conjugating mapping g we have

$$g(c_0) = g(f_{s+1}^{k_0+j+2}(a)) < f_{s+1}^{2(k_0+j+2)+i+2}(a) = f_{s+1}^{k_0+j+i+4}(c_0) = f_{s+1}^{k_1}(c_0) = b_2$$

and, since $l = 2^{s+1-e} \geqslant 2$,

$$g(c_1) = g(f_{s+1}^{l+k_0+j+2}(a)) > f_{s+1}^{2(l+k_0+j+2)+i}(a) = f_{s+1}^{2l-2}(b_2) \geqslant f_{s+1}^{l}(b_2) = b_3.$$

Note that $c_1 - c_0 \leqslant 2^{-\mu(e)}$ since c_0 and c_1 belong to the interval $[b_1, b_2]$, but $g(c_1) - g(c_0) > b_3 - b_2 = 2^{-e}$, which contradicts the fact that μ is a modulus of continuity of g, so g cannot conjugate f_{s+1} and f_{s+1}^2, and P_e is satisfied. Let $r_{s+1} = b_3$ so the above inequalities hold for all subsequent approximations f_t.

Construction. *Stage 0.* Let $r_0 = 0$ and end the stage.

Stage $s+1$. Pick a requirement P_e with the least index $e < s+1$ that requires attention but has not been met yet, if there are any. Proceed as prescribed in the P_e-strategy above. End the stage.

Verification. It must be clear from the description of the P_e-strategy that it successfully does its job and satisfies P_e. It remains to note that if the P_e-strategy is invoked at a stage $s+1$, then it operates on the interval $[r_s, r_{s+1}]$ of length $r_{s+1} - r_s = b_3 - r_s \leqslant 2^{-s+1} + 2^{-e}$. Combined, all strategies will take up an interval of length at most $\sum_{s+1\in\omega} 2^{-s+1} + \sum_{e\in\omega} 2^{-e} = 4\sum_{s\geqslant 1} 2^{-s} + 2 = 6$, i.e., a subinterval of $[0,6]$.

4   Appendix: Proof of Theorem 7

As noted earlier, proof of this theorem is a direct adaptation of the proof of a similar fact for the group $\mathrm{Aut}_c(\mathbb{Q})$, Theorem 6.1 of [5]. Proofs of technical lemmas below will often completely coincide with their counterparts from [5], references given in parentheses, the only difference being that now we should consider computable real numbers and computable sequences of them instead of rational numbers and their computable sequences. In this case we will omit the proof of the lemma, and the reader can consult the cited result. We keep the proof of Lemma 5 for an illustration.

The proof will be split into the following claims. First we show that if $f \notin L_c(\mathbb{R}) \cup R_c(\mathbb{R})$ then the normal closure of f coincides with $\mathrm{Aut}_c(\mathbb{R})$. Then we prove that the normal closure of $f \in L_c(\mathbb{R}) \setminus R_c(\mathbb{R})$ coincides with $L_c(\mathbb{R})$, and dually for $R_c(\mathbb{R})$. Finally, we show that the normal closure of any element of $B_c(\mathbb{R})$ coincides with $B_c(\mathbb{R})$.

We say that positive orbitals of f are *cofinal (coinitial, coterminal)* if the set $\{x \in \mathbb{R} \mid f(x) > x\}$ is unbounded above (resp. below, or on both sides).

Lemma 5. (Lemma 6.3 of [5]). *If $f \in \mathrm{Aut}_c(\mathbb{R})$ has coterminal positive orbitals, then there is a $g \in \mathrm{Aut}_c(\mathbb{R})$ such that $f^g f$ is an unbounded positive bump.*

Proof. Choose a computable sequence $(z_n)_{n \in \mathbb{Z}}$ of computable reals coterminal in $\mathbb{R}$ such that $z_n < z_{n+1}$ and $f(z_{2n}) = z_{2n+1}$ for all $n \in \mathbb{Z}$. Using Lemma 1, define a computable automorphism g such that $g(z_n) = z_{n+1}$ for all n. Then $f^g(f(z_{2n})) = z_{2n+2}$ for all n, which implies that $f(x) > x$ for all $x \in \mathbb{R}$.

Lemma 6. (Lemma 6.4 of [5]). *Suppose that $f \notin L_c(\mathbb{R}) \cup R_c(\mathbb{R})$, its positive orbitals are cofinal but not coinitial. Then there is a g in the normal closure of f whose positive orbitals are coterminal.*

Now, suppose that $f \notin L_c(\mathbb{R}) \cup R_c(\mathbb{R})$. By Lemmas 5 and 6, there is an unbounded positive bump in the normal closure of f. Consider an arbitrary $h \in \mathrm{Aut}_c(\mathbb{R})$. By Lemma 4, there is a $p \in \mathrm{Aut}_c(\mathbb{R})$ such that p and ph are unbounded positive bumps. By the effective Holland's criterion, p and ph belong to the normal closure of f, thus so does h.

We now turn to the case $f \in L_c(\mathbb{R}) \setminus R_c(\mathbb{R})$.

Lemma 7. (Lemma 6.6 of [5]). *If $f \in L_c(\mathbb{R}) \setminus R_c(\mathbb{R})$, then there is a $g \in L_c(\mathbb{R})$ in the normal closure of f such that the positive orbitals of g are coinitial, g has a greatest orbital that is positive, and $\sup(spf)$ is computable.*

Lemma 8. (Lemma 6.7 of [5]). *Suppose that $f \in L_c(\mathbb{R}) \setminus R_c(\mathbb{R})$ has coinitial positive orbitals, a greatest orbital that is positive, and a computable $\sup(spf)$. Then the normal closure of f contains a positive bump $g \in L_c(\mathbb{R}) \setminus R_c(\mathbb{R})$ such that $\sup(spg)$ is computable.*

Proof. Let $a = \sup(spf)$. Choose a computable coinitial decreasing sequence $(z_n)_{n \in \omega}$ of computable real numbers such that $f(z_{2n+1}) = z_{2n}$ for all $n \in \omega$ and z_0 belongs to the greatest orbital of f. Define an $h \in \mathrm{Aut}_c(\mathbb{R})$ such that $h(z_{n+1}) = z_n$ for all n and $h(z_0) = a$. Let $g = f^h f$. It is easily checked that $g(z_{2n+3}) = z_{2n+1}$ for all n and $g(z_1) = z_0$. Suppose $x \in (z_1, a)$. Then $f(x) \in (z_0, a)$, $h(f(x)) > a$, so $g(x) = f(x) > x$. Finally, $g(x) = x$ for $x \geqslant a$. This means that g has one positive orbital $(-\infty, a)$.

Lemma 9. (Lemma 6.8 of [5]). *If $f \in L_c(\mathbb{R})$, then there exists a $p \in L_c(\mathbb{R})$ such that both p and ph are positive bumps unbounded below and $\sup(spp)$, $\sup(spph)$ are computable.*

Take an arbitrary element $f \in L_c(\mathbb{R}) \setminus R_c(\mathbb{R})$. We need to show that the normal closure of f is $L_c(\mathbb{R})$. By Lemmas 7 and 8, there is a positive bump $g \in L_c(\mathbb{R}) \setminus R_c(\mathbb{R})$ in the normal closure of f whose upper boundary point is computable. By Lemma 9 and the effective Holland's criterion, for any $h \in L_c(\mathbb{R})$ there is a $p \in L_c(\mathbb{R})$ such that p and ph are conjugate to g. Thus, h is in the normal closure of f.

It remains to consider the case $f \in B_c(\mathbb{R})$.

Lemma 10. (Lemma 6.10 of [5]). *Suppose that $f \in B_c(\mathbb{R})$, $f \neq e$. Then there is a g in the normal closure of f that has exactly two nontrivial orbitals, these orbitals are of different parity and are separated by a single neutral orbital (consisting of a computable point). Moreover, $\sup(spg)$ and $\inf(spg)$ are computable.*

Lemma 11. (Lemma 6.11 of [5]). *For any $h \in B_c(\mathbb{R})$, there is a $p \in B_c(\mathbb{R})$ such that both p and ph have exactly two nontrivial orbitals, these orbitals are of different parity, are separated by a single neutral orbital, and their boundary points are computable.*

Take a nontrivial $f \in B_c(\mathbb{R})$ and fix an $h \in B_c(\mathbb{R})$. By the two lemmas above and the effective Holland's criterion, there is a $p \in B_c(\mathbb{R})$ such that p and ph belong to the normal closure of f. Hence, so does h. This finishes the proof of Theorem 7.

Acknowledgement. The work is supported by the Mathematical Center in Akademgorodok under the agreement No. 075-15-2022-282 with the Ministry of Science and Higher Education of the Russian Federation.

References

1. Holland, Ch.: The lattice-ordered groups of automorphisms of an ordered set. Michigan Math. J. **10**(4), 399–408 (1963). https://doi.org/10.1307/mmj/1028998976
2. Weinberg, E.C.: Embedding in a divisible lattice-ordered group. J. London Math. Soc. **42**, 504–506 (1967)
3. Glass, A.M.W.: Ordered Permutation Groups. Cambridge Univ. Press, Cambridge (1981)
4. Morozov, A., Truss, J.: On computable automorphisms of the rational numbers. J. Symb. Log. **66**(3), 1458–1470 (2001). https://doi.org/10.2307/2695118
5. Lempp, S., McCoy, C., Morozov, A., Solomon, R.: Group theoretic properties of the group of computable automorphisms of a countable dense linear order. Order **19**, 343–364 (2002). https://doi.org/10.1023/A:1022878003199
6. Kreitz, Ch., Weihrauch, K.: Theory of representations. Theoret. Comput. Sci. **38**, 35–53 (1985)
7. Weihrauch, K.: Computable analysis. An introduction. Springer, Berlin (2000)
8. Ershov, Yu. L.: Theory of numberings. In: Griffor, E. R. Handbook of computability theory (Stud. Logic Found. Math., 140), Amsterdam, Elsevier, pp. 473–503 (1999)
9. Melnikov, A.G.: Computably isometric spaces. J. Symbolic Logic **78**(4), 1055–1085 (2013)
10. McNicholl, T.: Computable copies of ℓ^p. Computability **6**(4), 391–408 (2017)
11. Ershov, Yu., Goncharov, S.: Constructive models. Kluwer Academic Pub. New York (2000)
12. Ash, C., Knight, J.: Computable Structures and the Hyperarithmetical Hierarchy. Elsevier, Amsterdam (2000)
13. Goncharov, S.: Autostability of models and abelian groups. Algebra Logic **19**, 13–27 (1980)
14. Harrison-Trainor, M., Melnikov, A., Ng, K.M.: Computability of polish spaces up to homeomorphism. J. Symb. Log. **85**(4), 1–25 (2020)

15. Hoyrup, M., Kihara, T., Selivanov, V.: Degree spectra of homeomorphism types of Polish spaces. J. Symb. Log
16. Melnikov, A.: Computable topological groups and Pontryagin duality. Trans. Amer. Math. Soc. **370**(12), 8709–8737 (2018)
17. Ko, K.: Reducibilities on real numbers. Theor. Comput. Sci. **31**, 101–123 (1984)
18. McCleary, S.: Groups of homeomorphisms with manageable automorphism groups. Comm. Algebra **6**(5), 497–528 (1978). https://doi.org/10.1080/00927877808822256

A Diamond Embedding Theorem in the Quotient Structure $\mathbf{R}/NCup$

Hong Hanh Tran[1] and Guohua Wu[2(✉)]

[1] Mathematics Department, FPT University, Education Zone, Hoa Lac Hi-Tech Park, Km29 Thang Long Boulevard, Thach That, Hanoi, Vietnam
hanhth12@fe.edu.vn
[2] School of Physical and Mathematical Sciences, Nanyang Technological University, 21 Nanyang Link, Singapore 637371, Singapore
guohua@ntu.edu.sg

Abstract. Li, Wu, and Yang constructed two incomplete cuppable c.e. degrees $\mathbf{a}, \mathbf{b}$ such that there is no incomplete c.e. degree which cups both $\mathbf{a}, \mathbf{b}$ to $\mathbf{0}'$. This result can be interpreted as the existence of a minimal pair in $\mathbf{R}/NCup$, the quotient structure of upper semilattice of computably enumerable degrees modulo the ideal of noncuppable degrees. In this paper, we will prove a stronger result by constructing $\mathbf{a}$ and $\mathbf{b}$ such that $\mathbf{a} \cup \mathbf{b} = \mathbf{0}'$ and no incomplete c.e. degree can cup both of them to $\mathbf{0}'$. In other words, the diamond lattice can be embedded into $\mathbf{R}/NCup$ preserving 0 and 1.

1 Introduction

A c.e. degree $\mathbf{a}$ is called *cuppable* if there is an incomplete c.e. degree $\mathbf{b}$ such that $\mathbf{a} \cup \mathbf{b} = \mathbf{0}'$, and *noncuppable* otherwise. Sacks' Splitting Theorem implies the existence of incomplete cuppable degrees. Yates (unpublished) and Cooper [2] provided the existence of noncuppable degrees. In [5], Li, Wu and Zhang proposed a hierarchy of cuppable c.e. degrees $\mathbf{LC}_1 \subseteq \mathbf{LC}_2 \subseteq \mathbf{LC}_3 \subseteq \cdots$, where for each $n \geq 1$, $\mathbf{LC}_n$ denotes the class of low$_n$-cuppable degrees, and proved that $\mathbf{LC}_1$ is properly contained in $\mathbf{LC}_2$. Recently, Greenberg, Ng and Wu proved in [3] that there is an incomplete cuppable degree which can only be cupped to $\mathbf{0}'$ by high degrees (in fact, superhigh), showing that $\cup_n \mathbf{LC}_n$ does not exhaust all of the cuppable degrees.

In this paper, we look at the ideal generated by noncuppable degrees, and consider the structure of $\mathbf{R}/NCup$. Here $NCup$ denotes the ideal of noncuppable degrees in $\mathbf{R}$. In [4], Li, Wu, and Yang constructed two incomplete cuppable c.e. degrees $\mathbf{a}, \mathbf{b}$ such that there is no incomplete c.e. degree cupping both $\mathbf{a}, \mathbf{b}$ to $\mathbf{0}'$. Consequently, the corresponding equivalent classes $[\mathbf{a}], [\mathbf{b}]$ form a minimal pair in $\mathbf{R}/NCup$. Li, Wu, and Yang claimed that it is possible to have such

G. Wu—is partially supported by MOE Tier 1 grants RG111/19 and RG102/23, Singapore.

L. Levy Patey et al. (Eds.): CiE 2024, LNCS 14773, pp. 420–430, 2024.
https://doi.org/10.1007/978-3-031-64309-5_33

a diamond lattice embedding into $\mathbf{R}/NCup$. However, no writing of this claim has been done. In this paper, we apply the techniques developed in [1] (different from the one in [4]) to prove this diamond embedding theorem.

Theorem 1. *There are two incomplete c.e. degrees* $\mathbf{a}$ *and* $\mathbf{b}$ *such that* $\mathbf{a} \cup \mathbf{b} = \mathbf{0}'$ *and there is no c.e. degree cupping both* $\mathbf{a}$ *and* $\mathbf{b}$ *to* $\mathbf{0}'$.

For c.e. degrees $\mathbf{a}$ and $\mathbf{b}$ in Theorem 1, the corresponding equivalence classes $[\mathbf{a}]$ and $[\mathbf{b}]$ in $\mathbf{R}/NCup$ satisfies $[\mathbf{a}] \vee [\mathbf{b}] = [\mathbf{0}']$. We now show that $[\mathbf{a}] \wedge [\mathbf{b}] = [\mathbf{0}]$.

Let $[\mathbf{w}]$ be an element below both $[\mathbf{a}]$ and $[\mathbf{b}]$ in $\mathbf{R}/NCup$. We let $\mathbf{e}_1, \mathbf{e}_2 \in NCup$ such that $\mathbf{w} \leq \mathbf{a} \cup \mathbf{e}_1$ and $\mathbf{w} \leq \mathbf{b} \cup \mathbf{e}_2$. Suppose that $[\mathbf{w}] \neq [\mathbf{0}]$, i.e. $\mathbf{w}$ is cuppable. We let $\mathbf{u}$ be an incomplete c.e. degree such that $\mathbf{0}' = \mathbf{w} \cup \mathbf{u}$. We then have that $\mathbf{e}_1 \cup \mathbf{e}_2 \cup \mathbf{u}$ cups both $\mathbf{a}$ and $\mathbf{b}$ to $\mathbf{0}'$, which gives that $\mathbf{e}_1 \cup \mathbf{e}_2 \cup \mathbf{u} = \mathbf{0}'$. As $\mathbf{e}_1 \cup \mathbf{e}_2$ is in $NCup$, we have $\mathbf{u} = \mathbf{0}'$, a contradiction. Thus, $[\mathbf{w}] = [\mathbf{0}]$ and $[\mathbf{a}] \wedge [\mathbf{b}] = [\mathbf{0}]$.

Theorem 2. *The diamond lattice can be embedded into the quotient structure* $\mathbf{R}/NCup$ *preserving 0 and 1.*

Our notation and terminology are quite standard and generally follow Soare [6]. A parameter p is defined to be fresh at a stage s if $p > s$ and p is the least number not mentioned so far in the construction.

2   Proof of Theorem 1

We now construct two computably enumerable degrees wanted in Theorem 1. We construct c.e. sets A, B, D, F, and partial computable functionals Γ, Ω_i's, satisfying for all $e, i = \langle i_1, i_2, e \rangle$, the following requirements:

$$S : K = \Gamma^{A \oplus B},$$

$$P_e : D \neq \Phi_e^A,$$

$$Q_e : D \neq \Phi_e^B,$$

$$N_i : \Psi_{i_1}^{A \oplus W_e} = \Psi_{i_2}^{B \oplus W_e} = K \oplus F \rightarrow K = \Omega_i^{W_e}.$$

Here, K is a fixed complete c.e. set. We fix an effective enumeration $\{K_s\}_{s \in \omega}$ of K such that there is at most one number entering K at each stage. We fix an effective list of partial computable functionals Φ_e's and Ψ_e's. We will sometimes omit the indices i_1, i_2 in the requirement N_i in order to simplify notations, if it is clear from the context.

Here, the requirements $\{P_e\}_{e \in \omega}$ and the requirement $\{Q_e\}_{e \in \omega}$ imply that A and B are incomplete, and the requirement S ensures that $\deg(A) \vee \deg(B) = \mathbf{0}'$. The requirements $\{N_i\}_{i \in \omega}$ ensure that there is no incomplete c.e. set cupping both A and B to K.

The S-Strategy. To satisfy the S-requirement, we will define a partial computable functional Γ such that $\Gamma^{A \oplus B}$ is total and computes K correctly. The S-strategy works as follows: at a stage s,

S1. if there is some n such that- $\Gamma^{A\oplus B}(n)[s] \downarrow \neq K_s(n)$, then enumerate $\gamma(n)[s]$ to $A \cup B$, undefining $\Gamma^{A\oplus B}(y), y \geq n$.

S2. if there is no such n,- then for the least number n with $\Gamma^{A\oplus B}(n)[s] \uparrow$, define $\Gamma^{A\oplus B}(n)[s]$ as $K_s(n)$, with the use $\gamma(n)[s]$ as a fresh number.

The use function γ has the following properties:

(1) When $\gamma(n)$ is defined, it is defined as a fresh number;
(2) If $\Gamma^{A\oplus B}(n)[s] \downarrow$, then $\gamma(n)[s] \notin A_s \cup B_s$;
(3) For $m < n$, if $\gamma(n)[s] \downarrow$, then $\gamma(m)[s] \downarrow$ and $\gamma(m)[s] < \gamma(n)[s]$;
(4) $\Gamma^{A\oplus B}(n)$ is undefined at a stage $s+1$ iff $\gamma(m)[s]$ is enumerated into A or B at stage $s+1$ for some $m \leq n$;
(5) If $\Gamma^{A\oplus B}(n)[s] \downarrow$ and n enters K at stage $s+1$, then $\gamma(m)[s]$ is enumerated in A or B at stage $s+1$ for some $m \leq n$;

If the construction of Γ satisfies rules (1–5) and $\Gamma^{A\oplus B}$ is total, then $\Gamma^{A\oplus B}$ computes K correctly.

The P,Q-Strategies. Fix α as a P_e-strategy. α works in the standard way.

P1. Pick a fresh number k first and proceed to P2. In the construction, whenever a number $i \leq k$ enters K, goes to P2. We will say that α is reset when i enters K and we call k a killing point of α.

P2. Pick a fresh witness $x > k$.

P3. Wait for $\Phi_e^A(x)[s] \downarrow = 0$.

P4. Put $\gamma(k)[s]$ into B, x into D, and stop.

If at a stage s, P4 happens and $\gamma(k)[s]$ is enumerated into B, then $\Gamma^{A\oplus B}(n)$, $n \geq k$, are all undefined, and when $\gamma(n)$ is defined later, they are defined as numbers larger than $\phi_e^A(x)[s]$. This means that $\Phi_e^A(x)$ is preserved as $\Phi_e^A(x)[s]$, which is equal to 0. Consequently, $\Phi_e^A(x)$ remains as 0, which is different from $D(x)$, until α is reset (some number $i \leq k$ enters K). Note that as k is fixed, such a process of resetting can happen at most $k+1$ times and α is eventually satisfied.

The outcomes of P_e are:

w: wait at P3 forever for some x. In this case, $D(x) = 0 \neq \Phi_e^A(x)$,

s: stop at P4 forever from some stage s onward for some x, and no number $i \leq k$ enters K after stage s. In this case, $\Phi_e^A(x) \downarrow = 0 \neq D(x) = 1$.

A Q_e-strategy β acts similarly to α, by swapping A and B correspondingly.

Note that if α has priority higher than β, then when α acts and enumerates $\gamma(k)[s]$ into B (P4), β is initialized. This kind of injuries from α can happen at most finitely many often, and after a stage large enough, β will not be injured anymore and will be satisfied in its own manner.

The N-Strategies. Fix an N_i-strategy η, where $i = \langle i_1, i_2, e \rangle$. We would like to construct a partial computable functional Ω_η such that if $\Psi_{i_1}^{A\oplus W_e} = \Psi_{i_2}^{B\oplus W_e} =$

$K \oplus F$, then $\Omega_\eta^{W_e}$ is total and computes K correctly. Recall that at an η-stage s, the *length of agreement for* η is

$$l(\eta, s) = \max\{x < s : \forall y < x[\Psi_{i_1}^{A \oplus W_e}(y)[s] = \Psi_{i_2}^{B \oplus W_e}(y)[s] = K_s \oplus F_s(y)]\}.$$

Say that a stage s is η-*expansionary* if $s = 0$ or $l(\eta, s) > l(\eta, t)$ for any η-expansionary stage $t < s$. So at an η-expansionary stage s, for $x < l(\eta, s)$, let

$$\psi(x)[s] := \max\{\psi_{i_1}^{A \oplus W_e}(x)[s], \psi_{i_2}^{B \oplus W_e}(x)[s]\}.$$

We will define $\Omega_\eta^{W_e}$ at η-expansionary stages. For instance, at an η-expansionary stage s, if there is the least number p that $2p + 1 < l(\eta, s)$ and $\Omega_\eta^{W_e}(p) \uparrow$, we define $\Omega_\eta^{W_e}(p)[s] := K_s(p)$ with the use $\omega(p)[s]$ as a fresh number. After that, the computation $\Omega_\eta^{W_e}(p)$ is undefined only if W_e changes below $\psi(2p+1)[s]$. So, if p enters K after stage s, making $\Omega_\eta^{W_e}(p)[s] \downarrow \neq K(p)$, we need an appropriate change on W_e to undefine $\Omega_\eta^{W_e}(p)$.

The outcomes of N_i are:

i: i for the case that there are infinitely many η-expansionary stages. *In this case,* $\Omega_\eta^{W_e}$ *will be total and computes K correctly.*

f: for finitely many η-expansionary stages. *In this case,* $\Omega_\eta^{W_e}$ *will be partial.*

When the P, Q-Strategies are Involved, the following problem arises. Assume that $\Omega_\eta^{W_e}(p)[s] = K_s(p) = 0$ is defined at stage s, with use $\omega(p)[s] > \psi(2p+1)[s]$ and also assume that W_e never changes below $\omega(p)[s]$ after stage s. It may happen that at an η-expansionary stage $s' > s$, a lower priority P-strategy $\alpha \succeq \eta^\smallfrown\langle i\rangle$ puts a number below $\psi(2p)[s]$ into B, and later a Q-strategy puts a number below $\psi(2p)[s]$ into A, followed by the enumeration of p into K. Then at the next η-expansionary stage s'' after s',

$$\Psi^{A \oplus W_e}(2p)[s''] = \Psi^{B \oplus W_e}(2p)[s''] = K_{s''} \oplus F_{s''}(2p) = K_{s''}(p) = K(p) = 1;$$

then the computation $\Omega_\eta^{W_e}(p)[s] \downarrow = 0 \neq 1 = K(p)$ may not be redefined correctly.

To solve this problem, we enumerate prepared numbers into F, another (auxiliary) set being constructed. That is, when $\alpha \succeq \eta^\smallfrown\langle i\rangle$ picks a witness x and a killing point k, it also takes an *attached* number z not in F and we say that a stage $t > s_0$ is η-expansionary if the length of agreement $l(\eta, t) > 2z + 1$. This delays the construction for a while but it does no harm if there are infinitely η-expansionary stages. With this, when $\Omega^{W_e}(p)$ is defined at stage t, we let $\omega(p)[t] > \psi(2z+1)[t]$. Thus, when α is ready to put x into D and $\gamma(k)$ into B [to undefine $\Gamma^{A \oplus B}(k)$], it also puts z into F. Then at the next η-expansionary stage $s_2 > s_1$, we have W_e has changes below $\psi^{A \oplus W_e}(2z+1)[s_1]$ (hence below $\omega(p)[t]$), and $\Omega^{W_e}(p)$ has no definition at stage s_2, and the reason for this is that while we enumerate the number $\gamma(k)$ into B, we enumerate no numbers into A, and hence the computations $\Psi^{A \oplus W_e}(2z+1)[s'_2]$ and $\Psi^{A \oplus W_e}(2z+1)[s_1]$ are different, which is caused by changes of W_e below $\psi^{A \oplus W_e}(2z+1)[s_1]$. The idea of using enumerating numbers z into F has been fully described in [1,4].

The S-Strategy Again. We consider the interaction between the S-strategy and the N-strategies, also P, Q-strategies, of course. In [1,4], making A and B cuppable is easy, as we are constructing incomplete c.e. sets C and D such that C cups A and D cups B, to K respectively, and when K changes, we mostly just enumerate the corresponding γ, δ-uses into C and D respectively. Here, in our construction, we want A cups B to K via the partial computable functional Γ and we need to consider into which sets, A or B, should we enumerate $\gamma(k)$, which turns out to be subtle and makes our construction more complicated.

Again, we assume that $\alpha \succeq \eta^\wedge \langle i \rangle$ enumerates x into D, $\gamma(k)$ into B and z into F, then we see n enters K at a later stage. If $n \geq k$, then we enumerate $\gamma(n)$ into A, as $\gamma(n)$ is undefined when $\gamma(k)$ is enumerated into B, and when $\gamma(n)$ is defined again, this new $\gamma(n)$ is defined as a big number and the enumeration of it into A will not change the computations $\Psi^{A \oplus W_e}(y)$. For the case when $n < k$, we enumerate $\gamma(n)$ into B, as $\gamma(k)$ is also enumerated into B (the B-side computations are changed), and the only side we can preserve is the A-side. This will keep our idea of forcing W_e to change below $\omega(p)[t]$ to keep $\Omega_\eta^{W_e}(p)[s]$ always correct, when defined. We will say that the enumeration of $\gamma(n)$, $n < k$, is directed to B by α in this simple situation.

Similarly, the enumeration of $\gamma(n)$, $n < k$, is directed to A, if the corresponding strategy is a Q-strategy, β.

In general, for a number m, the enumeration of $\gamma(n)$, $n < m$, is directed into A or B depending on the priority of the corresponding strategies. Precisely, we assume without loss of generality that $[0, k_1)$ is directed to B by a P-strategy α and $[k_1, k_2)$ is directed to A by a Q-strategy β where β has priority lower than α, which means that α acts first and put the direction of enumeration of numbers into B, and β acts later and put the direction of enumerations into A. If a number j less than k_1 enters K later, by α's direction, $\gamma(j)$ is put into B, and as β is initialized, β's direction becomes invalid. If a number $i \in [k_1, k_2)$ enters K later, by β's direction, $\gamma(i)$ is put into A. Note that when α acts, $\gamma(k_1)$ is enumeratd into B, and numbers enumerated into A by β's directions are large and will not affect those η-strategies with $\eta^\wedge \langle i \rangle \subseteq \alpha$. On the other hand, when β is initilized, the direction of enumerations of $\gamma(i)$, $i \in [k_1, k_2)$ will be handed over to other strategies, τ say. In particular, τ might direct the enumeration of $\gamma(i)$ into B. Here is the point: when τ is active to be eligible to direct enumerations, τ should be visited first, and for those η with $\eta^\wedge \langle i \rangle \subseteq \beta, \tau$, the corresponding W already have changes to undefine the involved $\Omega^W(p)$ (through the number z selected by β).

We are ready to provide the full construction.

3   The Construction

We first set up the priority tree of strategies for P, Q, N-requirements as follows. We don't put S on the tree as it is a global requirement. Let $\Lambda = \{i < f < s < w\}$ as the set of outcomes and $\Lambda^{<\omega}$ with the lexicographical ordering induced from the order in Λ. We effectively list all P, Q, N-requirements and assign to each node $\tau \in \Lambda^{<\omega}$ of length e the e-th requirement, for every $e \in \omega$. Here, the root λ is assigned to the requirement P_0. The priority tree of strategies T is a subtree of $\Lambda^{<\omega}$, where each node $\tau \in T$ is considered as a strategy of its corresponding requirement, and τ has nodes $\tau^\frown \langle o \rangle$ (with o ranging over all possible outcomes of τ) as its immediate successors.

In the construction, a strategy can have a couple of parameters attached. In particular, each P-strategy α has parameters $k(\alpha)$, $x(\alpha)$, $z(\alpha)$ corresponding to the killing point k, the witness x and the number z for forcing changes of W, respectively. Similarly, a Q-strategy β has parameters $k(\beta)$, $x(\beta)$, $z(\beta)$. An N-strategy η will be attached with a parameter $l(\eta)$ for measuring the length of agreements. If a strategy is initialized, we set its parameters as undefined and invalidate the corresponding direction of putting numbers into A (by a Q-strategy) or into B (by a P-strategy).

The construction is as follows.

Stage 0. Let all sets be empty and all strategies be initialized.

Stage $s + 1$.

(a) Working for the S-strategy. Let n be the number enters K at this stage.
S1. Find the corresponding strategy τ which direct the enumeration of $\gamma(n)$. Enumerate $\gamma(n)$ into A or B accordingly. Initialize all strategies with priority lower than τ.
S2. If there is no such a τ, then find a strategy ζ with the highest priority such that $n < k(\zeta)$. Enumerate $\gamma(n)$ into A to undefine $\Gamma^{A \oplus B}(y)$ for all $y \geq n$, and initialize all strategies with priority lower than ζ.
S3. Otherwise, find the least number p with $\Gamma^{A \oplus B}(p)[s + 1]$ not defined yet, define $\Gamma^{A \oplus B}(p)[s + 1] = K_{s+1}(p)$ with use $\gamma(p)[s + 1]$ fresh.
(b) Working on the priority tree for P, Q, N-strategies.

Compute the current true path TP_{s+1} inductively: $\tau_0 = \lambda$; if $\tau \preceq TP_{s+1}$ is of length $s + 1$, let $\tau = TP_{s+1}$, initialise all strategies to the right of TP_{s+1} and go to the next stage; otherwise, initialise all strategies to the right of τ and compute its immediate successor $\tau \prec \tau' \preceq TP_{s+1}$ as below.

There are three cases.
Case 1. τ is a P_e-strategy α. Proceeds as follows.

$\alpha 1.$ If $k(\alpha) \uparrow$, set it as fresh. Go to $\alpha 2$.
$\alpha 2.$ If $x(\alpha) \downarrow$, go to $\alpha 3$.
Otherwise, set $x(\alpha) \uparrow$ as fresh, and choose its attached sequence $z(\alpha) = (z_1, \cdots, z_{k(\alpha)})$. Let $\alpha^\frown \langle w \rangle = \tau' \preceq TP_{s+1}$ and initialise all lower priority strategies.
$\alpha 3.$

- If $\Phi_e^A(x(\alpha))[s+1] \downarrow = 0$, and $x(\alpha) \in D$, then let $\alpha^{\hat{}}\langle s \rangle = \tau' \preceq TP_{s+1}$,
- If $\Phi_e^A(x(\alpha))[s+1] \downarrow = 0$, and $x(\alpha) \notin D$, then put x into D, put $\gamma(k(\alpha))$ into B, and declare that when $n \in [q, k(\alpha))$ enters K, $\gamma(n)$ is enumerated into B. Here q is the current such that all numbers less than q have been directed by strategies with priority higher than α. Let $\alpha^{\hat{}}\langle s \rangle = \tau' \preceq TP_{s+1}$, initialize all lower priority strategies, and go to the next stage.
- Otherwise, let $\alpha^{\hat{}}\langle w \rangle = \tau' \preceq TP_{s+1}$.

Case 2. τ is a Q_e-strategy β. β works in a way similar to α.
Case 3. τ is an N_e-strategy η. η works as follows.

- If $s+1$ is an expansionary stage for η, then for the least $p \leq l(\eta, s+1)$ such that $\Omega_\eta^{W_e}(p)$ has not been defined yet, set $\Omega_\eta^{W_e}(p)[s+1] = K_{s+1}(p)$ with use $\omega(p)[s+1]$ fresh. let $\eta^{\hat{}}\langle i \rangle = \tau' \preceq TP_{s+1}$.
- Otherwise, let $\eta^{\hat{}}\langle w \rangle = \tau' \preceq TP_{s+1}$.

This completes the construction.

4   Verification

We let $TP = \liminf_{s \to \infty} TP_s$. The following lemma shows that TP is infinite.

Lemma 1. *For each node $\tau \prec TP$,*

(i) *There is a stage s_0 after which τ is not initialised and for any stage $t \geq s_0$, either $\tau \prec TP_t$ or $\tau < TP_t$. As a consequence, no node to the left of τ is accessible after stage s_0.*
(ii) *The node τ is accessible at infinitely many stages.*
(iii) *If τ is a P, Q-strategy then there is a stage s_0 after which $k(\tau)$ never changes and τ never acts by enumerating numbers into A, B, D or F.*
(iv) *There is unique $o \in \Lambda$ (the true outcome of τ) such that $\tau^{\hat{}}\langle o \rangle \prec TP$.*

Proof. We prove the lemma by induction on the length of $\tau \prec TP$.

First consider the root λ. As λ has the highest priority on the tree and $\lambda \preceq TP_s$ for all $s \geq 0$, so λ is never initialised after stage 0. Hence for λ, (i) and (ii) is satisfied.

We have that λ is a P_0-strategy with killing point k. Since λ never is initialized, $k(\lambda)$ never changes. Denote it by k. Clearly, λ is injured only at most $k+1$ times when a number $n \leq k$ enters K. Hence, from some stage $\bar{s}$ onward, there is no number less than or equal to k entering K, and λ eventually reaches its true outcome o at a stage $s_0 \geq \bar{s}$. If $o = s$, λ acts at stage s_0, by putting $\gamma(k(\lambda))$ into B, x into D, and $z(\lambda)$ into F and never puts numbers into these sets after stage s_0. If $o = w$, then λ will never act, and no number is put into A, B, D or F after stage s_0. (iii) holds for λ. We also have that $\lambda^{\hat{}}\langle o \rangle \prec TP_t$ for any $t > s_0$ and (iv) also holds for $\lambda^{\hat{}}\langle o \rangle$.

Suppose inductively that the nodes $\lambda = \tau_0 \prec \tau_1 \prec \cdots \prec \tau_{n-1} \prec TP$ satisfy $(i) - (iv)$, where $\tau_{i+1} = \tau_i\hat{\ }\langle o_i \rangle$ with $o_i \in \Lambda$ is the true outcome of τ_i for any $0 \leq i \leq n-1$. We will prove that $\tau_n = \tau_{n-1}\hat{\ }\langle o_{n-1} \rangle$ also satisfies $(i) - (iv)$.

Let s be the first stage at which τ_n is accessible at s and after stage s,

(a) if $\zeta \leq \tau_n$ is a P, Q-strategy, then $k(\zeta)$ never changes and no number is enumerated into A, B, D or F by ζ (set $k_0 := \max\{k(\zeta) : \zeta \leq \tau_n\}$);
(b) no node to the left of τ_n is accessible;
(c) there is no number $n \leq k_0$ entering K.

There are three cases.

Case 1. τ_n is a P_e-strategy α. Clearly, α will never be initialised after stage s and hence, $k(\alpha) \downarrow = k(\alpha)[s^+]$, where s^+ is the next α-stage of s. Since $\alpha = \tau_{n-1}\hat{\ }\langle o_{n-1} \rangle \prec TP$, (i-ii) holds for α. In addition, α is only injured at most $k(\alpha)[s^+]+1$ times, whenever a number $n \leq k(\alpha)[s^+]$ enters K. Let $s' \geq s$ be a stage after that there is no number $n \leq k(\alpha)[s^+]$ entering K. Clearly, eventually at a stage $s'' \geq s'$, α has the true outcome o, i.e. $\alpha\hat{\ }\langle o \rangle \prec TP$. If $o = w$, it never acts and hence, no number is put into A, B, D or F after stage s''. If $o = s$, after putting $\gamma(k(\alpha))$ into B, $x(\alpha)$ into D, and $z(\alpha)$ into F, α satisfies its P-requirement forever and never puts numbers into these sets after stage s''.

Case 2. τ_n is a Q_e-strategy β. Similarly to case 1, β finally has the true outcome o, and satisfies $(i) - (iv)$.

Case 3. τ_n is an N_e-strategy η. Then η is not initialised after stage s. We have:

- either η has true outcome f: $\eta\hat{\ }\langle f \rangle$ is accessible at stage $s_0 \geq s$ and for any stage $t > s_0$, $\eta\hat{\ }\langle f \rangle \prec TP_t$.
- or it reaches the true outcome i at infinitely many η-stages: let $t_0 \geq s$ be the first stage that $\eta\hat{\ }\langle i \rangle$ is accessible, we have that $\eta\hat{\ }\langle i \rangle \preceq TP_t$ for any η-expansionary stage $t \geq t_0$ and for any $t > t_0$ at which $\eta\hat{\ }\langle i \rangle$ is not accessible, we have that $\eta\hat{\ }\langle i \rangle < TP_t$.

Lemma 2. *For every $\tau \prec TP$, the requirement corresponding to τ is satisfied.*

Fix $\tau \prec TP$ of length e. From Lemma 1, let $\tau\hat{\ }\langle o \rangle \prec TP$ and s_0 be the first stage such that

(a) $\tau\hat{\ }\langle o \rangle \preceq TP_{s_0}$ is accessible at stage s_0 and $\tau\hat{\ }\langle o \rangle$ is never initialized after stage s_0,
(b) no strategy to the left of $\tau\hat{\ }\langle o \rangle$ is accessible after stage s_0,
(c) no P, Q-strategy $\alpha \preceq \tau$ puts numbers into A, B, D or F during or after stage s_0,

(d) there is no number $n \leq k_0$ entering K during or after stage s_0, where $k_0 = \max\{k(\zeta) : \zeta \leq \tau\}$.

There are two cases:

Case 1. τ is a P, Q-strategy α.

Without loss of generality, suppose that α is a P_e-strategy. Clearly, $k(\alpha) \downarrow = k(\alpha)[s_0]$, $x(\alpha) \downarrow = x(\alpha)[s_0]$. If $\alpha^\frown\langle w \rangle \prec TP$, then $D(x(\alpha)) = 0 \neq \Phi_e^A(x(\alpha))$. If $\alpha^\frown\langle s \rangle \prec TP$ then $D(x(\alpha)) = 1 \neq 0 = \Phi_e^A(x(\alpha))$. Thus, P_e is satisfied.

Case 2. τ is an N_e-strategy η.

Suppose that $\Psi^{A \oplus W_e} = \Psi^{B \oplus W_e} = K \oplus F$. Then there are infinitely many η-expansionary stages and $o = i$. We will prove by induction on $p \in \omega$ that for every $p \in \omega$, $\Omega_\eta^{W_e}(p) \downarrow = K(p)$. Hence, $\Omega_\eta^{W_e}$ is total and computes K correctly.

For $p = 0$, from the choice of s_0, we have that at the end of stage s_0, $\Omega_\eta^{W_e}(0)[s_0] = K_{s_0}(0)$ has been already defined with the use $\omega(0)[s_0]$ as a fresh number. If 0 never enters K, this computation remains correct, i.e. $\Omega_\eta^{W_e}(0) \downarrow = \Omega_\eta^{W_e}(0)[s_0] = K_{s_0}(0) = K(0)$. Otherwise, if 0 enters K at stage $t > s_0$, let $s_1 \geq t$ be the next η-expansionary stage. We have

$$\Psi^{A \oplus W_e}(0)[s_0] = \Psi^{B \oplus W_e}(0)[s_0] = K_{s_0} \oplus F_{s_0}(0) = K_{s_0}(0) = 0, \tag{1}$$

and

$$\Psi^{A \oplus W_e}(0)[s_1] = \Psi^{B \oplus W_e}(0)[s_1] = K_{s_1} \oplus F_{s_1}(0) = K_{s_1}(0) = 1. \tag{2}$$

Since all parameters chosen by $\zeta \succeq \tau^\frown\langle i \rangle$ are larger than $\psi(l(e, s_0))[s_0]$, no number less than or equal to $\psi(0)[s_1]$ is put into A or B by $\zeta \succeq \tau^\frown\langle i \rangle$ during stages between s_0 and s_1. Moreover, the strategy S only puts small numbers into one side (it is A if no $\zeta \succeq \tau^\frown\langle i \rangle$ directs the side of enumerations or it is the side directed by $\tau^\frown\langle i \rangle$) during these stages. Hence, at stage s_1, equation (2) is achieved because W_e has changed below $\omega(0)[s_0]$, allowing $\Omega_\eta^{W_e}(0)[s_0]$ to be undefined. At the next η-expansionary stage $s_2 > s_1$, $\Omega_\eta^{W_e}(0)[s_2]$ will be redefined as $1 = K(0)$ with use $\omega(0)[s_2]$ as fresh. This computation will be remained correctly forever. So, we have $\Omega_\eta^{W_e}(0) \downarrow = \Omega_\eta^{W_e}(0)[s_2]$.

Suppose that $\Omega_\eta^{W_e}$ correctly computes K up to $p - 1 \geq 0$, i.e. there is a stage $s \geq s_0$ such that for any $q \leq p - 1$,

$$\Omega_\eta^{W_e}(q) \downarrow = \Omega_\eta^{W_e}(q)[s] \downarrow = K_s(q) = K(q).$$

Let $t_1 \geq s_0$ be the smallest such stage. From the construction, we have that at the end of stage t_1, $\Omega_\eta^{W_e}(p) \uparrow$. At the next η-expansionary stage $t_2 > t_1$, we define $\Omega_\eta^{W_e}(p)[t_2] = K_{t_2}(p)$ with a fresh use $\omega(p)[t_2]$.

If p never enters K after stage t_2, this computation is correct, i.e., $\Omega_\eta^{W_e}(p) \downarrow = \Omega_\eta^{W_e}(p)[t_2] = K_{t_2}(p) = K(p)$. Otherwise, suppose that p enters K at stage

$s' > t_2$. Let $t_3 \geq s'$ be the next η-expansionary stage. We will prove that W_e has changed below $\omega(p)[t_2]$ at a stage s, where $t_2 < s \leq t_3$, allowing $\Omega_\eta^{W_e}(p)$ to be undefined at stage t_3. At the next η-expansionary stage $t_4 > t_3$, we then redefine $\Omega_\eta^{W_e}(p)[t_4] = 1 = K(p)$ and this computation will be correct forever. Indeed, we have

$$\Psi^{A \oplus W_e}(2p)[t_2] = \Psi^{B \oplus W_e}(2p)[t_2] = K_{t_2} \oplus F_{t_2}(2p) = K_{t_2}(p) = 0, \qquad (3)$$

and

$$\Psi^{A \oplus W_e}(2p)[t_3] = \Psi^{B \oplus W_e}(2p)[t_3] = K_{t_3} \oplus F_{t_3}(2p) = K_{t_3}(p) = 1. \qquad (4)$$

Note that the computations in (3) are only affected by the changes in W_e or by actions of the strategy S and P, Q-strategies $\zeta \succeq \tau^\frown\langle i \rangle$ that take parameters before stage t_2. At an η-expansionary stage, at most one P, Q-strategy can put numbers into A or B. Moreover, if $n \geq p$ enters K at a stage $t > t_2$, the strategy S puts $\gamma(n)$ into side A or B determined by only one P, Q-strategy which captures the interval $[m, r)$ containing n. Hence, for the least $q \geq p$ such that the computations $\Psi^{A \oplus W_e} \upharpoonright (2q+1)[t_2] = \Psi^{B \oplus W_e} \upharpoonright (2q+1)[t_2] = K_{t_2} \oplus F_{t_2} \upharpoonright (2q+1)$ has been changed from 0 to 1 during two consecutive η-expansionary stages between t_2 and t_3, W_e has been changed below $\min\{\gamma(q), \psi(2q+1)\} \leq \omega(p)[t_2]$ during these stages. This allows $\Omega_\eta^{W_e}(p)[t_2]$ to be undefined, and at stage t_3, we can redefine $\Omega^{W_e}(p)$ correctly. This completes the inductive step.

Lemma 3. *The requirement S is satisfied.*

Proof. We prove it by induction on n that $\Gamma^{A \oplus B}(n) \downarrow= K(n)$ for all n.

For $n = 0$, at the beginning of stage 1, we define $\Gamma^{A \oplus B}(0)[1]$ and $\gamma(0)[1]$. After that, all killing points are chosen as fresh large numbers and will not affect $\Gamma^{A \oplus B}(0)[1]$. Therefore, the computation $\Gamma^{A \oplus B}(0)[1]$ remains unchanged and computes $K(0)$ correctly unless 0 enters K at a stage $s > 1$. If the latter happens, then $\gamma(0)[1]$ is enumerated into A or B and $\Gamma^{A \oplus B}(0)$ is undefined at the beginning of stage s. At stage $s + 1$, $\Gamma^{A \oplus B}(0)$ will be redefined correctly forever, i.e. $\Gamma^{A \oplus B}(0) \downarrow= \Gamma^{A \oplus B}(0)[s + 1] = K(0)$.

Suppose that $\Gamma^{A \oplus B}(m) \downarrow= K(m) \forall 0 \leq m < n$. Let s be the first stage at which $\Gamma^{A \oplus B}(m) \downarrow= \Gamma^{A \oplus B}(m)[s] \downarrow= K_s(m) = K(m)$, $\forall m < n$. From the construction, at the end of stage s, we have $\Gamma^{A \oplus B}(n) \uparrow$. At the beginning of stage $s + 1$, we define $\Gamma^{A \oplus B}(n)[s + 1] = K_{s+1}(n)$ with $\gamma(n)[s + 1]$ as a fresh number. We have that no $\gamma(m)[s]$ (for any $m < n$) will be put into A or B after stage s. From the construction, $\gamma(n)[s+1]$ is enumerated into A or B at a stage $t > s + 1$ only if $n \in K_t \setminus K_{t-1}$. In addition, only the P, Q-strategy which takes its killing point $k = n$, may put $\gamma(n)$ into B or A, and this action occurs at most two times. Hence, there is a stage $s' \geq s + 1$ such that $\gamma(n)$ is not enumerated into B by a P-strategy (or into A by a Q-strategy) after s'. If at stage $s' + 1$, $\Gamma^{A \oplus B}(n) \uparrow$, then in step S2 we define $\Gamma^{A \oplus B}(n)[s' + 1] = K_{s'+1}(n)$. So, without loss of generality, we can suppose that $\Gamma^{A \oplus B}(n)[s' + 1] \downarrow= K_{s'+1}(n)$ and there is no P, Q-strategy which puts $\gamma(n)[s' + 1]$ into B or A after stage $s' + 1$. Then the computation $\Gamma^{A \oplus B}(n)[s' + 1]$ remains unchanged unless n enters K at a stage $s'' > s' + 1$. If the latter happens, $\Gamma^{A \oplus B}(n)$ will be rectified at stage $s'' + 1$ and will be correct forever. Thus, $\Gamma^{A \oplus B}(n)$ is defined and is equal to $K(n)$.

References

1. Bie, R., Wu, G.: A minimal Pair in the quotient structure $M/NCup$. In: Cooper, S.B., Löwe, B., Sorbi, A. (eds.) CiE 2007. LNCS, vol. 4497, pp. 53–62. Springer, Heidelberg (2007). https://doi.org/10.1007/978-3-540-73001-9_6
2. Cooper, S.B.: On a theorem of C. E. M. Yates, Handwritten Notes (1974)
3. Greenberg, N., Ng, K.M., Wu, G.: Cupping and jump classes in the computably enumerable degrees. J. Symbolic Logic 5(4), 1499–1545 (2020)
4. Li, A., Wu, G., Yang, Y.: On the quotient structure of computably enumerable degrees modulo the noncuppable ideal. In: Cai, J.-Y., Cooper, S.B., Li, A. (eds.) TAMC 2006. LNCS, vol. 3959, pp. 731–736. Springer, Heidelberg (2006). https://doi.org/10.1007/11750321_69
5. Li, A., Wu, G., Zhang, Z.: A hierarchy for cuppable degrees. Illinois J. Math. 44(3), 619–632 (2000)
6. Soare, R.I.: Recursively Enumerable Sets and Degrees. Perspectives in Mathematical Logic. Springer, Berlin (1987)

The Decision Problem for Undirected Graphs with Reachability and Acyclicity

Domenico Cantone[1]([✉]), Andrea De Domenico[2], and Pietro Maugeri[1]

[1] University of Catania, Catania, Italy
{domenico.cantone,pietro.maugeri}@unict.it
[2] Vrije Universiteit Amsterdam, Amsterdam, The Netherlands
a.de.domenico@vu.nl

Abstract. We address the decision problem for a theory about undirected graphs with reachability and acyclicity predicates, denoted UGRA, encompassing graph and node variables, the basic Boolean set operators ∪, ∩, \, singleton graphs, and predicates for acyclicity and reachability. By drawing from the well-established techniques of Computable Set Theory, we prove the decidability of the theory UGRA by showing that it enjoys the following *small model* property: every satisfiable formula of UGRA of size n admits a finite model of size $\mathcal{O}(n^8)$. Such a property will also allow us to prove that the decision problem for UGRA is NP-complete.

Keywords: Decision Problem · Undirected Graphs · Reachability and Acyclicity · Small Model Property · NP-completeness · Computable Set Theory

1 Introduction

Graphs find natural applications in numerous fields of computer science, serving as essential tools for modeling and solving diverse problems. Whether establishing equivalence between complexity classes [11] or representing the architecture of networks [7], graphs have proven to be invaluable tools. Acyclicity and reachability instances are desirable properties of graphs, of significant relevance in several applications. To mention just two examples, acyclic graphs are essential in analyzing networks, such as Bayesian Networks [12], and in verifying memory ordering enforcement for concurrent programs [9]. On the other hand, reachability plays an important role in program verification using SMT (Satisfiability Modulo Theories) solvers [8,10].

In this paper, we address the decision problem for the theory UGRA(*undirected graphs with reachability and acyclicity*), encompassing graph and node variables, the basic Boolean set operators (∪, ∩, \), singleton graphs, and predicates for acyclicity and reachability. In particular, by drawing from the well-established techniques of Computable Set Theory [2,4,5], we prove that the theory UGRA enjoys the following *small model* property: every satisfiable

© The Author(s), under exclusive license to Springer Nature Switzerland AG 2024
L. Levy Patey et al. (Eds.): CiE 2024, LNCS 14773, pp. 431–446, 2024.
https://doi.org/10.1007/978-3-031-64309-5_34

formula of UGRA of size n admits a finite model of size $\mathcal{O}(n^8)$. Such a property will allow us to prove that the decision problem for UGRA is NP-complete.

We will use an *edge-centric* representation of graphs, where they are depicted as collections of unordered pairs of *distinct* nodes (representing edges). Compared to the classical representation of graphs, namely as pairs of their node and edge sets, this alternative representation simplifies the solution of the decision problem for UGRA, although it disallows self-loops and isolated nodes in graphs. However, our approach could be extended to readmit self-loops and isolated nodes, albeit with added technicalities. For instance, our graph representation could be extended to admit singletons intended to depict self-loops. Thus, for example, $\{\{a\}, \{a, b\}, \{b, c\}\}$ would describe a graph with two edges ($\{a, b\}$ and $\{b, c\}$) and a self-loop on node a. Clearly, the decision procedure to be presented in Sect. 4 would need to be revised accordingly.

The decision problem for UGRA was already tackled in [1], using the classical graph representation. However, a major flaw in the proof was identified, as pointed out in [6], leaving the solution provided therein incomplete. Consequently, the decision problem for UGRA has remained unresolved up to now.

The ideas presented in [1] were nonetheless adapted in [6] to demonstrate the NP-completeness of the decision problem for the companion theory DGRA, which concerns directed graphs with reachability and acyclicity predicates.

Asserting acyclicity and reachability for directed graphs differs somewhat from asserting the same properties for undirected graphs. For example, reachability is bidirectional in the undirected case but unidirectional in the directed one. Additionally, acyclic directed graphs can be characterized as having no vertex reachable from itself via a non-null path, while acyclic undirected graphs are characterized by not containing any path with at least two edges and an edge connecting the endpoints of that path. For this reason, the decision problem for UGRA cannot trivially be reduced to that for DGRA by converting undirected graphs into directed ones, simply by replacing each undirected edge u, v with the pairs $\langle u, v \rangle$ and $\langle v, u \rangle$.

Here, we propose a new edge-centric approach that enables us to better identify and manage the hidden criticalities of the problem. This approach will help us prove a small model property for UGRA, which in turn will allow us to establish the NP-completeness of its decision problem.

The paper is organized as follows. In Sect. 2, we introduce some useful preliminary notions. The syntax and semantics of the language UGRA are then presented in Sect. 3, whereas the decision problem for UGRA is addressed in Sect. 4 and in an appendix. Finally, we provide some plans for future research.

2   Preliminary Notions

For convenience, we adopt an edge-centric view of undirected graphs, wherein self-loops and isolated nodes are not admitted. While disregarding these constraints may introduce certain technical complications, it does not compromise the decidability and complexity results presented in the remainder of the paper.

The aforementioned constraints allow us to represent (UNDIRECTED) GRAPHS as sets of edges, where each edge is an unordered pair of distinct nodes. In this perspective, the set of nodes of a graph $\mathcal{G}$ is equal to $\bigcup \mathcal{G}$, where $\bigcup$ denotes the unary union operator defined as $\bigcup S := \{s \mid s \in \sigma, \text{ for some } \sigma \in S\}$ for every set S.

A SIMPLE PATH π in a graph $\mathcal{G}$ is a *nonempty* finite set of edges $\big\{\{\nu_i, \nu_{i+1}\} \mid 0 \leq i < n\big\} \subseteq \mathcal{G}$, such that $\nu_i \neq \nu_j$ for $0 \leq i < j \leq n$. In this case, the nodes ν_0 and ν_n are the ENDPOINTS of π (and we put $\mathsf{ends}(\pi) := \{\nu_0, \nu_n\}$), whereas the nodes $\nu_1, \ldots, \nu_{n-1}$, if any, are the INTERNAL nodes of π. Finally, $\{\nu_0, \nu_1\}$ and $\{\nu_{n-1}, \nu_n\}$ are the EXTREMAL edges of π. The LENGTH of a simple path π is just its cardinality $|\pi|$, and its SUPPORT is the set $\bigcup \pi$ of all nodes incident to some edge in π. A SUBPATH of a simple path π is any simple path π' contained in π, namely such that $\pi' \subseteq \pi$. A SIMPLE CYCLE is a collection of edges of the form $\pi \cup \{\mathsf{ends}(\pi)\}$, where π is any simple path *of length at least* 2. Given any nodes ν_0, ν_1 in a graph $\mathcal{G}$, the node ν_1 is STRICTLY REACHABLE from ν_0 (in $\mathcal{G}$) if there exists a simple path in $\mathcal{G}$ whose endpoints are ν_0 and ν_1. Hence, no node is strictly reachable from itself. A graph is ACYCLIC if it contains no simple cycle.

A path in a graph is BASIC with respect to a set N of nodes if (a) it is a simple path with at least two edges; (b) its endpoints belong to N, while none of its internal nodes belongs to N. Basic paths relative to some set of nodes will be of central importance in our subsequent developments.

For simplicity, throughout the remainder of the paper, when we mention graphs, paths, and cycles, we are referring to undirected graphs, simple paths, and simple cycles, respectively.

3 Syntax and Semantics of UGRA

Syntax: The theory UGRA is quantifier-free. Its language is two-sorted and comprises:

- variables of sorts node and graph;
- the constant $\varnothing$;
- the Boolean operators $\setminus, \cup, \cap$ (of sort graph × graph → graph);
- the singleton operator $\{\{\cdot, \cdot\}\}$ (of sort node × node → graph);
- the binary predicates of equality $\cdot = \cdot$ and of graph inclusion $\cdot \subseteq \cdot$;
- the predicates $\{x, y\} \in G$, $x \in nodes(G)$, *strictly-reachable*(x, y, G), and *acyclic*(G), where x, y stand for node-variables and G for a graph-variable;
- the propositional connectives $\neg, \wedge, \vee,$ and $\longrightarrow$.

UGRA-FORMULAE are propositional combinations of well-sorted atoms, each involving one of the predicate symbols listed above.

Given a UGRA-formula φ, we denote with $\mathcal{V}_{\varphi,\mathsf{node}}$ and $\mathcal{V}_{\varphi,\mathsf{graph}}$ the collections of variables of sorts node and graph occurring in φ, respectively, and put $\mathcal{V}_\varphi = \mathcal{V}_{\varphi,\mathsf{node}} \cup \mathcal{V}_{\varphi,\mathsf{graph}}$. When the formula φ is understood, we will simply write $\mathcal{V}$,

$\mathcal{V}_{\text{node}}$, and $\mathcal{V}_{\text{graph}}$ in place of $\mathcal{V}_{\varphi}$, $\mathcal{V}_{\varphi,\text{node}}$, and $\mathcal{V}_{\varphi,\text{graph}}$. Additionally, to improve readability we will adopt the following abbreviations:

$$G(x,y) := \{x,y\} \in G, \qquad G^+(x,y) := \textit{strictly-reachable}(x,y,G),$$
$$\neg G(x,y) := \{x,y\} \notin G, \qquad \neg G^+(x,y) := \neg\textit{strictly-reachable}(x,y,G).$$

Semantics: A UGRA-assignment over a set of variables $\mathcal{V} := \mathcal{V}_{\text{node}} \cup \mathcal{V}_{\text{graph}}$ is a pair $(\mathcal{A}, \mathfrak{A})$ such that $\mathcal{A}$ is a nonempty graph, called the DOMAIN GRAPH of the assignment, and $\mathfrak{A}$ is a two-sorted interpretation fulfilling the following conditions:

- each node-variable x in $\mathcal{V}_{\text{node}}$ is mapped into a node $x^{\mathfrak{A}}$ of the domain graph $\mathcal{A}$, namely $x^{\mathfrak{A}} \in \bigcup \mathcal{A}$;
- each graph-variable G in $\mathcal{V}_{\text{graph}}$ is mapped into a subgraph $G^{\mathfrak{A}}$ of the domain graph $\mathcal{A}$, namely into a subset of $G^{\mathfrak{A}}$;
- the constant $\varnothing$, the function symbols $\cup, \cap, \setminus, \{\{\cdot,\cdot\}\}$, and the relation symbols $\{\cdot,\cdot\} \in \cdot$ and $\cdot \subseteq \cdot$ are interpreted according to their standard meaning over sets of unordered pairs of elements in $\bigcup \mathcal{A}$, (thus, for instance, for any term $G \setminus H$ it is not required that $H \subseteq G$ must hold.);
- $[\textit{strictly-reachable}(x,y,G)]^{\mathfrak{A}} = \textbf{true}$ if and only if there exists a simple path π in $G^{\mathfrak{A}}$ whose endpoints are $x^{\mathfrak{A}}$ and $y^{\mathfrak{A}}$;
- $[\textit{acyclic}(G)]^{\mathfrak{A}} = \textbf{true}$ if and only if the graph $G^{\mathfrak{A}}$ is acyclic.

We[1] put $\mathcal{V}^{\mathfrak{A}}_{\text{node}} := \{x^{\mathfrak{A}} \mid x \in \mathcal{V}_{\text{node}}\}$ and $\mathcal{V}^{\mathfrak{A}}_{\text{graph}} := \{G^{\mathfrak{A}} \mid G \in \mathcal{V}_{\text{graph}}\}$.

A UGRA-formula φ is SATISFIABLE, if there exists an assignment $(\mathcal{A}, \mathfrak{A})$ over the variables in φ that makes φ true (according to the above rules), in which case we say that $(\mathcal{A}, \mathfrak{A})$ is a MODEL for φ and write $(\mathcal{A}, \mathfrak{A}) \models \varphi$ (or, more simply, we just say that $\mathfrak{A}$ is a model for φ, written $\mathfrak{A} \models \varphi$).

A UGRA-formula is VALID, if it is satisfied by any UGRA-assignment.

Two formulae are EQUISATISFIABLE, if both formulae are satisfiable (possibly by distinct assignments) or both are not.

Here are two examples of UGRA-conjunctions, where the notational conventions provided above are used:

Example 1. The conjunction

$$H \subseteq G \;\wedge\; L = H \setminus \{\{z,w\}\} \;\wedge\; H^+(x,y) \;\wedge\; \neg L^+(x,y) \tag{1}$$

yields that the graph G contains a simple path connecting the nodes x and y, with the path passing through the node z. Indeed, (1) forces the existence of a subgraph H of G in which x and y are connected by some path π (since, because of the literal $H^+(x,y)$ in (1), the nodes x and y must be distinct). However, upon removal of the edge $\{z,w\}$ from H, the connection between x and y is lost. Hence, the path π must include the edge $\{z,w\}$ and, consequently, z.   □

---

[1] Non-strict reachability can be expressed by the disjunction

$$\textit{strictly-reachable}(x,y,G) \;\vee\; (x = y \;\wedge\; x \in \textit{nodes}(G))$$

Example 2. The conjunction

$$\bigwedge_{1\leq i\leq 3}\left(\overline{H}_i = G\setminus H_i \,\wedge\, H_i \subseteq G \,\wedge\, \neg H_i^+(x,y) \,\wedge\, \neg\overline{H}_i^+(x,y)\right) \,\wedge\, \bigwedge_{1\leq i<j\leq 3} H_i\cap H_j = \varnothing$$

$$(2)$$

implies that all the paths in G from x to y, if any, must contain at least three distinct edges. Indeed, (2) forces G to contain three mutually disjoint subgraphs H_1, H_2, and H_3 in which x and y are not connected, just as in their complements $\overline{H}_1$, $\overline{H}_2$, and $\overline{H}_3$ with respect to G. Therefore, any path in G from x to y must include at least one edge from each of H_1, H_2, and H_3. Given that H_1, H_2, H_3 are mutually disjoint, such paths must contain at least three distinct edges.

Similar formulae can be devised to enforce all the paths in a graph connecting two designated nodes to have length at least k, for any fixed constant $k \geq 2$. $\square$

The SATISFIABILITY (or DECISION) PROBLEM (s.p., for short) for the fragment UGRA is the problem of algorithmically establishing whether or not any given UGRA-formula is satisfiable. Any algorithmic solution to the s.p. for UGRA is called a DECISION PROCEDURE.

The s.p. for UGRA-formulae can be reduced in nondeterministic linear time to the s.p. for conjunctions of UGRA-LITERALS, namely UGRA-atoms or their negation. Indeed, if φ is any satisfiable UGRA-formula, then in nondeterministic linear time one can construct a satisfiable UGRA-conjunction φ_0 involving the same atoms as φ and such that the implication $\varphi_0 \to \varphi$ is a propositional tautology (hence, *a fortiori*, a valid UGRA-formula).

A further step allows us to reduce, again in nondeterministic linear time, the s.p. for UGRA-conjunctions to the s.p. for NORMALIZED UGRA-CONJUNCTIONS. These are conjunctions of UGRA-literals of specific types, as follows:

$$x = y, \qquad\qquad G = \{\{x,y\}\}, \qquad\qquad G = H\setminus L,$$
$$G^+(x,y), \qquad\qquad \neg G^+(x,y), \qquad\qquad acyclic(G).$$

Indeed, compound terms can be flattened in linear time by means of newly introduced variables. For example, a literal of the form $G_1 = G_2 \cup (G_3 \setminus G_4)$ is equisatisfiable with the conjunction $G_1 = G_2 \cup \boldsymbol{G} \wedge \boldsymbol{G} = G_3 \setminus G_4$, where $\boldsymbol{G}$ stands for a newly introduced graph-variable. In addition, by means of the following rewrite rules, in nondeterministic linear time we can reduce to normalized UGRA-conjunctions:

$$\begin{aligned}
x \neq y &\rightsquigarrow G(x,y) \\
x \in nodes(G) &\rightsquigarrow G(x,\boldsymbol{y}) \\
G \neq \varnothing &\rightsquigarrow G(\boldsymbol{x},\boldsymbol{y}) \\
G = \varnothing &\rightsquigarrow G = G \setminus G \\
G \neq H &\rightsquigarrow \boldsymbol{L} \neq \varnothing \ \wedge \ (\boldsymbol{L} = G \setminus H \ \vee \ \boldsymbol{L} = H \setminus G) \\
G \subseteq H &\rightsquigarrow G \setminus H = \varnothing \\
G = H &\rightsquigarrow G \subseteq H \ \wedge \ H \subseteq G \\
G = H \cap L &\rightsquigarrow G = L \setminus (L \setminus H) \\
G = H \cup L &\rightsquigarrow G \setminus L = H \setminus L \ \wedge \ L \setminus G = G \setminus G \\
\{x,y\} \in G &\rightsquigarrow \{\{x,y\}\} \subseteq G \\
\neg acyclic(G) &\rightsquigarrow \boldsymbol{L} \subseteq G \ \wedge \ G(\boldsymbol{x},\boldsymbol{y}) \ \wedge \ \neg L(\boldsymbol{x},\boldsymbol{y}) \ \wedge \ \boldsymbol{L}^+(\boldsymbol{x},\boldsymbol{y}),
\end{aligned}$$

etc., where boldface variables stand for newly introduced fresh variables.[2]

For instance, the validity of the latter rewrite rule can be understood from the observation that a graph G contains a cycle if and only if it meets two conditions:

(i) G possesses an edge $\{\boldsymbol{x},\boldsymbol{y}\}$, expressed by the literal $G(\boldsymbol{x},\boldsymbol{y})$;
(ii) G contains a path from $\boldsymbol{x}$ to $\boldsymbol{y}$ that does not include the edge $\{\boldsymbol{x},\boldsymbol{y}\}$ itself. This condition is equivalent to the existence of a subgraph $\boldsymbol{L}$ of G that does not include the edge $\{\boldsymbol{x},\boldsymbol{y}\}$ (expressed by $\neg \boldsymbol{L}(\boldsymbol{x},\boldsymbol{y})$) and where $\boldsymbol{y}$ is reachable from $\boldsymbol{x}$ (expressed by $\boldsymbol{L}^+(\boldsymbol{x},\boldsymbol{y})$).

Consequently, the following result holds:

Lemma 1. *The s.p. for UGRA-formulae is equivalent to the s.p. for conjunctions of normalized UGRA-literals.*

4   The Decision Problem for the Theory UGRA

In this section, we establish the decidability of the s.p. for UGRA and prove its NP-completeness.

The NP-hardness of the s.p. for UGRA can be proved by reducing to it the problem 3-SAT, much along the same lines of [3, *Sect. 3.2*] for the fragment MST$(\setminus, \notin)$.[3]

Here is an outline of a reduction of the problem 3-SAT to UGRA-conjunctions (and therefore to UGRA-formulae).

Let $F := \bigwedge_{i=1}^{m} C_i$ be an instance of 3-SAT, where $C_i = \ell_{i1} \vee \ell_{i2} \vee \ell_{i3}$ is a disjunction of literals over the propositional variables $P_1, \ldots, P_n$. Also, let

---

[2] Nondeterminism is called for because of the fourth rule, which contains a disjunction.
[3] The fragment MST$(\setminus, \notin)$ consists of conjunctions of literals of the form $s \notin t$, where s and t stand for set terms involving only set variables and the set operator '$\setminus$'.

$H, G^*, G_1, \ldots, G_n$ be $n + 2$ distinct graph-variables, and x, y be two distinct node-variables. For $i = 1, \ldots, m$ and $j = 1, 2, 3$ put:

$$T_{ij} := \begin{cases} G_k & \text{if } \ell_{ij} = \mathsf{P}_k, \text{ for some } k \in \{1, \ldots, r\} \\ G^* \setminus G_k & \text{if } \ell_{ij} = \neg \mathsf{P}_k, \text{ for some } k \in \{1, \ldots, r\}; \end{cases}$$

and for $i = 1, \ldots, m$ let $\mathcal{C}_i := ((G^* \setminus T_{i1}) \setminus T_{12}) \setminus T_{i3}$. Finally, let $\varphi_F := H(x, y) \wedge H = (\ldots ((G^* \setminus \mathcal{C}_1) \setminus \mathcal{C}_2) \ldots) \setminus \mathcal{C}_m$. Then, we have:

Lemma 2. *([3, Theorem 14]) The instance F of 3-SAT is propositionally satisfiable if and only if its corresponding UGRA-formula φ_F is satisfiable.*

Furthermore, by observing that $|\varphi_F| = \mathcal{O}(|F|)$, the preceding lemma implies:

Lemma 3. *The satisfiability problem for normalized UGRA-conjunctions and therefore for UGRA-formulae is NP-hard.*

To demonstrate that the s.p. for UGRA belongs to the class NP is a much more challenging task. This will be a consequence of the *small model property* for UGRA stated in the next theorem, whose proof will be unveiled in the remainder of this section.

Theorem 1 (Small model property). *Every satisfiable normalized UGRA-conjunction φ admits a "small" model $(\mathcal{S}, \mathfrak{S})$ over a set of nodes $\bigcup \mathcal{S}$ whose size is $\mathcal{O}(|\varphi|^4)$. More precisely, it holds that*

$$|\bigcup \mathcal{S}| \leq 2|\mathcal{V}_{node}|^2 \cdot |\mathcal{V}_{graph}|^2 + |\mathcal{V}_{node}|^2 \cdot |\mathcal{V}_{graph}| + |\mathcal{V}_{node}|.$$

4.1 Shortening Paths

Explicit nodes and explicit edges will play a central role in the proof of Theorem 1. These are defined as follows.

Definition 1 (Explicit nodes and edges). *Given a normalized UGRA-conjunction φ and a model $(\mathcal{A}, \mathfrak{A})$ for φ, the nodes in $\mathcal{V}_{node}^{\mathfrak{A}}$ are said to be* EXPLICIT. *Similarly, the edges in $\mathcal{A}$ whose endpoints belong to $\mathcal{V}_{node}^{\mathfrak{A}}$ are termed* EXPLICIT.

Given a normalized UGRA-conjunction φ and a model $(\mathcal{A}, \mathfrak{A})$ for it, roughly speaking, our strategy will consist in removing from the domain graph $\mathcal{A}$ all the non-explicit edges, and then accurately restoring the lost connections with paths of bounded length, while maintaining the satisfiability of φ.

Hereafter, when referring to a basic path π, it is understood that π is basic with respect to the collection of explicit nodes in the current model of the UGRA-conjunction under examination.

Let φ be a satisfiable normalized UGRA-conjunction, and let $\mathcal{V}_{node}$ and $\mathcal{V}_{graph}$ be the sets of variables (of type node and graph, respectively) occurring in φ.

Also, let $(\mathcal{A}, \mathfrak{A})$ be any model for φ. We describe a procedure, comprising six main steps, to 'extract' from the model $(\mathcal{A}, \mathfrak{A})$ a "small" model $(\mathcal{S}, \mathfrak{S})$ for φ.

The following elementary property is crucial for our purposes: *Every simple path whose endpoints are explicit is a (finite) concatenation of basic paths and explicit edges.*

Based on this property, we put forward the following approach towards a positive solution to the s.p. for UGRA.

For each pair $(\{x, y\}, G)$, where x, y are node-variables in φ such that $x^{\mathfrak{A}}$ and $y^{\mathfrak{A}}$ are distinct nodes, and $G \in \mathcal{V}_{\text{graph}}$, we select a basic path in $G^{\mathfrak{A}}$ with endpoints $x^{\mathfrak{A}}$ and $y^{\mathfrak{A}}$, if it exists (this is just Step 1 in the definition process below). Let $\mathcal{E}^*$ be the set of the edges (both explicit and non-explicit) belonging to any of the selected basic paths. It is an easy matter to check that the restricted interpretation $\mathfrak{A}^*$, defined as follows, still satisfies our conjunction φ:

- $x^{\mathfrak{A}^*} := x^{\mathfrak{A}}$, for every $x \in \mathcal{V}_{\text{node}}$,
- $G^{\mathfrak{A}^*} := G^{\mathfrak{A}} \cap \mathcal{E}^*$, for every $G \in \mathcal{V}_{\text{graph}}$.

However, while the number of selected basic paths is clearly $\mathcal{O}(|\varphi|^3)$, the number of edges in $\mathcal{E}^*$ does not admit any bound in $|\varphi|$, let alone a polynomial bound, since the selected basic paths can be arbitrarily long. In other words, the restricted interpretation $\mathfrak{A}^*$ cannot yet be considered "small".

A way to limit the length of the selected basic paths is just to shorten them. This can be achieved by selecting a limited number of "relevant" edges within each path (these are the SELECTED edges in Step 2 below), discarding the non-relevant edges, and adding suitable by-pass edges (see Step 3) to turn each collection of relevant edges into a path of length at most $2|\mathcal{V}_{\text{graph}}| + 2$, having the same endpoints as the basic path from which it originates. But then, to which graphs should the by-pass edges belong? The most natural answer to this question would be to add any by-pass edge introduced in the process of shortening a certain selected basic path π to the graphs $G^{\mathfrak{A}^*}$ such that $\pi \subseteq G^{\mathfrak{A}}$.

If every by-pass edge belonged to just one shortened path, then it could be shown that the restricted interpretation $\mathfrak{A}^*$ so extended would still be a model for our conjunction φ. However, if this is not the case, the interpretation $\mathfrak{A}^*$ could fail to model correctly the literals in φ of the following types:
$$\neg G^+(x, y), \qquad acyclic(G), \qquad G = H \setminus L.$$
Indeed, a by-pass edge could be added to the wrong graphs with the result of creating a forbidden path from $x^{\mathfrak{A}^*}$ to $y^{\mathfrak{A}^*}$ in a graph $G^{\mathfrak{A}^*}$ (where the conjunct $\neg G^+(x, y)$ is present in φ), or of creating a forbidden cycle in a graph $G^{\mathfrak{A}^*}$ (where the conjunct $acyclic(G)$ appears in φ). The case of conjuncts in φ of type $G = H \setminus L$ is a little more involved. Let us assume that the same by-pass edge $\bar{e}$ is introduced in connection to two distinct selected basic paths π_1 and π_2, where $\pi_1 \subseteq G^{\mathfrak{A}}, H^{\mathfrak{A}}$ and $\pi_2 \subseteq L^{\mathfrak{A}}$. Then, as a result of our strategy, the edge $\bar{e}$ would belong to all three graphs $G^{\mathfrak{A}^*}$, $H^{\mathfrak{A}^*}$, and $L^{\mathfrak{A}^*}$, and therefore the conjunct $G = H \setminus L$ would not be modeled correctly by $\mathfrak{A}^*$.

All the problems outlined above can be resolved by replacing each shortened basic path with a "clone", ensuring that no two distinct clones share a common edge. We also need to ensure that:

– a clone of a selected edge belongs to the same graphs as the selected edge;
– a clone of a by-pass edge belongs to the same graphs as its predecessor (which turns out to always be the clone of a *selected* edge) in the cloned path.

These actions will be carried out in Steps 3–6 of the following definition process.

STEP 1 (Set of selected basic paths). *For each pair $(\{x,y\}, G)$, where $x, y \in \mathcal{V}_{node}$ are such that $x^{\mathfrak{A}} \neq y^{\mathfrak{A}}$ and $G \in \mathcal{V}_{graph}$, we select, if any, a basic path in $G^{\mathfrak{A}}$ (with respect to the set of nodes $\mathcal{V}_{node}^{\mathfrak{A}}$) with endpoints $x^{\mathfrak{A}}, y^{\mathfrak{A}}$. We denote by $\Pi_{\varphi}^{\mathfrak{A}}$ the collection of all the basic paths so selected at this step.*

Plainly, the size of $\Pi_{\varphi}^{\mathfrak{A}}$ is bounded by $|\mathcal{V}_{node}|^2 \cdot |\mathcal{V}_{graph}|$ and since the cardinality of each of the sets $\mathcal{V}_{node}$ and $\mathcal{V}_{graph}$ does not exceed the size n of φ, it holds that $|\Pi_{\varphi}^{\mathfrak{A}}| \leq n^3$.

However, keeping just a polynomial number of basic paths in our interpretation is not enough to prove Theorem 1. In fact, as already noticed, in general selected basic paths may be arbitrarily long, although finite. Hence, in order to preserve satisfiability, we must choose for each path in $\Pi_{\varphi}^{\mathfrak{A}}$ a collection of edges to keep.

STEP 2 (Set of selected edges). *For each basic path $\pi \in \Pi_{\varphi}^{\mathfrak{A}}$, we select one extremal edge ϵ_π of π. In addition, for each graph-variable $H \in \mathcal{V}_{graph}$ such that $\pi \nsubseteq H^{\mathfrak{A}}$, we select any edge $\alpha_{\pi,H}$ in $\pi \setminus H^{\mathfrak{A}}$. We denote by $S(\pi)$ the set of the edges selected in π at this step, namely*

$$S(\pi) := \{\alpha_{\pi,H} \mid H \in \mathcal{V}_{graph} \wedge \pi \nsubseteq H^{\mathfrak{A}}\} \cup \{\epsilon_\pi\}.$$

Plainly, for each $\pi \in \Pi_{\varphi}^{\mathfrak{A}}$ we have:

$$|S(\pi)| \leq |\mathcal{V}_{graph}| + 1 \leq n + 1. \tag{3}$$

Given any basic path $\pi \in \Pi_{\varphi}^{\mathfrak{A}}$, the set of edges $S(\pi)$ is not guaranteed to form a path in the graph $\mathcal{A}$, let alone a basic path, as it generally consists of the union of mutually disjoint paths. To turn each $S(\pi)$ into a prospective path, we need to introduce new edges, called BY-PASSEDGES, to restore the lost connections.

STEP 3 (Indexing and by-pass edges). *Preliminarily, for each basic path $\pi \in \Pi_{\varphi}^{\mathfrak{A}}$, we establish an indexing $\{\nu_i^\pi\}_{0 \leq i \leq m_\pi}$ of the nodes in $\bigcup S(\pi) \cup ends(\pi)$, where $m_\pi := |\bigcup S(\pi) \cup ends(\pi)|$, ensuring that:*

– $\{\nu_0^\pi, \nu_{m_\pi}^\pi\} = ends(\pi);$
– $\epsilon_\pi = \{\nu_0^\pi, \nu_1^\pi\}$, *where we recall that ϵ_π is the extremal edge selected in π at Step 1;*
– $S(\pi) \subseteq \{\{\nu_i^\pi, \nu_{i+1}^\pi\} \mid 0 \leq i < m_\pi\}.$

Each pair $\{\nu_i, \nu_{i+1}\}$, with $0 \leq i < m_\pi$, not belonging to $S(\pi)$ is dubbed a BY-PASSEDGE for the basic path π. We denote by $P(\pi)$ the collection of the by-passedges for π, namely $P(\pi) := \{\{\nu_i^\pi, \nu_{i+1}^\pi\} \mid 0 \leq i < m_\pi\} \setminus S(\pi)$. Plainly, we have $|S(\pi) \cup P(\pi)| = m_\pi$.

Given a path $\pi \in \Pi_\varphi^{\mathfrak{A}}$, a possible way to construct such an indexing $\{\nu_i^\pi\}_{0 \leq i \leq m_\pi}$ of $\bigcup S(\pi) \cup \mathsf{ends}(\pi)$ consists of letting ν_0^π be the explicit node in ϵ_π, and then proceeding to index the remaining nodes in $\bigcup S(\pi) \cup \mathsf{ends}(\pi)$ in the order they appear along the path π.

Notice that, in general, $P(\pi)$ does not need to be a subset of π. Additionally, $S(\pi) \cup P(\pi) = \{\{\nu_i^\pi, \nu_{i+1}^\pi\} \mid 0 \leq i < m_\pi\}$ forms a basic path (with respect to $\mathcal{V}_{\mathsf{node}}^{\mathfrak{A}}$), with the same endpoints as π, in the (temporarily defined) AUGMENTED GRAPH $\mathcal{A}^+$, where

$$\mathcal{A}^+ := \mathcal{A} \cup \bigcup \{P(\pi') \mid \pi' \in \Pi_\varphi^{\mathfrak{A}}\},$$

obtained by adding all by-passedges to the domain graph $\mathcal{A}$.

We call $S(\pi) \cup P(\pi)$ the SHORTENED BASIC PATH ASSOCIATED WITH π.

It is useful to define a π-PREDECESSOR MAP prd_π over $P(\pi)$ by setting $prd_\pi(\{\nu_j^\pi, \nu_{j+1}^\pi\}) := \{\nu_{j-1}^\pi, \nu_j^\pi\}$ for each $\{\nu_j^\pi, \nu_{j+1}^\pi\} \in P(\pi)$ and refer to $\{\nu_{j-1}^\pi, \nu_j^\pi\}$ as the π-PREDECESSOR of the by-passedge $\{\nu_j^\pi, \nu_{j+1}^\pi\}$ in the basic path π.[4]

As shown in Lemma 4, the predecessor of any by-passedge for π is an edge in $S(\pi)$, namely one of the edges selected at Step 1.

Lemma 4. *Let $\pi \in \Pi_\varphi^{\mathfrak{A}}$, and let $\{\nu_i^\pi\}_{0 \leq i \leq m_\pi}$ be the indexing fixed for $\bigcup S(\pi) \cup \mathsf{ends}(\pi)$. The π-predecessors of all by-passedges for π belong to $S(\pi)$.*

Proof. Let $\{\nu_j^\pi, \nu_{j+1}^\pi\}$ be a by-passedge for π. Since $1 \leq j < m_\pi$ (see Footnote 4), we have $\nu_j^\pi \in \bigcup S(\pi)$. Hence, either $\{\nu_j^\pi, \nu_{j+1}^\pi\}$ or $\{\nu_{j-1}^\pi, \nu_j^\pi\}$ belongs to $S(\pi)$, and since $\{\nu_j^\pi, \nu_{j+1}^\pi\} \in P(\pi)$, it must be the case that $\{\nu_{j-1}^\pi, \nu_j^\pi\} \in S(\pi)$. □

For every $\pi \in \Pi_\varphi^{\mathfrak{A}}$, each selected edge in π can be the π-predecessor of at most one by-passedge for π; hence, since each by-passedge has a π-predecessor in $S(\pi)$, the number of by-passedges for π cannot exceed the number of selected edges. Thus, by (3), we have

$$|S(\pi) \cup P(\pi)| \leq 2 \cdot |S(\pi)| \leq 2 \cdot |\mathcal{V}_{\mathsf{graph}}| + 2, \tag{4}$$

which readily yields

$$m_\pi = \left|\bigcup S(\pi) \cup \mathsf{ends}(\pi)\right| = |S(\pi) \cup P(\pi)| + 1 \leq 2 \cdot |\mathcal{V}_{\mathsf{graph}}| + 3. \tag{5}$$

4.2   The Small Model

Our ultimate goal is to identify an alternative assignment that satisfies our conjunction φ, while having a polynomial size relative to φ.

While it is true that each by-passedge for a given basic path π has exactly one π-predecessor in the shortened path, the same edge can simultaneously serve as a by-passedge for more than one basic path. Consequently, a by-passedge can

---

[4] Notice that if $\{\nu_j^\pi, \nu_{j+1}^\pi\}$ is a by-passedge of π, then $1 \leq j < m_\pi$, since $\{\nu_0^\pi, \nu_1^\pi\} \notin P(\pi)$.

have different predecessors for each of them, and it could even be a selected edge for some basic path. We address this issue by suitably cloning non-explicit nodes and edges of the shortened basic paths so that the resulting paths become pairwise edge-disjoint.

STEP 4 (Cloning nodes and edges). *For each basic path $\pi \in \Pi_\varphi^\mathfrak{A}$ and each node $\nu \in \bigcup(S(\pi) \cup P(\pi)) \setminus \text{ends}(\pi)$—namely, each non-explicit node ν in the path $S(\pi) \cup P(\pi)$ in the augmented graph $\mathcal{A}^+$—we introduce a* CLONED NODE (ν, π), *which is distinct from every other node or cloned node already present. We also define a map f_π over the set of nodes $\bigcup(S(\pi) \cup P(\pi))$ by setting*

$$f_\pi(\nu) := \begin{cases} \nu & \text{if } \nu \text{ is an explicit node} \\ (\nu, \pi) & \text{otherwise.} \end{cases}$$

In other words, for a basic path $\pi \in \Pi_\varphi^\mathfrak{A}$, the map f_π maps each internal node ν in $S(\pi) \cup P(\pi)$ to its CLONE (ν, π) *relative to π, while leaving unchanged the endpoints of $S(\pi) \cup P(\pi)$. In addition, the map f_π can be naturally extended over edges $\{\nu, \mu\} \in S(\pi) \cup P(\pi)$ and sets of edges $\sigma \subseteq S(\pi) \cup P(\pi)$ by putting, respectively:*

$$f_\pi(\{\nu, \mu\}) := \{f_\pi(\nu), f_\pi(\mu)\} \quad \text{and} \quad f_\pi(\sigma) := \{f_\pi(\{\nu, \mu\}) \mid \{\nu, \mu\} \in \sigma\}.$$

We refer to $f_\pi(S(\pi) \cup P(\pi))$ as the CLONE *of the path $S(\pi) \cup P(\pi)$ (in $\mathcal{A}^+$) and denote by Π_φ^{cln} the set of the clones of all the basic paths in $\Pi_\varphi^\mathfrak{A}$, namely:*

$$\Pi_\varphi^{cln} := \left\{ f_\pi(S(\pi) \cup P(\pi)) \mid \pi \in \Pi_\varphi^\mathfrak{A} \right\}.$$

As expected, no two distinct cloned paths can share the same edge, as shown in the following lemma.

Lemma 5. *All distinct paths in Π_φ^{cln} are edge-disjoint.*

Proof. Let $\pi_1^* = f_{\pi_1}(S(\pi_1) \cup P(\pi_1))$ and $\pi_2^* = f_{\pi_2}(S(\pi_2) \cup P(\pi_2))$ be any two distinct members of Π_φ^{cln}, where π_1, π_2 are distinc basic paths in $\Pi_\varphi^\mathfrak{A}$, and let $\{\nu^*, \mu^*\}$ be any member of π_1^*. To prove the lemma, it suffices to show that $\{\nu^*, \mu^*\} \notin \pi_2^*$.

Since no edge in π_1 is explicit, at least one node between ν^* and μ^*, say ν^*, must have the form (ν, π_1), for some non-explicit node ν in $\bigcup(S(\pi_1) \cup P(\pi_1))$. In contrast, each edge in π_2^* contains either explicit nodes or pairs of the form (ρ, π_2), where $\rho \in \bigcup(S(\pi_2) \cup P(\pi_2))$. Hence, recalling that π_1 and π_2 are distinct basic paths, we conclude that $\{\nu^*, \mu^*\} \notin \pi_2^*$, thereby establishing the lemma. $\square$

From Lemma 5, it follows that clones of by-passedges can be put into a one-to-one correspondence with their predecessors, as will be elaborated in the following step.

STEP 5 (Predecessor map). *Let Cln_φ^S and Cln_φ^P be the disjoint collections of the clones of the selected and of the by-passedges, respectively, appearing in the cloned paths in Π_φ^{cln}, namely*

$$Cln_\varphi^S := \bigcup_{\pi \in \Pi_\varphi^{\mathfrak{A}}} f_\pi(S(\pi)), \qquad Cln_\varphi^P := \bigcup_{\pi \in \Pi_\varphi^{\mathfrak{A}}} f_\pi(P(\pi)).$$

We define a map pred: $Cln_\varphi^P \to Cln_\varphi^S$ *that associates each by-passedge in Cln_φ^P with its corresponding predecessor in Cln_φ^S. Specifically, let e^* be any by-passedge in Cln_φ^P. Then, by Lemma 5, there uniquely exist a basic path $\pi \in \Pi_\varphi^{\mathfrak{A}}$ and a by-passedge $e \in P(\pi)$ such that $e^* = f_\pi(e)$. We put*

$$\mathsf{pred}(e^*) := f_\pi(prd_\pi(e)).$$

We are now ready to define a model $(\mathcal{S}, \mathfrak{S})$ for φ and whose size is polynomial in the size of φ.

STEP 6 (Construction of the small model). *To begin with, for each $x \in \mathcal{V}_{node}$, we put*

$$x^{\mathfrak{S}} := x^{\mathfrak{A}}. \tag{6}$$

Next, for each variable $G \in \mathcal{V}_{graph}$, we denote by $E(G^{\mathfrak{A}})$ the set of the explicit edges in $G^{\mathfrak{A}}$ and by $S(G^{\mathfrak{A}})$ the set of the clones of by-passedges with predecessor in $G^{\mathfrak{A}}$, namely

$$E(G^{\mathfrak{A}}) := \{\{x^{\mathfrak{A}}, y^{\mathfrak{A}}\} \mid x, y \in \mathcal{V}_{node} \wedge \{x^{\mathfrak{A}}, y^{\mathfrak{A}}\} \in G^{\mathfrak{A}}\}$$
$$S(G^{\mathfrak{A}}) := \bigcup_{\pi \in \Pi_\varphi^{\mathfrak{A}}} f_\pi(G^{\mathfrak{A}} \cap S(\pi)).$$

Then, for each $G \in \mathcal{V}_{graph}$, we define:

$$G^{\mathfrak{S}} := E(G^{\mathfrak{A}}) \cup S(G^{\mathfrak{A}}) \cup \mathsf{pred}^{-1}[S(G^{\mathfrak{A}})].$$

It is possible that some nodes in $\mathcal{V}_{node}^{\mathfrak{S}} := \{x^{\mathfrak{S}} \mid x \in \mathcal{V}_{node}\}$ are not connected to any other nodes in any of the graphs $G^{\mathfrak{S}}$, where $G \in \mathcal{V}_{graph}$. To comply with our definition of assignments, we introduce a new "dummy"node $\overline{\nu}$ and the edge $\{\nu, \overline{\nu}\}$ in the domain graph, for each such "disconnected" node $\nu \in \mathcal{V}_{node}^{\mathfrak{S}}$, namely such that $\nu \notin \bigcup(\bigcup_{G \in \mathcal{V}_{graph}} G^{\mathfrak{S}})$.

Specifically, we define the domain graph $\mathcal{S}$ of the assignment under construction by putting: $\mathcal{S} := \bigcup_{G \in \mathcal{V}_{graph}} G^{\mathfrak{S}} \cup \{\{\nu, \overline{\nu}\} \mid \nu \in \mathcal{V}_{node}^{\mathfrak{S}} \setminus \bigcup(\bigcup_{G \in \mathcal{V}_{graph}} G^{\mathfrak{S}})\}$.

It turns out that the assignment $(\mathcal{S}, \mathfrak{S})$ defined at Step 6 satisfies our conjunction φ, as stated in the following lemma, whose detailed proof sketch is deferred to Sect. A of the appendix.

Lemma 6 (Main lemma). $\mathfrak{S}$ *satisfies the UGRA-formula φ.*

4.3   Complexity Analysis: Completion of the Proof of Theorem 1

We already know, from Lemma 6, that the assignment $(\mathcal{S}, \mathfrak{S})$ defined at Step 6 satisfies our conjunction φ. Now, we assess the size $|\bigcup \mathcal{S}|$ of the node set of its domain graph $\mathcal{S}$.

First, notice that the number of explicit nodes in $\mathcal{S}$ does not exceed the number $|\mathcal{V}_{\mathsf{node}}|$ of node-variables in φ. Concerning the non-explicit nodes in $\mathcal{S}$, we recall that all of them belong to $\bigcup \Pi_\varphi^{\mathsf{cln}}$. By construction, the set $\Pi_\varphi^{\mathsf{cln}}$ contains the same number of paths as $\Pi_\varphi^{\mathfrak{A}}$, whose size is at most $|\mathcal{V}_{\mathsf{node}}|^2 \cdot |\mathcal{V}_{\mathsf{graph}}|$, as remarked just after Step 1. By (4), the number of edges in each shortened basic path $S(\pi) \cup P(\pi)$ (for $\pi \in \Pi_\varphi^{\mathfrak{A}}$), and therefore in each cloned path in $\Pi_\varphi^{\mathsf{cln}}$, is at most $2|\mathcal{V}_{\mathsf{graph}}| + 2$. Thus, each path in $\Pi_\varphi^{\mathsf{cln}}$ contains at most $2|\mathcal{V}_{\mathsf{graph}}| + 3$ nodes, two of which are explicit. Finally, by taking into account also the dummy nodes $\overline{\nu}$ introduced for all 'disconnected' nodes $\nu \in \mathcal{V}_{\mathsf{node}}^{\mathfrak{S}} \setminus \bigcup (\bigcup_{G \in \mathcal{V}_{\mathsf{graph}}} G^{\mathfrak{S}})$, which are at most $|\mathcal{V}_{\mathsf{node}}|$, we obtain that the overall number of non-explicit nodes in $\bigcup \Pi_\varphi^{\mathsf{cln}}$ is at most

$$2|\mathcal{V}_{\mathsf{node}}|^2 \cdot |\mathcal{V}_{\mathsf{graph}}|^2 + |\mathcal{V}_{\mathsf{node}}|^2 \cdot |\mathcal{V}_{\mathsf{graph}}| + |\mathcal{V}_{\mathsf{node}}| = \mathcal{O}(|\varphi|^4),$$

as asserted in Theorem 1.

Based on Theorem 1, we have the following trivial decision procedure for normalized UGRA-conjunctions:

procedure UGRA-satisfiability-test(φ);
   1. $n := |\varphi|$;
   2. **for all** graphs $\mathcal{G}$ with $2n^4 + n^3 + n$ nodes **do**
   3.   **for all** interpretations $\mathfrak{S}$ of the variables in φ over the graph $\mathcal{G}$ **do**
   4.   **if** $\mathfrak{S} \models \varphi$ **then**
   5.   **return** "φ is satisfiable in $(\mathcal{G}, \mathfrak{S})$";
   6. **return** "φ is unsatisfiable";
end procedure;

Regarding the complexity of the above satisfiability test, when presented with a UGRA-conjunction φ of size n, the following considerations apply:

- the size of a graph $\mathcal{G}$ with $2n^4 + n^3 + n$ nodes is $\mathcal{O}(n^8)$;
- the size of any interpretation $\mathfrak{S}$ over a graph $\mathcal{G}$ of size $\mathcal{O}(n^8)$ is $\mathcal{O}(n^{16})$;
- the time needed to check whether a UGRA-assignment over a graph of size $\mathcal{O}(n^8)$ satisfies the conjunction φ is $\mathcal{O}(n^9)$.

Hence, for a satisfiable UGRA-conjunction φ of size n, the procedure UGRA-satisfiability-test has a nondeterministic $\mathcal{O}(n^{16})$-time complexity. Thus, we have:

Lemma 7. *The s.p. for normalized UGRA-conjunctions belongs to the complexity class* NP.

The above result can be easily generalized to UGRA-formulae that are not necessarily normalized conjunctions:

Lemma 8. *The s.p. for UGRA-formulae belongs to the complexity class* NP.

Combining Lemmas 3, 7, and 8, we finally obtain:

Theorem 2. *The s.p. for UGRA-formulae and for normalized UGRA-conjunctions is NP-complete.*

5 Conclusion and Future Directions

We have proven that the theory UGRA for undirected graphs with reachability and acyclicity predicates enjoys a small model property. This result not only establishes the decidability of UGRA but also allows one to demonstrate that the decision problem for UGRA is NP-complete.

Building upon this result, our plan is to develop a tableau-based decision procedure for UGRA-formulae, inspired by the approach in [6]. Additionally, we aim to expand the language of UGRA by introducing new features, including a predicate $connected(G)$ to express graph connectivity and a function $nodes(G)$ to denote the set of nodes in G. Finally, we intend to extend the applicability of Boolean set operators $\cup, \cap, \setminus$, and the equality predicate also to sets of nodes.

Acknowledgements. We gratefully acknowledge partial support from project "STORAGE—Università degli Studi di Catania, Piano della Ricerca 2020/2022, Linea di intervento 2", and from ICSC-Centro Nazionale di Ricerca in High-Performance Computing, Big Data and Quantum Computing. The first author is member of INdAM-GNCS.

A   Detailed Proof Sketch of Lemma 6

The proof of Lemma 6 consists of various cases, and relies on some propositions. Due to space limits, we only state those relevant to the cases presented here.

Proposition 1. *The basic paths in the graph S (with respect to $\mathcal{V}_{node}^{\mathfrak{S}} = \mathcal{V}_{node}^{\mathfrak{A}}$) are exactly the paths in Π_φ^{cln}.*

Proposition 2. *For all $\pi \in \Pi_\varphi^{\mathfrak{A}}$ and $G \in \mathcal{V}_{graph}$, we have:*

$$\pi \subseteq G^{\mathfrak{A}} \iff f_\pi(S(\pi) \cup P(\pi)) \subseteq G^{\mathfrak{S}}.$$

Lemma 6 (Main lemma). $\mathfrak{S}$ *satisfies the UGRA-formula φ.*

Proof (Detailed sketch). Recalling that $\mathfrak{A} \models \varphi$, we prove that $\mathfrak{S}$ satisfies all the literals in φ of types $x = y$, $G = \{\{x,y\}\}$, $G^+(x,y)$, $\neg G^+(x,y)$, and acyclic(G), omitting only the case of literals of type $G = H \setminus L$ due to space limitations.

Literals of type $x = y$:   Let the literal $x = y$ be in φ, so that $x^{\mathfrak{A}} = y^{\mathfrak{A}}$ holds. Then, by (6), we readily have

$$x^{\mathfrak{S}} = x^{\mathfrak{A}} = y^{\mathfrak{A}} = y^{\mathfrak{S}},$$

proving that $\mathfrak{S}$ satisfies the literal $x = y$.

Literals of type $G = \{\{x, y\}\}$:   Let us now consider the case of a literal in φ of the form $G = \{\{x, y\}\}$. Since $\mathfrak{A}$ satisfies φ, we have $G^{\mathfrak{A}} = \{\{x^{\mathfrak{A}}, y^{\mathfrak{A}}\}\}$, where $\{x^{\mathfrak{A}}, y^{\mathfrak{A}}\}$ is an explicit edge. Thus, by (6), $E(G^{\mathfrak{A}}) = \{\{x^{\mathfrak{S}}, y^{\mathfrak{S}}\}\}$. In addition, since $G^{\mathfrak{A}}$ consists of just one explicit edge, it follows that $S(G^{\mathfrak{A}}) = \mathsf{pred}^{-1}[S(G^{\mathfrak{A}})] = \emptyset$. Hence $G^{\mathfrak{S}} = \{\{x^{\mathfrak{S}}, y^{\mathfrak{S}}\}\}$, proving that $\mathfrak{S}$ satisfies the literal $G = \{\{x, y\}\}$.

Literals of type $G^{+}(x, y)$:   Assume that φ contains a literal of the form $G^{+}(x, y)$. Since $\mathfrak{A}$ satisfies it, there must exist a simple path π in $G^{\mathfrak{A}}$ with endpoints $x^{\mathfrak{A}}$ and $y^{\mathfrak{A}}$. Let $E(\pi)$ be the set of the explicit edges in π. The remaining edges in π, if any, can be partitioned into mutually edge-disjoint basic paths $\pi_1, \pi_2, \ldots, \pi_r$. Firstly, we have $E(\pi) \subseteq E(G^{\mathfrak{A}}) \subseteq G^{\mathfrak{S}}$ by definition. For each $i = 1, \ldots, r$, we can select a basic path $\tilde{\pi}_i \subseteq G^{\mathfrak{A}}$ from $\Pi_{\varphi}^{\mathfrak{A}}$ with the same endpoints as π_i. Define $\tilde{\pi}_i^* := f_{\pi_i}(S(\pi_i) \cup P(\pi_i))$, which is a basic path (relative to $(\mathcal{S}, \mathfrak{S})$ and φ) with the same endpoints as π_i by Proposition 2, and is contained in $G^{\mathfrak{S}}$. Therefore, $E(\pi) \cup \bigcup_{1 \leq i \leq r} \tilde{\pi}_i$ forms a simple path in $G^{\mathfrak{S}}$ connecting $x^{\mathfrak{A}} = x^{\mathfrak{S}}$ and $y^{\mathfrak{A}} = y^{\mathfrak{S}}$, thus demonstrating that $\mathfrak{S}$ satisfies the literal $G^{+}(x, y)$.

Literals of type $\neg G^{+}(x, y)$:   Let $\neg G^{+}(x, y)$ be a literal in φ, indicating the absence of any path in $G^{\mathfrak{A}}$ connecting $x^{\mathfrak{A}}$ and $y^{\mathfrak{A}}$. Assume, for the sake of contradiction, that $\mathfrak{S}$ instead satisfies $G^{+}(x, y)$, implying the existence of a simple path π^* in $G^{\mathfrak{S}}$ with endpoints $x^{\mathfrak{S}} = x^{\mathfrak{A}}$ and $y^{\mathfrak{S}} = y^{\mathfrak{A}}$. Let $E(\pi^*)$ be the set of explicit edges in π^*. As $S(G^{\mathfrak{A}})$ and $\mathsf{pred}^{-1}[S(G^{\mathfrak{A}})]$ contain no explicit edges, it follows that $E(\pi^*) \subseteq E(G^{\mathfrak{A}}) \subseteq G^{\mathfrak{A}}$. If there are any edges in $\pi^* \setminus E(\pi^*)$, they can be partitioned into a sequence $\pi_1^*, \pi_2^*, \ldots, \pi_s^*$ of mutually edge-disjoint basic paths (relative to $(\mathcal{S}, \mathfrak{S})$ and φ), which, by Proposition 1, must belong to $\Pi_{\varphi}^{\mathsf{cln}}$. Thus, for each $i = 1, \ldots, s$, there exists $\pi_i \in \Pi_{\varphi}^{\mathfrak{A}}$ such that $\mathsf{ends}(\pi_i) = \mathsf{ends}(\pi_i^*)$ and $\pi_i^* = f_{\pi_i}(S(\pi_i) \cup P(\pi_i))$. By Proposition 2, each π_i is contained in $G^{\mathfrak{A}}$, so $\bigcup_{1 \leq i \leq s} \pi_i \cup E(\pi^*)$ is a (simple) path in $G^{\mathfrak{A}}$ connecting $x^{\mathfrak{A}}$ and $y^{\mathfrak{A}}$, contradicting the absence of such a path in $G^{\mathfrak{A}}$. We can therefore conclude that $\mathfrak{S}$ satisfies the literal $\neg G^{+}(x, y)$.

Literals of type $\mathsf{acyclic}(G)$:   Let the literal $acyclic(G)$ occur in φ, so that the graph $G^{\mathfrak{A}}$ is acyclic. For a contradiction, suppose that $G^{\mathfrak{S}}$ contains a simple cycle γ. If γ contains at most one explicit node, then γ would be contained within $f_{\pi}(S(\pi) \cup P(\pi))$, for some basic path $\pi \in \Pi_{\varphi}^{\mathfrak{A}}$. Consequently, it would be isomorphic to a simple cycle within $S(\pi) \cup P(\pi)$. However, this is impossible, since $S(\pi) \cup P(\pi)$ is a basic path (in the augmented graph $\mathcal{A}^{+}$).

On the other hand, if the cycle γ contains at least two explicit nodes, it can be split into two edge-disjoint simple paths, denoted π_a^* and π_b^*, which share the same (explicit) endpoints. Following a similar reasoning as in the previous case, it becomes evident that the graph $G^{\mathfrak{A}}$ would contain two edge-disjoint paths connecting the endpoints of π_a^* and π_b^*, whose union is a simple cycle. However, the presence of such a cycle would contradict the acyclicity of $G^{\mathfrak{A}}$, thus demonstrating that the graph $G^{\mathfrak{S}}$ must also be acyclic. This establishes that $\mathfrak{S}$ satisfies the literal $acyclic(G)$.

Literals of type $G = H \setminus L :$ This case is omitted due to space limitations. $\square$

References

1. Cantone, D., Cincotti, G.: The decision problem in graph theory with reachability related constructs. In: Baumgartner, P., Zhang, H. (eds.), Proceedings of Third International Workshop on First-Order Theorem Proving (FTP 2000), pp. 68–90, Universität Koblenz-Landau (2000)
2. Cantone, D., Ferro, A., Omodeo, E.G.: Computable set theory. Number 6 in International Series of Monographs on Computer Science, Oxford Science Publications. Clarendon Press, Oxford, UK (1989)
3. Cantone, D., Maugeri, P., Omodeo, E.G.: Complexity assessments for decidable fragments of set theory. II: A taxonomy for 'small' languages involving membership. Theor. Comput. Sci. **848**, 28–46 (2020)
4. Cantone, D., Omodeo, E.G., Policriti, A.: Set theory for computing - From decision procedures to declarative programming with sets. Monographs in Computer Science. Springer-Verlag, New York (2001)
5. Cantone, D., Ursino, P.: An Introduction to the Technique of Formative Processes in Set Theory. Springer, Cham (2018). https://doi.org/10.1007/978-3-319-74778-1
6. Cantone, D., Zarba, C.G.: A tableau-based decision procedure for a fragment of graph theory involving reachability and acyclicity. In: Beckert, B. (ed.) TABLEAUX 2005. LNCS (LNAI), vol. 3702, pp. 93–107. Springer, Heidelberg (2005). https://doi.org/10.1007/11554554_9
7. Kivelä, M., Arenas, A., Barthelemy, M., Gleeson, J.P., Moreno, Y., Porter, M.A.: Multilayer networks. J. Complex Netw. **2**(3), 203–271 (2014)
8. Lahiri, S., Qadeer, S.: Back to the future: revisiting precise program verification using SMT solvers. SIGPLAN Not. **43**(1), 171–182 (2008)
9. Lustig, D., Sethi, G., Martonosi, M., Bhattacharjee, A.: Coatcheck: verifying memory ordering at the hardware-OS interface. SIGARCH Comput. Archit. News **44**(2), 233–247 (2016)
10. Rakamarić, Z., Bruttomesso, R., Hu, A.J., Cimatti, A.: Verifying heap-manipulating programs in an SMT framework. In: Namjoshi, K.S., Yoneda, T., Higashino, T., Okamura, Y. (eds.) ATVA 2007. LNCS, vol. 4762, pp. 237–252. Springer, Heidelberg (2007). https://doi.org/10.1007/978-3-540-75596-8_18
11. Savitch, W.J.: Relationships between nondeterministic and deterministic tape complexities. J. Comput. Syst. Sci. **4**(2), 177–192 (1970)
12. van Beek, P., Hoffmann, H.-F.: Machine learning of bayesian networks using constraint programming. In: Pesant, G. (ed.) CP 2015. LNCS, vol. 9255, pp. 429–445. Springer, Cham (2015). https://doi.org/10.1007/978-3-319-23219-5_31

Isometric Sets of Words and Generalizations of the Fibonacci Cubes

M. Anselmo[1], G. Castiglione[2], M. Flores[2(✉)], D. Giammarresi[3], M. Madonia[4], and S. Mantaci[2]

[1] Dipartimento di Informatica, Università di Salerno, Fisciano (SA), Italy
manselmo@unisa.it
[2] Dipartimento di Matematica e Informatica, Università di Palermo, Palermo, Italy
{giuseppa.castiglione,manuela.flores,sabrina.mantaci}@unipa.it
[3] Dipartimento di Matematica, Università di Roma "Tor Vergata", Rome, Italy
giammarr@mat.uniroma2.it
[4] Dipartimento di Matematica e Informatica, Università di Catania, Catania, Italy
madonia@dmi.unict.it

Abstract. The hypercube Q_n is a graph whose 2^n vertices can be associated to all binary words of length n in a way that adjacent vertices get words that differ only in one symbol. Given a word f, the subgraph $Q_n(f)$ is defined by selecting all vertices not containing f as a factor. A word f is said to be isometric if $Q_n(f)$ is an isometric subgraph of Q_n, i.e., keeping the distances between the remaining nodes. Graphs $Q_n(f)$ were defined and studied as a generalization of Fibonacci cubes $Q_n(11)$. Isometric words have been completely characterized using combinatorial methods for strings.

We introduce the notion of isometric sets of words with the aim of capturing further interesting cases in the scenario of isometric subgraphs of the hypercubes. We prove some combinatorial properties and study special interesting cases.

Keywords: Isometric sets of words · Hamming distance · Hypercubes · Generalized Fibonacci Cubes

1 Introduction

A hypercube Q_n, also known as an n-dimensional cube or an n-cube, is a geometric figure that extends the concept of a square or a cube into higher dimensions.

Partially supported by INdAM-GNCS Project 2023, FARB Project ORSA229894 of University of Salerno, TEAMS Project and PNRR MUR Project PE0000013-FAIR University of Catania, PNRR MUR Project ITSERR CUP B53C22001770006 and FFR fund University of Palermo, MUR Excellence Department Project MatMod@TOV, CUP E83C23000330006, awarded to the Department of Mathematics, University of Rome Tor Vergata.

L. Levy Patey et al. (Eds.): CiE 2024, LNCS 14773, pp. 447–460, 2024.
https://doi.org/10.1007/978-3-031-64309-5_35

Each one of its 2^n vertices can be named by a binary string (or word) of length n that describes its position in the n-dimensional space. This establishes a perfect correspondence between the distance of two vertices, taken as distance in the graph (i.e., number of edges in a minimal length path), and the distance between the associated words taken as the *Hamming distance* for similarity of strings. For this reasons, hypercubes are a contact point that allows the attack of some graph theoretical problems with combinatorial methods for strings, and vice versa.

Hypercubes are not just abstract mathematical entities; they have practical applications in computer networks, parallel processing, and error-correcting codes (see [17] for a survey). However, hypercubes have a critical limitation due to the fact that they have an exponential number of vertices. For this, a relevant role is played by their subgraphs that are *isometric*; that is the distance of any pair of vertices in such subgraphs is the same as the distance in the complete hypercube. With this aim, in 1993, Hsu introduced the *Fibonacci cubes* [18]. They are isometric subgraphs of Q_n obtained by selecting only the vertices whose corresponding words do not contain 11 as a factor. They have many remarkable properties also related to Fibonacci numbers and their recursive nature.

Inspired by those cubes, in 2012, generalized Fibonacci cubes $Q_n(f)$ were introduced as the subgraphs of Q_n keeping only vertices associated to binary words that do not contain word f as a factor. Note that, in order to get an isometric subgraph of Q_n, the avoided word should satisfy some special conditions; if this is the case, then the word is said isometric. Indeed, a binary word f is *isometric* (or Ham-isometric) when, for any $n \geq 1$, $Q_n(f)$ can be isometrically embedded into Q_n, and *non-isometric*, otherwise [22].

The structure of binary Ham-isometric words has been characterized in [20,22,25,28,29] by means of combinatorial methods for strings and related to a special property of their overlaps. The definition in [20] refers to binary strings to which the operation of replacement of a symbol can be applied at each position. The distance of two strings u and v is the minimal number of replacement operations needed to transform u into v. This corresponds to the classical Hamming distance between words; we indicate it as $\text{dist}_H(u, v)$. Given a word f, a word u is f-free if it does not contain f as factor. A word f is *isometric* if for any pair of f-free words u and v, there exists a sequence of length $\text{dist}_H(u, v)$ of symbol replacement operations that transforms u into v where all the intermediate words are also f-free.

The notion of isometric word combines the distance notion with the property that a word does not appear as factor in other words. Note that this property is important in combinatorics as well as in the investigation on similarities, or distances, on DNA sequences, where the avoided factor is referred to as an absent or forbidden word [10,12,13,15].

The research on Hamming isometric words is still very active [7,9,16,26,27]. Furthermore, very recently some generalizations have been proposed by enlarging the alphabet, by considering different edit distances, and by moving to two-dimensional words as in [1–6,8,11]. In this paper we restart from the notion of generalized Fibonacci cube $Q_n(f)$ prompted by some major questions that immediately come to mind.

– Not all the isometric subgraphs of the hypercube are $Q_n(f)$ for an isometric word f. Can we characterize them by means of an intersection of several $Q_n(f_i)$?
– Assume we are given a generalized Fibonacci cube $Q_n(f)$ with a non-isometric word f. Then $Q_n(f)$ is not an isometric subgraph of the original hypercube. Can we delete some more vertices in $Q_n(f)$ to make it isometric to Q_n?
– Similarly, assume that f is isometric, and then $Q_n(f)$ is an isometric subgraph of Q_n. How can we delete some vertices in $Q_n(f)$ and keeping it isometric to Q_n?

Then, it seems worth to consider some subgraphs $Q_n(f_i)$, for some words f_i, and study the cases when their intersection, say $H = Q_n(f_1) \cap Q_n(f_2) \cap \cdots \cap Q_n(f_k)$, is an isometric subgraph of the n-hypercube. The graph H contains all the vertices that avoid any word in $M = \{f_1, f_2, \ldots, f_k\}$ and therefore the set M can be investigated in a string combinatorial context.

In this paper, we introduce the notion of *isometric set of words* as it comes naturally when going from an element to a finite set of elements. The results are quite surprising and challenging.

First of all, the subgraph $Q_n(M)$ whose vertices avoid words in M can be either an isometric or a non-isometric subgraph of the whole hypercube Q_n, but this is not directly related to the isometricity of single words in M. In particular, we show an example of a set $M = \{f, g\}$ that is non-isometric with f and g that are isometric words. But we have also an example of a set $M = \{f, g\}$ that is isometric with f isometric and g non-isometric words. Moreover, other combinations are possible. Bringing this on the hypergraph setting this means that the property of being isometric or not of the graphs $Q_n(f)$ and $Q_n(g)$ does not say much on the same property for $Q_n(f) \cap Q_n(g)$. This implies that the property of being isometric for a set of words has to be inferred from the mutual relationships among the words.

A set M of words is isometric if, for all pairs of words u and v that avoid words in M, there is a sequence of symbol replacement operations that transforms u into v such that all the intermediate words in the transformation also avoid M. As for the classical case of a single string, to prove that a set is non-isometric, it suffices to exhibit a pair of words that contradicts the definition. We prove a necessary condition for a set to be non-isometric that is based on the notion of 2-error overlap among them. Unfortunately, the complete characterization seems quite hard to get.

The paper includes several examples of isometric sets. In particular, we present two notable ones, by proving the isometricity with ad-hoc argument. We show that the subgraph $Q_n(11) \cap Q_n(101) \cap \cdots \cap Q_n(10^{h-1}1)$, mentioned in [14] in the context of Hasse diagrams of powers of paths in a graph, is isometric. Actually, the authors there propose this as a generalization of the Fibonacci cube. The corresponding set of words $D_h = \{11, 101, 1001, \ldots, 10^{h-1}1\}$ contains the Fibonacci (isometric) word 11, while all the other words are non-isometric.

Interestingly, if we take a proper subset of D_h then it is not isometric. Another intriguing example is the set $S_n = \{1^n, 01^{n-1}, 101^{n-2}, \cdots, 1^{n-1}0\}$ that we call the *star*. We prove that it is isometric, we show that it can be recursively constructed and provide the recursive function that counts the number of its nodes. We conclude the paper with a glimpse into the future problems we plan to investigate.

2 Preliminaries

Let Σ be a finite alphabet. In this paper, the alphabet is $\Sigma = \{0, 1\}$, although many of the definitions and results can be stated and hold for a general alphabet. A word (or string) w of length $|w| = n$ is $w = a_1 a_2 \cdots a_n$, where $a_1, a_2, \ldots, a_n$ are symbols in Σ. The set of all finite words over Σ is denoted Σ^* and the set of all words over Σ of length n is denoted Σ^n. Finally, ε denotes the *empty word* with length zero and $\Sigma^+ = \Sigma^* \backslash \{\varepsilon\}$. A subset X of Σ^* is *uniform* if all the words in X have the same length. For any word $w = a_1 a_2 \cdots a_n$, the *reverse* of w is the word $w^{rev} = a_n a_{n-1} \cdots a_1$. If $x \in \{0, 1\}$, we denote by $\overline{x}$ the opposite of x, i.e. $\overline{x} = 1$ if $x = 0$ and vice versa. Then we define the *complement* of w as the word $\overline{w} = \overline{a}_1 \overline{a}_2 \cdots \overline{a}_n$.

Let $w[i]$ denote the symbol of w in position i, i.e., $w[i] = a_i$. Then, $w[i..j] = a_i \cdots a_j$, for $1 \le i \le j \le n$, is a *factor* of w that occurs in the interval $[i..j]$. The *prefix* (resp. *suffix*) of w of length ℓ, with $1 \le \ell \le n - 1$ is $\text{pre}_\ell(w) = w[1..\ell]$ (resp. $\text{suf}_\ell(w) = w[n - \ell + 1..n]$). When $\text{pre}_\ell(w) = \text{suf}_\ell(w) = u$ then u is an *overlap* of w of length ℓ and *shift* $r = n - \ell$; it is also referred to as *border*, or *bifix*. If $w, f \in \Sigma^*$, w is f-*free* if w does not contain f as a factor; we also say that w *avoids* f.

The *replacement (operation)* on $w = a_1 a_2 \ldots a_n$ at position i with a character $x \ne a_i$, transforms $w = a_1 \ldots a_{i-1} a_i a_{i+1} a_n$ into $R_{i,x}(w) = a_1 \ldots a_{i-1} x a_{i+1} \ldots a_n$. When $\Sigma = \{0, 1\}$, the replacement on w in a position i corresponds to a flip of the bit in that position; so we write $R_i(w)$ instead of $R_{i,x}(w)$. Given two equal-length words $u = a_1 \cdots a_n$ and $v = b_1 \cdots b_n$, they have a *mismatch* at position i if $a_i \ne b_i$; a mismatch is also called an *error* and i is referred to as an *error position*. Then, the *Hamming distance* $\text{dist}_H(u, v)$ is the number of positions where u and v have a mismatch.

Definition 1. *Let $u, v \in \Sigma^*$ be words of equal length and $\text{dist}_H(u, v) = d$. A transformation τ from u to v is a sequence of $d + 1$ words $(w_0, w_1, \ldots, w_d)$ such that $w_0 = u$, $w_d = v$, and for any $k = 0, 1, \ldots, d - 1$, $\text{dist}_H(w_k, w_{k+1}) = 1$. Moreover, τ is f-free if for any $i = 0, 1, \ldots, d$, the word w_i is f-free.*

Definition 2. *A word f is isometric if for any pair of f-free words u and v, there exists an f-free transformation from u to v. It is non-isometric otherwise.*

The word w has a q-*error overlap* (q-eo, for short) of shift r and length $\ell = n - r$ if $\text{pre}_\ell(w)$ and $\text{suf}_\ell(w)$ have q mismatches [20]. We say that w has a q-error overlap if w has a q-eo of shift r for some $1 \le r \le n - 1$. The following characterization of isometric words is given in [25].

Proposition 3. *A word f is isometric if and only if f has no 2-error overlap.*

The proof that a word f having a 2-eo is non-isometric is given in [25] by associating to any 2-eo of f a pair of words witnessing that f is non-isometric. In most of the cases, such pair of words is the pair $(\alpha_r(f), \beta_r(f))$ as in the following definition. We name them *standard witnesses*.

Definition 4. *Let $f \in \Sigma^n$ have a 2-eo of shift r with error positions i, j, with $1 \leq i < j \leq n - r$. The words $\alpha_r(f)$, $\beta_r(f)$ corresponding to that 2-eo are:*

$$\alpha_r(f) = pre_r(f)R_i(f) \text{ and } \beta_r(f) = pre_r(f)R_j(f).$$

As an example, $f = 1001$ has a 2-eo of shift 1 with error positions 1 and 3, so $\alpha_1(f) = pre_1(f)R_1(f) = 10001$ and $\beta_1(f) = pre_1(f)R_3(f) = 11011$. Then, $\alpha_1(f)$ and $\beta_1(f)$ are f-free and no f-free transformation exists from $\alpha_1(f)$ to $\beta_1(f)$; this witnesses that $f = 1001$ is non-isometric.

Let $G = (V(G), E(G))$ be a graph. The distance of two nodes $u, v \in V(G)$, denoted by $\text{dist}_G(u, v)$, is the length of the shortest path connecting u and v in G. A subgraph S of a (connected) graph G is an *isometric subgraph* of G if for any $u, v \in V(S)$, $\text{dist}_S(u, v) = \text{dist}_G(u, v)$.

The *n-hypercube*, or binary n-cube, Q_n, is a graph with 2^n vertices, each associated to a binary word of length n. Two vertices u and v in Q_n are adjacent when their associated words differ in exactly one position, i.e., when $\text{dist}_H(u, v) = 1$. The vertices are often identified with the associated word. Therefore, $\text{dist}_{Q_n}(u, v) = \text{dist}_H(u, v)$. The *Fibonacci cube* F_n of order n is the subgraph of Q_n whose vertices are all the binary words of length n avoiding the factor 11. It is well known that F_n is an isometric subgraph of Q_n (cf. [21]). Generalized Fibonacci cubes, or hypercubes avoiding a word, have been defined by giving the possibility to avoid any binary word, as in the following definition [19].

Definition 5. *The n-hypercube avoiding a word f, denoted $Q_n(f)$, is the subgraph of Q_n obtained by removing those vertices which contain f as a factor.*

Note that in the context of hypercubes, the definition of isometric word can be reformulated as follows. A word $f \in \Sigma^*$ is *isometric* if and only if for all $n \geq |f|$, $Q_n(f)$ is an isometric subgraph of Q_n.

3 Isometric Sets of Words and Uniformization

In this section we propose the notion of *isometric set* of words and state the correspondence with the notion of (isometric) hypercube avoiding a set of words. Some examples and preliminary results are shown. Then, we prove that the investigation on the isometricity of sets can be restricted to uniform sets, i.e., sets of words of same length. In what follows, M always denotes a finite subset of $\{0, 1\}^*$.

Definition 6. *A word w is M-free, or w avoids M, if w does not contain any word in M as a factor.*

The definition of isometric set of words comes out as a natural generalization of the classical one (see Definitions 1 and 2). Nevertheless, some care is due to the length of the words in the set. To illustrate this, consider for example the word $f = 101$. It is a non-isometric word and (u, v), with $u = 1001$ and $v = 1111$, is a pair of witnesses for f; in fact u and v are f-free words and no f-free transformation exists from u to v. Consider now a set $M = \{f, g\}$ where $f = 101$ and g is any word longer than 4. Then, the previous words $u = 1001$ and $v = 1111$, are still M-free words and still no M-free transformation exists from u to v, independently from g. To make sense, witnesses are defined to be long enough. Indeed the property of being M-free should not rely on the fact that witnesses are too short to contain words in M.

Definition 7. *Let $M \subseteq \{0, 1\}^*$ be a finite set of words and* max *be the length of a longest word in M. Then, M is* isometric *if for any pair of M-free words u and v with $|u| = |v| \geq$ max, there exists a transformation from u to v such that all its intermediate words are M-free.*

Definition 8. *A set M is* non-isometric *if it is not isometric. If M is non-isometric, a* pair of witnesses *for M is a pair (u, v) with $|u| = |v| \geq$ max, such that each transformation from u to v contains a word that is not M-free.*

Proposition 9. *The following statements are equivalent:*

- *M is isometric*
- *$\{\overline{x} \mid x \in M\}$ is isometric*
- *$\{x^{rev} \mid x \in M\}$ is isometric*

The proof of previous proposition is immediate. Let us now introduce the definition of the hypercube avoiding a set of words, as a generalization of Definition 5.

Definition 10. *The n-hypercube avoiding a set M, denoted $Q_n(M)$, is the subgraph of Q_n obtained by removing those vertices which contain a word in M as a factor.*

Note that if $M = \{m_1, m_2, \ldots, m_k\}$, then $Q_n(M) = Q_n(m_1) \cap Q_n(m_2) \cap \cdots \cap Q_n(m_k)$, that is the intersection of the hypercubes avoiding each word in the set, respectively.

The following proposition, whose proof follows from the definition, generalizes to isometric sets the analogous property of a single isometric word; it is a major motivation to look for a characterization of isometric sets.

Proposition 11. *Let $M \subseteq \{0, 1\}^*$ and let* max *be the length of a longest word in M. For any $n \geq$ max, $Q_n(M)$ is an isometric subgraph of Q_n iff M is an isometric set of words.*

In our investigation we bumped into a remarkable example given in [14] in the context of Hasse diagrams of powers of paths in a graph. Putting it in our notation, it consists in the intersections of graphs $Q_n(11) \cap Q_n(101) \cap \cdots \cap Q_n(10^h 1)$ for any $h \geq 0$. It is there introduced as a generalization of the Fibonacci cube, with no interest in its isometricity to the hypercube Q_n. Then, let us define the sets $D_h = \{11, 101, \ldots 10^h 1\}$, for any $h \geq 0$. Note that $D_0 = \{11\}$.

Proposition 12. *The set D_h is isometric, for all $h \geq 0$.*

Proof. A word w is D_h-free if either contains at most one 1, or any two consecutive occurrences of 1 are separated by at least $h + 1$ consecutive occurrences of 0. Let u and v be two D_h-free words. We prove that there always exists a transformation from u to v where all intermediate words are D_h-free. Consider all the 1's of u that mismatch with the corresponding character in v (if any), and change them one by one into 0's. All intermediate words are D_h-free because the distance between two consecutive 1's increases. Then, change all the 0's that mismatch with the corresponding character in v into 1's, and all the intermediate words are again D_h-free, since v is D_h-free. $\qquad\square$

The examples that follow show that the isometricity of a set does not rely on the isometricity of the single words in the set. The first one shows an isometric set that contains an isometric word and some other non-isometric words; the second one shows a non-isometric set composed by two isometric words.

Example 13. The set D_h is isometric, for every $h \geq 0$ (cf. Proposition 12). Note that 11 is an isometric word, whereas all the words of the form $10^i 1$, $1 \leq i \leq h$, are non-isometric because they have a 2-eo (cf. Proposition 3). This shows that $Q_n(D_h) = Q_n(11) \cap Q_n(101) \cap \cdots \cap Q_n(10^h 1)$ is an isometric subgraph of Q_n, although $Q_n(11)$ is isometric and all $Q_n(10^i 1)$ with $1 \leq i \leq h$ are not.

Example 14. The set $M = \{111, 100\}$ includes two isometric words, but it is non-isometric since (u, v) with $u = 1011$ and $v = 1101$ is a pair of witnesses. Indeed, u and v are M-free and $\mathrm{dist}_H(u, v) = 2$. Then, the only transformations from u to v are $\tau = (1011, 1111, 1101)$ and $\tau' = (1011, 1001, 1101)$, and 111 is a factor of 1111 and 100 is factor of 1001, respectively. This shows that although $Q_n(M) = Q_n(111) \cap Q_n(100)$ is the intersection of two isometric subgraphs, it is not an isometric subgraph of Q_n.

In this last part of the section we prove that our investigation on isometricity can be restricted to sets of words of the same length, referred to as uniform sets of words.

Definition 15. *Let M be a set of words and* max *be the length of a longest word in M. Then, the uniformization of M is $M^U = \Sigma^* M \Sigma^* \cap \Sigma^{\max}$.*

Remark 16. Let max be the length of a longest word in M, and $w \in \Sigma^*$. If $|w| \geq$ max, then w is M-free iff w is M^U-free. On the other hand, if $|w| <$ max then w is trivially M^U-free, but it can be either M-free or not.

The non-equivalence between M-freeness and M^U-freeness of a word stated in the previous remark does not affect the isometricity property of the sets M and M^U, as shown in the following proposition.

Proposition 17. *M is isometric iff M^U is isometric.*

Proof. Let max be the length of a longest word in M and note that max is also the length of a longest word in M^U. From definition, M is isometric iff for any pair of M-free words u and v with $|u| = |v| \geq$ max, there exists a transformation from u to v such that all its intermediate words are M-free. Applying Remark 16 to u, v and all the words in the transformation, which are of same length $|u| \geq$ max, such words are M-free iff they are M^U-free. Hence, this holds iff M^U is isometric. $\qquad\qquad\square$

As an application, consider the following example.

Example 18. Let $D_1 = \{11, 101\}$ be the isometric set as in Proposition 12, with $h = 1$. Then, max $= 3$ and the uniformization of M is $M^U = \{111, 011, 110, 101\}$. According to Proposition 17, M^U is isometric.

4   Isometric Sets of Words and 2-Error Overlaps

In this last part of the paper we concentrate only on uniform sets of words. We first extend the notion of q-error overlap to a pair of words. We do this because we know from Proposition 3 that the characterization of isometric words relies on the presence of some 2-error overlap. Refer to Fig. 1 for a graphical representation of a 2-error overlap.

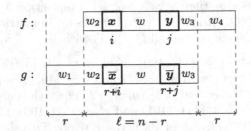

Fig. 1. A 2-error overlap of f on g.

Definition 19. *Let $f, g \in \{0,1\}^n$, f has a q-error overlap (or q-eo) on g of shift r and length $\ell = n-r$, with $0 \leq r < n-q$, $0 < \ell < n$, if $\text{dist}_H(\text{pre}_\ell(f), \text{suf}_\ell(g)) = q$. The positions $i_1, \ldots i_q$ in f in which $\text{pre}_\ell(f)$ and $\text{suf}_\ell(g)$ mismatch are called the error positions of the q-eo. As a notation, we say that f has a q-eo on g of type $[r; i_1, \ldots, i_q]$.*

By definition, if i is an error position of f on g of shift r then $f[i] = \overline{g[r+i]}$. Note that the existence of a q-eo of f on g does not imply the existence of a q-eo of g on f, i.e. the definition is not symmetric. In particular, if $g = f$ the above definition coincides with the classical definition of q-eo of a word.

The following result connects non-isometricity to the existence of a 2-eo between two words in M. It has already been stated in [11].

Theorem 20. *Let $M \subseteq \{0,1\}^n$. If M is non-isometric then there exist $f, g \in M$ (possibly $f = g$) such that f has a 2-eo on g.*

Proof. Let M be a non-isometric set and (u,v) be a pair of witnesses for M with minimal distance $d = \text{dist}_H(u,v)$. Let V be the set of all error positions. The minimality of the distance d implies that, when applying to u a replacement operation, then a word of M appears as a factor. Such an occurrence must disappear in the transformation from u to v, because v is M-free. Then, for any $i \in V$, $R_i(u)$ has an occurrence of a word of M in a certain interval $[k_i..k_i + n - 1]$ and such interval must contain i and another error position. The finiteness of V implies that, there exist $s, t \in V$, such that both $I_s = [k_s..k_s + n - 1]$ and $I_t = [k_t..k_t + n - 1]$ contain s and t. Suppose that $g \in M$ occurs in $R_s(u)$ in I_s $f \in M$ occurs in $R_t(u)$ in I_t and $k_s < k_t$. Then, a prefix of f occurs in $R_s(u)$ and a suffix of g in $R_t(u)$ both in $I_s \cap I_t$. Then, f has a 2-eo on g. $\square$

Corollary 21. *Let $M \subseteq \{0,1\}^n$. If for all pairs of words $f, g \in M$, f does not have any 2-error overlap on g, then M is isometric.*

Note that if $M = \{f\}$, the vice versa of Theorem 20 holds true (cf. Proposition 3) and this characterizes non-isometric words. In fact, if f has a 2eo, it is possible to construct from it a pair of witnesses with a standard technique (see Definition 4). When we consider sets of words, one can similarly construct a pair of witness candidates based on some 2-eo. For the pair to truly be a pair of witnesses, however, it is necessary that *no* words in M be a factor. The possible situations are illustrated in the next two examples. In particular, Example 23 proves that the reverse of Theorem 20 does not hold. Example 24 shows an application of Corollary 21.

Example 22. The set $M = \{00101, 11010\}$ is non-isometric. Indeed, 00101 has a 2-eo on 11010 with shift $r = 2$. From this 2-eo, $u = 1101101$ and $v = 1100001$ can be constructed with the standard technique. Since u and v are M-free, (u, v) is a pair of witnesses for M.

Example 23. In some cases, the pair of witness candidates, constructed by the standard technique, fails because the words are not M-free. Example 18, in fact, shows an isometric set $M = \{11, 101\}$ that contains the non-isometric word 101 with a 2-eo of type $[1; 1, 2]$. The pair $(\alpha_1(101), \beta_1(101)) = (1001, 1111)$ is not a pair of witnesses since 1111 is not M-free.

Example 24. The set $M = \{0010101, 1110110\}$ is composed of two isometric words and M is isometric, in view of Corollary 21. In fact the word 0010101 has no 2-eo on 1110110 and vice versa.

Let us introduce another remarkable family of isometric sets.

Definition 25. *The star of order $n \geq 1$ is the set*

$$S_n = \{1^n, 01^{n-1}, 101^{n-2}, \cdots, 1^{n-1}0\}.$$

Note that in S_n the word 1^n has distance 1 from all the other words in the set and this is the reason for its name. The star is an interesting example since it can be viewed as a further generalization of the Fibonacci cube. The star $S_2 = \{11, 10, 01\}$ is the complement of $\{00\}$, that defines the Fibonacci cube. This case is anyway extreme, since it shrinks the isometric hypercube $Q_n(S_2)$ to the single node 0^n.

Proposition 26. *The star S_n is an isometric set, for all $n \geq 1$.*

Proof. A word w is S_n-free if in every window of length n there are at least two 0's. Let u and v be two S_n-free words. We prove that there always exists a transformation from u to v where all intermediate words are S_n-free. Consider all the 1's of u that mismatch with the corresponding character in v (if any), and change them one by one into 0's. All intermediate words are S_n-free because the number of 0's in each window of length n does not decrease. In the word obtained from this transformation, change all the 0's that mismatch with the corresponding character in v into 1's, then all the intermediate words are again S_n-free, since v is S_n-free. □

We now investigate the structure of the hypercube avoiding the star S_3 and compare it with the Fibonacci cube and with the hypercube avoiding 111. See hypercubes $Q_4(111)$ and $Q_4(S_3)$ in Fig. 2. Denote by f_n the n-th Fibonacci number, defined by $f_1 = 1, f_2 = 1$ and $f_i = f_{i-1} + f_{i-2}$, for $i \geq 3$. The Fibonacci cube $Q_n(11)$ can be recursively constructed and the number of its vertices is equal to f_{n+2} (cf. [18,21,23]). Let us start with $Q_n(111)$, and state a preliminary lemma that suggests a recursive construction of $Q_n(111)$ and the consequent recurrence for the number of its vertices.

Lemma 27. *Let w be a word of length $n \geq 5$. Then*

- *$w0$ is 111-free iff w is 111-free.*
- *$w1$ is 111-free iff w is 111-free and w ends either with 0 or with 01. Furthermore, if $w = z0$ then w is 111-free iff z is 111-free; if $w = z01$ then w is 111-free iff z is 111-free.*

Proposition 28. *Let T_n be the number of vertices of $Q_n(111)$. Then, $T_3 = 7, T_4 = 13, T_5 = 24$ and for all $n \geq 6$,*

$$T_n = T_{n-1} + T_{n-2} + T_{n-3}.$$

It is the sequence of Tribonacci numbers (cf. Sequence A000073 in [24]).

Let us come to the recursive construction of $Q_n(S_3)$.

Lemma 29. *Let w be a word of length $n \geq 5$. Then*

- *$w0$ is S_3-free iff w is S_3-free*
- *$w1$ is S_3-free iff w is S_3-free and w ends with 00.*
  Furthermore, if $w = z00$ then w is S_3-free iff z is S_3-free.

Proof. If w is S_3-free, the addition of 0 in the end would generate a suffix in S_3 only if w ends with 11. But in such a case, since $|w| \geq 5$, the factor 11 is preceded either by 1 or by 0, and in both cases w would be not S_3-free, contradiction. The other direction of the proof is straightforward.

If w is S_3-free, the addition of a 1 in the end of w is S_3-free only if w ends with 00. In fact in all the other cases ($w = u01$, $w = u10$, $w = u11$) the addition of a 1 in the end generate a suffix that is in S_3 (011, 101 or 111). Now, let $w = z00$, if w avoids S_3, trivially, z avoids S_3, vice versa if z avoids S_3, since $|z| \geq 3$, the addition of 00 at the end does not create an occurrence of a factor of S_3. $\qquad\square$

Proposition 30. *The n-hypercube $Q_n(S_3)$ can be recursively defined, for $n \geq 3$.*

Proof. If $n = 3$, $Q_3(S_3)$ has vertices $\{000, 100, 010, 001\}$. If $n = 4$ the hypercube $Q_4(S_3)$ has vertices $\{0000, 0001, 1000, 0100, 0010, 1001\}$. If $n = 5$, $Q_s(S_3)$ has vertices $\{00000, 00010, 10000, 01000, 00100, 10010, 00001, 10001, 01001\}$. The edges of the hypercubes connect vertices having distance 1. Let $n > 5$ and suppose $Q_i(S_3)$ defined for all $i < n$. Let $x \in \Sigma^+$; denote with $Q_i^x(S_3)$ the copy of $Q_i(S_3)$ where each vertex v is replaced with vx. By Lemma 29, the only vertices of Q_{n+1} that avoid S_3 are the vertices of $Q_n^0(S_3)$ and $Q_{n-2}^{001}(S_3)$. Hence, the vertices of $Q_{n+1}(S)$ are obtained by considering all and only the vertices of $Q_n^0(S_3) \cup Q_{n-2}^{001}(S_3)$. The edges of $Q_{n+1}(S)$ are the edges of $Q_n^0(S_3) \cup Q_{n-2}^{001}(S_3)$ togeter with, for all u, vertex both of $Q_n(S_3)$ and $Q_{n-2}^{00}(S_3)$, we add an edge $(u0, u1)$, where $u0$ is in the copy $Q_n^0(S_3)$ and $u1$ is in the copy $Q_{n-2}^{001}(S_3)$. $\qquad\square$

Corollary 31. *Let V_n be the number of vertices of $Q_n(S_3)$. Then, $V_3 = 4, V_4 = 6$, $V_5 = 9$ and for all $n \geq 6$*

$$V_n = V_{n-1} + V_{n-3}.$$

(cf. Sequence A000930 in [24]).

Here we discussed the construction of $Q_n(111)$ and $Q_n(\{111, 011, 101, 110\})$. Similarly to $Q_n(D_h)$ (cf. Proposition 12), they can be viewed as possible generalizations of Fibonacci cube $Q_n(11)$ in two directions, the first one by extending the avoided word ($11 \rightarrow 111$), the second one by immersing 111 in a set ($111 \rightarrow \{111, 011, 101, 110\}$). The recurrences on the number of vertices confirm that generalized Fibonacci cubes based on sets can be "smaller" than the ones based on a single word, as expected from the fact that they can be obtained as intersection of generalized Fibonacci cubes of the single words in the set.

Further examples of families of isometric sets can be constructed generalizing the previous ones. For example, one can define the *generalized star* of order n and radius k, with $n \geq 1$ and $1 \leq k \leq n$, as the language $S_{n,k} = \{w \mid |w| = n, |w|_0 \leq k\}$, where $|w|_0$ denotes the number of 0's in w. Using the proof technique of Proposition 26 the following holds.

Proposition 32. *The generalized star $S_{n,k}$ is an isometric set for all $n \geq 1$ and for all $1 \leq k \leq n$.*

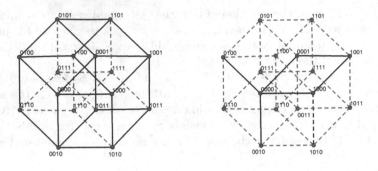

Fig. 2. $Q_4(111)$ and $Q_4(S_3)$

5   Conclusions and Future Work

In this paper we dealt with subgraphs of the hypercubes Q_n that are defined by selecting vertices that avoid the words in a given set M. The idea was to investigate the cases when such subgraphs result to be isometric to Q_n by studying some combinatorial properties of the set of words M. The context resulted to be very challenging. Next step will be considering the special case of sets of two words, classified with respect to the distance between the words. From the algorithm side, we plan to design an efficient algorithm to test whether a set of words is isometric.

Acknowledgments. We thank the anonymous referees, whose suggestions and comments contributed to improving the paper.

References

1. Anselmo, M., Castiglione, G., Flores, M., Giammarresi, D., Madonia, M., Mantaci, S.: Isometric words based on swap and mismatch distance. In: Drewes, F., Volkov, M. (eds.) Developments in Language Theory, DLT 2023, LNCS, vol. 13911, pp. 23–35. Springer, Cham (2023). https://doi.org/10.1007/978-3-031-33264-7_3
2. Anselmo, M., Castiglione, G., Flores, M., Giammarresi, D., Madonia, M., Mantaci, S.: Hypercubes and isometric words based on swap and mismatch distance. In: Bordihn, H., Tran, N., Vaszil, G. (eds.) Descriptional Complexity of Formal Systems, DCFS 2023, LNCS, vol. 13918, pp. 21–35. Springer, Cham (2023). https://doi.org/10.1007/978-3-031-34326-1_2
3. Anselmo, M., Flores, M., Madonia, M.: Quaternary n-cubes and isometric words. In: Lecroq, T., Puzynina, S. (eds.) WORDS 2021. LNCS, vol. 12847, pp. 27–39. Springer, Cham (2021). https://doi.org/10.1007/978-3-030-85088-3_3
4. Anselmo, M., Flores, M., Madonia, M.: Fun slot machines and transformations of words avoiding factors. In: Fun with Algorithms. LIPIcs, vol. 226, pp. 4:1–4:15 (2022)
5. Anselmo, M., Flores, M., Madonia, M.: On k-ary n-cubes and isometric words. Theor. Comput. Sci. **938**, 50–64 (2022)

6. Anselmo, M., Flores, M., Madonia, M.: Density of Ham- and Lee- non-isometric k-ary words. In: ICTCS'23 Italian Conference on Theoretical Computer Science. CEUR Workshop Proceedings, vol. 3587, pp. 116–128 (2023)
7. Anselmo, M., Flores, M., Madonia, M.: Computing the index of non-isometric k-ary words with hamming and lee distance. In: Computability, IOS Press, pp. 1–24 (2024). https://doi.org/10.3233/COM-230441
8. Anselmo, M., Giammarresi, D., Madonia, M., Selmi, C.: Bad pictures: some structural properties related to overlaps. In: Jirásková, G., Pighizzini, G. (eds.) DCFS 2020. LNCS, vol. 12442, pp. 13–25. Springer, Cham (2020). https://doi.org/10.1007/978-3-030-62536-8_2
9. Azarija, J., Klavžar, S., Lee, J., Pantone, J., Rho, Y.: On isomorphism classes of generalized Fibonacci cubes. Eur. J. Comb. **51**, 372–379 (2016)
10. Béal, M.-P., Mignosi, F., Restivo, A.: Minimal forbidden words and symbolic dynamics. In: Puech, C., Reischuk, R. (eds.) STACS 1996. LNCS, vol. 1046, pp. 555–566. Springer, Heidelberg (1996). https://doi.org/10.1007/3-540-60922-9_45
11. Castiglione, G., Flores, M., Giammarresi, D.: Isometric words and edit distance: main notions and new variations. In: Manzoni, L., Mariot, L., Roy Chowdhury, D. (eds.) Cellular Automata and Discrete Complex Systems. AUTOMATA 2023, LNCS, vol. 14152, pp. 3–16. Springer, Cham (2023). https://doi.org/10.1007/978-3-031-42250-8_1
12. Castiglione, G., Mantaci, S., Restivo, A.: Some investigations on similarity measures based on absent words. Fundam. Informaticae **171**(1–4), 97–112 (2020)
13. Charalampopoulos, P., Crochemore, M., Fici, G., Mercas, R., Pissis, S.P.: Alignment-free sequence comparison using absent words. Inf. Comput. **262**, 57–68 (2018)
14. Codara, P., D'Antona, O.M.: Generalized Fibonacci and Lucas cubes arising from powers of paths and cycles. Discret. Math. **339**(1), 270–282 (2016)
15. Epifanio, C., Gabriele, A., Mignosi, F., Restivo, A., Sciortino, M.: Languages with mismatches. Theoret. Comput. Sci. **385**(1), 152–166 (2007)
16. Epifanio, C., Forlizzi, L., Marzi, F., Mignosi, F., Placidi, G., Spezialetti, M.: On the k-hamming and k-edit distances. In: ICTCS 2023 Italian Conference on Theoretical Computer Science. CEUR Workshop Proceedings, vol. 3587, p. 143 - 156 (2023)
17. Harary, F., Hayes, J., Wu, H.: A survey of the theory of hypercube graphs. Comput. Math. Appl. **15**(4), 277–289 (1988)
18. Hsu, W.J.: Fibonacci cubes-a new interconnection topology. IEEE Trans. Parallel Distrib. Syst. **4**(1), 3–12 (1993)
19. Ilić, A., Klavžar, S., Rho, Y.: Generalized Fibonacci cubes. Discrete Math. **312**(1), 2–11 (2012)
20. Ilić, A., Klavžar, S., Rho, Y.: The index of a binary word. Theor. Comput. Sci. **452**, 100–106 (2012)
21. Klavžar, S.: Structure of Fibonacci cubes: a survey. J. Comb. Optim. **25**(4), 505–522 (2013)
22. Klavžar, S., Shpectorov, S.V.: Asymptotic number of isometric generalized Fibonacci cubes. Eur. J. Comb. **33**(2), 220–226 (2012)
23. Munarini, E., Salvi, N.Z.: Structural and enumerative properties of the Fibonacci cubes. Discrete Math. **255**(1–3), 317–324 (2002)
24. Sloane, N.: On-line encyclopedia of integer sequences. http://oeis.org/
25. Wei, J.: The structures of bad words. Eur. J. Comb. **59**, 204–214 (2017)
26. Wei, J.: Proof of a conjecture on 2-isometric words. Theor. Comput. Sci. **855**, 68–73 (2021)

27. Wei, J., Yang, Y., Wang, G.: Circular embeddability of isometric words. Discret. Math. **343**(10), 112024 (2020)
28. Wei, J., Yang, Y., Zhu, X.: A characterization of non-isometric binary words. Eur. J. Comb. **78**, 121–133 (2019)
29. Wei, J., Zhang, H.: Proofs of two conjectures on generalized Fibonacci cubes. Eur. J. Comb. **51**, 419–432 (2016)

Author Index

L. Levy Patey et al. (Eds.): CiE 2024, LNCS 14773, pp. 461–462, 2024.
https://doi.org/10.1007/978-3-031-64309-5

Printed in the United States
by Baker & Taylor Publisher Services

Printed in the United States
by Baker & Taylor Publisher Services